ABOUT THE AUTHORS

Tim Newby is Professor of Educational Technology at Purdue University. He teaches introductory courses in educational technology, as well as advanced courses in foundations of instructional design theory, instructional strategies, and motivation and instructional design. He is a member of the university's Teaching Academy and was inducted into its "Book of Great Teachers." His primary research efforts are directed toward examining the impact of learning and instructional strategies on students' learning and toward defining/investigating instructional conditions that foster and support the development of expert learners. Tim is particularly interested in the use of Web 2.0 technologies and their potential impact on learning.

Don Stepich is currently Associate Professor in the Instructional and Performance Technology Department at Boise State University, where he teaches courses in instructional design, learning theory, and needs assessment. As an instructional designer, Don is interested in the use of interactive strategies to help students learn and in the improvement of instructional materials through continuous evaluation. He is particularly interested in how individuals become experts in a professional discipline, case-based instruction, and the use of analogies in learning. In a former life, Don was a professional social worker in a variety of mental health and private counseling practices. In fact, it was his counseling work that led him into education. He found that he was spending a lot of time teaching assertiveness, active listening, and communication skills, which led him back to school to study learning and instructional design.

Jim Lehman is Professor of Educational Technology and currently serves as the Associate Dean for Discovery and Faculty Development in the College of Education at Purdue University. He teaches classes on the educational applications of computers, integration and management of computers in education, interactive multimedia, and distance learning. He is a member of the university's Teaching Academy and was inducted into its "Book of Great Teachers." His research interests include integration of computer technology into science education, interactive multimedia design, and online learning. He directed a PT3 implementation project at Purdue focused on enhancing preservice teachers' preparation to use technology, and he has been involved in projects related to online learning, STEM education, and computer science education. In his spare time, Jim likes to bike, garden, and do home repairs.

Jim Russell is Professor Emeritus of Educational Technology at Purdue University and former Visiting Professor at Florida State University. Jim started his teaching career as a high school mathematics and physics teacher. The Purdue University Teaching Academy has recognized him as a fellow and has honored him for exemplary work. He is also a member of Purdue's "Book of Great Teachers." His specialty areas are presentation skills and using media and technology in classrooms. Jim enjoys building plastic models and operating his HO-scale model railroad in his spare time. His wife, Nancy, is a nurse; their married daughter, Jennifer, is a high school guidance counselor; and their son-in-law, Lance, works for Lilly Pharmaceuticals. Jim and Nancy's granddaughter, Lauren, is a true joy in their lives.

Anne Ottenbreit-Leftwich is Assistant Professor of Instructional Systems Technology at Indiana University. Anne's research focuses primarily on learning about the values that motivate teachers to use technology and how they are trained to use technology. Her primary role at Indiana University is coordinating, supervising, and teaching preservice teacher technology courses. Anne has been working with the international Organisation for Economic Co-operation and Development to compare how teachers are prepared to use technology across the globe. She loves working with teachers and showing them the possibilities of technology in the classroom. Anne enjoys running, movies, and relaxing with her husband (Luke) and puppy (Andie).

BRIEF CONTENTS

nal Technology
for Teaching and Learning

Fourth Edition

Educational Technology for Teaching and Learning

Fourth Edition

Timothy J. Newby
Purdue University

Donald A. Stepich
Boise State University

James D. Lehman
Purdue University

James D. Russell
Purdue University

Anne Ottenbreit-Leftwich
Indiana University

Boston   Columbus   Indianapolis   New York   San Francisco   Upper Saddle River
Amsterdam   Cape Town   Dubai   London   Madrid   Milan   Munich   Paris   Montreal   Toronto
Delhi   Mexico City   Sao Paulo   Sydney   Hong Kong   Seoul   Singapore   Taipei   Tokyo

Senior Acquisitions Editor: Kelly Villella Canton
Editorial Assistant: Annalea Manalili
Vice President, Director of Marketing: Quinn Perkson
Senior Marketing Manager: Darcy Betts
Production Editor: Gregory Erb
Editorial Production Service: S4Carlisle Publishing Services
Manufacturing Buyer: Megan Cochran
Electronic Composition: S4Carlisle Publishing Services
Interior Design: S4Carlisle Publishing Services
Photo Researcher: Annie Pickert
Cover Designer: Jodi Notowitz

This is a special edition of an established title widely used by colleges and universities throughout the world. Pearson published this exclusive edition for the benefit of students outside the United States and Canada. If you purchased this book within the United States or Canada, you should be aware that it has been imported without the approval of the Publisher or the Author.

Credits and acknowledgments borrowed from other sources and reproduced, with permission, in this textbook appear on appropriate page within text.

10 9 8 7 6 5 4 3 2 1

ISBN-10:   0-13-706333-4
ISBN-13: 978-0-13-706333-8

CONTENTS

PREFACE

VISION AND GOALS OF THE TEXT

The vision of this textbook is to **provide the foundations** for **enhanced learning experiences** through the **meaningful integration of technology.** The first part of this vision is to provide a solid foundation to help you understand the research and background that support the selection, integration, and implementation of specific technologies and techniques for learning. This foundation provides the supporting structure to help you understand when and how to best utilize technology for learning. Second, in today's information society, the enhancement of learning experiences is essential, because lifelong learning has become the norm for almost everyone. We need to discover how we can make learning more effective and efficient, influence a wider diversity of learners, encourage transfer of learning, and induce higher levels of learner motivation. The third part of our vision is the meaningful integration of technology. This text introduces and explains not only the different types of technologies available but, more important, the conditional knowledge of when and why they should be used. When integrated in a meaningful way, technology can greatly facilitate the learning process. However, there will be times when limited use of technology is the optimal course of action. Knowing what to use and when to use it are skills all teachers need.

After using this text, readers will:

1. Be proficient in selecting, modifying, and designing instructional materials.
2. Be able to plan instruction that addresses and solves complex learning problems for individual students.
3. Have a repertoire of instructional methods and media to select from and use to effectively and efficiently influence student learning.
4. Be able to use the computer to develop and manage instructional materials, and as a learning tool for students.

NEW TO THIS EDITION

This is the fourth edition of *Educational Technology for Teaching and Learning.* For this edition, we have two major goals. First, this edition updates the technology

discussed in the book and the ways that you can use that technology for teaching and learning. Educational technologies change rapidly, and we are constantly finding new ways to use current and emerging technologies in the classroom and beyond. So, our first goal in this revision is simply to ensure that you, the reader, can learn about the latest developments in educational technology. Specific examples of new content are cited following. Second, the book is streamlined. We have shortened the book by one chapter, labeled all figures for ease of reference, and reduced the number of in-chapter features. We hope these changes will make it easier for you to use the book and enhance your learning from it.

The following aspects of the book are new to this edition.

- *Updated educational technology content.* Information about new and emerging technologies has been added to this edition. Examples include: expanded coverage of assistive technologies (Chapter 3); examples of productivity software available on the Web (Chapter 3); serious games (Chapter 9); Web 2.0 technologies such as social networking, blogs, and wikis (Chapter 10); and new distance education technologies such as podcasts, webinars, and voice over IP (VoIP) (Chapter 11).
- *PIE Checklist.* A new PIE (plan, implement, evaluate) Checklist feature has been introduced for use in conjunction with the extended lesson plan example (Kevin Spencer's Civil War Unit). The PIE Checklist provides a tool for students to use in implementing the PIE model, and a completed example used with the extended lesson plan will help students to see how to analyze learners and learning environments, develop objectives, develop activities, and select materials, methods, and media.
- *Simplified model of applications of computers in education.* A simplified model of computer applications in education, focusing on just two major categories—computer as teacher and computer as assistant, is introduced in Chapter 3 and revisited in Chapter 9. Computer as teacher applications include the various types of computer assisted instruction. Examples of computer as assistant applications include word processing, graphics packages, spreadsheets, databases,

presentation software, and now multimedia authoring packages.

↗ *Chapter reduction.* This edition has one fewer chapter than the third edition of the text. Readers felt that the historical content formerly placed in Chapter 14 would be better at the beginning of the text. So, that material is now included in Chapter 1. Other content from the former Chapter 14, including trends and the future of educational technology, has been combined with content on issues in the field in Chapter 13 to create a new, expanded Chapter 13 that deals with both issues and trends in educational technology.

↗ *Revised NETS Connection.* In 2008, the International Society for Technology in Education (ISTE) released new National Educational Technology Standards for Teachers (NETS-T), a significant revision of the standards for teachers first released in 2000. In order to help you think about how you will address these new standards and to understand how the content of this textbook will assist you in addressing the standards, a new NETS Connection feature has been placed in Appendix C. Use these activities to monitor your own development and guide your understanding of the standards and what you as teacher should know about educational applications of technologies.

↗ *Chapter Introductions and Technology Coordinator's Corner.* New and revised chapter introductions, focusing on issues faced by teachers in the classroom, are used at the beginning of chapters. These introductions act as advance organizers to help the reader focus on key questions to be answered while reading the chapter. Problems or issues that are raised in the introductions, in many cases, are revisited in the Technology Coordinator's Corner, found at the end of each chapter. The latter feature, introduced in the third edition, provides perspectives on the teachers' issues from various school technology coordinators who provide advice on what must be considered to overcome challenges and successfully integrate technology.

ORGANIZATION OF THE TEXT

The text is integrated around three components: the principles of designing instruction, the selection and use of methods and media, and the effective use of computers. To facilitate this integration, the text is designed around the PIE—*P*lan, *I*mplement, *E*valuate—model. Chapters 1–3 provide the needed background on learning, learning theories, and the computer. Chapters 4–8 help the reader discover how to **plan** effective and efficient instruction. This section provides guidance on gathering the needed information about the learner,

learning goals, instructional setting (Chapter 4), and the essential elements and activities needed to create an instructional plan (Chapter 5). It introduces the most commonly used instructional methods (Chapter 6) and media (Chapter 7), as well as how to select and/or create instructional materials (Chapter 8). This section emphasizes how technology can be integrated to enhance the learning experience and influence the overall learning that occurs.

The **implementation** phase focuses on how students actually experience instructional materials and activities. Here, we discuss proper integration and implementation of the computer (Chapter 9), the Internet (Chapter 10), and various forms of distance education (Chapter 11). Each chapter emphasizes when, why, and how these technologies should be integrated to enhance learning.

Chapter 12 examines both the assessment of student performance and the **evaluation** of instructional materials. We examine how teachers can use evaluation to continuously improve not only the abilities and skill of their students but also the effectiveness of their instruction. The role of the computer in storing, organizing, analyzing, and managing evaluation data is discussed.

The final section focuses on the key issues confronting the field today, trends, and future directions for educational technologies and their role in teaching and learning (Chapter 13).

STRUCTURING A COURSE USING THIS TEXT

Traditionally, preservice teachers have taken separate courses in instructional planning and design, media utilization, and computing to gain needed skills and competencies. *Educational Technology for Teaching and Learning,* Fourth Edition, is a single, integrated source that is designed to introduce preservice and in-service teachers to the basic principles of effective instructional material planning and development; to different types of methods and media and how to best utilize them; and to the computer as a powerful tool in planning, developing, delivering, and evaluating effective instruction.

There are at least three ways courses can be structured to accomplish these goals:

↗ *Emphasize the development and use of the instructional plan.* Covering the text's chapters in sequence will accomplish this task. Begin with the general chapters on learning, educational technology, theory, and the computer as a tool to develop and execute the plan. The remaining chapters (based on the steps of the PIE model) show how one can *plan, implement,* and continually *evaluate* to effectively teach and learn.

- *Emphasize the learning experience itself.* You may want to begin with the chapters that focus specifically on methods and media (Chapters 6 and 7) and their role in the learning process. This can be followed by how the computer, the Internet, and distance education (Chapters 3, 9, 10, and 11) can facilitate the learning experience. Finally, the chapters on designing (Chapters 4 and 5), developing (Chapter 8), and evaluating (Chapter 12) can be addressed to help your students learn how to develop and improve such learning experiences.
- *Emphasize the computer as a powerful tool that can improve learning.* You might begin by looking at background materials on the computer (Chapter 3), and how and why the computer can be effectively used by both teachers and learners (Chapters 3 and 9). You may then wish to investigate the "power of the computer" through the Internet and distance education (Chapters 10 and 11). Coupled with a lab component, this gives extra emphasis to the computer as a key tool for students and teachers, and demonstrates its effectiveness within the classroom setting.

OTHER FEATURES OF THIS TEXT

The following features are also found in each chapter.

- *Key words and objectives* outline the sequence of the information, how it is structured, and when it will be presented. The desired learning outcomes outline what you should be able to do once you have studied the materials within the chapter. Several key words and concepts that may be new to you are found in the glossary.
- *Toolboxes* throughout the text present relevant, useful pieces of information. These toolboxes present various tips, tools, techniques, and resources that relate to content in specific chapters. A toolbox might include information about computer hardware such as an electronic whiteboard, specific tools such as Internet search engines, or Internet links to find additional information on a topic.

SUPPLEMENTS AND RESOURCES FOR STUDENTS AND TEACHERS

The following ancillary materials have been created for the fourth edition. The instructor supplement is available for download from the password-protected Instructor Resource Center at www.pearsonhighered.com/irc. Please contact your local Pearson representative if you need assistance.

- *MyEducationKit.* Online resources, including video cases and Web-based activities related to the content of the text, are available for further exploration and study. Relevant activities are identified at pertinent locations within each chapter, and students can also test their knowledge of the content of each chapter using the Study Plan available in *MyEducationKit.*
- *Instructor's Manual/Test Bank.* An accompanying instructor's manual is available to professors using this text. The guide includes (a) identification of the key chapter concepts and principles, and ideas for introducing each of the main concepts; (b) strategies for teaching the chapter content; (c) ideas for assessment and feedback; (d) sample lesson outlines; (e) reference and supplemental resources, and (f) a question bank.
- *Live Telelectures and Internet Chat Sessions.* The authors are available for live telelectures or Internet chat sessions if you so desire.

PEARSON
myeducationkit

Dynamic Resources Meeting Your Needs

MyEducationKit is a dynamic website that connects the concepts addressed in the text with effective teaching practice. Plus, it's easy to use and integrate into assignments and courses. Whenever the MyEducationKit logo appears in the text, follow the simple instructions to access a variety of multimedia resources geared to meet the diverse teaching and learning needs of instructors and students. Here are just a few of the features that are available:

- Online study plans, including self-assessment quizzes and resource material.
- Gradetracker, an online grade book.
- A wealth of multimedia resources, including classroom video, expert video commentary, rubrics, and weblinks.

Study Plan   A MyEducationKit Study Plan is a multiple choice assessment with feedback tied to chapter objectives. A well-designed Study Plan offers multiple opportunities to fully master required course content as identified by the objectives in each chapter:

- *Chapter Objectives* identify the learning outcomes for the chapter and give students targets to shoot for as they read and study.
- *Multiple Choice Assessments* assess mastery of the content. These assessments are mapped to chapter objectives, and students can take the multiple choice quiz as many times as they want. Not only do these quizzes provide overall scores for each

objective and text excerpts for sections of the book related to the objective, but they also explain why responses to particular items are correct or incorrect.

Assignments and Activities   Designed to save instructors preparation time and enhance student understanding, these assignable exercises show concepts in action (through video and web links). They help students synthesize and apply concepts and strategies they read about in the book.

Multimedia Resources   The rich, media resources you will encounter throughout MyEducationKit include:

Videos: The authentic classroom videos in MyEducationKit show how real teachers handle actual classroom situations. Discussing and analyzing these videos not only deepens understanding of concepts presented in the text, but also builds skills in observing children and classrooms.

Web Links: On MyEducationKit you don't need to search for the sites that connect to the topics covered in your chapter. Here, you can explore web sites that are important in the field and that give you perspective on the concepts covered in your text.

General Resources on MyEducationKit   The Resources section on MyEducationKit is designed to help students pass their licensure exams, put together effective portfolios and lesson plans, prepare for and navigate the first year of their teaching careers, and understand key educational standards, policies, and laws. This section includes:

↗ *Licensure Exams*: Contains guidelines for passing the Praxis exam. *The Practice Test Exam* includes practice multiple-choice questions, case study questions, and video case studies with sample questions.

↗ *Lesson Plan Builder*: Helps students create and share lesson plans.

↗ *Licensure and Standards*: Provides links to state licensure standards and national standards.

↗ *Beginning Your Career*: Offers tips, advice, and valuable information on:

  ↗ Resume Writing and Interviewing: Expert advice on how to write impressive resumes and prepare for job interviews.

  ↗ Your First Year of Teaching: Practical tips on setting up a classroom, managing student behavior, and planning for instruction and assessment.

  ↗ Law and Public Policies: Includes specific directives and requirements educators need to understand under the No Child Left Behind Act

and the Individuals with Disabilities Education Improvement Act of 2004.

Visit *www.myeducationkit.com* for a demonstration of this exciting new online teaching resource.

CONTACTING THE AUTHORS

We believe wholeheartedly in communication and feedback. If you have a question or suggestion, let us know. Both students and professors are encouraged to send us e-mail messages and to visit the Companion website.

Tim Newby
E-mail: newby@purdue.edu
Telephone: (765) 494-5672 (office)

Don Stepich
E-mail: dstepich@boisestate.edu
Telephone: (208) 426-2339

Jim Lehman
E-mail: lehman@purdue.edu
Telephone: (765) 494-0019 (office)

Jim Russell
E-mail: jnan@att.net
Telephone: (317) 826-0599

Anne Ottenbreit-Leftwich
E-mail: aleftwic@indiana.edu
Telephone: (812) 856-8486

ACKNOWLEDGMENTS

We would like to thank all those who have contributed to this edition. In particular, our students, colleagues, and the scores of in-service teachers who have offered examples and insights need to be given special thanks. Through their timely advice we were able to identify areas to add, adapt, and improve. Also, thanks to Kelly Villella Canton (Acquisitions Editor), Annalea Manalili (Editorial Assistant), and Gregory Erb (Production Editor) of Pearson Education for their guidance, edits, and general assistance.

Finally, we thank our reviewers for their ideas and suggestions: Sherry Allen, University of Southern Indiana; J. Michael Blocher, Northern Arizona University; Ana Cruz, St. Louis Community College-Meramec; David Pratt, Purdue University North Central; and Jana M. Willis, University of Houston-Clear Lake.

We hope this text will provide both preservice and in-service teachers with a solid foundation for planning, implementing, and evaluating instruction. By integrating the principles of instructional design, by selecting and utilizing relevant instructional methods and media, and by making appropriate use of the computer, the teaching-learning process can become more effective, efficient, and appealing.

INTRODUCTION TO EDUCATIONAL TECHNOLOGY

Read Me First!

Frequently, when opening a new appliance or piece of hardware/software, you may have noticed that a booklet entitled "READ ME FIRST," has been included because the manufacturer wants to tell you about the product *before* you head off into some trial-and-error learning process. In similar fashion, we think it is important for you to know some essential information about this text before you dive into the initial chapters.

First, it would be helpful to know *why* this textbook was developed. We believe that many individuals, especially those within teacher education, need to know (1) how learning experiences and especially instruction are designed, developed, and improved; (2) the types and uses of different media formats—especially the personal computer; and (3) how the design of the instruction and the media are integrated to promote student learning. Meeting these needs requires integrating the three general areas of instructional design, educational media, and educational computing. Traditionally, these have been taught through individual texts and separate courses; however, teachers must apply them in an integrated fashion to have maximum impact on student learning.

Second, it is useful to know that this text is organized around a simple Plan, Implement, Evaluate (PIE) model. The main sections of the text (Sections II, III, and IV) are all based on this model. The different aspects of instructional design, media, and computing are discussed within this structure.

Third, there are a number of special features within this text designed to facilitate your learning. This text focuses on educational technology, specifically on the tools that can increase the effectiveness, efficiency, transfer, impact, and appeal of instruction. We have created a "toolbox" feature, which highlights important hardware, methods, techniques, and other tips. In addition, chapter objectives,

key words and concepts, as well as a chapter summary have been incorporated to help structure the information in a readily useable manner. Finally, we have also included a full example of the instructional planning process in one appendix (i.e. Kevin Spencer's lesson plan) and we have included within a separate appendix an "Addressing the Standards" feature that allows you to examine and reflect on how, when, and why the educational technology standards should be addressed.

Of special interest within this text is the emphasis on the integration of technology within the learner-centered classroom environment. We include various sections within each chapter to address the benefits, challenges, and solutions to integration. In addition, we have included a feature to review each chapter's content from the unique perspective of school technology coordinators. Looking through their eyes helps to keep the issues of integration interesting, practical, and on target with what actually happens in the typical school setting.

Throughout this text, we frequently ask questions, present ideas for you to ponder, and describe problems that need thoughtful analysis and synthesis in order to be adequately worked through. This is our attempt to get you involved and to help you to remember and apply the information.

IF WE WERE STUDYING THIS TEXTBOOK, WE WOULD . . .

A few years ago, one of our students asked, "If you were going to study for this exam, how would you go about it?" In response, we created a set of notes that began with the statement, *If we were studying for this exam, we would . . .* The goal was not to provide a list of specific items to memorize; rather it was to guide them so they could draw their own conclusions. These notes worked so successfully, we decided to include a similar set here. So, *if we were studying this textbook, we would . . .*

↗ *Read and reflect on the vision of the text.* As stated here, (and also within the Preface and Chapter 1) the vision of this text is: "To **provide the foundations** for **enhanced learning experiences** through the **meaningful integration of technology.**" The purpose, therefore, is to help you discover and explore the key principles and foundations of educational technology that allow the effective integration of technology tools to successfully select, adapt, and create exceptional, meaningful learning experiences. Fully understanding this vision helps you to realize and prepare for where the text is headed and what you will experience. Read and ponder this vision frequently as you venture through each section of this text.

↗ *Pay close attention to the plan, implement, and evaluate model.* Whenever you approach learning (from either a teacher's or learner's perspective) you need to think about how the planning will occur, how the learning will be experienced, and how the assessment measures will indicate what worked and what needs improvement.

↗ *Reflect on how the textbook material can be applied to your own experiences.* We have included hundreds of examples throughout the text. It is our hope that you will review what is offered and then determine how they match with your own experiences and how your experiences can expand your understanding.

↗ *Learn to appreciate the power of the computer as a teaching and learning tool, but do not be overwhelmed by it.* Do not fall into the trap of thinking that the computer is the savior of education. The computer is not the most important tool in *all* learning situations. It is one of many tools that can facilitate your work. In addition, do not think that the computer is such a complex tool that you cannot master it.

↗ *Reflect and question.* Take time to reflect on what is presented in this text and, more important, how you can *use* it. When a principle is presented, imagine how, when, and why you might apply it. In all cases, think about how the information can be applied in your situation.

↗ *Be excited about learning!* Learning should be a marvelous adventure, whether you accomplish it personally or assist in helping others experience it. As you learn about educational technology and begin to see its potential, we hope you will become as excited as we are.

OVERVIEW: SECTION I

This first section of the text, entitled "Introduction to Educational Technology," is an introduction to the field of educational technology and the supporting contributions of instructional design, media, and computing. Central to Chapter 1 is the concept of learning and how you can enhance it through the integration of technology.

In Chapter 2, we explore the theoretical foundations of teaching and learning. We look at learning from a number of different angles to enable you to consider which teaching and learning orientation might be best, given a particular topic, situation, and/or type of learner. To increase the usefulness of this theoretical background, realize that the emphasis is not simply on knowing the different perspectives of learning, but on understanding how each perspective applies to real students in actual classrooms.

Finally, we have designed Chapter 3 to supply important prerequisite information about the computer and how it can be used to enhance learning. The computer is a powerful machine, and it is intricately involved in the design, development, implementation, and evaluation of learning experiences.

Introduction to Learning and Technology

Source: Shutterstock

KEY WORDS AND CONCEPTS

Learning
Technology
Educational technology
Instructional design
Educational computing

Educational media
Cognitive overload
Transfer
Instruction
Instructional plan

CHAPTER OBJECTIVES

After reading and studying this chapter, you will be able to:

- Describe and give examples of learning and what constitutes "an enhanced learning experience."
- Evaluate given learning scenarios and determine how, when, and why each learning experience could be "enhanced."
- Describe examples of technology and educational technology.

- Describe how technology can potentially impact learning in a meaningful manner and generate examples of how this could occur.
- Describe the contributions of instructional design, educational computing, and educational media to educational technology.
- Discuss the evolution of the fields of instructional design, educational media, and educational computing, and describe the contributions of prominent individuals or projects to the development of those fields.

3

WELCOME

Welcome to *Educational Technology for Teaching and Learning*. We want you to know from the opening pages that we are excited about this book's contents. Demands on teachers and their students have never been higher. At the same time, we live in an era when phenomenal tools allow for rapid access to and manipulation of information. The need as well as the potential for learning is great. In this text we will explore ways to design instruction incorporating computers and related technology that can have a positive impact on learning.

In this chapter, we will share the vision of the book – where we are going and why. We will define and provide examples of learning and technology, and more importantly, we will begin to discuss the integration of the two. As we begin this chapter, review the following situation that involves a technology task force created by a newly hired school district superintendent. In particular, review the questions that are being posed. These will be the guiding questions that will direct our focus as we go through this chapter and the chapters that follow.

A technology task force   Mr. Clive Jackson was recently hired as the superintendent of a school district in a large southern state. Almost immediately, he felt the need to ascertain the level of technology availability and, more importantly, the quality of its use within his district. To get the information he needed, he set up a task force of interested administrators, teachers, students, and parents representing most of the district's schools. At the first meeting of the task force, Mr. Jackson gave the following set of questions to consider, discuss, investigate, and answer before reporting back to him:

↗ What types of technology are currently available at each of the schools?
↗ How are the different forms of technology being used in the classrooms?
↗ At what level, or to what degree, (e.g., heavy daily use, frequent weekly use, occasional monthly use, not being used) are these various types of technology being used?
↗ Which types of technology have the greatest impact on learning for the students of the district?
↗ Are there important technologies currently needed/desired but not available within the district?
↗ What are the challenges being faced by teachers and students when it comes to the effective use of technology?

Let us suppose you've been asked to serve as a member of this task force. How would you go about answering each of the questions? Identifying the hardware that is available in each school may take some time, but the procedure may be a fairly straightforward form of counting inventory. The more important and interesting questions come when trying to perceive which of the technologies are being used effectively in a manner that actually impacts student learning and where the challenges lie when learning is lagging. This text is about how we answer these important questions. That is, coming to understand what learning is and how it can and should be impacted by the strategic use of technology. *Strategic use* is a key phrase – understanding the types of technology is important; however, understanding *when* and *why* it should be used gives you the capability of reliably impacting the learning of your students.

VISION OF THE TEXT: WHERE ARE WE GOING?

The vision of *Educational Technology for Teaching and Learning* is contained in the following statement:

> To provide the foundations for enhanced learning experiences through the meaningful integration of technology..

This vision provides three key elements. First, it highlights the importance of a solid *foundation* of when, why, and how learning can be produced. When you construct such a foundation, you can more readily select methods, techniques, and strategies, as well as technologies that will support consistent and reliable learning. Instead of just trying to use only those techniques perceived as most familiar, easiest, or most available, a solid foundation gives you the ability to strategically select and use learning strategies that have consistent and reliable results. A foundation of learning research coupled with practical experiences allows you to know and understand how and why learning occurs, as well as what methods, techniques, activities, and strategies should be used in order to maximize learning outcomes.

The second element of the vision focuses on the *enhanced learning experience*. Here, the vision deals with what the learner will experience and how that experience is effectively designed, implemented and evaluated. Closely aligned with this is the third vision element of *meaningful integration of technology*. Beyond merely designing learning experiences, we want to integrate technology in a meaningful way in order to enhance what is actually experienced and what is ultimately learned. Technology integration can help us attain learning that is at a higher level, faster, more readily transferred, and is often more appealing.

From this vision, first and foremost will be an emphasis on designing learning experiences. We will examine what is required, as well as how it is accomplished, applied, and evaluated. Moreover, the strategic selection, integration, and use of technology will provide a means to examine potential learning enhancements. In sum, our vision is for you to become an instructional expert capable of helping others learn. To begin, we examine learning itself, and the key elements of the learning process.

 LEARNING

Based on the text's vision, a central focus is on human learning and how it is accomplished. Even though most of us are quite familiar with the "learning experience" and we know we have "learned" in the past, there are still key questions to address so that we are in the best position possible to truly impact what is learned.

- ↗ What exactly is learning?
- ↗ How does learning typically occur?
- ↗ Why is the study of learning important?
- ↗ How can the learning experience be enhanced?

What Exactly Is Learning?

It is relatively easy to cite examples of learning. For instance, reflect on the past few days or weeks and think about something you learned. Maybe it was something that required concerted time and effort, such as learning how to write a specific type of research paper. Or, you learned something that needed less effort or time, such as the location of the closest parking facility for your new night class. Or, possibly your learning occurred without consciously realizing it, such as when you learned two full verses of an obnoxious jingle from a television commercial. The time, effort, and purpose involved in each of these examples varied considerably. However, in each case, learning occurred.

Learning is a broad concept and occurs across such a variety of subjects that defining it concisely is not simple. However, here are some definitions with consistent terminology.

- ↗ Learning is "a relatively permanent **change** in someone's knowledge based on the person's **experience**" (Mayer, 2008, p. 7).
- ↗ Learning is "a persisting **change** in performance or performance potential that results from

experience and interaction with the world" (Driscoll, 2005, p. 1).
- ↗ "Learning is an enduring **change** in behavior, or in the capacity to behave in a given fashion, which results from practice or other forms of **experience**" (Schunk, 2008, p. 2).

Note that within each of these definitions, *change* is brought about through *experience* or some form of interaction with the environment. To *learn* is to change (or have the capacity to change) one's level of ability or knowledge in a permanent way. Typically, learning is measured by the amount of change that occurs within an individual's level of knowledge, performance, or behavior. To qualify as learning, experience plays a key role. Ormrod (2008) explains, "Learning is a change as a result of experience, rather than the result of physiological maturation, fatigue, use of alcohol or drugs, or onset of mental illness or dementia" (p. 4). Therefore, growing taller or developing freckles, does not qualify as learning. However, as novice piano players begin to read music faster and hit the keys with greater accuracy, we can then infer that their interaction with the environment (repeated use of the piano keyboard; repeated matching of written musical notes on a scale with keys on the keyboard) has resulted in a positive change in their piano playing skills. Thus, we can say that learning has occurred. Figure 1–1 compares examples and non-examples of learning. Note the need for change to occur due to experience. More than 70 years ago, Thorndike (1931) emphasized the importance of change by writing, "Man's power to change himself, that is, to learn, is perhaps the most impressive thing about him" (p. 3).

How Does Learning Typically Occur?

Learning may occur in a number of ways. For example, it may come about through: (a) direct experience (e.g., touching a hot stove and learning about the pain associated with such a touch); (b) vicarious experience (e.g., learning by watching someone else go through an experience such as touching a hot stove); (c) instructional

---

Examples:

- ↗ Executing a perfect kickboxing "round house kick" on command
- ↗ Reciting a J. R. R. Tolkien quote from memory
- ↗ Deriving and using an equation to solve a novel math problem
- ↗ Choosing not to drink milk that "smells funny"

Non-examples:

- ↗ Gaining weight or growing taller (results of maturation or physiological changes)
- ↗ Demonstrating perceived heightened interpersonal skills brought on by high levels of alcohol consumption (or drug use) that are generally of short duration

FIGURE 1–1   Examples and non-examples that illustrate the accomplishment of learning.

Direct experience is one way that children learn to avoid touching a hot stove surface.
Source: Heiko Wolfraum/Corbis.

presentation (e.g., learning through a presentation, reading, etc.,) to recognize, identify, and properly be wary of hot surfaces; and (d) a combination of any or all of the ways previously mentioned.

The selection of the optimal format of learning depends on several factors. Each factor must be considered before selecting the type of learning experience. The factors to consider include the learner, the learning environment, and the content that is to be learned (see Chapter 4 for extended discussions on each of these factors). Learners vary greatly in their ability to understand a learning experience whether it is derived from direct, vicarious, or instructional presentation types of experiences. Developmental level, learning styles, gender, ethnicity, intelligence, etc., all impact the degree to which a learner gains from a specific type of learning experience. Likewise, the learning environment will allow and restrict the type of learning experience that can be selected and used. Allowing students to have a direct experience using a flight simulator may be readily accomplished with a small group of students who live near a flight school. But, large classes of hundreds of students will not have ready

access to this type of direct experience because of the numbers involved or the location of the simulator. Finally, there is some content that lends itself to direct experience and other content that does not. Learning about writing a research paper is content that frequently lends itself to individuals gaining direct experience; whereas, learning about different management styles within major investment corporations may be more readily accomplished through a more presentation-oriented learning experience.

Why Is the Study of Learning Important?

Learning is complex. It may occur across all types of tasks (e.g., changing a car tire, falling in love, delivering a speech, identifying cell anomalies), for all types of learners (e.g., a newborn child, a business CEO, a high school student, a 90-year-old violin player), and in various environments (e.g., in the mountains, on a production line floor, in a small group of students, sitting at a computer). Moreover, it may occur today for a specific person, in a specific location, covering a specific topic; however, tomorrow (or even later today), it may not be as readily achieved.

The study of learning focuses on identifying and describing general conditions and principles that facilitate and/or inhibit learning and determining how they can be best utilized to promote reliable learning. If learners and those who guide the learning of others (e.g., teachers, trainers, parents) understand these key principles, then the chance of facilitating the learning process may be enhanced. Through the study of learning, we can come to identify specific theories and principles that allow us to predict certain situations that will facilitate (or hinder) certain learning for specific individuals.

As highlighted in the given definitions of learning, experience plays a key role. This indicates that the quality of the experience potentially enhances (or inhibits) what is actually learned. Specific activities, methods, media, techniques, technologies, etc., employed within a learning experience can be used to enhance the learning. ***Thus, the study of learning helps learners, and those who guide learning, to strategically identify, select, implement, and evaluate key elements of an experience that will ensure reliable changes in desired behavior.***

As an illustration, review the contributions of Mayer (2008). His research on the Cognitive Theory of Multimedia Learning indicates, for example, that individuals have a limited capacity to attend to and process incoming information through a single sense modality (e.g., auditory). That is, only a certain amount of information can be heard, understood, and processed efficiently by a learner at any one time. More than the restricted amount will not be retained because a form of **cognitive overload** may occur. However, if a second

Increased levels of:

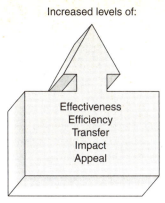

Effectiveness
Efficiency
Transfer
Impact
Appeal

FIGURE 1–2   The study of learning can lead to increased levels of several key benefits.

channel (e.g., visual) is utilized to convey additional information, then the limited capacity for processing new information by learners can be expanded to some degree. Through the use of multimedia, for example, the impact of the learning experience may be significantly enhanced. By studying the research of Mayer and others, we can come to see how learning experiences can be designed and structured to enhance overall learning.

Benefits, as shown in Figure 1–2, that are directly connected with the study of learning include:

- ↗ Increased **effectiveness.** In this case, students actually learn in a better way than they would without the experience. The study of learning helps to identify how to increase the encoding, retention, depth of understanding, and recall of needed information and skills.
- ↗ Increased **efficiency.** Here, the focus is on time. Through the study of learning we can identify ways to organize and deliver learning experiences in a manner that helps students obtain the information or skills in a more rapid and timely manner.
- ↗ Increased **transfer**. Through the study of learning, we may identify how to better generalize what is learned so that it can be utilized in different but related contexts or content areas. For example, learning how a specific problem-solving technique can be used across a wide variety of problems increases its value and usefulness to the learner.
- ↗ Increased **impact.** Identifying and implementing techniques that allow a greater diversity of learners to be positively influenced by the learning experience can also be achieved through the study of learning.
- ↗ Increased **appeal.** Identifying ways to enhance learner motivation for a specific learning experience can increase the possibility that students will devote time and energy to the learning task as well as the likelihood they will return to review and work on

the material at other times. Appeal is strongly associated with learners' attitudes toward the information and their motivation for investing effort.

How Can the Learning Experience Be Enhanced?

Let us imagine that you recently bought a used car. After driving it for several days, you may come to the conclusion that there are several improvements that could be made to enhance your purchase. For example, you might think about increasing its gas mileage by having the engine tuned or enhancing the overall ride by adding new tires, a wheel alignment, or even new shocks. Additionally, you may want to enhance the car's outward appearance by having it painted a new color. Similarly, the learning experience may be enhanced in various ways in order to increase effectiveness, efficiency, transfer, impact, and appeal. Let's examine the following example of how a lesson focused on multicultural education could be experienced within a normal classroom setting:

Situation A: Suppose you were teaching a class on multicultural education. For one lesson within the course, you design a discussion about the unique differences between rural versus inner-city classroom structure and students. To facilitate the discussion, you have the students read the textbook chapters that cover the content and explore some readings from various sources you have selected. Finally, you give them key questions to reflectively think about prior to coming to the class.

Now review the following situation involving the same lesson that has been adapted in a number of ways.

Situation B: Suppose you are teaching the same class as described in Situation A. However, in this case, before the discussion, you also have students access, read, and comment on two different teachers' blogs that focus on what they are currently experiencing within their classrooms. One of the blogs is from a teacher in a large urban school, and the other is a blog from a teacher at a small rural school. Your students have the opportunity to read what is going on within the schools and gain inside information about the daily joys and challenges faced within the classroom. In addition, you make arrangements for your class to be linked via a two-way interactive video so that the students can monitor visually and aurally a class of students at both an inner-city and rural school location. Your class then discusses a comparison between the two locations.

Reflect on the following questions:

- ↗ What are the key differences between how the information was experienced in the first learning situation versus that of the latter?

Toolbox: Tools, Tips, and Techniques

As you venture through this text, note that we have inserted special short features called "Toolboxes." Just as a cabinetmaker's toolbox holds valuable things that allow "cabinetmakers' toolboxes . . ." to successfully complete their job, our toolbox contains items that will play a role in your success as both teacher and learner.

Similar to the builder's toolbox, the ones in this text contain a variety of items. Each one might focus on a "tool," a "tip," or a "technique." Toolboxes appear strategically throughout the text because of our desire for you to immediately see their value and worth. Instead of giving you a long list of tools in an appendix, for example, our goal was to locate individual toolboxes where their need was apparent and where we could illustrate an example of its use. In that manner, you can read about the tool, tip, or technique in the inserted toolbox on the same page that you can see its value and potential usefulness. Some toolboxes will focus on hardware or software that you will find helpful in specific situations. We might, for example, discuss scanners, digital cameras, or graphic software that could help as you develop instructional materials. Other toolboxes will be devoted to giving you insight on specifics the authors and others have learned through experience that warn you of potential problems and help you teach in a more professional and efficient manner. Examples include "How to use visuals in instructional materials" and "Care of computer systems." Still other toolboxes will be devoted to different types of instructional techniques that have been shown effective in improving learning such as mnemonics, analogies, reflection, and debriefings.

We could not, of course, include everything you will need for all learning situations. We had to be very selective. This is our way of helping you begin to develop a toolbox of your own. Some of these items you may need and use daily; others you may use only on a very limited basis. It is important for you to understand that this is just a beginning. Throughout this text and as you venture on through your career, you will continue to add relevant tools, tips, and techniques to your learning toolbox.

↗ What could potentially be the key differences in the quality of the discussion students have within your course from those that participated in the second situation versus those that participated in the first?

↗ What are some benefits and challenges of each of these situations for both the students and the instructor?

Although the quality of the learning experience can be enhanced in a number of ways (e.g., quality of the text information, how the questions are asked within the discussion, use of attention-getting devices to focus the learner's attention) based on the vision of this text, we will concentrate on how to enhance the learning experience through the meaningful integration of various technologies both for the learner and for the individual who will be creating the learning experience. Throughout this text, we will highlight the use of these various technology tools, methods, and media and how they impact the design, development, delivery, and evaluation of the learning experience.

TECHNOLOGY

Technology has been referred to as "the systematic application of scientific or other organized knowledge to practical tasks" (Galbraith, 1967, p. 12). In other words, it is "the application of science to industry" (Mehlinger & Powers, 2002, p. 10). Note the emphasis on *application* within these definitions.

Technology is the manner in which research is applied to solve practical problems. As depicted in Figure 1–3, technology performs a bridging function between research and theoretical explorations provided by science on one side and the real-world problems faced by industry and various practitioners on the other.

The space industry offers a good example. Numerous practical problems have been encountered as humans traveled into space (e.g., How does one breathe in a place devoid of oxygen?). To solve such problems, contributions from physics, materials science, and other fields of research had to be translated to practical application. In many cases, the results were tangible products such as the space shuttle, space suits, and advanced telecommunications capabilities. In other situations, the resultant tools and products have taken not-so-tangible forms such as enhanced safety procedures, formulas for reentry projections, and backup contingency plans. In each instance, scientific knowledge was reviewed and applied to answer specific practical problems. Figure 1–4 highlights several other examples of practical problems faced by various industries and the resultant applications tools.

In each instance, technology served as the application bridge between the scientific research/knowledge and the practical problems.

What Exactly Is *Educational* Technology?

Just as technology has been used to address practical problems in communication, medicine, sports, construction, and so on, it has also been used to address practical problems involved in human learning. Formally stated, **educational technology** is the "application of technological processes and tools which can be used to solve problems of instruction and learning" (Seels &

FIGURE 1–3 The bridge of technology between research and practical problems.

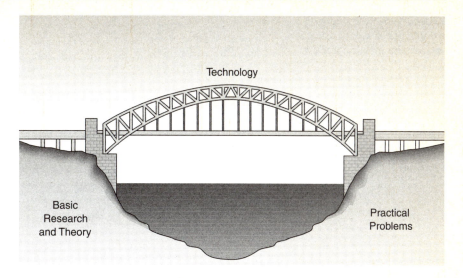

FIGURE 1–4 Examples of Problems and Application Tools Used within Various Industries.

Various Industries	Sample Practical Problems	Resultant Application Tools
Communications	Need for relatively easy and inexpensive communication between individuals across wide distances	Cell phones, Internet, video conferencing equipment
Publishing	Desire to deliver various forms of media in a cost-efficient and timely manner	Printing presses, digital pictures, online publications
Sports	Need to protect players in contact sports	Lightweight, flexible, protective jackets, braces, helmets, face guards, etc.
Medicine	Need to better diagnose internal disease and injury	X-ray, MRI, and CAT scans

Richey, 1994, p. 4). As depicted in Figure 1–5, it serves as the bridge between those who conduct research on human learning (e.g., psychologists, linguists) and those students and teachers who face practical learning challenges. Resultant application tools include principles, processes, and products that teachers and students use to enhance learning.

Educational technology utilizes application tools to accomplish the overall goal of constructing and delivering optimal learning experiences.

How Is Educational Technology Utilized?

Consider the following situations:

➤ A small high school desires to offer an advanced chemistry class for several capable students; however, a qualified teacher is not available.

➤ Two middle school teachers (one from the English department and one from social studies) desire to create a combined unit on explorers of North America.

➤ An art teacher at the elementary school level wants students to study insects and create their own bug art.

To utilize the tools of educational technology in such situations, the following should be considered:

a. How should the learning experience be constructed?

b. How should it be delivered/experienced?

c. How can we evaluate it to know if it worked and how it should be improved?

Within this text, we will expand on each of these questions. Using research on human learning, for example, various techniques, methods, strategies, and activities (e.g., organization and structure of the materials, the use of analogies, cooperative learning groups, tutorials, discovery learning, and discussions) will be examined and integrated with the content to create an optimal learning experience. Moreover, how the experience is planned, implemented, and evaluated will be examined in detail. In addition, various tools in the forms of computers, distance learning equipment, the Internet, and other forms of media will be examined in order to determine how the

FIGURE 1–5 The bridge of technology between learning research and practical learning problems.

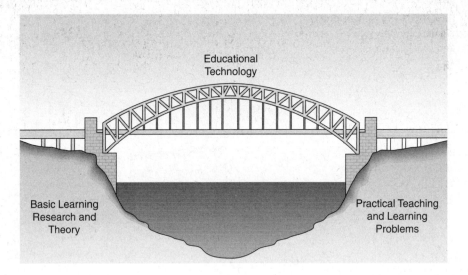

learning event should be received and experienced by each learner.

What Is the Meaningful Integration of Technology?

The meaningful integration of technology is knowing when, why, and how specific tools should be used to facilitate overall learning. It requires both the ability to plan and select the optimal application tools, as well as the knowledge and skill to implement and evaluate their effectiveness. Meaningful integration means that the use of the technology allows for an experience that otherwise would not have been fully experienced. It allows something to be seen that otherwise wouldn't have been seen (e.g., a microscope). It allows someone to participate that otherwise may have been left out (e.g., assistive technology, distance education); it allows someone to think at a deeper or higher level than otherwise possible (e.g., simulations involving complex problems).

Humans are noted for the use of tools in attempts to make their lives better in some way. Within education, examples of integration can take many forms. For instance:

↗ A preschool teacher who helps her students grasp the concept of small living organisms may incorporate the use of a magnifying glass or a microscope in order to accomplish the learning goals.

↗ Teachers in art and language may find their learning goals better served by having students reflect and write about examining the paintings and sculptures from historic masters after they have visited (virtually) several of the world's most prestigious art galleries.

↗ A head nurse may find that her new nurse trainees may begin to analyze and critique newborn babies with higher levels of proficiency following the review of an interactive DVD that highlights key new baby evaluation procedures and how to detect abnormalities.

As illustrated from these examples, the meaningful integration of technology requires more than just presenting a tool to a potential learner and saying, "Go forth and learn!" It requires knowledge of the learners and the content, as well as an understanding of how the technology can be used to help accomplish the learning goals. In each of these examples, the learners are learning *with* the technology instead of just learning *from* the technology. As pointed out by Jonassen, Howland, Marra, and Crismond (2008, pg. 7), "If technologies are used to foster meaningful learning, then they will not be used as delivery vehicles. Rather, technologies should be used as engagers and facilitators of thinking."

So why study technology? Because technology offers solutions to problems. Those solutions, however, do not just magically appear. Through study, we are able to refine what and how the optimal solutions are determined, selected, and implemented. This helps us identify the alternatives, select the best option, and evaluate and readjust as needed. Additionally, through study, it helps us come to understand what technology is available, when and why it should be used, and how it is effectively adapted, integrated, evaluated, and adjusted.

PEARSON **myeducationkit**™ Go to the Video Tutorials section of Chapter 1 in MyEducationKit to view the video clip entitled "Student Achievement Increases." As you watch the video, think about the ways that this teacher sees the use of technology contributing to student achievement and the ways she uses technology in her own teaching.

PEARSON **myeducationkit**™ Go to the Assignments and Activities section of Chapter 1 in MyEducationKit and complete the activity entitled "National Standards." As you explore these websites, review the content standards, think about the principles that underlie them, and consider examples that you might use as you begin to think about planning your own lessons.

Toolbox: The Technology Standards

Standards are tools for guidance and measurement. They are developed to help determine needed levels of skill proficiency as well as a comparison stick to measure the quality of skill attainment. Most professions have well-established standards they use to make judgments about current performance. For example, medical doctors must meet or exceed specific standards in order to practice their profession. Standards help to ensure that individuals have the competencies necessary to complete critical tasks.

Within educational technology, standards have been developed for both students and teachers. These standards are known as the National Educational Technology Standards (NETS) and they have been developed in conjunction with the International Society for Technology in Education (ISTE). The NETS standards for students as well as teachers can be found on the ISTE website (http://www.iste.org/NETS/). For your convenience, we have reproduced the standards for teachers in Appendix A.

To help facilitate your understanding of the standards and how they can be used to guide your perception of technology and learning, we have included an additional feature, called Meeting the Standards, within Appendix A. This feature includes activities that highlight one or more relevant standards and guide you to reflectively consider how to interpret the standard, as well as what should be considered in order for it to be properly addressed. Complete these activities to reflect on how the standards can be used to inform and guide your own level of understanding of educational technology.

PLAN, IMPLEMENT, EVALUATE (PIE): A RELIABLE MODEL TO IMPACT LEARNING

The study of learning is important for both those who will be learning and those who will be guiding the learning of others, because specific actions, techniques, and technologies can have an impact on the quantity and quality of what is learned. By understanding learning we can better design and develop strategic learning experiences.

Our emphasis is on what learners and teachers can do to positively impact learning. As shown in Figure 1–6, such things relate to the following:

↗ The *planning* required that ensures instruction is developed and sequenced in a manner to effectively promote learning

↗ *Implementing* the instruction

↗ *Evaluating* the instruction, including assessing the student's learning

In planning, the focus is on what students are to learn, as well as when, why, and how it might best be accomplished. The result is an outline, lesson plan, or blueprint of the learning experience that will bring about the desired goal. This plan helps to delineate learners' *present* knowledge and abilities, as well as what their knowledge and skills *should* be, and it suggests ways to reduce the difference between the two. This plan influences the manner in which you develop and present information and the learner experiences it. Section II of this text (Chapters 4–8) focuses on planning.

Implementation focuses on putting the plan into action based on what situational constraints exist, using selected instructional materials and activities. For learners, implementation is when, where, and how they experience learning. For the teacher, implementation includes monitoring and managing the instruction, groups of learners, and individuals with special needs. Section III (Chapters 9–11) explores implementation in greater detail.

The emphasis during evaluation is on the assessment of the effectiveness of the materials. This is a time to reflect on what was accomplished, to compare that with your desired goal, to suggest changes in future planning and implementation, and to complete suggested revisions and fix-ups. Section IV (Chapter 12) focuses on evaluation.

The planning, implementing, and evaluating process (we refer to as the PIE model) helps to guide us to systematically structure our approach to developing effective learning experiences. Refer again to Figure 1–7 and note that each of the stages within the model is

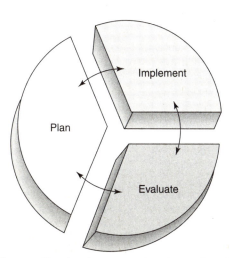

FIGURE 1–6   Plan, implement, and evaluate. The phases of learning.

	The Teacher	The Learner	Educational Technology
Plan	• What task must the students be able to do, and how can I determine when it has been accomplished? • What do the students already know that will assist in learning this task? • What resources, facilities, and equipment are available and accessible? • What information should be included in the instructional materials or activities? • What is the most effective, efficient, and appealing manner in which the to-be-learned task can be acquired by the students? • In what order should the learning activities be sequenced? • What are the best methods and media to assist students in learning the new information? • What can be done to help this learning be transferred to similar situations? • Are there relevant instructional materials (or parts thereof) that already exist? Which materials will need some adaptation? Which materials will need to be created?	• What is the goal of this task (i.e., What am I supposed to learn?)? • What will I need to learn from this task (e.g., learning strategies, assistance from others, time, effort)? • In what ways can my previous learning experiences help? • What obstacles and problems could hinder me from learning this task? • How will my motivation and effort in this task be generated and maintained (e.g., Am I good at this kind of task? Do I like this kind of work?)? • How should I attempt this task in order to effectively learn the materials while maintaining my motivation and overcoming presented obstacles (e.g., Does this type of activity require a great deal of concentration?)?	• In what ways can educational technology effectively impact how a student addresses a learning task? • In what ways can technologies effectively impact how a teacher designs and creates instructional materials? • How can students and/or teachers improve learner attention and motivation through the use of technology? • How can instructional technology improve the efficiency of student learning and/or teacher preparation?
Implement	• How will the instructional experience and activities be managed? • How will I manage groups of learners as well as individuals with special needs during their learning experience? • During the learning process, how will I maintain the students' attention and motivation?	• How do I assemble or create what is needed to carry out the plan? • How do I begin and follow the planned learning strategies? • Is this going the way I planned? • Do I understand what I am doing? • What outside materials or resources should be added? • What should I look for in order to tell if learning is occurring? • How can I tell if my task motivation is being maintained?	• In what ways can technology assist and impact the manner in which the student experiences? the instruction? • In what ways can teacher efficiency during the delivery of instruction be increased through the use of educational technology?
Evaluate	• How can I determine to what degree the students have learned the material? • What types of remediation or enrichment activities may be necessary for my students? • In what ways can these instructional materials and activities be improved for repeated or adapted use? • How will needed changes throughout the learning experience be monitored? • How will student self-evaluation and regulation be learned and encouraged?	• Was the quality and quantity of learning at the needed level? • What did I do when the selected tactics and learning strategies didn't work? • What obstacles were encountered, and what strategies were or were not effective in overcoming those problems? • What have I learned from this experience that could be used at other times for different tasks? • What improvements could I make for future learning tasks?	• How can technology be used to determine the degree of student learning that has occurred? • How can technology be used to generate teacher and student feedback? • In what ways can technology be used to measure the effectiveness, efficiency, and appeal of the implemented instructional materials?

FIGURE 1–7   Instructional Process: What Questions Should be Asked?

highly interactive with each of the other stages. For example, the planning impacts both how the instruction is implemented and how it is evaluated. The implementation feeds information back to the planning for future reference and updates and also helps dictate how and when evaluations can take place. Likewise, the evaluation gives critical feedback to how future instruction is planned, as well as how it is best implemented.

To help you understand how the PIE model functions, work through the following scenario. Imagine that you find yourself in the following situation. You have been asked to help students in a high school biology class learn about the impact of commercial fishing on the seal population in Alaska's Maritime National Wildlife Refuge during the last 30 years. From the *perspective of the teacher,* review the questions in the first column of Figure 1–7 and see if they help you grasp what needs to be considered when such an experience is being planned, implemented, and evaluated.

Once you have reviewed this task from the perspective of the teacher, do it again from the potential *learner/student perspective.* Review the questions in the second column of Figure 1–7 and see how the different elements of the PIE model should also be considered by students as they approach a learning task.

Finally, after reviewing the teacher and student perspectives, review the final column of questions. Think of ways in which **technology** could be used to facilitate that which is required of students and teachers during each of the PIE stages. These questions help to set the stage for the role of technology within the teaching/learning process.

 ## THE ROLE OF THE TEACHER
The Teacher as an Instructional Expert

An integral part in most educational settings is the teacher. Although classroom instructors frequently serve a variety of roles from administrator to surrogate parent (Kauchak & Eggen, 2008, p. 13), the most important function is that which Woolfolk (1990) refers to as the "instructional expert." In this capacity teachers are actively involved in several aspects of the instructional learning process. The instructional expert's involvement can range from little actual interaction with students (e.g., when devoting time and effort to developing learning activities) to a high amount of group or individual interaction (e.g., when presenting new materials to students in a lecture or discussion format).

Teachers take on several roles as they plan, implement, and evaluate instructional learning experiences.
Source: Anthony Magnacca/Merrill Education.

Over the years, the functions of teachers as instructional experts have remained relatively constant. Whether direct or indirect, good or bad, teachers heavily influence what students experience and subsequently learn in the classroom. Even in situations where students have more control (e.g., a discovery/exploratory environment, individualized instruction), the teacher selects or arranges the activities and gives guidance and clarification. Because of this critical role, *this text will focus on what you as an instructional expert should know and do so that your students can learn.*

Using the plan, implement, and evaluate model, the expertise of the teacher is shown to be needed in each of these areas. During planning, teachers identify students' instructional needs by recognizing existing gaps between current and desired levels of skills and knowledge and then selecting instructional methods and strategies to meet those needs. Other considerations at this time include the type of learners they are dealing with and the teacher's own personal style of teaching. The principal result is a plan or blueprint of instruction that includes learning content, which strategies and activities to use, when to use them, and how to structure them. Throughout this process, teachers need to be familiar with the tools of technology that can assist the planning of the learning experience.

After teachers assemble or produce needed instructional materials, they then become "directors of learning activities" (Ausubel, Novak, & Hanesian, 1978). This may require the teacher to personally disseminate information through some form of expository lecture, inquiry discussion, or demonstration; to serve as manager of other learning vehicles (e.g., video presentation, small-group discussion); or to become a guide/coach who encourages and helps students experience learning on their own. The primary outcome is that the student experiences the instruction. Likewise, knowledge of technology tools can be utilized to facilitate how the instructional experience is delivered and how the students come to experience the learning activities.

The final role for the instructional expert is that of **evaluator** of student learning, as well as the overall learning experience. Teachers traditionally have done this by examining how well students completed the lesson and by determining if they have attained the desired level of performance. Increasing attention is now being focused on providing continuous evaluation throughout all stages of learning (Stiggins, 2005). Evaluation should also be a time to reflect on successes achieved and problems encountered. The evaluation's result is a description of the strengths and weaknesses of the program, which teachers may then use for instructional improvement. Knowledge and use of technology during this process may aid in the manner in which evaluative information is gathered, analyzed, and reported. Teachers may come to find that technology can be used to examine closely what works and what does not within the learning experience,

as well as assess how well students are gaining the desired knowledge and skills.

For most teachers, planning, implementing, and evaluating instruction are all ongoing processes. On any given day, a teacher may plan and develop several future lessons, monitor current topics to ensure that they are being properly addressed, and reflect on completed lessons and the results they produced.

 ## THE ROLE OF INSTRUCTION

Instruction is "the deliberate arrangement of learning conditions to promote the attainment of some intended goal" (Driscoll, 2005, pp. 352–353). When it is effective, instruction helps learners gain the experiences needed in order for a desired change (or potential change) to be produced and thus learning to occur. In order for this to be accomplished in a reliable and consistent fashion, several key questions need to be addressed:

a. How is the instruction planned?
b. How will the instruction be experienced?
c. What tools will be needed in order to successfully design and deliver the instruction?

In many cases, individuals take specific courses to learn how to design and develop instructional materials, other courses to learn about different forms of media and how they are used to deliver the instructional experience, and even additional courses that focus on ways of using technology to facilitate the design, development, delivery, and evaluation of the instruction. Although such a disjointed approach may give students a solid background in all three individual areas of study (i.e., instructional design, media, and computing), it may limit their ability to see how each may expand the effectiveness of the others. We feel that such an approach can be improved by emphasizing the relationships among these areas. It is only through an integrated approach that teachers can identify and solve the more difficult problems of human learning. Through such an integrated approach, for example, teachers may readily see how computers can contribute to designing the instructional plan and developing the instructional materials, how the design directs the media selection, and, likewise, how using the media affects students' interpretation and acceptance of the designed instructional message. Although you could study instructional design, media, and computing independently, viewing them as an interrelated whole magnifies their potential for teacher and student alike.

Instructional Design (How is the instruction planned?)

Instructional design is "the systematic and reflective process of translating principles of learning and instruction into plans for instructional materials, activities, information resources, and evaluation" (Smith & Ragan, 2005, p. 4). The emphasis is on creating a plan for developing instructional materials and activities that increase an individual's learning. Reigeluth (1983) compared this task with that of an architect. The architect produces a blueprint or plan that effectively integrates the needs of those who will purchase and use the facility, the environment in which it will exist, the costs involved, the appropriate materials, and other design specifications for functionality, safety, and aesthetics. Similarly, instructional experts incorporate learning principles into plans for instructional materials and activities based on analyses of the learners, the situation, and the task or content to be learned.

Although a builder may attempt to construct a facility without using the architect's plan or blueprint, he or she may encounter problems that could have been avoided by using a plan—walls may be in the wrong location, electrical outlets forgotten or misplaced, or improper materials purchased. As with any plan, the major benefit of an instructional plan is the guidance it gives. This does not mean that all instruction should be designed based on a single set of plans (like a subdivision of one-style homes), but rather that specific principles can be used to solve different instructional problems and to produce unique solutions in a variety of situations.

Power of the Plan   The overall **instructional plan** plays a critical role in directing the selection and use of all other tools within the learning environment. The teacher and learners should use the plan to determine the methods, techniques, and media they will use. Additionally, the plan helps to determine how and when to present specific sets of information and when additional information is required.

Even though a plan provides teachers with direction, it should not be perceived as a rigid structure that dictates regimented, systematic procedures. Whenever learning is required, different types of learners, tasks, and situations all interact, requiring flexibility. The plan provides a means to review alternative possible solutions to instructional problems, assess their potential, and then confidently select the best. If and when those alternatives do not produce desired levels of learning, the plan can be revised and additional alternatives selected. The power of the instructional plan is that it suggests alternatives and a means whereby they can be investigated and evaluated before investing time and money in developing the final products.

Aspects of instructional design include:

↗ *the overall instructional plan*—what to include and how to arrange the components

↗ *various analysis techniques and methods* that help determine both learners' current skill levels and those needed to accomplish the task

↗ *a repertoire of methods, techniques, and activities* that can be used to increase student learning (see Figure 1–8)

↗ *strategies for sequencing instructional media and materials* so that learners get the proper amount of information when needed

↗ *an emphasis on evaluation* to ensure that the instructional materials and procedures resulted in students achieving the desired goals

This text explains how to design instruction so that learners and teachers all may benefit. Figure 1–8 lists instructional tools that aid in instructional design. These include instructional methods, techniques, and activities teachers may use to create and augment successful instructional materials. We discuss these technologies in greater detail throughout the text.

Specific chapters have been devoted to the discussion of instructional methods (Chapter 6) and instructional activities (Chapter 5). Instructional techniques are integrated throughout Section II within the various Toolbox features.

Educational Media (How will the instruction be experienced?)

A **medium** "refers to anything that carries information between a source and a receiver" (Smaldino, Lowther, & Russell, 2008, p. 6). In addition, Smaldino, et al. (2008) explain, if those messages contain information with an instructional

FIGURE 1–8 Types of Instructional Tools: Methods, Techniques, and Activities.

Instructional Methods	Instructional Techniques	Instructional Activities
Cooperative learning	Focusing questions	Motivation activities
Discovery	Highlighting	Orientation activities
Problem solving	Analogies	Information activities
Instructional games	Mnemonics	Application activities
Simulation	Imagery	Evaluation activities
Discussion	Concept maps	
Drill and practice	Embedded questions	
Tutorial	Feedback	
Demonstration	Case studies	
Presentation	Role-playing	

purpose, they are considered **educational media**. In one case, the selected educational medium may be a video; in another, it may be an audiotape, in still another it may be computer software, or even a diagram. Each educational medium represents a means of connecting learners, the teacher, and the instructional content. Figure 1–9 lists several forms of media, each with its own set of unique attributes. Important questions involving the manner in which learners experience information include the following:

↗ What forms of media are available?
↗ What impact do the different media formats have on learning?
↗ Under what conditions can this potential impact be altered and enhanced?
↗ How are various media formats most effectively used?

When investigating the answers to these and similar questions, research in the areas of perception, cognition, communication, and instructional theory comes to the forefront. For every learner and teacher, the central concerns are how information is structured and what happens once individuals have perceived and experienced it. Research shows that various forms of media and their respective selection and utilization processes directly impact what learners perceive and how they retain and recall information (Kozma, 1991).

Educational media for teachers and learners can be used to:

↗ present materials in a manner learners can readily assimilate (e.g., a video can clearly illustrate how cells divide in the early stages of reproduction)
↗ deliver materials independently of the teacher, thus allowing students some control over how much of the material they will experience and when (e.g., students

can rewind or fast-forward portions of a video- or audiotape to match their own learning needs)
↗ allow learners to experience materials through various senses (e.g., seeing projected visuals, reading textual materials, hearing a verbal description of the same content)
↗ provide learners with repeated and varied experiences with subject matter to help them construct their own understanding and meaning
↗ gain and maintain learners' attention on the subject matter
↗ motivate students toward a goal
↗ present information in a manner that individual learners otherwise could not experience (e.g., events can be speeded up or slowed down, objects can be decreased in size [e.g., the universe] or increased in size [e.g., an atom])
↗ accommodate varying sizes of audiences

Power of the Learning Experience   Review the list of media formats presented in Figure 1–9. Teachers can use all of these to help students learn. The question is, "Why do we need all the different types of media?" For example, isn't an overhead projector an effective medium for delivering information to students? Why then are videos, computer software, textbooks, and other media also used? The answer lies with the learning experience itself. Various levels of content, types of learners, and learning situations dictate that some media formats are at times better suited or more feasible than other formats.

Each medium has its own set of unique characteristics, and how people interact with a message is shaped by the medium's particular attributes. For that reason, it is important to understand what each medium can contribute

Educational Medium	Key Attributes	Examples
Real objects and models	Actual item or three-dimensional representation	A living animal A plastic model of the human eye
Text	Written words	Biology textbook Written material from an electronic encyclopedia
Video	Moving pictures	Instructional video on the procedures to insert memory chips in a computer Video on how to seek shelter during a tornado
Audio	Sound	Audio CD of an inspirational speech Audiotape of directions for completing a process
Visuals (graphics, slides, overhead transparencies)	Pictures, line drawings, maps	Projected overhead transparency of the state of South Carolina Map of the organizational structure of a school corporation
Multimedia	Combination of various media forms	Computer program on comparative culture that incorporates pictures, textual descriptions, native music, and short videos of individuals speaking different languages

FIGURE 1–9   Types of Media with Attributes and Examples.

to the learning experience. For example, readers make use of the stable quality of information presented in the traditional textbook. When they encounter a difficult passage, learners can slow down, reread portions, skip back and forth, refer to pictures or diagrams, and so on. As learners struggle to create meaning from information in a textbook, their interaction with the *text* is dependent, to a great extent, on the characteristics of that medium.

Throughout this text, we will emphasize the importance of correctly selecting and utilizing these various forms of media. *It is critical to keep in mind that no matter how good the medium, learning will be hindered if the message is poorly designed. Learning also will be obstructed if the message is well designed but delivered in such a fashion that the learner cannot understand or interpret it correctly.* The media format dictates how the instruction will be delivered and how learners will subsequently experience it. Clearly, media play a critical role in the overall learning process.

Educational Computing (What tools will be needed in order to successfully design and deliver the instruction?)

The computer has made a tremendous impact throughout our society, and that impact has been particularly strong within the field of education. **Educational computing** is defined as the use of the computer in the teaching and learning process. The computer's power within education is due to its versatility as both a production and a presentation tool. Although it is a form of media and should be considered as such, the computer's capability to be *both* a presentation and production tool sets it apart from other media formats (e.g., text, videos). For example, in a single day, a classroom computer may be used to write a creative short story about a character from the Wild West, monitor on the Internet the current shape and velocity of a tropical storm off the coast of Florida, store scores from the last social studies assignment, and look up information on Nelson Mandela and listen to parts of his major speeches. These examples illustrate the power of the computer in teaching and learning.

Because of its current impact and tremendous potential, it is imperative that classroom teachers understand the power of the computer and how they can use and adapt it for learning. Throughout this text, we devote sections to explaining how you may use the computer, when and why it is a valuable asset, and how to integrate it in the classroom to ensure the maximum effect on your teaching and on your students' learning.

Educational computing for teachers and learners can be used to:

↗ enhance the quality of instructional materials using the electronic capabilities of the computer
↗ reduce the time required to design, produce, and reproduce instructional materials

↗ increase the overall effectiveness of instructional materials through enhanced presentations
↗ combine graphics, video, audio, and textual forms of media into single, integrated instructional presentations
↗ store and quickly access huge amounts of information and data
↗ communicate with others at both near and distant locations
↗ function as a productivity tool, in which the student uses the computer to complete a task or to solve a problem
↗ function as an instructional expert, in which the computer makes decisions about levels of student learning, suggests media and learning experiences to students, and then selects and presents those media and experiences

Power of the Machine   The real power of the computer is in its versatility. At times, it becomes an assistant, helping to manage classroom and instructional development efforts. Other times, it can become the actual way through which students experience the instructional activities and learn content. In still other cases, it becomes the means by which students attempt to solve complex problems. This versatility, coupled with its power to store, access, and manipulate huge amounts of information, is why so much attention has been devoted to computers in education.

FOUNDATIONS OF EDUCATIONAL TECHNOLOGY: A BRIEF HISTORY

Within the vision of this text, a need to understand the basic foundations is highlighted. Toward this end, it is important to understand the history of educational technology in order to understand fully where we are currently and to predict what the future holds.

The roots of educational technology run deep, and a complete exposition of the history of the field is well beyond the scope of this text. For the historical account that follows, the authors are indebted to the work of Anglin (1991), Gagné (1987), Shelly and Cashman (1984), and particularly Saettler (1990). Interested readers are encouraged to consult these references for more information.

The beginnings of educational technology can be traced back as far as the ancient Greeks. Indeed, the word *technology* comes from the Greek *technologia,* meaning systematic treatment or craft. While we can see the basis for educational technology in the ideas of the ancient Greeks, the modern history of the field is one that falls largely within the twentieth century. Figure 1–10 presents an overview of developments in instructional design, educational media, and educational computing in the twentieth century. We begin here by looking briefly at the foundations of each of these three component disciplines.

18

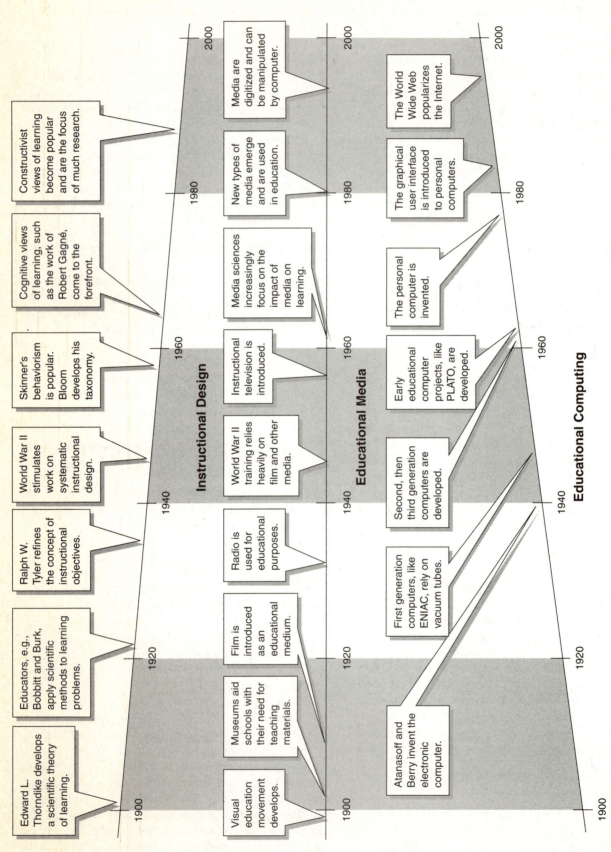

FIGURE 1–10 Converging time lines of developments in instructional design, educational media, and educational computing.

Instructional Design Roots

One of the single most influential figures in the early history of the instructional design field was Edward L. Thorndike, who joined the faculty of Teachers College of Columbia University in 1899. Thorndike conducted scientific investigations of learning, first on animals and then on humans, and developed what is considered by many to be the first scientific theory of learning. Thorndike's view of learning was founded on the basic notion that organisms establish a connection between stimulus and response. Every action has a consequence, and that consequence influences whether or not the action will be repeated. In a nutshell, when a particular action yields a satisfying result, it is more likely to be repeated in similar circumstances. When an action leads to a dissatisfying or unpleasant consequence, repetition is less likely. From an educational standpoint, Thorndike's work suggested that teachers needed to make explicit appropriate connections (e.g., between the stimulus $2 + 2$ and the response 4), reward students for making the proper connections, and discourage inappropriate connections. These concepts are evident in classrooms even today. Refer to the discussion of behavioral learning theory in Chapter 2.

John Dewey, among the most influential thinkers in the history of education, was also at Teachers College Columbia in the early part of the twentieth century. Dewey's view of learning in many ways contrasted with that of Thorndike. Whereas Thorndike focused on stimulus and response, a somewhat mechanistic view of learning, Dewey believed that organisms consciously interact with their environments through self-guided

activity. He viewed experience, interaction, and reflection as central to the learning process. While some of Dewey's progressive ideas fell out of favor during the mid-twentieth century, his emphasis on learning-by-doing has enjoyed a rebirth today, and many of Dewey's ideas are considered foundational to the constructivist view of learning (see Chapter 2) that is popular today.

In the 1930s, Ralph W. Tyler focused on the use of objectives to describe what students were expected to learn. He refined the process of writing instructional objectives and established that instructional objectives could be clearly stated in terms of student performance and that the use of clearly specified objectives made it possible to formatively evaluate instructional materials.

In 1956, Benjamin Bloom and his colleagues published the *Taxonomy of Educational Objectives,* a hierarchical scheme for categorizing educational objectives that is now familiar to most students of education. Initially, behavioral perspectives such as B. F. Skinner's theory of operant conditioning dominated instructional design. In the 1960s, the work of cognitive scientists, such as Robert Gagné gained more attention. Researchers and developers began to focus on instructional systems, and instructional design emerged as a discipline in its own right.

The decades after the 1960s gave rise to refinements and expansions of the field. Cognitive theories of learning, and later constructivist perspectives, came to the forefront of the field. Increased attention was given to student-centered perspectives of learning including discovery learning (e.g., Jerome Bruner), situated cognition (e.g., Brown, Collins, and Duguid), and social learning (e.g., Albert Bandura, Lev Vygotsky). Instructional design proliferated in military and business training, and its influence began to infiltrate K–12 classrooms. At the beginning of the twenty-first century, instructional design is a recognized field of endeavor with widespread applications, an active research community, and evolving perspectives.

Educational Media Roots

Educational media and instructional design developed along separate but converging pathways. Although the use of real objects, drawings, and other media has been a part of instruction at least since the dawn of civilization, the history of educational media, like that of instructional design, is mostly confined to the twentieth century. In North America, museums had a significant early influence on educational media. In 1905, the St. Louis Educational Museum became the first school museum to open in the United States. A forerunner of what is now called a media center (in 1943, it was renamed the Division of Audio-Visual Education), the museum housed collections of art objects, models, photographs, charts, real objects, and other instructional materials

Edward L. Thorndike (left) developed one of the first scientifically based theories of learning and is often viewed as the "father of instructional technology."
Source: Corbis.

gathered from collections around the world. These materials were placed at the disposal of teachers in St. Louis schools, who could request weekly deliveries of instructional materials that were first accomplished by horse and wagon and later by truck.

Visual instruction or visual education, based on the idea that pictures could better represent real objects than words, was popular in the late nineteenth and early twentieth centuries. Magic lanterns that projected slides, and stereopticons, early 3-D visual display devices, were popular means of illustrating public lectures and could be found in some schools. These were the first of many forms of media and new media technologies that were appropriated for educational use. Films came into classrooms early in the twentieth century and radio was the focus of a number of educational experiments from the 1920s through 1930s. In the 1950s, television took center stage as an important new medium on the educational scene. Later came overhead projectors, VCRs, DVD players, and, of course, personal computers.

The educational media field began to increasingly focus on the role of media in schools. Systematic studies were undertaken to establish how the attributes or features of various media affected learning. A convergence of audiovisual sciences, communication theories, learning theories, and instructional design began. This marked the beginnings of educational technology as we have defined it in this book.

Educational Computing Roots

The first all-electronic digital computer was invented in 1939 by John Atanasoff and Clifford Berry at Iowa State University. The first large-scale, general-purpose electronic digital computer, called ENIAC, was put into service by John W. Mauchly and J. Presper Eckert at the University of Pennsylvania in 1946. First-generation computers, such as ENIAC, relied on vacuum tube technology. The second generation, which emerged in the late 1950s and early 1960s, was based on transistors. The third generation followed rapidly on the heels of the second in the 1960s; it used solid-state technology or integrated circuits (ICs) that replaced discrete transistors and other electrical components with circuits etched onto tiny wafers of silicon called *chips*. The fourth generation, which arrived in the 1970s, relied on large-scale integration and very large-scale integration such as the *microprocessor,* a single silicon chip that included all of the key functions of a computer, first developed by engineers at Intel Corporation. This development made possible the invention of the personal computer in the late 1970s and early 1980s.

The first efforts to use computers for education date to the 1960s. At Stanford University, Patrick Suppes and his associates initiated a computer-assisted instruc-

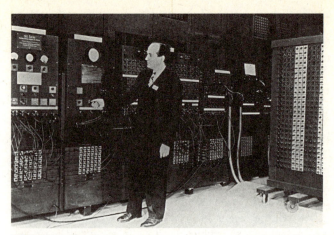

ENIAC was the first large-scale, general-purpose electronic digital computer.
Source: Courtesy of the Library of Congress.

tion (CAI) project. The PLATO (Programmed Logic for Automatic Teaching Operation) project, the largest CAI effort in history, was initiated at the University of Illinois. Much of the CAI software developed for the PLATO and similar projects was ultimately translated for personal computers.

In the 1970s, Seymour Papert and his associates at MIT began work on the Logo computer language, which brought powerful computing ideas to young learners and for a time became very popular in schools. The Minnesota Educational Computing Consortium (MECC), one of the first large-scale state initiatives involving educational uses of computers, was launched. Then, the personal computer was developed in the late 1970s with ready-to-run models from Apple, Commodore, and Tandy/Radio Shack. The personal computer quickly became the focus of educational efforts involving computers.

In the 1980s, there was a dramatic rise in the number of computers in U.S. schools. Initially, there were few productivity tools and little educational software, so much early educational use focused on programming and learning about computers. The concept of computer literacy, analogous to reading and writing literacy, was put forth. As the use of computers proliferated and their capabilities grew, more software became available. CAI programs in various subject areas appeared, and productivity applications such as word processors, electronic spreadsheets, and database managers were developed. By the end of the 1980s, most experts in educational computing had abandoned the idea of computer literacy as a separate field of study and instead had adopted a more comprehensive view of curricular integration that included the use of computers and computer tools in authentic subject-area contexts. Today, computers are viewed as just one educational tool, albeit one with capabilities and flexibility never before seen.

Toolbox: Discovering the Roots of Educational Technology

Learn more about key theorists and researchers in the history of educational technology. What were the important contributions of some of the major figures from the history of educational technology such as Albert Bandura, Jerome Bruner, John Dewey, Robert Gagné, Seymour Papert, Patrick Suppes, Edward L. Thorndike, and Lev Vygotsky? Use the following websites to learn more about these influential figures in educational technology.

What were the seminal ideas from each of these important figures in the history of educational technology? In what ways are these ideas important in education today? What additional resources can you locate on the Internet that provide information about these individuals and others who have made important contributions to the field of educational technology?

Site	URL
Classics in the History of Psychology, York University	http://psychclassics.yorku.ca
The Encyclopedia of Informal Education, Learning Theory	http://www.infed.org/biblio/b-learn.htm
Theory into Practice Database by Greg Kearsley	http://tip.psychology.org/

EDUCATIONAL TECHNOLOGY TODAY

Today, educational technology is the focus of great attention. A number of professional organizations are devoted strictly to the issues and concerns that confront educational technology (Figure 1–11). Schools are investing millions of dollars in the "nuts and bolts" of educational technology—computers and allied technologies. But the influence of educational technology on K–12 education remains an open question. Are we getting a return on our investment? In the remainder of this text, we will explore the processes and tools of educational technology, and you can make up your own mind about the value of this field for teaching and learning.

PEARSON **myeducationkit** Go to the Assignments and Activities section of Chapter 1 in MyEducationKit and complete the web activity entitled "Educational Technology Organizations." As you explore the websites, think about the resources these organizations provide for teachers and students that might support you in your classroom or school.

Organization	Publications	Web Address
AACE (Association for the Advancement of Computing in Education)	• AACE Journal • International Journal on E-Learning • Journal of Computers in Mathematics and Science Teaching • Journal of Educational Multimedia and Hypermedia • Journal of Interactive Learning Research • Journal of Technology and Teacher Education • Information Technology in Childhood Education Annual	http://www.aace.org/
AECT (Association for Educational Communications and Technology)	• Tech Trends • Educational Technology Research and Development	http://www.aect.org/
ALA (American Library Association)	• American Library Association Archives	http://www.ala.org/
ASTD (American Society for Training and Development)	• Training & Development Magazine • Technical Training Magazine	http://www.astd.org/
ISPI (International Society for Performance Improvement)	• Performance Improvement Journal • Performance Improvement Quarterly	http://www.ispi.org/
ISTE (International Society for Technology in Education)	• Learning & Leading with Technology • Journal of Research on Computing in Education	http://www.iste.org/
ITEA (International Technology Education Association)	• The Technology Teacher • Technology and Children • The Journal of Technology Education	http://www.iteawww.org/

FIGURE 1–11   Professional Organizations in the Field of Educational Technology.

TECHNOLOGY COORDINATOR'S CORNER

Background In order for you to begin to see how the information provided within the chapters of this text can be used in the real classroom setting, we will include in each chapter a short section based on the perspective of a school technology coordinator. In this section, we will highlight situations and problems commonly encountered by the coordinator and how those challenges were addressed. These problems will be presented to the coordinator by teachers with varying degrees of technology expertise who are dealing with a wide variety of students and content. You will read stories of success, frustration, excitement, and apprehension. Some teachers will provide insightful ideas that need further exploration and expansion; while others will need encouragement and help to find the proper direction for their efforts.

Each chapter's **Technology Coordinator's Corner** will integrate and illustrate the application of the key information from within that specific chapter. At times, simple, straightforward answers will be readily apparent. At other times, there may be several potentially relevant responses. In some cases, little help will be offered by the tech coordinator. All of these situations were designed to help you see the relevance of the material found within the chapter pages.

The Superintendent's Task Force Remember in the opening paragraphs of this chapter you were asked to be a member of Mr. Jackson's task force that was assembled to help the new superintendent better grasp the impact of technology being used within his school district? As a member of that group, you were asked to investigate how the technology was impacting the learning of the students within your selected school. You quickly found out that your school's tech coordinator didn't have all the answers – but she did offer some interesting insights. For example, in comparing computer use in the school a few years ago with the computer use of today, she indicated some slow, but dramatic shifts have occurred. In years past, the focus of the learning experience was on the technology itself. That is, students came to the lab to learn *about* the computer or to learn *from* the computer via content programs (e.g., math and reading tutorials). Today however, she sees many instances where the focus is on working *with* the computer in order to solve some desired problem. The focus of the students' interaction with the technology has changed to some degree. The technology is now more readily viewed as a means to get to a desired answer and not as the answer in and of itself. This shift in how the computer is viewed has had an impact on how teachers are now designing their lessons and learning experiences. In many cases, now the computer lab is a place of research and where groups of students come in to creatively discuss projects and work on solutions. Overall, the amount of time spent working on computers probably hasn't changed that much, but in some cases, there have been dramatic shifts in regard to what is being done on those computers.

SUMMARY

In this chapter, we have introduced several initial key concepts. We defined *learning* as a change, or potential to change one's level of skill or knowledge, and it is of central concern for both students and teachers. We emphasized that the design and use of effective, efficient, and appealing instruction can enhance learning.

Learning is difficult to measure and to consistently achieve because of the inherent differences in learners, content, and contexts. Facilitating learning requires an active knowledge of a variety of tools and techniques plus an understanding of how, when, and why they should be appropriately used. Educational technology includes tangible tools (high-tech hardware such as computers, and instructional media such as podcasts and videos) as well as other technologies (methods, techniques, and activities) for planning, implementing, and evaluating effective learning experiences.

Learners, teachers, and instruction all play key roles in the learning process. Furthermore, each of these roles shift as the instructional focus changes from planning, to implementing, and to evaluating instruction.

PEARSON **myeducationkit**™ To check your comprehension of the content covered in this chapter, go to the MyEducationKit for this book and complete the Study Plan for Chapter 1. Here, you will be able to take a chapter quiz, receive feedback on your answers, and then access resources that will enhance your understanding of chapter content.

SUGGESTED RESOURCES

Print Resources

Bransford, J. D., Brown, A. L., and Cocking, R. R. (2000, eds.). *How people learn: Brain, mind, experience, and school.* Washington, DC: National Academy Press.

Bruer, J. T. (1993) *Schools for thought: A science of learning in the classroom.* Cambridge, MA: The MIT Press.

Carr-Chellman, A. (2010). *Instructional design for teachers: Improving classroom practice.* Routledge.

Christensen, C., Johnson, C., & Horn, M. (2008). *Disrupting class: How disruptive innovation will change the way the world learns.* New York: McGraw-Hill.

Clark, R. C., & Mayer, R. E. (2008, 2nd ed.). *E-Learning and the science of instruction.* San Francisco, CA: Pfeiffer.

Driscoll, M. P. (2005). *Psychology of learning for instruction* (3rd ed.). Boston: Allyn & Bacon. (Chapter 1)

Harasim, L. (2009). *Learning theory, design and educational technology.* Routledge.

Jonassen, D. H., Peck, K. L., & Wilson, B. G. (1999). *Learning with technology: A constructivist approach.* Upper Saddle River, NJ: Merrill/Prentice Hall. (Chapter 1)

Jonassen, D., Howland, J., Marra, R. M., & Crismond, D. (2008). *Meaningful learning with technology* (3rd ed.). Upper Saddle River, NJ: Pearson/Merrill/Prentice Hall.

Kauchak, D. & Eggen, P. (2008, 3rd ed.). *Introduction to teaching: Becoming a professionnal.* Upper Saddle River, NJ: Pearson/Merrill/Prentice Hall.

Matzen, N. & Edmunds, J. (2007). Technology as a catalyst for change: The role of professional development. *Journal of Research on Technology in Education, 39*(4), 417–430.

Mayer, R. E. (2008, 2nd ed.) *Learning and Instruction.* Upper Saddle River, NJ: Pearson/Merrill/Prentice Hall.

Ormrod, J. E. (2008). *Human learning (5th ed.).* Upper Saddle River, NJ: Pearson/Merrill/Prentice Hall.

Reigeluth, C. (1999). Instructional design: What is it and why is it? In C. Reigeluth in *Instructional design theories and models: An overview of their current status* (pp. 3–24). Lawrence Erlbaum.

Seels, B. B., & Richey, R. C. (1994). *Instructional technology: The definition and domains of the field.* Washington, DC: Association for Educational Communications and Technology. (Chapter 1)

Schunk, D. H. (2008, 5th ed.). *Learning theories: An educational perspective.* Upper Saddle River, NJ: Pearson/Merrill/Prentice Hall.

Smaldino, S. E., Lowther, D. L., & Russell, J. D. (2008, 9th ed.). *Instructional technology and media for learning.* Upper Saddle River, NJ: Pearson/Merrill/Prentice Hall.

Smith, P. L., & Ragan, T. J. (2005, 3rd ed.). *Instructional design.* San Francisco: John Wiley & Sons/Jossey-Bass.

Spector, J., & Merrill, M. (2008). Editorial. *Distance Education, 29*(2), 123–126.

Woolfolk, A. E. (2010, 11th ed.). *Educational psychology.* Upper Saddle River, NJ: Pearson/Merrill/Prentice Hall.

Zheng, R. (2008). *Cognitive effects of multimedia learning.* Information Science Reference.

Electronic Resources

http://shifthappens.wikispaces.com/
(Shift Happens: Wikispaces)

http://www.edutopia.org/tech-integration
(Edutopia | Why Integrate Technology?)

http://techlearning.com/section/Bestpractices
(Tech & Learning | Best Practices: New Articles)

http://coe.sdsu.edu/eet/
(SDSU | Encyclopedia of Educational Technology)

http://en.wikipedia.org/wiki/Student-centered_learning
(Wikipedia | Student-centered learning)

2 Theory into Application

Source: Bob Daemmrich/PhotoEdit.

KEY WORDS AND CONCEPTS

Theory
Learning theory
Antecedent
Behavior
Learner-centered instruction

Consequence
Attention
Encoding
Retrieval

CHAPTER OBJECTIVES

After reading and studying this chapter, you will be able to:

↗ Explain theory and describe its practical value.
↗ Describe learning and how it occurs from three (behavioral, cognitive information processing, and constructivist) theoretical perspectives.

↗ Discuss the role of the instructional expert from three theoretical perspectives on learning.
↗ Discuss the role of technology from three theoretical perspectives on learning.

This chapter focuses on the concept of learning. In Chapter 1, we defined learning and discussed how understanding it will make us all better learners and better teachers. In this chapter, we discuss learning from three different perspectives: behavioral, information processing, and constructivist. We take a practical approach, describing applications of each learning theory.

 INTRODUCTION

The students in Ms. Moreno's sixth grade Spanish class are working at computer terminals on a vocabulary lesson. The computer presents students with increasingly difficult sentences in Spanish. Each sentence contains a blank space and students are asked to enter a Spanish word or phrase that fits into the sentence, such as the following:

¿ _____ te llamas?

¿ _____ viva Maria?

¿ _____ Ud. de Mexico, senora?

After students respond, the computer gives them feedback about the appropriateness of their chosen word or phrase. The computer allows for a number of "correct" responses for each sentence. When the response is correct, students move on to the next sentence. When the response is incorrect, the computer gives them a hint regarding how to translate the sentence and asks again for a response. If the response is again incorrect, the computer translates the sentence and provides several appropriate responses.

Down the hall, the students in Mr. Patrick's sixth grade Spanish class are corresponding with pen pals in Barcelona, Spain. The students work in small groups to write a letter describing current events, the history of their city, or other topics of common interest. The letter is then sent, via e-mail, to a group of students in Barcelona, who respond with a letter about the same topic. The students must then translate the letter from the Spanish students and send a reply. Because the students in Barcelona are learning English, the students correspond in Spanish for a month, in English for the following month, and so on.

Is one of these classes better than the other? No. But they are taking a very different approach to the instruction, based, in large part, on different views of how students learn and how technology can be used to support that learning. Recall from Chapter 1 that **learning** refers to a change in an individual's level of knowledge, performance, or behavior resulting from interaction with his or her environment. **Instruction** refers to the deliberate arrangement of learning conditions to maximize learning. **Educational technology** refers to the application of scientific knowledge about human learning to the practical tasks of instruction and learning. **Instructional expert** refers to an individual who uses his or her knowledge to plan, implement, and evaluate instructional activities.

This chapter will combine those concepts, using learning theory as the glue that holds them together. There are four essential points to keep in mind throughout the chapter:

↗ The purpose of teaching is learning.
↗ The teacher's primary role in learning is that of instructional expert.
↗ Educational technology can be used to help carry out that role.
↗ Learning theory should inform the use of educational technology.

 THE VALUE OF THEORY

A **theory** is an organized set of principles explaining events that take place in the environment (Schunk, 2008). Theories evolve from observations. As observations about causes and their effects accumulate, a theory attempts to explain those observations. Based on that explanation, the theory makes predictions, or hypotheses, in the form of "If x, then y" statements that can be tested, resulting in more observations, which lead to additional predictions, and so on (see Figure 2–1).

As an example, the theory of immunity was Edward Jenner's attempt to explain why milkmaids in early nineteenth-century England were less likely to catch smallpox than were most other people (Asimov, 1984). Jenner noticed that the milkmaids were *more* likely to catch cowpox, a similar but relatively minor disease. He hypothesized that individuals exposed to cowpox develop a natural protection against the disease that also protects them from smallpox. To test his theory, Jenner injected a young boy with cowpox. Two months later, he injected the same boy with smallpox. The boy did not get sick, which confirmed Jenner's theory.

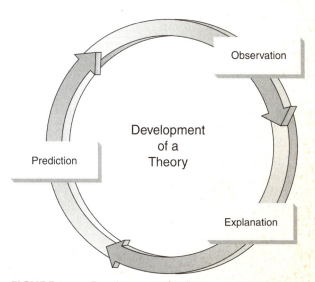

FIGURE 2–1 Development of a theory.

Edward Jenner's experiments confirmed a theory of immunity.
Source: Science Photo Library/Photo Researchers, Inc.

That is what a theory is. But the question is, "What is the practical value of theory?" First, theories offer a way to organize research studies and data. According to Schunk (2008, p. 3), theories provide "overarching frameworks" to which data can be linked. Second, theories also provide explanations for observations. For example, when Jenner observed that those who first were exposed to cowpox frequently did not contact smallpox, his theory provided a possible explanation for that observation. Third, as suggested by Ormrod (2008, p. 3), theories often generate empirically testable hypotheses and assumptions. Thus they can provide directions for asking questions, potential research objectives, and possible research methodologies that can be used to conduct further investigations.

Finally, effective professional practice requires more than knowing what tools and techniques are available and how to use them. The hallmark of professional practice is the ability to select and use tools and techniques to devise a solution that meets the demands of a particular situation. This requires the flexibility and adaptability that come from understanding at the level of theoretical principle rather than at the more superficial level of technique.

Theory informs practice in every profession. For example, thanks to Edward Jenner, physicians now routinely provide vaccinations as protection against infectious diseases such as diphtheria, measles, and the flu. The relevant principle from biology is that the body naturally develops immunity to many of the diseases it encounters.

Similarly, theory informs practice in the classroom. For example, students in a Spanish class will often practice their conversational skills together. Their progress may be slow because of their inability to give one another good feedback. The relevant principle from learning theory is that students learn best when they have frequent practice followed by *immediate* and *accurate* feedback. An instructional expert can implement this principle in live practice in the classroom or build it into a multimedia CD-ROM that encourages students to practice frequently and gives them accurate feedback for each practice.

In summary, theory is not simply a collection of abstractions that aren't relevant to the real world. Theory has *practical* value for teachers. As with other professions, the principles that form the theoretical foundation of teaching can be translated into practical guidelines. For the remainder of this chapter, we describe theories that inform instructional practice and discuss practical guidelines derived from them.

Before we begin, however, we have two caveats. First, we have not tried to include all of the theories that inform teaching practice. We focus on learning theory. Although motivational theory, communication theory, and others are important, we believe learning theory is critical because the way we teach is governed by what we know about how people learn. Second, our purpose here is *not* to provide a definitive statement of any theory. We want to outline some key features of several learning theories, and emphasize how they inform instructional practice. Thus, we will describe each theory in terms of four central questions: (1) What is learning? (2) What is the learning process? (3) What is the role of the instructional expert? and (4) What role can technology play?

LEARNING THEORY

A **learning theory** is an organized set of principles explaining how individuals learn, that is, how they acquire new knowledge and/or abilities. But we cannot describe learning theory as a single entity. Learning has been studied for hundreds (perhaps thousands) of years, and many theories have been proposed to explain it (see Driscoll, 2005; Gredler, 2009). Of these theories, we have selected three broad theoretical perspectives: behavioral, information processing, and constructivist.

These perspectives represent major trends or themes in the way learning is conceptualized and inform practice in different ways. They have different views on what learning is, how it occurs, how the instructional expert can facilitate learning, and what role technology can play. The perspectives are described briefly in Figure 2–2 and in more detail in the following sections.

It is important to note that we present these perspectives in roughly historical order rather than in order of importance. Each perspective is alive and well today and has both theoreticians and practitioners as adherents.

Behavioral Perspective

Behaviorism began in the early part of the twentieth century with the argument that "the subject matter of human psychology is the behavior *or activities of the human being*" (Watson, 1924, p. 3, italics in the original), rather

	Behavioral Perspective	Information Processing Perspective	Constructivist Perspective
What is learning?	A change in the probability of a behavior occurring	A change in knowledge stored in memory	A change in meaning constructed from experience
What is the learning process?	Antecedent → behavior → consequence	Attention → encoding → retrieval of information from memory	Continuous process of experience and reflection, often done in a group
What is the teacher's primary role?	Arrange external contingencies	Arrange conditions to support memory processes	Model and guide
What can the teacher do to carry out that role?	• State objectives • Guide student behavior with cues • Arrange reinforcing consequences to immediately follow students' behavior	• Organize new information • Link new information to existing knowledge • Use a variety of attention, encoding, and retrieval cues	• Provide opportunities to solve realistic and meaningful problems and to reflect on those experiences • Provide group learning activities • Model and guide the process of constructing knowledge within the context of mutual problem solving
What role can technology play?	Organize different kinds of materials (text, audio, video) and exercises into an instructional "program"	Help students organize new information, link it to their existing knowledge, and encode it into memory	Facilitate collaborative communication among students, instructors, and other experts Provide a variety of complex, realistic, and safe problem-solving environments
What is the student's primary responsibility?	Respond to cues	Actively synthesize information	Explore like a scientist

FIGURE 2–2   Comparing the three theoretical perspectives of learning.

than the mental phenomena, such as consciousness, that had been the subject of study during the latter part of the nineteenth century. In education, behaviorism is most closely associated with the work of B. F. Skinner. In contrast to other forms of behaviorism (such as Pavlov's classical conditioning), Skinner focused on the voluntary, deliberate behaviors that he believed made up most of an individual's behavioral repertoire. These behaviors, which he termed "operants" because they are the individual's way of operating on, or influencing, the environment, are affected by what follows them, as well as what precedes them. Understanding this type of behavior, therefore, involves understanding all of the environmental events surrounding it. Skinner developed his theory during the 1930s and began applying it to an increasingly broad array of human problems, including education, during the 1950s. He believed that, by applying behavioral principles, "the school system of any large American city could be so redesigned, at little or no additional cost, that students would come to school and apply themselves to their work with a minimum of punitive coercion and, with very rare exceptions, learn to read with reasonable ease, express themselves well in speech and writing, and solve a fair range of mathematical problems" (Skinner, 1984, p. 948).

What Is the Behaviorist Definition of Learning?

Learning has been defined in various ways. But, as we point out in Chapter 1, a central idea in those definitions is *change*. In considering these theoretical perspectives, the question becomes, "Change in what?" A primary assumption of the behaviorist perspective is that we must focus on the *behavior* of the learner and that, like other behaviors, learning is largely determined by the external environment. Within the behavioral perspective, learning is described as a change in the probability that a person will behave in a particular way in a particular situation (Ertmer & Newby, 1993).

What Is the Behaviorist Learning Process?

An A → B → C model can be used to explain how behaviorists view the learning process. The environment presents an **antecedent** (A) that prompts a **behavior** and (B) that is followed by some **consequence** (C) that then determines whether the behavior will occur again (Woolfolk, 2010). Learning is said to have occurred when students consistently behave in the desired way in response to the specific antecedent, that is, when A consistently results in B.

Students can learn without instruction, but instruction provides "special contingencies which expedite learning" (Skinner, 1968, p. 64). These contingencies are the antecedents and consequences that influence individuals' behaviors. To *shape* a behavior, teachers gradually and carefully adjust the environmental contingencies to encourage students to behave in ways that are progressively closer to the goal. For example, when learning to parallel park a car, a driving instructor may begin by asking students to park in a space that is much longer than a car. Gradually, the instructor will reduce the size of the space until students can park in a space that is only slightly longer than a car. According to Skinner (1968), well-designed instruction allows teachers to concentrate on those aspects of the learning situation that are "uniquely human": diagnosing learning needs and providing encouragement, support, and guidance.

What Is the Role of the Instructional Expert in Behaviorism?
This A → B → C framework emphasizes the influence of the external environment on learning. Instruction, then, refers to the environmental conditions presented to the students. Within the behavioral perspective, the primary responsibility of the instructional expert is to arrange these environmental conditions (antecedents and consequences) in a way that will help the students learn. This can be done by:

1. Stating instructional objectives as specific learner behaviors (B) that, when successfully performed, will indicate that learning has occurred. This involves identifying the goal and breaking that goal down into a set of simpler behaviors that can be combined to form the desired behavior.
2. Using cues (A) to guide students to the goal. Initially providing a cue will help ensure students' success by guiding them to the desired behavior. The cue can be gradually withdrawn to make sure the behavior is linked to the appropriate antecedent.
3. Using consequences (C) to reinforce desired behavior. Using consequences effectively involves two tasks. The first is to select reinforcers. Unfortunately, this is not always easy. Reinforcement is defined solely in terms of its effects on a student's behavior and, as a result, can often be determined only after the fact. In addition, different things reinforce different students and, to make matters even more complicated, the same student may be reinforced by different things at different times. Common reinforcers include praise, tangible rewards (good grades, certificates, etc.), and time spent on enjoyable activities. The second task is to arrange the selected consequences so that

they reinforce the desired behavior. Timing is critical. To be effective, the consequences should immediately follow the behavior they are meant to reinforce. Otherwise, it may reinforce an unintended behavior that does not help students progress toward the goal.

What Role Can Technology Play in Behaviorism?
Technology can be used to create an effective instructional "program." An instructional program is made up of a logical sequence of units, often called "frames." Each frame includes information along with a question, problem, or exercise that calls for a response. Students receive immediate feedback for their responses and move through the program at their own pace. The knowledge needed to move from one frame to the next is purposely kept small in order to increase the frequency of correct responses and, therefore, the frequency of reinforcement. Before the advent of the digital computer, instructional programs were built into programmed learning textbooks and mechanical teaching machines. But modern computers allow the development of instructional programs that are much more flexible and powerful. This is because computers allow us to:

- Incorporate different kinds of materials. Frames can include audio and video as well as text and pictures.
- Incorporate different kinds of exercises. Short simulations can be included along with more traditional questions.
- Monitor each student's progress. Information can be stored in the computer and retrieved at any time.
- Provide feedback that is immediate and geared to the student's response. They allow branching based on a student's response and can incorporate remedial information, if necessary.
- Set up the instruction so the students can start and stop whenever they like.

Note that a very simple version of integrating technology from a behavioral perspective would contain each of these key elements. For example, each of you will probably have some experience with the low-level flashcard-type technology. As shown in Figure 2–3, one side of the flashcard shows some type of antecedent (in this case, a term from human anatomy). When using the cards, this side of the card is presented to the student and then, after making a response, the student can turn over or flip the card and see the answer. This is very simple technology—but it easily illustrates the idea behind presenting an *antecedent* (A) to the learner (e.g., a description of an anatomical feature that must be identified), which is followed by a *behavioral response* (B) from the learner (e.g., a response in the form of the student generating a proper name that matches the description of the anatomical

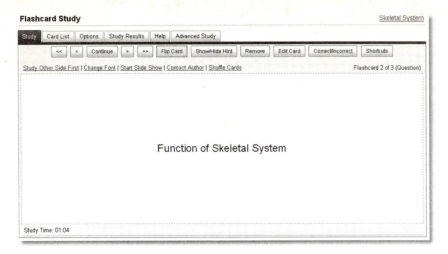

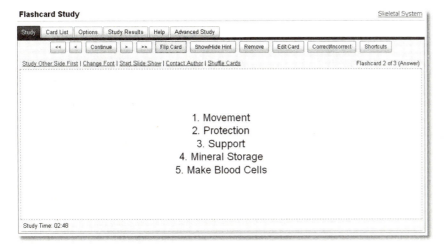

FIGURE 2–3 Electronic flash cards used to study elements of human anatomy.

Source: Reprinted with permission of the Tuolumne Technology Group, Inc.

feature), which is followed by a *consequence* (C) (e.g., turning over the card and matching the proper answer with the response that was generated – if correct the feedback is rewarding).

These same simple principles are also reflected in most computer-assisted instructional programs. For example, review the screen of the math program shown in Figure 2–4. Note the stimulus that is presented (equation on the submarine captain's table), the required behavioral response by the learner (identify the correct answer on one of the fish and click it with the mouse), and then the immediate feedback that is supplied. In addition, this program can increase its power by adding a number of sophisticated features. For example, performance levels of the learner can be electronically monitored and as mastery of simple problems is achieved, more challenging problems can be automatically introduced. Conversely, if continual mistakes are made with a certain type of problem, additional review problems can be interjected by the program. If the individual needs to stop work for a period of time, the computer program can remember where the student was and return to that location immediately upon his/her return. Even more sophisticated computer assistance can be shown in

programs that monitor the types of mistakes that are being made and give tailored feedback to help a student overcome a specific learning difficulty. An element might also be added allowing the software to monitor when a specific type of problem has been mastered and automatically introduce problems at the next level of difficulty. However, it also periodically reintroduces the "mastered" problems in order to help the learner maintain high levels of retention. Additionally, motivational incentives can be added (scoring elements that give students additional levels of achievement to obtain, rewards, etc.) that help the learner invest greater amounts of effort and maintain attention to the task for longer periods of time.

Using the computer's power, these types of sophisticated drill and practice elements can be added to other tutorial, simulation, and problem-solving programs so that learners can be taught independently, in a self-paced learning fashion that may include all types of needed enrichment and/or remediation activities. Behavioral principles illustrated within the simple flashcard-type drill and practice activity have become quite powerful when teamed with the power of the computer.

FIGURE 2–4 A screen from Stickybear Math Splash, a popular drill and practice computer program.

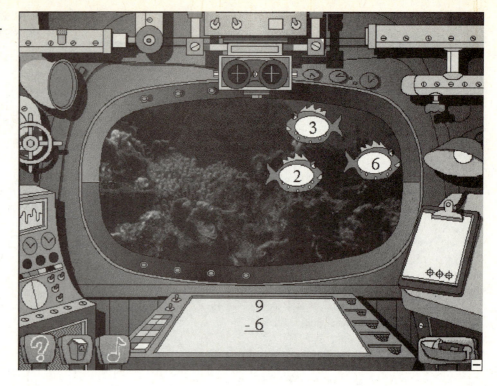

Source: Stickybear's Math Splash, Optimum Resources, Inc.

Information Processing Perspective

Behaviorism developed as a reaction to the study of mental phenomena, such as consciousness, that had characterized nineteenth-century psychology. In a similar way, cognitive psychology developed as a reaction to behaviorism. Cognitive psychology "was officially recognized around 1956" (Gardner, 1985, p. 28), in large part because of a growing dissatisfaction with behaviorism's inability to adequately explain complex behaviors such as language acquisition. For example, at a 1948 symposium on "Cerebral Mechanisms in Behavior," Karl Lashley argued that when people use language, their behavior is so rapid and continuous that it could not possibly be controlled by external prompts alone, as behaviorism would suggest (Gardner, 1985). Their behavior must be organized and planned in advance, using processes that occur internally in the mind. Lashley used language as his primary example, but he argued that most human behavior is similarly complex and governed by mental processes.

The perceived limitations of behaviorism led to a search for new ways of explaining human learning. At the same time, rapid technological advances led to the development of the high-speed computer as a mechanism for swiftly manipulating large amounts of information. As these two trends came together, one result was the development of the information processing view of human cognition, using the computer as a model for the way humans think. While this view is not the only one that has developed from cognitive psychology (see Driscoll, 2005, for descriptions of other cognitive theories of learning), it has been a prominent view that has influenced instructional practice. The cognitive information processing perspective suggests that, like a computer, the mind takes information in, organizes it, stores it for later use, and retrieves it from memory. With the growth of cognitive psychology the focus was again on the mind, as it had been before the advent of behaviorism. However, using computer models and other laboratory methods (e.g., reaction-time tests), cognitive scientists were able to quantify mental functions with much more scientific rigor than before.

What Is the Information Processing Definition of Learning?   The behavioral perspective emphasizes the influence of the *external* environment. In contrast, the information processing perspective has an *internal* focus. Learning is described as a change in knowledge stored in memory. The central principle is that most behavior, including learning, is governed by internal memory rather than external circumstances. Understanding learning, therefore, requires understanding how memory works.

What Is the Information Processing Learning Process?   Human memory is active rather than passive. That is, it does not simply receive information. It actively synthesizes and organizes information, integrating it with knowledge already stored in memory. As shown in Figure 2–5, this involves three processes: attention, encoding, and retrieval (Driscoll, 2005). **Attention** refers to the process of taking in some information from the environment while ignoring other information. **Encoding** refers to the process of translating information into some meaningful, memorable form. **Retrieval**

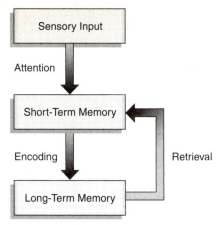

FIGURE 2–5 Role of attention, encoding, and retrieval in human memory.

refers to the process of recalling information for a particular purpose. Learning is said to have occurred when individuals encode information in a way that allows them to easily recall that information from memory and effectively use it in a particular situation.

As a way of understanding how these memory processes work, imagine a library receiving new books and subsequently making them accessible to its patrons (Stepich & Newby, 1988). A library continually receives information about new books and selects some of those books for addition to its collection (attention). New books that are selected are cataloged using a classification scheme such as the Dewey Decimal System (encoding). This places the new books into coherent categories and allows related books to appear on the shelves near one another. It also provides a search cue (a catalog number) to help someone find the books later. To locate a particular book in the library, an individual begins with the search cue and searches the shelves for the desired book, perhaps at the same time scanning the shelves for other relevant books (retrieval).

Memory works in a similar way. Humans are constantly bombarded with information from the environment and select only some of it to remember (attention). New information is considered in light of what is already known and integrated into existing knowledge whenever possible (encoding). This creates a coherent organization that makes new information more meaningful and allows related information to be linked together. It also provides a search cue that makes it easier to find information at a later time. In order to recall information from memory, an individual begins with the search cue and searches memory for the desired information, perhaps at the same time scanning memory for other relevant information (retrieval).

There is, of course, at least one significant difference between memory and a library. A library keeps physical objects (books) in specific places (shelves). In contrast, the facts and ideas that make up memory are not physical objects, and we cannot yet pinpoint where in the brain specific memories reside. However, the processes of attention, encoding, and retrieval are similar.

What Is the Role of the Instructional Expert in Information Processing? The emphasis of the information processing perspective is on students' cognitive processes and on the critical role memory plays in helping them translate new information into a form that they can remember and use. Instruction, then, involves a deliberate effort to help students make this translation. Within the information processing perspective, the primary responsibility of the instructional expert is to create conditions that will support these cognitive processes. This involves:

- Organizing new information. Because humans actively seek order in information as a way of making sense of it, new information will be easier to encode if it is organized in some explicit way.
- Carefully linking new information to existing knowledge. This linking makes information more meaningful and, thus, more easily learned.
- Using various memory aids (such as highlighting, mnemonics, analogies, and imagery)—techniques designed to help students attend to important information, encode that information into a memorable form, and retrieve that information when needed.

What Role Can Technology Play in Information Processing? Again, the behavioral perspective focuses heavily on getting passive learners to respond in appropriate ways through the environment providing structured cues and associated contingencies. From the information processing perspective the view is of a much more active learner who continually seeks ways to better organize and assimilate new information with that which is already known and experienced by the learner. From this perspective, technology can be useful by providing means to facilitate the organization, chunking, linking, assimilation, and accommodation of new information within memory. For example, software that is used to help chunk large amounts of information and perhaps put it into some readily usable outline would be useful to the learner. Inspiration is a type of software that allows individuals to quickly brainstorm ideas, organize one's thoughts in a visual manner, and show relationships between key elements. Figure 2–6 shows a small concept map that was created using this software to help the learner recognize the key elements within the targeted concept.

Another example would be how individuals learn to gather and use information from the Web. The Web, at times, can become overwhelming because of all the information that one can access. Software, such as that included as part of the WISE science project at the

FIGURE 2–6 Example of a concept map (controlling bleeding) created with brainstorming software (e.g., Inspiration).

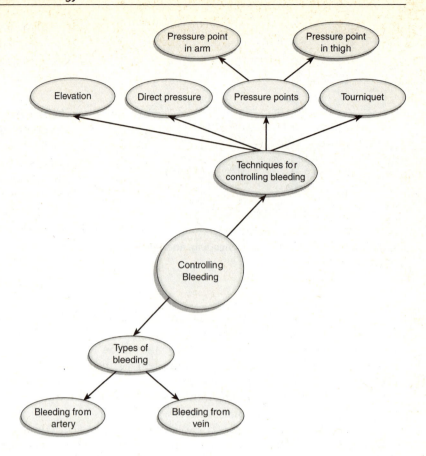

University of California at Berkeley (Williams & Linn, 2002), guides students through basic information pages that give the overall content, but then also facilitates information processing by providing tools that offer hints on how to organize, places to make journal entries for student reflections, and other tools to facilitate discussions between students, the visualization of data, and how to assess the information they have gathered. Each of these tools has been designed to help the learner organize and process information (see Figure 2–7).

There are other technology tools that are also closely aligned with this perspective. For example, tools that help a student visualize data (e.g., charts in a spreadsheet program) or help a student see information in a different or perhaps more relevant way (e.g., tables created within a word processing program). As an example, review Figure 2–2 on page 27. This contains a wealth of comparison information about the three different learning theory perspectives. Use of a word processing function that allows for such a table to be constructed facilitates the learning of those creating the table, as well as helping structure it in a fashion that may be readily encoded by those using the table to acquire and assimilate/process the presented information. As the technology has allowed for easier development, revision, and publishing of such table features, there has been a significant increase in its use.

Multimedia programs that incorporate audio, textual, as well as pictorial information are also programs that help learners more readily recognize meaningful prior learning and how the new information relates. A multimedia software program (see Figure 2–8) about the history of the civil rights movement, for example, may include pictures of relevant individuals, sound clips from important speeches, video clips of key events and news stories, and music and sounds from the era. Providing students with the opportunity to "experience" the civil rights movement from a number of different perspectives should allow them to make needed connections.

One note should be made. A technology tool may include elements of the behaviorist perspective, along with the information processing perspective. For example, the civil rights multimedia experience may include a tutorial or drill and practice piece that incorporates an antecedent that prompts a behavior that is followed by a consequence. This kind of combination of elements is often seen within various types of educational software.

Constructivist Perspective

Constructivism is a relatively recent term used to represent a collection of theories, including (among others) generative learning (Wittrock, 1990), discovery learning (Bruner, 1961), and situated learning (Brown, Collins, & Duguid, 1989). The common thread among these theories is the idea that individuals actively construct knowledge by working to solve realistic problems, usually in collaboration with others (Duffy, Lowyck, & Jonassen, 1993).

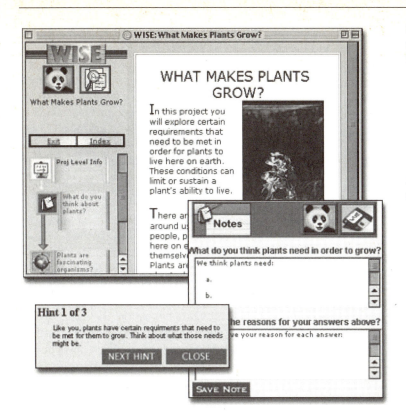

FIGURE 2–7   A screen showing how the WISE website guides students as they gather and process information.

Source: Reprinted with permission from University of California, Berkeley.

FIGURE 2–8   Use of multimedia software to facilitate learning from multiple sources such as visuals, audio, and text materials.

Source: Reprinted with permission from ABC-CLIO.

While the label is relatively recent, the ideas that make up constructivism have been around for a long time. As early as 1897, for example, Dewey argued that "education must be conceived as a continuous reconstruction of experience" (1897, p. 91) that occurs through "the stimulation of the child's powers by the demand of the social situations in which he finds himself" (1897, p. 84). In the middle of the twentieth century, the idea that knowledge is constructed through social collaboration can be found in the theories of Piaget, Bruner, and Vygotsky (Driscoll, 2005).

What Is the Constructivist Definition of Learning?

The constructivist perspective describes learning as a change in meaning constructed from experience. On the surface, this seems the same as the information processing definition of learning. But there is a critical difference in the way the two perspectives define knowledge (Jonassen, 1991). The information processing perspective defines knowledge as an *objective representation* of experience, whereas the constructivist perspective defines it as a *subjective interpretation* of experience.

An analogy will help illustrate this critical difference. In the information processing perspective, the mind is like a mirror, accurately reflecting the objects and events in our experience. The assumption is that knowledge is objective and can be described as separate from the knower. In other words, regardless of whose mirror is used, the picture in the mirror is essentially the same. Learning, then, refers to the *acquisition* of new representations. In the constructivist perspective, on the other hand, the mind is like a lens. When we look through our lens, some aspects of our experience are in sharp focus, some are fuzzy, and some cannot be seen at all. The assumption in the constructivist perspective is that knowledge cannot be separated from the knower. In other words, the picture we see is determined by the lens we use. Learning, then, refers to the construction of new interpretations.

Thus, knowledge construction is a process of thinking about and interpreting experience. And because each individual has a unique set of experiences, seen through a unique lens, each individual constructs a unique body of knowledge. Learning is said to have occurred when our knowledge is changed in a way that allows us to interpret our experience in a more complete, complex, or refined way, that is, when our lens allows us to see something that we could not see before or to see things in sharper focus.

What Is the Constructivist Learning Process? A basic premise underlying constructivism is that knowledge is constructed as learners try to make sense of their experiences. Learning, then, is a continuous process of experience and reflection in which learners create, test, and refine mental models that will synthesize their experience. Mental models are dynamic. As a learner's experience grows, his/her mental models become richer, meaning that they incorporate a wider range of experience. In addition, mental models do not necessarily correspond to any objective, external reality. What is important is that a mental model is useful and viable, that is, that it represents the individual learner's existing experience in a way that makes sense to him/her at the time.

There is some debate about exactly how this knowledge construction occurs (Phillips, 1995). Some constructivist theories (sometimes referred to as radical constructivism) focus on the individual learner, suggesting that constructing knowledge is a matter of individual interpretation. Other theories (sometimes referred to as social constructivism) focus on social interaction among individuals, suggesting that constructing knowledge is a matter of dialog leading to a shared interpretation. In general, however, this is a matter of degree and most constructivist theories incorporate both individual and social perspectives.

What Is the Role of the Instructional Expert in Constructivism? According the constructivist perspective, learning is determined by the complex interplay among students' existing knowledge, the social context, and the problem to be solved. Instruction, then, refers to providing students with a collaborative situation in which they have both the means and the opportunity to construct "new and situationally-specific understandings by assembling prior knowledge from diverse sources" (Ertmer & Newby, 1993, p. 63). From a constructivist perspective, the primary responsibility of the instructional expert is to create and maintain a learning environment that has two essential characteristics: learning in context and collaboration.

Learning in Context. According to the constructivist perspective, knowledge is like a muscle: It grows when it is used. Therefore, constructivist instruction asks students to put their knowledge to work within the context of solving realistic and meaningful problems. The idea is that when they work to apply their knowledge to a specific problem, students will naturally explore their knowledge and this will, in turn, lead to the continual refinement of that knowledge. However, not all problems are equally effective. To be effective, a problem should:

↗ Be seen by students as relevant and interesting.
↗ Be realistically complex.
↗ Require students to use their knowledge.

Collaboration. From the constructivist perspective, students learn through interaction with others. This collaboration has two basic aspects. The first involves relationships among students. Students work together as peers, applying their combined knowledge to the solution of the problem. The resulting dialog provides students with ongoing opportunities to explore alternative interpretations and to test and refine their understanding. The second aspect of collaboration involves the role of the teacher. Constructivist instruction has been likened to an apprenticeship in which teachers participate *with* students in solving meaningful and realistic problems (Collins, Brown, & Holum, 1991; Rogoff, 1990). This does not mean that the teacher knows "the answer" to the problem. In fact, the problem may be just as new to the teacher as it is to the students. However, teachers are probably more familiar with the processes of solving problems and constructing knowledge. Teachers, therefore, serve as models and guides, showing students how to reflect on their evolving knowledge and providing direction when they are having difficulty. Learning is shared. Teachers are likely to learn as much as students. Responsibility for instruction is also shared. As much as possible, students determine their own learning needs, set their own goals, and monitor their own progress. The amount of guidance teachers provide depends on students' knowledge level and experience.

What Role Can Technology Play in Constructivism? With the advancement of technology, we have moved from an industrial to a more informational age (see Reigeluth, 1999, Chapter 1). Technology has allowed us to gain greater access to more types of information than ever before. As this shift has developed, a need has been created for individuals who can more readily process information and make decisions based on that information. Instead of a focus on memorizing standard procedures, our world now requires us to access information, analyze it, and synthesize it in order to create novel solutions to problems that are often "ill-defined" (problems that don't have clear, easy solutions). With the access to more information has come a greater demand for higher-level problem solving by a greater number of individuals. Technology has created an environment in which more (higher levels of learning and problem solving) is expected from the learner.

Not only has the advancement of technology generated new types of demands on learners, but in many ways it has also begun to be used as a means to teach and educate learners to accomplish those higher-order tasks. Let's take a look at several ways that technology has been used to accentuate key constructivist elements.

First, a key element within this perspective is **social interaction.** Technology now allows for groups of students to interact with each other face-to-face, as well as across great distances. For example, recently a course at Purdue University was taught by preservice teachers observing and participating in a class of fifth-grade students at a school that had a high number of non-English-speaking students. This was a very good experience for the preservice teachers to see how such a class was organized and how the teachers worked with the various students. However, the preservice teachers were located 70 miles away from the classroom they were observing. Through the use of two-way live video and audio technology, connections were established and students in both classes could see, ask questions, and exchange ideas with those in the other class (Phillion, Johnson, & Lehman, 2004). Instead of just reading about the benefits and challenges of such a classroom situation, as shown in the photo of this page, this technology allowed the students to experience what it was like to actually be there and exchange ideas on what works and what needs to be refined.

Synchronous interchange between students at two different locations via distance education technology.
Source: Bob Daemmrich/PhotoEdit.

Other forms of communication (e.g., e-mail, instant messaging, social networking) have also opened up new ways of having students interact at a greater level than ever before. Students, for example, have greater access to content experts and can gain from their insights and thoughts. For example, e-mail exchanges between students and subject matter experts such as scientists, authors, politicians, sports stars, etc., are now readily accomplished. The technology has made it relatively easy and fast to gain access to individuals who previously would not have had the time or means to respond and offer their expertise. In addition, this same technology allows for ready access to one's classroom teacher and to fellow students. Social interaction within small-group exercises can also be enhanced as students can discuss and share ideas even when they are not in the same location.

Second, the constructivist perspective views the learner as **actively creating meaning** from what is encountered in the environment. Active participation is a key to learning. The use of technology has facilitated this participation in a number of ways. For example, hypermedia software allows students to actively create projects. Instead of just reading about the Serengeti plains in Africa, students can create multimedia programs about this part of the world. Use of the Internet to explore current research, photos, and videos can help students not only learn about it but also retain what they learn. Students learn about the Serengeti and about planning a project, working cooperatively with others, developing skills with various forms of software, presenting information in a way that others can understand, and so on.

The construction of meaning can also be enhanced through learners interacting with models and working within apprenticeships. Technology has allowed students more ready access to models of specific types of behaviors and skills. Think about how the high school art teacher within a summer apprenticeship program may be able to work closely with a master sculptor—even though the master may be in another part of the world. Through technology, the learner can monitor and observe the master's techniques, attempt various new skills, and ask for direct feedback on his or her creations. It may not be a perfect substitution for actually having the master in the same studio, but it will provide a greater degree of learning than if no contact was possible.

Finally, from the constructivist perspective, meaningful learning occurs within an environment that resembles the real world, which is often a very **complex environment.** Finding such a complex environment that is conducive to the needs of the learner is often difficult, if not impossible. For example, training firefighters about the complex nature of fighting high-rise fires is difficult unless one is actually working on such a fire. Teaching student drivers to react appropriately to small children running in front of them as they drive down a suburban street is also difficult and dangerous to achieve in a

planned learning environment. Technology has been introduced to meet such learning needs. Simulations have been helpful in creating similar complex environments that may be more convenient, reliable, and less dangerous for the participants. Advanced flight simulators, for example, allow pilots to be repeatedly exposed to all types of mechanical, weather, or passenger-related problems, without incurring the severe cost of time, money, and health risks that could be imposed in a real-world environment. In the classroom environment, many types of instructional simulations have been developed for students to learn about such topics as solving problems of drug abuse, prejudice, the environment, as well as what it would be like to be a participant in such events as the Revolutionary War, the gold rush of 1849, or even to be a New York City resident on September 11, 2001. An example is "Decisions, Decisions Online" from Tom Snyder Productions (see Figure 2–9). This software asks students

FIGURE 2–9 Screen shots showing how technology can be used to present students with complex problems.

Source: Reprinted with permission from Tom Snyder Productions, www.tomsnyder.com

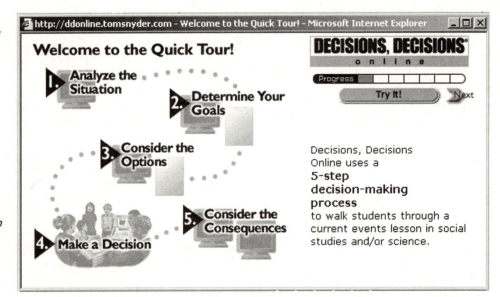

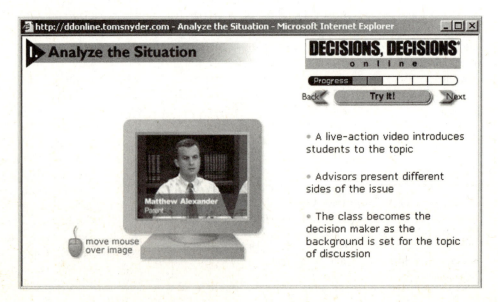

to work together, following a five-step process, to find a solution to a complex social issue, such as Internet censorship, television violence, or cloning. Throughout the process, the software provides live-action video access to advisors who help to explain the issues and the implications of the solution the students have chosen. Using technology in this way leads to greater levels of meaningful learning, allowing students to acquire knowledge and experience that previously took years in the real world to acquire.

PEARSON **myeducationkit**™ Go to the Assignments and Activities section of Chapter 2 in MyEducationKit and complete the activity entitled "Authentic Learning with Technology." As you view the video for this activity, think about how these activities were organized to engage and challenge students. Consider the theoretical principles underlying this approach.

A SHIFT IN THE ROLES OF TEACHERS AND STUDENTS

An important question is, "Why do we have or need different learning theories?" To come to an understanding of why different theories have evolved, think about the "traditional" classroom setting. For most, this will conjure up thoughts of a room with rows of desks and chairs. The traditional view of teaching and learning is one in which the teacher stands and delivers the content, while students sit and receive.

This view places the control of all learning in the hands of the teacher. It assumes only a slight diversity in the manner in which most students assimilate information. For some types of learning, mostly those dealing with basic rote skills, this traditional approach has proven quite efficient.

In today's world, however, demands on the learner have increased substantially. Where once it may have been sufficient to learn rote responses within given working environments, now the real world demands individuals use social collaboration, team work, and high-order reasoning skills to solve complex problems. Access and accountability for solving complex problems are no longer left to the few; all individuals, whether they are working on an assembly line or in a corporate think tank, need problem-solving skills. As stated by Driscoll (2005), no longer should learners be viewed as "empty vessels waiting to be filled, but rather active organisms seeking meaning" (p. 387). Learners must now be viewed as proactive participants in learning, actively seeking ways to analyze, question, interpret, synthesize, and understand their ever-changing environment.

From another viewpoint, think about the average classroom from 90 years ago and the demands placed on the classroom teacher. The majority of students, and

teachers as well, came from homogeneous backgrounds (e.g., grew up in the same town, raised in two-parent families, one parent was home to raise the children, less mobility). Today, the diversity among class members is much greater. With that diversity comes the challenge of different learning styles, greater differences in background experiences, varied home life settings, and so on. Classrooms of today are much more diversified, leading to more complex learning challenges for teachers and students alike (Kauchak & Eggen, 2008, pp. 24–25).

The Role of Technology in the Shift to More Learner-Centered Instruction Today we live in an age of lightning-fast information transfer. Technology has allowed individuals to obtain, assemble, analyze, and communicate information in more detail and at a much faster pace than ever before possible. One consequence of this is the ever-increasing demand on education to help all learners acquire higher-level skills that allow them to more readily analyze, make decisions, and solve complex "real-world" problems. According to Bruer (1993), learners must rise above the rote, factual level to begin to think critically and creatively. These increased demands dictate changes in the way teachers interact with students; moreover, these changes must be grounded in an understanding of how a diverse population of individuals learns.

Throughout this text, we give examples of many techniques, methods, and technologies for helping learners acquire new knowledge. We understand that at times you will engage your students in lower-level, rote learning, and as needed we describe techniques to help learners acquire factual information. (For example, we highlight the use of mnemonics or specific drill and practice techniques for basic-level learning.) In such cases, the teacher-centered "traditional" view of teaching may prove most efficient and effective.

Of particular importance, however, will be teaching the higher-order skills and the manner in which students acquire them. A major emphasis must be on problem solving and transfer. We emphasize the use of such methods as simulations, discovery, problem solving, and cooperative groups for learners to experience and solve real-world problems. In these cases, you will note a shift in the manner in which the learning experience is planned and carried out. Instead of the traditional teacher's total control and manipulation, the importance of the learner's role in planning, implementation, and self-evaluation will be emphasized. Learners engaged in **learner-centered instruction** proactively engage with various sources of potential information (e.g., peers, the teacher, technology, parents, media) to gain insights into a problem and its possible solutions. The teacher's role shifts to one of guide and facilitator who assists learners in achieving understanding and their ultimate learning goals.

Figure 2–10 highlights several key changes in the roles of the teacher and the learners within a

For the STUDENT	
A Shift From:	A Shift To:
Passively waiting for the teacher to give directions and information	Actively searching for needed information and learning experiences, determining what is needed, and seeking ways to attain it
Always being in the role of the learner	Participating at times as the expert/knowledge provider
Always following given procedures	Desiring to explore, discover, and create unique solutions to learning problems
Viewing the teacher as the one who has all of the answers	Viewing the teacher as a resource, model, and helper who will encourage exploration and attempts to find unique solutions to problems
For the TEACHER	
A Shift From:	A Shift To:
Always being viewed as the content expert and source for all of the answers	Participating at times as one who may not know it all, but desires to learn
Being viewed as the primary source of information who continually directs it to students	Being viewed as a support, collaborator, and coach for students as they learn to gather and evaluate information for themselves
Always asking the questions and controlling the focus of student learning	Actively coaching students to develop and pose their own questions and explore their own alternative ways of finding answers
Directing students through preset step-by-step exercises so that all achieve similar conclusions	Actively encouraging individuals to use their personal knowledge and skills to create unique solutions to problems

FIGURE 2–10   Key role changes in a learner-centered environment.

learner-centered environment. As you reflect on these changing roles, imagine the impact they have on the manner in which you plan and carry out instruction. We want to emphasize that because of the diversity in both learners and information, a single approach to all instruction will not always work: A number of different methods and media exist for designing and developing learning experiences, and the roles of learner and teacher shift based on the situation, the content, and the special needs of the individuals involved.

 ## SELECTING THEORETICAL PRINCIPLES

Learning theory has been defined as an attempt to explain how people acquire new knowledge and skills. We have presented three perspectives on learning and, because these three perspectives view learning in distinctly different ways, you might ask, *Which theory is best?* While this is a natural question, we believe it isn't the right one to ask. It is similar to asking, *Which food is best?* The inevitable answer is that no one food is best. We should eat a variety of foods, because each one contributes something to good nutrition. Similarly, we believe that teachers should understand a variety of theoretical perspectives because each perspective contributes something to good instruction.

Principles from the different theories can be applied to virtually any learning situation. For example, reinforcement (from the behavioral perspective), organized

information (from the information processing perspective), and learning from one another (from the constructivist perspective) are principles that will be useful in virtually every instructional situation. At the same time, however, some theories fit some learning situations better than others. Ertmer and Newby (1993) suggest that this fit depends on two critical factors: students' knowledge level and the amount of thought and reflection required by the learning task. As Figure 2–11 shows, students with little content knowledge are likely to benefit most from learning strategies based on the behavioral perspective. As students' knowledge grows, the emphasis may shift to the information processing perspective and then the constructivist perspective. In the same way, learning tasks requiring little thought and reflection (e.g., memorizing facts, following a rote procedure) are also likely to benefit most from behavioral learning strategies. As the amount of thought required by the learning task increases (e.g., finding unique solutions to "old" problems, inductive reasoning, creative thinking), the emphasis may shift to the information processing and then the constructivist perspective.

The shift from behavioral to information processing to constructivist strategies involves an important shift in the extent to which the students direct their own learning. With behavioral strategies, responsibility lies almost entirely with the teacher (i.e., a more teacher-centered approach–see Figure 2–11). Students learn by responding to cues the teacher builds into the environment. In contrast, with constructivist strategies, the teacher and students share

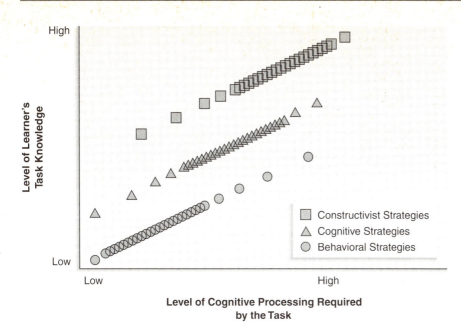

FIGURE 2–11   A heuristic guide for selecting principles from the three theoretical perspectives on learning.

Note: Copyright 1993 by the Learning Systems Institute, Florida State University, Suite 4600 University Center, Bldg. C. Tallahassee, FL 32306-2540. Reprinted by permission from Performance Improvement Quarterly.

responsibility for directing learning (i.e., a more learner-centered approach–see Figure 2–11). Students learn by collaborating with one another and with the teacher to solve mutually determined problems. Information processing strategies occupy a middle ground. Teachers may present the cognitive supports that facilitate effective information processing or students may develop these supports for their own use.

TECHNOLOGY COORDINATOR'S CORNER

Lexy Bowman was getting increasingly bored as she sat in the media center reviewing advertisements for newly released software. As her mind wandered, she began to listen in on a nearby conversation between a couple of student teachers who were currently in the middle of their teaching assignment at the high school. Both were in the media center looking for materials for an upcoming unit they were teaching in their government classes. They were worried that it was going to be difficult to get high school students interested in the traditional legislative process. Having them actually learn the key concepts and the steps of the process was going to be even more challenging.

Lexy listened for a while and then offered a few suggestions that the young teachers might want to consider. Above all else, she suggested, the students needed to become active participants in the learning process. One suggestion might be to use an available software simulation that allowed small groups of students to take on different insiders' roles within the U.S. government (e.g., a senator's aide, a researcher for a specific lobbying group, a presidential cabinet member) and then experience what is required to promote a good idea into a law. Learning about procedures, negotiations, and compromise are outcomes that often result from this experience. Past students have reported that these case studies helped them to appreciate the complexity involved in the whole legislative process.

A second idea was to have the students identify a local problem and get involved with the city government to try to promote a solution. Reducing property damage caused by skate boarders and inline skaters might be one possibility the students could find personally relevant and of interest. Groups could be formed to research what other cities have done to curb the problem, the city council representative with whom they would discuss this problem, how to develop and present a proposal for a solution, and so on. Lexy offered to assist the classes with the use of technology such as the Internet sites to access relevant information, brainstorming and flowcharting software to formulate ideas on what could be done and how to proceed, and other software needed to write proposals, make the formal contacts, create awareness in the community, and create and deliver presentations about their solutions. Lexy acknowledged that such a plan would take additional time and effort to implement, but the benefits for the students in what they recall later and how they use and transfer that information to other complex real-world problems should make this time well spent.

SUMMARY

As a teacher, your primary role, that of instructional expert, is based on a theoretical foundation. In every profession, including teaching, theory informs practice. This means that theory offers a set of consistent principles teachers may use to create solutions to a variety of unique problems. As in other professions, understanding theory allows teachers to select the tools and techniques that will work best with specific students and learning goals, apply those principles in a coherent manner, and adapt instruction as students' needs change.

Instructional practice is built on a diverse theoretical foundation, with learning theory as the critical cornerstone. In this chapter, we have described three broad categories of learning theory—behavioral, information processing, and constructivist—in terms of their central principles, their applications to your role of instructional expert, and the part technology can play in carrying out that role. Just as different foods contribute to good nutrition, different learning theories contribute to good instruction.

PEARSON **myeducationkit** To check your comprehension of the content covered in this chapter, go to the MyEducationKit for this book and complete the Study Plan for Chapter 2. Here, you will be able to take a chapter quiz, receive feedback on your answers, and then access resources that will enhance your understanding of chapter content.

SUGGESTED RESOURCES

Print Resources

Bigge, M., & Shermis, S. (2003). *Learning theories for teachers.* Allyn & Bacon.

Cronje, J. (2006). Paradigms regained: Toward integrating objectivism and constructivism in instructional design and the learning sciences. *Educational Technology Research and Development, 54*(4), 387–416.

Driscoll, M. P. (2005). *Psychology of learning for instruction* (3rd ed.). Boston: Allyn & Bacon.

Ertmer, P. A., & Newby, T. J. (1993). Behaviorism, cognitivism, constructivism: Comparing critical features from an instructional design perspective. *Performance Improvement Quarterly, 6*(4), 50–72.

Jonassen, D. (Ed.). (2004). *Handbook of research for educational communication and technology.* Mahwah, NJ: Lawrence Erlbaum Associates.

Orey, M. (Ed.). (2001). Emerging perspectives on learning, teaching, and technology. Retrieved June 9, 2009 from http://projects.coe.uga.edu/epltt/

Woolfolk, A. (2010). *Educational Psychology (11th ed.).* Upper Saddle River, NJ: Merrill.

Electronic Resources

http://tip.psychology.org/
(Theory into Practice)

http://my-ecoach.com/idtimeline/learningtheory .html
(Instructional Development Timeline: Learning Theory)

http://www.innovativelearning.com/teaching/ teaching_methods.html
(Innovative Learning: Teaching Theories)

http://carbon.cudenver.edu/~mryder/itc_data/ idmodels.html
(Martin Ryder, University of Colorado at Denver: Instructional Design Models)

http://www.emtech.net/learning_theories.htm
(Learning Theories: Links to articles and descriptions)

http://carolyn.jlcarroll.net/LearnThrySite.html
(Learning Theory MindMap Site: Study Aids for Visual Learners)

http://www.sjsu.edu/depts/it/mcgriff/kbase/ theory.html
(Steven J. McGriff: Knowledgebase – Theories)

http://en.wikipedia.org/wiki/Learning_theory_ (education)
(Wikipedia: Learning theory)

3

Computers and Computer Tools for Teaching and Learning

Source: Peter Skinner/Photo Researchers, Inc.

KEY WORDS AND CONCEPTS

Hardware
Software
Personal computer
Processor
Memory
Ergonomics
Word processor

Graphic
Spreadsheet
Database
Presentation software
Authoring software
Assistive technology

CHAPTER OBJECTIVES

After reading and studying this chapter, you will be able to:

↗ Identify and describe the functions of the main hardware components of a computer system (processor, internal memory, mass storage, input and output devices).

↗ Define software, and identify examples of systems software and applications software.

↗ Discuss factors to consider when evaluating computer systems.

↗ Describe basic troubleshooting techniques to use to resolve routine computer hardware and software problems that can occur in the classroom.

↗ Describe ways to maintain a healthy and safe environment for using computers.

- Describe educational applications in which the computer can be used as a teacher or an assistant.
- Describe each of the major categories of software productivity tools discussed in this chapter (word processor, graphics, database, spreadsheet, presentation software, multimedia/hypermedia authoring package, telecommunication tool).

- Describe three examples of teacher and/or student uses of each of the major computer productivity tools discussed in this chapter.
- Describe how assistive technology can be used to assist students with special needs.

In Chapters 1 and 2, we introduced you to educational technology, and we presented fundamental concepts of learning and the theories that help us to understand it. In this chapter, we introduce the computer, a multifaceted tool that can be of benefit to you and your students in many different ways. Common computer productivity tools that you can use to design, develop, and evaluate instruction are described. In Chapter 4, we will move on to look at the instructional planning process.

INTRODUCTION

Mary Jordan is a veteran sixth grade teacher at Spring Valley Middle School. Just before the start of the school year, she got a letter from the school district's technology coordinator, Bob Jones, informing her that the district was installing new computer hardware and software throughout the building. Brand new systems equipped with the latest editions of Microsoft *Windows* and *Office* would be installed in the computer lab, and each classroom would now have several computers including one dedicated to the teacher's use. All the computers would be equipped with the latest productivity applications including word processor, spreadsheet, presentation software, and more. The letter emphasized that teachers were expected to learn how to take care of the hardware and use the software effectively for their own work and for students' learning. An in-service workshop was planned for the week before the start of school to orient the teachers to the new computers and productivity software.

Mary had a sense of unease as she finished reading the letter. Though she knew she should be happy that the district was providing new computers, she was anxious about the changeover to new equipment and software. She had reached a certain level of comfort with the old computers and software, but she felt overwhelmed by what she would have to learn. She had heard from colleagues in other schools that the new *Office* was significantly different from the version she was used to, and, like many teachers, she felt she did not have the time to learn how to use new computers and applications on top of everything else she had to do. Many questions ran through her mind. What will I need to know about the computers? Will I be able to deal with any problems that might arise? What are the key computer applications I should know? How can I use the computer both for myself and with my students?

As you read this chapter, imagine that you are in Mary's shoes. As a future teacher, what will you need to know about computers and computer software? This chapter provides basic information about computers and computer hardware as well as information about computer software and those productivity applications that teachers use most often. This information will provide the basic foundation that you will need as we go forward in this book to examine the design and development of learning experiences that integrate technology to enhance the learning experience for students.

UNDERSTANDING COMPUTER SYSTEMS

In popular terms, the word *computer* refers to a machine that processes information according to a set of instructions. A **personal computer**, also known as a *PC* or *microcomputer,* is intended for use by an individual, and since PCs proliferated in the 1970s and 1980s, they have become the focus of most of the computing industry. When we use the term *computer* in this book, we almost always refer to a personal computer, whether that be a desktop computer, a notebook or laptop computer, a *tablet PC* or a *netbook*, a new class of inexpensive notebook computers designed primarily to access Web-based applications. We emphasize the personal computer, because it is such a useful tool for teaching and learning.

When people picture a computer, they may envision elements such as a keyboard, a box with a disk or CD/DVD

Personal computers, like this tablet PC, are intended for use by individuals.
Source: Shutterstock

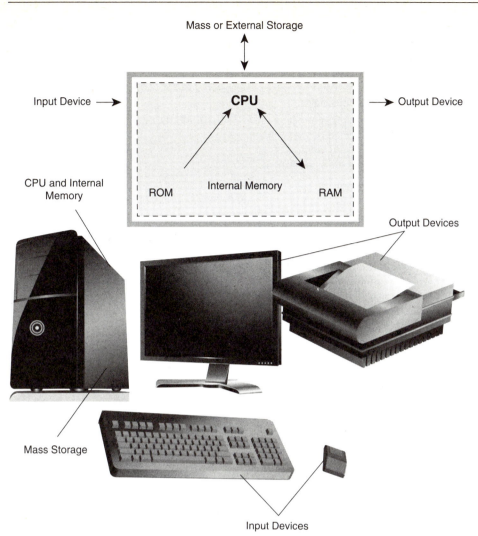

FIGURE 3–1 Diagrammatic and pictorial representation of a typical computer system. (Note: The dashed box represents the computer proper in the computer system.)

drive, and a display screen. This is actually a computer system, a collection of components that includes the computer and all of the devices used with the computer to realize or extend its capabilities. The computer's capabilities are defined, enabled, and constrained by the **hardware** (physical components) and **software** (programs) that comprise a particular computer system. The hardware sets absolute limits on what the computer can do, while the software unlocks the capabilities of the hardware. Figure 3–1 shows diagrammatic and pictorial representations of a personal computer system. Let's take a closer look at its components.

Hardware

Hardware is the term for the physical components of a computer system that perform the basic functions that make everything work. See Figure 3–2 for a summary of the functions of the basic components. A brief discussion of these components follows.

The **processor** is like the brain of the computer; it controls everything. In most personal computers, the processor is a single computer chip, a thumbnail-sized square of silicon with millions of microscopic electronic circuits etched onto it. The processor works with digital data, the bits (individual 0s and 1s) and bytes (collections of bits that code for letters, numbers, and symbols) that represent the various kinds of information (e.g., text, visuals, audio, video) that we use.

Input devices allow us to put information into the computer, and **output devices** allow us to get information from the computer. Common input devices include the keyboard, mouse, and microphone. Common output devices include the display, speakers, and printer. The display is usually a flat panel often based on **LCD** (liquid crystal display) technology, but older computers may use a television-like display called a **CRT** or monitor. The printer is usually one of two types: an **ink-jet printer** that yields very good print quality and supports color printing at moderate cost, or a **laser printer** that produces excellent print quality (600 dots per inch or more) but may not do color. Input and output devices often communicate with the computer through what is called an interface or port; the **USB** (universal serial bus) port is a popular standard today.

Hardware Component	Function	Examples
Processor	Acts as the "brain" of the machine; controls the functions of the rest of the system and manipulates information in various ways.	Intel Core 2 Duo, Intel Centrino, AMD Opteron, AMD Athlon
Internal or Main Memory	Stores instructions (programs) and information where they can be readily accessed by the processor. The computer's working memory is where your programs and data are stored when you use the computer.	RAM, SDRAM, DDR
Input Devices	Put information into the computer.	Keyboard, Mouse, Microphone
Output Devices	Get information from the computer.	Display (LCD or CRT), Printer (ink-jet or laser), Speakers
Mass or External Storage	Stores information over long periods of time; acts as a "library" of readily accessible software and personal work that can be copied into working memory when needed.	Hard disk, Floppy disk, CD-ROM, CD-R/RW, DVD-ROM, DVD-R/RW, Flash drive

FIGURE 3–2   Computer System Components and their functions.

Information inside the computer is stored in the internal or main **memory**. Working memory, sometimes called RAM (random access memory), is your personal workspace inside the computer. The power of RAM is its flexibility to be used for different purposes at different times as need dictates. The capacity of RAM is usually described in terms of the kilobytes (KB) or thousands of bytes, megabytes (MB) or millions of bytes, and gigabytes (GB) or billions of bytes of storage. A single page of text requires about 2 kilobytes (KB) of storage; digital video files, on the other hand, often require many megabytes (MB).

Mass storage (also called *external storage*) refers to devices and media that maintain a "library" of readily accessible software and personal work and bring it into working memory when needed. Large storage requirements are met by the computer's **hard disk** or *hard drive*, which has a storage capacity measured in gigabytes (GB). The operating system and commonly used software are kept on the computer's hard disk for ready access. Some computers today still rely on 3.5" **floppy disks** (or diskettes) to meet small-scale, portable storage needs, but computer manufacturers are beginning to phase out floppy disk drives. Today, most computer users meet portable storage needs with a USB **flash drive** or jump drive which stores information in flash memory, a special type of computer memory. A flash drive plugs into a computer's USB port and acts like an extra disk drive on the computer. Flash drives can store megabytes to gigabytes of data, depending on the specific model, and can be transported from one computer to another to meet portable mass storage needs.

A flash drive is a small device that plugs into the computer's USB port and allows data to be stored and transported from one computer to another.
Source: Shutterstock

Optical storage technologies also address mass storage needs. Most computers come with a CD-ROM or DVD-ROM drive often with recording capability. A **CD-ROM** can store 650 MB of data, and a **DVD-ROM** can store 4.7 GB or more of information. Prerecorded information, such as electronic encyclopedias and computer software, are often distributed on CD-ROMs or DVD-ROMs. Recordable versions of these media, CD-R/RW and comparable DVD formats, allow for archiving of information. To make a music CD or your own data CD, your computer system must be equipped with a CD or DVD recorder, or what is sometimes called a "burner." These accessories are popular options for recording, archiving, and transporting music, photos, videos, and other types of personal computer data.

While personal computers can do much work as stand-alone devices, today they are often linked via wired or wireless connections to other computers to form networks. Within a laboratory or school building, computers may be linked together to create a **LAN (local area network)** that supports the sharing of resources such as printers and software applications. LANs, in turn, can be linked together to form a **WAN (wide area network)**; the Internet is the most extreme example of a WAN. In order to function on a network, a personal computer must be equipped with a network adapter or card that supports communication with other computers on the network.

Software

Software consists of computer programs, sets of instructions to the computer's processor that tell it how to perform a particular task, such as editing text or presenting a computer-based lesson. Programs are loaded from disk into memory for use as needed. There are two basic categories of software: systems software and applications software.

Systems software is the basic operating software that tells the computer how to perform its fundamental functions. The main systems software is called the **operating system (OS)**. The OS acts as the master control program for the computer managing common machine functions such as copying files or opening an application programs such as a word processor or *iTunes*. Key components of the OS are loaded from disk into memory when the computer starts up; other components

are accessed from disk as needed. The most widely used operating systems in education today are Microsoft *Windows*, the latest version of which is *Windows 7*, and Apple *MacOS*, the latest version of which is called *OS X Leopard*. A relative newcomer to the scene that is gaining popularity is *Linux*, an open-source operating system derived from UNIX. Most popular OS's today use a **graphical user interface** (GUI) in which graphical symbols called **icons** are used to represent programs, disks, and other aspects of the computer system (see Figure 3–3).

Applications software includes programs designed to perform specific functions for the user, from processing text to doing calculations to presenting a lesson on the computer. Thus, applications software includes common computer productivity tools (word processors, databases, etc.) as well as educational software. Although applications software interacts frequently with the OS, it is through the applications software that people do most of their real work. The most commonly used applications are discussed later in this chapter.

Computer Operation

When your computer operates, it carries out a complex set of actions that involves interplay among the various components of the system and you. Suppose that you wish to use your word processing software to compose a lesson plan. When you sit down at your computer and turn it on, the computer's basic startup information is retrieved from built-in memory, a brief check of all systems is conducted to make sure everything is operating properly, and your operating system is loaded into memory and assumes control of your computer.

FIGURE 3–3 Microsoft *Windows 7* is a popular operating system in education.

Source: Microsoft product screen shot reprinted with permission from Microsoft Corporation.

To begin your word processing session, you might use your mouse to click on the icon for the software. This input passes to the processor and on to the OS, which instructs the computer to copy the word processing program from your computer's hard disk into working memory. The word processing program then assumes control of your interactions with it.

As you begin to type, each keystroke sends a signal to the processor. The word processing software working with the OS keeps the information in memory and shows the contents of your document on the computer's display. When you finish, you select the print option in the word processor. The OS sends a copy of your document to your printer, and the hard copy emerges. Finally, you select Save, and the OS stores a copy of your document on disk for later reference or editing. The computer system, operating system software, and word processing software work in concert to carry out the desired actions. The whole process involves a complicated interplay of many different components. Fortunately, most of the time, this process works so well that we never even notice it is happening.

COMPUTER SYSTEM EVALUATION AND ACQUISITION

Suppose that you, like Mary Jordan, go into a school with all new computers. You might want to get your own new computer for home to become more familiar with the new software and to use for work at home, or you might be asked by your school's principal to be on the technology committee that selects the new computers for the school. What should you consider when evaluating a computer system for possible purchase? Today, the education marketplace is dominated by two main groups of computers: (1) those designed to run the *Windows* operating system using Intel and compatible processors, often called "Wintel" machines for short, manufactured by companies including Dell, HP, Sony, and others; and (2) Apple Macintosh computers that run the MacOS operating system. Both groups of computers are popular in education, although the *Windows* platform is far and away the most widely used in homes and the workplace.

See Figure 3–4 for factors you should consider when selecting computer system hardware. It is important

Factor	Issues/Considerations
Software Availability	↗ What do you want to be able to do with the computer system? Identify software that can meet your needs, and acquire a computer system that can operate the software.
	↗ Both Wintel and Macintosh computers feature easy to use operating systems, but some people prefer the way one operates over the other.
	↗ Many popular applications are available for both platforms, but some applications may be available for only one or the other. If a key application you need is available only for one platform, that may be an overriding consideration.
Processor	↗ How much processing power do you need? Generally, newer processors are capable of more processing power and faster operations than their predecessors, although there are exceptions. When comparing processors, look for the results of benchmarking tests, well-defined sets of processing tasks used by testing labs to rate the performance of different processors.
	↗ When all else is equal, look for faster processing speeds (more gigahertz). Faster processor speeds contribute to faster overall performance.
Internal Memory	↗ How much memory will you need? Newer operating systems generally need at least 2 gigabytes (GB) for basic operations.
	↗ Special applications, such as multimedia development or digital video editing, usually benefit from significantly more memory than needed for the basics.
Keyboard and Mouse	↗ How important are input devices to you? For people who do a lot of typing, the layout and feel of the keyboard may be an important consideration. Pay special attention to notebook or tablet PC keyboards where limited space can restrict layout and functions.
	↗ Wintel system mice have two buttons, while single button mice are standard on Macintosh computers. Do you have a preference for one or the other?
Display	↗ Will you need a lot of "screen real estate"? Do you want a standard display or a widescreen display? Display size is measured diagonally like televisions. Most desktop personal computers feature displays of 15 to 22 inches. Notebook or tablet PC displays range from 10 to 17 inches.
	↗ Consider screen resolution, which refers to how many dots or pixels can fit onto the screen. Most displays today support at least 1024 by 768 pixels; with more pixels, you can better see detail.
	↗ Color capability is another display factor. So-called true color, capable of millions of hues, requires 24 to 32 bits of color information for each pixel. The computer's graphic card must have adequate display memory to support true color at the highest resolutions.

FIGURE 3–4 Computer System Evaluation Considerations.

Factor	Issues/Considerations
Sound	↗ Is sound important to you? Digital sound capability is standard on most computers today, but quality can vary. ↗ A good sound card and high-quality speakers are needed to support high-fidelity sound.
Printer	↗ What kind of printer will you need? Ink-jet printers are usually inexpensive and offer color capability, but ink cartridges are costly. Laser printers tend to be more expensive, most lack color, but they offer excellent performance for the cost. ↗ Other printer factors include speed (pages printed per minute), resolution (dots printed per inch), paper-handling capability, and ability to operate on a network.
Mass Storage	↗ How much and what kind of mass storage will you require? A hard disk is an essential feature of all PCs. Capacity and speed of access to data distinguish different models. A fast hard drive can greatly enhance overall system speed. ↗ For most systems, a CD-ROM or DVD drive is a key mass storage option. For archiving data and making music or video CDs, a CD or DVD recorder, or "burner," is a required option. ↗ Some systems still include a floppy disk drive, but many vendors are phasing out this small-scale storage option.
Interfaces	↗ Built-in Internet connectivity capability, through a wired Ethernet port and a modem for dial-up access, is common on most computers today. For notebook or tablet PCs, especially, is wireless Internet connectivity available? ↗ What ports are available for connecting peripherals? USB ports are now nearly universal on personal computers, but the number of available ports varies. If you hope to work with digital video, you may also want to look for an IEEE-1394 (also called Firewire or iLink) port; it is often used to connect digital video camcorders.
System Expandability	↗ Expansion slots permit components to be added to the system. How many expansion slots does the computer have? Are all available, or are some used by existing components? ↗ Increasing memory is a common system upgrade. Will the system support additional memory without modification? Can you add memory without removing existing memory?
Warranty and Service	↗ How long is the warranty and what does it cover? Look for the most comprehensive coverage. ↗ If service is needed, what are your options (e.g., on-site service, carry-in service, mail-in service)?
Cost	↗ What are you willing to spend? Today's computer systems can range anywhere from a few hundred to thousands of dollars. ↗ A good basic computer system for school use can generally be purchased for less than $1,000 to about $1,500.

FIGURE 3–4 (Continued)

Toolbox: Pricing School Computers

You can use available vendor websites to determine the educational prices for popular computer models. Assume that your school has been given the funding to equip a computer lab with 25 computers. Use available vendor resources on the Web to determine the configuration and approximate cost of the 25 computers. Determine how each computer will be equipped given two different scenarios. (1) In scenario 1, assume that the school board, while not providing a blank check, has stressed that the lab should be well-equipped to meet students' needs for advanced applications such as multimedia production and digital video editing. (2) In scenario 2, assume that the school sees cost as a major consideration and wants to be sure that the total cost of the lab is under $25,000.

Use the following vendor websites to get cost estimates.

Vendor	Online Store
Apple	http://store.apple.com
Dell	http://www.dell.com
HP	http://www.hp.com/go/computing

Consider the following questions as you do your research:

↗ Are special prices, discounts, or incentives available for purchases by schools or individual educators?
↗ In addition to the cost of the computers themselves, what other costs would be involved in outfitting a school computer laboratory?
↗ Where could you find more information about additional needs and costs?

to consider each component that makes up the computer system. To select a personal computer system, carefully investigate these factors. Compare competing brands. Talk to users. Visit vendors and try out the machines. In the end, make your decision based on how well you believe a particular computer system will meet your specific needs.

TROUBLESHOOTING COMPUTER PROBLEMS

Computer systems are complex devices, and problems do arise. In many school districts, such as Mary Jordan's school described at the beginning of this chapter, there are few technical support personnel and those that are available may be so busy with networking and computer installation issues that they have limited time to help teachers solve routine computer problems in the classroom. So, it is important for teachers to be able to troubleshoot basic computer problems to keep things working.

Computer troubleshooting is not an easy task, especially for beginners. There are many possible causes of problems—hardware, software, network, user error—and interactions among the various components can complicate matters. For example, suppose that you try to print a document from an application, but nothing happens. There are many possible causes of such a problem. Your printer's ink or toner cartridge might be empty, or your printer cable might have come loose (hardware problems). Your printer may not be selected within the operating system, or your printer software may not work properly with the application (software problems). If you use the printer on a network, your network connection to the printer might be "down," i.e. not functioning (a network problem). You may have accidentally clicked Cancel instead of OK in the print dialog box (user error). How can you sort out the problem?

While you may not be able to solve all the problems that you encounter, it is possible to develop some basic troubleshooting proficiency, so that minor problems do not become major obstacles. Here are some fundamental troubleshooting guidelines and tips.

Identify the problem. While this may seem obvious, the first step is just to identify the problem as specifically as possible.

- What is the extent of the problem? For example, have you lost all computer function, or is the problem something more limited in scope such as an inability to print from an application?
- Under what circumstances does the problem occur? Does the problem occur all of the time, only in specific applications, or only at specific times?

- Can you repeat the problem or is it something that occurs intermittently? Repeatable problems tend to be more easily identified. Intermittent problems may result from a difficult-to-observe combination of conditions.

Look for possible causes.

- Begin by checking the obvious. If you've apparently lost all computer function, is the computer still plugged in and is the power switch turned on? If you are unable to print, is the printer still connected, receiving power, and switched on?
- Try restarting the computer. Many times, a simple restart will correct problems that have arisen.
- Read your computer documentation. Make certain that you are using the computer and applications correctly.
- Consider whether you have made any changes to your computer system recently. Problems with computers often arise as a result of changes in one part of the system that affect other parts of the system. For example, if you recently installed a new piece of software, it might have changed your system (e.g., installed new printer software or changed control panel settings) in ways that affect other applications.
- Use diagnostic software to check for problems. For example, use virus protection software to scan for a virus. Viruses, often accidentally downloaded from e-mail or other online sources, can wreak havoc with your system. Use a utility (e.g., *Windows Scandisk,* Apple's *Disk First Aid,* or Semantec's *Norton Utilities*) to check for problems with your files/disks. Disk errors can lead to many problems.

Use a process of elimination to identify the specific problem.

- Localize the problem by determining what *does* work as well as what *does not* work. For example, if you are having trouble printing from an application, try to print from another application. If you can print from another application, then the problem is not a generalized printing problem. If you are unable to receive e-mail, check to see if you can access a website. If you can access a website, the problem is not a general network connection problem.
- Check the control panels in your system to make certain that all of the settings are correct. See Figure 3–5 for an example.
- If you suspect a problem with a particular component, substitute a known working component. For example, if you are having trouble with your printer, replace it with one known to be

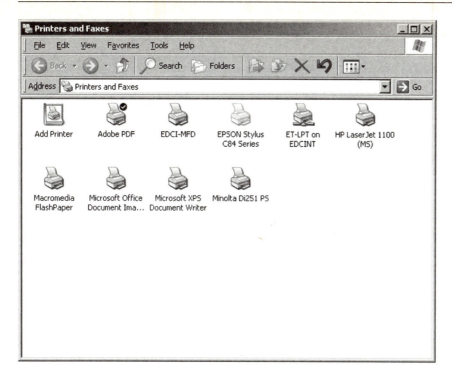

FIGURE 3–5 An incorrect setting within an operating system control panel, such as the printer control panel shown here, can be the source of a computer problem. For example, if the wrong printer is set as the default, your document may not print.

Source: Microsoft product screen shot reprinted with permission from Microsoft Corporation.

working. If the problem persists, the printer is not at fault. If the problem is resolved, then the printer was faulty.

↗ Check one thing at a time. When trying to identify a problem, be systematic about checking first one thing and then another. If you change more than one thing, it may obscure the source of the problem and make it harder to find a solution.

Resolve the problem or seek assistance.

↗ If you are able to identify the specific problem, try to correct it by making any necessary changes.

↗ If you are unable to identify the specific problem or you determine that the problem is beyond your ability to resolve, then seek assistance. Ask friends or associates, or check on the Web, to see if others have had a similar problem and know how to correct it. If all else fails, call for professional assistance. In a school setting, contact your technical support staff. For a home computer, contact an authorized service center or the telephone support line for your computer brand.

Take preventative measures to avoid future problems.

↗ Make sure that you install anti-virus software, and keep it up-to-date by regularly updating your virus definitions.

↗ Regularly use software to check for and correct file/disk errors. Defragment your hard disk periodically using software designed for that

purpose (e.g., *Windows Defrag* or *Norton Utilities Speed Disk*). Over time, files on your hard disk can become split into pieces or fragments, and defragmenting consolidates the pieces to make your computer operate more efficiently.

↗ Make and keep an emergency start-up disk for your computer to use in the event of serious system failure. (Macintosh users can boot from the system CD-ROM in an emergency.)

↗ Keep your system up-to-date. Regularly check for and install operating system upgrades (especially critical or security-related upgrades) and the latest drivers for your peripherals. Manufacturers usually release updates on their websites that fix known problems. Before installing new applications or upgrading existing applications, check the system requirements to make certain that they will work with your system.

COMPUTER AS TEACHER AND ASSISTANT

The computer is a powerful machine with a many different uses in education. The growing breadth and diversity of computer applications in education makes categorization difficult. However, to bring some order to this range of possibilities, we have elected to present the educational applications of computers here in two broad categories: computer as teacher and computer as assistant. Each category is summarized in Figure 3–6.

Computers can be used to present instruction directly to students. In this mode, the computer engages in

Toolbox: Healthy and Safe Use of Computers

In recent years, it has become clear that improper placement and/or use of a computer can pose a threat to your health. To minimize your risks, follow the guidelines below.

↗ Repetitive stress injuries, such as carpal tunnel syndrome, have become increasingly common among those who use computers extensively. Proper application of **ergonomics**, the study of the physical interaction of humans with machines, can help to limit problems. For example, use adjustable furniture. The keyboard should be placed at the proper height for typing, usually about 27 to 29 inches from the floor, so that your elbows are at a 90° angle when typing. The mouse should be next to the keyboard at the same height or slightly higher. When typing, your wrists should be level; if necessary, use wrist rests for support. Your chair should be comfortable and provide good support for your back. Keep your posture straight but relaxed and your feet flat on the floor. Finally, take regular breaks from computer work to stretch and rest.

↗ CRT-type computer monitors can emit radiation that might pose a health risk. (Flat panel displays do not have this problem.) While monitors are shielded to reduce emissions and the extent of the danger is unclear, it is wise to be cautious. It is recommended that you sit at least 28 inches from the front of a monitor; maintain a distance of at least 48 inches from the sides or rear of a monitor, which may emit more radiation.

↗ Lengthy viewing of computer displays can cause eyestrain, headaches, and vision problems. The computer display should be placed at eye level. Reduce ambient lighting in the room if it is bright. Minimize glare off the screen by positioning the computer display away from direct sunlight and lighting fixtures; anti-glare coatings or screens can be used if repositioning is not enough to reduce glare. Text should be easily viewable when you are seated the proper distance from the screen. Adjust the font size in your application to make it easily readable, if necessary. If you wear eyeglasses or contact lenses, consider getting a special prescription for computer work. Finally, take regular breaks to allow your eyes to rest.

In addition to using computers in ways that are healthy, you need to be sure that you use computers in ways that are safe and protect your personal information.

↗ To avoid falling prey to a computer virus or other "malware," always use anti-virus and anti-spyware software and keep it up-to-date. Install operating system upgrades, especially critical or security-related upgrades, because these often patch identified vulnerabilities in the software. Use firewall software to protect your computer from outside intrusion over the Internet. Never open e-mail attachments unless you are expecting an e-mail with an attachment from a trusted source. When Web browsing, do not click on advertising or download freeware as these may install unwanted and possibly malicious software on your system.

↗ Never divulge your personal information online except when you know you are visiting a trusted site with a secure connection. You could fall victim to theft of your personal information. Avoid falling for "phishing" scams, legitimate looking e-mail messages or websites that seek to entice you to divulge valuable personal information.

↗ Use strong passwords for accessing your computer accounts. Use a mixture of upper and lower case letters, numbers, and symbols. Do not include names, words, or other easy-to-guess information in passwords. If you must write down your password, keep it in a secure place away from your computer. Never give your computer password to someone else.

↗ Always keep backups of your important documents and files. If your computer does become infected with a virus, or your hard drive fails, you'll be able to recover your work if you have a backup.

Proper computer placement and ergonomics will help you to stay comfortable and healthy when using the computer.
Source: David Young-Wolff/PhotoEdit.

Computer's Role	Description	Examples
Teacher	The computer, functioning like a human teacher or tutor, presents instruction, provides instructional materials or activities, quizzes or otherwise requires interaction from learners, evaluates learner responses, and provides feedback. As a teaching machine, the computer can be highly interactive, individualized, and infinitely patient.	• computer-based instruction (CBI) • computer-assisted instruction (CAI) • computer-assisted learning (CAL)
Assistant	The computer functions as a productivity tool to aid the teacher or learner in performing a variety of work tasks such as writing, drawing, calculating, storing information, presenting information, creating multimedia materials, and/or communicating with others. Teachers may employ computers as labor-saving devices to produce instructional materials and manage their instruction. Learners may employ the computer to help with their schoolwork.	• word processor • graphics package • spreadsheet • database • presentation software • multimedia/hypermedia authoring tool • telecommunication tool

FIGURE 3–6   Computer as teacher and assistant.

activities traditionally associated with human teachers or tutors. It presents instruction, provides instructional activities or situations, quizzes or otherwise requires interaction from learners, evaluates learner responses, provides feedback, and determines appropriate follow-up activities. As teaching machines, computers can be highly interactive, individualized, and infinitely patient. Applications that utilize the computer for teaching are usually labeled computer-based instruction (CBI), computer-assisted instruction (CAI), or computer-assisted learning (CAL). There are a number of common categories of computer-based instruction: drill and practice, tutorial, simulation, instructional game, and problem solving. We will discuss these in more detail in Chapter 9.

As an assistant, the computer serves as a productivity tool aiding the teacher or learner in performing various work tasks. It can function as a typewriter, an artist's canvas, a financial worksheet, a filing system, a slide projector, a multimedia kit, a communication tool, and much more. Software applications for these uses include word processors, graphics packages, spreadsheets, databases, presentation software, multimedia/hypermedia authoring tools, e-mail packages, and many others. Teachers often employ computers as labor-saving devices to produce instructional materials (e.g., printed matter, pictures, multimedia), present information (e.g., in-class presentation, website), communicate with students and parents (e.g., e-mail, Web), and manage the instructional process (e.g., maintain records, calculate student grades, assess student progress). Of course, learners can also employ the computer as an assistant. Students can use the computer to produce materials (e.g., term papers, graphs, presentations, multimedia), communicate with the teacher and fellow students (e.g., e-mail, Web), and help with other tasks while learning (e.g., perform calculations, do online research). In this chapter, we introduce the computer as an assistant so that you have an understanding of some of the most important applications available to help you as you learn to plan and design instruction in the coming chapters. We will look in more detail at applications of the computer as a teacher and as a tool for learning when we discuss integrating computers into learning experiences for students in Chapter 9. We will talk more about the role of the Internet in education in Chapters 10 and 11.

COMPUTER PRODUCTIVITY TOOLS

In the role of assistant, the computer is a productivity tool. When computers are used in the workplace, they are most often used as a tool to assist the worker. Secretaries prepare documents using word processors, businesspeople store customer records in databases, accountants use spreadsheets to calculate balance sheets, graphic artists use drawing programs, and these are only a few examples. Therefore, it makes sense that teachers and students use computers in schools in the same ways that they are used in the workplace. Students can use computers as assistants when doing schoolwork. Teachers, like Mary Jordan, can use the same tools to prepare instructional materials and manage the instructional process. We introduce these tools here so that as you continue in this text and begin to learn how to plan for the effective integration of technology in your own teaching, you will be aware of the key computer tools that are available to help you with the task of planning instruction and preparing educational materials and learning experiences for your students. What follows are descriptions of some of the most common computer applications for assisting teachers and learners as well as examples of how both teachers and students can use them.

Word Processors

Word processors are the most widely used computer personal productivity tools. A **word processor** is a computer application that allows you to enter, edit, revise, format, store, retrieve, and print text. Word processors today also permit you to include graphic and tabular materials along with text. Nearly all word processors have spelling checkers; some correct spelling "on the fly" as you enter text, and some do basic grammatical and syntactical checking (e.g., subject-verb agreement).

Popular word processors for personal computers include Microsoft *Word* and Corel *WordPerfect* as well as the *Pages* word processor in Apple's *iWorks* integrated suite of applications. Other word processing programs are available via the Internet. For example, *OpenOffice.org Writer* (http://www.openoffice.org) is an open source word processor that is growing in popularity, Thinkfree *Office Online* (http://www.thinkfree .com/) is suite of tools that includes a word processor, and *Google Docs* (http://docs.google.com) is another Web-based set of tools, from the popular Google website, that includes a word processor. See Figure 3–7.

> **PEARSON myeducationkit** To learn more about using word processors go to the Video Tutorials section of Chapter 3 and watch the video tutorial entitled either "MS Word for PC" or "Ms Word for Mac." As you watch the video, consider how you and your students can use the word processor for your work.

> **PEARSON myeducationkit** To learn more about *Google Docs* go to the Video Tutorials section of Chapter 3 and watch the video tutorial entitled "Google Docs." As you watch the video, think about how you can use these Web-based tools for your own work and how your students can use them for their class projects.

Word Processor Uses for Teachers

- ↗ Preparing lesson plans, handouts, worksheets, and other instructional materials
- ↗ Recording ideas during in-class brainstorming sessions
- ↗ Creating quizzes, tests, and other forms of student assessment
- ↗ Writing letters, permission slips, newsletters, and other forms of communication with parents, students, and administrators

Word Processor Uses for Students

- ↗ Writing papers and other assigned written work
- ↗ Performing prewriting activities such as brainstorming, note taking, and idea collection
- ↗ Typing handwritten notes to reinforce learning or when studying for an exam

Graphics Tools

While word processors are primarily tools for manipulating text, graphics tools handle pictorial information. Any computerized pictorial representation of information—drawing, chart, graph, animated figure, or photographic reproduction—is called a **graphic**. On a computer screen,

FIGURE 3–7 A screen from Microsoft *Word* showing features including text formatting, a two-column layout, and an embedded graphic.

Source: Microsoft product screen shot reprinted with permission from Microsoft Corporation.

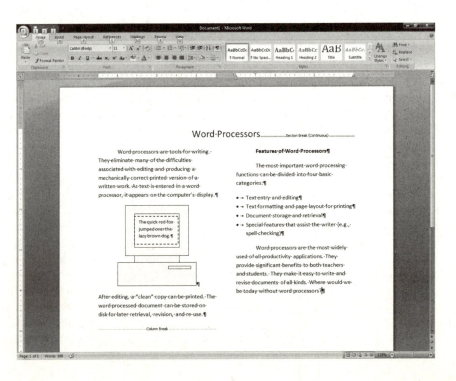

Graphic Format	Description
BMP—Windows Bitmap	The standard *Windows* bit-mapped (raster) graphic format.
GIF—Graphic Interchange Format	A format originally developed for CompuServe that stores images with up to 256 colors. It is widely used on the Web for icons, clip art, and other limited color images. It also supports a form of animation that is popular on the Web.
JPG or JPEG—Joint Photographic Experts Group	A format widely used for photographic images on the Web. It can support images with millions of colors and offers varying levels of compression to reduce storage size.
PICT—Macintosh graphic	The standard Apple Macintosh graphic format capable of storing both bit-mapped and vector (draw) images.
PNG—Portable Network Graphic	A Web image format designed as a replacement to the proprietary GIF format. It supports up to millions of colors and better compression than GIF.
TIF or TIFF—Tagged Image File Format	A widely supported format for bit-mapped images that is often used with images in printed materials. Scanners often store scanned images in this format.

FIGURE 3–8   Common Graphic File Formats.

graphic images are composed of many tiny dots, much like photographs in a newspaper. Each screen dot is referred to as a picture element or **pixel** for short. Some types of computer images, called bit-mapped or raster graphics, keep track of the individual pixels, while others, called vector or draw graphics, store the lines and shapes that make up the image. There are many different graphics file formats (that is, ways of storing graphic information in a computer file). Some of the most common graphic file formats are shown in Figure 3–8.

Computer-based graphic tools can create or manipulate images, generate graphs/charts, and so forth. For creating or manipulating images, most graphics applications let you use the mouse as a pencil, paintbrush, color fill bucket, or eraser. You can draw lines, circles, and polygons, as well as curves and irregular shapes. You can move or rotate portions of graphics as well as cut, copy, and paste them. You can select and control colors, and fill shapes with colors and/or patterns. Advanced graphics applications let you apply special effects such as blurring, textures, and the illusion of embossing. Popular graphics packages include Adobe *Photoshop, Illustrator,* and *Fireworks,* Corel *Paint Shop Pro* and *Draw,* and Microsoft *ExpressionPaint.* See Figure 3–9. Graphics packages oriented for elementary students' use include Brøderbund's *Kid Pix* and Knowledge Adventure's *Kid Works.* Inspiration's *InspireData* is tool that lets students visually represent data in various ways. There are also graphic programs available via the Internet such as GIMP (http://www.gimp.org/), Picasa (http://picasa.google.com/) and Inkscape (http://www.inkscape.com/), which are downloadable programs, as well as Web-based graphical editing applications such as

Splashup (http://www.splashup.com/) and Picnik (http://www.picnik.com), which allows you to edit images online.

PEARSON **myeducationkit** To learn more about using graphics software go to the Video Tutorials section of Chapter 3 and watch the video tutorial entitled "PhotoShop". As you watch the video, think about how you can use graphics software for your own work and how your students can use it for their work.

Graphic Tool Uses for Teachers

↗ Creating images for handouts, worksheets, and other instructional materials for student use
↗ Creating signs or other graphical material for classroom display
↗ Maintaining graphical information (e.g., pictures of students) in a class database
↗ Designing and producing a class newsletter to send home to parents

Graphic Tool Uses for Students

↗ Making drawings for mini-books, reports, and other illustrated material
↗ Editing photos for reports, presentations, and other kinds of school work
↗ Producing major school works such as the school newspaper or yearbook
↗ Creating a graph of data collected in the science laboratory

FIGURE 3–9 A screen from Adobe *PhotoShop,* a popular program for editing digital photos and creating graphic images.

Source: Reprinted with permission from Adobe Systems, Inc.

FIGURE 3–10 A sample worksheet in Microsoft *Excel* for calculating students' grades. Cell H2, which is highlighted, includes a formula to calculate a student's overall percentile.

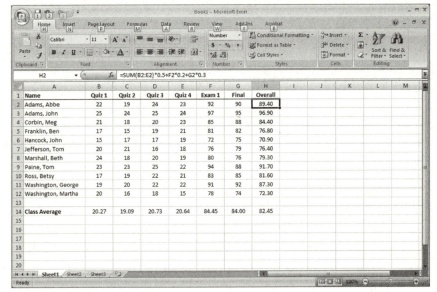

Source: Microsoft product screen shot reprinted with permission from Microsoft Corporation.

Spreadsheets

Spreadsheets are general-purpose calculating tools derived from the paper worksheets once used by accountants. A spreadsheet is like a large piece of paper marked off into rows and columns to form a grid. Each intersection of a row and column, a single block in the grid, is called a **cell**. Individual columns and rows are labeled (e.g., lettered and numbered) for reference. Thus, each cell can be uniquely identified by its column and row reference. A cell normally contains one of three types of information: a number, text, or a formula. Numbers are the basic components with which spreadsheets work. Text may be used to label parts of the spreadsheet or as part of a database (see discussion below). **Formulas** are mathematical expressions that direct the spreadsheet to perform various kinds of calculations or operations on the data entered in the cells. Formulas work on values in the spreadsheet by referring to the cells where the values are located. See Figure 3–10.

Spreadsheets usually offer a wide variety of built-in mathematical functions (e.g., basic statistics, trigonometric functions, common financial functions) to facilitate calculations. They support data entry, editing, formatting, printing, and usually graphing of data. Spreadsheets often include basic database functionality. Popular spreadsheets include Microsoft *Excel,* Lotus *1-2-3,* and Quattro *Pro.* In addition, spreadsheets are found in integrated application suites such as Microsoft *Works* and Apple *iWorks.* Knowledge Adventure's *The Cruncher* is a spreadsheet program designed especially for school use. Spreadsheets available via the Internet include *OpenOffice.org Calc* (http://www.openoffice.org/product/calc.html), an open source spreadsheet, and the Web-based spreadsheet in *Google Docs* (http://spreadsheets.google.com/).

> **PEARSON myeducationkit** To learn more about using spreadsheets go to the Video Tutorials section of Chapter 3 and watch the video tutorial entitled either "MS Excel for PC" or "MS Excel for Mac." As you watch the video, think about how you can use spreadsheets for your own work and how your students can use them for their work.

Spreadsheet Uses for Teachers

↗ Creating a gradebook to maintain students' grades and track student assessment information

↗ Keeping other student records (e.g., a physical education teacher might store students' performances in various exercises or sporting activities)

↗ Tracking costs of classroom materials (e.g., a chemistry teacher could maintain information about the costs of chemicals used in laboratory exercises)

↗ Demonstrating complex calculations to a class (e.g., a business teacher might build loan amortization tables varying by interest rate as a class illustration)

Spreadsheet Uses for Students

↗ Maintaining financial records of a student organization (e.g., tracking candy sales by members of the pep band)

↗ Entering and analyzing data from science experiments

↗ Using the chart function to make a visual representation of a set of data

↗ Performing "what if?" simulation or hypothesis-testing activities (e.g., What would happen to my monthly cost of operating a car if an accident doubled my insurance rates?)

Databases

A **database** is nothing more than a collection of information. We are familiar with many examples of databases that are *not* computerized: a telephone book, a recipe file, a collection of old magazines. Computer databases offer significant advantages because they can store large amounts of information, can be readily searched for information by category, and are relatively easy to set up and maintain.

Most computer databases are structured in similar ways. For example, suppose you want to computerize your name and address book. See Figure 3–11.

Each entry in the address book corresponds to an individual. Within each entry are various items of information: name, address, telephone number, e-mail address, and so on. In computer terminology, each individual category of information that is recorded is called a **field**. So there might be a name field, a street address field, a city field, a telephone number field, and so on. The whole collection of fields that corresponds to one individual is called a **record**. Each record contains the same collection of fields. All of the records are collected into a **datafile**. The datafile corresponds to the entire address book. In simple cases a database consists of only a single datafile. In more complex cases the database may be a collection of datafiles that are inter-related in some way (e.g., a name and address file that is cross-referenced with an employee records file in a company). **Relational databases** allow multiple datafiles to be accessed and interrelated. Popular database management programs include Microsoft *Access,* *dBASE,* and *FileMaker* as well as the database components of integrated products such as Microsoft *Works* and Apple *iWorks. OpenOffice.org Base* (http://www.openoffice.org/product/base.html) is a downloadable open source database program, and, popular computer spreadsheets such as Microsoft *Excel* include basic database functionality.

Database Uses for Teachers

↗ Creating and maintaining basic information (e.g., name, address, parents' names) about students

↗ Keeping records of books, media, or other materials available in the classroom or media center to support the curriculum

↗ Tracking student performance data to assist in student assessment

↗ Building a collection of test or quiz questions referenced by topic, book chapter, objective, and possibly other identifiers, such as level of Bloom's taxonomy

↗ Storing compilations of teaching methods, strategies, and lesson plans

Database Uses for Students

↗ Locating information in prepared databases such as the school's electronic card catalog or a database of U.S. presidents

↗ Developing problem-solving and higher-order thinking skills by investigating the answers to complex questions through searching databases

↗ Developing original databases as class projects to research various topics (e.g., U.S. states, class members' pets, dinosaurs, elements of the periodic table)

Presentation Software

Presentation software allows users to produce and display computer text and images, usually for presentation to a group. It replaces the functions typically associated with

FIGURE 3–11   Components of a computer database.

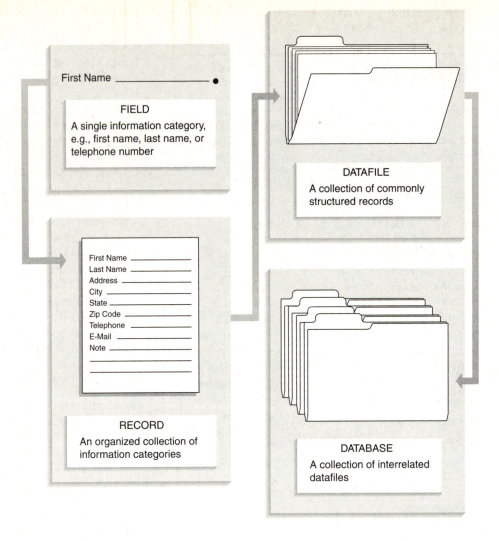

older media presentation tools such as slides and overhead transparencies. Most presentation software is built around a slide concept, with predesigned slide templates, special effects to transition from one slide to another, ability to sort and order slides, and ability to add multimedia elements to slides. Like other computer-based tools, it offers advantages over its traditional counterparts. Information is easily entered, edited, and presented. There is no need to set up or fumble with traditional media and equipment such as slides and slide carousels. With a presentation package, it is easy to produce professional looking presentations complete with multimedia elements. Popular presentation packages include Microsoft *PowerPoint,* Apple *Keynote,* and Corel *Presentations.* There are also presentation applications available via the Internet such as *OpenOffice.org Impress* (http://www.openoffice.org/product/impress.html), an open source presentation program, and *Google Docs* (http://docs.google.com), which includes a presentation program as part of its suite of Web-based tools. See Figure 3–15.

PEARSON **myeducationkit**™ To learn more about using presentation software go to the Video Tutorials section of Chapter 3 and watch the video tutorial entitled either "MS PowerPoint for PC" or "MS PowerPoint for Mac." As you watch the video, think about how you can use presentation software for your own work and how your students can use it for their work.

Presentation Software Uses for Teachers

↗ Supporting lectures or other presentations in the classroom, at professional meetings, or in other settings

↗ Displaying information at events such as parent open house nights; most presentation packages support timed or auto-run features that allow slide shows to run unattended

↗ Preparing notes, pictures, or other material that can be printed, transferred to photographic slides, or converted for placement on the Web

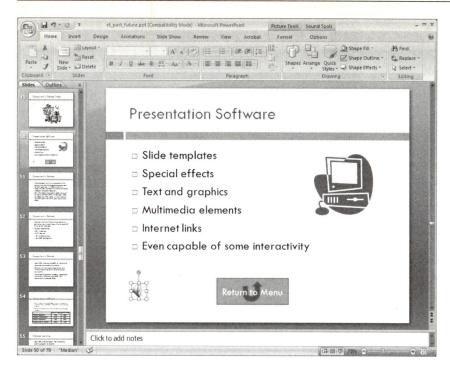

FIGURE 3–12   A screen from Microsoft *PowerPoint* showing media elements including bulleted text, clip art, sound, and an action button.

Source: Microsoft product screen shot reprinted with permission from Microsoft Corporation.

Presentation Software Uses for Students

↗ Making in-class presentations
↗ Developing multimedia reports or projects
↗ Creating a simple multimedia portfolio

Multimedia/Hypermedia Authoring Software

Authoring software is the term for programs used to develop multimedia and/or Web applications. The world that we live in is a complex environment of sights and sounds, and increasingly computer applications can reflect the complexity and richness of the real world by incorporating multimedia. **Multimedia** involves the use of a variety of media formats (e.g., text, visuals, audio, video) in a single presentation or product. **Hypermedia**, a distinct but closely related term, refers to multimedia information representation in which the information is stored digitally in interlinked chunks called *nodes*. The World Wide Web is the best example of hypermedia today.

Authoring software allows teachers or students to develop multimedia or hypermedia applications, which can be stand-alone products or networked Web pages. In many authoring tools, a single node of hypermedia information is like a card in a stack (think of a stack of index cards) or a page in a book (like a traditional print book). The user can view the contents of one card or page at a time. The author can put information of various sorts (text, pictures, sounds, videos) on one card/page, and each card/page can be linked to one or more other cards/pages of related information. Unlike a print book, nodes in a hypermedia application are often linked to other nodes in a nonlinear fashion. Users can jump from node to node to view the multimedia information by clicking on navigation buttons or links.

Many multimedia/hypermedia authoring tools are available for use in schools. Microsoft *PowerPoint*, though often used as a linear presentation tool (see above), can also be used to create nonlinear multimedia/hypermedia. Adobe *Acrobat Professional*, while known primarily as a tool for creating portable document format (PDF) documents, likewise can be used as a tool for multimedia creation. Packages specifically designed for multimedia/hypermedia authoring include Roger Wagner's *HyperStudio*, SAFARI Video Networks *eZedia*, Tech4Learning *MediaBlender*, and Adobe (formerly Macromedia) *Director*. For authoring Web-based materials, available products include Adobe (formerly Macromedia) *Dreamweaver* and *Flash* and Microsoft's *SharePoint Designer* and *Expression Web*. See Figure 3–13.

Authoring Software Uses for Teachers

↗ Creating interactive, multimedia instructional materials for student use
↗ Developing an informational presentation or website for parents, students, or others
↗ Creating a teaching portfolio

Authoring Software Uses for Students

↗ Developing multimedia reports or projects
↗ Creating interactive instructional materials for other students to access
↗ Creating a multimedia portfolio

FIGURE 3–13   A screen from Adobe *Flash*, a popular tool for authoring Web-based multimedia.

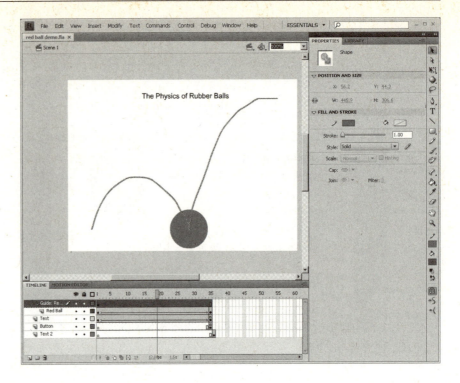

Source: Reprinted with permission from Adobe Systems, Inc.

Telecommunications Tools

Telecommunications tools permit people to communicate with one another via the computer. Today, we live in an era of global interconnectivity that brings a whole world of information to the personal computer user through networking and telecommunication. By accessing the Internet, you can instantly locate up-to-date information, communicate with others, and explore the far corners of cyberspace.

The **Internet** is the vast collection of computer networks that links millions of computers and tens of millions of people worldwide. It provides teachers and students with unprecedented access to up-to-date information and resources, and it supports many forms of communication, such as electronic mail, instant messaging, blogs, wikis, and video conferencing.

Electronic mail (e-mail) is the most widespread form of computer telecommunications. It allows messages to be sent from individuals to other individuals or from individuals to groups. Popular programs for composing, sending, and receiving e-mail include Microsoft *Outlook* and *Outlook Express* and Mozilla *Thunderbird* as well as the Webmail clients associated with Web-based services such as *Hotmail, Gmail*, and *Yahoo!*. For K-12 students, Web-based programs such as Gaggle (http://www.gaggle.net) and ePals (http://www.epals.com) are both free and provide teacher monitoring while students communicate.

Another popular form of communication with others is **instant messaging** (IM). It allows two users on the Internet to type messages back and forth to one another in real time, sort of like having a telephone conversation in print. Recently, many instant messaging services have begun to include video conferencing and

voice over IP (VoIP) features. Common instant messaging programs include *AOL Instant Messenger (AIM), Jabber, EBuddy, Skype*, and *Yahoo! Messenger*.

The **World Wide Web** (WWW or just the Web) is the hypermedia wing of the Internet. Today, much of the action on the Internet takes place on the Web, and the Web is home to many new and exciting features such as blogs, wikis, social networks, virtual worlds, and more. A software application used to access the Web is known as a **browser**. Browsers allow users to navigate the Web, bookmark favorite sites, control how Web pages are displayed, and manage the behind-the-scenes interactions that take place when retrieving Web information. Popular Web browsers include Microsoft *Internet Explorer*, Mozilla *Firefox*, Apple *Safari*, Netscape *Navigator*, and *Opera*. See Figure 3–14.

Telecommunication Tool Uses for Teachers

↗ Gathering up-to-date content to plan and carry out lessons

↗ Communicating with other teachers in similar positions to exchange ideas and reduce teacher isolation

↗ Communicating with students and parents about class activities and assignments

Telecommunication Tool Uses for Students

↗ Accessing up-to-date information on the Internet to research a paper, prepare a speech, or write a report

↗ Using e-mail for pen-pal exchanges with students at other locations to learn more about other places and cultures or to practice a foreign language

↗ Using a website such as a wiki to co-construct a project with other students

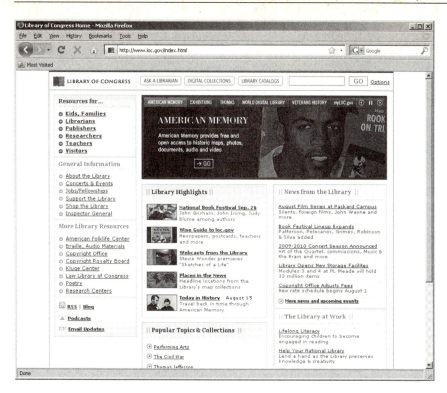

FIGURE 3–14   A screen from Mozilla *Firefox*, a popular Web browser, showing the Library of Congress website (http://www.loc.gov).

Source: Reprinted with permission of Mozilla.

Other Tools

The computer tools listed earlier are among the most popular and widely used computer applications. However, this list just begins to scratch the surface of what is available to teachers and learners for doing work of all kinds. For example, when one needs a finer degree of control over text and graphic layout than is available in typical word processors, teachers and students can turn to desktop publishing programs. Examples include Microsoft *Publisher*, Broderbund *Printshop,* Adobe *Pagemaker* and *InDesign*, and Quark *Xpress* as well as online tools such as *LetterPop* (http://letterpop.com). Mary Jordan began to use *Publisher* to make a newsletter to send home to parents, and her students used the program to create fliers about school recycling and renewable energy sources.

There are also many other graphics tools besides general drawing and painting programs. For example, to create technical drawings, there are programs such as *AutoCAD* and *TurboCAD*. To create graphic organizers, such as concept maps and flowcharts, one can turn to software such as *Inspiration* and the elementary-friendly version called *Kidspiration*. Mary Jordan used *Inspiration* to create concept maps for lesson planning, and her students used the program to create a dichotomous key for classifying tree leaves for a unit in life sciences.

Multimedia is becoming popular in schools today. Digital audio can be created and edited using programs such as Adobe *Soundbooth, Audacity, Goldwave* and Sony *ACID* and *Sound Forge*. Digital video can be produced as a component of multimedia programs or for making stand-alone videos. Products for capturing and editing digital video include Apple *iMovie* and *Final Cut Pro*, Microsoft *Windows Live Movie Maker*, Adobe *Premiere*, Ulead *VideoStudio*, and Sony *Vegas Movie Studio*. See Figure 3–15. Mary Jordan learned that one of her colleagues used *Movie Maker* to edit a video of her class to show at parent open house night, and her colleague's students used the program to edit videos of interviews with older people, such as their grandparents, as part of a unit on local history.

PEARSON **myeducationkit** To learn more about some of these tools go to the Video Tutorials section of Chapter 3 and watch one or more of the following video tutorials: "MS Publisher for PC", "iMovie", or "Movie Maker." As you watch the videos, think about how you can use this software for your own work and how your students can use it for their work.

Our point here is just to emphasize that the computer is truly a multifaceted educational tool. As the examples illustrate, computer applications exist to support almost any kind of work or production of media that one can imagine, and there will be new applications developed in the future that will allow us to do even more with our computers. Throughout the book, we will mention other computer tools of interest to the topics being discussed. However, always keep in mind that the list of computer tools will continue to grow and expand, and in the future you are likely to be limited in the classroom only by your own imagination.

FIGURE 3–15 A screen from Microsoft *Windows Live Movie Maker*, software for editing digital movies.

Source: Microsoft product screen shot reprinted with permission from Microsoft Corporation.

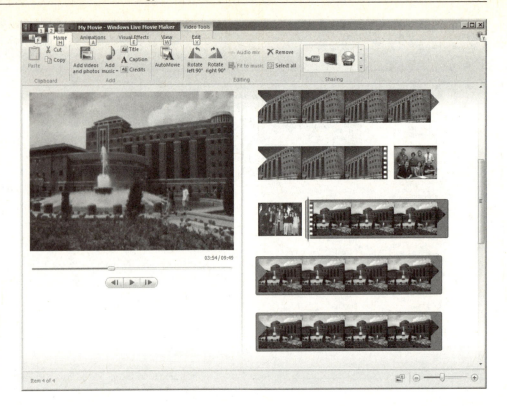

Toolbox: Assistive Technology

Mary Jordan has several students with special needs in her class, and as a teacher you probably will too. **Assistive technology** refers to any item, piece of equipment, or product system that is used to increase, maintain, or improve the functional capabilities of an individual with a disability. You can think of assistive technology devices as mechanical aids that can either substitute for or enhance the function of an ability that is impaired. While some forms of assistive technology are very low-tech (e.g., pencil grip, book holder, highlighter, non-electronic communication board), computer-based hardware and software often play an important role in assisting individuals with disabilities. When planning instruction for students with special needs, it is important for teachers to be aware of available options and to make available appropriate assistive technology. Computer hardware and software can empower all students, but they may be especially important to individuals with disabilities. Many types of computer-based assistive technology are available today. Some of the most common are described here and categorized by the types of functions they address. If you have a student who might benefit from assistive technologies, consult with your school's special education teacher. Availability of these technologies can make a world of difference to a student with special needs.

Computer access In order to take advantage of what the computer has to offer, the student must first be able to access it. For students with certain limitations, special hardware

may be needed to allow the students to work with the computer. For a student with motor difficulties, for example, special input devices and software may be required for the student to be able to interact with and control the computer. As long as the student has some voluntary control of movement, even if it is very small (e.g., finger, eyebrow, head, mouth), this movement can be used to operate systems that provide access to the computer. Specialized input devices for individuals with limited motor control include:

- oversized keyboards or special keyboard layouts such as the Dvorak Simplified Keyboard, which has the most commonly used keys more easily accessible
- StickyKeys feature of Microsoft *Windows,* which allows an individual to type characters requiring a modifier key (Shift, Ctrl, Alt) without having to simultaneously hold down the modifier key
- trackballs, joysticks, touch pads, and touch screens
- head, finger, eyebrow, or sip and puff switches

These input devices can be coordinated with software that allows for selection of options, such as menu management software or alphabet scanning software for text entry, to facilitate manipulation of the computer. Once the user has access to the computer, it can then be used for communication, environmental control, or many other functions.

(continued)

Toolbox: Assistive Technology (*continued*)

Assistive technology, such as adaptive hardware, can help students with disabilities to improve their functional capabilities.
Source: Elizabeth Crews/PhotoEdit.

myeducationkit Go to the Assignments and Activities section of Chapter 3 in MyEducationKit and complete the activity entitled "Adaptive Technology." As you watch the video and answer the accompanying questions, think about how the adaptive keyboard and software allow this student with special needs to more fully participate in learning activities.

Augmentative communication Students who are nonverbal or who have difficulty being understood may benefit from using an augmentative or alternative communication device. Examples of such devices include: digital communication and picture boards, type and talk devices, pocket communicators, speech synthesizers and digitizers, and similar devices. These electronic tools give a voice to individuals who might otherwise have difficulty communicating.

Visual aids For visually impaired learners, there are numerous solutions available. With mild visual impairment, simply enlarging the fonts on the computer may help, and screen

An electronic communication board can help students with speech difficulties to communicate.
Source: Rhoda Sidney/The Image Works.

enlargers or magnifiers are available to further enlarge what appears on the computer's display. For individuals with more significant visual impairment, screen readers with speech synthesizers can convert what appears on the computer screen into spoken language. The use of scanners with optical character recognition (OCR) software or stand-alone reading aids can allow print materials to be accessed. In addition, Braille printers and tactile Braille output devices are available for personal computers.

Auditory aids There are also devices available to assist students with hearing impairments. A telecommunications device for the deaf (TDD), sometimes referred to as a teletypewriter (TTY), is an electronic device that permits hearing impaired individuals to communicate via text over telephone lines. Closed captioning is an assistive technology that allows hearing impaired individuals to acquire information in textual form from video programming.

Cognitive aids In addition to physical limitations, some students may have learning difficulties. Assistive technologies can also help such students. Computer-based instruction, for example, may help students with learning difficulties to practice essential skills in a format that may allow repetition and mastery. Multimedia software may assist students by providing alternative representations of concepts and allowing alternate ways for students to respond to exercises and learning activities. Devices for students with physical disabilities, such as text to speech converters, may also be useful for students with some learning disabilities. There are many available options to help students who have learning challenges.

myeducationkit Go to the Assignments and Activities section of Chapter 3 in MyEducationKit and complete the Web activity entitled "Assistive Technology Training." As you explore this website, think about the diverse needs of your students, how they might benefit from the use of assistive technologies, and why this is important.

(continued)

Toolbox: Assistive Technology (*continued*)

Like students with special needs themselves, assistive technologies are increasingly becoming part of the mainstream today. According to the tenets of **Universal Design** (UD), a philosophy that embraces good design for all, products and environments should be designed to be as usable as possible by all people regardless of their abilities and situations. Universal design arose, in part, out of the development of assistive technologies, and it is a movement that is growing. We should recognize that the world can be a better place if we all think about making design universal. So, as you learn to develop instructional materials and learning environments in this textbook and beyond, always keep in mind how you can design your lessons to be accessible to all of your students.

PEARSON
myeducationkit™ Go to the Assignments and Activities section of Chapter 3 in MyEducationKit and complete the video activity entitled "Universal Design." As you watch the video, think about the way that this university has helped apply concepts of Universal Design to technology use and the potential benefits for students.

TECHNOLOGY COORDINATOR'S CORNER

At the beginning of this chapter, we introduced you to Mary Jordan, a veteran teacher at Spring Valley Elementary School who was concerned about having to learn to use new computer hardware and software in her school. Just before the beginning of the school year, the school district's technology coordinator, Bob Jones, conducted an in-service workshop to orient Mary and the other teachers to the new computers and software applications. During a break in the workshop, Bob sat down with Mary to chat about the anxiety she was feeling about having to learn new technologies.

Bob counseled Mary on how to approach the use of the new computers. First, he suggested that she develop a basic familiarity with the hardware. He shared basic hardware troubleshooting guidelines similar to those presented in this chapter, but he assured Mary that his staff would be available whenever she had hardware problems she couldn't handle on her own. Next, he suggested that Mary take it one step at a time when learning about the available applications. He recommended that Mary start with the basics, such as using *Word* to prepare handouts and other materials for her students. He also recommended *PowerPoint* and *Inspiration,* applications that most teachers find pretty easy to use. After getting comfortable with those, he suggested that Mary think about *Excel* for organizing information. He urged her to take her time and add new software to her repertoire gradually. He also told her to not be afraid to try new things, to use the help feature of the applications to learn how to do new things, and, of course, to ask another teacher or him for help if needed. He noted that teachers do not need to know everything to get started.

Bob also suggested that Mary consider using students as helpers in the classroom. He commented that the teacher doesn't always have to be the expert when it comes to technology. Students and teachers can be co-learners. He noted that students often pick up technology very quickly, and they may enjoy the chance to share their computer expertise with others. A classroom strategy that can facilitate this approach is having small groups of students work together on a project, such as using *PowerPoint* to prepare reports. When the students work together in a group, they help one another learn to use the software and take some of the burden off the teacher.

Bob congratulated Mary on developing a spirit of adventure and openness, which is the best attitude to have when working with computers. He told Mary, "As you learn and grow, you will become more comfortable with the technology, and you will find more and more ways that computers and software can be of benefit both to you and to your students."

SUMMARY

In this chapter, we examined computer systems and computer tools for teaching and learning. Computer systems consist of several components including the CPU, internal memory, mass storage, and input and output devices. These components work together to allow us to perform useful tasks with the computer. When evaluating computer systems for possible acquisition, one should consider these components in light of the desired uses of the system. When using the computer, one should always endeavor to maintain a safe and healthy working environment. Finally, if difficulties arise, follow some basic guidelines to troubleshoot problems with computer systems.

The computer can be used in education as a teacher or as an assistant. In the role of an assistant, commonly used computer productivity tools include word processors, graphics tools, spreadsheets, databases, presentation packages, authoring tools, and computer telecommunications tools among others. We described common features of each type of software and presented typical applications for both teachers and learners. In addition, we described assistive technology, a special class of hardware and software designed to assist individuals with disabilities to use computers and computer applications.

We hope that this chapter has given you many ideas about how you might begin to use the computer for your own productivity (i.e., to design, develop, and evaluate instruction) and as a tool in your own classroom. Keep in mind that the computer with appropriate software is just a tool, albeit a very versatile one. However, it is not appropriate for everything. For example, the computer is not particularly effective in many learning situations ranging from helping students learn handwriting to assisting with some types of complex reasoning and problem solving. While the computer can do a lot, it is not right for everything. In teaching and learning, it is important to know when and how to use available tools appropriately. As we look closely throughout this text at the best ways to plan and implement instruction to help your students learn, we will highlight ways that computers can be useful tools for you and for your students.

PEARSON **myeducationkit**™ To check your comprehension of the content covered in this chapter, go to the MyEducationKit for this book and complete the Study Plan for Chapter 3. Here you will be able to take a chapter quiz, receive feedback on your answers, and then access resources that will enhance your understanding of chapter content.

SUGGESTED RESOURCES

Print Resources

Lewis, P. (2006). *Spreadsheet magic*. Washington DC: ISTE Books.

Lewis, P. (2007). *Database magic*. Washington DC: ISTE Books.

Lewis, P. (2008). *PowerPoint magic*. Washington DC: ISTE Books.

Newby, T. & Lewandowski, J. (2009). *Teaching and learning with Microsoft Office 2007 and Expression Web: A multilevel approach to computer integration (2nd ed.)*. Boston, MA: Pearson Education.

Roblyer, M. D. (2010). *Integrating educational technology into teaching* (5th ed.). Upper Saddle River, NJ: Pearson Education.

Shelly, G. B., Cashman, T. J., Gunter, R. E., & Gunter, G. A. (2008). *Teachers discovering computers: Integrating technology and digital media in the classroom* (5th ed.). Boston, MA: Thompson Learning.

Smaldino, S. E., Lowther, D. L., & Russell, J. D. (2008). *Instructional technology and media for learning* (9th ed.). Upper Saddle River, NJ: Pearson.

Taylor, R. (2003). The computer in the school: Tutor, tool, and tutee. *Contemporary Issues in Technology and Teacher Education, 3*(2), 241–252.

White, R., & Downs, T. (2008). *How computers work* (9th ed.). Indianapolis, IN: Que Publishing.

Electronic Resources

http://www.abledata.com/
(AbleData information about assistive technology)

http://www.actden.com/
(Digital Education Network online tutorials for popular software)

http://computer.howstuffworks.com/
(How Stuff Works: computers)

http://www.healthycomputing.com
(Healthy Computing)

http://www.microsoft.com/learning/
(Microsoft Learning site)

http://www.internet4classrooms.com/k12links.htm
(Internet 4 Classrooms – Helping teachers use the Internet effectively)

http://edcommunity.apple.com/ali/
(Apple's Learning Exchange)

PLANNING THE TECHNOLOGY-ENHANCED LEARNING EXPERIENCE

Webster's *New World Dictionary* defines a *plan* as "any detailed method, formulated beforehand, for doing or making something." Planning is a natural part of life. We plan in order to exercise some influence over future events and to increase the likelihood that things will turn out the way we want. Although a plan does not guarantee success, not having a plan often ensures failure. Plans can take various forms:

↗ A recipe helps us to make sure the food we are preparing includes the necessary ingredients and cooks for the right amount of time.

↗ An itinerary helps us to make sure our vacation trip includes all the things we want to see and do, given our limited amount of time.

↗ A budget helps us to make sure our income both covers our expenses and also allows us some spending money.

↗ A grocery list helps us to make sure we purchase the necessary items when we go shopping.

This section is about planning for instruction and learning. Our purpose is twofold: to convince you that effective planning is a vital part of effective instruction, and to provide you with some practical guidelines for effective planning.

This is the first part of the PIE model described in Chapter 1. Your instructional plan directs what takes place during the implementation and evaluation stages of instruction. Once you have a plan for your instruction, you can move on to implement the instruction outlined in the plan. Once you have implemented your instruction, you can evaluate its effectiveness in helping

your students learn. Planning instruction is made up of three parts:

1. *Developing the plan.* This involves (Chapter 4) identifying the important characteristics of your learners, specifying your intended objectives for the instruction, and specifying the relevant features of the learning environment. In addition, developing instructional activities that will ensure learning is discussed within Chapter 5.

2. *Identifying methods and media.* A variety of instructional methods (Chapter 6) and media (Chapter 7) exist that can impact how learners experience the learning situation. With the variety of content, as well as differences in learners and the practical constraints of time and budget, it is imperative that you become aware of the different methods and media available. We discuss these options, the advantages and limitations of each, and how one goes about selecting the most appropriate option.

3. *Selecting, adapting, and/or producing instructional materials.* We explore in Chapter 8 the process of assembling and/or developing the instructional materials you will need to carry out your plan. We address the practical aspects and issues (e.g., copyright) related to preparing instructional materials within your time and budget constraints.

In this exciting section of the book we encourage creativity, problem solving, and reflection. For many, the art of teaching is embedded in planning and developing what students will experience and how they will learn from those experiences. This section focuses on how you can create learning experiences that will ensure your students' success.

Technology and Instructional Situations: Understanding Learners, Learning Objectives, and Learning Environments

Source: Tom & Dee Ann McCarthy/Index Stock/Jupiter Images.

KEY WORDS AND CONCEPTS

Socialization
Socioeconomic status
Culture
Ethnicity
Prerequisite
Motivation
Learning style

Special needs
Technology literacy
Objective
Performance
Conditions
Criteria
Learning environment

CHAPTER OBJECTIVES

After reading and studying this chapter, you will be able to:

↗ Outline a process for instructional planning.
↗ Identify the important characteristics of a group of students and how those characteristics may influence your use of instructional technology.

↗ Describe how diversity can be used as an asset in instructional planning.
↗ Specify the objectives for a lesson of your choice.
↗ Identify the relevant characteristics of a learning environment.

INTRODUCTION

In the next several chapters, we will describe the components of the instructional planning process, with each chapter describing a different component of the process. To begin, we would like to introduce you to a teacher, Kevin Spencer, who teaches social studies in a suburban middle school. He has been a teacher for a number of years and has taught at his present school for the past seven. Kevin enjoys working with the students and the students seem to like him. He knows his subject and is good at creating lessons that get the students working with one another and that include a variety of interesting activities.

When Kevin was in college, instructional technology was still relatively new. But he has seen some of his colleagues do exciting things with the use of technology by their students. Instructional technology has become better and easier to use, and Kevin has come to the conclusion that this would be a good time for him to incorporate more technology into his teaching. His plan is to begin with his sixth-grade social studies class.

We will return to Kevin at the end of the chapter. But first, we will provide an overview of the instructional planning process and describe the first three components of that process: students, objectives, and the learning environment. These three components are considered the foundation for instructional planning. Instruction usually involves helping particular students accomplish particular learning objectives within a particular learning environment. So, information about students, objectives, and the learning environment will allow teachers to develop plans that are matched to their particular situations in which they are working. We will use Kevin's work as an example of the role this planning process can play in your own efforts to design technology enriched learning experiences.

 OVERVIEW OF INSTRUCTIONAL PLANNING

Recall from Chapter 1 that *learning* is the process of acquiring new knowledge and skills through experience. *Instruction* is the process of helping students learn through the deliberate arrangement of information, activities, methods, and media. *Instructional design* is the process of developing plans for instruction through the practical application of theoretical principles (some of which are described in Chapter 2).

Designing instruction is often viewed as a set of systematic, rational steps that are put in place in a prescribed order, beginning with the goals and objectives of the instruction (Gagne, Wager, Golas, & Keller, 2005). However, practicing teachers do not always follow an objectives-first order when they plan their instruction.

They may begin by specifying objectives. But they are just as likely to begin by:

- ↗ Creating a practice activity
- ↗ Outlining the content to be covered
- ↗ Identifying students' existing knowledge
- ↗ Developing a test
- ↗ Selecting a relevant computer activity

Teachers are likely to follow an equally varied order in developing the remaining elements of their plans. To mirror this flexibility, we suggest that instructional planning is like assembling a jigsaw puzzle. The pieces of the puzzle must fit together to complete the picture, but the order in which the pieces are put in place is not particularly important. As shown in Figure 4–1, we suggest a planning process made up of nine key pieces.

This "jigsaw puzzle" illustrates four important principles of instructional planning:

1. Instructional planning is a systematic process. It is a logical, methodical process in which each element of the plan is considered and carefully linked to the other elements.
2. Instructional planning is a flexible process. The order in which the elements are considered is likely to vary from one situation to the next.
3. Instructional planning is a dynamic, interactive process. Decisions made while developing one element of the plan will affect decisions about other elements. This may mean reconsidering, even changing, decisions you have already made.
4. The result of the process is a coherent plan made up of elements that work together to promote learning.

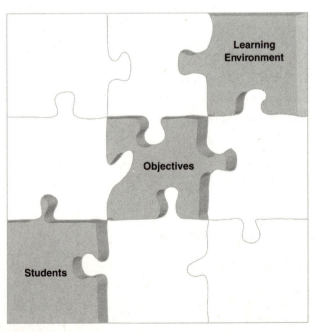

FIGURE 4–1 The pieces of the instructional planning "puzzle."

In Chapter 1 of this text, the Plan, Implement, and Evaluate (PIE) model was introduced (see page 11). Each piece of this model was described, and a table listing a series of questions pertaining to each component was given (see Figure 1-6). Within that introduction, it was explained that teachers and students address each of these components of the model to facilitate a reliable and effective learning experience. In the next nine chapters of this text, we will describe in detail what should occur in order to successfully plan, implement, and evaluate an effective learning experience and how technology can be successfully integrated and utilized within that process. As shown in Figure 4–2, we have developed a checklist of the key steps that should be considered within each of the PIE components. This checklist can be utilized in a number of ways:

1. To provide an advance organizer that helps you to identify what will be essential within the respective chapters and how those elements fit together;
2. To provide a simple structure whereby we can demonstrate and show examples of how each of the steps works within practical learning settings; and
3. To provide you with a tool that can be used in the years to come to help you recall and apply each of the elements that are needed in order to successfully develop reliable instructional learning experiences.

Briefly review the full checklist shown in Figure 4–2. For ease of use, a full version of the checklist is also listed in Appendix C. Within each of the chapters using this checklist, specific parts of the checklist will be highlighted and discussed as you proceed through the PIE chapters of this text.

LEARNERS

We begin our discussion with the learners because the purpose of instruction is to help them learn. As shown in Figure 4–1, knowledge of your students is a key piece in the planning puzzle. Likewise, within the PIE Checklist (see Figure 4–2 on pages 70–71), the initial component is designed to focus your attention directly on the learners/students. As a teacher, your challenge is to help **all** students reach desired learning goals. However,

developing an instructional plan will be easier if you first consider the characteristics of your students, including:

- Gender
- Socioeconomic status
- Culture and ethnicity
- Existing knowledge of the content
- Motivation
- Learning style
- Special needs
- Technology literacy

Extensive discussion of these characteristics is beyond the scope of this book, but we briefly touch on each one here. Our purpose is to briefly describe student characteristics that might affect your instructional planning. More information can be found by referring to the resources listed at the end of the chapter.

Gender

When they are young, boys and girls are more similar than different. However, as they mature, some differences appear. For example, beginning at puberty (approximately 11 or 12 years of age), boys tend to be taller and have more muscular strength; boys tend to be more physically aggressive, while girls tend to be more affiliative, concerned with social relationships; and boys tend to explain their successes in terms of ability ("I'm smart") and their failures in terms of effort ("I didn't try very hard"), while girls tend to explain their successes in terms of effort ("I kept trying until I got it") and their failures in terms of ability ("I'm not very good in science") (Deaux, 1984; Ormrod, 2006).

These differences are partly the result of biology (Boys become stronger because of increased levels of the hormone testosterone). However, they are mostly the result of **socialization**—the process by which we learn the rules, norms, and expectations of the society in which we live. In general, boys and girls are treated differently by parents, peers, teachers, and mass media. As a result, they learn that some things are appropriate for males, while others are appropriate for females. For example, boys may be reinforced for being independent, competitive, and logical. As a result, they may be drawn to school subjects such as science and to occupations such as engineer and electrician. In contrast, girls may be reinforced for being cooperative, sympathetic, and artistic. As a result, they may be drawn to school subjects such as social studies and to occupations such as librarian and nurse.

These gender-related stereotypes have been decreasing during the past 25 years, but they still exist and affect students at all grade levels. However, it is important to note that, even as they mature, few substantial differences in academic ability exist between boys and girls. As a group, their scores on IQ tests are

Planning Phase

1. Learners – Chapter 4
   ☐ Give a general description of your learners (e.g., age, gender, culture, socioeconomic status).
   ☐ Describe the general background knowledge, skills, and attitudes they already possess about the to-be-learned content.
   ☐ Describe each of the following characteristics of your learners that could impact their learning:
   Level of motivation
   Level of technology literacy
   Learning style
   Special needs

   Other: _____

2. Objectives – Chapter 4
   ☐ Briefly describe what you want your learners to know or do. That is, what is the goal of the learning experience?
   ☐ Explain how your learners will demonstrate that the needed learning has actually occurred.
   ☐ Develop and list each of the learning objectives.

   *NOTE: include the 3 key elements of *conditions, performance,* and *criteria* (e.g., Given the (*conditions*), the students will be able to (*performance*), based on (*criteria*).

3. Learning Environment – Chapter 4
   ☐ Describe where the learning is designed to occur.
   ☐ List and describe what resources are available within the selected learning environment (e.g., technology available, equipment, furniture).
   ☐ Describe any ways that this learning environment could hinder/challenge learning from occurring (e.g., high level of noise or other distractions, improper heating/cooling/lighting, location).

4. Developing the initial draft outline – Chapter 4
   ☐ Complete background research (e.g., review relevant research, Internet sites, previously published instructional materials).
   ☐ Based on each objective:
   Complete a draft outline
   Develop a set of planning/storyboard cards
   Develop a flowchart

5. Instructional Activities – Chapter 5
   ☐ For each of the following instructional activities, review the questions and reflectively consider how the various activities and strategies can be incorporated within the instructional materials:

   Motivation Activities
   What strategies will you use to hold students' attention throughout the lesson?
   What strategies will you use to help students see the relevance of the information?
   What strategies will you use to increase students' confidence in learning?
   What strategies will you use to increase students' satisfaction in learning?

   Orientation Activities
   What will you do to help students understand the objectives of the current lesson?
   What will you do to link the lesson to previous lessons?
   What will you do to form transitions?
   What will you do to summarize the lesson and link it to future lessons?

   Information Activities
   What major content ideas will you present? In what sequence? Using what examples?
   What will you do to help students understand and remember those ideas?
   What will you do to help students see the relationships among the ideas?
   What will you do to help students understand when and why the ideas will be useful?

   Application Activities
   What will you do to give students an opportunity to apply their new knowledge or skill?
   How much guidance will you provide and what form will that guidance take?
   In what way will you give students feedback about their performance during practice?

   Evaluation Activities
   What will you do to determine whether students have achieved the learning objectives?
   How will you give students feedback about their performance during the evaluation?

   ☐ Create additional planning cards that include and explain the selected activities and include those within the previously developed set.

FIGURE 4–2 The PIE Checklist.

6. Instructional Methods – Chapter 6
   ☐ Select all instructional methods that apply to the instruction and provide a short description of how each selection will be used.

Check Methods to Incorporate.	Provide Short Description.
☐ Presentation	
☐ Demonstration	
☐ Discussion	
☐ Drill & Practice	
☐ Tutorial	
☐ Instructional Games	
☐ Cooperative Learning	
☐ Simulations	
☐ Discovery	
☐ Problem Solving	

    ☐ Indicate within the planning card set what method, as well as when each of the selected methods will be integrated within the instruction.

7. Instructional Media – Chapter 7
   ☐ Select all instructional media that apply to the instruction and provide a short description of how each selection will be used.

Check Media Used.	Provide Short Description.
☐ Video	
☐ Visuals	
☐ Audio	
☐ Text	
☐ Real Objects and/or Models	
☐ Multimedia	

    ☐ Indicate within the planning card set which media, as well as when each of the selected media will be integrated within the instruction.

8. Instructional Materials – Chapter 8
   ☐ Identify ways in which technology could be integrated to facilitate the development of the instructional materials.
   ☐ Outline the steps involved to develop the draft instruction.
   ☐ Based on your planning cards, outline, and flowchart develop the initial draft of your materials.
   ☐ Review your draft materials for any possible copyright infringement.
   ☐ Have members of the target audience and other stakeholders (e.g., teachers, content experts) review and evaluate the draft materials.

Implementation Phase

1. Instructional Delivery – Chapters 9, 10, and 11
   ☐ Identify the various ways that the instruction may be delivered (e.g., face-to-face, computer-based, online).
   ☐ Determine the optimal manner for delivering your instruction.
   ☐ Revise your instruction to be delivered in the proper manner.
2. Instructional Management – Chapters 9, 10, and 11
   ☐ Describe the role of the teacher and the learners before, during, and after the learning experience.
   ☐ Determine and describe the procedures needed to effectively implement the instructional experience.
   ☐ Revise your instruction so it can be managed properly.

Evaluation Phase

1. Continuous Cycle of Improvement – Chapter 12
   ☐ Implement the revised instructional materials with a selected group of target learners.
   ☐ Review the revised materials with both content and teaching experts (e.g., subject matter experts and other teachers).
   ☐ Based on the data collected from those reviewing the draft instruction, describe what went well, as well as what difficulties were encountered.
   ☐ Based on the evaluation data, complete a "final" version of the instructional materials.

FIGURE 4–2 (Continued)

comparable. While socialization may lead boys and girls to prefer different subject areas and different instructional methods, they have the same *ability* to *learn* in all content areas.

Socioeconomic Status

Socioeconomic status (SES) encompasses a variety of factors, including family income, parents' occupations, and the amount of formal education parents have completed. In general, the more education parents have completed, the more "professional" their occupations, and the more money they earn, the higher the family's SES. SES is worthy of our attention because it is consistently related to "success" in school, as measured by things such as standardized test scores, grades, truancy, and dropout rates (Macionis, 1997). This is largely because of the nature of the parent-child interactions that occur within families. In general, high SES parents are more likely to provide their children with a variety of educational experiences outside of school (e.g., travel, music lessons, museum visits), be involved in their children's school and extracurricular activities, and value education and communicate that value to their children. SES may also affect the experience with technology that a student brings to school.

However, it is important to note that these are broad generalizations that aren't limited to high SES families. It can be easy to stereotype low SES parents as unable and/or unwilling to support their children's education. But this would frequently be inaccurate. Many low SES parents maintain high educational standards, actively participate in their children's school activities, take their children to museums, and encourage their children to participate in a variety of extracurricular activities. In addition, all families have "historically accumulated and culturally developed bodies of knowledge and skills essential for household or individual functioning" (Moll, Amanti, Neff, & Gonzalez, 1992, p. 133). Though the content may differ, these "funds of knowledge" can be used to help children learn by connecting school experiences with home experiences. For example, children from farm families may have access to information about plants and animals that would be relevant in a science class. Children whose parents are police officers may be familiar with laws and courts in a way that would be relevant in a social studies class.

The point is that understanding these varied "funds of knowledge" can be helpful in instructional planning by enabling teachers to:

1. Tap into unique learning experiences that naturally occur in the home.
2. Provide opportunities for parents to become directly involved in their children's education through their day-to-day activities.

3. Help students maintain a sense of pride in their families and the contributions they make to the community.
4. Provide diverse approaches to subject matter that enriches the learning for all students in a class.

Culture and Ethnicity

Culture refers to the attitudes, values, customs, and behavior patterns that characterize a social group (Banks, 2006). Part of culture is **ethnicity**, which refers to "the way individuals identify themselves with the nation from which they or their ancestors came" (Kauchak & Eggen, 2008, p. 76). Within the United States, there are a number of ethnic groups, including African American, Hispanic, Asian American, Native American, and various immigrant groups, including Italian, Polish, Israeli, Indian, and many others.

For the most part, schools in the United States are based on a white, middle-class, American majority culture. Students from different cultural backgrounds are likely to experience a "cultural mismatch" (Ormrod, 2006), in which important discrepancies appear between their home culture and the school culture. This may result in confusion about what to expect or what is expected of them, which may, in turn, result in reduced achievement for these students. Teachers sometimes contribute to this cultural mismatch through the natural human tendency to view student behaviors through their own cultural windows. The resulting misinterpretations may lead teachers to conclude that minority students lack ability and/or motivation. They may very well be wrong. Consider the following examples:

↗ During a conversation with the teacher, a student looks down rather than maintaining eye contact. The teacher interprets this to mean that the student is bored and is not paying attention. However, the student may come from a culture in which eye contact with an adult is a sign of disrespect.

↗ A student seems to wait a long time before responding to a question. The teacher interprets this to mean that the student does not understand the question or know the answer. However, the student may speak a language other than English at home and need time to translate the question.

As with SES, knowing about your students' culture and ethnicity can facilitate instructional planning because it will help you understand and accommodate the attitudes, experiences, and "funds of knowledge" students bring to school. For example, cultural mismatch can be particularly prominent with some cultures. Ogbu (1992) distinguishes between ethnic groups who immigrated to the United States voluntarily (such as Irish or Vietnamese) and groups who were brought to the United States against their will (such as African Americans) or were conquered (such as Native Americans). Students from these "involuntary minorities" may form "resistance cultures" (Ogbu & Simons, 1998) in which school success is perceived as a rejection of their native culture. As a result, these students often experience low grades, disciplinary problems, and high dropout rates. To counter these effects, teachers may have to work harder to build trust with the students, provide instruction that is culturally responsive, and involve parents and members of the cultural community in the children's education.

Existing Knowledge of the Content

Existing knowledge of the content refers to what students already know when they begin a lesson. There are two related questions: Are the students ready to begin the lesson? Have they already achieved the desired goals? To understand the first question, it is important to understand the concept of **prerequisites**. As we will see in the next section, objectives define the knowledge students should have at the *end* of a lesson. Prerequisites, on the other hand, define the knowledge students should have at the *beginning* of the lesson. When students don't have the necessary prerequisites, they will, at best, have a difficult time succeeding in the lesson. Learning is cumulative, and this means two things. First, it means that virtually every lesson has prerequisites. The objectives of one lesson often form the prerequisites for the next. Second, it means that finding out what the students already know will help with instructional planning because it will allow you to create instruction that builds on that existing knowledge.

Imagine that you are planning a lesson on long division. The prerequisites for long division are subtraction and multiplication; to learn long division effectively and efficiently, students must be able to subtract and multiply. Students lacking these prerequisite skills cannot learn long division. Figure 4–3 illustrates the order in which these prerequisites lead up to long division. It represents three students who differ in what they already know. The first student, Tom, has mastered subtraction, but not multiplication. Long division is over his head; he is not ready yet because he does not have all the prerequisites. He is likely to be frustrated and lost. The second student, Becky, has all the prerequisites. She knows how to subtract and multiply but does not yet

know how to do long division. She is ready to begin. The third student, Polly, has gone beyond the prerequisites. She knows how to subtract and multiply, and she knows how to do long division, at least in some situations. Like Tom, Polly is likely to be frustrated, but for a different reason; she is likely to be bored because the instruction is presenting something she already knows.

Motivation

Motivation refers to a "process whereby goal-directed activity is instigated and sustained" (Schunk, Pintrich, & Meece, 2008, p. 4). It can be distinguished from ability in that it defines what people *will* do rather than what they *can* do (Keller, 1983). Motivation is a common influence on human activities. We are motivated to pursue certain relationships, enter certain careers, go to certain places, or engage in certain activities. Motivation makes a direct contribution to learning by focusing students on certain desired learning goals and increasing the effort they expend in reaching those goals.

Motivation can be categorized as intrinsic or extrinsic. *Intrinsic* motivation is generated by aspects of the experience or task itself (such as its novelty or the challenge it presents). *Extrinsic* motivation is generated by factors unrelated to the experience or task (such as grades or recognition). Intrinsic and extrinsic motivation are often thought of as opposite ends of a single continuum. But they are actually two separate dimensions, as shown in Figure 4–4.

As Figure 4–4 shows, it is possible for a student to show high, medium, or low intrinsic motivation and high, medium, or low extrinsic motivation on a given activity. Motivation will also vary from student to student and from activity to activity. For example, John and Mary may participate in school debates. John participates because he enjoys it (intrinsic motivation), but Mary participates

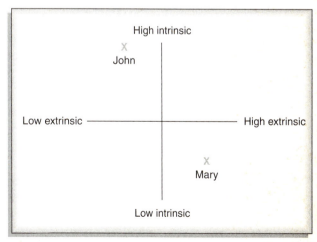

FIGURE 4–4 Intrinsic and extrinsic dimensions of motivation.

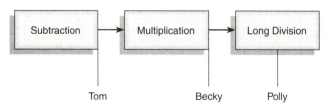

FIGURE 4–3 An example of the concept of prerequisites.

because she thinks it will look good on college applications (extrinsic motivation). At the same time, John participates in every environmental debate he can, but is less interested in debates about social policy issues. Both intrinsic and extrinsic motivation are useful. But, in general, intrinsic motivation is more effective in learning. Students who are intrinsically motivated will work harder and learn more because of their natural interest in the material.

Knowing something about your students' motivation will help with instructional planning, because it will help you add to the extrinsic and intrinsic appeal of the instruction. More specifically, it will help you determine what kinds of reinforcers (Chapter 2) might work with individual students (extrinsic motivation). It will also help you create intrinsically motivating instructional activities including (Eggen & Kauchak, 2010):

↗ Challenge—Adjusting the difficulty level of activities and providing feedback that is immediate and matched to needs of the individual student.
↗ Control—Allowing students to regulate their own learning by adjusting the pace of an activity and varying the amount and kind of assistance they receive.
↗ Curiosity—Presenting students with a variety of situations that are unique, surprising, or inconsistent with their existing ideas.
↗ Confidence—Providing students with guidance and assistance that will help them succeed, develop their confidence in their own abilities, and increase their interest in other, more difficult activities.

Learning Style

Learning style refers to students' approaches to learning, problem solving, and processing information (Morrison,

Ross, & Kemp, 2007). There are a number of ways to categorize learning style. One simple way to think about learning style is to consider the sensory channel a student prefers for taking in new information—visual, auditory, or kinesthetic. As shown in Figure 4–5, knowing your students' preferred sensory channels can help in planning your instruction.

Now that we have presented this information, a couple of important cautions are in order. First, the categories aren't mutually exclusive. Each student will use all three sensory channels, though one channel may be stronger or used more frequently than the others. Second, no value judgment should be made about these learning styles. For example, visual learners are not smarter or better than auditory learners. They are simply different. In fact, these learning styles should not be used to label or categorize students (Susie is an auditory learner). Instead, they should serve as reminders:

↗ Students are not alike. They differ from one another in the sensory channel they prefer. Perhaps as important, they differ from us. The sensory channel we prefer will not be the sensory channel that all of the students prefer.
↗ We should vary our instruction to accommodate those differences. This is where instructional technology can be an asset. Technology is particularly good at using multiple sensory channels. It allows us to combine text, graphics, audio clips, video, and "hands on" activities to help all students learn.
↗ We should help students understand how they learn best. This may involve helping them understand which sensory channel is most effective for them and helping them develop the other sensory channels.

	Characteristics	Technology Ideas
Visual Learners	↗ Learn best what they see ↗ Are good at spatial relations ↗ Will often use images or color to remember information	Present information in the form of graphs, pictures, animations, video clips, and other types of visuals
Auditory Learners	↗ Learn best what they hear ↗ Have strong language skills ↗ Will often sound things out or talk as a way of understanding something	Use audio to explain ideas or narrate
Kinesthetic Learners	↗ Learn best what they do ↗ Are often well-coordinated ↗ Will often physically explore his/her environment	Ask students to manipulate items

FIGURE 4–5 Learning style characteristics and ideas for technology use.

Special Needs/Exceptionalities

Students are individuals, and differ from one another in a variety of ways. Sometimes students are different enough from their peers that they require special educational services to help them reach their potential. In recent years there have been increasing efforts for *inclusion* of these students—to educate them as much as possible in regular classrooms with other students who do not have **special needs/exceptionalities**—to ensure that all students have the same educational opportunities. Inclusion focuses on providing a web of services that includes placing students with special needs into the regular age- and grade-appropriate classroom with needed support for their special needs (Kauchak & Eggen, 2008). At the same time, there have been increasing efforts to identify their special needs in order to provide them with school experiences that will enable them to reach their individual learning potentials.

Students may require special educational services for a variety of reasons, which can be classified into several categories:

- Learning disabilities, such as attention deficit/hyperactivity disorder (AD/HD), in which a student has difficulty concentrating on a single task for any length of time
- Behavior disorders, which include both "acting out," marked by aggressive or disruptive behavior, and "acting in," marked by anxiety and withdrawal (Eggen & Kauchak, 2001)
- Communication disorders, such as stuttering, in which a student repeats a sound while pronouncing words
- Perception problems such as loss of vision or hearing
- Motor problems such as those associated with cerebral palsy or epilepsy
- Health problems such as asthma or diabetes

For each of these types of special needs, we must reemphasize that students are individuals, as different from one another as they are similar. For example, visually impaired students are similar in that they all have a functional limitation. Like other students, however, they are likely to differ in terms of their cultural background, motivation, and learning styles. For a thorough discussion of special needs students and the issue of inclusion, see Salend (2005). For a discussion of assistive technologies, which can assist students with special needs, refer to the Toolbox: Assistive Technologies on pages 60–62 of Chapter 3.

There is another category of special needs/exceptionalities that is often not thought of as a "problem," but that requires special attention—giftedness. *Giftedness* refers to an exceptional talent or ability in one or more areas. Students may be gifted in any academic area—science, music, creative writing, and so on. Gifted students are often frustrated or bored in school and may become isolated from other students because of differences in their interests that may seem impossible to reconcile. Gifted students may benefit from planned instructional activities that challenge them and help them to develop their special talents.

Technology Literacy

Traditionally, literacy has meant the ability to read and write. However, with the growth of the information age, the definition of literacy has expanded to include visual literacy, information literacy, and technology literacy. **Technology literacy** refers to "computer skills and the ability to use computers and other technology to improve learning, productivity, and performance" (U.S. Department of Education, 1996, p. 7). This includes the variety of technology tools described in Chapter 3: word processors, graphics tools, presentation software, computer databases and database management systems, electronic spreadsheets, multimedia/hypermedia authoring tools, and computer telecommunications and the Internet.

Knowing the technology literacy of your students has obvious benefits for instructional planning. If you are planning a lesson that asks the students to use a word processor, an electronic bulletin board, or a search engine, then it is a good idea to find out how familiar the students are with that technology.

Technology literacy is likely to vary in a particular class, depending on the students' ages, prior experience with computers, and access to computers outside of school. One way to assess technology literacy is to ask your students (or a sample of students) a series of questions about their computer skills, such as shown in Figure 4–6. This figure shows an excerpt from a survey used to assess the technology skills among a group of high school students. You can easily adapt the questions to fit the grade level of your students.

The figure shows a relatively formal assessment of technology skills. But it does not have to be done formally. It can be just as useful to ask students about their technology skills as part of short, informal "chats." In any case, the purpose is to find out how much your students know about technology so you can choose appropriate hardware and software, consider the value of creating familiarization activities for the students, and determine how much technology support the students will require during the lesson.

Diversity as an Asset

Clearly, we have only scratched the surface of the dimensions that describe students. However, even these brief descriptions illustrate the important role student characteristics

Can you edit, copy, cut, and paste a block of text within a document?	☐ I can do this ☐ I can probably do this ☐ I would have difficulty doing this ☐ I would not be able to do this
Can you create a table with 3 rows and 4 columns?	☐ I can do this ☐ I can probably do this ☐ I would have difficulty doing this ☐ I would not be able to do this
Can you insert a picture and wrap the text around it?	☐ I can do this ☐ I can probably do this ☐ I would have difficulty doing this ☐ I would not be able to do this
Can you change the size, color, font, and style of text?	☐ I can do this ☐ I can probably do this ☐ I would have difficulty doing this ☐ I would not be able to do this
Can you insert a formula that computes and reports sums, averages, and high and low scores?	☐ I can do this ☐ I can probably do this ☐ I would have difficulty doing this ☐ I would not be able to do this
Can you change the format of a number within a cell?	☐ I can do this ☐ I can probably do this ☐ I would have difficulty doing this ☐ I would not be able to do this
Can you select a range of rows and columns of data and create a chart?	☐ I can do this ☐ I can probably do this ☐ I would have difficulty doing this ☐ I would not be able to do this
Can you sort and filter data?	☐ I can do this ☐ I can probably do this ☐ I would have difficulty doing this ☐ I would not be able to do this

FIGURE 4–6 A sample set of technology literacy survey questions focusing on word processing and spreadsheet capabilities.

play in instructional planning. For example, Figure 4–7 shows how the use of technology can be influenced by student characteristics. This is because virtually every group of students will be diverse in ways that are both apparent (gender, race) and hidden (learning style, motivation). For example, one in three students in elementary and secondary school belongs to a racial or ethnic minority; one in five lives in poverty; 11 percent are classified as disabled; and more than 50 percent will live in a single-parent home before they turn 18 (Sapon-Shevin, 2001). This diversity can be confirmed by looking into any classroom. Even in groups that are homogeneous on one dimension (e.g.,

single-sex classes), the students are likely to vary on other dimensions (e.g., SES, ethnicity, learning style).

PEARSON **myeducationkit™** Go to the Assignments and Activities section of Chapter 4 in MyEducationKit and complete the activity entitled "Teaching to Multiple Intelligences." As you watch the included video, think about the differences exhibited by the various children in the classrooms and how considerations within the learning experience must be taken into account for this diverse set of learners.

Dimension	Characteristics	Possible Technology Implications
Gender	Boys may be more aggressive and dominate available equipment (Swain & Harvey, 2002).	Develop procedures to ensure equitable access.
	Girls may focus more on the social functions of technology (Brunner & Bennett, 1997).	Choose software that emphasizes simulation and collaboration.
	Girls may feel less confident in their ability to use and learn from technology.	Provide more guidance and feedback.
SES	Low-SES children are likely to have less experience with technology than high-SES children (U.S. Department of Education, 2006).	Provide remediation or familiarization activities for low-SES students.
Culture and ethnicity	African American and Hispanic children are likely to have less experience with technology than white children (U.S. Department of Education, 2006).	Provide remediation or familiarization activities for minority children.
Learning preferences	Students with a visual preference learn best what they see.	Ask students to use drawing software to create concept maps for new information.
	Students with an auditory preference learn best what they hear.	Use video conferencing and other types of communication tools to have students interact with experts.
	Students with a kinesthetic preference learn best what they do.	Ask students to visit websites and scroll for information.
Special needs	Students with impaired vision may not be able to read information on a monitor.	Provide a screen reader that will read aloud text and names of icons.
	Students with motor problems may have difficulty with the fine motor coordination required to use a keyboard or mouse.	Provide switch-accessible software that allows them to control the keyboard or cursor with a head nod or puff of air.

FIGURE 4–7 Diversity and technology.

This diversity has benefits. For example, Terenzini and colleagues (2001) investigated the relationship between racial/ethnic diversity and student learning among college students. They found that students in diverse classes reported greater gains in both problem-solving ability and group skills. Similarly, in a review of research, Milem (2003) reports that college students who interacted with diverse people and ideas showed greater intellectual engagement and academic motivation, along with greater gains in critical thinking.

Thus, classroom diversity is both inevitable and valuable. The question is how to deal with it. Traditionally, diversity has been viewed as a deficit—something that is lacking in students who don't fit the "norm." However, we propose a "difference" approach to diversity (Villegas & Lucas, 2002). A difference approach suggests that a particular student's problems can often be attributed to a mismatch between the school experience and some characteristic of the student, rather than to something that is wrong with the student (a deficit). For example, using verbal descriptions to teach mathematics concepts may present a mismatch for students with a more visual learning style.

Putting this kind of difference approach into practice involves five basic principles that should be incorporated into your instruction.

1. Recognize that, like your students, you are an individual. That is, you are a man or woman who has certain cultural and socioeconomic characteristics, learning styles, and motivational interests.
2. Get to know your students as individuals. Identify and support their specific cultural backgrounds, talents, accomplishments, and interests. These first two principles help us avoid the "ethnocentric" assumptions that our students are all alike and that they are all like us.
3. Teach each of your students as an individual, as much as possible. This means teaching each student to read, write, and solve mathematics problems. It also means teaching them to respect one another and to value their diversity.
4. Use teaching methods that incorporate their diversity. For example, Sapon-Shevin (2001)

suggests three teaching strategies that make use of students' diversity:

- ↗ Cooperative learning—This involves putting students into groups to work on a shared learning task and making sure that the groups are diverse in one or more dimensions.
- ↗ Peer tutoring—This involves asking students to teach one another. An important consideration is making sure to allow all students to be the teacher at one time or another so that no one is permanently identified as less able.
- ↗ Multilevel teaching—This involves creating instruction that focuses on an essential idea and includes a variety of learning tasks to accommodate students with different cultural backgrounds, learning styles, and existing knowledge.

5. Represent diversity in the examples, stories, posters, and other classroom materials that you use. A key here is to make sure that each gender, race, and cultural group is represented in a positive light.

Following these guidelines will make it easier to understand any problems or concerns particular students are having and to plan instruction that will help overcome those problems. For example, you'll be able to:

- ↗ Encourage boys and girls in subject areas that do not fit traditional gender-related stereotypes
- ↗ Adjust instructional methods to allow for responses that are appropriate in students' home cultures
- ↗ Provide additional support (social and emotional as well as educational) for students (and their parents) from low-SES families
- ↗ Organize new information and plan instructional activities based on students' learning styles
- ↗ Develop strategies to increase students' intrinsic motivation
- ↗ Help identify students' special needs and obtain services to help meet those needs

 OBJECTIVES

Imagine that you are taking a vacation trip. You will want to know where you're going so you can:

- ↗ Make reasonable decisions about what routes and means of transportation to take, what you might want to see along the way, what you'll need to take with you, and so on
- ↗ Manage your budget
- ↗ Monitor your progress and manage your time
- ↗ Tell concerned others (family and friends) where you're going and what your itinerary is so they will know where you are

A lesson is an instructional "trip," and, like a vacation trip, you'll want to know where you're going so you can:

- ↗ Make reasonable decisions about what instructional methods and media to use, how long your students will take to reach the "destination," what else you might want them to learn along the way, what materials, facilities, and equipment you'll need, and so on
- ↗ Manage your budget
- ↗ Monitor students' progress and manage the time allotted for the lesson
- ↗ Tell concerned others (students, parents, principals, other teachers, etc.) where you're going and what your itinerary is so they know where you'll be.

So, **objectives** are important because they define where you're going—the knowledge or skills the students should have at the end of the lesson. Refer again to Figure 4–1 and note that "Objectives" are critical piece of the puzzle within the planning process. Note also within the PIE checklist (see Figure 4–2), that early on within the instructional planning process, you need to consider what exactly will be learned. What is it that your learners will do to show that they have acquired the knowledge, skills, and abilities? Knowing this information allows you to know where your instruction is going–and it lays the ground work for understanding what your learners need to experience in order to acquire that information.

Sources of Objectives

There are a number of sources that you can refer to help you identify lesson objectives:

- ↗ *Curriculum guides*—General objectives are often provided in curriculum guides, competency lists, and content outlines that are set forth by state education departments, school districts, or professional organizations. You may then translate these general course objectives into objectives for specific lessons.
- ↗ *Textbooks and instructional activities*—Textbooks and commercially produced instructional activities often include suggested objectives that identify what students should learn. These objectives may appear in an accompanying instructor's guide.
- ↗ *Tests*—Objectives can be derived from the tests used in a course. When the objectives, instruction, and tests are parallel, tests will indicate what the students should have learned. This is true for standardized tests as well as for tests you develop. The general principle is that if it is important enough to be on the test, it is probably important enough to specify as a lesson objective.

↗ *Internet*—More and more lesson plans and instructional activities can be found on the Internet. Through the use of search engines, lesson plans and their associated objectives can be readily found for all types of content and across all age levels.

↗ *Your own ideas*—You will often have your own ideas about what students should learn from a lesson, especially if you have taught the lesson before or are familiar with the particular students.

Specifying Lesson Objectives

Objectives specify what the teacher wants the students to learn. Various methods for specifying objectives have been described (Gronlund & Brookhart, 2008). We suggest the method Mager (1997) describes, in which objectives include three components:

Performance: what students will do to indicate that they have learned

Conditions: the circumstances under which the students are expected to perform

Criteria: the standard that defines acceptable performance

Specifying the objectives for a lesson involves specifying each of these three components.

Specifying the Performance

What will students do or say that will indicate they have learned? We suggest specifying the performance first because it is often the easiest component to identify. Teachers usually know what they want their students to learn in a lesson, even if they have not thought out all the details. The key is to specify a performance that is an observable indicator of students' capabilities.

Observable Indicator. Assessing learning almost always involves inference. In some situations (e.g., learning to solve arithmetic problems) the inference is relatively straightforward, while in other situations (e.g., learning to think critically) the inference is more difficult. But in virtually every situation, students must do something before you can infer their level of learning. To

facilitate this inference, the objective should specify an observable performance. This will allow both you and the students to tell whether learning has occurred. One way to ensure the specification of an observable performance is to use verbs that describe observable actions—things you can see or hear students do. Figure 4–8 lists some observable action verbs, along with verbs you should avoid, because they are not observable actions. These lists are not exhaustive, but will give you an idea of the kinds of verbs to use when specifying lesson objectives.

Student Capability. Teachers are naturally focused on what is going to happen during the lesson (Sardo-Brown, 1990). One result of this is a tendency for the teacher's plans to focus on the activities (either the teacher's or the students') that will take place during the lesson. Developing these activities is an important aspect of planning. But the purpose of specifying objectives is to clearly identify the results, or destination, of the lesson rather than the route students will follow to reach that destination. What should students learn? One way to make sure you describe a student capability is to use the phrase "the students will be able to," before the action verb. Using this phrase will remind you that the objective of the lesson is a future capability of the student.

Specifying the Conditions

What are the circumstances under which students will be expected to perform? What will they be given to work with? The key is to specify conditions that will be in place *at the time of the expected performance.* One way to specify the conditions is to think about the questions students are likely to ask about the expected performance. Their questions can be grouped into four categories:

Setting: Where will they be expected to perform?
People: Will they be working alone? With a team? Under supervision?
Equipment: What tools or facilities will they have to work with?
Information: What, if any, notes, books, checklists, or models will they have to work with?

FIGURE 4–8   Use observable action verbs in objectives.

Use Verbs Such As			Avoid Verbs Such As	
compare	construct	operate	understand	believe
translate	create	adjust	appreciate	become familiar with
describe	explain	replace	think	become aware of
measure	repair	compose	know	be comfortable with
identify	define	compute	recognize	
draw	administer	solve		

For example, imagine that you want your students to describe the use of symbolism in *Macbeth*. The students might ask: Will we have to come up with the examples ourselves, or will we describe examples you give us (information)? Will this be an in-class assignment, or can we take it home (setting)? Can we use our books (information)? Can we work together (people)?

As shown in the following example, you can include your responses to these questions in the objective by using a word such as *given* or *using*:

↗ Given a scene from *Macbeth*, individual students will be able to describe the use of symbolism in the scene.

Specifying the conditions often helps you define what is important in the performance. For example, if you want your students to describe symbolism in *Macbeth*, you might consider the following questions: Is it important that they recall instances of symbolism, or is it enough that they can describe the identified symbolism? Is it important that they be able to perform under pressure, as in the classroom, or is it enough that they can perform in the more private and relaxed setting of home?

Specifying the Criteria What is the standard that defines desired performance? How well must students perform? Some might argue that specifying criteria for students' performance is part of developing a test. However, criteria, like conditions, are an important component of an objective, because they help you identify what is important in the performance. Consider wanting your students to describe symbolism in *Macbeth*. Will you accept just any description? Probably not. You want students' answers to be "correct" in some way. Thinking about what "correct" looks like will help you devise a lesson that will guide students to the objective. There are a number of possible ways of defining a "correct" performance. As Figure 4–9 indicates, these can be classified

Category	Description	Example
Time		
Time limits	Specifies the time limits within which the performance must take place.	Given a "victim" with no pulse or respiration, the student will be able to begin one-person CPR *within 15 seconds.*
Duration	Specifies the length of the performance.	Given a "victim" with no pulse or respiration, the student will be able to maintain one-person CPR *for at least 15 minutes.*
Rate	Specifies the rate or speed at which the performance must take place.	Given a "victim" with no pulse or respiration, the student will be able to administer one-person CPR *at a steady rate of 12 compressions per minute.*
Accuracy		
Number of errors	Specifies the maximum acceptable number of errors.	Given a topic, the student will be able to compose a letter that contains *no more than two errors* in spelling, grammar, or syntax.
Tolerances	Specifies the maximum acceptable measurement range.	With the aid of a dial gauge, the student will be able to measure the lateral roll-out on a disc *to within 0.002 inch.*
Quality		
Essential characteristics	Specifies the characteristics that must be present for the performance to be considered acceptable. Often signaled by words such as "must include."	Without reference to books or notes, the student will be able to describe the causes of the American Revolution. The description *must include at least two of the significant events leading up to the war.*
Source	Specifies the documents or materials that will be used as a gauge of the performance. Often signaled by words such as "according to," or "consistent with."	Given a computer with a hard drive and a new software application, the student will be able to install the software onto the hard drive *according to the procedure described in the software manual.*
Consequences	Specifies the expected results of the performance. Often signaled by words such as "such that" or "so that."	Given a flat bicycle tire, a patch kit, and a pump, the student will be able to patch the tire *so that it holds the recommended air pressure for at least 24 hours.*

FIGURE 4–9 Categories of criteria for defining acceptable performance.

	Guidance	Communication
Teacher	Guides selection and development of lesson content and activities. Guides selection and development of assessment instruments.	Reminds the teacher of the expected outcomes.
Students	Guides students' studying.	Tells students what will be expected of them.
Others	Guides the development of the overall curriculum into which the lesson or course fits. Guides the delivery of instruction by substitutes.	Tells interested others (e.g., principals, parents, substitutes) what the students are learning and what is expected of them.

FIGURE 4–10 The practical benefits of specifying lesson objectives.

into three broad categories: time, accuracy, and quality (Mager, 1997). Of course, not all of these criteria will be relevant in every situation. The key is to identify those that are critical for successful student performance in your particular lesson.

Of course, an objective may use more than one type of criterion, as in the following example:

↗ Given a topic, the student will be able to compose a letter that contains no more than two errors in grammar or syntax (accuracy: number of errors). The letter must be at least one page in length (time: duration) and contain a combination of simple and complex sentences (quality: essential characteristics).

Composing Objectives

Once you have considered each of the three components of an objective, you can put them together. You can simply list the components of the objective, as in the following example:

Performance: Solve simultaneous algebra equations
Conditions: Graphing calculators
Criteria: Accurate to two decimal places

Or, you can combine the components into a coherent sentence or two, as in the following example:

↗ With the use of graphing calculators, students will be able to solve simultaneous algebra equations. Solutions must be accurate to two decimal places.

PEARSON myeducationkit™ Go to the Assignments and Activities section of Chapter 4 in MyEducationKit and complete the web activity entitled "Planning for Instruction." On the website given within that activity, explore the section titled, "Writing objectives?" and then complete the "Interactive practice" section to test your skill when writing instructional objectives. Think about the different ways that objectives can be written and still be effective.

Benefits of Objectives

Figure 4–10 summarizes the practical benefits of specifying lesson objectives. As this figure shows, objectives provide a useful communication tool as well as practical guidance for teachers, students, and others. However, researchers have raised questions about the value of specifying objectives in advance (Reiser & Dick 1996; Yelon, 1991). Following are several of the most common criticisms, together with our responses.

Criticism: Objectives dehumanize the instruction by focusing on the requirements rather than the students.
Response: Contrary to this common misperception, the purpose of objectives is to specify the knowledge and skills that are important for the students to acquire. This allows you to plan a way for *each* student to accomplish what you want him or her to. In addition, clearly stated objectives tell students where they will be going. This helps motivate them, guides their studying, and allows them to plan and monitor their own progress.
Criticism: Specifying objectives takes up valuable time.
Response: Time spent specifying objectives is an *investment* rather than an expenditure. As with any other investment, clearly stated objectives have a significant dividend: They help ensure that your instructional plan will match your students' needs.
Criticism: Objectives cannot be specified for complex or intangible skills, such as problem solving or critical thinking. The result is a focus on low-level skills, such as memorization, which are easy to describe and measure but are not always the skills the students should be learning.
Response: It is easier to specify objectives for low-level skills such as memorization. However, objectives can be specified for all types of learning, including complex, high-level skills like problem solving or critical thinking. In fact, because of the greater complexity of high-level skills, specifying objectives for them may be more important than for low-level skills.
Criticism: Specifying objectives in advance "locks in" the curriculum and makes it difficult to change.

Response: Explicitly stating objectives does not necessarily mean they are written in stone. You can modify them as easily as you write them. Good teachers review their objectives periodically so they can modify those that are no longer relevant.

Criticism: Specifying objectives in advance leads to a rigid, mechanistic approach to teaching that reduces the teacher's ability to respond creatively and spontaneously to students and to the "teachable moments" that often occur in the classroom.

Response: When you're taking a vacation trip, having a destination doesn't necessarily mean that you can't or won't take side trips to explore other interesting places. Similarly, on an instructional "trip," having objectives does not mean that you cannot or will not explore other interesting ideas.

Criticism: Specifying objectives in advance results in a tendency to "teach to the test."

Response: If your test accurately assesses your objectives, as it should, and you have designed your instruction to achieve your objectives, as you should, then your instruction will also help students succeed on the test.

LEARNING ENVIRONMENT

Simply stated, the **learning environment** is the setting or physical surroundings in which learning is expected to take place. At first glance this may seem obvious: Learning takes place in the classroom. It is more complicated than that, however, for two reasons. First, classrooms are different; they vary in size, layout, lighting, and seating, among other things. Second, learning takes place in a variety of settings besides the classroom: the laboratory (computer lab, science lab, or language lab), playground, beach, backstage at a theater, or at home. In fact, learning typically involves some combination of environments. As highlighted in the PIE checklist (see Figure 4–2), you need to consider where the learning will occur and how it could impact what the learner experiences.

We said earlier that instruction should match the students for whom it is intended and the goals defined in the objectives. It is equally true that instruction should match the environment in which it will occur. If it does not, the instruction may be theoretically valid but practically impossible (Tessmer, 1990). Sometimes this is obvious, as in the following example:

↗ A biology lesson that includes a laboratory experiment in which the students use microscopes to identify the structures of the cell requires enough lab equipment and supplies for all students. When lab equipment is limited, it may be necessary to change the experiment to a group activity. When lab equipment is severely limited, it may be necessary to use a demonstration as the instructional method.

Sometimes this problem is not as obvious, as in the following example:

↗ A mathematics lesson on solving algebra equations that includes a commercial computer-based tutorial requires a site license authorizing use of the tutorial at multiple workstations. Without a site license, the students may have to use the tutorial one at a time, requiring a reorganization of the lesson.

Instructional planning, therefore, involves asking several questions about the setting:

↗ Where will learning occur? A classroom? A laboratory? Some other area of the school? On a field trip? Or at home?

↗ What are the characteristics of those environments? In a classroom, how large is the space in relation to the number of students? How are the seats arranged? Can they be moved easily? How much noise do you anticipate in the setting? What other distractions are there? Is the lighting adequate? Can you adjust the lighting?

↗ How will these characteristics influence your instruction? Can the setting be modified to accommodate the instruction you're planning? If not, what constraints will the setting impose on the instruction?

Bringing it all together: Starting the initial drafts of the instructional learning experience

Now that you have identified the who, what, and where of your instructional experience, the next step is outlining the initial draft. This can be done in a number of ways. First, search for examples of what may already be available. Locate materials that might have similar goals and objectives and/or have been developed to work with similar target students. It always helps in the development of materials to see what has previously been successfully developed and used. An Internet search for specific lesson plans that focus on one or more of your objectives can be helpful in this regard. Second, focus on each objective and develop a rough outline for the key steps needed to get the learner from his or her current level of performance to the desired level of performance described in that objective. Based on the type of instruction and the level of complexity, it is

Toolbox: Using Planning Cards

Planning Cards (frequently referred to as *Storyboard Cards*) are a simple, inexpensive method to generate an initial draft of instructional materials. The cards generally consist of 3 by 5 inch or 4 by 6 inch pieces of paper (generally on stiffer card stock paper). Although small scraps of paper can work as planning cards, we have found that a heavier card stock type paper is generally preferred because of frequent changes that are made on the cards and for the ability to pickup, handle, and move them quickly. Lined note cards generally work quite well.

To use the cards, begin by listing one of your lesson objectives on one of the cards. After reviewing that objective, ask yourself, "For my target learners to successfully achieve that objective, what do they need to know and how do they need to perform?" Generate as many answers as possible and list each on a separate note card. At this point don't go into great detail, just list the basic thoughts and ideas. Discuss your ideas and cards with other content experts, teachers, etc. and add new cards as they generate additional thoughts and ideas. Once a stack of cards listing the brainstormed ideas has been generated, go to a large flat area (e.g., a kitchen table works well) and lay out all of the cards for one specific objective. Push the cards around on the table with some of the cards becoming major topics and other cards becoming subtopics. The cards should allow for easy placement of the ideas and thoughts. Place the

cards in some logical order based on when specific items should be experienced by the learner. When holes in the process are noted, add in cards with your ideas on them. Embellish information on some of the cards in order to help clarify what is to occur at that specific point. After some work on the order and placement has occurred, a structure to the cards should begin to be revealed. This is the beginning outline for the instruction for that specific objective. As you think of new items, new cards can readily be added, and as things are deleted, the cards can readily be removed.

The key idea here is that the cards are quick, readily adapted, and very cheap. At this point, we do not want to focus on making the instruction pretty – we just want to get the basic ideas down. We are attempting to develop the first rough draft of what the instructional learning experience will be. After aligning the cards in the proper order, additional information can be written on the cards that may include information about types of instructional activities, methods, media and even specific information about where available media could be accessed, etc.

The general philosophy behind the cards is to help you brainstorm, organize, and produce the outline of the initial draft of your instructional experience. Once a stack of the cards has been produced, you should be able to use the stack to guide you in the actual development of the instructional materials.

often helpful to use a planning or storyboard card method to further develop this process. This method is inexpensive, quick to begin, and allows for immediate alterations. Review the Toolbox Technique: Planning Cards on this page for further information on how planning cards can be utilized. The goal with planning cards is to produce a quick, basic draft of what the instructional experience will be. In addition, the cards will provide you with a means to begin adding information about other elements of the experience that will need to be considered (e.g., type of methods and media to use) within your materials. The idea is to produce an initial draft of the materials so that you know who your target audience is, what they will be learning, and where the learning will occur. As we work through the remaining chapters of this text, we will explore how to adjust and embellish the plan and then to implement and evaluate it in order to ensure its success.

 ## KEVIN SPENCER'S LESSON PLAN

As mentioned in the introductory paragraphs of this chapter, Kevin Spencer is a sixth-grade social studies teacher, and he has decided to design and develop a new lesson that deals with the Civil War unit of his class. His work can be used as an example of how one designs an integrated lesson plan. One of the first steps that Kevin needed to review was information on his learners, the content, and the learning environment. Here is a sample of that information:

Information about the target learners

- 23 sixth-graders in a suburban public school in a predominantly blue-collar neighborhood
- Gender—13 boys and 10 girls
- Ethnicity—10 white, 6 African American, 2 Asian, and 5 Hispanic
- SES—7 students qualify for free or reduced price lunch (definition of low SES)
- Learning preferences—16 primarily visual, 5 primarily auditory, and 2 primarily kinesthetic
- Special needs—1 visually impaired student; 1 student with epilepsy, controlled by medication; and 1 student who works with a reading teacher 1 hour a week
- Technology literacy—Students are all able to use MS Word, PowerPoint, and Internet Explorer

The content objectives

1. Given a WebQuest containing information about the Civil War, students will be able to create a journal that (1) is written in the first person from the perspective of the assigned character, (2) uses historically accurate language, and (3) refers to historically important events.

2. Given a WebQuest containing information about the Civil War and working with a small group of peers, students will be able to create either a story-telling PowerPoint presentation or a script for a play that (1) is at least 5 minutes long, (2) tells a story from the perspective of the assigned character, (3) uses historically accurate language, and (4) refers to historically important events.

Information about the learning environment

↗ A traditional classroom with 25 movable student desks, arranged in 5 rows of 5 with a teacher's desk at the front of the room.

↗ A teacher's computer, at the front of the room, is connected to a data projector.

↗ Against the back wall are 4 computers with broadband Internet connections.

↗ Along one side of the room is a bank of windows with book shelves underneath. Along the opposite side is a bulletin board covering the wall. A chalkboard covers the wall behind the teacher's desk. Two pull-down maps are located above one side of the chalkboard. A pull-down screen is located above the center of the chalkboard.

Review what Mr. Spencer has generated and then evaluate how they may be improved or adapted. Review the PIE checklist with Mr. Spencer's lesson in mind. Ask yourself the following questions about each of the elements.

Students

1. Do you think Mr. Spencer has done enough to accommodate the characteristics of his students? If not, what other accommodations would you suggest?

2. Is there anything more you would want to find out about these students? What and how would this information help you in developing the instructional plan?

Objectives

3. Do the listed objectives include each of the three components described in the chapter? If so, label those components within each objective. If not, add the components that are missing.

Learning Environment

4. Do you think this plan is workable within the described learning environment? If not, in what ways is there a mismatch and what might you do to resolve this mismatch?

Appendix B (page 289) lists the full lesson plan developed by Mr. Spencer. Review that full plan and note the role of the Learner Analysis, Objectives, and the Learning Environmental Analysis. As we work through other chapters of this text we will focus on how other sections of that lesson plan were also developed.

TECHNOLOGY COORDINATOR'S CORNER

Kevin Spencer recently went to a national education conference where he listened to a seminar about celebrating the diversity in the classroom. He walked away wondering how he could integrate technology into his classroom in order to celebrate the diversity of the students in his, as well as other, classrooms. Mr. Spencer approached Sara Gillespie, the technology coordinator for his school district, to see if she had any ideas. Sara suggested a couple of ways in which technology could support the diversity of the students. She recommended that he have his students create a database or spreadsheet of student information. This could be done through a survey of questions the students create themselves. It could comprise noninvasive information such as likes and dislikes of food, colors, hobbies, and so on, or could be more personal such as gender, hair color, eye color, heritage, and so on. The students could then graph the information and, using a chart, see the differences easily. To enhance this lesson, the students could converse with a school across the country in a different type of environment, such as rural versus an inner-city school, survey those students, and compare the results.

As Mr. Spencer was considering these suggestions, he also began to ponder on how a similar student database could be used to impact how he designed his own lessons. Although it might get overwhelming to concentrate on all the differences among his students, Sara suggested that he might also look over the list and notice those things that were similar. Identifying the differences could help to show the variety needed in order to help all individuals accomplish the learning objectives; however, seeing the similarities would help identify the common ground that would allow him to build the confidence of the students by relating things to their common experiences, attributes, and so on. He quickly came to realize that understanding both differences and similarities of the students allows you to plan much more effective instructional lessons. In both cases, the technology facilitates how the information is gathered, stored, analyzed, and later accessed for use.

SUMMARY

An instructional plan is like a jigsaw puzzle. It describes the pieces of the instruction and how they fit together to create a coherent lesson. This chapter began our description of the instructional planning process by describing the first three elements of a plan: students, objectives, and learning environment.

First are the students. Individual students invariably bring to any instructional situation a unique set of characteristics and a major part of the teacher's task is to fit the instruction to the students. This means gathering information about their background, what they already know about the content, their motivation for learning, and any special needs they may have. Second are the objectives. Objectives specify the intended results of the instruction: They define what the students should be able to do following the instruction. Objectives have three components: a performance, conditions under which that performance is expected, and criteria that define acceptable performance. Third is the learning environment. It is as important to match the instruction to where learning will occur as it is to match the instruction to who will be learning (the students) and what is to be learned (the objectives).

PEARSON **myeducationkit™** To check your comprehension of the content covered in this chapter, go to the MyEducationKit for this book and complete the Study Plan for Chapter 4. Here you will be able to take a chapter quiz, receive feedback on your answers, and then access resources that will enhance your understanding of chapter content.

SUGGESTED RESOURCES

Print Resources

Achinstein, B., & Barrett, A. (2004). (Re)framing classroom contexts: How new teachers and mentors view diverse learners and challenges of practice. *Teachers College Record, 106*(4), 716–746.

American Society for Training and Development. (2008). *Instructional design & implementation: The tools for creating training program curriculum (vol 2)*. Danvers, MA: Infoline and ASTD Press.

Bonk, C., & Zhang, K. (2006). Introducing the R2D2 model: Online learning for the diverse learners of this world. *Distance Education, 27*(2), 249–264.

Brown, A., Green, T., & Bray, M. (2004). *Technology and the diverse learner: A guide to classroom practice*. Thousand Oaks, CA: Corwin Press.

Coyne, M., Kame'enui, E., & Carnine, D. (2007). *Effective teaching strategies that accommodate diverse learners* (3rd ed.). Merrill.

Deason, C. (2007). *Culturally sensitive computer environments for pedagogy: A review of the literature*. In C. Crawford et al. (Eds.), Proceedings of Society for Information Technology and Teacher Education International Conference 2007 (pp. 1965–1967). Chesapeake, VA: AACE.

Gronlund, N., & Brookhart, S. (2008). *Gronlund's writing instructional objectives* (8th ed.). Prentice Hall.

Hill, M., & Epps, K. (2009). Does physical classroom environment affect student performance, student satisfaction, and student evaluation of teaching in the college environment? *Proceedings of the Academy of Educational Leadership, 14*(1), 15–19. Retrieved on June 9, 2009 from http://www.alliedacademies.org/public/Proceedings/Proceedings24/AEL%20Proceedings.pdf

Kizlik, B. (2009). How to write learning objectives to meet demeanding behavioral criteria. *Education Information for New and Future Teachers*. Available at http://www.adprima.com/objectives.htm

Kizlik, B. (2009). A rationale for learning objectives that meet demanding behavioral criteria. *Education Information for New and Future Teachers*. Available at http://www.adprima.com/objectives2.htm

Kizlik, B. (2009). Examples of student activities using behavioral verbs. *Education Information for New and Future Teachers*. Available at http://www.adprima.com/examples.htm

Marzano, R., & Kendall, J. (2008). *Designing and assessing educational objectives: Applying the new taxonomy*. Thousand Oaks, CA: Corwin.

Smith, G., & Throne, S. (2007). *Differentiating instruction with technology in K-5 classrooms*. Washington, DC: International Society for Technology in Education.

Electronic Resources

http://equity.4teachers.org/index.php
(4Teachers.Org: Equity Index)

http://www.wested.org/pub/docs/tdl/research.htm
(West Ed: Research Base on Using Technology to Support Diverse Learners)

http://oct.sfsu.edu/design/outcomes/index.html
(San Francisco State University: Design Learning Objectives)

http://www.go2itech.org/HTML/TT06/toolkit/design/outcomes.html
(Training Toolkit | Design Learning Objectives & Outcomes)

http://www.edutopia.org/re-designing-learning-environments#
(Edutopia: Re-designing learning environments: Improved schools improve education)

http://www.newhorizons.org/strategies/learning_environments/front_lrnenvironments.html
(Environments for Learning: School Sites and Learning Communities)

5

Technology and Instructional Planning: Identifying the Plan's Key Activities

Source: Michael Newman/PhotoEdit, Inc.

KEY WORDS AND CONCEPTS

Instructional activity
Declarative information
Structural information
Conditional information

Reinforcing feedback
Corrective feedback
Heuristic

CHAPTER OBJECTIVES

After reading and studying this chapter, you will be able to:

↗ Specify the instructional activities for a lesson of your choice.

↗ Describe the practical benefits of an instructional plan.

↗ Develop an instructional plan for a lesson of your choice.

INTRODUCTION

In Chapter 4, we introduced the instructional planning puzzle and described the first three pieces of that puzzle—students, objectives, and learning environment. Those pieces provide the foundation for instructional planning by describing *who* we are teaching, *what* we want them to learn, and *where* the instruction will take place. In this chapter, we will begin describing *how* to present the instruction to the students by putting into place the next piece of the puzzle—instructional activities (see Figure 5–1).

 ## DEVELOPING INSTRUCTIONAL ACTIVITIES

Simply put, an **instructional activity** refers to something that is done during a lesson to help students learn. Any lesson is made up of a collection of instructional activities intended to stimulate the students' curiosity, present new content, provide opportunities for practice, and so forth. Instructional activities can be thought of as the key pieces of the "script" for the instruction. In a play, the script directs the action, telling the actors what to do as the play progresses. The various instructional activities serve much the same purpose for a teacher. Taken together, they tell the teacher what to do as the lesson progresses. Various ways to organize this instructional script have been described (Gagne, Wager, Golas, & Keller, 2005). We are going to use the five types of instructional activities proposed by

Yelon (1996). Yelon suggests that every instructional plan should include:

- ↗ Motivation activities
- ↗ Orientation activities
- ↗ Information activities
- ↗ Application activities
- ↗ Evaluation activities

We will describe each of these types of instructional activity separately.

> **PEARSON** **myeducationkit™** Go to the Assignments and Activities section of Chapter 5 in MyEducationKit and complete the video activity entitled "Using Learning Centers." As you review the video, identify as many of the instructional activities (i.e., motivation, orientation, information, application, and evaluation) that you can.

Motivation Activities

As described in Chapter 4, motivation refers to the internal interests that lead students to want to learn and to put in the effort required for learning. The purpose of a **motivation activity** is to gain the students' attention and maintain it throughout the lesson. The "and" is critical. It is, perhaps, obvious that generating interest in learning is important at the start of a lesson—to get the students' attention and help them focus on the lesson at hand. But, it is just as important to hold their interest throughout the lesson—to maintain their focus and encourage their active participation.

One valuable approach to increasing student motivation is Keller's (1983, 2008) ARCS model. Keller describes four essential aspects of motivation using the mnemonic ARCS (the mnemonic has given its name to the model):

Attention refers to whether students perceive the instruction as interesting and worthy of their consideration.
Relevance refers to whether students perceive the instruction as meeting some personal need or goal.
Confidence refers to whether students expect to succeed based on their own efforts.
Satisfaction refers to the intrinsic and extrinsic rewards students receive from the instruction.

One of the benefits of the ARCS model is that Keller and his colleagues (1987) have described a variety of techniques that can be used throughout a lesson to increase each aspect of motivation. Some of these techniques are shown in Figure 5–2.

To develop the motivation activities for a lesson, consider the following questions:

↗ What will you do at the beginning of the lesson to gain the students' attention?

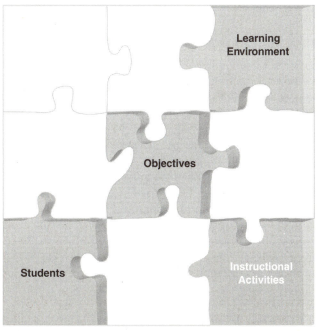

FIGURE 5–1   Instructional activities as the next piece of the puzzle.

To Increase:	Use One or More of These Motivational Techniques:
Attention	↗ Introduce an idea that seems to contradict the students' past experience ↗ Vary the format of the instruction according to the attention span of the students ↗ Build in problem-solving activities at regular intervals
Relevance	↗ Find out what the students' interests are and relate the instruction to those interests ↗ Ask students to relate the instruction to their own future goals ↗ Provide meaningful alternative methods for accomplishing a goal
Confidence	↗ Explain the criteria for evaluation of performance ↗ Organize materials on an increasing level of difficulty ↗ Teach students how to develop a plan of work that will result in accomplishing a goal
Satisfaction	↗ Allow a student to use a newly acquired skill in a realistic setting as soon as possible ↗ Provide informative feedback when it is immediately useful ↗ Provide frequent reinforcements when a student is learning a new task

FIGURE 5–2   Techniques to increase student motivation.

↗ At what points in the lesson will it be useful to build student motivation?

↗ What can you do throughout the lesson to increase each aspect of motivation: attention, relevance, confidence, and satisfaction?

Orientation Activities

In general, orientation refers to knowing where you are in relation to your intended destination. If you took a course about orienteering, you would study maps and how to use them to find specific locations. In instruction, orientation refers to knowing where you are in terms of the intended objectives. The purpose of an **orientation activity** is to help students see where they have been (what they have previously learned), where they are now (what they are currently learning), and where they are going (what they will subsequently learn). It is like looking at a map, highlighting your current position as well as the desired location and then determining the direction you need to travel to get from here to there. As a teacher, you will use orientation activities to introduce a lesson and link it to preceding lessons, to move from one part of a lesson to the next, to help students monitor their progress, and to summarize a lesson and link it to subsequent lessons. To develop an orientation activity for an instructional plan, consider the following questions:

↗ What will you do to help students understand the objectives of the current lesson?

↗ What will you do to link the lesson to previous lessons?

↗ What will you do to provide smooth transitions within the lesson?

↗ What will you do to summarize the lesson and link it to future lessons?

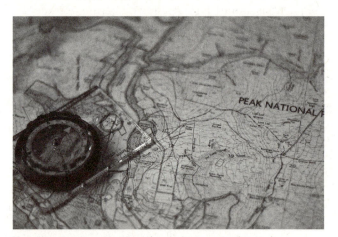

Knowing your current location helps you to determine the next proper steps to be taken.
Source: Shutterstock.

Information Activities

Instruction generally includes some new ideas (facts, concepts, principles, procedures, etc.) and an opportunity for students to practice using those ideas. The purpose of an **information activity** is to help students understand and remember those new ideas. To be effective, information activities should focus on three different types of information—declarative, structural, and conditional. **Declarative information** refers to the new ideas themselves (e.g., Boyle's Law states that . . .). Declarative information is important, but by itself is not enough. **Structural information** refers to the relationships that exist among those ideas (e.g., Boyle's Law is one of several laws meant to explain . . .). Structural information is important because it provides an organizing framework for the new ideas. This makes them easier to understand and remember because they are seen as part of a coherent whole rather than as isolated facts. Finally, **conditional information** refers to information about the potential usefulness of the new ideas (e.g., Boyle's Law can be used to explain . . .). Conditional information helps students internalize what they learn and transfer it to a variety of situations by showing them when the new ideas will be useful (the types of situations) and why they should use the new ideas (how they will help).

To develop the information activities for a lesson, consider the following questions:

↗ What major content ideas will you present? In what sequence? Using what examples?
↗ What will you do to help students understand and remember those ideas?
↗ What will you do to help students see the relationships among the ideas?
↗ What will you do to help students understand when and why the ideas will be useful?

Application Activities

Application activities involve practice, guidance, and feedback. First, the purpose of an application activity is to provide students with an opportunity to practice using what they are learning. Practice serves a diagnostic function. If students practice successfully, they can move on to evaluation. If, on the other hand, they have trouble, they might either repeat the practice, perhaps in a simpler form, or go back over the information, clarifying it as needed. To serve as an effective diagnostic tool, an application activity should ask students to demonstrate the performances called for in the objectives under the same conditions described in the objectives.

Second, an application activity may include varying amounts of guidance. In guided practice, students are given clues that suggest how they should proceed. In unguided practice, students must decide for themselves how to proceed. The amount of guidance that can be provided exists on a continuum and should be regulated to meet the needs of individual students. In general, practice that includes more guidance is less difficult than practice that includes less guidance. As a result, students who progress easily might benefit most from relatively unguided practice, while those who are having trouble might need more structured practice.

Finally, feedback is an essential component of an application activity. **Feedback** refers to giving students information about how well they are doing when they practice (for a review on feedback and its impact on learning see Hattie & Timperley, 2007). Feedback comes in two forms: reinforcing feedback and corrective feedback. **Reinforcing feedback** is like a pat on the back (e.g., saying "Good job" or "I like the way you . . ."). You use it to acknowledge good performance and encourage continued effort. **Corrective**

feedback, as its name implies, tells students specifically what they can do to correct or improve their performance (e.g., saying "What if you . . ." or "Next time try . . ."). These two forms of feedback are often used together, reinforcing what students have done well and correcting what they could do better. Practice and feedback are inseparable, or at least should be. Practice without feedback has limited value because it does not tell students whether they are progressing toward the objectives or what they can do to improve their progress. To develop the application activities for a lesson, consider the following questions:

↗ What will you do to give students opportunities to practice using their new knowledge or skill?
↗ At what points will you build those opportunities into the lesson?
↗ How much guidance will you provide and what form will that guidance take?
↗ What will you do to give students both reinforcing and corrective feedback about their performance during the practices?

PEARSON **myeducationkit**™ Go to the Assignments and Activities section of Chapter 5 in MyEducationKit and complete the video activity entitled "Collaborative learning through WebQuests." As you review the video, think of the various ways in which WebQuests and similar activities can be used as application activies to practice and use new information and skills.

Evaluation Activities

In Chapter 12, we define evaluation as the process of gathering information about what students have learned and describe a variety of techniques that can be used

Applying what has been learned is facilitated by guidance and feedback.
Source: The Charlotte Observer, David T. Foster III/AP Images.

Toolbox: Using Questioning, Examples, and Feedback Effectively

Within each of the instructional activities, you can use a variety of techniques to enhance the activity's overall effectiveness. In particular, materials should incorporate questions, examples, and feedback. Listed below are several suggestions and guidelines for incorporating these techniques.

QUESTIONING

You can use questions to gain attention, maintain focus, pique interest, probe for depth of understanding, increase relevance for a topic of focus, or evaluate the quality of the instructional materials. Questions may be generated by the teacher or student, and answers can range from simple, to difficult, to unknown.

Several guidelines can help you incorporate productive questions into your instructional lessons (Dallmann-Jones, 1994; Wasserman, 1992).

When planning and developing questions:

- ↗ Determine why you will ask the question. Make sure each serves an important purpose.
- ↗ Use "who," "what," "when," and "where" questions to check information for review purposes. "Why" and "how" questions encourage higher levels of thought. Ask students to provide in-depth explanations or additional examples.
- ↗ Frame questions to invite, rather than intimidate. Help students feel safe to express their thoughts. Questions and responses should be respectful, nonthreatening, and productive.

When using questions:

- ↗ Sample class responses randomly; that is, ask questions of all students equally.
- ↗ Take time to pause after asking a question; provide students with time to think.
- ↗ Listen to students' responses before formulating your own so you can accurately reflect their ideas.
- ↗ Respond positively to appropriate responses, but never belittle incorrect answers.
- ↗ Allow students the chance to formulate questions in response to comments from you or from other students.
- ↗ When a student repeatedly provides incorrect answers, coach that individual during one-on-one sessions. Provide the student with opportunities to answer questions that you have previously discussed during your session.

EXAMPLES

Research has shown that examples are very effective in helping learners understand concepts and applications. Examples can highlight key characteristics and information about concepts, make ready comparisons, and illustrate how things are applied and generalized across different situations. Guidelines for using examples include the following:

- ↗ Begin with simple examples so students can readily identify their critical attributes. Simple examples can also increase your learners' confidence.
- ↗ Present examples in different formats, such as flowcharts, pictures, live demonstrations, and real objects.
- ↗ Use nonexamples (negative examples) to help highlight examples' critical attributes. Nonexamples may have some of the same attributes of the examples but vary on those features that make the critical difference. For example, to teach the concept "red," you may present learners with an example of a red ball. To make sure they understand the critical attribute of color, introduce nonexamples such as a blue ball and an orange ball. All of the attributes in the examples and nonexamples are the same, *except* for the critical attribute of color. The nonexample helps to identify the critical attribute.
- ↗ Gradually increase the difficulty level of the examples until you end with more difficult ones that approximate the real-world cases that students will encounter.

FEEDBACK

We are all familiar with the phrase "practice makes perfect," but is it true? With a short addition we can capture a more accurate picture—"Practice makes perfect, *as long as feedback is provided.*"

Feedback, according to Foshay, Silber, and Stelnicki (2003, p. 28), "follows logically from practice. Feedback lets learners know how well they've done in applying the new knowledge, what problems they are having, and why they are having those problems." Feedback can serve two functions: (1) it can inform students about *how much* of the task they have completed, thus encouraging them to continue working; and (2) it can inform students *how well* they are performing and indicate what they can do to improve their performance.

As you design and implement instruction, it is important to make provisions for delivering feedback to students. Without timely, reliable feedback, students may not know if their work is correct. Without some form of feedback, students could potentially continue practicing errors over and over. Use the following guidelines when designing practice and feedback exercises (adapted from Leshin, Pollock, & Reigeluth, 1992):

- ↗ Effective feedback should be delivered immediately (or as soon as reasonably feasible) after practice is completed.
- ↗ Well-designed feedback can motivate students to greater levels of performance.
- ↗ Informative feedback should function like a good example.
- ↗ Corrective feedback should require learners to think. Give hints but do not provide the correct answer immediately.

before, during, and after instruction. This is the purpose of an **evaluation activity.** Like practice, evaluation serves a diagnostic function. Students who "pass" the evaluation are ready for the next lesson, while those who don't "pass" may need some additional instruction before they proceed. We have purposely put quotation marks around the word "pass" to make a point. We often think of evaluation in terms of traditional paper-and-pencil tests. But there are a variety of ways to evaluate how well students have learned, and the meaning of "pass" will be different for these different evaluation methods.

To develop an evaluation for an instructional plan, consider the following questions:

↗ What will you do to determine whether students have achieved the learning objectives?
↗ How will you give students feedback about their performance during or after the evaluation?

 ## INSTRUCTIONAL PLANS AS HEURISTIC GUIDES

We've suggested an instructional "script" that is flexible and adaptable to a variety of teaching and learning situations. Remember that an instructional plan, like a script, is a decision-making guide. It helps you decide what actions to take and how to combine those actions to help your students learn. The instructional plan we have presented is designed to provide you with a set of **heuristic** guidelines; that is, it is a set of general rules that you can adapt to fit each situation, rather than a rigid procedure that you must follow in the same way every time. Our goal is to provide you with guidelines that are flexible enough to use with a variety of situations, yet structured enough to provide practical guidance. However, you must keep in mind that *there is no one "correct" instructional plan.* Instructional situations differ in terms of students' needs, interests, and experiences; the structure of the content; the available resources; and your preferences, interests, and experiences. Your task is to create a unique solution for the unique problem of helping your students learn; that is, you must develop a plan that helps your particular students learn the particular content. There are several ways in which instructional plans may vary from one situation to the next.

Combining Instructional Activities   We think the five instructional activity categories (motivation, orientation, information, application, and evaluation) are basic ingredients that you should include in every lesson. However, that doesn't necessarily mean that each activity must be a separate entity in every lesson. For example, the purpose of an application activity is to allow students to try out their new knowledge or skill, and the purpose of an evaluation activity is to determine whether they have mastered the intended objectives. It is possible to present a sequence of application activities that

Toolbox: Case Studies

The case study is a teaching approach that requires students to actively participate in real or hypothetical problem situations that reflect the types of experiences actually encountered in the discipline under study. After you read the following case study examples, reflect on the type of problem-solving lesson you could generate by using them.

↗ You are a botanist working to preserve the waters of Everglades National Park in Florida, the nation's third-largest national park, established in 1947. You have already documented the extent of the damage from surrounding farm chemicals that run off into the Everglades' vast swamps, saw grasses, and coastal mangrove forest. But recent attempts to reach agreement on the part of government and farmers' organizations have failed. How can you work to preserve these natural wonders of the country? (Barell, 1995, p. 126)
↗ Aurora is experiencing an increase in the crime rate. Currently, 30 percent of the cases admitted to hospital emergency rooms are victims of violent crimes, compared with a rate of 25 percent two years ago. What steps should the city take to find a solution to the problem? (from Gallaher, Stepien, & Rosenthal, 1992, as cited in Barell, 1995, p. 126)

The case "report" contains relevant (but not conclusive) data. You may present it to students, or they may develop it themselves. Individual or group work follows the case presentation, allowing students to analyze data, evaluate the nature of the problem(s), decide on applicable principles, and recommend a solution or course of action. A case discussion follows, which is useful in developing critical-thinking, problem-solving, and interpersonal skills. Although case methods may have strategies in common with other teaching techniques (particularly simulations and instructional games), the focus in all case methods is a specific set of circumstances and events. Whereas case methods are generally motivating to students due to the high level of involvement and can help bridge the gap between the "real" world and life in the classroom, they tend to be time consuming and require good management skills on the part of the discussion leader.

Toolbox: Role-Playing

Role-playing is a type of instructional simulation. It is like a drama in which each participant is assigned a character to depict, but must improvise their performance. Examples include learning how to interview for a job, managing a situation in which a hostile student threatens a teacher, discussing a questionable call with an umpire during a championship baseball game, and establishing a personal relationship.

Role-playing encourages creativity and allows students to express their feelings and attitudes. It is an effective means to develop and practice social skills, and it can help students learn to organize thoughts and responses instantly while reacting to a situation or question.

Consider the following guidelines when designing and implementing role-play in the classroom (see Dallmann-Jones, 1994; McKeachie & Svinicki, 2006):

- ↗ Design the situation in sufficient detail prior to class.
- ↗ Define participants' roles in terms of the situation.
- ↗ Ask for volunteers rather than choosing participants—volunteers are less likely to feel put on the spot.
- ↗ Allow participants a short time to get their thoughts together.
- ↗ Brief all students before role-play begins. Describe the situation and indicate what nonparticipants should look for.
- ↗ Don't let the role-play "run" too long. Three to six minutes is usually sufficient.
- ↗ Stop the role-play and reverse roles if a "hot" topic is encountered and emotions begin to get out of hand.
- ↗ Conduct follow-up discussion to analyze the performance. To avoid defensiveness, allow players to discuss their perceptions and emotional reactions first.

Toolbox: Using Analogies

In Chapter 1 we compared the instructional design planning process to that of an architect's process of developing a structure's blueprint. This is an example of the instructional technique of analogy. Its purpose is to help you learn by comparing a new concept with something familiar. An analogy consists of four parts:

1. the information to be learned (the subject)
2. the familiar thing to which the new information is compared (the analog)
3. the means by which the subject and analog are compared (the connector)

4. a description of the similarities and differences between the subject and analog (the ground)

In the architect's blueprint analogy, we used the key steps that are involved in creating a blueprint (the analog) to describe the similar steps involved in designing effective instructional materials (the subject).

Analogies have repeatedly been found to be effective in learning all types of subject matter (West, Farmer, & Wolff, 1991). To facilitate your own use of analogies, consider the following ABCDE method of constructing an analogy (adapted from Kearny, Newby, & Stepich, 1995).

A	Analyze the subject.	What is it you most want the learners to understand about the subject?
B	Brainstorm potential analogs.	What concrete items share the important feature(s) you have identified?
C	Choose the analog.	Which candidate analog has the best combination of the following characteristics:

- ↗ Familiarity—Will learners recognize the analog?
- ↗ Accuracy—Does the analog accurately reflect the identified feature?
- ↗ Memorability—Is the analog vivid; will learners remember it?
- ↗ Concreteness—Is the analog something learners can directly perceive?

D	Describe the ground.	How are the subject and analog alike? How are they different?
E	Evaluate the analogy.	Does the analogy work with the intended audience?

will help determine whether students have mastered the objectives. In this case, you combine evaluation and application. The point to keep in mind is that each instructional activity has an important purpose in each lesson. Sometimes you can accomplish those purposes with greater efficiency by combining two or more instructional activities.

Emphasizing an Instructional Activity   Instructional activities are not all necessarily of equal importance in every lesson. For example, one lesson may present a lot of information and provide limited time for application, while another lesson on the same content may present a small amount of information and allow a lot of time for application.

The Manager of an Instructional Activity   The manager of an instructional activity is the person or entity that is primarily responsible for carrying out that activity, dictating the pace of the activity, controlling the flow of information, and determining what to do next. We say "primarily" because learning is always a collaboration among students, the teacher, and instructional materials, and all are likely to influence each instructional activity. However, to what extent do students, the teacher, and materials control the pacing, flow of information, and decision making? Note that the manager may vary from one activity to the next. For example, in a given lesson the teacher may manage the orientation while the material manages the information and the students control the application.

Encouraging students to manage their own learning is a powerful technique (refer to the discussion of constructivist learning theory in Chapter 2). Students often learn more from an instructional activity when they manage it themselves. However, this is an acquired skill, and students—especially younger or less-sophisticated ones—may require instruction and practice before they are able to do it well. Although teaching students to manage their own learning is beyond the scope of this book, we refer readers who are interested in learning more about this topic to Schunk and Zimmerman (1998).

The Amount of Detail or Structure in the Plan   You may describe an activity within an instructional plan with more or less detail or structure, depending in part on your experience with the technique being used. Teachers who are relatively inexperienced or who are using a new technique may want their plans to provide a lot of structure and will, therefore, describe activity content and materials in great detail. On the other hand, teachers using familiar techniques may need less structure and may, therefore, sketch out their activities rather than describe them in detail. Note that we are talking about individual activities rather than an entire plan. Different activities within a plan may be described at different levels of detail. For example, a teacher who has developed a new way to introduce a familiar topic may develop detailed motivation and orientation activities while briefly outlining the familiar information.

The Order and Number of Activities   We have listed instructional activities in an order that seems logical, but that is not the only "correct" order. For example, you may decide to place an orientation activity at the beginning of the lesson as a natural introduction. Alternatively, you may decide to place an orientation activity after an information activity as a way of clearly connecting the new information to previously learned information. Or you may decide that an orientation activity would be useful in both places.

This last point highlights the idea that a lesson often contains more than one of each type of activity and that the activities may be clustered together or spread throughout the lesson. As shown in Figure 5–3, a lesson may include multiple motivation activities, information activities, and/or application activities in various configurations.

Instructional Activities and the PIE Checklist   In Chapter 4, we discussed the use of the Plan, Implement, and Evaluation (PIE) checklist (see Appendix C for the full checklist). As shown in Figure 5–4, an important part of the checklist focuses on the selection and development of the various instructional activities and the key questions that should be considered when developing each. From a practical standpoint, the checklist helps the teacher make sure nothing is missed or forgotten. At times when in the middle of developing a lesson, it is easy to focus on the information, for example, and forget to consider the need for orientation or motivational type activities. By knowing each of these activities you are in a much better position to ensure the structure of the lesson will be complete.

A.   Orientation >>> Motivation >>> Information >>> Application >>> Evaluation

B.   Motivation >>> Information >>> Orientation >>> Information >>> Application >>> Evaluation

C.   Orientation >>> Information >>> Motivation >>> Information >>> Application >>> Application >>> Evaluation

D.   Application >>> Orientation/Motivation >>> Information >>> Application >>> Evaluation

---

FIGURE 5–3   Varying sequences of instructional activities.

5. Instructional Activities – Chapter 5

❏ For each of the following instructional activities, review the questions and reflectively consider how the various activities and strategies can be incorporated within the instructional materials:

Motivation Activities

What strategies will you use to hold students' attention throughout the lesson?
What strategies will you use to help students see the relevance of the information?
What strategies will you use to increase students' confidence in learning?
What strategies will you use to increase students' satisfaction in learning?

Orientation Activities

What will you do to help students understand the objectives of the current lesson?
What will you do to link the lesson to previous lessons?
What will you do to form transitions?
What will you do to summarize the lesson and link it to future lessons?

Information Activities

What major content ideas will you present? In what sequence? Using what examples?
What will you do to help students understand and remember those ideas?
What will you do to help students see the relationships among the ideas?
What will you do to help students understand when and why the ideas will be useful?

Application Activities

What will you do to give students an opportunity to apply their new knowledge or skill?
How much guidance will you provide and what form will that guidance take?
In what way will you give students feedback about their performance during practice?

Evaluation Activities

What will you do to determine whether students have achieved the learning objectives?
How will you give students feedback about their performance during the evaluation?

❏ Create additional planning cards that include and explain the selected activities and include those within the previously developed set.

FIGURE 5–4   PIE checklist for instructional activities.

In addition to the reflective questions to consider about each of the instructional activities, this part of the checklist also reminds the user about developing planning cards for each of the activities. These cards will prove beneficial as the overall sequence of the lesson is developed. Using such cards allows the designer to readily add, remove, or alter the placement of specific activities (review Toolbox: Using Planning Cards, page 83 in Chapter 4 for more details on how this occurs).

Instructional Activities and the Integration of Technology   During the planning portion of the learning experience, technology is often used by the designer to access and structure information about the various activities. Discovering examples that can guide how to identify and implement specific activities are now readily found on the Internet. Simple use of a search engine (e.g., Google) with search terms such as "lesson plans" will generate various websites to explore with large repositories of example plans. Many of these plans will not identify specific instructional activities, however, once reviewed many ideas can be generated on how to present specific types of content, as well as how to orient, motivate, practice, and assess the learning. In addition, designers often use technology to identify and contact other individuals who may have experience with specific information or other types of activities. Through e-mails, professional blogs, and other social networking means, access to individuals who may be able to offer insights and guidance on how to structure specific instructional activities may occur.

As the plan begins to develop (e.g., a set of planning cards has been created) and the individual activities begin to be embellished and developed, various uses of technology may also be identified. Chapters 6 and 7 will focus on instructional methods and media

	Example A—Congruent	**Example B—Not Congruent**
Objective	Be able to solve algebra equations	Be able to solve algebra equations
Information Activity	Description of the notation used in algebra equations, followed by a demonstration of how to solve various types of algebra equations	Description of the historical development of algebra as a branch of mathematics
Application Activity	Problems asking the students to solve the types of algebra equations presented in the information activity	Problems asking the students to interpret various types of algebraic notation
Evaluation Activity	A set of algebra equations to solve	Questions about the importance of knowing how to solve algebra equations

FIGURE 5–5 Congruent Components in the Instructional Plan.

which will specifically look at various technologies that can be integrated within the activities to enhance the learning experienced by the students.

Making Plans Congruent

Instructional plans are flexible, designed to guide decision making rather than dictate the way to present a lesson to students. However, one thing should be true of every instructional plan: The components of the plan should be congruent with one another. That is, the objectives should match the instructional activities, and the instructional activities should match one another. For example, the objectives should accurately represent the knowledge and skills described in any information activities and measured in the evaluation activities. Similarly, the evaluation activities should measure the knowledge and skills described in the information activities and represented by the objectives. Students should be motivated to learn, and should be applying the knowledge and skills they will be evaluated on, and so on through all the combinations of instructional activities.

To illustrate the concept of congruent plans, consider the brief examples in Figure 5–5. In Example A, the objectives, information, application, and evaluation are all congruent. They all relate directly to learning how to solve algebra equations. In Example B, however, the objectives, information, application, and evaluation are all aimed at different aspects of algebra. Although they are all important, they are not parallel to one another.

How might you combine instructional activities to form a congruent instructional plan for a specific situation? The following two sample instructional plans will help answer that question. The situations are related, but begin with a different planning component. As a result, the plans are different. Look over each of the two sample plans. What differences do you notice? How might you explain those differences? What does this suggest about the flexibility of the instructional plan?

Scenario A: Ms. Heinrich teaches a beginning Spanish class for fourth-graders. A curriculum guide distributed by the school district specifies that students should be able to carry on simple conversations in Spanish and be able to use Spanish greetings (see Figure 5–6).

Scenario B: Mr. Delgado teaches a beginning Spanish class for fourth-graders in a different school. His objective is also to have students be able to use Spanish greetings. He has read about cooperative learning techniques, and he likes what he has read. He wants to try cooperative learning in his class (see Figure 5–7).

 ## PRACTICAL BENEFITS OF PLANS

An instructional plan is a decision-making guide. It allows you to make sensible decisions about how to carry out instruction, respond to the changing needs of students and the situation, and make continual improvements in the instruction you provide. The practical benefits of having a plan can be described in terms of the functions the instructional plan serves before, during, and after the instruction (Borko & Livingston, 1992; Kauchak & Eggen, 1989; Reynolds, 1992).

Before Instruction

Bridge The instructional plan serves two important linking functions. First, it is the *link between the curriculum goals and the students*. The plan is the vehicle you use to decide how to tailor the curriculum, which is often predetermined, to the needs of your particular students. Second, the plan is the *link among the objectives, instructional activities, and evaluation*. It is the means by which you can decide how to adapt the objectives, instructional activities, and/or evaluation to ensure that they match one another. The way these links are made depends on (1) the particular curriculum, (2) the students,

Students: Fourth Grade Spanish I   Topic(s): Greetings

Objectives:

↗ Say the Spanish equivalent to a given English greeting.
↗ Say the appropriate Spanish greeting when meeting someone.
↗ Say an appropriate Spanish response when greeted in Spanish.

Learning environment: Classroom Activities

1. **Combined motivation–orientation activity**
   Present a series of situations, in English, calling for a greeting. Ask students what they would say. Show similar situations in Spanish on videotape. Present the objectives as steps toward being able to converse in Spanish. Emphasize the importance of practice.

   Method: presentation
   Medium: videotape

2. **Information activity**
   Demonstrate common Spanish greetings and responses (both formal and informal) for morning, afternoon, and evening. Write the words on the chalkboard, say them several times. Emphasize the greeting/response pairs. During the demonstration, clearly explain when each greeting and response would be used.

   Method: demonstration
   Medium: chalkboard

3. **Orientation activity**
   Before starting the practice activity, ask students when greetings are generally used and why. Then ask them when they would use the different types of greetings and why. Use this discussion to decide whether to review any of the previous information.

   Method: discussion
   Medium: audio (conversation)

4. **Combined application–evaluation activity**
   Pair the students up with an audiotape recorder. Instruct students to practice on the tape and to listen to the tape to see how they sound. Spend a few minutes with each pair after they have recorded a practice greeting and response. Listen to the taped practice with students (ask them to evaluate what they hear on the tape). Point out specific strong points in their pronunciation and give specific pointers for improving pronunciation.

   Method: drill and practice
   Medium: audiotape

FIGURE 5–6   Instructional plan for teaching Spanish greetings and responses.

and (3) your knowledge of the content, level of experience, beliefs about students and how they learn, and knowledge about teaching methods that will help students learn. By making these links, you can ensure students meet the prescribed learning goals, thus making your instruction more accountable.

Checklist   The instructional plan encourages you to anticipate the specific materials, facilities, and equipment needed, as well as when you will need them. This helps you make sure that there will be enough materials on hand for all students.

Schedule   The instructional plan allows you to decide what activities you will use to help students learn, to put them in a logical sequence, and to allocate sufficient time to the different activities.

During Instruction

Road Map   The instructional plan describes the destination you want to reach and the routes you plan to follow to get there. This road map function helps you make adjustments in the plan. This is important for two reasons. First, interruptions in the classroom are inevitable (e.g., because of student absences, school assemblies). The instructional plan *helps you keep the instruction on track,* monitor students' progress toward the destination, and ensure that the prescribed content is covered in the face of these inevitable interruptions. It does this by marking your place so you can return after the interruption. Second, students' needs and interests may change, and unanticipated learning opportunities may arise. *The instructional plan allows you to respond to these changing needs, interests, and opportunities* while continuing to progress

Students: Fourth Grade Spanish I   Topic: Greetings

Objectives:

↗ Say the Spanish equivalent to a given English greeting.
↗ Say the appropriate Spanish greeting when meeting someone.
↗ Say an appropriate Spanish response when greeted in Spanish.

Learning environment: Classroom Activities

1. **Combined motivation–orientation activity**

    Greet students in English. Explain that all languages use similar greetings. Their task will be to learn greetings in Spanish. Each student will learn 1 greeting from audiotape and teach it to classmates. This is the beginning of being able to talk with people in Spanish. Once they have learned the greetings, they will be able to move on to other parts of conversation.

    Time: 5 minutes   *Add written materials showing*
    Method: presentation   *the words*
    Medium: audio (conversation)

2. **Information activity**

    Divide class into 3 equal groups for morning, afternoon, and evening greetings. Give each group an audiotape with the greeting and response for their time of day recorded on it. Review how to use the tape recorder.

    Directions—Each group is to practice their greeting and response so they can teach it to 2 classmates. Group members should listen to one another and help one another with pronunciation. ◄— *Encourage them to practice as much as they can*

    In about 15 minutes, the groups will switch around, and each student will teach their greeting to the students in their new group. Ask if they need help. Circulate around the room. Keep students on track.

    Time: about 15 minutes
    Method: tutorial
    Medium: audiotaped Spanish greetings

3. **Orientation activity**

    Reorganize class into groups of three—one member from each of the previous 3 groups.

    Directions—Your task now is to teach as much as you can. Help one another out. Everyone in the group is to learn each greeting and response. After about 15 minutes start calling students to the front of the room in pairs to show what they have learned.

    Time: about 15 minutes
    Method: cooperative learning
    Medium: audio (conversation)

4. **Evaluation activity**

    Call students to the front in pairs. Give first student an English greeting on a card. The student is to greet his or her partner with the corresponding Spanish greeting. Partner is to respond in Spanish.

    Time: 15 minutes ◄—   his or her
    Method: drill & practice   *Find an alternative. Students*
    Medium: Spanish/English flash cards   *need more time for practice*

5. **Information activity**
    Debrief the lesson:

    ↗ Recall when each greeting and response is used.
    ↗ Ask who else students might teach these greetings to (parents, friends, etc.).
    ↗ Suggest using the greetings with one another around school.

    Time: 15 minutes
    Method: discussion
    Medium: audio (conversation)

FIGURE 5–7   Instructional plan for teaching Spanish greetings and responses using cooperative learning.

toward the destination. The plan is designed to be flexible and to allow you to improvise based on the students' responses.

Outline   The instructional plan provides a set of guidelines to follow in the classroom, allowing the teacher to concentrate on interacting with the students rather than trying to remember what comes next.

Compass   The instructional plan provides you with a clear sense of direction, and this helps to increase your confidence and reduce the uncertainty and anxiety that often accompany not knowing where you're going. This may be especially important if you are relatively inexperienced and need guidance.

After Instruction

Diary   The instructional plan provides you with a place to record what happened during the instruction (McCutcheon, 1980). It is also a place to record your observations and comments about what worked and what didn't. You can then use these notes to improve your instruction.

Briefing Book   It is often important that others know what is happening in the classroom. The instructional plan provides a convenient way to do this. For example, the plan will tell substitute teachers what parts of a lesson have been completed and what is yet to be done. Similarly, the plan will help principals keep track of what is happening in all classrooms in their buildings.

Kevin Spencer's Lesson Plan

As highlighted in Chapter 4, a new lesson on the Civil War is being designed and developed by Kevin Spencer, a sixth-grade social studies teacher. After identifying his target students, the lesson objectives, and the learning environment, Mr. Spencer's next step is to identify and develop the key instructional activities that need to occur during his new lesson. Based on his knowledge of his students, the content, and the learning environment, he begins to develop a lesson script by identifying and outlining the type, sequence, and number of activities that will be needed within his lesson. For example, he knows that motivational activities will be critical as many of his students may not invest the needed effort into the lesson without first understanding its relevance within their own personal lives. Using the PIE Checklist (see Appendix C), he focuses on the different types of instructional activities and addresses the reflective questions posed within the checklist. Using planning cards, he highlights the key activities, puts in a brief description and then begins the process of sequencing the cards in order to get an overall script or structure for his lesson. At first, the activities may be very sketchy and lack detail; however, as each is reviewed more detail (and often more cards) can be added.

As shown in Figure 5–8, Mr. Spencer will begin his Civil War lesson with a motivation activity that focuses on having the students learn about what life was like for all kinds of people during the Civil War. Other selected activities include repeated orientation and information activities to ensure the students know the direction the lesson is going and what information is critical for their understanding and also various application and evaluation activities to practice using what they have learned and to get the needed feedback for their efforts.

Introduction to the lesson

Motivational Activity

- ↗ Show photographs of a variety of people (e.g., different ages, different professions, locations) from the Civil War era.
- ↗ For each photo — ask:
  - ○ What do you think life was like for this person?
  - ○ How do you think the war affected him/her?
  - ○ In what ways do you think life was different than for the previous person?
- ↗ Explain that this lesson will explore what life was like for various people during the Civil War.

In Appendix B, the full lesson plan developed by Mr. Spencer is presented. Review each of the instructional activities he has included, and note what is described as well as the sequence of its occurrence within the lesson. All of the activities together give the lesson its needed structure. Based on your review of his selected activities, what do you think will work well and what changes would you suggest? It should be noted that this is one view of how the Civil War lesson should be structured; however, you may have other ideas and thoughts about how different activities could/should be included. Review the section again of the PIE Checklist (see Appendix C) that focuses specifically on the instructional activities. Using those questions, can you see ways in which these activities could be improved/enhanced? Is there a better way to sequence the activities so that the learning experience will be more effective, efficient, and/or appealing?

FIGURE 5–8   Sample motivation activity from Mr. Spencer's lesson on the Civil War.

TECHNOLOGY COORDINATOR'S CORNER

The cross-curriculum theme at Lakeside Elementary this year has been "Cultures of the World." In keeping with this theme, two fifth-grade teachers, John Babcock and Rosie Avila, have recently finished the first draft of a new instructional website called "Traditional Japanese Holidays and Festivals." Before using it with their students, they asked several teachers including Michelle Asay, the school technology coordinator, to go through the website and offer suggestions. After a few days, they received the following e-mail message from Michelle.

March 23

John and Rosie,

Thanks for the opportunity to look over your website on Japan. I learned things that I had never known. Here are my brief comments about your work:

↗ Getting and maintaining the attention of students as they work through the website is critical. Your use of a variety of colored pictures and graphics should help in this regard. You may also want to think about helping the students understand how big the site is and how much they have to do. I have found that this helps to orient the student and it gives them an understanding of what they are to do – basically, where they are going and what they are trying to accomplish. I have found that once they know this, they gain confidence that they can get it accomplished. Otherwise some might give up before getting to some critical parts of the site. In this regard, you may want to create a "site map" on the index/home page that should give students an overview of what they will experience plus it provides them direction as to where they need to go and what they have already covered.

↗ You have provided a lot of information about the holidays. Most of it is good information; but some students may see it as overwhelming and confusing. One suggestion would be to help them organize the information in some way. For example, you could group the holidays based on the season of the year. In this way the student begins to chunk them into groups that are more manageable. In addition (and perhaps more important), they may more readily make comparisons between the holidays/festivals of Japan and those with which they are more familiar. Adding "helps" for them to recognize the structure (e.g., simple but relevant pictures, graphics, and perhaps even music) is relatively simple within such Web pages and it would provide the students with some interesting and memorable cues of your content.

↗ Finally, one element that I really think is lacking in your website is helping the students see how the information

they are receiving can be applied and used. Knowing this, they should be able to retain it to a greater degree. One thought that I had is that since they will already be on the Web, why not have a page where they link to a school site in Japan where they may be able to interact with students of their same age. Yes, the language may become somewhat of a barrier, but I have found school sites where students are trying out their English writing skills and they would be thrilled to have students from our school interact with them in some fashion. You could have our students begin by sharing what we know about their traditional holidays and then ask questions such as which holiday they like the best, tell them about similar things we do here, and so on. Hopefully this interaction will develop into the students' learning about other similarities and differences in the cultures. After all, isn't that the goal of the school's theme this year?

I would be happy to brainstorm more with you about what could be done and how to get it accomplished. Thanks for allowing me to review your work.

Michelle

SUMMARY

An instructional plan is like a script. It describes the activities that will take place during the instruction, indicates how those activities are to be combined for a particular lesson, and is used as a flexible decision-making guide. Instruction is made up of varying combinations of five types of instructional activities: motivation, orientation, information, application, and evaluation. In instructional planning, the order in which components appear is not as important as developing a plan whose parts are congruent. Such a plan offers a number of benefits before, during, and after instruction.

PEARSON myeducationkit™ To check your comprehension of the content covered in this chapter, go to the MyEducationKit for this book and complete the Study Plan for Chapter 5. Here you will be able to take a chapter quiz, receive feedback on your answers, and then access resources that will enhance your understanding of chapter content.

SUGGESTED RESOURCES

Print Resources

Gagne, R., Wager, W., Golas, K., & Keller, K. (2005). *Principles of instructional design* (5th ed.). Belmont, CA: Wadsworth.

Hattie, J., & Timperley, H. (2007). The power of feedback. *Review of Educational Research, 77*(1), 81–112.

Jones, F., Jones, P., Lynn, J. (2007). *Fred Jones tools for teaching: Discipline, instruction, motivation.* Fredric H. Jones & Associates.

Keller, J. (2008). First principles of motivation to learn and e3-learning. *Distance Education, 29*(2), 175–185.

Merrill, M., Barclay, M., & van Schaak, A. (2008). Prescriptive principles for instructional design. In J. Spector, M. Merrill, J. vanMerrienboer, & M. Driscoll. Handbook of research on educational communications and technology (3rd ed.). New York: Lawrence Erlbaum Associates. (pp. 173–184).

Simmons, C., & Hawkins, C. (2009). *Teaching ICT: Developing as a reflective secondary teacher.* London: Sage.

Sims, R. (2006). Beyond instructional design: Making learning design a reality. *Journal of Learning Design,* 1(2), 1–7. http://www.jld.qut.edu.au/

Steel, N., & Dijkstra, S. (2004). Curriculum, plans, and processes in instructional design: International perspectives. Mahwah, NJ: Lawrence Erlbaum.

Tileston, D. (2004). *What every teacher should know about learning, memory, and the brain.* Thousand Oaks, CA: Corwin.

Vercauteren, D. (2008). *Teacher feedback to primary school students: Do they get the message?* VDM Verlag.

Electronic Resources

http://www.4teachers.org/intech/lessons/
(4Teachers.org: Teacher Tacklebox)

http://www.lessonplanbuilder.org
(Stanislaus County Office of Education: Lesson Plan Builder)

http://www.thinkfinity.org/home.aspx
(Thinkfinity: Free Lesson Plans and Educational Resources)

http://ericir.syr.edu/Virtual/Lessons/
(The Educator's Reference Desk: Lesson Plans)

http://teachers.net/lessons/
(Teachers.Net: Lesson Plans)

http://school.discoveryeducation.com/lessonplans/
(Discovery Education: Lesson Plan Library)

http://school.discoveryeducation.com/schrockguide/edles.html
(Kathy Schrock's Guide for Educators: Lesson Plans and Thinking Skills)

http://www.teachervision.fen.com/lesson-plan/resource/5775.html
(TeacherVision: Lesson Planning Center)

6

Instructional Methods: Identifying Ways to Involve Learners

Source: Shutterstock.

KEY WORDS AND CONCEPTS

Presentation
Demonstration
Discussion
Games
Simulations

Cooperative learning
Discovery
Problem solving
Drill and practice
Tutorials

CHAPTER OBJECTIVES

After reading and studying this chapter, you will be able to:

↗ Define instructional methods and justify their importance in teaching and learning.
↗ Describe each method discussed in this chapter including examples with your description.

↗ Demonstrate the correct procedures for using each method discussed in this chapter.
↗ Discuss techniques for selecting and combining methods for instructional purposes.

INTRODUCTION

Sally Lopez, a fourth-grade teacher at Fair Oaks Consolidated School, is discussing instructional methods with colleagues in the break room. They are discussing techniques with which Sally is not familiar. She remembers studying them when she was an undergraduate, but they are ones she has rarely implemented in her classroom. As her colleagues continue the conversation, she wonders what they see in these methods.

As Sally listens to her colleagues enthusiastically share the various methods that work for them, she begins to think that she may want to experiment with some of these techniques: cooperative learning, problem solving, simulation, discovery, and tutorials. She already uses discussion, games, drill and practice, demonstration, and presentation.

Sally realizes during the discussion that her approaches are very teacher-centered. The other teachers are using terms like "student-centered" and "learner driven." As you read this chapter, consider Sally's concerns. Which of the methods do you consider teacher-centered and which are student-centered? Study the descriptions and examples of the various methods. Can you think of other examples that would apply to your teaching? Carefully consider the principles for using each of the methods. This chapter will give you the basic information for applying ten methods, so you can use each more appropriately to enhance the learning experiences of your students.

As is shown in Figure 6–1, the instructional methods represent another piece of the planning puzzle. Chapter 5 began the discussion of how to present the instruction

to the students through various instructional activities. In this chapter we expand that discussion to include the means and procedures that are used for the learner to experience those learning activities.

Figure 6–2 shows the portion of the PIE Checklist related to methods. A full version of the checklist is included in Appendix C.

WHAT ARE INSTRUCTIONAL METHODS AND HOW CAN WE USE THEM?

As described in Chapters 5, instructional activities are done during a lesson to help students learn. They may provide motivation, orientation, information, application, or evaluation. Instructional activities incorporate methods along with media (discussed in the next chapter). Together they assist the learners in getting from where they are before the lesson (previous knowledge, skills, and attitudes) to where you want them to go (mastery of objectives).

Traditionally, instructional methods have been described as "instructional techniques" such as lecture and discussion. Your methods are the procedures and actions used to help students achieve the stated lesson objectives. In Chapter 1, we introduced ten different types of methods (refer to Figure 6–3). We discuss each of them in this chapter, beginning with the more teacher-centered approaches and proceeding to the more student-centered approaches. (See the "Sample Lesson Plan" in Teacher Resource B on page 289.)

You should use a variety of methods in your teaching. However, some methods seem better suited for certain content or certain learners. You will learn which method or combination of methods is most effective only by trying them with actual students. You will undoubtedly find yourself using a variety of methods to keep instruction interesting.

Methods of instruction vary in their interactivity and typical group size. Presentations and demonstrations tend to be less interactive, while drill and practice and tutorials are highly interactive. While most methods lend themselves to small-group instruction, presentations and demonstrations are more effective for larger groups. Tutorials and drill and practice tend to work best with individuals.

The purpose of this chapter is to help you identify the methods most appropriate for your planned instructional activities. Methods can be used to present information and to actively involve the learner. They are an integral part of learning and consequently of your learning plan.

We now look briefly at each method, including examples and guidelines for using it. The methods are discussed in order of their increasing interactivity. Of course, the amount of interactivity can vary greatly for each

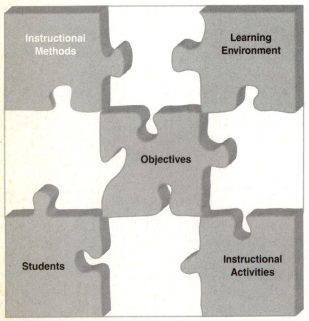

FIGURE 6–1 Instructional methods as the next piece of the planning puzzle.

Planning Phase

1. Learners — Chapter 4
2. Objectives — Chapter 4
3. Learning Environment — Chapter 4
4. Developing the Initial Draft Outline — Chapter 4
5. Instructional Activities — Chapter 5
6. Instructional Methods — Chapter 6
   ❏ Select all instructional methods that apply to the instruction and provide a short description of how each selection will be used

Check Methods to in-corporate.	Provide Short Description.
❏ Presentation	
❏ Demonstration	
❏ Discussion	
❏ Drill and Practice	
❏ Tutorial	
❏ Instructional Games	
❏ Cooperative Learning	
❏ Simulations	
❏ Discovery	
❏ Problem Solving	

   ❏ Indicate within the planning card set what method, as well as when each of the selected methods will be integrated within the instruction

7. Instructional Media — Chapter 7
8. Instructional Materials — Chapter 8

Implementation Phase

1. Instructional Delivery — Chapters 9, 10, and 11
2. Instructional Management — Chapters 9, 10, and 11

Evaluation Phase

1. Continuous Cycle of Improvement — Chapter 12

FIGURE 6–2   Methods Portion of PIE Checklist.

Cooperative learning	Discussion
Discovery	Drill and practice
Problem solving	Tutorial
Games	Demonstration
Simulation	Presentation

FIGURE 6–3   Instructional Methods.

method, depending upon the actual situation and how it is implemented.

Presentation

In a presentation, a source relates, dramatizes, or otherwise provides information to learners. The source may be a textbook, audio, video, online via e-learning tools, a teacher, a student, and so on. This method makes use of verbal information and/or visual symbols to convey material quickly. Presentations typically provide students

Students share their knowledge through classroom presentations.
Source: Anthony Magnacca/Merrill Education.

with essential background information. A presentation can also introduce a new topic, provide an overview, and motivate students to learn. It is a one-way communication method controlled by the source, with no immediate response from, or interaction with, the audience.

In a presentation, the content can be presented verbally by the teacher or a student and the "audience" listens and takes notes. Video-, audio-, and computer-based presentations can also be used, either as the main way of presenting new material or as a supplemental approach for covering a specific topic in more detail.

Presentation Examples

1. In Jill Sanchez's sixth-grade class, a small group of students design and produce a mediated presentation on the origin and meaning of the Bill of Rights to summarize the content studied during a lesson. The presentation is given to the rest of the class.
2. The website from a major food company lists the nutritional information for all its products. Wanda Elliott's food and nutrition class learns the pros and cons of eating each of the products.
3. Ralph Watson's social studies class watches a DVD of the television news coverage of the same story from four different cultures (United States, United Kingdom, Spain, and Israel). Students then compare and contrast the nature of coverage, length of coverage, content, and depth of coverage of the same news story from four different perspectives.

Principles for Using Presentations

↗ Inform students of the purpose of the presentation by providing them with an agenda or outline.
↗ Highlight the critical points of the presentation by showing a visual that illustrates a key point, by repeating the key points several times, by using voice

inflection to emphasize important points, and by simply declaring a point as one of central importance.

↗ Make the presentation relevant. Learners need to be able to relate the information from the presentation to their own experiences. You can accomplish this by asking questions such as the following: How does this relate to you? Have you ever had a similar kind of experience? How could you use this information now or in the future?
↗ Use variety to maintain attention. Add variety by introducing graphics or other forms of media, by asking questions, by incorporating relevant personal experiences, or even by making a simple change in your volume or rate of speech.

Demonstration

Demonstrations show students how to do a task as well as why, when, and where it is done. In this method, students view a real or lifelike example of a skill or procedure. Verbal explanations become more concrete by illustrating ideas, principles, and concepts. In addition, demonstrations can set performance standards for student work. By demonstrating how to properly perform a task, you establish the criteria you expect students to meet. You may use recorded demonstrations played back by means of a video or computer. Two-way interaction or student practice with feedback requires either a live instructor or a computer. The desired outcome may be for the student to imitate a physical performance, such as swinging a golf club or changing the oil in a car, or to adopt the attitudes or values exemplified by a respected person.

In a demonstration an individual performs a procedure in order to highlight an important principle or process. Demonstrations may be done live or recorded on a media format, such as videotape, Web-based video, or DVD.

You may use demonstration to illustrate how something works, to show how to perform a task, or to teach safety procedures. Demonstrations are essential when teaching a psychomotor procedure (such as jumping rope) or an interpersonal skill (such as participating in an interview).

Demonstration Examples

1. Molly Calhoun, a kindergarten teacher, demonstrates on the whiteboard how to form the capital and lowercase "letter of the week." The students then practice on their worksheets as Ms. Calhoun circulates throughout the classroom.
2. Jason LaJoy, the physical education teacher, demonstrates how to perform a forward flip on the trampoline as students watch. He describes each step and then demonstrates them in sequence. Next, each student is given an opportunity to practice the forward flip with feedback from Mr. LaJoy.

Toolbox: Classroom Response Technologies

Although presentations typically involve one-way communication of information with limited opportunities for interaction, there are ways to involve students, even large groups, in a presentation. A relatively new technology that supports interactivity during group presentations is the use of clickers. **Clickers**, also known as classroom or audience response systems, are devices similar in appearance to TV remotes that allow students to respond to questions during a presentation. In a typical scenario, the teacher embeds questions, often in multiple choice format, to test students' comprehension or poll students' opinions at key points during the presentation. When the question appears, students use their clickers to transmit a response (e.g., A, B, C, or D in answer to a multiple choice question) to a receiving station connected to the teacher's computer. Clickers typically use an infrared or radio frequency signal, and each clicker generates a unique signal so that individual responses can be linked back to individual students (so that clickers can be used to take attendance in large groups). The receiving station captures all of the students' responses and software on the teacher's computer provides a summary chart or graph showing how many students selected each answer. If a number of students select incorrect answers, the teacher can immediately stop and go over the material again to help clear up any misunderstandings. Opinion questions can also be used to stimulate discussion and help students see how their views compare with others in the class. Similar technologies are being developed that allow students to use cell phones, laptops, and other devices to respond to teacher questions; at Purdue University, new software called *HotSeat* allows students to respond to and even send comments to the teacher through any Web-enabled device. With clickers and related technologies, presentations can become a more interactive instructional method.

3. A computer program demonstrates how to deal with sexual harassment between students. The program dramatizes a variety of ways to deal with sexual harassment. Following the demonstration, students role-play how to deal with unwanted sexual advances.

Principles for Using Demonstrations

↗ While planning, preparation, and practice are important for all instructional methods, they are especially critical for demonstrations if you are going to be manipulating materials and equipment that you do not use regularly.

↗ Ensure that all can see and hear.

↗ Present the demonstration in small, sequential steps.

↗ Allow the audience to practice. It is often motivational for learners to watch a demonstration and then attempt to complete it themselves.

Students learn content and communication skills by participating in discussions.
Source: Anthony Magnacca/Merrill Education.

Discussion

Discussion is a dynamic method that encourages classroom interaction and actively involves students in learning. Discussion involves a group of individuals sharing information about a topic or problem. Students talk together, share information, and work toward a solution or consensus. They are given the opportunity to apply principles and information. This method introduces students to different beliefs and opinions, encouraging them to evaluate the logic of, and evidence for, their own and others' opinions. A major benefit of the discussion method is the amount of interaction that occurs and the learning that results from that interaction. It provides the teacher with immediate feedback on your students' understanding of course material.

Three important skills are associated with the discussion method: (1) asking questions, (2) managing the flow of responses to your questions, and (3) responding to students' questions. Discussions teach content as well as processes such as group dynamics, interpersonal skills, and oral communication. Discussion among students or between students and teachers can make significant contributions throughout students' learning. It is a useful way of assessing the knowledge and attitudes of a group of students. Discussion can foster collaborative and cooperative learning. In combination with written forms of student assessment, you also may use discussion to evaluate the effectiveness of your instruction.

Discussion Examples

1. A third-grade teacher leads a discussion on the meaning of Thanksgiving Day when preparing his students to attend a Thanksgiving play presented by high school students. A discussion after the play helps to answer students' questions and ensures that everyone understands the performance.

2. After reading different news articles, Jolene Moller's social studies students contemplate a current political issue or hot topic in the news through discussions and debates. Students then write their own viewpoint on the topic based on the discussion.

3. Officer Richardson from the local police department shows a picture of a mangled car resulting from an auto accident involving a drunken driver to gain a student group's attention before discussing the problems of drug and alcohol abuse. She asks the students to discuss the consequences of drunk driving, particularly as it has affected their family and friends.

Principles for Using Discussions

➤ Provide motivation before beginning a discussion by using a common reading, a picture, an audio recording, or a short video to secure the interest and attention of the students.

➤ Encourage active participation from each group member. The exchange of ideas among group members is a critical factor in learning from discussions.

➤ Questions are needed to stimulate discussion and should be prepared beforehand. Either you or your students may prepare the questions.

➤ Summarize and/or synthesize the different viewpoints of various small groups discussing aspects of a specific topic.

Games

Instructional **games** provide an appealing environment in which learners follow prescribed rules as they strive to attain a challenging goal. It is a highly motivating approach, especially for repetitive content. Games often require learners to use problem-solving skills or demonstrate mastery of specific content such as math facts or vocabulary words.

Games have two key attributes—rules and competition or challenges. First, a clearly defined set of rules outlines how the game will be played, what actions are and are not allowed, what constitutes winning the game, and what the end result will be for a winning performance. Second, elements of competition or challenge provide players with an opportunity to compete against themselves, against other individuals, or against a standard of some type.

Spelling bees and speed math facts (e.g., students are given a number of problems to solve during a short time period; points are awarded for accuracy and speed) are common instructional games used in elementary classrooms to teach basic skills. You may easily adapt other games, such as Trivial Pursuit and Jeopardy, to contain relevant subject-matter content and at the same time retain the benefits of the game structure. Today, there is growing interest in the use of video and computer games for learning. See the Toolbox: Serious Games on page 166 in Chapter 9.

Instructional games provide a challenging approach to experiencing a variety of activities.
Source: Scott Cunningham/Merrill Education.

Toolbox: Presentations, Demonstrations, and Discussions

Presentations, demonstrations, and discussions are instructional methods commonly used within classroom instruction. At this point in your learning career, you have probably experienced these methods literally hundreds of times. From those experiences, compile a list of evaluation criteria that you could use to determine the quality of these methods used within a classroom learning experience. With your list, assess three different classes that use one or more of these methods. Based on your criteria, what went well, what needed improvement, and what types of suggestions/recommendations could you offer? Did you find that you needed to adapt your evaluation criteria as you were using them to evaluate the quality of the methods? Are there ways in which to improve your set of evaluation criteria?

Game Examples

1. Where in the World is Carmen Sandiego? is a popular computer game that develops students' understanding of geography and world culture (see Figure 6–4). Students assume the roles of detectives who must track down a thief who has stolen a national treasure from somewhere in the world. By gathering clues and conducting research, players are able to track the thief around the world, learning about geography as they go.

2. The religious education students in Reverend McCullan's class of middle school students enjoy playing Jeopardy. Rev. McCullan generates answers each week based on the reading assignment. The student teams actively participate to come up with the correct questions.

3. A group of high school chemistry students is given the assignment to memorize 15 element names and their associated numbers and symbols from the periodic table. The teacher has designed a board game in which four teams of two students each compete to complete the "experiment" by answering questions related to the 15 elements.

Principles for Using Games

↗ Students must have a clear concept of the instructional goal of the game. Ask yourself, "What do students need to learn, and how will a game help accomplish that?" Make sure to communicate the answer to these questions to your learners.

↗ Students must understand the procedures and rules for how the game, will proceed and how all scoring will occur. With a new game, it always helps to have written rules.

↗ Make sure the game is structured so active involvement is maintained at the highest possible level for all participants. If groups are too large and long waits occur between "turns," the effectiveness of the game will wane. Allow enough time to play but not so much that students grow tired of the game.

↗ Include a debriefing or discussion following the game's conclusion. This should focus on the instructional content and value of the game and why it was played. Make sure the students understand that their participation in the game had an instructional purpose, and summarize what they should have learned from it.

Simulation

Using simulation, learners confront realistic approximations of real-life situations. Simulation allows realistic practice without the expense or risk involved in real situations, such as driving and flight simulators. The simulation may involve participant role-play, handling of materials and equipment, or interaction with a computer. This method promotes skills that emphasize accuracy and speed. Simulations also allow students to practice cooperation and team work, and can help foster leadership skills. Simulations can promote decision making and build positive values and attitudes by putting

FIGURE 6–4   A screen from *Where in the World is Carmen Sandiego?*, a popular educational computer game.

Source: Where in the World is Carmen Sandiego?®, © 1999. The Learning Company, Inc.

students in unfamiliar roles (see "Toolbox: Role-Playing" page 92 in Chapter 5).

Laboratory experiments in the physical sciences are popular subjects for simulations because simulations avoid the risks and costs of real experiments. Sim City is a popular computer simulation. The program allows students to simulate the management of a city, including such elements as budget, construction of infrastructure, traffic, pollution, and crime. Students can build their own city from scratch or manage one of several well-known cities around the world.

Simulation Examples

1. The sixth-graders in Judy Krajcik's class learn about surviving in the inner city by playing a computer simulation about life downtown in a large city. She introduces the simulation to the entire class, then divides the students into groups of four and assigns each group to one classroom computer. She moves among the groups to answer questions, to monitor the progress of each group, and to discuss students' feelings about the conditions in the inner city.

2. Students in John Morales's middle school social studies class learn about the operations of government by participating in a role-playing simulation about creating and passing new legislation. John circulates around the room and lets the simulation progress at the students' pace. He takes extensive notes for a debriefing at the conclusion of the "legislative session."

3. High school students in Family Studies pretend that they are taking care of a baby. They are assigned a computerized doll that requires feeding, changing, and other baby functions. These simulated experiences give them insight into how they might respond in similar real-life situations.

Principles for Using Simulations

➤ Explain the purpose and procedures for the simulation. Make students aware of over simplifications implicit in the simulation. Explain the goal to be achieved and, where appropriate, the role of each student.

➤ Simulations can be confusing, and students may need guidance or direction in order to benefit from them. Questions, activities, and scenarios can fill this guidance role.
➤ Allow participants to play out their roles with minimum input from you.
➤ Conduct follow-up discussions or debriefing with students to maximize the benefit from the simulation. Provide feedback following the simulation.

Cooperative Learning

Many educators have criticized the competitive atmosphere that dominates some classrooms. They believe that pitting student against student in achieving teacher-assigned grades creates an adversarial relationship between students and teachers and is contrary to later on-the-job teamwork. Some teachers feel competition in the classroom can interfere with learning.

Cooperative learning involves small groups of students working together to learn collaborative and social skills while working toward a common academic goal or task. This method is specifically designed to encourage students to work together, drawing on their individual experiences, skills, and levels of motivation to help each other achieve the desired result. The central idea is that cooperation and interaction allow students to learn from several sources, not just the teacher, while also providing each student opportunities to share their own abilities and knowledge.

Each student in the group is accountable to the group for a different and specific aspect of the content. Individual students cannot complete the task on their own, but must rely on others in the group. In this method, students apply communication and critical-thinking skills to solve problems or to engage in meaningful work together. A growing body of research supports the claim that students learn from each other when they work on projects as a team.

Cooperative groups have several uses including learning course content, promoting positive interactions and interdependence among groups of students, and teaching important social and communication skills. Another important reason for using such an approach is

Toolbox: Simulations

Simulations of all varieties can be found on the Internet to download and explore. One example is a popular simulation known as Roller Coaster Tycoon (for a free trial, go to http://www.searchamateur.com/Tycoon-Games/Tycoon-Game-Download.htm). Additional simulations can be found by completing a search (e.g., using Google) with the search term simulation game demo. Locate a simulation such as Roller Coaster Tycoon and preview the software. From your experience with the software:

a. Identify and describe the simulation aspects of the program;
b. Identify and describe the game aspects of the program; and
c. Describe how this program could be used within an educational setting.

Students learn interpersonal skills through cooperative learning.
Source: Tom Watson/Merrill Education.

to teach individual accountability. When a group's success depends on the input of each individual in it, individuals learn to be accountable for their actions.

Cooperative Learning Examples

1. Recently the members of the fifth-grade Ecology Club and their advisor went on a field trip to view a creek near their school. Upon close observation of the creek, the students noticed patches of oil floating on the slow-moving water. After further investigation, the club advisor decided it would be a good project for the club to research what was occurring and to determine what could be done about it. He divided the students into four-person teams. Each team member was given a specific task. One student was to determine who should be contacted at the public health department. Another was to find out what the oily substance was and determine how it could have been introduced to the creek. Still another was in charge of identifying potential ways of publicizing what was occurring and determining the potential impact on the animals and community. The fourth was to review what the club could do to raise public awareness.
2. In the science lab, groups of middle school students work together as "detectives" to determine the nature of an unknown substance. In each group, one student is assigned to search the Internet, another goes to the public library for background research, others focus on designing and running experiments on the substance, while others work to locate someone who may be familiar with the substance. Together they pool their information to come to a combined, cooperative solution.
3. In a high school art appreciation class, groups of students were assembled to learn about the different forms of creative art. Each group was composed of three students: one who was accomplished at a musical instrument, another who had the ability to paint, and a third who had the ability to sculpt. The group's task was to learn about the different art forms and their relationships.

Principles for Using Cooperative Learning

↗ Build an atmosphere that encourages participation and cooperation. Help students realize the advantages of working together as a team. This can be facilitated by requiring that all members of the group have roles to fill that are necessary for the group's success.

↗ Teach group processes to the students. Effective group cooperative efforts do not happen by chance.

↗ Learn to facilitate, not dominate. It is important for you to take on the role of monitor, facilitator, and guide instead of director.

PEARSON **myeducationkit** Go to the Assignments and Activities section of Chapter 6 in MyEducationKit and complete the activity entitled "Cooperative Learning with Handhelds." As you view the video and answer the accompanying questions, consider the benefits of cooperative learning and think about how you might use such an activity in your own classroom.

Discovery

The **discovery** method enables and encourages students to find "answers" for themselves. A principle of discovery learning is that students learn best by doing, rather than by just hearing and reading about a concept. With this method, your role is to arrange the learning environment so that "discovery" can occur.

Implementing a discovery method places students in a situation where they can learn through personal experience. Such experiences generally require learners to develop and use observation and comparison skills. Moreover, like detectives, students must learn to follow leads and clues and record findings in order to explain what they experience.

Discovery uses an inductive, or inquiry, approach to learning; it presents problems students must solve through trial and error. The aim is to develop a deeper understanding of the content through active involvement with it. For discovery learning in the physical sciences, students might view a video in which the narrator states a set of relationships and then go to the lab to discover the principles that explain those relationships. For example, after hearing the narrator say, "Air has weight," the students may then experimentally weigh a balloon before and after filling it with air, thus discovering that the statement is true.

Discovery Examples

1. Judy Lewis gives her first-graders a variety of watercolors and encourages them to mix any two colors together and see what color is produced. Judy uses the activity to teach color names. She has printed the color names on large cards along with a sample of the color. She also used cards with plus signs and equal signs to form equations such as "Blue + Yellow = Green." The activity allows students to "discover" the results of various combinations of colors. In addition, they learn to read the names of colors and are introduced to the basics of addition.

2. To help her middle school science students discover the relation between time and distance, Linda Harrison has them "experiment" with remote-control cars measuring the time it takes to go specific distances. Linda has the laboratory lesson carefully planned, but does not tell students what the result "should be." The students work in pairs and each lab pair manipulates the data with the aid of a computer, which constructs graphs of their data. Each pair shares their results with the entire class. Often, individual pairs' data do not show the function. However, when the class pools the data, the relationship among the variables becomes evident to everyone.

3. High school economics students "play" the stock market with $100,000 in pretend money. Students work in teams to gain the most from their "investments." Their success or failure is determined by the rise and fall of the real stock market during the time they are "investing." Students discover how outside forces, such as the Federal Reserve, impact the value of stocks.

Principles for Using Discovery

↗ Be prepared for all types of "discoveries." Combining unique students with unique learning environments often leads to unique results. Be prepared for all types of standard and not-so-standard findings when students are allowed to make their own observations and draw their own conclusions.

↗ Encourage students to share their discoveries. Through the experience of discovery, students often gain both great insights into their subject and great enthusiasm for what they have learned. These important insights and feelings should be shared with other individuals.

↗ Make sure students understand that "one right answer" may not exist. They may need instruction and examples on how to observe, compare, and evaluate phenomena.

↗ Constantly encourage and reward students for being inquisitive, for asking questions, and for trying new approaches.

PEARSON myeducationkit Go to the Assignments and Activities section of Chapter 6 in MyEducationKit and complete the activity entitled "Promoting Innovative Thinking, Creativity, Collaboration and Inventiveness through WebQuests." As you view the video and answer the accompanying questions, consider how this activity has been structured to foster innovative thinking and cooperative learning.

Problem Solving

The real world is filled with problems that need resolution. Some problems may be very well defined (e.g., determining if purchasing a new outfit is within one's current monetary means; finding the shortest route to travel to a near by art museum). Other problems may be less well defined (e.g., determining how to increase neighborhood safety and finding the "best" postsecondary education). To fully participate in this world, students need to be able to analyze problems, form tentative hypotheses, collect and interpret data, and develop some type of logical approach to solving the problem.

In the problem-solving method, learners use previously learned content and skills to resolve a challenging problem. **Problem solving** is often based on the scientific method of inquiry. The usual steps are (1) define the problem and all major components, (2) formulate hypotheses, (3) collect and analyze data, (4) formulate conclusions and/or solutions, and (5) verify conclusions and/or solutions. Learners must define the problem clearly (perhaps state a hypothesis), examine data (possibly with the aid of a computer), and generate a solution. Through this process, learners are expected to arrive at a higher level of understanding of the content under study.

One way to distinguish problem solving from discovery is that in problem solving students are using previously learned content and skills to solve problems while in discovery students are learning the content and skills.

Problem-Solving Examples

1. A computer program called Thinkin' Things makes use of various problem-solving strategies, such as working backwards, analyzing a process, determining a sequence, and thinking creatively (see Figure 6–5). The software provides the user with a factory that produces creative-looking feathered friends. The preschool-aged child selects from a set of options in order to create the next appropriate bird in the sequence.

2. Sister Anne is a sixth-grade science teacher at St. John's Catholic School. During a recent unit in science, she wanted her students to directly experience the impact of human population on the environment. She posed the following problem: "Does acid rain have an impact on the environment?"

FIGURE 6–5 *Thinkin' Things* allows the student to create a feathered friend based on a specific pattern and sequence.

Source: Thinkin' Things, Edmark Corporation. Reprinted with permission.

She quickly felt the need to clarify and redefine the question at her students' level, so she revised her question to, "In what ways does acid rain affect the growth patterns of common outdoor plants?" She asked her students to design an experiment that would provide an answer to that question.

3. Students in a business class are given information about a situation at a small manufacturing firm and asked to design a solution for a problem of low production. After gathering more data, they determine whether the solution should involve training or, perhaps, changing the environment or attitudes of the workers.

Principles for Using Problem Solving

↗ Clarify the problem when necessary. Especially with less mature students, one of the most difficult parts of problem solving is getting a true, accurate picture of the problem itself. In the initial stages of problem solving, your role often involves helping students in identifying and outlining the specific problem. Be careful, however, to not overdo the clarification. If you explain the problem too thoroughly, the students won't have to work for the answer.

↗ Use additional resources and materials when necessary. It is important that students have access to additional resources, as well as instruction on how to use those resources most effectively.

↗ Keep groups small. Because of the uniqueness of the potential solution paths to the problems and the time required to complete the various steps, it is

often essential to have a smaller number of students.

↗ Help students understand the need for generalization. Students must recognize that problem solutions are generally unique and that no single answer works for all problems. This connotes an emphasis on learning general problem-solving strategies and procedures and adapting them as each new situation dictates.

Drill and Practice

Drill and practice is frequently beneficial when students need to memorize and recall information. During drill and practice, students are led through a series of practice exercises designed to increase proficiency in a newly learned skill or to refresh an existing one. To be effective, drill and practice exercises should include feedback to correct errors students might make along the way.

Drill and practice is a common classroom method for helping individual learners master basic skills or knowledge through repetitive work. Drill and practice is not designed to introduce new content. It is assumed that the skill or knowledge has already been introduced and, thus, its purpose is to give learners the opportunity to master the material at their own pace.

Drill and Practice Examples

1. To learn math facts to a level of automatic recall, students employ flash cards. On one side of the card is a simple arithmetic problem; on the other,

the answer. Students attempt to answer the problem and then flip the card and compare their answer to the correct solution. This format can be used to learn states and their capitals, the names of animals and their young (e.g., goose and gosling, kangaroo and joey), foreign words and their translation, and other paired information sets.

2. Students in Wilber Groves's seventh-grade geography class work on their map-recognition skills using printed worksheets. He circulates throughout the classroom to monitor each student's work as they practice their skills in recognizing countries from their outline map. He also makes sure to give them feedback as to the correctness of their answers.

3. Mary Owens uses a tutorial program on the computer to help her high school French students practice their vocabulary skills. Ms. Owens uses the quizzing ability of a voice recognition program that gives her students immediate feedback on their vocabulary pronunciation.

Principles for Using Drill and Practice

↗ Introduce content prior to the drill and practice session.

↗ Use many short drill and practice sessions instead of a few longer ones. Use both individual and group activities.

↗ Use competition (against self or others) to make drill more interesting.

↗ Make sure students are practicing the correct information or procedures. Only correct practice makes perfect!

↗ Provide opportunities for students to apply what they master through drill and practice.

Tutorial

Tutorials convey content from a tutor to a learner and may include instructor and student, student and student, computer and student, and print and student. The computer can play the role of tutor because of its ability to quickly deliver a variety of responses to different student inputs. Tutorials can be used for learning all types of content. Unlike drill and practice, which simply goes over previously presented information again and again, you can use tutorials to introduce new material to the student.

A tutor—in the form of a person, computer, or special print materials—presents content, poses a question or problem, requests student response, analyzes the response, supplies appropriate feedback, and provides practice until learners demonstrate a predetermined level of competency. Tutoring is most often done one to one and is frequently used to teach basic skills such as reading and arithmetic, although you may use it to teach higher-level skills as well.

Tutorial Examples

1. John Johnson uses a tutorial, in the form of an illustrated storybook on local history, as a makeup activity for his fourth-grade students who were absent when the topic was covered in class. He monitors their progress to check their understanding and learning.

2. A middle school math teacher uses a tutorial to teach her class how to calculate the area of a rectangle. First, she helps them recall relevant information from previous lessons (e.g., the concepts of rectangle, length, height, and multiplication). Then, she introduces and explains the concept of area as the product of the length of the rectangle multiplied by its height. She then demonstrates and shows a number of examples of determining the area of different sizes of rectangles. The students then attempt novel problems using the same format. The teacher gives them feedback on their performance, and they continue practicing until all students can successfully calculate a rectangle's area.

3. Jill Day, an industrial arts teacher, uses a video-based tutorial on shop safety as a prelude to having her students work with power equipment. The video shows each step of shop safety procedures and poses questions for students to answer.

Principles for Using Tutorials

↗ Present an overview of the material. Prompt students through content or skills, then release them to demonstrate content or skills on their own. Provide opportunities for students to apply what they have learned.

↗ Present content or skills one step at a time.

↗ Ask questions of the student, and encourage the student to ask questions.

↗ Plan for varying rates of completion. Monitor students' progress regularly to ensure that they are on task and learning.

Kevin Spencer's Lesson Plan

1. Refer to Teacher Resource B. This teacher resource describes the instructional plan Mr. Spencer has developed for his sixth-grade social studies class. Read over the plan and identify several of the instructional methods that have been incorporated within the plan.

2. With a partner, discuss the strengths and weaknesses of several of the selected methods. Convince your partner of an alternative method that should work effectively within Kevin Spencer's lesson plan. Justify your selection with information from Figures 6–6 and 6–7.

Instructional Method	Advantages	Limitations
Presentation	Can be used with groups of all sizes	Requires little student activity
	Gives all students the opportunity to see and hear the same information	Makes assessment of students' mental involvement difficult
	Provides students with an organized perspective of lesson content (i.e., information is structured and relationships among concepts are illustrated)	Doesn't provide feedback to students; by definition, presentation is a one-way approach
	Can be used to efficiently present a large amount of content	
Demonstration	Utilizes several senses; students can see, hear, and possibly experience an actual event	May be difficult for all students to see the demonstration
	Has dramatic appeal if the presenter uses good showmanship techniques, such as demonstrating an unexpected result or a discrepant event	Is time consuming if demonstrations are done live
		Demonstrations may not go as planned
Discussion	Allows students to actively practice problem-solving, critical-thinking, and higher-level thinking skills	Students must have a common experience (reading a book, viewing a video, participating in an activity) in order to meaningfully participate and contribute
	Is interesting and stimulating for teachers and students alike	
	Can change attitudes and knowledge level	Teacher must prepare and possess discussion-leading skills for the method to be effective
	Makes effective use of students' backgrounds and experiences	
Games	Actively involves students and encourages social interaction through communication among players	May involve students with competition more than content
	Provides the opportunity for practice of skills with immediate feedback	Can be impossible to play if pieces are lost or damaged
	Can be incorporated into many instructional situations to increase student motivation	Can be time-consuming to set up if games have many components
	Helps students learn to deal with unpredictable circumstances	
Simulation	Provides practice and experimentation with skills	Can cause deep emotional involvement (e.g., students in veterinary school get very attached to "sick" animals they diagnose and attempt to "save," even though the animals exist only within the simulation)
	Provides immediate feedback on actions and decisions	
	Simplifies real-world complexities and focuses on important attributes or characteristics	
	Is appealing, motivates intense effort, and increases learning	Both setup and debriefing can be time-consuming
Cooperative Learning	Promotes positive interdependence, individual accountability, collaborative and social skills, and group processing	Requires a compatible group of students (this may be difficult to form)
	Encourages trust building, communication, and leadership skills	Takes more time to cover the same amount of content than other methods
	Facilitates student learning in academic as well as social areas	Is less appealing to individuals who prefer to work alone
	Involves students in active learning	
Discovery	Encourages higher-level thinking; students are required to analyze and synthesize information rather than memorize low-level facts	Allows for the discovery of "incorrect" or unintended information
	Provides intrinsic motivation (where merely participating in the task itself is rewarding) to discover the "answer"	Can be time-consuming
	Usually results in increased retention of knowledge; students have processed the information and not simply memorized it	
	Develops the skills and attitudes essential for self-directed learning	

FIGURE 6–6   Advantages and Limitations of Instructional Methods.

Problem Solving	Increases comprehension and retention; students are required to work with everyday problems and to apply theory to practice	Limits the amount of content covered; can be time-consuming
	Involves higher-level learning; students cannot solve problems by simple memorization and regurgitation	Selecting, modifying, and/or designing effective instructional problems can be time-consuming
	Provides students with the opportunity to learn from their mistakes	Requires teachers to have good management skills to coach students without giving them the "answer"
	Develops responsibility as students learn to think independently	
Drill and Practice	Provides repetitive practice in basic skills to enhance learning, build competency, and attain mastery	Students can perceive it as boring
	Promotes psychomotor and low-level cognitive skills Helps build speed and accuracy	Does not teach when and how to apply the facts learned
Tutorial	Provides optimum individualized instruction; all students get the individual attention they need	May be impractical in some cases because appropriate tutor or tutorial material may not be available for individual students
	Provides the highest degree of student participation	
	Expands the number of "teachers" in the classroom by using students or computers as tutors	May encourage student dependency on human tutor; students may become reluctant to work on their own
	Frequently benefits student tutors as much as, or more than, the tutees	
	Introduces new concepts in a sequenced, interactive way	

FIGURE 6–6 (Continued)

3. With the selection of your alternative method, what alterations (if any) would have to be made for the selected instructional activities?

 WHICH METHOD(S) TO USE?

It is important to note that you may use multiple or mixed methods within a single lesson. In many instructional situations one method will not do the job. For example, you can combine a tutorial with drill and practice to strengthen the newly learned skills. The combination of methods may be more powerful and result in more learning than either method used alone. The key is to focus on what will work best to help your students learn your content. Try various methods with actual students to help determine which method or combination of methods is most effective and consider using a variety of methods to keep the instruction interesting. The advantages and limitations of the methods we have just discussed are listed in Figure 6–6. These advantages and limitations provide a foundation for choosing methods for a particular lesson.

We have compiled the advantages of the various instructional methods into a checklist, shown in Figure 6–7. This table will help you select your method(s) for a particular lesson. The checklist will help you remember the factors to consider when selecting instructional methods. Without such a list, it is easy to make choices based

only on what you like best or are most comfortable with. The list will remind you that there are other important considerations. It is not meant to replace your professional judgment, but to supplement or support it. We recommend that you use the checklist to narrow your choices and then rely on your experience and judgment to make a final decision. This will, of course, become easier as you gain teaching experience.

Kevin Spencer's Lesson Plan

As begun in Chapter 4, we are tracing the development of Kevin Spencer's sixth-grade social studies lesson plan that deals with the Civil War. As part of the Planning Phase, Kevin decides upon the methods he might use (see Figure 6–8).

SUMMARY

This chapter discussed different types of methods for learning. We presented the ten most widely used instructional methods, gave examples, and listed advantages and limitations of each method. You will need to select the appropriate method(s) for your students. Keep in mind that methods can be used in combination. There is no one best method for any instructional situation. For each lesson you will have to consider your objectives, your students, and your comfort level with each method.

Which Methods Should I Choose?

The Methods Selection Checklist will help you select the method or methods that will best fit your lesson. Each method has advantages, listed in the first column of the table. There are ten additional columns, one for each instructional method. To use the checklist, place a "√" in all the white spaces that best describe your instructional needs or situation. For example, if you think learning will be enhanced by allowing students to learn on their own, go to item 4 and place a "√" in the four columns that contain a white space. Continue this process for each of the items in the first column. When you have gone through the entire checklist, determine which column has the most "√s."

If most of the "√s" are in:	Select		If most of the "√s" are in:	Select
P	Presentation		CL	Cooperative Learning
DM	Demonstration		DY	Discovery
DN	Discussion		PS	Problem Solving
G	Games		DP	Drill and Practice
S	Simulation		T	Tutorial

It is possible that you will have more than one column with the same number of "√s." In that case, you will need to choose which method is best or consider using multiple methods for your lesson.

Student learning will be enhanced by instructional methods that

	P	DM	DN	G	S	CL	DY	PS	DP	T
1. Are predominantly student centered	▓	▓	▓							
2. Are predominantly teacher centered				▓	▓	▓	▓	▓	▓	▓
3. Provide a high level of interactivity	▓	▓								
4. Allow for students to learn on their own	▓	▓	▓	▓	▓	▓				
5. Allow several students (2–5) to be involved simultaneously	▓								▓	
6. Are appropriate for a small group (6–15)	▓						▓	▓	▓	▓
7. Are group oriented (16 plus)			▓			▓	▓	▓	▓	▓
8. Provide information and content				▓		▓			▓	
9. Provide practice with feedback	▓	▓								
10. Provide a discovery environment	▓	▓					▓			▓
11. Present situations requiring strategy	▓	▓							▓	▓
12. Can be completed in a short time (less than 20 minutes)					▓	▓	▓	▓		▓
13. Provide more content in a shorter time (are efficient)				▓	▓	▓	▓	▓		▓
14. Enhance skills in the high-level intellectual skills domain	▓		▓						▓	
15. Enhance skills in the low-level intellectual skills domain			▓		▓	▓	▓	▓		
16. Enhance skills in the psychomotor skills domain	▓		▓			▓		▓		
17. Enhance skills in the attitude domain	▓	▓					▓		▓	▓
18. Are appropriate for a noncompetitive environment	▓	▓	▓				▓			
19. Promote decision making	▓	▓						▓	▓	▓
20. Provide a realistic context for learning	▓						▓		▓	▓
21. Are highly motivating	▓	▓				▓			▓	
22. Enhance retention of information		▓								▓
23. Use the inductive or inquiry approach to learning	▓	▓							▓	▓

FIGURE 6–7 Method selection checklist.

Toolbox: Selecting Appropriate Instructional Methods

For practice, look over each of the following three scenarios. Decide what would be the best method for each situation. Then answer the following questions: What were the reasons you used to make your selections? Did you identify any potential problems with your selections? If so, what were those problems? What other methods could you also have selected? Under what conditions would you switch to those alternatives?

↗ *Scenario A:* The sixth-grade concert band instructor, Mr. Snyder, has decided that his students need to better discriminate between sharps, flats, and natural notes on the musical scale. He has 56 students currently in his band, and the instruction will take place in the band room, which is large enough to seat approximately 125 individuals.

↗ *Scenario B:* The instructor of an advanced survival training course needs to teach the six participants how to recognize edible versus nonedible desert plants found in the southwestern United States. Even though the course involves training for desert survival, it is being taught at a small college in Ohio.

↗ *Scenario C:* Mrs. Spence and her class of 25 tenth-grade students have been studying a unit on developing critical-thinking skills. One section of the content focuses on methods used to solve ill-defined problems and Mrs. Spence has decided that she wants to give the students practice using the different techniques they are studying.

To help you understand how factors such as the students, objectives, and learning environment might affect your choice of method in these scenarios, consider how your selections would change if the following aspects were different:

↗ *Scenario A:* Instead of being a band director, Mr. Snyder is a private flute teacher with 12 students of different ages who all come at different times during the day for individualized instruction. His goal is still to have the students increase their ability to discriminate between flats, sharps, and natural notes.

↗ *Scenario B:* The survival course takes place at the University of Nevada, Las Vegas, within minutes from large sections of desert.

↗ *Scenario C:* The focus of Mrs. Spence's class changes from being able to apply the problem-solving techniques to simply understanding them.

Refer to Teacher Resource B (see page 241) and review the sample lesson plan. Note the methods used for each of the sections. Would you consider using any different methods for any of the sections? Why or why not?

TECHNOLOGY COORDINATOR'S CORNER

At the beginning of this chapter, we introduced you to Sally Lopez, a fourth-grade teacher at Fair Oaks Consolidated School. She listened to her colleagues in the break room discussing various methods. Being more familiar with some of the methods than others, Sally decided to talk with her friend, the school's tech coordinator, Nikki Sharp. Nikki reminded Sally of a couple of things. First, learning is complex, and thus a number of different methods may be needed in order to attain maximum effectiveness. There would always be times when one method or another would be less appropriate. Second, the learners and the objective of the learning should dictate what types of methods are needed in order to accomplish the learning. It is important to understand different types of methods so that an optimal selection can be made. Finally, there will be times when technology is not needed as the primary means to attain learning; however, it may still play other important supporting roles to learning. For example, a debate may not involve any technology; however, technology can be used to facilitate gathering needed prerequisite information, to prepare the debaters to deliver their remarks effectively, and so on. Nikki said, "Often technology has its greatest impact on learning as a support to other effective instructional methods."

Nikki encouraged Sally to consider a wide variety of methods before deciding which one or ones to use. Consider your learners and the content. Use a variety of methods, not just the ones with which you are most familiar. Extend your range of expertise by trying them all during various lessons.

PEARSON myeducationkit   To check your comprehension of the content covered in this chapter, go to the MyEducationKit for this book and complete the Study Plan for Chapter 6. Here you will be able to take a chapter quiz, receive feedback on your answers, and then access resources that will enhance your understanding of chapter content.

Planning Phase

1. Learners — Chapter 4
2. Objectives — Chapter 4
3. Learning Environment — Chapter 4
4. Developing the Initial Draft Outline — Chapter 4
5. Instructional Activities — Chapter 5
6. Instructional Methods — Chapter 6

❏ Select all instructional methods that apply to the instruction and provide a short description of how each selection will be used

Check Methods to in-corporate.	Provide Short Description.
X Presentation	Show sample story-telling presentation; Overview of important events; Student presentations
❏ Demonstration	
X Discussion	Introduction; Orientation; Student presentations; Summary
❏ Drill and Practice	
❏ Tutorial	
❏ Instructional Games	
X Preparation of student presentations Cooperative Learning	
❏ Simulations	
X Discovery	Use WebQuest search for information
❏ Problem Solving	

X Indicate within the planning card set what method, as well as when each of the selected methods will be integrated within the instruction

7. Instructional Media — Chapter 7
8. Instructional Materials — Chapter 8

FIGURE 6–8   Methods Portion of PIE Checklist for Kevin Spencer's Lesson Plan.

SUGGESTED RESOURCES

Print Resources

Anderson, P. (2006). Psychology in learning and instruction. Upper Saddle River, NJ: Merrill/Prentice Hall.

Benjamin, A. (2005). Differentiated instruction using technology: A guide for middle and high school teachers. Larchmont, NY: Eye on Education, Inc.

Borich, G. (2007). Effective teaching methods: Research-based practice (6th ed.). Upper Saddle River, NJ: Pearson/Merrill/Prentice Hall.

Dieterle, E., & Clarke, J. (in press). Multi-user virtual environments for teaching and learning. In M. Pagani (Ed.), Encyclopedia of multimedia technology and networking (2nd ed.). Hershey, PA: Idea Group.

Forcier, R., & Descy, D. (2007). The computer as an educational tool: Productivity and problem solving (5th ed.). Prentice Hall.

Jacobsen, D. A., Eggen, P., & Kauchak, D. (2006). Methods for Teaching: Promoting Student Learning (7th ed.). Upper Saddle River, NJ: Merrill/Prentice Hall.

Joliffe, W. (2007). Cooperative learning in the classroom: Putting it into practice. London: Paul Chapman Publishing.

Kozma, R. B., Belle, L. W., & Williams, G. W. (1978). Methods of Teaching. Schooling, Teaching and Learning American Education. (pp. 210-211). St. Louis, Missouri: C.V. Mosby Co.

Lengel, J. G., & Lengel, K. M. (2006). Integrating technology: A practical guide. Boston: Allyn & Bacon.

Orlich, D., Harder, R., Callahan, R., Trevisan, M., & Brown, A. (2009). Teaching strategies: A guide to effective instruction. Boston, MA: Wadsworth.

Thorsen, C. (2008). Techtactics: Technology for teachers. (3rd ed.). Boston: Allyn & Bacon.

Westwood, P. (2008). What teachers need to know about teaching methods. Victoria, Australia: ACER.

Electronic Resources

http://www.educause.edu/ELI/LearningTechnologies/GamesSimulationsandVirtualWorl/11263

(Educause Learning Initiative: Games, Simulations, and Virtual Worlds)

http://simschoolresources.ed.greenriver.org/portal/simschoolresources/simulations

(SimSchool Resources: Simulations & Games in Education)

http://www.adprima.com/teachmeth.htm

(Instructional Methods: Advantages and Disadvantages)

http://www.teach-nology.com/teachers/methods/models/

(Teachnology: Methods and Theory Resources)

http://olc.spsd.sk.ca/de/pd/instr/index.html

(Saskatoon Public Schools: Instructional Strategies Online)

http://www.sasked.gov.sk.ca/docs/policy/approach/instrapp03.html

7 Instructional Media: Involving Multiple Senses of Learners

Source: Bob Daemmrich Photography.

KEY WORDS AND CONCEPTS

Medium (plural-media)
Text
Visuals
Printed visuals
Projected visuals
Overhead transparencies
PowerPoint
Displayed visuals

Audiotape
Compact disc (CD)
Videotape
DVD
Real objects
Models
Multimedia
Computer software

CHAPTER OBJECTIVES

After reading and studying this chapter, you will be able to:

↗ Distinguish among the concepts of methods, media, and materials.
↗ Define instructional media and justify their importance in teaching and learning.
↗ Describe each medium discussed in this chapter including examples with your description.

↗ Demonstrate the correct procedures for using each medium discussed in this chapter and/or discuss the guidelines for using each.
↗ Discuss techniques for selecting and combining media for instructional purposes.
↗ Select the most appropriate instructional media for a particular lesson.

INTRODUCTION

Joe Salvo, a new teacher at Kirkmont High School, is very proficient at using computers and other recent technology for instruction, but is not proficient at using the "older media." To Joe, "older media" include textbooks, printed visuals, overhead transparencies, audiotapes, videotapes, real objects, and models. He realizes that some of these, like textbooks, can be presented on a computer using e-books. However, Kirkmont does not have a lot of the new technology, like e-books.

Joe wonders how he can learn to use these "older media," because Kirkmont has a lot of them available in his teaching field. He decides to ask the Technology Coordinator, Brenda Walters, what he should do. During their initial meeting, Brenda points out, "After you define your needs, you should make yourself aware of the range of available media. Only after you learn the characteristics, advantages, and limitations of each are you prepared to choose the one that meets your needs."

In the last chapter, we introduced you to methods that are like roads. Media, discussed in this chapter, are like vehicles. They help you and your students carry the content (information) along the road (methods) to learning. Just as most vehicles can travel on most roads, most media can be used by most methods. In this chapter, you will learn how to select and use media to help your students learn.

To put these concepts into perspective, methods are procedures of instruction selected to help learners achieve objectives or understand content (e.g., presentation, simulation, drill and practice, cooperative learning). Media are channels of communication that carry messages and means by which information can be delivered to the learner (e.g., text, visuals, audio, video, multimedia). The specific items used in a lesson are called instructional materials (e.g., the World History textbook, *Where in the World is Carmen Sandiego?* computer software, the wall chart showing different types of insects).

As shown in Figure 7–1, a critical piece in the overall planning puzzle is that of the "instructional media." Just as there were a variety of instructional methods discussed within Chapter 6, the focus of Chapter 7 is to acquaint you with a variety of available media. The media help to determine how the instructional message is delivered and its overall impact on the learner. The strategic selection of media is based upon the needs of the learners, the desired outcome, and the constraints of the environment, as well as what methods and activities need to be supported.

 INSTRUCTIONAL MEDIA

Media are essential to good teaching and, to get the most from them, they must be selected properly and used effectively. In this chapter, we examine various

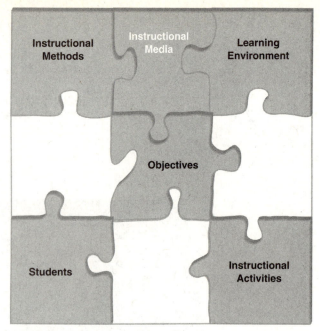

FIGURE 7–1   Instructional media as the next piece of the planning puzzle.

types of media, including descriptions and examples of each, along with how to use them.

A **medium** (plural-media) is a channel of communication. Media are "carriers of information between a source and a receiver" (Smaldino, Lowther, & Russell, 2008, p. 6). Examples of media include *PowerPoint* slides, videotapes, diagrams, printed materials, and computer software. These are considered instructional media when they carry messages with an instructional purpose. The purpose of instructional media is to facilitate communication and to enhance learning.

Media serve a variety of roles in education. Their primary role is to help students learn. One way they do this is by providing an information-rich environment. Media can provide simulated experiences. Students do not have to go to a foreign country to "see" it. Visuals give added meaning to words. Students can see what a new invention looks like, not just hear or read a verbal description of it. Video or a series of pictures can demonstrate a process. It is better if learners see a skill demonstrated before being asked to practice it. The demonstration can be live, videotaped, or presented through a series of photographs. In addition, color, sound, and motion can increase student interest and motivation to learn.

Another role of media, often overlooked, is their use in assessment. You can ask students to identify an object or parts of an object in a photograph or to describe the movements in a musical composition recorded on audiotape. Videotapes can present the events leading up to a problem situation, and you may have students describe their responses to the problem.

Media commonly used in elementary and secondary schools include text, visuals, audio, video, real objects and models, and multimedia. We discuss each of these, along with examples of classroom applications.

Text

The term **text** refers to letters and numbers, usually presented in the form of printed materials or on a computer screen. Examples include study guides, manuals, worksheets, textbooks, and computer displays. Textbooks, such as this one, have long been used in the learning process. You can use many of the other media and computer formats discussed in this book along with textbooks.

The most common application of text is to present information. Students read text to learn the content. They are given reading assignments and are responsible for the material during class discussions and on tests. Text can also complement your presentation. Students may use study guides and worksheets to enhance information you present verbally or through other media. Worksheets allow students to practice what they have learned and to receive feedback. Additionally, students may use text references in the library media center or search computer databases to find information on a specific topic. See "Preview Form: Text" in Appendix D, on page 300.

Text Examples

1. Jean Montgomery's fourth-graders are reading in their textbooks about the countries of Africa. Ms. Montgomery has taught them that reading is especially fun if you can share with others who are reading the same material. Students are working together in small groups, with each group studying a different country. The students take turns leading a discussion after reading a section of the text. Some students also refer to the encyclopedia on CD-ROM in the classroom to get additional information.
2. Students complete worksheets about the workings of an artificial heart after having viewed a videotape on the topic. The worksheet serves as viewing notes during the video. Each student practices applying the information presented and receives immediate feedback from the teacher.
3. Moderately handicapped industrial education students assemble a bicycle by following the directions in its accompanying pamphlet. The purpose of the activity is to promote reading and to encourage students to follow instructions. After assembling the bicycle, they disassemble it so other students can repeat the process.

Principles for Using Text

Textbooks and other text-based materials, such as those found on the Internet, should meet your students' needs rather than dictate what they do. As indicated in the PIE model (see Chapter 4), you should determine learning objectives and then select materials that will facilitate your students achieving them. Too often text is selected first, and then what the students learn and do is determined by what is in the text.

- Direct student reading with objectives and/or questions.
- Emphasize the use of visuals with text-based materials.
- Check the teacher's guide for additional materials and activities.
- Supplement text with other media.

Visuals

Visuals are two-dimensional materials designed to communicate a message to students. They usually include verbal (text or word) elements as well as graphic (picture or picture-like) elements. Figures and tables, such as the ones used in this book, are good examples of visuals.

We live in a very visual society. From pictures in the morning newspaper, to signs on the roadway, to graphics downloaded from the Internet, we constantly see visuals every day. Why are visuals used so frequently? Because they work! Visuals can increase instructional effectiveness by highlighting concepts through the use of graphs, illustrations, charts, and diagrams. They increase viewers' comprehension and understanding because they provide a summary or visual representation of the information presented in the text. For example, visuals can show real or abstract items, illustrate procedures, provide examples, identify parts and pieces, and draw attention to similarities and differences among various objects. Additionally, visuals can increase efficiency by representing, in a single form, what may take hundreds if not thousands of words to explain. Finally, visuals can increase appeal by attracting attention, as well as stimulating thought and inquiry. See "Preview Form: Visuals" in Appendix D, on page 301.

Visuals have numerous applications. For example, you may use photographs or drawings to illustrate specific lesson topics, especially those explaining a process. Visuals are helpful when students are learning to identify people, places, or things. You may use them to stimulate creative expression such as writing stories or composing poetry. They can provide an excellent way to review or preview experiences of past or future field trips. Visuals also serve to pique interest and provide specific information for testing and evaluation purposes.

Using Visuals in Instructional Materials

Your selection and use of visuals are important when adapting or creating instructional materials. Just as the proper visual may lead to increased instructional effectiveness, efficiency, and appeal, one that is not appropriate may cause learner difficulties and frustration. Ask yourself the following questions when selecting visuals to use with your instructional materials:

- ↗ Is the visual relevant to the instructional outcomes?
- ↗ Is the information depicted accurately?
- ↗ Is the information current?
- ↗ Is the information presented clearly and simply?
- ↗ Will learners comprehend what is depicted?
- ↗ Will it be big/small enough for the given purpose and size of audience?
- ↗ Is it aesthetically pleasing?

Several types of visuals are used in teaching and learning. We look at three types here: printed visuals, projected visuals, and displayed visuals.

Printed Visuals

Printed visuals include drawings, charts, graphs, posters, and cartoons. Sources of visuals include textbooks, reference materials, newspapers, and periodicals, as well as those created by teachers or students. Several types of visuals are used in teaching and learning.

Printed Visuals Examples

1. Tom Keller selects one of his students' favorite books, *Alexander and the Terrible, Horrible, No Good, Very Bad Day,* to read to a small group of second-graders. Before beginning the story, he shows students pictures from the book to preview the story. This will help the students focus on the plot of the story. After reading the story, students will create their own drawings based on the main points of the story.
2. Middle school science students are given a set of individual drawings showing the major steps involved in the production of oxygen by plants. As a group, they are to put the individual visuals into the proper sequence. Handling the visuals stimulates discussion and learning.
3. High school history students use geography maps to point out the difficulties an army would have if it attempted to invade Switzerland. Using topographic maps on a computer the students attempt to find possible routes before the teacher points out the routes actually used by invaders in the past.

Principles for Using Printed Visuals

A variety of pictures, drawings, charts, and other visuals are available or can be prepared for classroom use. Graphics are available in textbooks and other printed materials, in computer software and multimedia programs, and as separate paper-based visuals.

- ↗ Use simple materials that everyone can see.
- ↗ Provide written or verbal cues to highlight important aspects of visuals.
- ↗ Use one visual at a time except for comparison.
- ↗ Hold visuals steady.

Projected Visuals

Projected visuals include overhead transparencies and computer presentation software such as Microsoft's *PowerPoint.* **Overhead transparencies** are widely used in classrooms because of their many advantages. You can write on clear plastic with colored markers and print on clear plastic using a computer. In addition, you can project a variety of materials, including cutout silhouettes, small opaque objects, and many types of transparent objects.

Basically, the overhead projector is a box with a large "stage" on the top. The overhead projector is one of the easiest devices to use. With a little practice, anyone—including your students—can make a professional presentation using overhead transparencies (see Figure 7–2 showing an overhead projector).

The overhead has many group-instruction applications. Commercial distributors of transparencies have made materials available for virtually all curricular areas, from kindergarten through adult education .

PowerPoint is an example of presentation software used on a computer connected to a projector. It is possible for users without specialized training to create and project colorful and animated visuals. Students, as well as instructors, can use templates to produce very professional-looking presentations. *PowerPoint* allows the user to include text, draw pictures, produce diagrams, import digital photos, include music, and create animation.

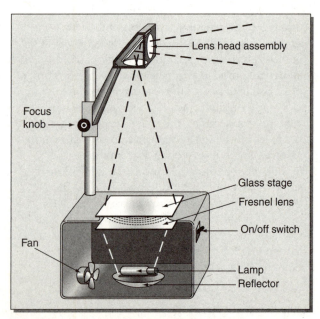

FIGURE 7–2 Key parts of the overhead projector.
Source: Smaldino, Sharon E.; Lowther, Deborah L. & Russell, James D. Instructional Technology and Media for Learning. 9e. *© 2008. Reprinted by permission of Pearson Education, Inc., Upper Saddle River, NJ.*

It is easy to use the overhead projector to show visuals to a group.
Source: Scott Cunningham/Merrill Education.

Projected Visuals Examples

1. The chalkboard and overhead projector make a good team for teaching problem solving in Dianna Williams's physics class. After she demonstrates how to solve acceleration problems, Dianna projects similar problems with the overhead projector. Prior to class time she had prepared the problems on transparencies, using an 18-point font so all students would be able to see and read the problems. The screen is in the front corner of the room so it will not block the chalkboard. She randomly selects several students to do a problem on the chalkboard, telling them to print large enough so that everyone in the room can see their work. The other students work on the same problem at their desks. When all students are finished, Dianna leads a discussion on the various ways to approach the problem. Students indicate errors they find in the techniques and the calculations of each other's problems.

2. Charles Miller divides his eighth-grade general science class into groups of four. Each group draws from a jar a topic that they are responsible to present to the entire class. They are encouraged to use Apple *Keynote* on school Macintoshes for their presentations. Because science lends itself so well to visuals and diagrams, the students are encouraged to create their own drawings or to take photographs with the school's digital camera. However, in some instances, Mr. Miller allows them to use material from the Internet, but they must properly cite their source.

3. Demetrius Brown uses a *PowerPoint* presentation that was developed by several local teachers to provide his fourth-graders with information and a "tour" of a local historical site. The old canal and locks could be visited as part of a field trip, but Demetrius would rather spend the available time and funds on another field trip, so he uses the multimedia presentation complete with sound

FIGURE 7–3 Transparency overlays can be used to build complex visuals step by step.

Source: Smaldino, Sharon E.; Lowther, Deborah L. & Russell, James D. Instructional Technology and Media for Learning. 9e. © 2008. Reprinted by permission of Pearson Education, Inc., Upper Saddle River, NJ.

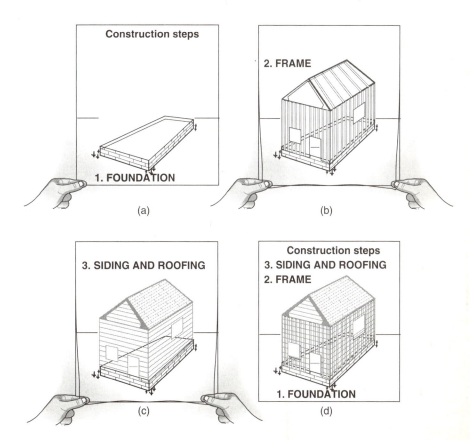

(narration and music) as well as animation (video shot by a local teacher) to introduce his students to the site. He also encourages his students to visit the site with their parents after the lesson.

Principles for Using Projected Visuals

↗ Focus the image so it fills the screen.

↗ Turn off lights over the screen if possible. The learners should be able to take notes and you should be able to see the class.

↗ Stand facing your class. Do not block the screen especially when using overhead transparencies.

↗ Use appropriate pacing. In most cases, do not show a projected visual for more than 20 to 30 seconds without adding to it or changing to the next transparency.

↗ Direct students' attention to the important parts of the projected visual.

↗ Summarize frequently. Every so often, assist your audience in their efforts to "see" the big picture. *PowerPoint's* "Summary Slide" features may be helpful for this.

PEARSON myeducationkit Go to the Assignments and Activities section of Chapter 7 in MyEducationKit and complete the activity entitled "Integrating Visuals into Portfolios." As you view the video and answer the accompanying questions, consider how and why visuals are integrated into the students' portfolios.

Displayed Visuals There are many surfaces in the classroom on which to display visual materials, including whiteboards, multipurpose boards, and bulletin boards. The most common medium in the classroom is the whiteboard.

Multipurpose boards (also called whiteboards or marker boards) have more than one purpose. Their smooth, white plastic surface requires a special erasable marker. The surface is also suitable as a screen on which you can project visuals. Materials cut from thin plastic, such as figures and letters, will adhere to the surface when rubbed in place. Some of these boards have a steel backing as well and can be used as a magnetic board for displaying visuals.

A bulletin board's surface is made of a material that holds pins, thumbtacks, staples, and other sharp fasteners without damage to the board. In practice, bulletin board displays tend to serve three broad purposes: decorative, motivational, and instructional. The decorative bulletin board is probably the most common in schools. Its function is to lend visual stimulation to the environment by using catch phrases or posters. Displaying student work illustrates the motivational use of bulletin boards. The public recognition offered by such displays can play an

important role in classroom life. It promotes pride in achievement, encouraging students to do a good job.

The third purpose of bulletin boards is instructional, complementing the educational objectives of the formal curriculum. Rather than merely presenting static informational messages, you can design displays to invite participation. Such displays ask questions and give viewers some means of manipulating parts of the display to verify their answers (e.g., flaps, pockets, dials, or movable parts). Learners can also take part in the actual construction of the display. For example, to introduce a unit on animals, an elementary teacher might ask each student to bring in a picture of a favorite animal. Students would then make a bulletin board incorporating all the pictures.

Displayed Visuals Examples

1. Three of Carl Shedd's fifth-grade students print an outline on the chalkboard for their class presentation on the characteristics of gorillas. After describing each characteristic, one student puts a checkmark at the appropriate place on the outline so the students in the class can easily follow the presentation.

2. Bonnie Johnson uses a marker board and a variety of colored markers to diagram the relationships among the various components of several computer software applications. She leaves these diagrams on the marker board during class so students can refer to them. She also puts key commands on the board for her students' easy reference.

3. Students classify various types of igneous, metamorphic, and sedimentary rocks displayed on platforms secured to a bulletin board. Then they check their responses against the correct answer provided under a movable flap. Because the display is available in the classroom during the entire unit, they can check and recheck themselves until they are confident that they know all the types of rocks.

4. Students sing the simple notes of the treble clef displayed on a multipurpose board. As the teacher adds sharps and flats, different colors draw students' attention to these special notes. The notes can be easily moved around the board.

Principles for Using Displayed Visuals In the classroom, the most widely used (and misused) tool is the chalkboard. Although chalkboards have been replaced by dustless multipurpose boards in some classrooms, the same simple techniques can increase the effectiveness of both.

↗ Check the visibility of the board from several positions around the room.

↗ Decide in advance how you plan to use the board.

↗ Print using upper- and lowercase, not all caps or in script.

➷ Face your audience; do not talk to the board with your back to the class.

Evaluating the Effectiveness of Visuals

1. Using the Preview Form: Visuals in Appendix D, review a chapter in one of your textbooks and evaluate the visuals that are incorporated within the chapter. Rate the chapter's visuals for each of the criteria (it may be easiest to develop a 1 (low) to 5 (high) rating scale). Include comments about which photos should serve as examples and non-examples for specific criteria rankings. What, if any, recommendations would you give the author for enhancing the visual quality of the chapter?

2. During the next lecture/oral presentation that you attend, use the Preview Form: Visuals in Appendix D. During the presentation, evaluate the quality of the visuals that are presented with the preview form criteria. What suggestions would you offer to the presenter in order for him/her to improve the presentation visuals?

Audio

In addition to the teacher's voice, there are numerous ways to bring sound (animal sounds, famous speeches, and foreign languages) into the classroom. The most common are the **audiotape** and **compact disc (CD)**.

Audiotapes allow both students and teachers to make their own recordings to share with the class. For hands-on learning, you can record a tape from which students can receive step-by-step instructions. To be efficient and effective in their work, these students must have both hands free and their eyes on their work, not on a textbook or manual. Audiotapes allow students to move at their own pace and leave you free to circulate around the classroom and discuss each student's work individually. Students with learning difficulties can revisit classroom presentations using audiotape.

The students practice their listening skills with CDs of recorded stories, poetry, and instructions. After the students have practiced their listening skills under your direction, you can evaluate them using a CD they have not heard before. See "Preview Form: Audio" in Appendix D, on page 302.

Audio Examples

1. The eighth-grade students at Fairfield Middle School are using cassette tape recorders to gather an oral history of their community. The project is a cooperative effort by all eighth-grade social studies teachers and their students. The teachers each chose to focus on an aspect of the community's history, such as transportation, government, business, industry, and recreation. Students spend

Students can share audio experiences.
Source: Scott Cunningham/Merrill Education.

many weeks deciding on important topics in the area assigned to their class, then work together to develop a set of questions to ask each individual they interview. Armed with tape recorders, students interview people from the community. Some of the citizens come to the school; the students visit others. Students edit the individual tapes into one tape that highlights important aspects of the community's history. The finalized copy is available for use by community groups and organizations.

2. High school students learn and practice Spanish conversation using audiotapes. The students enjoy recording and listening to the tapes. Using this technique, students learn conversational Spanish.

3. Students with visual impairments listen to recorded versions of novels being discussed in literature class. Other students also choose to listen to the tapes. All students, whether they read the novel or heard the CDs, then share their interpretations.

Principles for Using Audio   In formal education, a lot of attention is given to reading and writing, a little to speaking, and essentially none to listening. Like all skills, listening and learning from audio can be improved with practice.

➷ Cue the audio material before you and your students use it.

➷ Make sure that all students involved can hear and that other students aren't distracted.

➷ Use a handout or worksheet to maximize learning from audio media.

➷ Use a follow-up activity after each audio lesson.

PEARSON **myeducationkit**™ Go to the Assignments and Activities section of Chapter 7 in MyEducationKit and complete the activity entitled "How Can Digital Sound Capabilities Help Learners?" As you explore the websites, think about how digital audio might be useful in your classroom.

Video

Any media format that uses a television screen or monitor to present a picture can be referred to as **video**: videotapes, DVD, and webcasts. All these formats offer ways to store and display moving images accompanied by sound. As we will see, the formats differ considerably in cost, convenience, and flexibility.

The VHS half-inch **videotape** is one way to capture moving images. VHS can be used for amateur video production in education. However, it is rapidly being replaced by **DVD**.

DVD is a compact disc format for displaying motion video. It offers digital, optical recording, storage, and playback of full-motion video. The disc is the same physical size as an audio CD or a CD-ROM. Current DVDs can hold enough data for a full-length feature film—about two hours. Some DVD discs are able to hold about four times that amount. DVD has instant random access and is highly durable. Recordable DVDs are available. They have done for video what the CD did for music.

Both videotape and DVD have fast forward and reverse search capabilities. Video formats, particularly DVD, can be indexed, making it possible to locate specific sections of a program. Certain special effects, such as slow motion and still images, are available during the video presentation. Because the equipment is easy to operate, video lends itself to use by individual students.

Webcast is video distributed or "broadcast" on the Internet. They may be live events or prerecorded programs. See "Preview Form: Video" in Appendix D, on page 303.

Video Examples

1. Paige Ertmer's preservice teachers are viewing the acclaimed videotape *Good Morning, Miss Tolliver* in their mathematics methods course. Originally

DVDs and CD-ROMs allow learners to view full-motion video on a computer.
Source: Ellen B. Senisi/The Image Works.

shown on public television, the video is a fascinating look at how Kay Tolliver, an East Harlem math teacher, combines math and communication arts skills to inspire and motivate her students. Dr. Ertmer is hoping this videotape will inspire and motivate her students, who will be doing their student teaching next semester. She has distributed a set of questions to direct students' viewing of the videotape, asking them to look over the questions prior to seeing the tape and to take notes during the viewing. These questions will form the basis of a class discussion following the video.

2. By watching a golfing DVD, physical education students use slow motion and freeze-frame capabilities to practice imitating the grip and swing of a golf professional. Their coach is able to point out the critical parts of the pro's swing. Students can imitate the swing and also get feedback from their peers.

3. Students write a position paper after viewing a webcast presenting the opposing positions of the lumber industry and environmentalists on retaining the virgin forests of the northwestern United States. Viewing actual forests on video and hearing and seeing representatives of both sides of the issue stimulate the students to investigate the issue and to put their thoughts on paper.

Principles for Using Video   Video, regardless of its format, provides motion, color, and sound. Students are accustomed to viewing television passively at home. Therefore, you must prepare students for active viewing of video in the classroom.

↗ Check lighting, seating, and volume controls before the showing.
↗ Prepare students by reviewing previously learned content and by asking new questions.
↗ Stop the videotape at appropriate points for discussion.
↗ Highlight major points by writing them on the chalkboard or overhead.

Locate an instructional video (VHS, DVD, webcast). Check your school media center or on the Internet. How effective is the video in helping students learn? What does it do well? How could it be improved? How does the audio contribute to learning?

Real Objects and Models

Often not thought of as media, real objects and models can require learners to use all their senses—sight, hearing, smell, touch, and even taste! They bring the outside world into the classroom. **Real objects**, such as coins, tools, plants, and animals, are some of the most accessible resources available to promote student learning. **Models**

Toolbox: Microsoft's PowerPoint and Producer

Microsoft's *Office* suite of applications is one of the most popular collections of productivity software for both teachers and students. Within that suite, a popular application program is known as *PowerPoint*. To learn to use this application, complete the level 1 and level 2 activities in Chapter 5 of the book:

Newby, T. J. (2004). *Teaching and learning with Microsoft Office and FrontPage: Basic building blocks for computer integration.* Upper Saddle River, NJ: Merrill/Prentice-Hall.

Once you are familiar with creating *PowerPoint* presentations, go to the Microsoft website and examine and download their software known as *Producer. Producer* is a free video editor that was developed to work in conjunction with *PowerPoint*. With it, you can create a product that can incorporate audio, video, and *PowerPoint* slides simultaneously on the computer screen. See Figure 7–4 for an example of the *Producer* software editing screen and Figure 7–5 of a screen capture of the finished product.

To acquire information and to download the free *Producer* add-on to *PowerPoint*, visit Microsoft's website: http://www.microsoft.com/windows/windowsmedia/technologies/producer.mspx. For additional listings and updates on this and similar software, use your search engine with search terms such as "Microsoft *Producer*."

FIGURE 7–4   Microsoft *Producer* video editing software.

Source: Reprinted with permission from Microsoft Corporation.

FIGURE 7–5   An edited video created with MS *Producer*.

Source: Reprinted with permission from Microsoft Corporation.

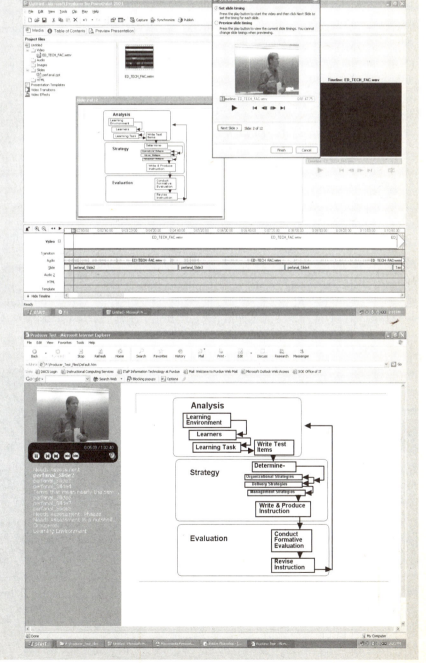

are three-dimensional representations of real objects and may be complete in detail or simplified for instructional purposes. Models of almost everything are available from teacher supply companies and toy stores.

Often you can introduce a new topic with a real object or a model. Invite the students to see and handle it. Both elementary and secondary students can learn about objects in their own environment and those from foreign cultures and other times. Real objects and models add relevance for the students and can generate interest and enthusiasm for a topic. If you cannot bring real things into the classrooms, a field trip can take students to them. Another effective use of these materials occurs during assessment as students classify objects, describe their functions, and identify their components. See "Preview Form: Real objects and Models" in Appendix D, on page 299.

Real Objects and Models Examples

1. Nancy Foust, an instructor in the high school vocational-technical program, is demonstrating how automobile carburetors work so her students can adjust and repair them. She brings several different carburetors into the classroom to arouse interest at the beginning of the class. The students can handle and look at them before the class begins, then she puts the carburetors away. Nancy uses a larger-than-life model of a carburetor to show how the internal parts operate. Some of the parts are made of clear plastic, and many are color coded for easy identification. Having seen and manipulated the actual carburetors, Nancy's students know how big they are and what they look like. The enlarged model allows all of her students to see the various parts as she describes their functions.
2. Elementary students create a terrarium to observe the water cycle. All students are excited when they place the plants and animals in the terrarium. They work together in teams under the teacher's direction to complete the terrarium.
3. Students in a multicultural course discuss the impact of various artifacts (real or replicas of tools, dishes,

etc.) on the lives of those from another culture. They then visit a museum. The artifacts hold the interest and attention of all the students. The real objects and models make the cultures "come alive."

Principles for Using Real Objects and Models   There are countless things in the environment that you and your students can use to learn from—leaves, globes, dolls, manipulatives (objects designed for educational use, such as letter blocks and counting rods), tools, and so on. However, real objects and models will be effective only if they are used properly.

↗ Familiarize yourself with the object or model.
↗ Make sure objects are large enough to be seen.
↗ Indicate actual size, shape, and color of objects represented by models.
↗ Avoid passing a single object around class. It can be distracting and students may play with it while you are trying to move on in the lesson.

Multimedia

Multimedia is the sequential of simultaneous use of a number of different media formats, including video, visuals, audio, text, and real objects and models (see Figure 7–6). These media can be used together as multimedia or can also be used individually. Multimedia are often under computer control. The computer—with its virtually instantaneous response to student input, its extensive capacity to store and manipulate information, and its unmatched ability to serve many individual students simultaneously—has wide application in instruction. The computer can also record, analyze, and react to student responses typed on a keyboard or input with a mouse. Some display screens react to the touch of a student's finger. See "Preview Form: Multimedia" in Appendix D, on page 305.

Objects and models can bring the real world into the classroom.
Source: Scott Cunningham/Merrill Education.

Students can learn from a variety of sources when using a multimedia kit.
Source: Bob Daemmrich/PhotoEdit.

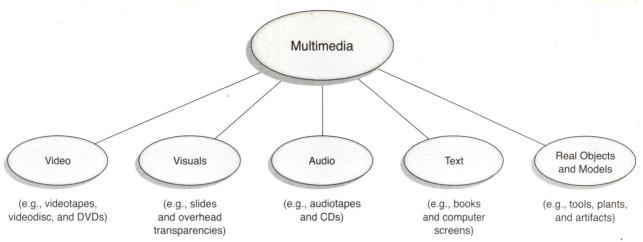

FIGURE 7–6   Multimedia is a combination of different media types.

Multimedia Examples

1. Picture a student in a Spanish conversation class seated in front of a multimedia system. It looks pretty much like a typical computer system, perhaps with a few additional pieces of equipment installed. The student reads the directions on the computer screen and clicks the mouse to get started. The lesson begins with a video clip showing a conversation between two native speakers of Spanish. The video not only allows the student to see and hear two native speakers, but also provides a cultural backdrop, as it was shot on location in Spain. As the lesson progresses, the student makes use of a Spanish dictionary stored on the computer that provides definitions and translations, as well as the actual aural pronunciation of each word and phrase. The computer allows the student access to all of this information and provides periodic review questions and feedback about her progress. This is just one example of how interactive multimedia can function.

2. Nancy Matson has selected a multimedia program from Tom Snyder Productions titled *Rainforest Researchers* (see Figure 7–7). The program provides introductory material for both Nancy and her students. A teacher's guide and student booklets direct lesson activity. The students continue their learning adventure for several class periods. Students consider how ecosystems change and what caused the changes. Nancy accesses for students by their individual worksheets and teamwork.

3. Students in George Morgan's middle school mathematics class are using the computer simulation *Hot Dog Stand* to develop a variety of mathematical and practical skills. The simulation requires planning and recordkeeping, as well as judgments based on computational skills, to make as much money as possible while managing a hot dog stand during a season of various types of concerts. Random generation of variables ensures that the same students can use the program again and again. Participating students are gathered around a computer in the corner of the classroom while other students are engaged in different activities. Mr. Morgan has checked to be sure that all can see the screen and interact without disturbing other students. The students record data, enter the data into spreadsheets, and generate graphs. There is friendly competition to see which group of students can "earn" the most money from its hot dog stand.

Principles for Using Multimedia   When you use multimedia materials, you should test all of the components of the multimedia system well in advance of your lesson. You want to make certain that everything will work when you are ready to use it. Make sure you have all adjunct materials, such as printed materials, for all students.

- ↗ Use a display technology (computer monitors and/or projection systems) that is appropriate for the number of students. Be sure that all students can see the computer images.
- ↗ Install and test all software in advance of the presentation.
- ↗ Encourage student participation through questioning and having students decide next steps.
- ↗ Provide a follow-up discussion at the end of the multimedia experience.

PEARSON **myeducationkit**™   Go to the Assignments and Activities section of Chapter 7 in MyEducationKit and complete the activity entitled "Multimedia Software Supports Instruction." As you view the video and answer the accompanying questions, think about how you might use PowerPoint for multimedia instruction and how it might benefit your students.

FIGURE 7–7 *Rainforest Researchers* is a multimedia instructional learning experience developed by Tom Snyder Productions. Students interact with various media to gain a greater understanding of the topic.

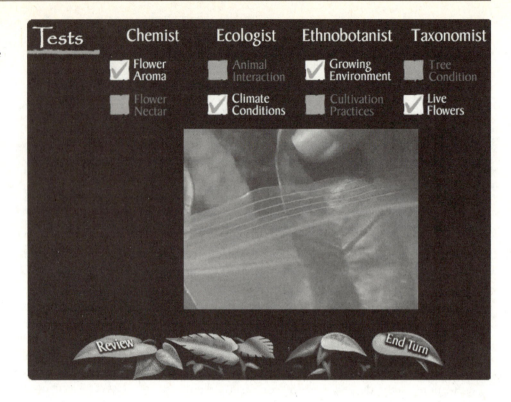

Source: Rainforest Researchers, Tom Snyder Productions.

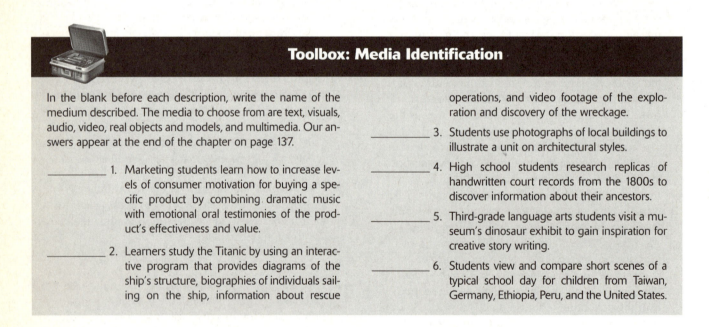

Toolbox: Media Identification

In the blank before each description, write the name of the medium described. The media to choose from are text, visuals, audio, video, real objects and models, and multimedia. Our answers appear at the end of the chapter on page 137.

_____ 1. Marketing students learn how to increase levels of consumer motivation for buying a specific product by combining dramatic music with emotional oral testimonies of the product's effectiveness and value.

_____ 2. Learners study the Titanic by using an interactive program that provides diagrams of the ship's structure, biographies of individuals sailing on the ship, information about rescue operations, and video footage of the exploration and discovery of the wreckage.

_____ 3. Students use photographs of local buildings to illustrate a unit on architectural styles.

_____ 4. High school students research replicas of handwritten court records from the 1800s to discover information about their ancestors.

_____ 5. Third-grade language arts students visit a museum's dinosaur exhibit to gain inspiration for creative story writing.

_____ 6. Students view and compare short scenes of a typical school day for children from Taiwan, Germany, Ethiopia, Peru, and the United States.

 ## WHICH MEDIUM?

A decision you must make is which instructional medium or media to use. You are now familiar with six types of media: text, visuals, audio video, real objects and models, and multimedia. To make a good decision about the type of medium to use, you must know the advantages and limitations of each. Figure 7–8 presents the main advantages and limitations of the media described in this chapter. These advantages and limitations provide your foundation for choosing which medium or media to use in a particular lesson. See "Preview Forms for review of instructional materials" in Appendix D, on page 299.

Instructional Medium	Advantages	Limitations
Text	*Readily available.* Printed materials are readily available in a range of topics and formats.	*Reading level of learners.* Many students are nonreaders or poor readers.
	Flexible. Printed materials may be used in any lighted environment. They are portable. Properly designed text organizes the content and is very user friendly.	*Memorization.* Some critics say textbooks promote memorization rather than higher-level thinking skills.
	Economical. Text can be used again and again by many students size.	*Passive.* Others contend that text promotes solitary learning rather than cooperative group processes. Textbooks may be used to dictate the curriculum rather than to support it.
Visuals Printed Visuals	*Realistic format.* Visuals provide a representation of verbal information.	Some visuals are simply too small to use with a large group and enlarging can be expensive. However, a document camera can project an enlarged image before a class.
	Readily available. Visuals are readily available in books, magazines, newspapers, catalogs, and calendars.	*Two-dimensional.* Visuals lack the three-dimensionality of the real object or scene. However, providing a series of visuals of the same object or scene from several different angles can address this limitation.
	Easy to use. Visuals are easy to use because they do not require any equipment.	*Lack of motion.* Visuals are static and cannot show motion. However, a series of sequential still pictures can suggest motion.
	Relatively inexpensive. Most visuals can be obtained at little or no cost.	
Projected Visuals	*Versatility.* Projected visuals can be used in normal room lighting. The projector is operated from the front of the room, with the presenter facing the audience and maintaining eye contact. All projectors are simple to operate.	*Instructor dependent.* The overhead projector cannot be programmed to display information by itself. The overhead system does not lend itself to independent study. The projection system is designed for large-group presentation.
	Instructor control. The presenter can manipulate projected materials, pointing out important items and highlighting them.	*Preparation required.* Except for the document camera, printed materials and other nontransparent visuals, such as magazine illustrations, cannot be projected immediately but must first be made into transparencies. This can be done using color copying machines.
	Readily available. Computer presentation software and overhead transparencies are readily available in classrooms and the school media center.	
Displayed Visuals	*Versatile.* Both students and teachers can use display boards for a variety of purposes.	*Commonplace.* Instructors often neglect to give display boards the attention and respect they deserve as instructional devices. Displays can quickly lose their effectiveness if left in place too long.
	Colorful. Display boards provide color and add interest to classrooms or hallways.	*Not portable.* Most display boards are not movable.
	Involvement. Students can benefit from designing and using display boards.	
Audio Audiotapes	*Student and teacher preparation.* Students and teachers can record their own tapes easily and economically, erasing and reusing them when material becomes outdated or no longer useful.	*Fixed sequence.* Audiotapes fix the sequence of a presentation, even though it is possible to rewind or advance the tape to a desired portion. It is difficult to scan audio materials as you would printed text.
	Familiarity. Most students and teachers have been using audiocassette recorders since they were very young.	*Lack of attention.* Students' attention may wander while they are listening to audiotapes. They may hear the message but not listen to or comprehend it.
	Verbal message. Students who cannot read can learn from audio media. Audio can provide basic language experiences for students whose native language is not English.	

FIGURE 7–8   Advantages and Limitations of Instructional Media.

	Stimulating. Audio media can provide a stimulating alternative to reading and listening to the teacher. Audio can present verbal messages more dramatically than can text. *Portable*. Audiocassette recorders are very portable and can even be used "in the field" with battery power. Cassette recordings are ideal for home study because many students have their own cassette players.	*Pacing*. Presenting information at the appropriate pace can be difficult for students with a range of skills and background experiences. *Accidental erasure*. Just as audiotapes can be quickly and easily erased when no longer needed, they can be accidentally erased when they should be saved.
CD	*Locating selections*. Students and teachers can quickly locate selections on CDs and can program machines to play any desired sequence. Information can be selectively retrieved by students or programmed by the teacher. *Resistance to damage*. There are no grooves to scratch or tape to tangle and break. Stains can be washed off and ordinary scratches do not affect playback.	*Limited recording capability*. Students and teachers cannot produce their own CDs as cheaply and easily as they can cassettes.
Video Videotape	*Motion*. Moving images can effectively portray procedures (such as tying knots or operating a potter's wheel) in which motion is essential. Operations, such as science experiments, in which sequential movement is critical, can be shown more effectively by means of videotape. *Real-life experiences*. Video allows learners to observe phenomena that might be dangerous to view directly—an eclipse of the sun, a volcanic eruption, or warfare. *Repetition*. Research indicates that mastery of physical skills requires repeated observation and practice. Video allows repeated viewing of a performance for emulation.	*Fixed pace*. Videotape programs run at a fixed pace; some viewers are likely to fall behind, while others are waiting impatiently for the next point. *Scheduling*. Teachers typically must order videos well in advance of their intended use. Arrangements also have to be made for the proper equipment to be available. The complexity of the logistics discourages some teachers.
DVD	*Storage capacity*. Each disc holds two to eight hours of full-motion video. *High-quality audio*. The audio is high fidelity, comparable to that on a compact disc. *Digital format*. Because DVD is a digital medium, it is directly computer compatible.	*Limited materials*. At this time, limited educational materials are available. *Few playback units available*. Many schools have few, if any, DVD players or player-equipped computers.
Real Objects and Models	*Less abstract and more concrete*. Real objects and models provide hands-on learning experiences and emphasize real-world applications. *Readily available*. Materials are readily available in the environment, around school, and in the home. *Attract students' attention*. Students respond positively to both real objects and their models.	*Storage*. Large objects can pose special problems. Caring for living materials such as plants and animals can take a lot of time. *Possible damage*. Materials are often complex and fragile. Parts may be lost or broken.
Multimedia	*Better learning and retention*. Interactive multimedia provides multiple learning modalities and actively involves learners. *Addresses different learning styles and preferences*. The incorporation of multiple modalities provides opportunities for teaching individual learners. For example, those with weak reading skills can use aural and visual skills to process verbal information.	*Equipment requirements*. The equipment requirements for multimedia can be an impediment. While basic systems may involve only the computer and its built-in components, more complex systems may involve external DVD players, CD-ROM players, audio speakers, and so on. These can be difficult to hook up and maintain.

FIGURE 7–8 (Continued)

Effectiveness across learning domains. Interactive multimedia instruction has been shown to be effective in all learning domains. It can be used for psychomotor training, such as learning CPR techniques; to present simulations that provide opportunities for problem-solving and higher-order thinking skills; and even to address affective components of learning.

Realism. Interactive multimedia provides a high degree of realism. Instead of merely reading about a speech by Dr. Martin Luther King, Jr., students can actually see and hear the speech as he originally gave it.

Motivation. Learners show consistently positive attitudes toward interactive multimedia. For today's MTV-conscious youth, multimedia instruction represents a natural avenue for exploring the information revolution.

Interactivity. The key element of computers is interaction with the user. The computer can present information, elicit the learner's response, and evaluate the response.

Individualization. The computer's branching capabilities allow instruction to be tailored to the individual. The computer can provide immediate feedback and monitor the learner's performance.

Consistency. Individualization results in different instructional paths for different learners. But it can be equally important to ensure that specific topics are dealt with in the same way for all learners.

Learner control. Computers can give the user control of both the pace and the sequencing of instruction. Fast learners can speed through the program, while slower learners can take as much time as they need.

Startup costs. Startup costs can be high. The computer itself can be expensive. Adding components and software may cost thousands of dollars.

Complexity and lack of standardization. Interactive multimedia systems can be quite complex. Sometimes it is a challenge just to get the individual components to work together. Novices may become hopelessly lost. This is complicated because there is currently little standardization in many facets of multimedia.

Compatibility. The lack of compatibility among the various brands of personal computers limits multimedia transportability. Developers cannot always create a single package that will work across all types of computers.

Limited intelligence. Most computer software is limited in its capacity for genuine interaction with the learner, and often relies on simple multiple-choice or true-false questions.

FIGURE 7–8   (Continued)

Selecting the appropriate materials for instruction is an important process.
Source: Bob Daemmrich/The Image Works.

As with instructional methods, we have compiled the advantages of the various media into a checklist, shown in Figure 7–9, that may facilitate your selection of the appropriate media for any particular lesson.

Kevin Spencer's Lesson Plan

1. Refer to Teacher Resource B. This teacher resource describes the instructional plan Mr. Spencer has developed for his sixth-grade social studies class.
2. Refer again to the Technology Coordinator's Corner for this chapter.
3. If Lizzy and Sally, the two ninth-grade multimedia developers, were asked by Mr. Spencer to review his lesson plan, do you think they might suggest some types of changes in the use of media within his plan? With what parts do you think they would

Toolbox: Media Selection

For practice, look over each of the following three scenarios. Decide what would be the best medium/media for each situation. Then answer the following questions: What were the reasons you used to make your selections? Did you identify any potential problems with your selections? If so, what would those problems be? What other media could you also have selected? Under what conditions would you switch to those alternatives?

↗ *Scenario A:* The sixth-grade concert band instructor, Mr. Snyder, has decided that his students need to better discriminate between sharps, flats, and natural notes on the musical scale. He has 56 students currently in his band, and the instruction will take place in the band room, which is large enough to seat approximately 125 individuals.

↗ *Scenario B:* The instructor of an advanced survival training course needs to teach the six participants how to recognize edible versus nonedible desert plants found in the southwestern United States. Even though the course involves training for desert survival, it is being taught at a small college in Ohio.

↗ *Scenario C:* Mrs. Spence and her class of 25 tenth-grade students have been studying a unit on developing

critical-thinking skills. One section of the content focuses on methods used to solve ill-defined problems and Mrs. Spence has decided that she wants to give the students practice using the different techniques they are studying.

To help you understand how factors such as the students, objectives, and learning environment might affect your choice of medium/media in these scenarios, consider how your selections would change if the following aspects were different:

↗ *Scenario A:* Instead of being a band director, Mr. Snyder is a private flute teacher with 12 students of different ages who all come at different times during the day for individualized instruction. His goal is still to have the students increase their ability to discriminate between flats, sharps, and natural notes.

↗ *Scenario B:* The survival course takes place at the University of Nevada, Las Vegas, within minutes from large sections of desert.

↗ *Scenario C:* The focus of Mrs. Spence's class changes from being able to apply the problem-solving techniques to simply understanding them.

Which Media Should I Choose?

As you begin planning your instruction, it is important to select a medium that will enhance your topic. The Media Selection Checklist will help you in the process.

Each type of media has a set of advantages (e.g., motion, realism) and a set of educational limitations (e.g., room size, group size). These specifications are listed in the first column of the table on the next page. There are seven columns next to the specifications. Place a √ in all the white spaces that best describe your instructional needs (or situations).

For Example

If it is important that you draw or write key words during your presentation, go to items #7 on the table (on next page) and put "√s" in the three columns to the right that are white. Continue the process for each requirement or item that best describes your instructional situation (needs). When you have gone through the entire table, determine which column has the most "√s" entered in the white spaces in the column. Select the media that has the most "√s".

If most of the "√s" are in:	Select the following media format:
T	Text (handouts, books, computer screen)
V-Print	Visuals-printed (graphics, photos, charts, diagrams)
V-Prj	Visuals-projected (overhead transparencies, *PowerPoint*-type slides)
A	Audio (tape, CD)
Vid	Video (DVD, tape, television)
RO	Real objects and models
MM/CS	Multimedia and other computer software

It is possible that you will have more than one column with most of the white spaces filled in. In that case, you will need to choose which medium is best or consider using multiple media formats in your presentation.

FIGURE 7–9   Media selection checklist.
Source: Adapted from © Claranne K. English, 1995 with permission.

Media Selection Checklist

Student learning will be enhanced by media that:	T	V-Print	V-Prj	A	Vid	RO	MM/CS
1. Enable students to see and/or touch actual objects	■	■	■	■	■		■
2. Allow materials to be taken from the classroom		■	■	■	■		■
3. Can be used after the lesson as a reference, guide, or job aid		■	■	■	■	■	■
4. Allow several participants to respond simultaneously		■	■	■	■	■	■
5. Can be easily erased/modified		■		■	■	■	■
6. Require minimal expense		■	■	■	■	■	■
7. Allow one to draw or write key words during the lesson	■	■		■			
8. Are appropriate for a small group (under 25)	■		■	■		■	■
9. Use visuals that are easy to prepare	■	■					
10. Allow advanced preparation of the visuals		■	■		■		■
11. Present word cues or a lesson outline		■	■				
12. Provide portability						■	■
13. Offer commercially prepared visuals					■	■	■
14. Allow the order of the material to be easily changed				■		■	
15. Allow the user to control pacing and/or to replay a portion of the presentation	■				■	■	
16. Are appropriate for students who have difficulty reading or understanding English	■		■		■		
17. Reproduce an exact sound	■		■	■	■		
18. Are easily used by teachers or students	■						
19. Present high-quality, realistic images (color/graphics/illustrations/visuals)	■		■		■	■	
20. Can be used independently of the instructor		■	■	■	■	■	■
21. Show motion, including sequential motion	■	■	■				■
22. Allow observation of dangerous process; real-life reenactments	■	■	■	■			
23. Provide a discovery learning environment	■	■	■	■			
24. Present problem-solving situations that lead to group discussions	■	■	■	■			
25. Shape personal and social attitudes	■	■	■	■		■	

Adapted from © Claranne K. English, 1995 with permission.

FIGURE 7–9 (Continued)

135

agree? What types of suggestions do you think they would make regarding the use of media? How do you think they could justify their recommendations?

TECHNOLOGY COORDINATOR'S CORNER

At the beginning of this chapter, we introduced you to Joe Salvo, a new teacher at Kirkmont High School, who was very proficient with computers, but not as proficient using "older media." He went to see Brenda Walters, the school's technology coordinator. Brenda pointed out that what Joe called "older media" were just as relevant and important today as always. She said, "Often these other media can complement the computer and other instructional technology. They also provide variety in your teaching and student learning activities." She pulled a book off her shelf that she had used as an undergraduate. It was titled *Instructional Technology and Media for Learning* (Smaldino, Lowther, & Russell, 2008). She loaned it to Joe and suggested that he let her know if he had any questions. Most of the media and technology described in the book were available in Kirkmont's Media Center.

SUMMARY

In this chapter, you learned to complete an instructional plan by selecting instructional media that will match your students, objectives, learning environment, and instructional activities. We looked at the advantages and limitations of various media and introduced the media selection checklist.

PEARSON myeducationkit™ To check your comprehension of the content covered in this chapter, go to the MyEducationKit for this book and complete the Study Plan for Chapter 7. Here you will be able to take a chapter quiz, receive feedback on your answers, and then access resources that will enhance your understanding of chapter content.

SUGGESTED RESOURCES

Print Resources

Alvarado, A. E., & Herr, P. R. (2003). *Inquiry-based learning using everyday objects: Hands-on instructional strategies that promote active learning in grades 3-8.* Thousand Oaks, CA: Sage.

Bell, A. (2005). *Creating digital video in your school: How to shoot, edit, produce, distribute, and incorporate digital media into the curriculum.* Worthington, OH: Linworth.

Bull, G. (2005). *Teaching with digital images: Acquire, analyze, create, communicate.* Washington, DC: International Society for Technology in Education.

Butzin, S. (2005). *Joyful classrooms in an age of accountability: The Project CHILD recipe for success.* Bloomington, IN: Phi Delta Kappa International.

Carlson, G. (2004). *Digital media in the classroom.* San Francisco: CMP Books.

Clark, R. C., & Lyons, C. (2004). *Graphics for Learning.* San Francisco: Pfeiffer.

Dockerman, D. (2003). *Great teaching with video: TSP's guide to using the VCR and videodisc player in the classroom.* Watertown, MA: Tom Snyder Productions.

Farkas, B. GT. (2006). *Secrets of podcasting.* (2nd ed.). Berkeley, CA: Peachpit Press.

Forcier, R. C., & Descy, D. E. (2007). *The computer as an educational tool: Productivity and problem solving* (5th ed.). Upper Saddle River, NJ: Merrill/Prentice Hall.

Holden, J., & Westfall, P. (2005). *An instructional media selection guide for distance learning.* United States Distance Learning Association. Available at www.usdla.org/html/resources/2._USDLA_Instructional_Media_Selection_Guide.pdf

Howell, D. D., Howell, D. K., & Childress, M. (2006). *Using PowerPoint in the classroom.* Thousand Oaks, CA: Corwin Press.

Lever-Duffy, J. and McDonald, J. B. (2008). *Teaching and learning with technology* (3rd ed.). Boston: Allyn & Bacon.

Moreno, R. (2006). Does the modality principle hold for different media? A test of the method-affects-learning hypothesis. *Journal of Computer Assisted Learning,* 22(3), 149-158.

Moreno, R. (2006). Learning with high tech and multimedia environments. *Current Directions,* 15, 63–67.

Muthukumar, S. (2005). Creating interactive multimedia-based educational courseware: Cognition in learning. *Cognition, Technology & Work,* 7(1), 46–50.

Rieber, L. (2005). Multimedia learning in games, simulations, and microworlds. In R. E. Mayer (Ed.), *The Cambridge Handbook of Multimedia Learning* (pp. 549–567). New York: Cambridge University Press.

Roblyer, M. D. (2010). *Integrating educational technology into teaching* (5th ed.). Upper Saddle River, NJ: Pearson Education.

Simkins, M., Cole, K., Tavalin, F., & Means, B. (2002). *Increasing student learning through multimedia projects.* Association for Supervision and Curriculum Development.

Smaldino, S. E., Lowther, D. L., & Russell, J. D. (2008). *Instructional technology and media for learning* (9th ed.). Upper Saddle River, NJ: Pearson.

Electronic Resources

**http://www.adobe.com/support/authorware/
basics/instruct/instruct02.html**

(Macromedia Authorware: Instructional Methods and
Instructional Media)

**http://learningforlife.fsu.edu/ctl/explore/
onlineresources/docs/Chptr9.pdf**

(Florida State University, Office for Distributed and
Distance Learning: Instructional media: Chalkboards
to videos)

http://www.k12imc.org/multimedia/

(K-12 Instructional Media Center: Multimedia)

**http://www.nowhereroad.com/gallery/
mmmodel/index.html**

(MMModel: A Simulation about Multimedia Design and
Dual-Coding Theory by Lloyd Rieber)

ANSWERS TO TOOLBOX EXERCISE:

Media Identification

1. Audio
2. Multimedia
3. Graphics
4. Text
5. Real objects and models
6. Video

Technology and Instructional Material Selection, Adaptation, and Creation

Source: Peter Skinner/Photo Researchers.

KEY WORDS AND CONCEPTS

Instructional materials
Formative evaluation
Copyright

Public domain
Fair use

CHAPTER OBJECTIVES

After reading and studying this chapter, you will be able to:

↗ Distinguish among the concepts of method, medium, and materials.
↗ Select the most appropriate instructional materials for a particular lesson.
↗ Identify sources of existing instructional materials.

↗ Select, modify, or design instructional materials for a particular lesson.
↗ Outline a procedure for acquiring computer software.
↗ Acquire instructional materials in a manner consistent with current copyright law.

INTRODUCTION

Imagine that you are the costume director for a high school's drama department. Each year the school puts on a winter play and a major spring musical. In each case, a unique set of costumes is required for those playing the various roles. Your job is to make sure that all costumes are suitable for the current production, that they fit appropriately, allow for the required movements and costume changes, and that their total cost is within the production's budget.

In order to accomplish your job, you need to ask two sets of key questions.

First set:

a. What types of costumes will match the needs of the production?
b. What special needs/requirements of each actor/actress should be considered (e.g., role of the character, size of each participant)?
c. What will the acts and scenes dictate that will impact the use of the costumes (e.g., movements that will require extra flexibility, rapid costume changes)?

Second set:

a. What costumes do we already have that will work for this production?
b. Do we currently have costumes that might be able to work if we can alter them appropriately?
c. What costumes will definitely need to be created?

The first group of questions focuses on the objectives of the production, as well as considerations for the actors and actresses and the stage/scene environment. The second set of questions focus on practical aspects of finding, adapting, and creating needed costumes given the budget constraints. All experienced costume directors know that answers to both sets of questions are critical for the success of the overall production.

The design and development of instruction requires the teacher to seek answers to similar questions. In order to effectively select and use proper instructional materials, the goal and objectives of the lesson, as well as the needs of the learners and the demands of the learning environment, must be clearly understood. In addition, just as there are practical constraints (e.g., budgets for time and money) placed on the costume director, those same types of constraints are always found within education and the development of the learning experience. As the teacher goes about developing the learning experience, specific instructional materials will be needed to accomplish the desired learning. Those materials may already be available and can be used in their current format. However, in some cases, the available materials may only work by adapting them in some fashion. In still other situations, the materials may not exist in any available form and must then be created. As with the costume director, creating is much more expensive in time and cost than using what is already available.

Within this chapter, we are going to finish the planning and development process. That will require us to look closely at the learning plan that was outlined in Chapter 5 and what was added in terms of methods and media in Chapters 6 and 7, respectively. We again add a piece to the puzzle as shown in Figure 8–1. This puzzle piece represents the need to add "meat" to the plan by identifying and including the proper instructional materials. To do so we

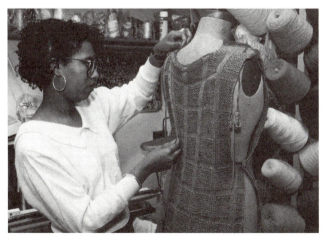

The process of determining whether to select, adapt, or create costumes for a drama production can be compared to the process teachers use to obtain needed instructional materials.
Source: Robert Brenner/PhotoEdit.

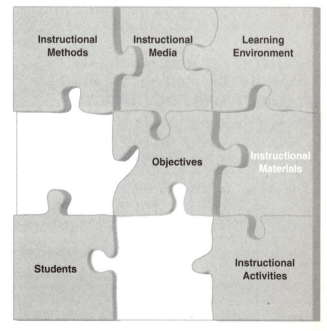

FIGURE 8–1   Instructional materials as another piece of the instructional planning puzzle.

must fully understand the objectives of the learning plan, the characteristics and needs of the learners, and the environment in which the learning will occur. Moreover, we must consider what is already available, how it can be identified and accessed, how it may need to be adapted, and if additional materials will be required. In addition, we also need to evaluate the materials to make sure they accomplish what the plan has envisioned.

 ## INSTRUCTIONAL MATERIALS

Instructional materials are the specific items experienced by students within a lesson that influence their learning. For example, a lesson for lower-elementary students may focus on learning simple addition problems. To accomplish this, a computer software program may be utilized that allows students to repeatedly experience the presentation of practice problems, generate a response to those problems, and receive feedback. The specific math problems and feedback experienced by the students through the use of this software are the instructional materials. Another example would be the chapter that you are currently reading. These instructional materials consist of the written information and exercises found on these pages.

The design and use of instructional materials is critical, because it is the interaction of the student with those materials that generates and reinforces actual learning. If the materials are weak, improperly structured, or sequenced in a poor manner, limited learning will occur. Powerful, well-designed instructional materials are experienced in such a way that they can be readily encoded, retained, recalled, and used in a variety of ways. These materials will be what the learners will remember, and they must be created, integrated, and presented in a manner that allows them to have the needed impact.

INSTRUCTIONAL MATERIALS, METHODS, AND MEDIA: HOW THEY WORK TOGETHER TO ENSURE LEARNING

For an effective learning experience to occur, instructional materials, media, and methods work together in a coordinated manner. For example, instructional materials may be delivered and experienced by the student via a number of different media (see Chapter 7). In one case, part or all of a set of instructional materials may be experienced by viewing a video; whereas, in another case, part of the materials may be experienced by reading a text, viewing a graphic, or even listening to an audio CD. Combining several media formats together is often required in order for a set of instructional materials to be effectively experienced by the learners.

In addition to media, various instructional methods (e.g., cooperative groups, drill and practice, simulations,

discussions; see Chapter 6) are incorporated within a lesson in order to adapt to levels of needed interactivity, size of the target group of learners, the learning environment, and so on. For example, in one instance, instructional materials may be needed as prerequisite information in order for a discussion to be successfully accomplished; whereas, in a different situation, the effectiveness of the instructional materials may be enhanced by providing the materials within a structured tutorial method.

Learners and learning situations can vary quite considerably. Consistent, meaningful learning requires well-designed instructional materials that are presented in a clear, motivating, and understandable manner. Integration and use of correctly selected and coordinated media and methods ensure that the materials impact students in the most effective, efficient, and appealing way.

Review the following classroom learning situation. Note how the methods, media, and materials are integrated to produce the final learning experience.

> Mr. Hughes wants to teach sentence structure to his eighth-grade English class, which meets right before lunch. He decides to use a game to make the topic interesting and to give his students a chance to practice their skills and receive feedback. Not able to find any instructional materials in his school, he decides to design his own board game in which students roll dice, draw a card, and advance if they can correctly identify the part of a sentence highlighted on the card.

Within this situation, the instructional *materials* are the content and exercises found on the individual cards within the game. This is the focus of the overall learning task. In order to deliver this in an interesting and appealing way, a game *method* was employed with rules and directions on how to advance and compete. Real objects in the form of a tangible game board and dice were the *media* used to deliver the instructional experience to the learners.

In order to gain a greater understanding of materials, methods, and media, read the following situation and reflect on the questions that follow:

> Ms. Roth, a fifth-grade teacher in the Midwest, wants to increase her students' awareness of the ways in which living things affect each other. She recently discovered software of a simulation titled *A Field Trip into the Sea* in the school library media center. After previewing it, she decided it matches the characteristics of her students and teaches the desired content. She is sure the software will motivate her students to develop an awareness of living things they have not seen.

- ↗ What constitutes the instructional materials that Ms. Roth's students will experience during this lesson?
- ↗ What principal instructional method is Ms. Roth going to use by implementing *A Field Trip into the Sea* software with her students?
- ↗ What is the primary medium that will deliver the instructional materials to the students?

↗ Could the students in Ms. Roth's class increase their understanding of the instructional materials if other instructional methods (e.g., discussions, cooperative groups, discovery learning) are included as additional parts to the overall lesson?

↗ What is the value of knowing a variety of methods and media and how they can be used with various types of instructional materials?

PEARSON **myeducationkit**™ Go to the Assignments and Activities section of Chapter 8 in MyEducationKit and complete the video activity entitled "Successful Technology Integration." Think about different ways that teachers need to consider the integration of technology as they identify, adapt, and/or create instructional materials. Review what the steps are that are outlined by this administrator and consider why teachers need to learn to integrate technology.

WHEN AND WHERE ARE INSTRUCTIONAL MATERIALS INCLUDED WITHIN THE LEARNING PLAN?

As highlighted in the PIE Checklist (see Appendix C, on page 295) and also illustrated within the example Civil War lesson learning plan in Appendix B, the learning plan consists of a number of key activities—each of which plays a role in what the student experiences and what ultimately the student learns. Although not all lessons have each of these activities, a majority of the elements are found within most effective learning experiences. You can incorporate instructional materials throughout these lesson activities outlined in your plan, from the motivation component through the evaluation activities. For example, if you were designing a physics lesson on the characteristics of light, you may have several components of the lesson that require instructional materials. Note that each set of instructional materials may be presented via a number of different media and integrated within a variety of instructional methods:

↗ *Motivation lesson activity.* Gain attention for the topic with instructional materials that illustrate the behavior of light given different environmental situations, for example by demonstrating the effect of a prism or having students view photographs that illustrate the bending of light caused by water or hot air.

↗ *Orientation lesson activity.* Materials may be incorporated to focus on identifying and explaining the learning goals for the lesson.

↗ *Information lesson activity.* Instructional materials may provide key points on how light can be reflected, or refracted, as well as give students experience in achieving different results working with various types of light sources.

↗ *Application lesson activity.* Materials provide guidance and instruction on how to manipulate and use various forms of lenses, mirrors, prisms, and lasers to solve a variety of problems involving light.

↗ *Evaluation lesson activity.* Materials may help students question their abilities, ask self-reflective questions, and look for ways to improve how they approach problems and attempt solutions.

DETERMINING THE VALUE OF INSTRUCTIONAL MATERIALS

Selecting and/or creating proper instructional materials should be based on several criteria. These criteria allow us to determine if the materials will actually accomplish what they are intended to do, for the right group of students, under the constraints of the given time and cost elements. Figure 8–2 highlights a set of key criteria to use when considering the selection and/or creation of instructional materials.

For an example of using these selection criteria, refer back to the case of Ms. Roth (see page 140) and her instructional materials that involved the use of a software simulation of ocean life. Before she selected that piece of software, she had to determine what she needed and if the selected software would deliver what she desired. To do so, she first needed to examine the overall objectives of the lesson and determine if what was offered by the software would actually help her to accomplish those objectives. If there was little or no match between the software materials and her objectives, she should have dismissed the software outright and continued to search for more relevant materials. Second, once she found some materials that matched her objectives, she needed to make sure that those materials would work well with her particular students. A critical criterion in this case would be if the language level within the instructional materials matched with what her students could understand. Additionally, was the material something that was not a total repetition of something they already knew—but yet was not so far ahead of their level of understanding that they would not be able to grasp what it was explaining? Third, she needed to consider where the selected instructional materials would be used. Would the learning environment be conducive to students learning the material? In her case, if she did not have access to a computer or computer lab, how effective would the software materials actually be? Finally, one should always consider time and cost of the materials. You can have a wonderful set of instructional materials, but if they take too long to use or they cost too much money to obtain, then they cannot be used.

There are three important points you should consider when thinking about such criteria. First, perfect matches between instructional materials and this set of criteria generally will not exist. Some will come closer than others, but there will always be some mismatches. In some cases, the instructional materials may be acceptable with some slight modifications at certain points. Second, there will be times when you find powerful instructional

Criteria	Questions to Consider:
Objectives	↗ What are the learning objectives for this lesson?
	↗ What types of learning are required (e.g., problem solving, concept learning, rote memorization)?
	↗ What level of cognitive demand will be placed on the students?
	↗ In what sequence should the content be presented?
Students	↗ What are their general characteristics (e.g., age, grade level, socioeconomic status, previous experience, special needs)?
	↗ What specific knowledge or skills do they already possess?
	↗ What are their learning styles and preferences?
	↗ How many students will participate in the learning experience?
Learning environment	↗ How large is the space?
	↗ What distractions could there be?
	↗ What types of technology are available/accessible?
Available resources	↗ What resources do you have at your disposal (including materials, equipment, funds)?
	↗ What constraints are there on what you can do?
	↗ How much time is there to produce the materials?
	↗ How much time is there to prepare and utilize the materials?

FIGURE 8–2   Criteria for Selecting and/or Creating Instructional Materials.

materials that you know will positively impact your students; however, they may not match your current learning objectives. In such a case, you may find yourself adapting your objectives in order to effectively incorporate the instructional materials. Finally, watch out for slick packaging of instructional materials. Make sure you look closely at the content and not get lost in the glitz and shine of the color pages, the bells and whistles of the program, and so on. First and foremost, make sure it has sound content.

> **PEARSON myeducationkit**™   Go to the Assignments and Activities section of Chapter 8 in MyEducationKit and complete the web activity entitled "Lesson Planning Ideas." Explore several of the linked lesson plan sites and select one lesson plan that you find interesting. Based on Figure 8-2, consider how your selected plan could be adapted for a specific audience of learners. What questions should you consider and how would you answer those questions given your selected audience and the lesson plan?

WHERE DO WE ACQUIRE INSTRUCTIONAL MATERIALS?

In the opening paragraphs of this chapter, the job of a costume director for a school musical was described. One major role of the costume director is to acquire the proper costumes for the actors and actresses. As explained at that point, the job is relatively easy and the cost is minimal if one can go to the school's storehouse of costumes and select the needed type and size of costume from an already existing inventory. However, for most high schools and local civic playhouses, the wardrobe

inventory is very small. In such a case, the next alternative is either to borrow what is needed or to use what one has access to and adapt it to fit the style and/or needed size. This alternative is more time-consuming and generally more expensive than the first alternative. Finally, if all else fails, the costume director may be left with creating specific costumes. This is, by far, the most expensive in terms of both time and overall monetary cost.

These alternatives are similar to what is faced by individuals seeking proper instructional materials. In some cases, the materials are close at hand and are readily available; in other cases, materials can be used but there is a need to adapt the originals. Finally, there are times when the only thing that works is to actually create the materials. Although each alternative has its drawbacks, each also offers some interesting learning possibilities.

SELECTING EXISTING INSTRUCTIONAL MATERIALS

As we noted at the beginning of the chapter, the simplest, most cost-effective way to incorporate instructional materials into a lesson is to use existing materials. Locating and selecting instructional materials involve the following steps:

1. *Determine needs.* What are you trying to accomplish? What needs might specific instructional materials address?
2. *Check a variety of sources.* There are a number of sources for instructional materials. Refer to the "Toolbox: Locating Relevant Instructional Materials" found in this chapter for several important ways to access relevant materials.

3. *Obtain and preview the materials.* Always preview all materials before using them to be certain they meet your needs and your students' needs. Go to Appendix D of this text to access the preview forms with which you can evaluate a single set of materials or compare two sets of materials.

4. *Try out the materials with students.* How well do they like the materials? How effectively do the materials help them learn?

5. *Compare any competing materials.* If you have located more than one set of applicable materials, repeat the preview and tryout process to compare their effectiveness and appeal to students.

6. *Make your selection.* Use the information you have gathered to select the instructional materials that you think will work best in your situation.

7. *Keep accurate records.* After you have chosen materials, make sure you follow up on their effectiveness. By keeping records you also can determine how effective the materials could be in other lessons.

If the content of the instructional materials you find does not match the objectives of your instructional plan, you have two alternatives: (1) modify the materials so they do meet your objectives, or (2) create new

Toolbox: Locating Relevant Instructional Materials

Literally thousands of instructional materials are available to use in various learning situations—if one can locate them. In some cases, gaining ready access to these materials is not difficult if you actually have an idea of where they can be found. Some suggestions to help in your search are:

At school: Most schools maintain a computer database in the school library or media center. Some school districts also maintain a central collection of instructional materials. In addition, districts sometimes combine their resources to form a regional media center or service center housing a collection of instructional materials.

In the neighborhood: Many local libraries (including school libraries) supply not only books but other forms of instructional materials to those who visit. In many cases, those materials are accessible online.

On the Internet:

a. The Web can be a valuable source of instructional materials. In addition, Figure 8–3 provides a number of popular teacher websites that contain downloadable instructional materials for various activities. Use of a general search engine should generate results when using the search terms "instructional materials" and your area of interest (e.g., "science").

b. Many museums and libraries have large collections of instructional materials. Searches of the websites for the Smithsonian museum, the Museum of Science and Industry, the Library of Congress, and so on will find significant portions of the sites devoted to education and provide ways for teachers to access and use their instructional materials when teaching a variety of different subject content and activities. For example, visiting the Smithsonian site (http://www.si.edu/) you will find a link to their teacher's site. In this location, you can find all types of lesson plans linked to materials and activities associated with items within their museum.

c. Several comprehensive databases are available through which you can locate instructional materials. The National Information Center for Educational Media

(NICEM), for example, provides an automated index of commercially available materials. With it, you can locate the distribution sources for thousands of educational, informational, and documentary materials recorded in a variety of media formats. The database covers a range of subject areas at grade levels from preschool to graduate and professional school. NICEM (www.nicem .com) is continually being updated based on information from producer and distributor catalogs, the Library of Congress, media centers, and many other sources. In addition, The Education Software Selector (TESS) is a comprehensive database that includes information about educational software at every level, from preschool to college, in a variety of content areas (www.epie.org/epie_tess.htm). Each piece of software is described in terms of subject, learning approach, grade level, computer platform, pricing, and publisher contact. Entries include evaluation citations from educational journals, state evaluation agencies, and technology journals.

Through professional organizations: Professional meetings and trade shows held at local, state, and national levels provide opportunities to talk with vendors and other teachers to find out what is available.

Commercial vendors:

a. Most school textbook companies now include ancillary materials with their textbooks including software, websites, workbooks, charts, lab manuals, and so forth, which can provide a wealth of additional materials to use within the classroom setting.

b. Commercial producers and distributors of instructional materials publish catalogs listing materials you can buy and, in some cases, rent. To obtain educational software, for example, use a search engine (e.g., Google) and search terms such as "Educational Software catalogs" to locate a number of websites that will list where and how to find commercial producers and distributors of materials. One such site, www. buyersindex.com, lists a huge number of commercial sites and catalogs—all online.

Site Name	Web Address	Printable	Lesson Plan	Online Activities	Professional Development	Tools
Scholastic Teacher	http://teacher .scholastic.com/	Graphic organizers, mini-books, worksheets, independent reading contracts, and many more printables to produce more effective and efficient learning.	Browse or search by subject, topic, and grade.	Interactive timelines, scholastic news, radio, and other resources for students to participate.	Teaching strategies, free programs and giveaways, newsletters and theories; this site has numerous links and information to assist in teacher development.	Lesson plan maker, planning calendar, test and quiz maker, presentation maker, website maker, and many more tools.
Teachers. Net	http:// teachers.net/	Tons of printables ranging from calendars to checklists, but no search function. (use CTRL-F to search for specific word)	Browse or search by subject, topic, and grade.	Discussion board and chat functions for teachers.	Monthly newsletters concerning educational practices. Searchable or subscribe to receive via e-mail.	No tools.
Education World	http://www .education-world.com	Many printables, but only available through specific lesson plans.	Browse lesson plans by subject area. There are excellent monthly aligned units. Lesson plans typically include national standards.	Message boards and bullet in boards available for teachers.	Lots of articles in a variety of subjects and topic areas. Reading rooms and virtual workshops target timely issues. This is a highlight for this site.	No tools to use.
Web for Teachers	http://www .4teachers.org/	There are no ready-made printables for teachers to use, but the tools provide teachers with their own customized printables.	Excellent lesson plans searchable by topic. They provide loads of good links to content information and innovative ideas.	Interactive educational games available through Academic Skill Builders. For teachers, the site has an online professional learning community (TeachStrong).	There are numerous links to websites and articles that will aid in professional development questions in specific timely areas.	Amazing tools ranging from RubiStar, PBL Checklists, Quiz Star, Web Poster Wizard, and many more!
Discovery Learning	http://school .discovery.com/	The tools allow you to create some custom printables; some downloadable worksheets are also available on specific topics. Clip art is also available for educational use.	Some lesson plans are linked to Discovery videos (available for purchase). Browse by grade level and subject topics.	Short educational videos for home use, WebMath scaffold to help with student homework, and interactive learning environments on specific content are provided.	There is more information on the Kathy Schrock section of this website. However, this is difficult to find and unless you know the link, there is no link from the home page.	A puzzle maker for students or teachers.
PBS	http://www.pbs .org/teachers/	No printables available.	Browse lesson plans and resources by grade level and subject areas.	Teacher discussion boards available to discuss each lesson plan.	There is a link to PBS TeacherLine online professional development, but a fee is required.	No tools available.

FIGURE 8–3 Education Websites with Instructional Materials.

ABC Teach	http://abcteach.com/	Many printables are organized by themes, although limited in scope for elementary.				
Teachnology	http://www.teachnology.com/	Many printables for teachers available.	Browse lesson plans by topic area, although most lesson plans are links to outside websites.	There are some games for students, but not all educational.	Tutorials, message boards, and different teaching ideas are provided by this website.	Tools available include work sheets, rubrics, venn diagrams, graphic organizers and more! Although not sophisticated, a wide variety.
A to Z Teacher Stuff	http://atozteacherstuff.com/	Printables are organized by themes, although limited in scope for elementary.	Lesson plans can be searched. They can also be sorted by grade level or subject area.	Different discussion forums are the only source of interaction.	Tips, articles, and discussion boards provide topics and ideas for teachers to develop within the profession.	Tools include: word shapes worksheet generator, word search maker, and hand writing worksheet generator.

FIGURE 8–3 Education Websites with Instructional Materials. (Continued)

Toolbox: Software Evaluation and Acquisition

We have examined issues related to selecting instructional materials in general and different media in particular. Here we discuss evaluating and selecting computer software.

In most school districts today, hardware decisions are centralized. An individual teacher cannot go out and select just any computer for his or her classroom. However, individual teachers often make software decisions. There is commonly an approval process that involves the technology coordinator, a technology committee, or an administrator, but software purchasing usually begins with the individual teacher. It is thus important for teachers to know how to evaluate and select software. Following are the steps involved:

1. *Determine needs.* As in any instructional activity, begin by assessing what you need. What needs might you address through the use of computer software?
2. *Specify desired software characteristics.* Your needs assessment should give you a general idea of the type of software you want. For example, if your students are having trouble adding mixed fractions, you may decide that you want a drill and practice program on this topic.
3. *Obtain or construct an evaluation form.* Many useful software evaluation forms are available from a variety of sources. We provide one for software evaluation within Appendix D of this text. Your school may have its own

evaluation form. Alternatively, you could design one geared to your specific needs.

4. *Survey available sources of software.* Software is available from a variety of sources. Look through publishers' catalogs. Read software evaluations published in journals and magazines. Talk to your colleagues. Visit vendors' booths at professional meetings. Check collections of shareware. It is relatively easy to contact, via the Web, individuals who have developed and/or used the software with their students. Getting insights from the developers and finding out how it has worked for students in other classrooms should provide needed insights into the value of the software for your classroom use.
5. *Obtain software for preview.* Many software companies provide special demonstration versions for preview. With these, if you like the software and buy it, the company provides you with a password that unlocks full access. Alternatively, you can often preview software via delayed-purchase-order billing. In that case, a purchase order for the product is submitted with the specification that it is for preview purposes. The vendor delays billing for a set period, usually 30 days. If you decide against purchase, simply return the software within the grace period, and the purchase order is canceled. Otherwise, keep the software,

(continued)

Toolbox: Software Evaluation and Acquisition (*continued*)

and the vendor processes the purchase order at the end of the grace period.

6. *Read the documentation.* Although there is a temptation to simply jump into a software program, you should always read the documentation first. It should indicate the recommended audience for the program, and it will provide directions for how to properly use the software.

7. *Run through the software several times.* The first time you go through the software, simply concentrate on using the program correctly. How does it work? For a second pass, make certain that the software is "bombproof"; that is, make certain it does not fail when something unexpected happens. Purposely test for problems; if the program indicates, "Enter a number between 1 and 4," see what happens if you enter 5.

Finally, run through the program with a pedagogical eye. Is the educational approach sound? Is it appealing? How does the software rate on the criteria given on the evaluation form you are using?

8. *Have students try out the program.* How do they like it? Do they learn from it?

9. *Complete the evaluation form.* Using the information gained from your review of the software, complete the evaluation form.

10. *Repeat the process for any competing products.* If you have more than one possible purchase, look at each competing product in the same way.

11. *Make your selection.* Select the desired software package. File your evaluation with the school, and be sure to enclose a copy of your evaluation with any product that is returned to the publisher.

---

instructional materials. We discuss these options in the next two sections.

Modifying Available Instructional Materials

If you cannot locate suitable materials, you may be able to modify what is available. In terms of time and cost, it is more efficient to modify available materials than to create new materials. It is also an opportunity for you to be creative. You can modify almost any type of instructional materials. For example, imagine that, for a piece of equipment being used in a middle school woodworking class, the only available visual is from a repair manual. The picture could be useful, but it contains too much detail and complex terminology for students. One possible solution would be to use the visual but modify the caption and simplify or omit some of the labels.

In another situation, the only video available for a specific needed concept shows a needed video sequence, however the audio is inappropriate because the vocabulary level is either too high or too low for your students. In such a case, you could show the video with the sound turned off and narrate it yourself. Videos can also be shown in segments. You can show a portion of a video, stop the DVD or VCR, discuss what has been presented, then continue with another short segment, followed by additional discussion.

Often, you can modify the audio portion of foreign-language materials (or English-language materials for a bilingual class). Narration can be changed from one language to another or from a more advanced rendition to a simpler one.

If you try out modified materials while they are still in more or less rough form, you can then make further modifications in response to student reactions until your materials meet their exact needs. A word of caution about modifying commercially produced materials: Be sure your handling and use of such materials does not violate copyright laws and restrictions. If you are in doubt, check with your school media specialist.

PEARSON **myeducationkit** Go to the Assignments and Activities section of Chapter 8 in MyEducationKit and complete the video activity entitled "Online Reading Supplement Textbooks." Review the video and note what the teacher has done to set up and support student learning during the activity. How have the materials been adapted to be successfully included and used?

Creating New Instructional Materials

Teachers have long been known for their creative use of available tools and resources to produce instructional materials. Classrooms are usually filled with a variety of teaching materials, from concrete objects to posters, bulletin boards, and printed material of every kind. For several decades the tools for producing instructional materials changed relatively little, with typewriters and ditto machines doing the bulk of the work. But times have changed.

Photocopying machines, long commonplace in society at large, are now standard equipment in schools. Compared to a mimeograph or ditto machine, preparing copies with a photocopier is much simpler. In addition, the tools for creating the master copies of instructional materials have improved by leaps and bounds. The reason, of course, is the computer. Computer-based tools make it much easier to produce high-quality, professional-looking materials.

How Are Effective Materials Created? For many teachers, creating ways to impact student learning is a key reason why they chose their profession. Creating materials allows you an opportunity to reflect on what is needed, use experiences from the past, synthesize new materials, and creatively bring together an effective learning experience. Is there a single recipe to creating effective instruction? Of course not. Just as there are different styles of learning, there are different ways to create learning experiences. Here is a general procedure that may help you in this process. It is a guideline only, and certainly not the *only* way to successfully construct instructional materials.

- Refer repeatedly to your instructional plan. The plan contains the direction and activities that you have determined your students need. Just as the general contractor of a large office building would not dream of beginning construction without the blueprints of the building, you should closely review your instructional plans.
- Within the plan, look closely at the overall learning objectives and the key activities that need to occur so that students meet them. Ask yourself, "What needs to be constructed so that the activities are successful?" For example, will the students need explanations, directions, examples, non-examples, or guided practice? Will feedback be needed, and if so, how quickly should you deliver it? (See "Toolbox Techniques: Using Questioning, Examples, and Feedback Effectively" on page 90 in Chapter 5.)
- Reflect on what you already know or have seen. If you determined that materials did not already exist, did you see pieces of different sets of materials that might give you insight into how to construct what you need? Can you talk with anyone who has taught these or similar concepts before?
- Put yourself in the "learner's shoes." What would you want to experience in order to effectively learn this material? Look for means to make materials relevant to students.
- Outline your materials. Have students review what you have thought through and determine what major changes need to occur.
- Construct a draft set of the materials. Incorporate the use of tools (e.g., copy machines, computers, clip art) to extend your creative development abilities.
- Review the materials to ensure that you make all needed changes. In most cases, you will not create perfect materials on the first attempt.

To practice creating new instructional materials, review the following section, visit the given website, and ponder answers to the reflective questions. *Integrating*

New Technologies Into the Methods of Education (In-Time) is a website that provides all kinds of online videos of teachers using technology within the classroom setting. An interesting part of the website is a tool that they have included that allows you to access and review the videos but more importantly to also create instructional materials/case studies that integrate the selected videos within your materials. For example, if you are creating some materials for a unit on brainstorming and problem solving, you could access via InTime relevant videos of teachers using brainstorming software within a classroom setting. With the use of their technology, clips of such relevant videos can be downloaded and adapted to be used within your lessons.

Go to the InTime website (http://www.intime.uni.edu/) and review the categories of the available videos. Access the section "Build Your Own Case Study" and walk through the process of selecting and identifying relevant information for a topic of your interest and how the materials can be selected and adapted for your use. Practice adapting one or more of your lesson plans with a video section provided by the website.

Think about the following questions:

- What additional materials will be needed to support the video in order to make it optimally effective?
- Within what types of instructional activities would the video be most effective?
- What issues of copyright will need to be resolved before such videos can be legally used within a classroom presentation?
- Are there other websites that may provide additional videos or additional materials from different content areas? How does one go about locating such sites?

How One Teacher Created Instructional Materials
Nancy Piggot has taught fifth grade at Glen Acres Elementary School for a number of years. Increasingly, Nancy has felt the need to enhance her students' learning experiences as they study their science unit "Insects." She has located a number of great sources of visuals and textual materials, but in most cases, they are above her students' level of understanding.

In reviewing and reflecting on her past "Insect" lesson plans, she noted that the different parts of the insect body consistently created problems for her students when it came to identification and descriptions. She determined that to facilitate learning she would assign her students live insects (large cockroaches from the local pet store) to care for. Students would observe their "pets" for a short time each day during the remainder of the insect unit. Students could name their pets and draw various pictures of them during the observation periods. In addition, her plan was to design and create a short multimedia program that would introduce students to their "pets" and show them things that they should observe. In particular, she planned for various pictures and drawings to explain how to identify the specific parts of the insect, highlight the body parts, and describe their functions.

During the development phase of the program, Nancy completed a number of interesting steps. First, she reviewed closely her overall lesson plan for the unit. She noted the weaknesses and the areas that she felt she could add to the instructional effectiveness. Through past experience, she knew that she would need to focus student attention via questioning, examples, practice, and feedback. Likewise, she knew it would be critical to use audio and visual stimulation techniques to effectively highlight key features. The multimedia software allowed her to include such features within a tutorial that students could review on their own. Nancy took one additional step to ensure the success of the program: She began by drawing out all of the key concepts on 3 by 5 inch cards (see Toolbox: Using Planning Cards, Chapter 4, p. 83). She used rough sketches to show how the actual program would look. After developing several of these cards, she asked a few of her students to tell her what they liked and did not like about them. Her students actually helped her determine when more explanation was needed and when she was giving too much. By the time she actually sat at the computer, she had a good idea of the length of the program and that it would be effective. Figure 8–4 contains examples of some of the screens that students viewed as they worked through this program.

From start to finish, this project took Nancy a number of hours to complete. In fact, every year when she gets to the "Insect" unit she finds herself adding new things based on her students' suggestions and new in-

formation she uncovers. She has found that this unit has really helped to increase her students' knowledge of insects and also has piqued their interest and motivation.

As illustrated by this story, one of the most creative, exciting, and rewarding activities for teachers and students is the development of effective instructional materials. It can be very satisfying to identify a specific learning need and then create some intervention that actually addresses that need and helps individuals to learn. That said, the development of instructional activities can also be time consuming, expensive, and totally frustrating. In order to ensure that success is achieved, it is important that key steps are taken (see the PIE Checklist in Appendix C on page 295). In the next section, evaluation will be introduced. Formative evaluation will help to make sure that the materials do what they are supposed to do and individuals learn the maximum amount from the experience.

FORMATIVE EVALUATION OF INSTRUCTIONAL MATERIALS

Any time you modify or create instructional materials, you should assess how effective they are in helping students learn *before* you put the materials to use. This is done via the process of formative evaluation. **Formative evaluation** is evaluation done during the planning or production of instructional materials to determine what, if any, revisions should be made to make them more useful. Formative evaluation can help identify aspects of the materials that are unclear, confusing, inconsistent, obsolete, or otherwise not helpful to students. Chapter 12 provides guidelines for a number of techniques that you

FIGURE 8–4 Instructional screens from a teacher-created "Insect" multimedia program.

Source: Contributed by Nancy Piggott, Glen Acres Elementary, Lafayette, Indiana.

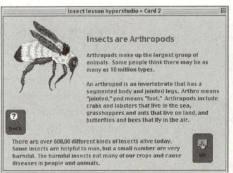
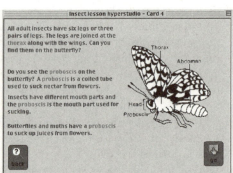
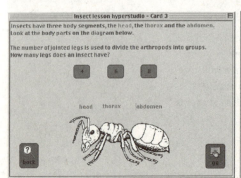
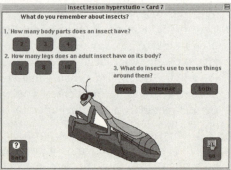

can use to carry out formative evaluation of instructional materials. The point we make here is that formative evaluation is a critical step in either modifying existing materials or creating new materials.

As an example, we noted earlier that one common way to modify existing materials is to show a video with the sound muted, providing separate narration that better matches your students' vocabulary level. In this situation, formative evaluation would involve checking the narration to make sure it is, in fact, consistent with students' vocabularies and to identify any further revisions you might make to make it more useful.

We also noted earlier that teachers commonly produce their own instructional materials. They may, for example, produce their own instructional game for a particular lesson. In this situation, formative evaluation would involve checking the game against students' needs and interests and against the lesson objectives. If the game matches both students and objectives, then it is ready for use. If, on the other hand, it does not match the students or objectives in some way, then it will be important to revise the game before using it.

LOCATING, ADAPTING, CREATING, AND EVALUATING INSTRUCTIONAL MATERIALS: HOW CAN TECHNOLOGY HELP?

Finding, selecting, adapting, and creating instructional materials all require time and effort. Can technology be used to help these processes in some way? Of course, there are a number of ways that technology can be used. First, think of the ways in which technology can **access needed materials.** With the use of Internet search engines, for example, huge amounts of already prepared materials can be located and reviewed (see Chapter 10 for more information on the Internet). Teachers are now able to use the Web to post materials they have found effective and others can then access, use, and adapt these materials for their own classroom situations. Moreover, once both websites and useable materials have been accessed, relevant information can be stored electronically in a way that can ensure rapid access in the future. Combining the use of large electronic storage devices (e.g., hard drives, CDs, and DVDs) with databases allows for the **storage of huge amounts of learning materials** and ways to immediately access them via keyword, subject, and grade level searches.

Second, think of how technology can be used to **create and/or adapt materials.** With the ability to electronically cut and paste within word processing and desktop publishing programs, you can quickly add visuals, change text, and alter needed sequences. Even the creation and editing of video and audio instructional materials have become relatively easy. Along with the

ease of using technology to create materials, the **publication of the materials** has also been simplified. Use of printers, copy machines, LCD projectors, and posting to the Web have all increased our ability to produce the materials and reach the students in a quicker, easier, and more cost-effective fashion.

Third, improvement of the learning experience should continually be sought through the **evaluation of materials.** Technology can be used to transfer information between users of materials to gain insights into when, why, and how the materials are best implemented. Additionally, simple stored comments, ratings, and rankings on the effectiveness, efficiency, and appeal of the materials can be quickly completed and stored for quick review before the next use of the materials.

PEARSON **myeducationkit**™ Go to the Assignments and Activities section of Chapter 8 in MyEducationKit and complete the video activity entitled "Assessing Technology-based Learning." Review the video and note the various strategies that this teacher uses to assess her instructional materials. Ask yourself, "In what ways could technologies be used to facilitate the assessment?" and "In what ways are the effectiveness of the technologies used within the instructional materials assessed?"

Figure 8-5 highlights a number of areas where the use of specific software may facilitate various steps in the process of finding and using instructional materials. After reviewing the ideas presented in Figure 8-5, read the following three different scenarios. Based on the materials within this chapter, determine which ways technology may be used to facilitate the access, storage, creation, publication, and evaluation of the needed instructional materials.

For each of the following situations, consider these questions:

↗ What should be your first considerations when determining how to obtain the proper instructional materials?
↗ In what ways could relevant materials be accessed, previewed, adapted, created, delivered, and evaluated?
↗ How could technology assist in the process of planning, adapting, producing, and delivering the instructional materials?

Situation A: A high school science teacher has the goal of having his students learn that common recycled materials (paper, plastic, glass) could be used in a number of different, productive ways. Currently, the students have a chapter in their science text that explains the need to recycle, but little is stated about adapting and using recycled materials. Could additional instructional materials be included into his lesson that would help his students attain the desired goal?

Planning for the Instructional Materials

What Is Needed	Potential Useful Software
Questionnaire development to get information from students	Word processing (e.g., MS *Word*), survey software (www.surveymonkey.com; www.zoomerang.com)
Means to assemble, sort, store, and analyze the collected information	Database (e.g., MS *Access*), spreadsheet (e.g., MS *Excel*), word processing
Determine potential types of materials needed by the students for the lesson	Brainstorming software (e.g., *Inspiration*)
Development of preliminary outlines, flowcharts, and/or planning cards of the needed materials	Flowcharting software (e.g., *Inspiration*, MS *PowerPoint*, MS *Word*)

Identifying and Accessing Potential Instructional Materials

What Is Needed	Potential Useful Software
Finding and reviewing potential materials	Internet browsers (e.g., MS *Internet Explorer*, Mozilla *Firefox*) Website search engines (e.g., *Google, Yahoo!*) Library search software
Reviewing critiques provided by others who have used the materials in the past	Internet browsers and search engines

Creating and Adapting Potential Instructional Materials

What Is Needed	Potential Useful Software
Adding text, questions, written examples, exercises, and directions for use	Word processing
Creating and integrating needed audio, visuals, graphics, and video	Word processing, graphics, video and audio editing software, scanning software, clip art software
Adding graphs	Spreadsheet
Creating actual presentations and/or publications	Presentation software (e.g., MS *PowerPoint*); desktop publishing (e.g., MS *Publisher*, Adobe *PageMaker*)

Delivering the Instructional Materials

What Is Needed	Potential Useful Software
Delivery of written materials	Word processing, desktop publishing
Delivery of Web-based materials	Web editing software (e.g., Adobe *Dreamweaver* and *Flash*)
Delivery of presentations	Presentation software

Evaluating the Instructional Materials

What Is Needed	Potential Useful Software
Complete reviews of the materials	Word processing
Comparison with results from other similar materials	Web search software
Storage of results for future access and use on revisions	Word processing, database

FIGURE 8–5 Instructional Materials and the Use of Technology.

Situation B: A teacher in the local middle school has a nice *PowerPoint* presentation that she gives to her science students that deals with the tides and phases of the moon. However, feedback from its previous use in other semesters indicates that some students are not able to fully grasp all of the concepts based on the presentation alone. The students seem to need more practice with the key concepts and they seem to falter when asked to explain how tides can be reliably predicted. In what way could additional instructional materials be included into this lesson?

Situation C: For an upper-elementary teacher, there was need for her health class students to develop ways to properly interact within small groups and also to help them learn about various forms of communicable diseases. By working together in small groups on a project about a specific type of disease, the students may be able to gain insights into their content, develop their research skills, learn to work cooperatively, and also develop skills for writing, producing, and presenting an effective learning experience for others. What are some basic instructional materials that would help the learning within these small groups to occur?

Developing Instructional Materials: Use of the PIE Checklist

As in the previous chapters dealing with planning the instructional materials, the PIE Checklist (see Appendix C on page 295, for the full checklist) helps to identify the steps that need to occur during the production process. In particular, it reminds you to use your planning cards and initial outlines and flowcharts to develop the full draft of the materials, incorporate technology effectively, and review the materials with students and other stakeholders (see Figure 8-6). One final checklist item deals with reviewing your materials for potential copyright infringements. This is critical for the success of your materials–and something that is often overlooked by classroom teachers. The next section of this text will explain the issues of copyright and fair use and why these are relevant to all classroom teachers and their students.

 ## COPYRIGHT ISSUES

One of the most important issues related to the acquisition or creation of instructional materials, especially in this age of computers and digital reproduction, is copyright.

8. Instructional Materials

☐ Identify ways in which technology could be integrated to facilitate the development of the instructional materials.

☐ Outline the steps involved to develop the draft instruction.

☐ Based on your planning cards, outline, and flowchart develop the initial draft of your materials.

☐ Review your draft materials for any possible copyright infringement.

☐ Have members of the target audience and other stakeholders (e.g., teachers, content experts) review and evaluate the draft materials.

FIGURE 8–6 PIE Checklist portion highlighting the instructional materials.

Copyright refers to the legal rights to an original work. Schools have an obligation, both under the law and from an ethical standpoint, to adhere to the law and to instruct students in proper behavior. The penalties for violation of copyright law can be severe, and, as a number of schools and businesses have found, publishers' groups are willing to take action against organizations that are in violation. To avoid problems, schools should establish clear copyright policies and make those policies known to both teachers and students.

The origin of copyright can be found in the U.S. Constitution. Article I, section 8 specifies: "[Congress shall have power] to promote the progress of science and useful arts, by securing for limited times to authors and inventors the exclusive right to their respective writings and discoveries." Current law governing copyright can be found in Title 17 of the U.S. Code (available online at: http://www.law.cornell.edu/uscode/17/). Although a complete discussion of copyright law is beyond the scope of this book, in this section we provide some basic guidelines. For more information, contact your school's library or media specialist or consult references on the subject.

In the following questions and answers, we cover some of the most important points of copyright law.

↗ What are copyrighted materials?

Copyrighted materials are original works of authorship that are fixed in any tangible medium of expression. This includes such things as written works, works of art and music, photographs, and computer software. Basically, any tangible authored work qualifies. Ideas, concepts, and procedures cannot be copyrighted. A work does not have to be registered to be protected under copyright law; such protection is automatically granted to the creator of the work when it is produced. This means the little copyright symbol © is a symbol of convenience, and it is not required to signify copyrighted materials.

↗ How long does copyright last?

Under current law, copyrighted works are protected for the life of the author plus 70 years. Works for hire are protected for 95 years from the date of publication or 120 years from the date of creation, whichever comes first. Similar rules apply to works created before 1978.

↗ What rights does the law give copyright owners?

The copyright owner is the person or entity that holds the copyright to a work. Usually, this is the creator of the work, except in the case of work for hire or when copyright is transferred (e.g., to a publisher). The owner of the copyright to a work has *exclusive* rights to:

↗ reproduce (copy) the work,
↗ create derivative works,
↗ sell or distribute the work, and
↗ perform or display the work in public.

↗ Are there any limitations or exceptions to copyright owners' rights?

The law spells out several specific exceptions to the exclusive rights of copyright owners. For example, libraries are allowed to make copies under certain circumstances, which allow us to enjoy things like interlibrary loans of materials. Also, works produced by the U.S. government cannot be copyrighted; they are in the **public domain**. This means that students or teachers can use things like NASA photographs (those deemed public domain) in their multimedia projects without special permission. There are also important exceptions related to software backup, teaching, and fair use of materials. Because these are so relevant to teachers and schools, we discuss them here in more depth.

Software Backup   Under copyright law, computer software may be duplicated when such duplication is essential to the use of the software on a particular computer or to create an archival backup copy of the software to be used if the original fails. Other copying of computer software, except as may be allowed by the license for a particular software product, is illegal. This applies to networks as well as to stand-alone computers. While a network file server actually holds only one copy of a particular program, multiple copies can be operated on the network. This is illegal if only a single copy of that software was purchased. Schools must purchase network licenses or multiple copies of the software to run multiple copies on a network, and the network must monitor use to prevent violations if the license is restricted to a specific number of copies.

Teaching   For some time, educators have been given some latitude under copyright law to publicly display copyrighted works for the purpose of face-to-face teaching. For example, a teacher may show a video in the classroom, even one labeled FOR HOME USE ONLY, as long as the video was legally purchased, is materially relevant to the subject being taught, and is used in face-to-face teaching at a nonprofit educational institution.

This particular exception in copyright law was, to some degree, recently extended to distance education through the Technology, Education and Copyright Harmonization Act (TEACH Act) of 2001. This means that an instructor within a distance education course now is allowed to transmit materials to students within the distance course. There are limitations; for example, "the TEACH Act covers works an instructor would show or play during class such as movie or music clips, images of artworks in an art history class, or a poetry reading. It does **not** cover materials an instructor may want students to study, read, listen to or watch on their own time outside of class" (Harper, 2001). These excluded works include items typically purchased by students (such as textbooks and course packs) for a

normal class. Additional restrictions on how the works are transmitted, which types of institutions and courses are eligible, and the length of retention for the materials are also specified within the Act. Crews (2003) offers a full discussion about the meaning and importance of the TEACH Act and its implications for teachers.

Fair Use   **Fair use** applies to situations involving criticism, comment, news reporting, educational use, and research associated with copyrighted material. Researchers, for example, can make single copies of articles from library journals as part of their research. A critic can excerpt dialogue from a book as part of a published review of the work. Fair use can also apply to education, and it is one of the most important exceptions for teachers and students. There are no absolute guidelines for determining what constitutes fair use in an education setting. Instead, four factors must be weighed:

↗ The purpose and character of the use (e.g., using a copyrighted work for an educational objective is more likely to be considered fair use than using it for commercial gain).

↗ The nature of the copyrighted work (e.g., if the work itself is educational in character, this would tend to support a judgment of fair use).

↗ The amount of the work used in relation to the whole (e.g., using a smaller amount of a total work is more likely to be fair use than using a larger amount).

↗ The effect of the use on the potential market for the work (e.g., if the use negatively impacts potential sales of the original work, this weighs against fair use).

Fair use guidelines must be applied case by case. However, guidelines on the subject suggest that educational use of a copyrighted work can meet fair use guidelines if (1) only a brief excerpt is used (e.g., an excerpt of less than 1,000 words or less than 10 percent of the whole written work), (2) it is a spontaneous use (e.g., a teacher

A teacher contemplates making copies of a textbook illustration for her students.
Source: Anthony Magnacca/Merrill Education.

could copy an article for a class if the decision to use it was on the spur of the moment, occurring too late to reasonably seek permission), and (3) there is no cumulative effect (e.g., the use does not occur in more than one course, it is not repeated, and it does not serve as a substitute for purchase). Other rules govern the use of specific media, such as taped television broadcasts. Consult with your media specialist for specific guidelines.

Digital Media. With the advent of digital media and the Internet, copyright issues have become even more important and more difficult to sort out. While it is possible to scan images or digitize audio and video and incorporate the digital representations into multimedia presentations or Web pages, is it legal? In most cases, the answer to that question is "Probably not," although matters are not altogether clear today. A number of groups around the country are working on revisions to copyright law, or interpretation guidelines for specific situations, that would clarify issues related to digital media and other new technologies. But, as of this writing, nothing has been settled.

The best advice is for teachers and students to treat digital media according to established fair use guidelines. That is, use of copyrighted material in digital format (text, graphics, audio, or video) is likely to be considered fair use when (1) the use is of an educational nature (e.g., part of classroom instruction, including student-created projects), (2) the material itself is educational in nature, (3) relatively little of the original material is used (and credit is given to the source of the materials), and (4) it is unlikely to detrimentally affect the market for the original materials. However, use or distribution beyond the classroom is a problem. So, for example, putting copyrighted materials on the Web without permission is almost certainly contrary to copyright law.

Avoiding Problems. There are several ways teachers and students can avoid problems with copyrighted material. One solution is to request permission to use the material. Publishers are often willing to permit copyrighted material to be used free of charge for nonprofit educational purposes in the classroom. Another solution is to obtain "royalty-free" collections of media. Many vendors now sell CD-ROMs that contain collections of images and sounds that can be used in presentations or other products without payment of royalties. Be sure to read the fine print, however. What is meant by "royalty-free" varies from one collection to the next. In some cases, there are almost no restrictions on the use of materials; in others, you may not be allowed to use the materials in any kind of electronic product.

Many collections of images and other materials are on the Web. While images available on the Web are often described as "public domain," they may not be. Use caution when acquiring materials this way. Some websites permit you to use materials from the site as long as you give proper attribution and create a link to the site on your web page. This can be a small price to pay for good material. Another way to "get" images or other materials on the Web is to create a link on your site to the original source. In this way your site provides access to the information without actually copying it. If you adopt this approach, it is considered polite to request permission from the source site to create a link, and you need to be alert to the possibility that your link may be broken if something changes on the source site.

For more information about copyright, or to track the latest developments in the debate about copyright law and new technologies, visit the websites shown in Figure 8–7.

Website	URL
Title 17 of the U.S. Code—copyright law. This is the law and how it is stated.	http://www.law.cornell.edu/uscode/17/
U.S. Copyright Office. U.S. government's official website dealing with copyright.	http://www.copyright.gov/
Stanford University Copyright and Fair Use site. One of the most comprehensive sites on copyright and education. Highly recommended.	http://fairuse.stanford.edu/
Copyright Quick Guide. Quick reference to the key questions about copyright and the issues involved with it. This is part of the Copyright Management Center.	http://copyright.columbia.edu/copyright-quick-guide
Copyright Crash Course. University of Texas tutorial and quizzes dealing with all aspects of copyright and fair use.	http://www.utsystem.edu/OGC/IntellectualProperty/cprtindx.htm

FIGURE 8–7   Websites related to Copyright and Fair Use.

FIGURE 8–8 Portion of Mr. Spencer's Civil War lesson plan highlighting the use of a WebQuest.

Introduction to WebQuest search (orientation activity)

Allotted time—20 minutes

Method—presentation

Media—Internet

Equipment and materials required—computer with Internet access and a data projector; scoring rubric on handouts (attached)

1. Use the following list and ask the student to pick the character they would most like to learn about. Students may choose a character that is not on the list, with teacher approval.

Southern farmer	Northern farmer
Southern plantation owner	Northern storekeeper
Southern belle	Northern woman
Southern newspaper reporter	Northern newspaper reporter
Female African American slave	African American freeman
Confederate infantry soldier	Union infantry soldier
Southern abolitionist	Northern railroad engineer

2. Introduce the WebQuest and demonstrate how to access it.

3. Describe the expectations for the journal assignment. Explain that this assignment is intended to help the students learn what it was like to live during the Civil War. They are to gather as much information as possible about their character and to write in their journals as though they were that person. They can also include drawings in their journals. Remind the students of the key events included in the timeline discussed previously and suggest that they look at these events from their character's point of view—how did it affect that character, what did it mean to that character?

4. Present the scoring rubric and explain it. Emphasize that the journals must use historically accurate language and historically accurate descriptions of events. Each day in the classroom will be one month during the Civil War.

PEARSON myeducationkit Go to the Assignments and Activities section of Chapter 8 in MyEducationKit and complete the web activity entitled "Academic Tools Online." Review the various online web resources that are given within this activity. Consider the following questions: a) If you accessed and used ideas and/or materials from one or more of these sites, how would you correctly cite that reference?; b) Would you need permission from the copyright owner of this material in order to use the desired materials within your classroom instructional materials? Why or why not?; and c) How would you go about obtaining the proper permissions to use materials from these sites in your materials?

Kevin Spencer's Lesson Plan

Throughout several of the previous chapters, we have shown how Mr. Spencer, a sixth-grade social studies teacher, has been developing a lesson plan about the Civil War (see Appendix B for the fully developed lesson plan). Following the development of objectives for the lessons (Chapter 4), the outline and sequencing of the instructional activities (Chapter 5), and the identification of the needed methods (Chapter 6) and media (Chapter 7) to be used within the lesson – it is now time to actually assemble and/or produce the materials the students will experience. For example, as shown in the lesson plan (see Figure 8-8), a key part of the learning experience will be the WebQuest journaling activity. A major portion of the learning that will occur for his students will be based on that WebQuest and the reflective journal writing that it will initiate. Based on information within this chapter, Mr. Spencer now needs to determine if an appropriate WebQuest actually exists. If one is identified, will it work in its current state or will it need to be adjusted in some way to fit his objectives, students, and learning environment? If an appropriate WebQuest does not exist, does he have the time and ability to create one that will work for his students? In either case, Mr. Spencer needs to formatively evaluate the WebQuest and its effectiveness with his students and also make sure that all required copyright permissions for use have been granted.

TECHNOLOGY COORDINATOR'S CORNER

Recently, Marion Parker, the tech coordinator at Durban Elementary, received a call from one of her second-grade teachers. Two weeks earlier, this teacher had created a class website that explained the activities occurring in her class, the important assignments for the kids, her teaching philosophy, and reports on several field trip activities in which her students participated. She had published her course site and had asked Marion to create a link on the school's website to her course site. Everything seemed to run fine—until last Friday. On that day, she had received a call from one child's grandparent. The child had called his grandmother and told her to visit his class's website to see what he and his class were doing in school. However, when Grandma visited the site, she was worried by what she saw. She first expressed concern about why a teacher would spend so much time creating the site. She thought it was pretty, but she did not see the educational value of the site, and she worried about the investment of time on the site and if that took away from classroom time she spent with her students. Second, and more importantly, she found several pictures of class members working on projects and her grandson and his name were prominently displayed below one of those pictures. Although she found it interesting to read about the activity, she was worried that the publication of her grandson's name, the school's address, and a picture broadcast to the entire world, via the Internet, would place him in danger in some way. She called the teacher to ask if she had permission to use her grandson's picture and if she was concerned about safety issues.

The second-grade teacher was not overly concerned about the grandmother's criticism of the value of the course website. In discussions with Marion, she had planned out what was to go within the site and what value it had. She had already witnessed in her own class how it helped students to remember assignments and how it helped parents to stay connected to their children's school activities and work. Furthermore, in the near future, she planned to add interactive activities, examples, and more practice exercises for her students. Each of these additions would extend the learning that was currently occurring in her classroom. Marion also suggested that to ensure those visiting the site fully understood its value, additional explanation of what the site contained and why it contained that material should be added to the opening (index) page. The other issue of safety, however, was something that Marion wanted to see addressed. In today's world, one can not be too careful. It is important that before publishing anyone's picture, permission is granted and, in the case of minors, they remain anonymous in pictures, such that identities and locations are not revealed. Marion suggests that she and the teacher review the site and remove or adapt any and all identifying pictures and names of her students.

SUMMARY

In this chapter, you learned to complete an instructional plan by selecting instructional materials that match your students' objectives, learning environment, and instructional activities. In acquiring instructional materials, select existing materials whenever possible. If appropriate materials are not available, try to modify existing materials to meet your students' needs. Only as a last resort should you attempt to create new materials. In all cases, whether selecting, modifying, or creating, you should follow established copyright guidelines.

PEARSON **myeducationkit** To check your comprehension of the content covered in this chapter, go to the MyEducationKit for this book and complete the Study Plan for Chapter 8. Here you will be able to take a chapter quiz, receive feedback on your answers, and then access resources that will enhance your understanding of chapter content.

SUGGESTED RESOURCES

Print Resources

Boss, S., & Krauss, J. (2007). *Reinventing project-based learning: Your field guide to real world projects in the digital age.* Washington, DC: International Society for Technology in Education.

Clark, R. (2008). *Developing technical training: A structured approach for developing classroom and computer-based instructional materials.* San Francisco, CA: Pfeiffer.

Clark, R., & Lyons, C. (2004). *Graphics for learning: Proven guidelines for planning, designing, and evaluating visuals in training materials.* San Francisco, CA: Jossey-Bass/Pfeiffer.

Crews, K. D. (2006). *Copyright Law for Librarians and Educators.* (2nd ed.). Chicago, Ill.: American Library Association, Davis, M. (2008). *The teacher's guide to copyright.* Buzzgig, LLC.

Dynarski, M., Agodini, R., Heaviside, S., Novak, T., Carey, N., Campuzano, L., et al. (2007). Effectiveness of reading and mathematics software products: Findings from the first student cohort. National Center for Education Evaluation and Regional Assistance, U.S. Department of Education: NCEE 20074005. Available at http://ies.ed.gov/ncee/pdf/20074005.pdf

Fenrich, P. (2005). *Creating instructional multimedia solutions: Practical guidelines for the real world.* Santa Rosa, CA: Informing Science Press.

Frei, S., Gammill, A., & Irons, S. (2007). *Integrating technology into the curriculum: Practical strategies for successful classrooms.* Huntington Beach, CA: Shell Education.

Ivers, K., & Barron, A. (2005). *Multimedia projects in education: Designing, producing, and assessing* (5th ed.). Libraries Unlimited.

Kim, D., & Gilman, D. A. (2008). Effects of text, audio, and graphic aids in multimedia instruction for vocabulary learning. *Educational Technology & Society, 11* (3), 114–126.

O'Grady, J., & O'Grady, K. (2008). *The information design handbook.* How.

Smaldino, S. E., Lowther, D. L., & Russell, J. D. (2008). *Instructional technology and media for learning* (9th ed.). Upper Saddle River, NJ: Pearson.

Taylor, J., Van Scotter, P., & Coulson, D. (2007). Bridging research on learning and student achievement: The role of instructional materials. *Science Educator, 16*(2), 44–50.

Thompson, N., & McGill, T. (2008). Multimedia and cognition: Examining the effect of applying cognitive principles to the design of instructional materials. *Journal of Educational Computing Research, 39*(2), 143–159.

Tondreau, B. (2009) *Layout essentials: 100 design principles for building grids.* Beverly, MA: Rockport.

Vaughan, T. (2008). *Multimedia: Making it work.* New York: McGraw-Hill.

Electronic Resources

http://www.thegateway.org/
(Gateway to 21st Century Skills: Search Over 50,000 Online Educational Resources)

http://www.free.ed.gov/
(Federal Resources for Educational Excellent: Teaching and Learning Resources from Federal Agencies)

http://www1.nasa.gov/audience/foreducators/index.html
(NASA: For Educators)

http://school.discoveryeducation.com/schrockguide/
(Kathy Schock's Guide for Educators: Subject Access)

http://www.pbs.org/teachers/
(PBS Teachers: Resources for the Classroom)

http://www.bcps.org/offices/lis/office/admin/selection.html
(Baltimore County Public Schools: Selection Criteria for School Library Media Center Collections)

http://www.portical.org/Presentations/McGann/fairuse/53928/index.html
(Primer on Copyright Law and Fair Use)

http://fairuse.stanford.edu/
(Standford Copyright and Fair Use Center)

http://www.pbs.org/teachers/copyright/
(PBS: Copyright and Fair Use)

http://www.teachersfirst.com/copyright.cfm
(Teachers First: Copyright and Fair Use)

http://www.edutopia.org/place-for-pbl-envision-schools-project-exchange
(EduTopia | A place for PBL: Envision schools's project exchange)

MEANINGFUL INTEGRATION OF TECHNOLOGY

Although we have covered a lot of ground to this point, our question now is, "If your students interact with your instructional materials, will they learn?" The answer is, "It depends." Moving to the "I" in the PIE model, in this section of the textbook we concentrate on how instructional materials are best *implemented*. We illustrate how you *must* couple an excellent plan and set of instructional materials with good integration and implementation strategies for your students to achieve the highest-level learning. Consider the last few times you experienced *poor* results from instruction. Was your learning inhibited by poorly planned materials, by the manner in which the materials were integrated and/or implemented, or by some combination? Were there, for example, distractions because of poor-quality video, inaccessible websites, uninterpretable audio, or visuals that were not relevant to the information being presented? What about class discussions which were unavailable to students who were absent, lab experiences that did not work because of limited software access, or network problems that slowed or halted Internet access?

The point is, you may have the best instructional plan ever developed and a wonderful set of instructional materials, but if you do not properly implement them, your students will not learn as they should.

In this section, we emphasize that learning is a function of both instructional content and the manner in which students interact with the content. There are principles of utilization that can help to ensure that learning occurs. It is not enough to know the different types of technology tools that are available and when they could be used; you must also know *how* to use them effectively.

To begin this section, Chapter 9 examines the computer specifically as a means to support student learning. This chapter is followed by Chapter 10, which deals with the Internet and how it can be integrated within the classroom setting to effectively impact both teaching and learning. This section on integration and implementation concludes with a focus on distance education in Chapter 11 and how it can be used to bring instructional to students from a distance and impact learning in a unique way.

Integration of Computers to Support Learning

Source: Bob Daemmrich Photography.

KEY WORDS AND CONCEPTS

Computer-assisted instruction
Serious games
Integrated learning systems
Digital storytelling

One-computer classroom
Multimedia
Hypermedia

CHAPTER OBJECTIVES

After reading and studying this chapter, you will be able to:

↗ Describe the characteristics and give at least one example of each common category of computer-assisted instruction – drill and practice, tutorial, simulation, instructional game, and problem-solving.

↗ Discuss ways that students can learn by using common computer productivity tools such as word processors, graphics tools, spreadsheets, databases, and presentation software.

↗ Discuss a rationale for having students learn through developing their own multimedia/hypermedia projects.

↗ Compare and contrast the benefits and limitations of using computers to promote student learning through computer-assisted instruction, use of productivity tools, and development of multimedia/hypermedia.

↗ Discuss ways to effectively use a single computer in the classroom and use a computer laboratory.

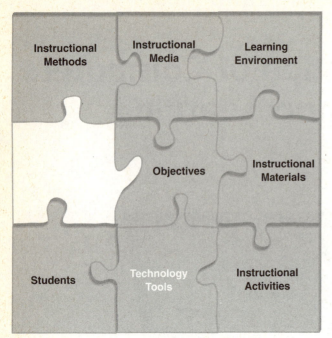

FIGURE 9–1   Technology tools are a piece in the development of the learning experience puzzle.

In this chapter, we begin to explore how to integrate technologies to enhance the learning experience (see Figure 9–1). This chapter focuses specifically on the computer and how you can use it in the classroom and laboratory to promote student learning. Recall that in introducing the computer and its uses in education in Chapter 3, we briefly explained two ways of using it: as a teacher and as an assistant. We revisit and expand that classification scheme in this chapter with a special focus on using the computer to promote student learning. In Chapter 10, we continue this section by looking specifically at the Internet and ways that you can use it in the classroom, and in Chapter 11 we examine ways to integrate distance education technologies to enhance learning.

 INTRODUCTION

Bonnie Anderson is a fourth-grade teacher at Washington Elementary School who has used computers in the classroom for a number of years. When she first started teaching, she viewed the computer mainly as a teaching machine. At the urging of her principal, she identified several computer-assisted instruction software packages that fit the fourth-grade curriculum and she felt comfortable using, and she designed ways to make them a part of the learning experience for students in her classroom. For the most part, the kids used the computers as learning stations for math and language arts exercises and an occasional science or social studies simulation. Bonnie felt that this use of the computers

helped her students to master basic skills while adding variety and making learning more motivating, and she was happy to help meet the school district's objective to integrate the use of computers in the curriculum.

Beginning a few years ago, Bonnie began incorporating other uses of computers in her class. With the availability of more computers in the school, she required her students to word process some of their writing assignments, and she introduced other assignments in which her students used *PowerPoint*. Both she and her students became increasingly comfortable doing work with the computers in her classroom and the school's lab. Given the success of these experiences, she is thinking about integrating additional computer-based learning activities, perhaps involving other productivity tools or even student development of hypermedia projects, in her class. As she ponders the possibilities, she asks herself a number of questions. How can the computer be used to promote student learning? What are the advantages and limitations of each approach? Are certain ways of using the computer effective for certain learning outcomes? Are there examples of what others have done that I can learn from? Given my own teaching style, how can I best use the computer to help my students learn?

As you read this chapter, think about Bonnie's situation. This chapter provides information about ways to use computers and computer software to help students learn. This information will help you as you implement technology-enhanced learning experiences for your own students.

 TECHNOLOGY INTEGRATION PROCESS: PREPARING TO INTEGRATE THE COMPUTER INTO THE LEARNING EXPERIENCE

This chapter explores options for integrating the computer in the classroom and laboratory to enhance the learning experience for your students. As you prepare to integrate the computer in learning activities, what should you consider? Remember the components of the PIE model.

First, when planning, consider the knowledge, skills, and dispositions of your students. What capabilities do your students possess as they come to the learning activity? At a minimum, to use today's computers students need to be able to use a mouse, select options from menus, and otherwise navigate the computer's interface. Detailed knowledge of specific applications is usually *not* necessary to get started using the computer. However, students do need to know the basics of whatever software they will use in order to get started. If students do not have the necessary technical knowledge and skills, you should plan on introducing them as part of your lesson.

Consider your objectives. What is it that you want your students to learn, and how can the computer be of benefit? As you will see in this chapter, the computer can help to address many learning objectives. However, it is certainly not appropriate for all. A computer is of limited value in helping students learn to distinguish different fruits by their smells or to estimate the length of a parking lot.

Of course, in order to use the computer, the learning environment must include at least one. In schools, available computer technology can range from a single computer in the classroom (see "Toolbox: One-Computer Classroom" on page 169) to a cluster of classroom or library computers to a computer laboratory where each learner has access to his or her own machine (see "Toolbox: Using Computer Laboratories" on page 175). Each configuration has its own opportunities and challenges; you must plan to effectively use what is available.

When using the computer with students, as with any instructional activity, be sure to prepare the instructional materials, prepare the learning environment, and prepare the learners. While preparing your learning environment, check that the computer or computers are working properly and any needed software is installed. Make sure that you are familiar with the software that you plan to use, whether that is a computer-assisted instruction package, an office application, or a multimedia authoring tool. Prepare your students for the activity. If necessary, introduce the basic operations of the software that they will need to complete the activity. Discuss the purpose (objectives) of the lesson, develop written instructions and supplemental instructional materials for the activity, and remind students of the rules for proper use of the computers.

During implementation of a computer-enhanced lesson, monitor individual students to check for understanding and to head off any problems they may encounter. Encourage students to use each other as resources if they have questions or problems. Be sure to integrate the use of the computer with other classroom methods and media so that the use of the computer builds upon and adds to the existing curriculum.

Of course, following a lesson, you and your students need to take time to evaluate how well it worked. Was the use of the computer helpful? How could the lesson be improved in the future?

 Go to the Assignments and Activities section of Chapter 9 in MyEducationKit and complete the web activity entitled "Teaching With Computers." As you explore these websites, consider ways that you might use computers in your classroom for teaching and learning.

STUDENT LEARNING WITH COMPUTERS

There are many ways to use computers and related technologies to promote student learning. You must understand the strengths of different computer applications so you can use them effectively to achieve your ultimate goal in the classroom—enhancing student learning. In Chapter 3, we introduced you to a simple but useful categorization scheme for educational applications of computers: computer as teacher and computer as assistant. In the first category, computer as teacher, the computer presents instruction to the learner much as a teacher or tutor might. In the second category, the student uses the computer to assist with learning-related tasks such as writing, calculating, or communicating with others. This involves using common computer productivity tools for work related to learning. In some cases when the computer is used as an assistant, the learner may actually take on the role of the teacher, using the computer to organize and present multimedia information for others to learn from. In this chapter, we revisit and expand upon this organizational scheme to help you better understand how you can use computers to promote student learning.

COMPUTER AS TEACHER

The computer in education, dating back to the early 1960s, is as a tool that presents instruction directly to students. Such use is usually termed *computer-assisted instruction (CAI)*, *computer-based instruction (CBI)*, or *computer-assisted learning (CAL)*. In this mode, the computer can present content information using various media (text, visuals, audio, video), provide instructional activities or situations, quiz or otherwise require interaction from learners, assess learner performance, provide feedback, and determine appropriate follow-up activities.

The chief advantage of the computer as teacher is its interactivity. Whereas a printed worksheet may leave space for a student's answer or an instructional video may pose a question for the viewer, there is no guarantee that the student will in fact respond. The computer can require a response; it can demand the learner's active involvement. When used as a teaching machine, the computer can be highly interactive, individualized, engaging, and infinitely patient. Early research analyses of studies comparing computer-assisted instruction with traditional methods suggested that it produces slightly superior achievement, often in less time, and may produce improved attitudes toward computers and sometimes toward the subject matter itself (Kulik & Kulik, 1991; Niemiec & Walberg, 1987). The positive effects are somewhat greater in the lower grades. More recent studies and analyses have been mixed, sometimes showing that instructional software is of little benefit but other times showing student learning gains (Bayraktar, 2001; Dynarski, et al., 2007; Hannafin & Foshay, 2008; Kulik, 2003), but evidence suggests that integration of instructional technology during the past decade has been more successful than earlier attempts.

CAI has a long history of use, and it remains a popular option in classrooms today, especially at the elementary level, such as in Bonnie Anderson's classroom described at the beginning of this chapter. Consider the scenario that follows. As you read, identify how Ms. Stanley uses the computer as a teacher.

Scenario: States and Capitals

Sue Stanley is a fifth-grade teacher at Riverside Elementary School. The school district's social studies curriculum guide calls for all students in the fifth grade to be able to name and correctly spell all 50 U.S. states and capitals from memory. To help her students meet this requirement, Ms. Stanley set up a series of learning activities stretching over several weeks.

At the beginning of the unit on U.S. geography, Ms. Stanley handed out a labeled U.S. map and a printed list of all fifty states and capitals to her students, and explained that each student would be responsible for learning the names and correct spellings of all 50 states and capitals. Realizing that this task could be daunting to fifth-graders, she looked for ways to make it easier and to give her students plenty of opportunities for practice.

First, she broke up the task into more manageable pieces. She divided her class of 24 students into four groups of six students each. Students in each group were assigned the task of becoming class "experts" on the states and capitals from one of four geographical regions of the United States: the Northeast, the South, the Midwest, and the West. Each student was responsible for learning information about the states and capitals in his/her region. Ms. Stanley set up the two computers in her classroom as learning stations. One station had a CD-ROM almanac that students could use to research each state, its major points of interest, population, and so forth. The other had a drill and practice program that allowed individuals to quiz themselves over the states and capitals. As students worked, Ms. Stanley circulated throughout the classroom, helping those students who needed assistance.

After giving the students time to develop their expertise, Ms. Stanley set up a classroom rotation where a student from one group was paired with a student from another group. The students took turns peer tutoring and drilling each other over the states and capitals in their respective regions, and, through the rotation schedule, they were able to practice all 50 states and capitals in a week. Each week, Ms. Stanley gave each student

a worksheet on a subset of states and capitals to complete, and gave a quiz over the subset each Friday.

To help students with learning difficulties, Ms. Stanley worked closely with Ms. Epstein, the school's special education teacher. Guided by the individualized education program (IEP) for each student, special practice activities were arranged and assignments were adjusted for special needs students. She also talked to Mr. McHenry, the music teacher, who was able to help by using music time to teach the class a song that helped everyone learn the names of the 50 states.

Ms. Stanley also scheduled the computer lab several times during the unit. On computer lab days, students played the educational game, *Where in the USA is Carmen Sandiego?* In this game, students use geographic clues about the United States to catch a criminal who has stolen a national treasure. At first, Ms. Stanley had students work in pairs on the game, because she found that students working in pairs were able to help each other learn the game and work through any problems. In later sessions, she had students work alone, so that she could get a sense of how well individual students were progressing.

After several weeks, most of the students became fairly proficient at writing the names of U.S. states and capitals from memory. Ms. Stanley was pleased with their progress, and gratified that her unit was successful in meeting the district objective. As a culminating activity, the class put on a "USA Day." Each student took one of the states and prepared a short oral presentation about it. Ms. Hopper, the art teacher, helped them create art work for their presentations. Some drew maps of their state, others drew pictures of famous places in the state, and one student even made a papier mâché model of Mount Rushmore for her presentation about South Dakota. Parents were invited, and everyone gave their presentations then sang the song they had learned to end the program. The day was a big hit with the kids and their parents, and it was a great way to wrap up the unit.

The computer is used as a learning station in many elementary classrooms.
Source: Shutterstock.

What can this scenario tell us about using the computer as a teacher? We can note the following:

↗ *CAI usually is used in a supporting or adjunct role.* In this example, educational software was one part of a broader strategy of classroom activities. Since the earliest uses of CAI, there has been an enduring myth that computers will become perfect teaching machines and one day will replace human teachers. This has not happened, and does not seem likely anytime in the foreseeable future. CAI is merely one tool at the teacher's disposal for helping students learn.

↗ *CAI is appropriate for certain learning goals.* In this example, the specific learning goal of the school district was to have every student memorize the fifty U.S. states and capitals, a largely rote task. The computer programs Ms. Stanley selected, a drill and practice program and an educational game, were appropriate to this learning goal. They could engage students' interest while providing opportunities for practice and repetition. While some forms of CAI are appropriate to higher-level learning goals, many CAI programs are designed for basic skills learning and draw on the behavioral learning perspectives discussed in Chapter 2 (i.e., they present a basic task or problem, require a learner response or behavior, and provide immediate feedback).

↗ *CAI can help students while freeing the teacher for other things.* Not only were students able to benefit from the software, but its use gave the teacher the opportunity to address individual learners' needs. When the learning stations were operating, Ms. Stanley could circulate to help those students who needed the most help. Later, when all of the students were playing the game, she could take time to assess the progress of individual students.

In Chapter 6, we introduced you to various instructional methods including the two employed in this example: a drill and practice program and an educational game. Other common methods often employed in CAI software include tutorial, simulation, and problem solving. While you can use the computer as a teacher in other ways that do not neatly fit these categories, and new types of CAI continue to be invented, these categories provide a useful framework for discussion. Let's look at these common categories of CAI, their characteristics, and examples.

Categories of Computer-Assisted Instruction

Drill and Practice   As you learned in Chapter 6, a drill and practice application is designed to help learners master already introduced basic skills or knowledge through repetitive work. Computer-based drill and practice is among the most popular of all applications of the computer as teacher, especially in the elementary grades.

Characteristics of computer drill and practice include:

↗ *Interactivity.* The computer can present many problems and require student responses.
↗ *Immediate feedback.* The computer can immediately inform the learner if an answer is right or wrong and, in a well-designed program, tell the learner why. Some drill and practice programs automatically recycle missed items until they are mastered.
↗ *Infinite patience.* A computer drill and practice program can go all day without getting tired or irritable.
↗ *Variable level of difficulty.* The computer can adjust the level of difficulty. This might be set by the teacher or the learner, or the program may adjust automatically based on the student's performance.

Examples. Drill and practice programs are best used for basic information and skills where factual learning or automatic student response is desired. In the classroom, drill and practice programs can be used to provide practice and repetition in addition to other techniques such as worksheets and problem sets. Common classroom strategies include individualized practice in a computer laboratory or rotation of individual students through learning stations so that each student is able to get at least 10 or 20 minutes of practice at a time. In the preceding scenario, Ms. Stanley used a drill and practice program on the states and capitals as one learning station in the classroom. Popular elementary level drill and practice programs include the *Stickybear Math* and *Reader Rabbit* series, which address the content areas of basic computation and beginning reading skills, respectively. Figure 9–2 shows a sample screen from *Stickybear Typing*, another title in the *Stickybear* line.

Tutorial   In a tutorial application, the computer assumes the primary instructional role of teacher or tutor. It presents new content and assesses learning. A tutorial typically contains an organized body of content, one or more pathways through that content, specific learning objectives, and built-in tests of student learning. While a poorly designed tutorial may be little more than a book on the computer screen, a well-designed one can be a highly interactive and effective form of instruction that responds to the needs or wants of individual learners.

Characteristics of computer-based tutorials include:

↗ *Dynamic presentation.* The computer can present information dynamically, such as by highlighting important text on the screen to capture the learner's attention, using images, depicting processes with animation, or employing audio and video.

FIGURE 9–2   A screen from *Stickybear Typing,* a popular drill and practice computer program.

Source: Stickybear Typing, Optimum Resources, Inc. Used with permission.

↗ *Embedded questions.* Tutorials on the computer, like drills, have the advantage of being interactive. Students must take an active role by answering embedded questions, and the computer provides immediate feedback.

↗ *Branching.* Computer tutorials can automatically branch, that is, adjust content presentation order according to the learner's responses to embedded questions or choices. Remediation or advancement can be built in to meet the needs of individual learners.

↗ *Record-keeping.* Computer tutorials can automatically maintain student records, which inform students of their progress. In addition, the teacher can check the records to ensure students are progressing satisfactorily.

Examples. Tutorials address verbal and conceptual learning in various subjects and grade levels. They are often used to supplement regular instruction or provide remediation, enrichment, or makeup work for selected students. Use of tutorials in the social and natural sciences has been found to be consistently effective (Kulik, 2003). *Science Smart* is an example of a tutorial program designed to teach key anatomy concepts (see Figure 9–3). *Rosetta Stone* is a popular tutorial series for foreign language learning. *World History* from ABC-CLIO provides a comprehensive treatment of historical developments from the 1500s to the present. In addition, tutorials are available to help

individuals learn to use many popular computer office applications and graphics software (see, for example, http://www.good-tutorials.com).

Simulation   A *simulation* is a representation or model of a real (or sometimes imaginary) system, situation, or phenomenon. In most cases, this representation is simplified to make learning easier. Most simulations are designed to promote application of information, thinking, and problem-solving skills.

Characteristics of computer simulations include:

↗ *Control of multiple variables.* Computers can manage multiple variables simultaneously. As a result, they can realistically depict complex phenomena, such as the growth and change of a city or the physics of bodies in motion. Learners can manipulate these variables to observe their effects on the system being modeled.

↗ *Dynamic presentation.* As with tutorials, the computer's ability to dynamically present information is important in simulation. Simulated instrumentation can change like the real thing, and processes such as plant growth can be graphically depicted.

↗ *Time manipulation.* The computer can contract or expand time to allow study of phenomena that are too slow (e.g., population growth) or too fast (e.g., chemical reaction) for normal classroom observation. The computer can also depict historical situations (e.g., a nineteenth-century wagon train).

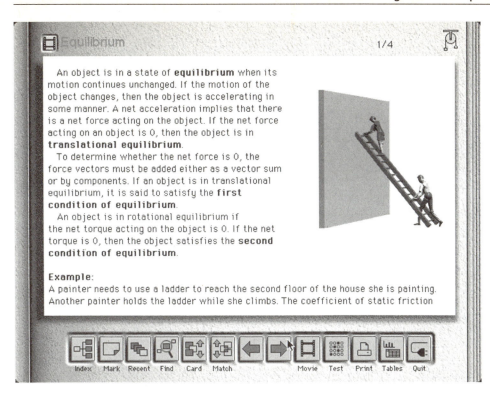

FIGURE 9–3   A screen from *Science Smart,* a popular tutorial program.

Source: The Princeton Review "Science Smart." Used with permission.

FIGURE 9–4   A screen from *The Oregon Trail,* a popular educational simulation.

Source: The Oregon Trail, ©1999. The Learning Company, Inc. Used with permission.

↗ *Effects of chance.* Many simulations include an element of chance or randomness that makes them even more realistic, allowing students to interact with them differently on different occasions.

Examples. Simulations have found their greatest use in the natural and social sciences. While evaluations of simulations' effectiveness have been mixed (Kulik, 2003;

Lee, 1999), there are many good examples of educational simulations, including *SimCity* (management of a growing city), *CatLab* (simulated cat breeding), *Decisions, Decisions* (social studies role-playing simulation series), and *The Oregon Trail* (travel by covered wagon). Figure 9–4 shows a sample screen from *The Oregon Trail.* Many educational simulations are now available online as well (http://www.simulations.com/). Effective use of simulations in the classroom requires that students have adequate content preparation, receive guidance during use of the simulation, and participate in follow-up after the simulation. For example, if use of *The Oregon Trail* is to be meaningful as a historical exercise, students need background about the westward expansion, the factors that promoted it, and life in a covered wagon in the nineteenth century so that they understand the context for the actions that they take during simulation play. Simulations vary in their time requirements; some may take only a few minutes while other may require many hours. Often, simulations can be used effectively by both individuals and small groups of students.

 PEARSON myeducationkit™ Go to the Assignments and Activities section of Chapter 9 in MyEducationKit and complete the activity entitled "Learning Chemistry in a Virtual Laboratory." As you view the video and answer the corresponding questions, think about how this sort of simulation supports student learning.

Instructional Game Instructional games add an element of fun to CAI. In many cases, games are modified versions of other types of CAI, such as drill and practice or simulation, to which gaming elements are added. Today, there is increasing interest in so-called *serious games*, games that use the appeal of video and computer games to help student learn content important to the school curriculum.

Characteristics of computer games include:

⤳ *Motivation.* The chief advantage of computer games is the variety of motivational elements they may employ, including competition, cooperation, challenge, fantasy, recognition, and reward.
⤳ *Game structure.* The game structure means that there are rules of play and an end goal.
⤳ *Sensory appeal.* Games on the computer often appeal through the use of graphics, animation, sound, and other sensory enhancements.

Examples. Games are available in a variety of subject areas and grade levels, and there is renewed interest in

Toolbox: Serious Games

The popularity of video games has led to renewed interest in the potential of gaming for education. Gee (2003) has argued that engaging video games incorporate good learning principles that are supported by research in cognitive science. While many computer and video games are not overtly educational, people do learn from them, and a growing number of educators are interested in tapping the motivational appeal of video and computer games for educational purposes. The term **serious games** is used to describe games that are used for overtly educational or training purposes, and a serious games initiative has been launched (http://www.seriousgames.org/).

Many new educational games that borrow concepts from the commercial video game realm have been developed. *Physicus* is a computer game that involves the application of principles of physics on a mysterious island. *Quest Atlantis* uses an immersive three-dimensional environment to engage students in various educationally relevant tasks, such as environmental investigations and studying other cultures. *River City* is a multi-user virtual environment (MUVE) in which students interact with virtual characters and interpret evidence to solve ecological problems in the city. *Darfur is Dying* is a Web-based game that focuses on the humanitarian crisis in the Darfur region of Sudan. *DimensionM* from Tabula Digita uses gaming to teach pre-algebra and algebra concepts (see Figure 9–5).

Traditional video and computer games are also being appropriated for educational uses. For example, *America's Army* is a popular online game, created for the U. S. Army as a recruiting tool, which teaches civilians about the Army and its operations using an entertaining gaming format. The popular video game *Dance Dance Revolution* and various games for

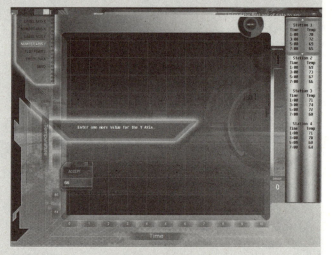

FIGURE 9–5 A screen from *DimensionM*, a computer game that teaches algebra concepts.
Source: DimensionM, © 2007, Tabula Digita, Inc. Used with permission.

the Nintendo *Wii*, which uses an innovative motion-sensing controller, are being used to promote physical fitness in schools and other settings. History-based games such as *Civilization* and *Age of Empires* are being used in some classrooms to help students learn about the past. Games hold great potential for learning, and we should not be surprised to see even greater use made of them in classrooms in the future.

the educational potential of games today (see "Toolbox: Serious Games", on page 166). *Zoombinis: Logical Journey* is a popular educational game that requires students to apply logical thinking skills to solve puzzles to help the Zoombinis along on a journey. In the classic computer game, *Where in the World is Carmen Sandiego?*, the student assumes the role of a detective who must use geography clues to track a thief around the world (see Figure 6–4 on page 107). In this role, the student experiences an element of fantasy, the challenge to locate the thief within a set amount of time using clues embedded in the game, and opportunities to compete against other students' times or cooperate with other students to solve the crime. *Where in the USA is Carmen Sandiego?*, mentioned in the previous scenario, is a spin-off game focused on U.S. geography.

Problem Solving   Some CAI applications are designed to foster students' problem-solving skills but do not fit into any of the previous categories. Problem-solving applications are often designed to promote students' higher-order thinking skills, such as logic, reasoning, pattern recognition, and strategies.

     Characteristics of computer problem-solving applications include:

- ↗ *Focus on specific types of problems*. Specific problem-solving programs often focus on specific skills (e.g., spatial ability, logic) or problem-solving in a specific discipline (e.g., mathematics, science).
- ↗ *Practice*. The computer can provide students with practice over a large number of problems in a short period of time, requiring interaction and providing feedback as in other forms of CAI.
- ↗ *Variety*. The computer is capable of presenting a variety of problems. This helps students to generalize their problem-solving skills.

Examples. Some teachers use problem-solving software to enhance students' problem-solving skills for their own sake. Sunburst's *The Factory Deluxe* allows students to develop planning and spatial reasoning skills while constructing products. Edmark's *Thinkin' Things* series allows young learners to do various kinds of problem-solving in a fun environment (see Figure 6–5). Other problem-solving programs link to relevant curricular areas such as mathematics or science. *Zoombinis Island Odyssey*, for example, focuses on reasoning and logic in science. *Geometric Supposer* allows students to explore geometry. *Alien Rescue* places students in a problem-based learning situation in which they must determine the environment in which alien life forms can survive; in performing this task, students learn about science and the solar system (see Figure 9–6).

FIGURE 9–6   A screen from *Alien Rescue*, a problem-solving computer program.
Source: Alien Rescue, University of Texas. Used with permission. (http://alienrescue.edb.utexas.edu)

Integrated Learning Systems

Integrated learning systems (ILSs) are the most complex and sophisticated computer systems that function as a teacher. They combine comprehensive computer-assisted instruction (CAI), any or all of the categories mentioned previously, and computer management features into a single networked computer delivery system. They are designed to provide a cycle of instruction, assessment, and prescription for a particular subject matter—all on the computer.

    ILSs are usually supplied by a single vendor that provides all of the hardware and software. Leading ILS producers today include Compass Learning and Pearson Digital Learning. While ILSs are expensive, they provide a lot for the money. The hardware consists of a local area network (LAN) of computers linked to a large file server that contains all of the software. The software includes a fully articulated curriculum in a particular subject area, such as mathematics or language arts, as well as software that tracks students and manages their progress.

    Students in schools that have ILSs typically use the system regularly, from daily to once or twice per week. The computer delivers instruction, most often tutorials and drill and practice exercises, and tests the students. Instruction, testing, and test scoring are all managed by the system. Because the curriculum is well integrated and spans a number of grade levels, students may work on the ILS over a period of years and progress at their own rate. Teachers like the fact that the instruction is individualized. In addition, because the computer handles both the instruction and the assessment, the teacher is freed to provide individualized assistance, plan ancillary learning activities, and guide the learning process.

Administrators like ILSs because they provide detailed information about the levels of mastery of the student body. A summary of the effects of using instructional technology in elementary and secondary schools by Kulik (2003) reported that the use of ILSs had an effect too small to be educationally meaningful on students' achievement in reading. However, the use of ILSs did have a positive effect on students' achievement in mathematics.

Problems and Pitfalls

We have emphasized the many advantages of using the computer as teacher here, and clearly CAI has much to offer. However, there are concerns that we must consider, as well. Critics charge that CAI is a low-level use of the computer that simply puts a new face on old busywork and that is not consistent with a view of learning as knowledge construction. In some cases this charge is surely justified. Some drill and practice programs are little more than electronic worksheets, and some tutorials are mere electronic workbooks. Early CAI programs were often developed from a behavioral learning perspective (see Chapter 2) that may not reflect more recent thinking about how people learn. But, that is changing. Newer software releases tend to make better use of the computer and what we know about learning. As with any type of instructional material, it is your responsibility as the teacher to see that CAI is used productively in the classroom to help students learn and not simply as busywork.

Classroom management is also an important consideration in the use of CAI. Effective use often requires special classroom management strategies. If you have only one or perhaps two computers in the classroom, you must devise mechanisms to ensure that each student gets access (see "Toolbox: One-Computer Classroom" on page 169). If a computer laboratory is available, you must plan computer activities well in advance in consultation with the school's technology or media coordinator. Laboratory settings, too, have their own challenges (see "Toolbox: Using Computer Laboratories" on page 175). You will need careful planning and structured activities to provide the direction required to keep students productively on task.

 ## COMPUTER AS ASSISTANT: USING PRODUCTIVITY TOOLS

In the role of assistant, the computer aids the learner in performing routine work tasks that may help facilitate learning. In Chapter 3, we introduced important computer applications that fall into this category including word processors, graphics tools, spreadsheets, databases, presentation software, multimedia/hypermedia authoring software, and telecommunication tools. These applications can be used in a variety of ways. In this section of the chapter, we focus on the use of computer productivity tools that can assist the student in learning.

This use of computers in the classroom is one of the most important and one of the most common as well. In many ways, this is only natural. When computers are used in the workplace, they are most often used as a tool to assist the worker. Writers prepare documents using word processors, businesspeople store customer records in databases, accountants use spreadsheets to make calculations, graphic artists use drawing programs, and so on. So, it makes sense that students should learn to use computers in schools in the same ways that they are used in the workplace.

In this section, we will revisit the popular computer applications that we introduced in Chapter 3. To begin, read the following scenario, looking for examples where students use the computer as an assistant.

Scenario: Stock Market Game

Bob Goins is an economics and social studies teacher at George Washington Carver High School. For the past several years, he has included a popular unit in his economics class in which his students "play" the stock market by creating and tracking a portfolio of investments. Bob uses the unit as a synthesizing activity in which students learn and apply information about investing, the market, and financial tracking. Here is how it went last year.

To ensure that his students were adequately prepared, Mr. Goins waited until the start of the second semester of his economics class to begin the game. Once started, however, the activity spanned the entire semester. At the beginning of the unit, the class was divided into teams of three or four students each. Each team was given an initial investment of $100,000 of play money. Teams were allowed to invest in the stock market in any way that they wanted, and they could change their investments during the semester by buying or selling stocks (taking sales commissions into account). Each team's goal was to have its initial investment grow as much as possible by the end of the game. The teams competed against one another to achieve the best overall performance, and Mr. Goins added an extra incentive by offering to treat the winning team to pizza at the end of the semester.

Before the teams actually made their first investments, Mr. Goins set aside three weeks for research. During this period, each team investigated stocks to purchase. Using computers available in the Business Department's lab, students used the Internet to do online research of various companies and mutual funds. Mr. Goins provided the class with the URLs of online brokerage houses and other sources of investment information on the Web. When teams identified promising investments, they requested more information online or used the lab's word processor to compose a letter requesting more

Toolbox: One-Computer Classroom

Despite the fact that millions of computers are now installed in U.S. schools, one-computer classrooms remain relatively common. What can be done with a single computer in the classroom? The answer is, a lot!

All of the methods of using computers in the classroom discussed in this chapter can apply to the one-computer classroom. Students can work on computer-assisted instruction, either individually or in small groups. The computer can be used as a productivity tool, for example, to create visuals or graph data from a science experiment. One computer can even be used, with appropriate management, for multimedia development activities in which students take on the role of teacher.

One simple but useful way to use limited hardware is to give individual students access to the computer in rotation. This model is especially popular at the elementary level, where the computer is often established as one of a number of learning stations through which students rotate. For example, primary-age learners working on basic arithmetic skills might rotate through several related learning stations featuring concrete manipulatives, traditional flash cards, and a computer drill and practice program. While time on the computer is necessarily limited in this approach, it does give each student in an entire class at least some access. You, the teacher, must effectively manage students' access to the computer to avoid conflicts and to keep those students who are not working on the computer productively engaged in other activities. Sign-up sheets, schedules, fixed time intervals, and other similar techniques can help with the management challenge.

Students can also use the computer in small groups. Research suggests that for many types of computer-assisted instruction there are benefits to having small groups, as opposed to an individual, work on CAI programs (Johnson, Johnson, & Stanne, 1985; Lou, Abrami, & d'Apollonia, 2001). Cooperating students can learn from and help one another, where a single student might become confused or stuck. Small groups can also use the computer to do such things as create presentations or develop hypermedia projects. Even whole-class use of a single computer is possible. Using an electronic whiteboard, LCD projector, or other whole-class display device, the teacher can lead a whole class through a session with a program such as *Where in the USA is Carmen Sandiego?*, calling on students to make decisions during each game turn. Some CAI programs are even designed to support whole-class use with a single computer. A notable example is Tom Snyder Productions' *Decisions Decisions* software line. The whole-class activities in these role-playing simulations are orchestrated by a single computer.

Finally, although the emphasis in this chapter is on students' learning, one should not overlook the single classroom computer as a tool for you, the teacher. A word processor is a great tool for producing printed material. With a single computer equipped with word processing software and a printer, you can produce printed instructional materials you can then copy for the whole class to use. Many textbooks today come with computerized question banks; you can make copies of selected questions to help guide review activities. You might use a database to keep student records, a spreadsheet to maintain student grades, and so on. As some experts have argued, if you have only one computer in a classroom, the most useful place for it is on your own desk!

---

information. Mr. Goins also invited a local stockbroker to talk to the students about investing and to provide some tips about possible investment selections. At the end of the three-week research period, each team made its mock purchases, and the game was under way!

To keep track of their investments, Mr. Goins required each team to maintain an investment spreadsheet. To help the students learn to use the software, Mr. Goins briefly demonstrated *Excel* during class, and provided a handout that covered the basics. However, he let the students figure out the details, and with some occasional help they seemed to do just fine. Mr. Goins required the students to design the team spreadsheet so that it listed each individual investment and calculated the total value of the portfolio. He required that each team update its spreadsheet weekly, though most teams were so engaged in the game that they checked their stocks daily. Each team created a graph from the spreadsheet to show the overall performance from the beginning of the game to the current week. These graphs were posted on the classroom bulletin board every Friday, so all of the teams knew where they stood. A few of the teams went further and used their spreadsheets to do projections—calculating what would happen if market conditions changed in certain ways. They used their projections to decide whether to buy or sell certain stocks.

As a final activity at the end of the semester, each team prepared a *PowerPoint* presentation to summarize their investments, the strategies they used during the game, and their results. The students were able to import graphs and data from their spreadsheet into their presentation. Finally, each team presented its report using the classroom computer and a portable LCD projector that Mr. Goins checked out from Ms. Habib, the technology coordinator. The unit went well, it was a favorite of the students, and Mr. Goins expects that it will be a part of the curriculum in his economics class for many years to come.

What can we learn about the use of the computer as an assistant from this scenario? Consider the following points:

↗ *Content comes first.* When the computer is used as an assistant, the computer and productivity software play a secondary role to the subject matter itself.

A team of students uses spreadsheet software on the computer to prepare a graph showing their investments as part of a stock market game lesson.
Source: Scott Cunningham/Merrill Education.

In this example, the goal of the activity was for students to learn economics. The computer tools simply helped them achieve this goal.

↗ *Computer productivity tools offer benefits.* The students in this example were able to easily create a graph of their investment history each week because they had the data in a spreadsheet. They could have done this by hand, but the computer made the job much quicker and easier, and the computer-generated graph was neater and more accurate than one created by hand. The initial time and effort needed to create the spreadsheet led to benefits later on.

↗ *Using computer productivity tools can help students achieve learning goals.* While some applications of productivity tools are relatively basic (e.g., totaling the value of the stock portfolio), others can foster more high-level learning (e.g., using a spreadsheet to do projections based on market changes, communicating information to an audience). See the discussion below for ways to use the various computer productivity tools.

↗ *Extensive software knowledge is not necessarily required.* Some teachers are reluctant to have students use the computer as an assistant unless the students (and the teacher too) have extensive knowledge of the software. But, as with Mr. Goins in the scenario, many teachers find that students are able to function adequately when they have just the basics, whether from prior exposure (e.g., a computer applications class) or, as in this example, from instruction such as a handout or in-class demonstration.

In Chapter 3, we introduced you to a number of the most popular computer productivity tools. Refer to the information there for their features and advantages. Here, we examine these tools—word processors,

graphics tools, spreadsheets, databases, and presentation software—to see how students can use them as assistants while learning. We consider multimedia/ hypermedia authoring in the next section.

Common Computer Productivity Tools

Word Processors   As we indicated in Chapter 3, word processors take much of the drudgery out of creating and editing written work. As a result, they are useful for a variety of student learning activities that involve literacy. Students can use word processors to:

↗ *Write papers, stories, poems, letters, and other in-class work.* The major emphasis today in helping students learn to write is on the process of writing. With almost any written work, students can use the word processor to practice creating a draft, editing the work, and producing a new draft. The ease with which they can do this encourages students to write more and do more revising. In the stock market game, students wrote letters to obtain information during their initial research. This is one way to encourage students to reach out beyond the classroom and connect with people in the community. Many teachers have students write to other students through pen-pal projects, which can be done electronically using e-mail.

↗ *Do writing-related activities.* The word processor can be useful for any type of writing-related activity. Students can use it singly or in groups to take notes, to record an experiment's or project's progress, or to collect ideas from a brainstorming session.

↗ *Do exercises or study.* Students can use the word processor, for example, to type spelling words, science vocabulary words, or other language exercises as a way of practicing these skills. They can type their own handwritten notes on a word processor to reinforce learning or study for an exam.

Research on the effectiveness of word processors in writing instruction, while not unequivocal, suggests that they can be beneficial if used appropriately. In a statistical review of 32 studies, Bangert-Drowns (1993) concluded that using word processors in writing instruction results in both longer documents and better-quality writing on average. However, the research is mixed, and you should not assume that any use of word processors in a classroom automatically results in better student performance. The effects of word processors in instruction derive from the teacher's methods and the classroom organization (Cochran-Smith, 1991). As a result, it is important to integrate word processors into a well-conceived process approach to writing, provide students with adequate opportunity to learn to use the software, and take into account the particular classroom environment where the word processor is used.

Graphics Tools   Graphics tools provide students with the capability to work with visuals of all types (e.g., photographs, clip art, charts, graphs). See Chapter 3 for basic information about these tools. Students can learn by using these tools for the following:

↗ *Creative drawing.* Students can use drawing or painting programs to produce original artwork. Computer drawing tools allow students to easily experiment when creating works, because they allow students to make changes or start over without using paint or other traditional art supplies.

↗ *Illustration of work.* Students can use drawing or painting programs and clip art to illustrate written stories, reports, or multimedia projects.

↗ *Charting or graphing.* As in the stock market game scenario, students can chart or graph data. This is especially applicable in data-rich subjects such as mathematics, science, and economics.

↗ *Concept maps and other organizational diagrams.* With appropriate software, such as *Inspiration* (or *Kidspiration* for younger students), *MindMapper*, or *FreeMind*, students can create concept maps, mind maps, or other diagrams to visually illustrate the relationships between ideas or concepts (see Figure 9–7).

While graphics tools reduce the effort it takes for students to produce visual materials, they still rely on users' abilities to effectively communicate ideas. Visuals can be used effectively to promote learning, but they can also be used ineffectively and in some cases can even interfere with learning (Rieber, 1994). When using graphics tools in the classroom, help your students find the best ways to visually present information.

PEARSON myeducationkit™ To learn more about concept mapping software go to the Video Tutorials section of Chapter 9 and watch either the video tutorial entitled *Inspiration* or *Kidspiration*. As you watch either the video, consider how you and your students can use such a tool in the classroom. For more about using these tools, go to the Assignments and Activities section of Chapter 9 in MyEducationKit and complete the activity entitled "Uses of Inspiration or Kidspiration." As you review the websites, consider how these programs support visual learners and promote conceptual understanding.

Spreadsheets   Spreadsheets, as we noted in Chapter 3, are tools for calculating. In many cases, they include database elements as well as the capability to graphically depict data. Students can use these versatile tools to do the following:

↗ *Manage financial information.* Spreadsheets first became popular tools for helping businesses manage finances. Students, likewise, can use them for tracking financial information ranging from personal budgets to the finances of student clubs and organizations to class projects such as the stock market game in the preceding scenario.

↗ *Keep records.* Although primarily calculating tools, spreadsheets can be used for simple recordkeeping, such as maintaining lists of information (e.g., names and addresses of classmates, list of resources such as websites) that can be quickly searched or sorted.

↗ *Create charts and graphs.* Spreadsheets are excellent tools for quickly producing a chart or graph from data. In the stock market game scenario, students graphed their investment data using a spreadsheet.

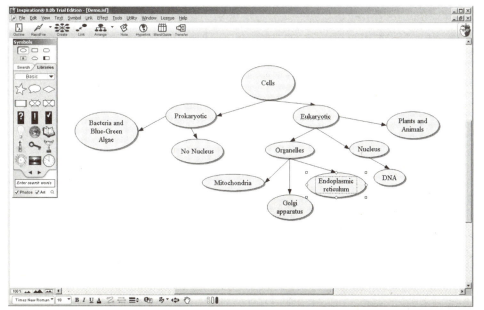

FIGURE 9–7 A screen from *Inspiration*, a tool for creating concept maps and other kinds of organizational diagrams.

Source: Inspiration, Inspiration Software, Inc. Used with permission.

↗ *Perform complex calculations.* Spreadsheets can quickly produce results involving complex calculations. For example, students in an economics or business class might generate loan amortization tables, while students in a trigonometry class could calculate trigonometric functions of various triangles.

↗ *Perform "what-if?" simulation or hypothesis-testing activities.* Spreadsheets allow students to investigate how changes in one factor impact other factors— "What will happen if I change . . ." Using a spreadsheet, students in a high school business class, for example, might examine the effects of changing insurance rates on the cost of owning and operating a car. Students in a biology class could explore the effects of changing birth and death rates on the growth of populations. Students in a geometry class could examine the relationship between perimeter and area in various geometric shapes.

Spreadsheets allow students to concentrate on real-world problems without becoming bogged down in the calculations. In a review of applications of spreadsheets in education, Baker and Sugden (2003) documented many applications of spreadsheets for student learning particularly in mathematically-related subject areas. When using spreadsheets in the classroom, make certain your students understand that the results from spreadsheets are only as good as the data and formulas entered in them. An incorrect formula or bad data can lead to erroneous results. The relevant expression in the computer world is "garbage in, garbage out." If what you start with is not correct, the computer cannot magically fix it. Spreadsheets are great tools, but like any other computer tool, they must be used properly.

Presentation Software   As we pointed out in Chapter 3, presentation software is designed for the production and display of computer text and images usually for presentation to a group. Appropriate presentation hardware is needed for group display; see "Toolbox: Presentation Hardware" on page 173 for more information. Students can use presentation software to:

↗ *Make in-class presentations or reports.* Presentation packages make it easy for students to create professional-looking electronic reports complete with multimedia elements.

↗ *Store and display electronic portfolios.* Because presentation packages are capable of handling multimedia elements, students can use them to assemble a portfolio of work including text, graphics, and even digital audio and video.

↗ *Transfer work to other media.* Many presentation packages provide a simple mechanism for converting electronic slides to print or Web pages. As a result, they can be used as multimedia authoring tools similar to the other

multimedia/hypermedia authoring tools discussed later in this chapter.

Presentation software, because of its multimedia capability, shares usage characteristics with graphics software as well as hypermedia authoring software. For all of these programs, it is important that students avoid becoming caught in the trap of form over substance. Emphasize to your students that *what* they are presenting is more important than *how* they are presenting it. Also, you and your students need to be aware of copyright regulations to avoid making improper use of copyrighted material in presentations or other multimedia products. See the discussion on copyright in Chapter 8 for more information.

Databases   As you have already learned, computer database software provides the capability for creating, editing, and manipulating organized collections of information. Students can use databases and database management software to do the following:

↗ *Locate information in prepared databases.* Given the widespread use of computer databases today, at a minimum, students should be able to use database software to find information (e.g., locate a book in the school library's electronic card catalog or find the name of the nineteenth president in a database of U.S. presidents). As students progress, they should learn to apply the Boolean (logical) operators AND and OR to narrow or expand searches, respectively.

↗ *Develop problem-solving and higher-order thinking skills.* Databases make excellent tools for the development of problem-solving and higher-order thinking skills. Using a database of U.S. presidents, for example, students might explore questions such as: "How does war impact presidential elections?" or "Is there a relationship between the rate of increase in federal spending and the political party of the president?"

↗ *Develop original databases.* Students can learn a great deal about research, information organization, and a particular content area by developing their own databases. For example, as a social studies class project, students might develop a database of historical sites within their community.

Research into the use of databases in the classroom suggests that students can acquire information from databases and can learn from them but that they often need assistance to do so effectively (Collis, 1990; Ehrman, Glenn, Johnson, & White, 1992; Maor & Taylor, 1995). Just because students have access to databases does not ensure that they will learn. Students often exhibit poor inquiry skills. They may have difficulty formulating appropriate questions and corresponding searches, and they may have difficulty interpreting

Toolbox: Presentation Hardware

To make the computer's display visible to a group, choose one of several hardware options. The most common choices include a large television or video monitor (often equipped with special computer-to-video conversion hardware), video projectors, and electronic whiteboards. We look at each of these options.

LARGE TELEVISIONS OR VIDEO MONITORS

Most schools possess large televisions or video monitors, often mounted in classrooms or available on carts, for use with VCRs, DVDs, or cable TV. For classroom use, sizes ranging from 21 inches to 35 inches are common. Large-screen televisions, although less common, can also be used for group presentations.

Today, most personal computers are incapable of working with older analog video monitors or televisions without special hardware. However, a number of vendors supply devices called *scan converters* that convert the computer's display output into standard analog video (often referred to as NTSC, the old U.S. video standard) for display on an older TV or monitor. A disadvantage of this approach is that analog video cannot reproduce the high resolutions found on most personal computers. As a result, when the computer image is converted to analog video, there is some degradation of the image such that it may become fuzzy and small text fonts may not be legible. To compensate for this loss of resolution, some scan converters support magnification of the image. If this is not an option, select larger text fonts (at least 18 point) when using a computer with a video scan converter.

Many newer digital high definition televisions are capable of accepting computer output and displaying it directly. Because they are digital and can display higher resolution images, such TVs are directly compatible with computers. As digital TVs become the norm, this will become an increasingly common option for the classroom.

VIDEO PROJECTORS

Video projectors provide the capability to project a video or computer image onto a screen. Most projectors today use a liquid crystal display (LCD), the same technology found in computer displays. Another technology now available is digital light processing (DLP); projectors using this technology rely on computer chips with thousands of tiny mirrors that control light to display the images. Because video projectors are capable of producing very large images—in some cases, 20 feet or more across—these devices provide an option for very large groups. Indeed, they are popular in classrooms, lecture halls, auditoriums, and other facilities that seat large numbers of people.

Different video projectors are distinguished by such features as the maximum screen resolution supported, the number of colors simultaneously displayed, and how rapidly the display is "refreshed" or renewed, an important consideration when tracking rapid motion such as the movement of a mouse cursor on the computer screen. Most projectors today can display video (e.g., from a DVD or VCR) as well as computer output from either *Windows*-based or *Mac OS*-based computers, usually with only an appropriate cable connection. Some video projectors are so bright that they can function effectively in fully lighted rooms. Many projectors are transportable; most weigh under 20 pounds and are usually equipped with a handle or carrying case. In a classroom, they can be mounted on the

An LCD projector.
Source: iStockphoto.

ceiling for a permanent installation or wheeled into the classroom on a cart. Many projectors come with their own speakers to support audio as well as video. Projectors are an especially attractive option for classroom display of computer images.

ELECTRONIC WHITEBOARDS

Electronic whiteboards are large classroom displays that allow teachers or students to interact with the computer through a touch sensitive board on which the computer screen is projected.

Electronic whiteboards resemble traditional whiteboards but have interactive capabilities. A computer image is projected onto the whiteboard, and the teacher or students can interact with the computer via special hardware and software that senses where the user is touching the projected image with a finger or a special electronic marker. So, computer software can be manipulated through the whiteboard (e.g., files can be opened, options selected, websites accessed), and whatever is written or drawn on the whiteboard can be captured and saved. With an electronic whiteboard, the teacher can orchestrate a whole-class interaction with the computer from the front of the classroom, keeping students engaged and directing their interactions with the computer.

Electronic whiteboards are manufactured by various vendors. They are distinguished by size and various features. Some electronic whiteboards rely on rear projectors while others have the projector in the front. The projector may be bundled with the board, or in some cases it may be purchased separately. The particular interactive features of the system will vary with more sophisticated systems tending to be more expensive. Because of their versatility and interactivity, electronic whiteboards have become a popular option for computer display in classrooms.

An electronic whiteboard.
Source: Najlah Feanny/Corbis.

results. You should help students understand the structure and organization of the database, and guide them through the process of using it.

Problems and Pitfalls

When using any of the productivity tools for computer as assistant discussed here, it is important to keep the learning objectives first and foremost. It is easy for students to become distracted by the features of the software and to spend too much time tweaking available options (e.g., fonts, colors, clip art) rather than focusing on the objectives of the learning activity. Also, help students understand the limits of what computer productivity tools can do. As noted earlier, the output of a computer spreadsheet is only as good as the formula that was constructed to perform a calculation, and while a word processor's spell checker may catch many errors the student still needs to know when to use "their" instead of "there" or "they're" in a sentence. Computer productivity tools are only as good as the people using them.

As with any instructional tool, the important thing to remember is that computer use should be appropriate to the specific instructional goals, the educational context, and the students. Keep in mind that you may need special hardware and/or software to meet the needs of students who have disabilities. See the section on assistive technology in Chapter 3 for more information.

COMPUTER AS ASSISTANT: MULTIMEDIA AUTHORING

As discussed in Chapter 3, multimedia/hypermedia authoring software allows students to develop their own multimedia applications. We present it here as a separate category of computer as assistant, because when using the computer in this way, the student often uses the computer to take on the role of "teacher." When creating a multimedia application, the objective is for the students to organize and present the content in such a way that others can learn from it. To achieve this objective, the students must develop their own knowledge and understanding of the content and then effectively present the information through the computer. This is a challenging and open-ended task that requires students to construct knowledge and apply organizational, logical thinking, and problem-solving skills to present it. As a result, this approach aligns well with the constructivist principles of learning described in Chapter 2, and many experts believe this is one of the most valuable ways to use a computer in education.

We look here at the ways that students can learn by creating multimedia products on the computer. Read the scenario that follows. Identify how the students use the computer to present content to others in this example.

Scenario: Multimedia Projects

Peggy Gambrel teaches eighth grade science in William McKinley Middle School. Last year, she modified an assignment that she had used in previous years to integrate technology. In the past, Ms. Gambrel had assigned her students the task of making a written report about a famous scientist or inventor (e.g., Marie Curie, Thomas Edison, Albert Einstein, George Washington Carver). For the new assignment, she assigned pairs of students the task of doing research and creating an interactive multimedia program about a famous scientist or inventor.

At the beginning of the two-and-a-half week activity, Ms. Gambrel made the assignment to her class and paired off the students. Each pair's initial task was to decide on the scientist or inventor for their report. To help them choose, Ms. Gambrel decorated her room by hanging pictures of famous scientists and inventors on the walls. With the help of the school librarian, Ms. Keck, she also gathered a number of relevant books and other print materials. After surveying the available materials, each team wrote the names of their top four preferred choices on a card and turned it in to Ms. Gambrel. By looking through all of the requests, Ms. Gambrel was able to assign a subject to each team so that there were no duplicates in the class, and every team was able to get its first, second, or third choice.

During the first week, students researched their choices. Ms. Gambrel set aside time each class period for students to go to the library. All of the students used the available print materials, and they were also able to go online to find information on the Web. To ensure that everyone had a chance to do online research, Ms. Keck set up a sign-up system where each team was assigned two 30-minute blocks during the week. She helped the students during their searches so that they were able to make productive use of the limited time.

During the second week, students created their multimedia programs using *PowerPoint*, the popular package, using the school's minilab as well as the three computers in their classroom to work on their projects. Ms. Gambrel didn't feel that she was an expert in using *PowerPoint* for multimedia herself, but she understood the basics, and Mr. Alvarez, the computer teacher, offered to help her students if they had problems. The students had learned to use *PowerPoint* in Mr. Alvarez's computer class earlier in the year, so Ms. Gambrel did not spend time teaching them how to use the software for this activity. The kids just dove right in! Ms. Gambrel gave them time each day to work on their reports.

Toolbox: Using Computer Laboratories

Computer laboratories are commonplace in most schools, and they offer the advantage that each student, or perhaps pair of students, is able to work on an individual machine. This makes it possible for an entire class to simultaneously use computer-assisted instruction software, work with an office application such as a word processor or spreadsheet, or do multimedia authoring. However, just as there are challenges in using a single computer in the classroom, working with an entire class of students in a computer laboratory brings its own set of challenges. How can you effectively make use of a computer laboratory?

First, be certain to plan in advance for use of a computer laboratory. Computer laboratories are shared resources within schools, and often a number of classes, perhaps even the entire school, may use a computer laboratory. In some schools, computer laboratories can be reserved for a specific period of time by making a request to the technology coordinator or media specialist. In other schools, a fixed rotation schedule may be utilized to allow each eligible class to have some time in the lab. Regardless of the particular method, it is likely that you will have only a limited amount of time, such as an hour a day for several consecutive days or perhaps only an hour once per week, in the lab. Be prepared to effectively utilize the laboratory by planning your lessons around the available times.

Sessions in computer laboratories have the potential to become chaotic because of the fact that many students are working on computers simultaneously and may need assistance at the same time. How can the teacher manage the laboratory environment so that time is productively spent? Employ the following tips to make best use of laboratory time.

↗ Obtain assistance, if possible. It never hurts to have more hands and eyes in the computer lab. The school's technology coordinator, a teacher's aide, parents, or others may be able to assist during laboratory activities.

↗ Prepare students for the laboratory experience. Complete preparatory work in the classroom before going to the lab. Make sure students know the rules for how to work in the lab (e.g., proper lab behavior, how to save work, how to print) and what they are to do when they go to the lab. Create instructions, worksheets, checklists, and other materials to guide students' activities. Discuss with students the amount of time their activities will entail, and schedule the lab accordingly.

↗ Monitor students during the laboratory activity to make certain that they are on task. Break down the laboratory activity into steps and require students to check in or complete work at each step to ensure that they make adequate progress throughout the assigned laboratory time.

↗ If you need to address all of the students in the lab, have the students turn off their computer monitors/displays so that they will focus their attention on you.

↗ Encourage students to help one another. "Ask three before me" is a laboratory rule used by many teachers that means students should ask three other students before asking the teacher if they have a question or problem. Develop student "experts" who are knowledgeable about particular computer applications and can assist others.

↗ Have students use visual signals to indicate when they need help. You can use colored cards or plastic cups for this purpose. For example, if students have noncritical questions or problems, instruct them to put a yellow card or cup next to the computer or on the monitor. If students have critical questions or problems, such that they cannot continue without help, instruct them to put a red card or cup on the computer or monitor. These visual signals make it easier for the teacher and aides to determine who is in need of immediate assistance.

All of the teams built *PowerPoint* projects consisting of text, images, animations, and interactive elements. Ms. Gambrel provided the general guidelines for the multimedia projects and shared her scoring rubric with the class, but each team had to determine exactly what content to include and how to present it. Ms. Gambrel was amazed at how hard the students worked—much harder, she thought, than when they did their usual written reports—and how creative they were. Each team included textual information about its subject, navigational buttons and Web links, interactive questions about the subject, and multimedia elements. Lauren and Katie, for example, scanned a picture from a book for their report on Jane Goodall, and they also added a sound clip of chimpanzees because they thought it sounded "cool."

Tim and Jim used a picture of Marie Curie that they found on the Internet for their project. Chris and Sean recorded their own narration and added it to their project. David and Nancy found a digital video clip of Albert Einstein for their report. No two projects were alike.

At the end of the unit, the class had a show-and-tell session. Ms. Gambrel used the electronic whiteboard in her classroom for showing the projects. Each team presented its multimedia project. The students really enjoyed the assignment, and they loved sharing their projects. During the school's science night, the students set up their projects in the school's computer lab so that their parents could stop by to see them. Ms. Gambrel was pleased with the new class activity and glad that she had tried it.

Students work on a multimedia project.
Source: David Young-Wolff/PhotoEdit.

What does this scenario tell us about having student author multimedia projects? There are several things to note:

↗ *Students must learn both the content and how to present it.* When students develop interactive multimedia projects, they take on the role of "teacher" and have a two-part task to both learn the content themselves and learn how to present it via the computer. This requires organization, logical thinking, and problem solving.

↗ *Students are actively involved.* Although it is certainly not the only way to accomplish this aim, having students create computer-based projects gets them actively involved in learning. It is motivating. It is consistent with a view of learning as construction of understanding (see Chapter 2).

↗ *There is more than one way to achieve success.* A characteristic of most situations in which students use the computer to assume the role of teacher is that there are many ways they can succeed. In this scenario, no two students' projects were the same, yet all met the goal. Just as in most "real-world" problem solving, different approaches can and do work.

↗ *Extensive prior knowledge is not necessarily required.* As with the use of other computer productivity tools, a little knowledge can go a long way in the classroom when it comes to developing multimedia. In this example, Ms. Gambrel did not feel she was expert with the software, but her students knew enough to get the job done with a little help from the computer teacher, Mr. Alvarez.

Students can create interactive multimedia using any one of a variety of tools. In the following section, we look at multimedia and hypermedia authoring options. Further information about authoring for the Web is discussed in Chapter 10.

Multimedia and Hypermedia Authoring

As noted in Chapter 3, **multimedia** refers to the use of a variety of media formats (e.g., text, visuals, audio, video) in a single presentation or program, while **hypermedia** refers to a system of multimedia information representation in which the information is stored digitally in interlinked chunks called *nodes*. In popular hypermedia systems, nodes are often referred to as *cards* in a *stack* (like a stack of index cards), *slides* in *presentation* (like an old slide carousel), *pages* in a *book* (like a traditional print book), or, on the Web, *web pages* in a *website.* You can think of each hypermedia node as a card or page on which you can put information of various sorts, and the card/page can be linked to one or more other cards/pages of related information. Unlike a print book, however, nodes in hypermedia are often linked to other nodes in a nonlinear fashion. Today, hypermedia has become commonplace because of its use for commercial reference materials (e.g., CD-ROM encyclopedias) and, of course, the World Wide Web.

The process of creating multimedia/hypermedia products is called *authoring.* When authoring a multimedia or hypermedia product, you can put onto a given card/page various "objects" including text, visuals, other media, and links to other nodes of information, which are often depicted as buttons or highlighted text. Because they work with media as objects, many multimedia and hypermedia authoring systems have the characteristics of what are known as *object-oriented programming systems* **(OOPS)**. In addition, to allow for interaction with users, they often are **event driven**, which means that they respond to events in the computer environment such as when the user clicks on a button or a *hot link* (an active link to another node often appearing as highlighted text), which triggers a *mouse click event.* The system can respond to this event with an action, such as navigating to another card or page.

Because of the growth and popularity of multimedia and hypermedia, many schools now teach students how to author multimedia and hypermedia works. Let's examine some of the options for doing this.

Multimedia/Hypermedia Authoring Tools With multimedia/hypermedia authoring tools, students can create multimedia products with relative ease. Typically, multimedia/hypermedia authoring tools require less technical knowledge than a traditional **programming language** such as BASIC, Logo, C, or Java. A number of options are available for students to author multimedia materials in the classroom.

Presentation software, such as Microsoft *PowerPoint*, though originally designed to create linear presentations, can also be used to create nonlinear multimedia/hypermedia as in the scenario above (see Figure 9–8).

FIGURE 9–8 Presentation software such as *PowerPoint*, shown here, supports hyperlinking and can be used to create nonlinear multimedia/hypermedia products.
Source: Microsoft product screen shot reprinted with permission from Microsoft Corporation.

Using presentation software, students can easily integrate multimedia such as text, visuals, sounds, and even video clips. It is also a simple matter to embed links to Web resources and to create nonlinear links to any slide in a presentation or to another presentation. Using these features, students can create hypermedia projects that include multimedia elements and even simple forms of interaction, such as multiple choice questions, where the nonlinear branching feature can be used to provide feedback.

PEARSON **myeducationkit**™ Go to the Assignments and Activities section of Chapter 9 in MyEducationKit and complete the video activity entitled "Multimedia and Project-Based Learning." As you view the video and answer the corresponding questions, think about how the use of PowerPoint, or other multimedia software, helps to supports the sorts of project-based learning activities presented here.

A number of products specifically designed for multimedia/hypermedia authoring are available for schools. These include Interactive Solutions *MediaWorks*, and Roger Wagner's *HyperStudio*. For more advanced multimedia/hypermedia authoring, there are products such as SumTotal Systems *Toolbook* and Adobe *Director*. *HyperStudio*, now available in a new version from Software MacKiev for both Windows and Macintosh computers, has been a popular hypermedia development tool in schools for many years. *HyperStudio* applications, called stacks, consist of multiple cards that can

contain text objects (known as *fields*), graphic objects (pictures or clip art), and *buttons* (objects used for navigation or to invoke actions). *HyperStudio* also provides a high level of multimedia support for playing digital sounds, movie clips, animations, and special actions such as a function that causes credits to roll up the screen like a movie. *HyperStudio* even contains a special version of the programming language, Logo, called HyperLogo, which can be used to script actions.

Video has become a particularly popular feature of multimedia today. Various forms of digital video have proliferated on the Web and elsewhere, including Apple *QuickTime*, *Windows Media Video*, *RealVideo*, MPEG, and *Flash Video*. While it was once difficult and time-consuming to create and edit video content, it is now easy to record digital video, edit it on the computer, and create digital video files for use on the Web. Popular digital video editing applications include Apple *iMovie* and *Final Cut Pro*, Microsoft *Windows Movie Maker*, Adobe *Premiere*, Ulead *VideoStudio*, and Sony *Vegas Movie Studio*. Using one of these tools, students can create their own video products as either stand-alone multimedia projects or for integration into a multimedia/hypermedia project created using one of the authoring tools discussed here. Websites such as YouTube (http://www.youtube.com), TeacherTube (http://www.teachertube.com), and SchoolTube (http://www.schooltube.com) provide a forum for students and teachers to share videos they create.

PEARSON **myeducationkit**™ Go to the Assignments and Activities section of Chapter 9 in MyEducationKit and complete the activity entitled "Student Created Video Supports Science Teaching and Learning." As you view the video and answer the corresponding questions, think about the skills students are learning and using in this activity, how this activity supports content learning, and how you might envision using such an activity to help student learn content in your classroom.

Because of the popularity of the Internet and World Wide Web, much of the attention in multimedia and hypermedia development today is focused on Web development tools. A number of programs specifically designed for Web content creation are available today. For basic Web authoring, programs such as Adobe *Dreamweaver* and Microsoft *Expression Web* allow students to design web pages in much the same way as creating a document in a word processor. For interactive multimedia on the Web, Adobe *Flash* has emerged as one of the most popular authoring tools. *Flash*, which was originally designed primarily for creating animated visuals on the Web, has become a de facto standard for

FIGURE 9–9   A screen from *Flash*, a popular multimedia authoring tool for the Web.

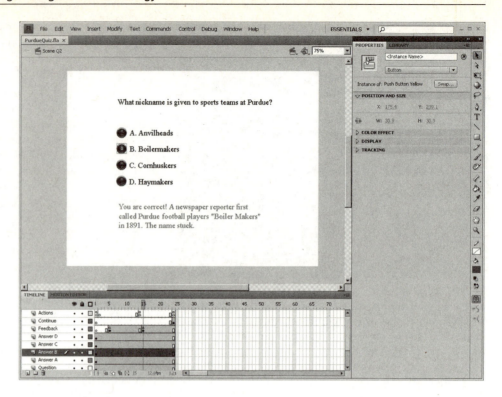

Source: Adobe Systems, Inc. Used with permission.

Web multimedia (see Figure 9–9). It supports text, visuals, animation, audio, and even its own format of digital video. In addition, *Flash* applications can be designed for a high level of interaction with the user, including the ability to customize interaction through its built-in scripting language, ActionScript, which resembles Javascript. Because the *Flash* plug-in is a popular browser add-on, *Flash* content can be viewed using most Web browsers. In Chapter 10, we will look at additional tools and techniques for authoring Web-based materials.

Multimedia/Hypermedia Authoring in the Classroom   As we noted in the discussion of the preceding scenario, the rationale for teaching students to author multimedia/hypermedia is that engaging in this process causes students to be actively involved and often highly motivated. Further, multimedia development is consistent with the view of learning as knowledge construction. To develop a multimedia project, the student must research, evaluate, organize, and present information in a variety of formats. Also, because multimedia/hypermedia is rapidly becoming the norm of the computer world, teaching students to author such materials prepares them for future study and work. In addition, not only is the creation of a hypermedia project a learning activity, but the process and the end product can serve as a form of assessment.

Student development of multimedia/hypermedia offers many opportunities for classroom activities.

↗ *Multimedia/hypermedia projects.* Perhaps the most common application of multimedia/hypermedia authoring in the classroom is student development of projects or reports. Multimedia/hypermedia projects allow students, either individually or in groups, to create reports that summarize a major effort such as a science experiment or interdisciplinary project. Rather than simply writing about it, students can include written work, pictures, sound clips, video, and links to further information. Students can include built-in questions and use hyperlinking to help other students link to further resources to learn more about the content.

↗ *Digital storytelling and fiction.* Multimedia and hypermedia can be used for special forms of writing and storytelling. **Digital storytelling** is the term for a relatively new form of storytelling that relies on short multimedia narratives, often created using a video format in the style of Ken Burns (creator of PBS documentaries *The Civil War* and *Baseball* among others), to tell compelling and often personal stories. Students can also use hypermedia authoring tools to write nonlinear fiction, where the branching capabilities of hypermedia are used to create stories that may have more than one ending.

↗ *Portfolios of student work.* Multimedia/hypermedia authoring tools are excellent for building portfolios of student work in many subjects. Students can assemble and link together many different documents or examples of work.

Problems and Pitfalls

There is evidence that students are motivated by and can benefit educationally from developing multimedia/hypermedia projects (Ayersman, 1996; Chen & McGrath, 2003). However, there are potential shortcomings. Multimedia/hypermedia project development can be very time-consuming in relation to the amount of curriculum coverage. As with other computer tools, students can easily become distracted by the options available and spend more time adding multimedia and creating special effects than learning and presenting the content information. Plus, students do not automatically possess the skills to design and develop multimedia materials that make effective use of visual and instructional design principles. As the teacher, you must plan and prepare in order for hypermedia development to pay dividends in the classroom.

When students develop hypermedia projects, structure and advance planning are important. Two forms of advance planning, often used by computer programmers and instructional designers, are helpful in getting students to think about their projects *before* getting on the computer. These two techniques are storyboarding and flowcharting. Software designers often use storyboarding, a technique originally borrowed from animators and filmmakers. **Storyboarding** is a way of illustrating, on paper, what computer displays or video frames will look like in a finished product. Students can design a *PowerPoint* or *Flash* project, for example, on index cards before making the real thing. They can redesign and rearrange the cards before making the effort to create the project on the computer. Programmers describe the logic of a program using **flowcharting,** a graphical means of representing the flow of a program. The flowchart illustrates where the links go in a hypermedia project or a web page. This can be especially important in a highly linked hypermedia project. Figure 9–10 shows samples of a storyboard card and flowchart for one page of a hypermedia project.

SUMMARY

In this chapter we explored ways that students can use computers for learning, examining two basic categories of computer use: computer as teacher and computer as assistant. Computer as teacher is often labeled computer-assisted instruction (CAI), where the computer delivers instruction to the student. Common forms of CAI include drill and practice, tutorial, simulation, instructional game, and problem solving. Computer as assistant refers to the use of the computer as a productivity tool for common tasks. Typical computer applications in this category include word processor, graphics tool, spreadsheet, database, and presentation software. One special category of

Storyboard Card

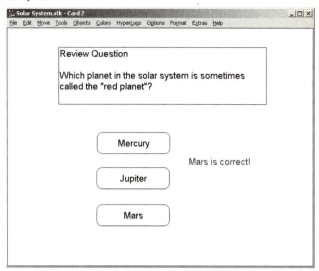

Flowchart of Card

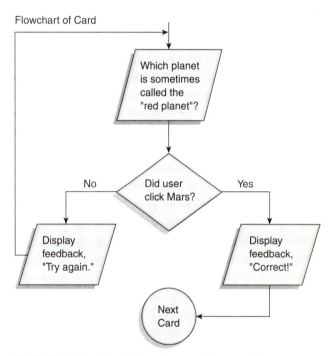

FIGURE 9–10 Sample flowchart and the resulting screen shot for an interaction question in a hypermedia project. *Source: Reprinted with permission from James D. Lehman.*

computer as assistant is when the student assumes the role of the "teacher" by creating multimedia or hypermedia products using an authoring tool. This use of the computer for learning requires that the student both develop content expertise and communicate it to others in an organized fashion.

TECHNOLOGY COORDINATOR'S CORNER

Recall the situation of teacher Bonnie Anderson described at the beginning of this chapter. After pondering her options, Bonnie decided to consult with her school's technology coordinator, Phyllis Parker. Bonnie talked with Phyllis about the range of options for using computers in her classroom.

After listening to Bonnie, Phyllis assured her that she was experiencing a natural progression in her thinking about computers in the classroom. She told Bonnie that many teachers, especially those who began teaching a number of years ago, started out focusing just on computer assisted instruction. She told Bonnie that even though there are many options today, CAI *can* still have a place in the classroom. For example, drill and practice programs can help learners to master basic skills, tutorials can help students to learn concepts or catch up after an absence, and simulations and problem-solving software give learners the opportunity to apply what they have learned to solve problems. However, Phyllis cautioned, CAI should be just one part of an overall instructional strategy in the classroom, and it should not be the only way that technology is used to help student learn.

Phyllis complimented Bonnie for going beyond CAI to have students work with productivity tools such as *Word* and *PowerPoint*. However, she encouraged Bonnie to stretch beyond her comfort zone and think about other productivity software might be of value in her class. She noted that *Inspiration*, for example, is a great graphics tool that can help students to organize their ideas, and *Excel* can be a good tool for managing data and graphing it. Phyllis reminded Bonnie to keep the focus on the learning task rather than on the software, which is just a tool to help achieve the learning goal.

Phyllis also suggested that Bonnie consider having her students try hypermedia authoring using *PowerPoint* or perhaps *HyperStudio*, a hypermedia authoring package available in the school. To get started, Phyllis recommended that Bonnie familiarize herself with the software by going through a tutorial or attending a workshop on it. Next, she advised Bonnie to introduce her students to the software through a warm-up activity such as creating a small project about their hobbies or pets. Phyllis assured Bonnie that the students would be quick to learn. Then, Phyllis suggested that Bonnie consider assigning a larger hypermedia project as part of favorite unit. Phyllis suggested that Bonnie have her students design their projects on note cards before ever going to the computer lab, and when they did begin work in the computer lab, Bonnie should designate student helpers who could assist when questions came up. In this way, Bonnie would be able to spend more of her time helping those students who needed it the most.

Bonnie thanked Phyllis for her advice, and agreed to try the suggestions. She headed back to her classroom with lots of new ideas for using computers to help her students learn.

PEARSON myeducationkit™ To check your comprehension of the content covered in this chapter, go to the MyEducationKit for this book and complete the Study Plan for Chapter 9. Here you will be able to take a chapter quiz, receive feedback on your answers, and then access resources that will enhance your understanding of chapter content.

SUGGESTED RESOURCES

Print Resources

Ayersman, D. (1996). Reviewing the research on hypermedia-based learning. *Journal of Research on Computing in Education, 28*(4), 500–526.

Baker, J. E. & Sugden, S. J. (2003). Spreadsheet in education– the first 25 years. *Spreadsheets in Education, 1*(1), 18–43.

Bayraktar, S. (2001). A meta-analysis of the effectiveness of computer-assisted instruction in science education. *Journal of Research on Technology in Education, 43*(2), 173–188.

Chen, P., & McGrath, D. (2003). Moments of joy: Student engagement and conceptual learning in the design of hypermedia documents. *Journal of Research on Technology in Education, 35*(3), 402–422.

Dynarski, M., Agodini, R., Heaviside, S., Novak, T., Carey, N., Campuzano, L., Means, B., Murphy, R., Penuel, W., Javitz, H., Emery, D. & Sussex, W. (2007). *Effectiveness of Reading and Mathematics Software Products: Findings from the First Student Cohort.* Washington, D.C.: U.S. Department of Education, Institute of Education Sciences.

Frazel, M. (2009). *Digital storytelling guide for educators.* Washington, DC: ISTE Books.

Gee, J. P. (2003). *What video games have to teach us about learning and literacy.* New York: Palgrave/St. Martin's.

Gee, J. P. (2007). *Good video games and good learning: Collected essays on video games, learning and literacy.* New York: Peter Lang Publishing.

Hannafin, R., & Foshay, W. (2008). Computer-based instruction's (CBI) rediscovered role in K-12: An evaluation case study of one high school's use of CBI to improve pass rates on high-stakes tests. *Educational Technology Research and Development, 56*(2), 147–160.

Johnson, R. T., Johnson, D. W., & Stanne, M. B. (1985). Effects of cooperative, competitive, and individualistic goal structures on computer-assisted instruction. *Journal of Educational Psychology, 77*(6), 668–677.

Jonassen, D. H. (2006). *Modeling with technology: Mindtools for conceptual change* (3rd ed.). Upper Saddle River, NJ: Allyn & Bacon.

Kafai, Y. (2008). How computer games help children learn. *Science Education, 92*(2), 378–381.

Ke, F. (2008). Computer game application within alternative classroom goal structures: Cognitive, metacognitive, and affective evaluation. *Educational Technology Research and Development, 56*(5/6), 539–556.

Kirschner, P., & Erkens, G. (2006). Cognitive tools and mindtools for collaborative learning. *Journal of Educational Computing Research, 35*(2), 199–209.

Kulik, C. C., & Kulik, J. A. (1991). Effectiveness of computer-based instruction: An updated analysis. *Computers in Human Behavior, 7,* 75–94.

Kulik, J. A. (2003). *Effects of using instructional technology in elementary and secondary schools: What controlled evaluation studies say.* Arlington, VA: SRI International.

Lee, J. (1999). Effectiveness of computer-based instructional simulation: A meta-analysis. *International Journal of Instructional Media, 26,* 71–85.

Lou, Y., Abrami, P. C., & d'Apollonia, S. (2001). Small group and individual learning with technology: A meta-analysis. *Review of Educational Research, 71*(3), 449–521.

Newby, T. & Lewandowski, J. (2009). *Teaching and learning with Microsoft Office 2007 and Expression Web: A multilevel approach to computer integration (2nd ed.).* Boston, MA: Pearson Education.

Niemiec, R., & Walberg, H. J. (1987). Comparative effects of computer assisted instruction: A synthesis of reviews. *Journal of Educational Computing Research, 3,* 19–37.

O'Bannon, B., Puckett, K., & Rakes, G. (2006). Using technology to support visual learning strategies. *Computers in the Schools, 23*(1/2), 125–137.

Paske, R. (2005). Hypermedia: A brief history and progress report. *Technological Horizons in Education.*

Rieber, L. P. (1994). Computers, graphics, and learning. Madison, WI: Brown & Benchmark.

Roblyer, M. D. (2010). *Integrating educational technology into teaching* (5th ed.). Upper Saddle River, NJ: Pearson Education.

Shelly, G. B., Cashman, T. J., Gunter, R. E. & Gunter, G. A. (2008). *Teachers discovering computers: Integrating technology and digital media in the classroom* (5th ed.). Boston, MA: Thompson Learning.

Taylor, R. (2003). The computer in the school: Tutor, tool, and tutee. *Contemporary Issues in Technology and Teacher Education, 3*(2), 241–252.

Vogel, J., Vogel, D., Cannon-Bowers, J., Bowers, C., & Wright, M. (2006). Computer gaming and interactive simulations for learning: A meta-analysis. *Journal of Educational Computing Research, 34*(3), 229–243.

Electronic Resources

http://www.adobe.com
(Adobe)

http://www.mackiev.com/hyperstudio/
(HyperStudio)

http://www.storycenter.org/memvoice/pages/intro.html
(Center for Digital Storytelling)

http://hypermedia.educ.psu.edu
(Hypermedia Technology Resources: Penn State University)

http://www.successmaker.com
(Pearson SuccessMaker: Integrated Learning System)

http://eduscapes.com/tap/tap4.htm
(Eduscapes | The Teacher Tap: Technology Tools)

http://www.internet4classrooms.com/on-line.htm
(Internet 4 Classrooms: Technology Tutorials)

10 Integration of the Internet to Support Learning

Source: AP Images.

KEY WORDS AND CONCEPTS

Internet
Electronic mail (e-mail)
Listserv
Chat
Instant messaging (IM)
Social networking
World Wide Web
Uniform Resource Locator (URL)

Bookmark
Browser
Podcast
Home page
WebQuest
Blog
Wiki
HTML

CHAPTER OBJECTIVES

After reading and studying this chapter, you will be able to:

↗ Discuss uses of the Internet in education that fall into the categories: (1) communication, (2) information retrieval, (3) information publishing, and (4) application platform.

↗ Describe forms of Internet communication and categorize them as synchronous or asynchronous.

↗ Discuss advantages and limitations of the Internet for information retrieval.

↗ Define WebQuest, and describe the common components of a WebQuest.

↗ Discuss advantages and limitations of using the Internet for information publishing.

↗ Define blog and wiki, and describe examples of how students and teachers can use these tools.

↗ Discuss advantages and limitations of the Internet as an application platform.

↗ Identify and discuss issues related to the use of the Internet in the classroom.

This chapter focuses on using the Internet and World Wide Web as tools to enhance the learning process. Chapter 9 examined the use of the computer as a tool that can be used as a teacher and as an assistant. Here, we extend that notion to include the use of the Internet. In Chapter 11, we will continue our look at technology integration by considering distance education technologies.

 ## INTRODUCTION

Phil Nelson and Linda Johnson are veteran high school social studies teachers. Phil has required students to use the Internet for information retrieval in his American History class for a number of years. Linda, on the other hand, uses e-mail and the Web herself but had never integrated student use of the Internet in her Government and Civics classes. Not long ago, the two teachers chatted about ways that they might make better use of the Internet in their classes.

Phil described to Linda lessons in which he had asked his students to use the Internet to find historical information about topics being discussed in class. As an example, he said he required his students to research various Native American tribes and the conflicts with European settlers when studying the history of the U.S. He found this to be an excellent use of the Internet, and he suggested to Linda that having her students use the Web to retrieve relevant information would be a relatively easy way to meaningfully integrate use of the Internet in her Government and Civics classes. Linda agreed that this sounded like a good way to get started. She also told Phil she was thinking about using e-mail as a way to communicate with local politicians and government officials who might be able to share their expertise with students even if they could not come to the school. Phil, for his part, said that he was happy with what he was doing but would like to have his students take their use of the Internet to "the next level," although he did not know himself just what that might be.

As you read this chapter, think about Phil and Linda and the use of the Internet in the classroom. What are the different ways that the Internet can be used as a tool for learning? What are the advantages and limitations of these uses of the Internet? What important issues should teachers be aware of related to the use of the Internet? What will you, as a future teacher, need to know to make effective use of the Internet in your own classroom?

TECHNOLOGY INTEGRATION PROCESS: PREPARING TO INTEGRATE THE INTERNET IN THE LEARNING EXPERIENCE

As with any instructional activity, when preparing to integrate the Internet in your classroom, begin by developing a plan. Consider the characteristics of your students, and give special attention to their abilities to use the Internet for communication, information retrieval, information publishing, or as an application platform. If your students do not have the necessary skills, you will need to teach them.

In specifying objectives for your students, determine if using the Internet will enhance their ability to meet the objectives. For example, the Internet may provide up-to-date information on the content the students are studying, or it may provide a means for them to communicate with others outside the classroom to meet their objectives. These are good reasons to use the Internet in the classroom. Avoid having students use the Internet just for its own sake or to find information readily available in the classroom. Instead, use it when it adds real value to your lesson.

Of course, in order to use the Internet, the learning environment must include access to a computer with an Internet connection. This could be one computer in the classroom or a computer lab where all students can access the Internet simultaneously. Be aware that the type of connection you have will dictate what you can do. A dial-up connection to the Internet can be slow, limiting what can be done in a class period. Even a relatively fast connection may slow to a crawl if a whole class of students attempts to access the same website at the same time.

If you plan to use websites as part of a lesson, be sure to preview them in advance. Selecting websites for a lesson is no different than selecting any instructional materials (textbooks, videotapes, audio recordings, etc.) as described in Chapter 8. There are countless websites for students and teachers, and we have included a few of our favorite examples in this chapter.

When using the Internet with students, follow the same general process as you would for any lesson implementation: Prepare the instructional materials, prepare the learning environment, prepare the learners, and proceed with the lesson. When preparing your materials, make sure the websites you plan to use are appropriate and available. Check the sites you plan to use a few days before you will use them at the same time of day that you plan to have students access them, if possible. Before the lesson begins, check that the computer or computers are working properly and have functioning Internet access. Schedule the computer laboratory if you plan to have many students access the Internet simultaneously. If you are going to demonstrate the Internet to a class, be sure that the computer projection equipment is working properly and that all students will be able to see the image. Prepare your students for the lesson activity whether it is to be done individually, in small groups, or as a class. Discuss the purpose (objectives) of the lesson, provide written guidelines for the activity, and remind students of proper procedures.

During a lesson involving the Internet, monitor individual students to keep them on task and to be sure that they are following the acceptable use guidelines for your school (see "Toolbox: Acceptable Use Policies" on page 205). Watch for students who might wander off into cyberspace; students can be easily distracted and end up visiting off-task or inappropriate sites when using the Internet.

Of course, following a lesson, you and your students should take time to evaluate how the Internet worked (or didn't work) within the lesson. You need to determine if the students learned from the experience. If the lesson was less successful than expected, think of ways in which you could improve on your use of the Internet in the future.

Have realistic expectations of the Internet. It will not answer all questions and solve all learning problems. The Internet is a learning tool (admittedly a powerful one), and like all tools, it has advantages and limitations. You cannot just turn students loose and hope for the best.

WHAT IS THE INTERNET AND HOW CAN IT BE USED?

Think about the library in your school or community. On its shelves, you can find a large collection of information resources of various types: books, reference collections such as encyclopedias, magazines, newspapers, and often other media such as music CDs and videos. A library contains a substantial collection of accumulated knowledge and information that has been brought to one location where you can browse through it, search for items of interest, and explore topics of interest to you.

In some ways, the Internet is like a vast library. The Internet brings information resources including text, pictures, sounds, and video from all over the world into your classroom. As in a library, you can browse through available information resources to pick and choose what you need to learn about a topic of interest or to create lessons and learning experiences for your students. The Internet is more than just a repository of information, however. It is also a communications tool that gives you and your students the capability to interact and collaborate with others around the world; a tool for information publishing that your students can use to make their own

materials available to others; and an application platform from which you can do word processing, edit images, develop spreadsheets for doing calculations, or do other kinds of work. This power and versatility make the Internet a truly revolutionary tool for learning.

As noted in Chapter 3, the **Internet** is a vast collection of computer networks that connects millions of computers and tens of millions of people around the world. The Internet is also referred to as the "Net," the "Information Superhighway," and "cyberspace." Today, almost all schools, most classrooms, and most homes in the United States are connected to the Internet.

A personal computer can access the Internet in various ways including through a wired network connection to a LAN, a wireless connection to a networked access point, a dial-up connection over telephone lines, or an always-on connection through a cable TV network or a telephone digital subscriber line (DSL). Your computer must be equipped with an appropriate wired or wireless network card to connect to the Internet via a network. To make a connection over telephone or TV cable lines, your computer must use a **modem** (short for modulator/demodulator), which converts your computer's digital information into a form suitable for transmission over the telephone or cable wires and converts incoming signals back into digital format for your computer.

The many different kinds of computers on the Internet communicate with one another by means of a standard communications *protocol* (a set of common rules) known as **TCP/IP** (Transmission Control Protocol/Internet Protocol). Every computer on the Internet has a unique address, expressed in numeric form, called its *IP address*. Computers communicate with other computers on the Internet by sending information to their IP addresses. Special computers called *domain name servers* (DNSs) act like the phone books of the Internet, automatically translating familiar written Internet addresses (www.yahoo.com) into their corresponding IP addresses (209.131.36.158). Information is sent through the Internet in **packets** (see Figure 10–1), little bundles of information. The packets of an individual message are sent along any available path through cyberspace and then reassembled when they arrive at their destination. A network device called a **router** regulates traffic on the Internet and determines the most efficient route for each packet. So, when you send an e-mail message, for example, the message is broken into packets, sent across your local area network (LAN) to a router, which then shunts the packets to their destination. Packets may travel through many computer networks on their journey, but because they travel at the speed of electricity the journey usually takes only seconds.

You and your students can use the Internet in a wide variety of ways. The most common uses can be grouped into four categories: communication, information retrieval,

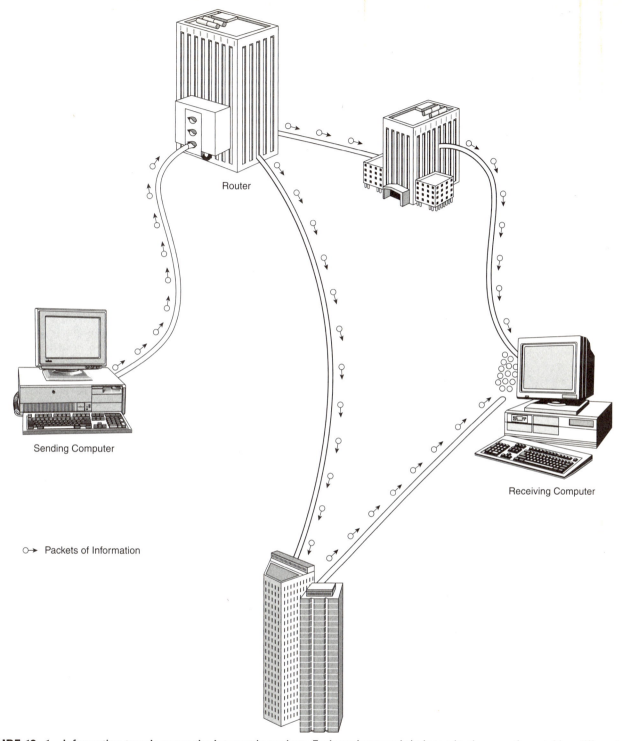

Router

Sending Computer

O→   Packets of Information

Receiving Computer

FIGURE 10–1   Information travels across the Internet in packets. Each packet travels independently, sometimes taking different paths, from one computer to another. The packets are reassembled at their destination.

information publishing, and application platform. We introduce them here and discuss them at length in the remainder of this chapter.

Communication. The Internet allows individuals to easily communicate with one another in various ways. Electronic mail (e-mail) is the most widely used service

on the Internet. Instant messaging (IM) is another popular form of Internet communication. Anyone with a computer connected to the Internet can instantly communicate with anyone else in the world who is also connected. Students can communicate with other students as well as with the teacher and individuals outside of the school to accomplish educational objectives.

Information Retrieval. There is a wealth of interesting and varied information available on the Internet for students and teachers. Most of this information is up-to-date, usually free of charge, and can be accessed in seconds. The Web has become a key information resource, perhaps *the* key information resource, on almost every topic imaginable.

Information Publishing. You and your students can publish material on the Internet. Publishing on the Internet is quicker and cheaper than publishing in traditional ways such as by reproducing a document with a copying machine or printing press and sending the copies through the mail. Students' work can, with parental approval, be posted on the Internet for the world to see.

Application Platform. Increasingly, the Internet is being seen as a platform for doing work of all types. Computer programs such as word processors, spreadsheets, and presentation software are now available on the Internet. These tools allow teachers and students to do work of all kinds as described in Chapters 3 and 8.

INTERNET APPLICATIONS FOR COMMUNICATION

One valuable aspect of the Internet is its capacity to facilitate human interaction and the exchange of data and ideas. You and your students can communicate via the Internet with other students, teachers, and experts in various fields in your community or around the world. Three common categories of Internet communication are e-mail and mailing lists, instant messaging and chat, and social networking. Communication by e-mail is analogous to writing a letter to one person. Mailing lists, also called listservs, are like bulk mailings. While e-mail is an **asynchronous** (not occurring at the same time) form of communication, instant messaging and chat support **synchronous** (occurring at the same time) communication. Social networking refers to various Internet applications that allow individuals to share information and communicate with others to form online communities. Social networking websites provide various communication tools, often both asynchronous and synchronous. We look here at each of these types of communication in more detail.

E-Mail and Mailing Lists

Any computer-stored communication sent from one individual or group to another over a computer network is called **electronic mail (e-mail)**. Today, most individuals have at least one unique e-mail address (see Figures 10–2 and 10–3). You can exchange e-mail with another teacher or student in your school or with a scientist in Antarctica. Because e-mail is transmitted over network lines, it reaches its destination in seconds, rather than in the days required for postal mail, even if that destination is halfway around the world. Like postal mail, e-mail waits in a

Author	E-mail Address
Tim Newby	newby@purdue.edu
Don Stepich	dstepich@boisestate.edu
Jim Lehman	lehman@purdue.edu
Jim Russell	jrussell@purdue.edu
Anne Leftwich	aleftwic@indiana.edu

FIGURE 10–2   The e-mail addresses of the authors of this text.

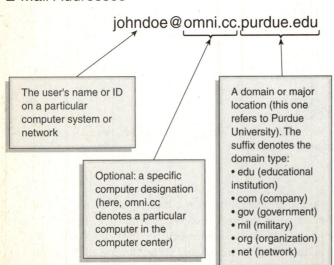

E-Mail Addresses

johndoe @ omni.cc.purdue.edu

The user's name or ID on a particular computer system or network

Optional: a specific computer designation (here, omni.cc denotes a particular computer in the computer center)

A domain or major location (this one refers to Purdue University). The suffix denotes the domain type:
• edu (educational institution)
• com (company)
• gov (government)
• mil (military)
• org (organization)
• net (network)

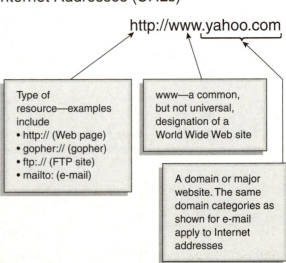

Internet Addresses (URLs)

http://www.yahoo.com

Type of resource—examples include
• http:// (Web page)
• gopher:// (gopher)
• ftp:.// (FTP site)
• mailto: (e-mail)

www—a common, but not universal, designation of a World Wide Web site

A domain or major website. The same domain categories as shown for e-mail apply to Internet addresses

FIGURE 10–3   Finding your way in cyberspace: the anatomy of e-mail addresses and URLs.

mailbox for the recipient to read it; so, it is an asynchronous form of communication. E-mail is usually a person-to-person communication, and you can provide "enclosures" (called **attachments**) as you would in a letter. In addition, you can send the same message to multiple individuals as you would copies of a letter sent by the postal service. Using e-mail, you and your students can communicate with one another as well as exchange information with people all over the world. Popular programs for composing, sending, and receiving e-mail include Microsoft *Outlook* and *Outlook Express*, Apple *Mail*, and Mozilla *Thunderbird* as well as the webmail clients associated with Web-based services such as *Hotmail, Gmail,* and *Yahoo!*. For K-12 students, Web-based programs such as Gaggle (www.gaggle.net) and ePals (www.epals.com) provide e-mail access but with teacher monitoring features for safety.

Mailing lists use e-mail to deliver topic-specific information to your computer on a regular basis. They are like electronic magazines. See Figure 10–4 for a small sample of mailing lists available for teachers and students. When a mailing list receives a message, a copy of the message is sent to everyone on the mailing list. In most cases, to subscribe to a mailing list, all you have to do is send an e-mail message to the **listserv** (the computer that controls, sorts, and distributes incoming information on a particular topic) with the word "subscribe," the name of the list to which you wish to subscribe, and your name (not your e-mail address) in the body of the e-mail. After you send the message, you will receive a confirmation from the listserv that you are subscribed; keep the welcome message that you receive because it will contain information about the list and how to unsubscribe if you decide to opt out later. You can distribute your own message to list subscribers by "posting" a message (sending an e-mail) to the list.

Instant Messaging and Chat

Whereas e-mail and newsgroups support asynchronous communication, **instant messaging (IM)** allows two users on the Internet to synchronously communicate by typing messages back and forth to one another in real time. IM resembles a telephone conversation, except that the conversation in most cases is written rather than spoken. However, recent developments in IM software permit audio and video communication as well as textual communication. Whereas it is possible to communicate with any other user who is online at the same time and using the same or compatible instant messaging software, most IM users maintain a list of particular users, or buddies, with whom they regularly communicate. Common instant messaging programs include *AOL Instant Messenger (AIM), Jabber, EBuddy,* and *Yahoo! Messenger.*

Chat, like instant messaging, is a form of synchronous communication in which users communicate mainly by typing messages to one another. However, in a chat room, you and your students can "chat" with one person or many people at the same time. Various software programs for Internet chat are available including the software built into popular course management systems such as *Blackboard, Moodle,* and *Angel*. Some chat software uses *avatars,* pictures that represent the individuals chatting. Like e-mail lists, chat rooms tend to be topic specific (see Figure 10–5). Although some people think chat is a time-consuming and confusing way to communicate, most younger people love it. It allows people who are far apart to communicate with each other in real time.

Because e-mail, instant messaging, and chat usually lack the cues of face-to-face conversation, conventions have been developed for conveying emotion via text.

List Resource	Internet Address	Description
Community Learning Network	http://www.cln.org/lists/home.html	Good source for locating educational mailing lists
The Teacher's Guide	http://www.theteachersguide.com/listservs.html	Reference for dozens of educationally oriented mailing lists
ACSOFT-L	listserv@wuvmd.wustl.edu	Educational software discussion
AERA-C	listserv@asu.edu	AERA Division C: Learning and Instruction
ECENET-L	listserv@postoffice.cso.uiuc.edu	Early childhood education discussion
EDINFO	listproc@inet.ed.gov	Updates from the U.S. Department of Education
EDNET	listproc@nic.umass.edu	Discussions about a variety of educational topics
EDTECH	listserv@msu.edu	Educational technology discussion
TEACHNET	listserv@byu.edu	Exchange of ideas, articles, research, experiences, and questions about teaching
WWWEDU	listproc@kudzu.cnidr.org	The World Wide Web in Education

FIGURE 10–4 Sample mailing lists for teachers and students.

Name	Web Address	Description
About.com	http://k6educators.about.com/mpchat.htm	Chat room for elementary school educators
Big Pond	http://bigpond.com/chat/rooms/default.asp	Chat rooms on a wide variety of topics
Dave's ESL Café for Students and Teachers	http://host8.123flashchat.com/eslcafe/	Chat room about English as a second language
Tapped In	http://tappedin.org	An international community of education professionals
Teachers.Net Teacher Chatboard	http://www.teachers.net/chatboard/	Dedicated to open discourse among teachers of the world

FIGURE 10–5   Examples and sources of chat rooms for teachers and students.

:-)	happy	:-D	laughing
:-(	sad	;-)	a wink
:'-(	crying	:-I	indifferent
:-X	writer's lips are sealed	:-O	surprised
:-/	skeptical or confused	:-&	tongue tied
BBFN	bye bye for now	BTW	by the way
FYI	for your information	<G>	grinning
IMHO	in my humble opinion	JK	just kidding
LOL	laughing out loud	ROF	rolling on the floor
TTYL	talk to you later	TY	thank you

FIGURE 10–6   Emoticons and Message Acronyms.

Emoticons are "e-mail body language" and are usually combinations of characteristics that resemble human faces when turned sideways (see Figure 10–6). They are used to indicate the writer's feelings because we can't see the writer or hear voice inflection in chat rooms or over e-mail. Acronyms are also commonly used in e-mail and instant messaging messages to convey emotion or simply as brief shortcuts for common expressions.

Social Networking

Social networking is the term for various Internet applications that allow individuals to share information and interests in an online community. The forms of Internet

Toolbox: Netiquette

The informal rules for appropriate etiquette on the Internet are often referred to as **netiquette**. The following guidelines apply anytime you or your students are using the Internet to send e-mail or other text messages (see Figure 10–7):

↗ Keep your message short and simple. Try to limit your message to *one* screen. Make it brief, descriptive, and to the point.

↗ Identify yourself as sender. Include your name, school's postal address, and school Internet address. Do not use your or your students' home addresses and telephone numbers.

↗ When replying to a message, include the pertinent portions of the original message.

↗ Do not write anything you would not want someone other than the receiver to read. E-mail can be intercepted and/or forwarded.

↗ Check spelling, grammar, and punctuation but be tolerant of others' language usage. In the world of Internet communication, spelling and grammar are often very informal.

↗ Avoid using all CAPITAL letters. It is the Internet equivalent of shouting.

↗ When joining a listserv or chat room, take some time to get acquainted with the topics and typical pattern of postings before contributing your own message. If a **FAQ** (frequently asked questions) file is available, read it. Consider yourself a guest on the system just as if you were in someone's home. In exchange for help and information you receive, be willing to answer questions and to share your resources.

↗ Be sensitive to other people. Treat them with respect and courtesy, especially in reference to social, cultural, and ethnic differences.

↗ Be careful with humor. When online, the reader does not have the benefit of your facial expressions, body language, or tone of voice and may misinterpret your comment. Use emoticons if you want to clarify the intention of your message (see Figure 10–6).

↗ Be certain that your students are aware of netiquette before they use the Internet.

(Continued)

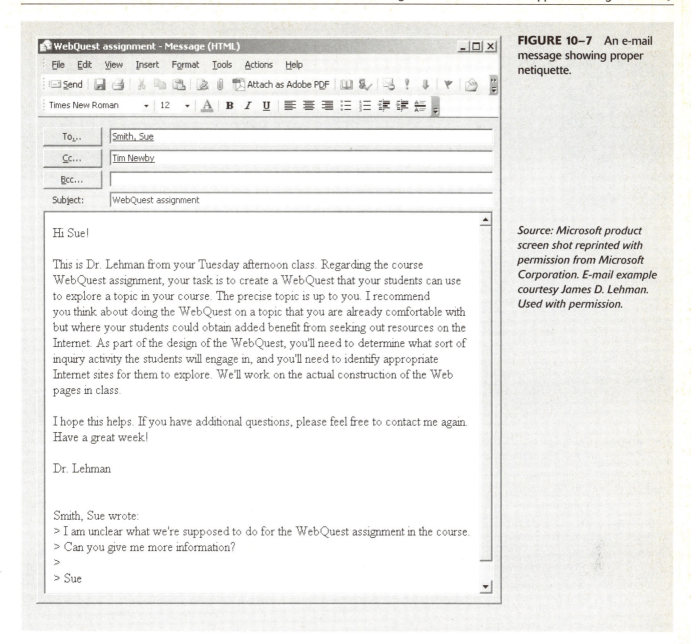

FIGURE 10–7   An e-mail message showing proper netiquette.

Source: Microsoft product screen shot reprinted with permission from Microsoft Corporation. E-mail example courtesy James D. Lehman. Used with permission.

communication we have already discussed such as e-mail, instant messaging, and chat can be used for social networking. However, many websites have arisen that allow individuals to share writing, photos, activities, and interests with other people. These are considered **Web 2.0 technologies**, an umbrella term for second-generation Web technologies that allow for communication and collaboration of people in Web-based communities. In addition to social networking, blogs, wikis, and Web applications discussed later in this chapter fall into this category. Among the most popular of the social networking sites are MySpace (www.myspace.com), Facebook (www.facebook.com), and Xanga (www.xanga.com) (see Figure 10–8). According to the Pew Internet and American Life Project (Lenhart & Madden, 2007), more than half of American youth ages 12–17 use online

social networking sites. Young people predominantly use the sites as a way of keeping in touch with friends. Girls tend to use social networking sites as places to reinforce pre-existing friendships, while boys often use the sites for flirting and making new friends.

Social networking sites allow individuals to create profiles that contain personal information and photos. Individuals can link to the profiles of other users in the online environment who share common interests and designate particular individuals as "friends." Through these linkages, one can be in contact with dozens to hundreds of friends and can make information openly available to all of the users of the system. While the sites can be fun and engaging forums for keeping in touch with others, teachers should help students be aware of the risks of such sites. Inappropriate behavior such as

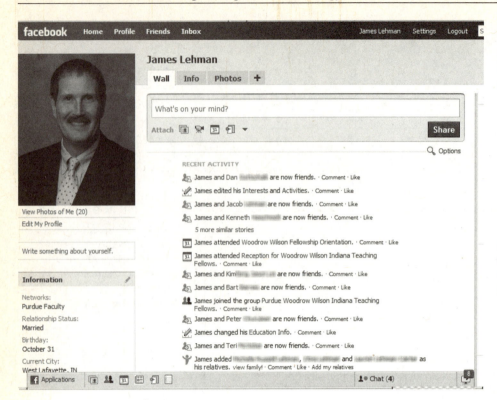

FIGURE 10–8 Social networking sites like Facebook (shown here) allow people to share information and develop online communities.

Source: Facebook. Used with permission. Profile page courtesy of James Lehman. Used with permission.

cyberbullying and risky sexual contacts may occur in these environments. In addition, the personal information that students disclose online is actually public and could be potentially damaging (e.g., a photo of underaged alcohol consumption could lead to prosecution). While most social networking is being discouraged in the school environment because it lacks an overt educational purpose, some attempts are being made to capitalize on students' interest in social networking for education. For example, Elgg.net (www.elgg.net/) is a new social networking site designed to support learning.

> **PEARSON myeducationkit**™ To learn more about social networking go to the Video Examples section of Chapter 10 and watch the video tutorial entitled "Social Networking." As you watch the video, consider possible educational applications of social networking.

Others

While much Internet communication is text-based, graphics, sound, and video can also be sent over the Internet. With a microphone and speakers connected to your computer you can communicate with someone whose computer is similarly equipped as you would during a telephone conversation and not have to pay long distance toll charges. Internet telephony, also called voice over IP (VoIP), is becoming increasingly popular, and a number of companies now offer services. Skype (www.skype.com/) is one of the most popular. Add an inexpensive camera to

each of your systems, and you have a "video phone" that can support the transmission of audio and video.

Another form of communication on the Internet is peer-to-peer (P2P) networking. In peer-to-peer networking, individual computers on the Internet connect directly with one another, without the need for a server, to exchange information. While P2P has gotten a lot of negative press because of its association with the illegal sharing of music files, the technology has great potential for enhancing Internet communication. Programs such as *Groove Virtual Office* from Groove Networks (www.groove.net) use P2P technology to allow individuals or groups to share data and work collaboratively on projects without the need for a central server to store documents and manage the communication.

Classroom Applications

Learning experiences can be enhanced in a number of ways through the communication applications of the Internet. Communicating with other individuals and groups allows for the exchange of ideas, insights, and cultures. The following are typical applications of the Internet for communication.

↗ Students communicate with e-mail "e-pals" or electronic pen pals to exchange ideas, cultures, and to learn about and from each other. This might occur between two 9-year-olds in different states or different countries, or might occur between a college preservice teacher and a group of fifth-grade students.

Go to the Assignments and Activities section of Chapter 10 in MyEducationKit and complete the activity entitled "Email in the Classroom." As you view this video, think about the strategies this teacher uses to have her students use e-mail to communicate.

↗ Student teachers use live chat discussions to discuss problems they are encountering within their current classroom settings with other student teachers or practicing teachers who have been through that experience.

↗ An e-mail list is used by the members of the Spanish club or an afterschool service organization to disseminate information rapidly to all members. For example, the next meeting time, topic of discussion, advance reading, and reflective questions could be posted on the Spanish club's listserv to allow all members to quickly receive the relevant information and make comments back to the listserv as they deem necessary.

↗ Teachers participate in a learning community using an e-mail list that allows them to explore with colleagues ways to creatively use technology to improve student learning.

↗ An Internet-based "video phone" session might be used to link a scientist in a local research laboratory with a science class or science club in your school. Have the students prepare questions ahead of time to pose to the scientist during the video conference.

INTERNET APPLICATIONS FOR INFORMATION RETRIEVAL

Both students and teachers can access valuable resources and a wealth of up-to-date information on the Internet. You are no longer limited to textbooks and resources in the library. Today you and your students have access to the latest, most up-to-date information located far beyond the walls of the schools building (see Figure 10–9). Like the library, as we discussed at the beginning of the chapter, the Internet makes available information resources from around the world. The information is available on the Web in the form of databases, documents, government information, online bibliographies, publications, videos, computer software, and more.

The **World Wide Web** (usually referred to simply as WWW or the Web) is a part of the Internet. Countless information resources (including text, images, sound, video, and even virtual reality) are stored on computers

Funbrain
http://www.funbrain.com

NASA
http://www.nasa.gov

FIGURE 10–9 Websites of interest to teachers and students for information retrieval from the Internet.

Online Frog Dissection
http://curry.edschool.virginia.edu/go/frog

Discovery School
http://school.discovery.com/

around the world in documents called **Web pages**. A **website** is a collection of Web pages maintained by a school, university, government agency, company, or individual. A **home page** is the first or main page in a website. A **Web server** is a computer connected to the Internet that makes Web pages and websites available to other computers.

Each Web page, and individually accessible component of a Web page, has a unique Internet address called a **Uniform Resource Locator (URL).** See Figure 10–3 for the components of a URL. Web pages are hypertext documents, which means they contain links (often highlighted text) that connect to other pages on the Web. Hypertext allows you to quickly move from one Web page or website to another.

A software program that allows you to move around the Web and locate specific information is a Web browser. A **browser** allows you and your students to navigate through information on the Web. Popular browsers include Microsoft *Internet Explorer,* Apple *Safari,* Mozilla *Foxfire,* and *Opera.* Most browsers are available free of charge or at low cost on the Web, and one or more is most likely already installed on your home or school computer.

While exploring the Web, you may find sites of interest and wish to return to them in the future without having to remember where you were or to retrace your path. A **bookmark** allows you to return to interesting sites without having to remember and retype the URL. Browsers allow you to create, store, organize, and retrieve bookmarks. The computer stores the website address and lets you easily recall it using a menu. Bookmarks may also be filed and divided into many different file folders for easier access if you have a lot of them. In school, you can speed access to the online resources you want students to use by setting up a folder of bookmarks in advance.

Another browser feature is image capture, which allows you and your students to "copy" images from others' Web pages. On a Windows machine, place the mouse cursor over the desired image and right-click; on a Macintosh, hold down the mouse button. A pop-up menu will appear with an option to save the image to your computer. A reminder about copyright is in order here. *Assume that all images on the Internet are copyrighted!* Although a number of websites make clip art or photographs available free of charge for certain purposes,

you should assume that you will need to obtain permission to use any image you download from the Internet—even for educational purposes (review the discussion on copyright in Chapter 8).

Plug-ins allow you and your students to display or play certain types of files on the Internet. A plug-in performs tasks the Web browser cannot perform on its own. You must install the appropriate plug-in before you can work with that particular file. For example, Adobe System's *Acrobat Reader* lets you view and print Portable Document Format (PDF) files. PDF files are an Internet standard for cross-platform distribution of formatted documents. *Shockwave* and *Flash* plug-ins let you view certain kinds of animations and multimedia via your Web browser. *Acrobat Reader* as well as *Shockwave* and *Flash* plug-ins are available free of charge at www.adobe.com/downloads/. In order to view some videos on the Web, you may need the *Quick Time* plug-in (www.apple.com/quicktime) or *RealPlayer* plug-in (www.real.com). There are literally hundreds of plug-ins available; plug-ins are often accessible through your browser's website or from specific product vendors.

Increasingly, Web resources are moving beyond just text and pictures to include multimedia such as audio and video. In education, there is growing interest in the use of podcasts. A **podcast** is a digital media file, most often audio, distributed via the Internet for playback on a portable media player, such as Apple's iPod, or a computer. Video podcasts, or *vodcasts*, are also available. Teachers can create podcasts of lectures or other content (e.g., foreign language pronunciation exercises) that students can download to study for an exam or do homework. You can find podcasts on many topics at sites such as Apple's iTunes Store (www.apple.com/itunes/store/podcasts.html), Podcast Alley (www.podcastalley.com/), and Podcast.net (www.podcast.net). The Education Podcast Network (www.epnweb.org) is a collection of podcasts on many subjects of interest to teachers and students.

Likewise, video is a very popular feature of the Internet today. While video is available on many sites on the Internet, YouTube (www.youtube.com) has become an enormously popular site that makes user-created videos available to others. YouTube has an area dedicated to K-12 education (www.youtube.com/group/K12), and TeacherTube (www.teachertube.com) is a newer site similar to YouTube that focuses on videos for teachers and education (see Figure 10–10).

Because the information resources available on the Internet are vast and often ill-structured, students should be provided with guidance and structure to make effective use of them. Students need to be able to use search engines to locate relevant information (see "Toolbox: Using Search Engines", on page 194). In addition, teachers can shape and guide

FIGURE 10–10 Users of YouTube, the popular website, have created a section devoted to K-12 education where teachers and students ages 13 and older can post their videos (http://www .youtube.com/group/K12).

Source: Google, Inc. Used with permission.

students' use of online resources by creating activities such as online scavenger hunts and WebQuests. Evaluating the quality of websites is discussed later in this chapter (see "Toolbox: Evaluating the Quality of Websites" on page 206).

There are also search engines, or subsets of existing search engines, that are specifically designed for use by children. These include Ask for Kids (www.askkids. com), KidsClick! (www.kidsclick.com), and Yahoo! Kids (kids.yahoo.com). These sites filter out websites that might have content inappropriate for children.

For more information about how to search the Internet, visit the listed search engines and view the guidelines associated with each. You can also visit any of a number of sites that provide information about how to use search engines and locate information on the Web, including Search Engine Watch (www.searchenginewatch. com/), Search Engine Showdown (www.searchengineshowdown.com/), and the UC Berkeley Library guide to the best search engines (www.lib.berkeley.edu/ TeachingLib/Guides/Internet/SearchEngines.html).

Scavenger Hunts

Scavenger hunts are one popular way to teach students how to find and use information resources available on the Internet. Like their real-life counterparts, online scavenger hunts involve searching for specific items. But rather

than searching in the real world, students search for items of information on the Web. Elementary students might search for facts about specific animals in the rain forest, middle school social studies students might search for information about American presidents, or high school students might investigate issues facing Native Americans.

Scavenger hunts are structured around a series of questions or searching tasks. To help the students locate information, the URLs for specific, relevant websites are provided by the teacher or scavenger hunt designer. The students must search through those sites to find the information needed to answer the questions or complete the tasks. Scavenger hunts can be fun and informative while helping students to practice their Web searching skills. They can be adapted to almost any grade level or curriculum area. See Figure 10–11 for some sites about scavenger hunts.

PEARSON
myeducationkit™ Go to the Assignments and Activities section of Chapter 10 in MyEducationKit and complete the activity entitled "Web Site Supports Learning." As you view this video, think about how the website in this example supports learning, and how you could use websites to support learning in your own classroom.

Toolbox: Using Search Engines

Search engines are websites designed to help people locate information of interest on the Internet. Search engines do not search the Internet in real time. Instead, each search engine maintains a database of information accumulated from the Internet. When you use a search engine and submit a query, the database is searched to yield web pages, and sometimes other sources of information (e.g., images), that fit the search criteria. These are returned as a list of "hits," rank-ordered according to criteria applied by the search engine. Different search engines maintain different databases of information. They apply different criteria to rank-order the list of potential sites. As a result, even though Google is the #1 search engine, it is a good idea to use a variety of search engines when you are looking for information, because different search engines will give you different results.

Although the specifics of searching for information vary from engine to engine, basic techniques apply across most. Search engines allow you to search for topics using key words. Pick relevant nouns or proper names as key words. Avoid broad terms that will return too many hits (e.g., education, computer), and omit common words (e.g., a, an, the). Use several key words together to narrow your search (e.g., lesson, biology, plant, elementary); this is equivalent to using the Boolean (logical) AND operator. Many search engines allow the Boolean operator OR to be used with key words to broaden searches (e.g., botany OR zoology). When you want to search for a specific term or phrase, enclose it in quotes (e.g., "lesson plan", "American history"). Many search engines allow you to include key terms with + and exclude other terms with a – (e.g., the key terms "recipe, cookie, +oatmeal, –raisin" would yield a search for cookie recipes containing oatmeal but not raisins).

Search Engine	URL
AllTheWeb	www.alltheweb.com
Ask	www.ask.com
Bing	www.bing.com
Dogpile*	www.dogpile.com
Google	www.google.com
Hotbot	www.hotbot.com
Live Search	www.live.com
Metacrawler*	www.metacrawler.com
Vivisimo	vivisimo.com
Yahoo!	www.yahoo.com

*meta-search engine, which returns results from more than one search engine.

Site	Web Address	Description
Education World	www.education-world.com/a_curr/curr113.shtml	Curriculum resources related to Internet scavenger hunts
LT Technologies Internet Hunts	hwww.lttechno.com/links/hunts.html	Information about scavenger hunts and examples in various curriculum areas
Internet Hunts by Cindy O'Hora	homepage.mac.com/cohora/ext/internethunts.html	A collection of Internet scavenger hunts arranged by curriculum areas
Vicki Blackwell's Internet Guide for Educators	www.vickiblackwell.com/hunts.html	A collection of Internet scavenger hunts on various topics for kids

FIGURE 10–11 Scavenger Hunt Websites.

WebQuests

WebQuests are inquiry-oriented activities in which some or all of the information used by learners is drawn from resources on the Web (see Figure 10–12). This approach was developed by Bernie Dodge and Tom March at San Diego State University, and it has become one of the most popular ways of using the Web in education. WebQuests ordinarily contain several specific components:

↗ Introduction—introduces the activity, sets the stage, and provides basic background information to engage the learner

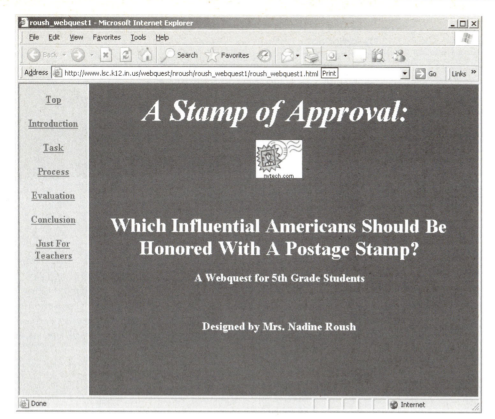

FIGURE 10–12   A screen from a WebQuest, a popular way for learners to use the Internet for inquiry-based learning in the classroom.

Reprinted with permission from Nadine Roush.

↗ Task—describes what the learner is to do and identifies the culminating performance or end product of the activity

↗ Process—outlines the steps the learner is to follow, identifies the resources to be used including specific websites, and provides guidance or scaffolding to assist the learner

↗ Evaluation—describes the evaluation criteria to be applied to the activity, often in the form of a rubric

↗ Conclusion—provides closure for the WebQuest and encourages the learner to reflect on the activity

↗ Teacher Page—provides key information about the WebQuest for other teachers (e.g., target learners, standards addressed, suggestions for implementation)

WebQuests are often designed as group activities with different students assuming different roles in the activity. This approach not only encourages cooperative learning but motivates the learners by giving them realistic scenarios as a context for the activity; a review of research on WebQuests suggests they may have a positive impact on collaborative working skills and learner attitudes (Abbitt & Ophus, 2008). The best WebQuests focus on developing students' higher-order thinking skills using Internet resources. Like scavenger hunts, WebQuests are available for or can be developed for almost any grade level or curriculum area.

See Figure 10–13 for some sites that have example WebQuests.

Consider developing a WebQuest if you will have the opportunity to help students learn about a particular topic in a subject area and grade level of your choice. After studying about WebQuests, design a WebQuest that the students could use to learn about the topic. Determine the introduction, task, process, evaluation, conclusion, and teacher page information. Identify at least three to five online resources that students could use during the WebQuest to obtain information about your topic. Once you have designed your WebQuest, consider actually developing it by using Web authoring software. See the section on Internet Applications for Information Publishing which follows for more information about Web authoring.

PEARSON myeducationkit™ Go to the Assignments and Activities section of Chapter 10 in MyEducationKit and complete the following activities: "Promoting Innovative Thinking, Creativity, and Collaboration through WebQuests," "Using the Web to Support Learning," and "Technology-Supported." Consider how each of these teachers uses a WebQuest to promote student learning of content.

Site	Web Address	Description
The WebQuest portal	webquest.org	Up-to-date news and information about WebQuests and a matrix of examples by grade level and curriculum area
BestWebQuests.com	bestwebquests.com/	A collection of the best WebQuests maintained by Tom March, one of the developers of the approach
WebQuest Direct	www.webquestdirect.com.au/	A searchable directory of thousands of teacher-reviewed and -rated Web-Quests
Teacher Tap	eduscapes.com/tap/topic4.htm	Links to information about WebQuests and collections of them

FIGURE 10–13 WebQuest Resources.

Classroom Applications

Information retrieval from the Internet offers exciting applications within all classrooms. With access to so much information, you and your students will need to develop skills to be able to effectively wade through all of the possibilities, find that which is most relevant, and determine its quality. Here are just a few ideas of how you can use access to this unlimited information to enhance students' learning experiences:

↗ Conduct online research using databases and other online resources. You and your students can access information on almost any topic, from a variety of sources, very quickly. Finding huge amounts of information on topics such as whales, tax laws, soccer rules, trigonometry equations, and kindergarten safety is no longer difficult. Additionally, this information frequently includes visuals, audio, and other media formats beyond text.

↗ Monitor current events through online newspapers and magazines. Access to the Internet allows you and your students to get up-to-the-minute information on critical news stories and read it from a variety of sources. Students can read what their local newspapers have to say about a current event and immediately compare that with what is being written by the national newspapers and even those from countries around the world.

↗ Use scavenger hunts or WebQuests to direct students' online explorations of particular aspects of the curriculum. A wide variety of existing activities are already available, and it is easy to develop your own.

↗ Access Web-based archives of teaching methods, instructional strategies, and lesson plans. Finding information on what to teach and how to teach is now easy. From hands-on science experiments to drama techniques, lesson plans are available to give ideas to both new and experienced teachers.

PEARSON **myeducationkit** Go to the Assignments and Activities section of Chapter 10 in MyEducationKit and complete the activity entitled "Discovering Online Resources." As you explore the website, look for resources you can use in planning instructional activities for your students.

↗ Retrieve information on possible job opportunities. Information on potential employment, contact personnel, and how to prepare (e.g., résumé development) for job interviews is readily available.

INTERNET APPLICATIONS FOR INFORMATION PUBLISHING

Everyone likes to see his/her writings in "print." You and your students can publish material on the Internet. The Internet is a quick and inexpensive method for sharing writing, images, and other content. Students' short stories, poems, science projects, or art work can, with parental approval, be posted on the Internet for the world to see. You can also share your teaching ideas with others in your discipline.

The explosive growth of the World Wide Web has led to widespread interest in Web page authoring and other forms of Web publishing in K–12 schools. Most schools now have their own home pages, and many individuals have personal home pages or blogs to present information about themselves and their interests. Wikis can be used for collaborative construction of documents or projects. A student's hypermedia project that once may have been seen only by her teacher and classmates may now be available for viewing by almost anyone. Realistically, the world will probably not beat an electronic path to every school Web page in cyberspace. However, the mere idea that the world can see their work is motivating to students, and making students' work available

Toolbox: HTML, the Language of the Web

HTML, Hypertext Markup Language, is the underlying "language" of all Web pages. Each Web page is derived from an HTML document; you can see the document that gives rise to any Web page by choosing the option to view the page source in your Web browser (This is a great way to learn HTML). HTML is not a language in the same sense as a computer programming language such as Java or BASIC. Rather, it is a set of conventions for embedding tags or markup labels within a text file. HTML documents are plain text files, which means you can create them with any text editor, including simple ones such as *Windows WordPad* (or the older *Notepad*), Apple's *SimpleText*, or any word processor that allows the document to be saved in plain text (or ASCII) format. While it is not necessary to know HTML to create web pages today, a little knowledge of HTML can be useful. Popular course management systems, such as *Blackboard* and *Moodle*, as well as other Web-based programs often allow individuals to use HTML tags to format text entered by the user.

HTML **tags** tell Web browsers how to interpret the text that is marked up. In most cases, the tags tell the browser how to display information on the computer's screen and how to do things like link to other Web pages. Most tags come in pairs, a beginning tag and an ending tag. For example, the tags <b> and </b> are used to bracket text that is to be boldfaced (e.g., <b>some text</b> would be displayed by a Web browser as **some text**). All tags are set off by angle brackets (< >). Capitalization of tags is ignored. Tags can be nested within other tags to create compound effects (e.g., <b><i>boldface and italics</b></i> would yield ***boldface and italics***). In addition to text formatting, tags also control text layout. For example, one can center or otherwise align page elements. In addition to formatting, tags are used to embed pictures and links to other web pages. The <IMG> tag is used to insert a graphic image. Links are accomplished using the anchor (<A>) tag. An example of a simple Web page with its corresponding HTML is shown in Figure 10–14.

For more information about the latest developments in HTML, visit the World Wide Web Consortium's website (www.w3.org/).

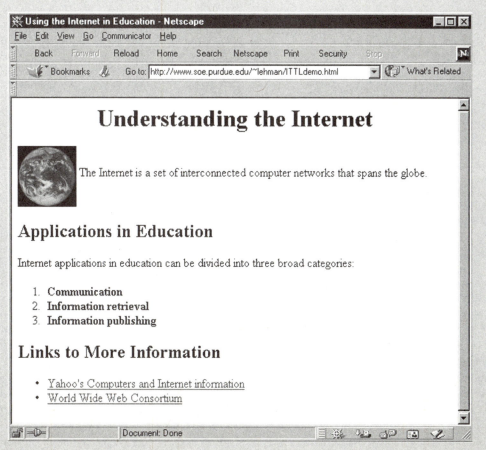

FIGURE 10–14 An example of a Web page and its corresponding HTML document.

Source: Web example courtesy of James Lehman. Used with permission.

(continued)

FIGURE 10–14
(Continued)

```
<HTML>
<HEAD>
<TITLE>Using the Internet in Education</TITLE>
</HEAD>
</BODY>
<CENTER><H1>Understanding the Internet</H1></CENTER>
<IMG SRC="apollo17_earth.gif" ALIGN=CENTER> The Internet is a set of interconnected
computer networks that spans the globe.
<H2>Applications in Education</H2>
<P>Internet applications in education can be divided into three broad categories:</P>
<OL>
<LI><B>Communication</B></LI>
<LI><B>Information retrieval</B></LI>
<LI><B>Information publishing</B></LI>
</OL>
<H2>Links to More Information</H2>
<UL>
<LI><A HREF="http://www.yahoo.com/Computers_and_Internet/">Yahoo's Computers and
Internet information</A></LI>
<LI><A HREF="http://www.w3.org/">World Wide Web Consortium</A></LI>
</UL>
</BODY>
</HTML>
```

on the Web does give parents, grandparents, and members of the community an opportunity to see what is happening in school.

The procedures for publishing on the Internet are becoming steadily easier. Let's examine popular ways of publishing information on the Internet including Web authoring, blogs, and wikis.

> **PEARSON myeducationkit™** Go to the Assignments and Activities section of Chapter 10 in MyEducationKit and complete the activity entitled "Web Use for Classrooms." As you view the websites for this activity, consider how these teachers use classroom websites and think about how you might develop a website for your own classroom.

Web Authoring

When the World Wide Web first burst onto the scene in the 1990s, tools for creating Web pages were limited. As a result, many people learned **Hypertext Markup Language (HTML)**, the underlying language of web pages. While there is still merit in understanding a bit about HTML (see "Toolbox: HTML, the Language of the Web" on page 197), today it is no longer necessary to know HTML in order to create functional and attractive Web pages. Web page authoring tools allow you to create pages without resorting to HTML coding.

Among the simplest to use of all the tools for creating HTML documents is a basic word processor. In addition to writing HTML code in a word processor, most popular word processors (e.g., Microsoft *Word,* Corel *WordPerfect*) provide the option to save documents as Web pages. Simply create your document onscreen as you would if you were writing any document, and select·the "Save as Web Page" or "Save as HTML" option. It is simple and easy. However, word processors were not designed specifically for Web page creation, and so they may not be as easy to work with or provide results as good as products designed for that purpose.

A number of programs specifically designed for web page creation are on the market today. Among the most popular Web authoring programs are Adobe (formerly Macromedia) *Dreamweaver,* Microsoft *Sharepoint Designer* and *Expression Web,* and Netscape *Composer.* These programs allow one to visually design and save individual Web pages (see Figure 10–15). More advanced features available in some packages include page design from templates, website management tools, sitewide spell checking, link testing, and search and replace. Today, better Web authoring products also provide support for the latest developments in Web creation including Java and JavaScript programming language support, cascading style sheets (CSS), dynamic content via databases, and extensible markup language (XML). There are also free website builders available to teachers

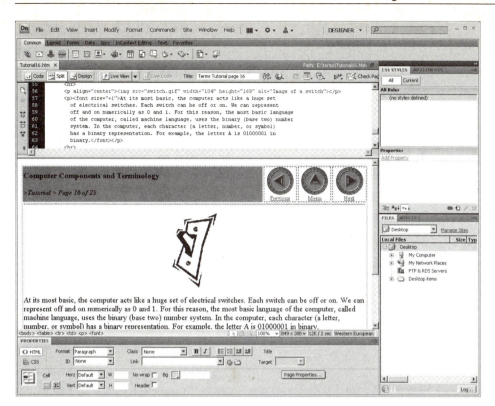

FIGURE 10–15 A screen from Adobe *Dreamweaver,* a popular Web authoring software tool.

Source: Reprinted with permission from Adobe Systems, Inc.

and students online. They typically provide templates and enable the user to quickly design a website. Some of the available website builders are EducatorPages (www .educatorpages.com), Google Sites (sites.google.com), Teachers.Net (teachers.net/sampler), and TeacherPage (www.teacherpage.com).

PEARSON myeducationkit™ To learn more about Web editing software such as *Dreamweaver,* go to the Video Examples section of Chapter 10 and watch the video tutorial entitled *"Dreamweaver."* As you watch the video, consider how you and your students can use *Dreamweaver* to create educational web pages.

When creating Web pages, students experience benefits and encounter difficulties similar to those associated with authoring other forms of hypermedia (see Chapter 9). To author Web pages, students must gather, evaluate, organize, and ultimately present information on a topic. This requires them to develop logical thinking and planning skills, and the process actively engages and often motivates the learners.

For teachers, it is important to help guard against students' tendency to want to jump right in and begin creating web pages without planning. As in other types of development efforts, a little planning at the beginning pays great dividends later on. In addition, as with other forms of visual expression, there is a need for students to adhere to good design guidelines (see Figure 10–16). Also, you and your students must remember that the Web is a public

medium of expression. A Web page may be seen by many people, and a mistake or inappropriate content could be very embarrassing. Students also have the potential to get into trouble with copyright infringement on the Web (see the discussion on copyright later in this chapter and in Chapter 8). A student who scans a picture from an encyclopedia for a report in class is probably protected under fair use guidelines, but displaying that scanned picture on the Web without permission would be a clear violation of copyright law. As a general rule, assume that material gathered from other sources, including the Web itself, is copyrighted and cannot be displayed on the Web without permission. When in doubt, err on the side of caution.

Blogs

A **blog**, short for web log, is a website in which entries on a topic are usually posted in reverse chronological order, i.e. most recent first (see Figure 10–17). Blogs are commonly used as a kind of Web-based personal journal in which the author provides commentary on topics such as news and current events, politics, a hobby or topic of interest, or just the author's personal life and activities. Authors of blogs are called *bloggers*. While most blogs convey information primarily in textual form, like other web pages they may include images, links to other websites, as well as audio and video.

Blogs are often made available to interested readers by means of **RSS** (Really Simple Syndication). RSS is a family of Web formats that is used to push frequently

Start with users.	Know who your users will be and what they are interested in learning.
Identify your purpose.	Describe in writing what you want your users to gain from the Web page/site to keep you on target as you design it.
KISS principle—Keep It Simple for Students.	Present information clearly and simply. Also, do not assume that users will have the latest and fastest technology to access your Web page/site.
Write clearly and succinctly.	Write in a clear, simple style that is easy for users to scan. Use headings to help organize content and make it easy for users to find what they want.
Limit information on each page.	A guideline is that pages should be no larger than about 50K to download reasonably quickly, usually in no more than about 10 seconds, using a 56K modem.
Use simple graphics that load quickly.	To keep pages small enough to load quickly, limit the number and type of graphics. Convert graphics designed for print to the lower resolution needed for viewing on the Web to reduce file size.
Follow guidelines for development of instructional materials.	See the section on creating new instructional materials in Chapter 8.
Limit number of links to other information.	Too many links without structure and guidelines can cause users to get lost in cyberspace.
Provide navigational support.	Use clear and consistent navigational elements. Do not assume users know as much about the site as you do. Use linking text that describes the destination; never use "click here" without explanation.
Avoid useless and annoying animation (blinking and movement).	Put your emphasis on the content, not the glitz.
Limit use of cutting-edge technology.	Minimize the use of technologies (e.g., video streaming) that require plug-ins and use a lot of bandwidth. Many users may be unable to utilize these technologies.
Make sure your pages are accessible.	Follow accessibility guidelines (see http://www.w3.org/WAI/) to ensure that your Web pages can be accessed by everyone.

FIGURE 10–16   Guidelines for designing Web pages/sites.

FIGURE 10–17   A blog, like the one shown here, allows an individual to easily create Web content without the need for specialized knowledge.

Source: David Wiley, opencontent.org/blog. Used with permission.

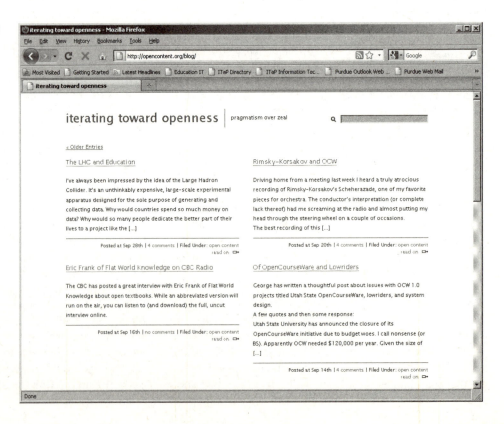

updated content out to interested readers automatically rather than requiring the readers to come to the website to view it. RSS documents, called feeds, are often used to distribute blog entries as well as other frequently updated content such as news headlines and podcasts. Interested readers can subscribe to the content feed much as one subscribes to a magazine or e-mail list. Then, whenever a new update is posted to the website, for example a blog, an RSS document is sent to the subscriber with either a summary of content from the originating website or the complete contents of the new posting. This RSS content is made available to the subscriber through software called a feed reader or aggregator, which can assemble information from multiple RSS feeds. This capability is built into popular e-mail clients (e.g., Microsoft *Outlook*, Apple *Mail*, Mozilla *Thunderbird*) and Web browsers (Microsoft *Internet Explorer*, Apple *Safari*, Mozilla *Firefox*, *Opera*) as well as through programs such as *SharpReader*, *NetNewsWire*, *mDigger*, and Web-based sites including *Google Reader* (www.google.com/reader), *AmphetaDesk* (www.disobey.com/amphetadesk/), and *Bloglines* (www.bloglines.com/).

A key feature of blogs for Web publishing is their ease of use. Using a blog host site (see Figure 10–18 for examples of sites that host free blogs), a teacher or student can easily create a website that can be used to post thoughts, resources, photos, and other information without the need to know HTML or even how to use Web editing software. Teachers can use blogs to distribute class information, homework tips, and other resources to students and parents. Blogs can also be used to share teaching ideas and lesson plans with other teachers. Students can use blogs to write reflections about in-class activities or readings, to publish class projects or other

works (again keeping in mind cautions about copyright), and to have discussions with others about topics of interest. Blogs simply make it easier to do Web publishing.

Twitter (twitter.com) is a popular micro-blogging site. Twitter allows individuals to post short text messages (only 140 characters), called tweets, that provide updates to friends and others via computer or cell phone. Although Twitter is primarily used as a social networking tool, allowing friends to keep in touch, it has potential educational applications. Twitter has been used to provide updates on ongoing legislative sessions, for example, and some teachers have begun to experiment with Twitter as a way to allow students to provide ongoing feedback about class activities.

> PEARSON
> **myeducationkit**™ To learn more about blogging go to the Video Examples section of Chapter 10 and watch the video tutorial entitled either "Blogs with *Wordpress*" or "Blogs with *Blogger*." As you watch the video, consider how you and your students can use blogging in the classroom.

Wikis

A **wiki**, like a blog, is software that allows users to create and edit Web pages using a Web browser. Wikis are generally used to create collaborative websites in which multiple individuals contribute to creating and editing the content. The best known example is *Wikipedia* (wikipedia.org), the free online encyclopedia that has been created and is maintained through the efforts of thousands of users. In education, wikis can be used to support collaborative work by a group of students. The term wiki comes from the Hawaiian word Wiki Wiki,

Site	Web Address	Description
Blogger	www.blogger.com	One of the most widely used sites for creating/hosting free blogs
WordPress	wordpress.com/	Another popular free blog hosting site
Edublogs	edublogs.org/	A site hosting over 100,000 free education blogs
Online Education Database	oedb.org/library/features/top-100-education-blogs	A list of 100 blogs on various aspects of education
Weblogg-ed	weblogg-ed.com/	A blog about using blogs in education
PBWorks	pbworks.com	A popular site for hosting free wikis for education and other uses
Wetpaint	www.wetpaint.com/	Another popular site for hosting free wikis in education
Wikispaces	www.wikispaces.com/	Another popular site for hosting free wikis in education
Education World: Information about Wikis	www.education-world.com/a_tech/sites/sites079.shtml	Information and links to resources about wikis for educators
Using Wiki in Education	www.wikiineducation.com	A wiki book about using wikis in education

FIGURE 10–18 Blog and Wiki Resources.

which means fast, and it conveys the idea that creating a website with a wiki is fast and easy.

The basic concept behind a wiki is that many minds are better than one. Wikis support collaborative construction of a website by many different individuals. Some wikis are completely open, allowing anyone to edit or add to the content on the site. Others, such as those commonly used in education, restrict content creation and editing to specific individuals through a login procedure. In either case, individuals who have access to the wiki can edit existing content on the site or add new content freely. Other users review these changes and additions and can make their own. Through this process, the community of users gradually builds up and refines the content of the site so that it comes to represent a consensus, of sorts, of the entire community. By relying on a large community of users, much can be accomplished; *Wikipedia* has over seven million entries (more than two million in English alone), which dwarfs the number of entries in traditional encyclopedias.

However, critics argue that quality is an issue with wikis. If anyone can edit or add to a site, how can quality be assured? Proponents of wikis point to two safeguards. First, wikis rely on many sets of eyes. If a user adds incorrect information to a wiki site, other users can catch the error and correct it. Second, wikis maintain records of previous versions of the site and any changes that have occurred. If, for example, someone maliciously erases all of the content on a wiki site, it is a simple matter for the site owner to restore the previous version of the site. While mistakes and site vandalism do sometimes occur with wikis, the system generally works well. A study comparing *Wikipedia* and the online *Encyclopedia Britannica* found that Wikipedia was nearly as accurate for selected science entries (Giles, 2005).

> **PEARSON myeducationkit** To learn more about wikis go to the Video Examples section of Chapter 10 and watch the video tutorial entitled "Wikis." As you watch the video, consider how you and your students can use wikis in the classroom.

There are many resources available for educators who would like to use wikis in the classroom (see Figure 10–18). A teacher can create a wiki to provide class information, collaborate with other teachers, or set up opportunities for students to collaborate with one another. Students can use a wiki to create a jointly authored paper or report, share ideas about common readings, work together on a common project such as a science fair investigation, or otherwise collaborate on class projects. Like blogs, wikis make it easy for teachers and students to be able to publish their work on the Internet.

Classroom Applications

Student publishing on the Web offers many opportunities for classroom activities that parallel those that we cited for hypermedia authoring packages in the last chapter. Typical applications of the Web for information publishing include the following:

- Students can create hypermedia projects or reports on the Web in much the same way as they would do hypermedia authoring as discussed in Chapter 9. Using Web authoring software, a blog, or a wiki, students can create Web materials that contain textual information, pictures, and other multimedia elements. Significantly, on the Web, they can also contain links to further information on the same website or other websites.

- The Web is a great tool for displaying examples of students' work. Parents and members of the community can get a sense of what goes on in the school by seeing posted work. Remember, always get permission from *both* students and their parents/guardians before displaying students' work on the Web.

- Learning how to develop web pages may be an educational goal in and of itself. Students, for example, might learn web page development skills by helping to construct or maintain a portion of the school's website. This "win-win" situation gives students experience and helps schools to maintain a Web presence by using an inexpensive pool of student labor.

THE INTERNET AS APPLICATION PLATFORM

In addition to its uses for information retrieval, communication, and information publishing, the Internet is emerging as an important application platform for work of all kinds. Traditionally, computer applications have been installed on personal computers from computer-readable media, such as diskettes or CD-ROMs. In some schools and businesses, applications have been stored on a server and accessed across a local area network (LAN). Today, an increasing number of applications are designed to be used over the Internet; in most cases, users access these applications by using a basic Web browser to interact with a website that has been designed to provide much of the same functionality as a stand-alone personal computer application (e.g., word processor, spreadsheet, graphics program). With these Web-based applications, the Internet can be a platform for doing productive work, reducing or perhaps even eliminating the need for dedicated applications on your computer. See Figure 10–19 for a small sampling of the many Web-based applications available.

Web-based applications have the advantage that they can be accessed anytime and from anywhere that the Internet is available. Further, in many cases, they can be used from any Internet-capable device including not just computers but also PDAs and mobile phones. The end user does not have to install software, other than a Web browser, to use them. The applications themselves are always up-to-date without the need to install software updates because the producer can simply upload the latest version to one source website, and all users

Application	Description	Web Address
30Boxes	Online calendar	www.30boxes.com
Backpack	Information organization tool that can manage notes, calendars, files, images, etc.	www.backpackit.com
Basecamp	Project management tool.	basecamphq.com
Document Converter eXPress	Converts many types of documents into PDF or image format.	www.convert.neevia.com
Eyespot	Web-based video editor.	eyespot.com
Google Docs	A suite of Web-based applications including a word processor, spreadsheet, and presentation package.	docs.google.com
NumSum	Online spreadsheet.	numsum.com
Picnik	Online photo editing application.	www.picnik.com
Thinkfree Online Office	A suite of online office tools including a word processor, spreadsheet, and presentation package.	www.thinkfree.com
Writeboard	Text editing/writing tool that supports collaborative document construction.	writeboard.com
Zoho	A suite of online tools including a word processor, spreadsheet, and presentation package.	www.zoho.com

FIGURE 10–19   Example Web-based Applications.

instantly have access to it. Best of all, many Web-based applications are free to use; the companies that produce them generally earn revenue from advertising rather than from the sale of the software itself.

However, there are disadvantages to Web-based applications. Most Web-based applications are not as full-featured as their stand-alone counterparts. So, you may be limited in what you can do. In addition, some people object to having to view advertising or sign up with a company to use an online application. Finally, if you cannot connect to the Internet to use the application or your Internet connection is temporarily down, you are effectively cut off from being able to do your work.

Classroom Applications

Classroom uses of Web-based applications are no different than those of their stand-alone software counterparts. Web-based productivity applications allow the computer to be used as an assistant to help teachers or learners to do their work. See the discussions in Chapter 3 and 9 for examples of the use of computer tools by teachers and students.

 PROBLEMS AND PITFALLS

The Internet is a rich source of information for students and teachers. It can also provide quick communication, be a place to share or publish materials, and serve as an application platform. However, these benefits can have a downside as well. For one thing, there is a financial cost to access the Internet. Costs can vary greatly from school to school depending on arrangements with local

Internet Service Providers (ISPs). Once the connection is there and paid for, there still may be problems with access. Websites may be busy or not available when you or your students want to access them. This can be especially true for popular educational sites during the school day. A school's connection to the Internet may be down. So, it is important to have backup plans when planning to use the Internet in the classroom.

The ease with which students can access information on the Internet, while generally thought of as an advantage, can sometimes be a detriment. Students doing research for a class paper may search the Internet only and assume that they have found all that there is to find. While the Internet is a great research tool, students still need to be able to use traditional library resources to find information. Further, Internet resources, more so than traditional print resources, can be inaccurate, biased, or misleading. Students need to understand how to evaluate the quality of the Internet resources that they do find. See the discussion later in this chapter about evaluating the quality of websites.

Educators also need to be vigilant when students use the Internet. Students may deliberately or accidentally gain access to inappropriate sites, they may choose to "play" on the Internet, or they may gain access to materials that are not relevant to lesson content, such as the "Hot Wheels" website or the "Barbie" website during a social studies lesson on local history. To discourage this—it can never be totally prevented—monitor students closely. It is also important to monitor students when they use the Internet for communication. Students may send inappropriate e-mails to others, or they may receive inappropriate messages from others. Any use of the Internet also introduces vulnerability to problems such as viruses, spam (unwanted e-mail advertisements), and computer attacks. Caution students against downloading files, which might contain malicious software. Advise them to avoid clicking on advertisements or responding to e-mail advertisements that they might receive. Also, make sure that they understand the importance of maintaining computer security. See the discussion below for more about security and information privacy.

ISSUES INVOLVED IN THE USE OF THE INTERNET IN THE CLASSROOM

In addition to the problems and pitfalls noted above, the use of the Internet in the classroom brings with it some special issues and concerns. Several of these key issues are identified and briefly discussed following.

Copyright and Fair Use of Materials on the Web

Teachers have an obligation to make students aware of copyright laws and how they apply to the Internet. *All* materials on the Internet are copyrighted! It is no different from materials published in a textbook. Just because something can be copied electronically doesn't mean it can be distributed legally without the copyright holder's permission. You and your students may use Internet materials personally, but you may not make copies, modify them, or incorporate them into commercial materials without the permission of the copyright holder.

Likewise, you should *not* post on a website any materials (stories, artwork, photographs, poems, etc.) created by your students or photographs of your students *without* the written permission of their parents or guardians. You should spend some class time discussing copyright rules and guidelines with your students. Check with your school administration about the local policies. Refer to the information on copyright in Chapter 8.

Security and Information Privacy

Always monitor your students when they are using the Web. Discourage students from exploring inappropriate websites either accidentally or deliberately. While many schools now use filtering software to prevent students from accessing inappropriate sites, students may still encounter unsuitable content. The amount and level of your monitoring will be determined by the maturity of your students and local school policies (see "Toolbox: Acceptable Use Policies" on page 205).

Make certain that students understand that computer security is important and personally meaningful. Instruct students to *not* give out personal information such as phone numbers and addresses on the Internet. If students are using the Internet for gathering information for a school project, instruct them to receive the information at school using the school's electronic address or postal address. It is also important to make students aware that their passwords must be kept private in order to keep school computers secure. Students and teachers should create hard-to-guess passwords (e.g., consisting of nonsensical mixtures of upper and lowercase letters and numerals) and change passwords often. Passwords should never be shared with others or written down where someone else might get them.

Spam, unwanted e-mail advertising, is becoming an increasing problem for all users of e-mail, including teachers and students. While spam cannot be completely eliminated, it can be limited. Use e-mail filters to catch spam before it gets to your inbox. Avoid giving out your e-mail address online; it may end up on a spam list. Avoid posting your and your students' e-mail addresses on a Web page; some spammers obtain e-mail addresses by scanning web pages for them. Never respond to spam; just delete it. Responding to spam verifies that your e-mail address is valid and just invites more spam.

To avoid problems with viruses, never allow students to download programs from the Internet. Even apparently innocuous programs, such as screen savers, may harbor viruses or **spyware**, programs that covertly gather information and transmit it to someone else over the Internet. Likewise, instruct students to never open e-mail attachments from unfamiliar sources or that contain executable files (in the Windows world, files with extensions such as exe, com, bat, pif, ocx, and vbs, among others). Of course, anti-virus software should always be installed and kept up-to-date.

To minimize problems with outsiders gaining access to school and home computers, Internet firewalls should be installed. Most schools now maintain **firewalls**, combinations of hardware and software that prevent outsiders from gaining access to private networks connected to the Internet. In addition to network-level firewalls, personal firewalls can be installed on individual computers to limit the danger from viruses and hackers.

Evaluating the Quality of Websites

We conclude our discussion of using the Internet in education by exploring *evaluation*—the E in our PIE model. As we noted at the beginning of the chapter, the Internet

Toolbox: Acceptable Use Policies

Some information on the Web is inappropriate for students. What you might consider appropriate might be considered inappropriate by parents or your school administration. It is the responsibility of your school board to establish acceptable use policies for your district. **Acceptable use policies** are signed agreements among students, parents/guardians, and the school administration outlining what is considered to be proper use of the Internet and Web by all persons involved (see Figure 10–20). Locate and read your local policies very carefully *before* you use the Internet or Web with your students. Protocol will vary from one community to another.

FIGURE 10–20 Sample statement of Acceptable Use Policy from Crawfordsville (IN) School Corp.

Source: Crawfordsville Community School Corporation, Crawfordsville, IN 47933.

Internet Use Agreement

The intent of this contract is to ensure that students will comply with all Network and Internet acceptable use policies approved by the District. In exchange for the use of the Network resources either at school or away from school, I understand and agree to the following:

A. The use of the network is a privilege which may be revoked by the District at any time and for any reason. Appropriate reasons for revoking privileges include, but are not limited to, the altering of system software, the placing of unauthorized information, computer viruses or harmful programs on or through the computer system in either public or private files or messages. The District reserves the right to remove files, limit or deny access, and refer the student for other disciplinary actions.

B. The District reserves all rights to any material stored in files which are generally accessible to others and will remove any material which the District, at its sole discretion, believes may be unlawful, obscene, pornographic, abusive, or otherwise objectionable. Students will not use their District-approved computer account/access to obtain, view, download, or otherwise gain access to, distribute, or transmit such materials.

C. All information services and features contained on District or Network resources are intended for the private use of its registered users. Any use of these resources for commercial-for-profit or other unauthorized purposes (i.e., advertisements, political lobbying), in any form, is expressly forbidden.

D. The District and/or Network resources are intended for the exclusive use by their registered users. The student is responsible for the use of his/her account/password and/or access privilege. Any problems which arise from the use of a student's account are the responsibility of the account holder. Use of materials, information, files, or an account by someone other than the registered account holder or accessing another person's account without permission is forbidden and may be grounds for loss of access privileges.

E. Any misuse of the account will result in suspension of the account privileges and/or other disciplinary action determined by the District. Misuse shall include, but not be limited to:

  1) Intentionally seeking information on, obtaining copies of, or modifying files, other data, or passwords belonging to other users.
  2) Misrepresenting other users on the Network.
  3) Disrupting the operation of the Network through abuse of or vandalizing, damaging, or disabling the hardware or software.
  4) Malicious use of the Network through hate mail, harassment, profanity, vulgar statements, or discriminatory remarks.
  5) Interfering with others' use of the Network.
  6) Extensive use for non-curriculum-related communication.
  7) Illegal installation of copyrighted software.
  8) Unauthorized downsizing, copying, or use of licensed or copyrighted software or plagiarizing materials.
  9) Allowing anyone to use an account other than the account holder.
  10) Using the Internet without a teacher's permission.
  11) Violating any local, state, or federal statutes.

is similar to a library, but the Internet has no librarian and no assurances of quality. Therefore, you must evaluate the resources that are brought to you via the Internet. How can you and your students determine if information on the Internet is credible and of quality? For most printed materials, especially textbooks, there are editors who review the materials and make sure what is presented is accurate. However, this is not the case for most sites on the Internet. You and your students need to understand that what you read on the Internet may not be correct. There is no guarantee that the information you may find is up-to-date, unbiased, and accurate.

One of the most important rules is to evaluate the content and to separate it from the glitz. It goes back to the old proverb, "Never judge a book by its cover." Many websites are pretty, but also pretty shallow in terms of content. Inaccurate and inappropriate content beautifully presented is still inaccurate and inappropriate! Examine the content of websites closely. Pay attention to indicators of quality and the qualifications of the

author. Typical criteria that can be used to judge Web resources include:

- ↗ Authority—Who is the author of the site? What information can you glean from the website itself about the person or organization that created the site? Do other reputable sites link to the site?
- ↗ Accuracy—Is the content of the site correct? How can you judge the accuracy of the content? Does the author document information sources? Do other reputable sites support the information?
- ↗ Currency—Is the site up-to-date? Were the pages last modified recently or long ago?
- ↗ Objectivity—Does the site present a biased or slanted point of view? How can you tell?
- ↗ Coverage—What is the scope of topic coverage on the site? For whom was the site written?

To practice judging the quality of websites, complete the "Toolbox: Evaluating the Quality of Websites" activity following.

Toolbox: Evaluating the Quality of Websites

Because of the lack of controls on the Internet, anyone can put anything on a website. Therefore, it is important for users to learn to judge the quality of information on the Web. Website evaluation is an important skill for teachers and students alike.

Some sites that provide information about website evaluation include:

- ↗ http://school.discovery.com/schrockguide/eval.html (Kathy Schrock's Guide for Educators)
- ↗ http://www.lib.berkeley.edu/TeachingLib/Guides/Internet/ Evaluate.html (Guidelines from the University of California at Berkeley Library)

- ↗ http://lib.nmsu.edu/instruction/evalcrit.html (Web evaluation criteria from the New Mexico State University Library)
- ↗ http://www.library.cornell.edu/olinuris/ref/research/ webeval.html (Web criteria and tools from the Cornell University Library)

Use the "Preview Form: Web Pages/Sites" in Appendix D to evaluate the websites listed below. Which of these websites do you think are or are not credible sources of information? Why?

Site	URL
Boilerplate: Mechanical Marvel	www.bigredhair.com/boilerplate/
Dihydrogen Monoxide	www.dhmo.org/
Faked Moon Landings	batesmotel.8m.com/
Gettysburg Address	www.loc.gov/exhibits/gadd/
Harriet Tubman and the Underground Railroad	www2.lhric.org/pocantico/tubman/tubman.html
Institute for Historical Review	www.ihr.org/
Martin Luther King	www.martinlutherking.org
Tobacco Control Archives	www.library.ucsf.edu/tobacco/index.html
U.S. Holocaust Memorial Museum	www.ushmm.org/

TECHNOLOGY COORDINATOR'S CORNER

At the beginning of this chapter, you met Phil Nelson and Linda Johnson, two social studies teachers who were talking about integrating the Internet into their classrooms. After chatting with each other, Phil and Linda sat down with Don Bauer, their school's computer coordinator, to explore options.

Don began by discussing the different ways that the Internet can be used in the classroom, from retrieving information to communicating across distances and from publishing information to using available Web-based applications. Don agreed with Phil's suggestion to Linda to start by having her students use the Web to retrieve up-to-date information. As one example, Don mentioned THOMAS, part of the Library of Congress website (thomas.loc.gov), which students could use to research and track current federal legislation online. He thought it might be a good resource for Linda's Government and Civics classes. Don suggested that Linda prepare for any Internet information retrieval activity by locating websites where her students could find relevant information. He suggested that she record the addresses of those websites on a worksheet for her students, or, better yet, save them in a bookmarks folder that could be put on the computers in the school's lab. With a bookmark file, Don explained, students could quickly access relevant sites, and this would help to keep them from wandering aimlessly or getting off task. Don also suggested that Linda consider locating an existing WebQuest that would work with one of her units. A WebQuest, he explained, would make sites available for student research within the context of some sort of inquiry activity. Don suggested that Linda might want to make her own WebQuest in the future, and he invited her to attend a WebQuest workshop that he was offering for teachers later in the month.

Don also encouraged Linda to explore her idea to use the Internet as a vehicle for communication between her students and experts outside of the school, such as politicians or government officials. He noted that students could get the electronic contact information for U.S. Senators and Congressional Representatives online at the websites for the Senate (www.senate.gov) and House of Representatives (www.house.gov). He suggested that Linda consider integrating e-mail communication into one of her units, perhaps for students to gather information (i.e. What do local Congressional representatives think of a pending piece of legislation?) or as a culminating activity (i.e. Having students send an e-mail to senators or representatives to encourage them to vote a certain way on a piece of legislation that the students had researched).

Don knew that Phil, unlike Linda, was experienced using the Internet for information retrieval in his class.

So, he suggested ways that Phil might go even further in making use of what the Internet could offer. Don suggested that Phil think about having his students focus on using primary source materials for an upcoming unit on the history of the civil rights movement. Don noted that the Web is a great repository of many original materials that would be relevant to the objectives of the planned unit. One example is the American Memory collection at the Library of Congress (memory.loc.gov), which has many excellent primary source materials. With students who are already fairly capable users of the Web, the task of finding primary source materials to do reports would be challenging but doable.

Don also suggested that another way for Phil to take his use of the Internet up a notch would be to have the students put the results of their research on the Web for others to see. Rather than just doing reports in class, the students could create Web reports using Web authoring software (e.g., *Dreamweaver*) or a blog or wiki. With student and parent permission, and after ensuring that the projects adhered to copyright law, the students' projects could be made accessible to the public on the Web. Since the public could access them, Don suggested that Phil consider inviting members of the community to provide feedback or evaluate students' projects. Don noted that students tend to work extra hard on projects when they know that people other than just the teacher will see and evaluate them. Phil agreed that these were interesting suggestions that he would consider. Linda and Phil thanked Don for his help and left to work on the new ideas for using the Internet in their classrooms.

SUMMARY

In this chapter, we examined uses of the Internet to enhance learning. Applications of the Internet in education can be put into one of four broad categories; communication, information retrieval, information publishing, and application platform. Asynchronous forms of communication include e-mail and mailing lists, while synchronous forms of communication include instant messaging and chat. These technologies allow for rapid communication between individuals or groups. Students and teachers can retrieve text, images, audio, and video information from the World Wide Web. Structured approaches for integrating information retrieval in educational lessons include scavenger hunts and WebQuests. The Internet can also be used for information publishing. Using Web authoring software, blogs, or wikis, students and teachers can create materials that can be accessed by others on the Internet. Finally, Web-based applications make the Internet a platform for doing work of all kinds.

Teachers and students need to be aware of issues related to the use of the Internet in the classroom. Copyright laws apply to materials on the Internet just as they do to materials in other media. Security and information privacy are of concern when using the Internet, and precautions should be taken to minimize problems. Finally, because information sources on the Internet can be inaccurate or biased, students need to understand how to judge the quality of websites.

> PEARSON **myeducationkit** To check your comprehension of the content covered in this chapter, go to the MyEducationKit for this book and complete the Study Plan for Chapter 10. Here you will be able to take a chapter quiz, receive feedback on your answers, and then access resources that will enhance your understanding of chapter content.

SUGGESTED RESOURCES

Print Resources

Abbitt, J., & Ophus, J. (2008). What we know about the impacts of WebQuests: A review of research. *AACE Journal 16*(4), 441–456.

Ackerman, E., & Hartman, K. (2002). *Learning to use the Internet and World Wide Web*. Wilsonville, OR: Franklin, Beedle, & Associates.

Blanchard, J., & Marshall, J. (2004). *Web-based learning in K-12 classrooms: Opportunities and challenges*. New York: The Haworth Press.

Chen, I., & Thielemann, J. (2008). *Technology application competencies for K-12 teachers*. Hershey, PA: IGI group.

Ertmer, P. A., Hruskocy, C., & Woods, D. M. (2003). *The worldwide classroom: Access to people, resources, and curricular connections*. Upper Saddle River, NJ: Prentice Hall.

Giles, J. (2005). Internet encyclopaedias go head to head. *Nature, 438,* 900–901.

Goodstein, A. (2007). Totally wired: What teens and tweens are really doing online. New York: St. Martin's Press.

Heide, A., & Stilborne, L. (2004). *The teacher's Internet companion*. Markham, Ontario: Trifolium Books.

Hendron, J. (2008). *RSS for educators: Blogs, newsfeeds, podcasts, and wikis in the classroom*. Washington D.C.: ISTE Books.

Herring, J. E. (2004). *The Internet and information skills: A guide for teachers and school librarians*. New York: Neal Schuman.

National School Boards Association (2007). Creating and connecting: Research and guidelines on online social – and educational – networking. Available at http://www.nsba.org/site/docs/41400/41340.pdf

Nielsen, J. (2000). *Designing Web usability*. Indianapolis, IN: New Riders Publishing.

November, A. (2008). *Web literacy for educators*. Thousand Oaks, CA: Corwin Press.

Project Tomorrow. (2007). *Speak Up 2007 for Students, Teachers, Parents & School Leaders*. Available at http://www.tomorrow.org/speakup/speakup_reports.html.

Provenzo, E. F. (2004). *The Internet and online research for teachers*. Boston: Allyn & Bacon.

Richardson, W. (2008). *Blogs, wikis, podcasts, and other powerful web tools for classrooms*. Thousand Oaks, CA: Corwin Press.

Roblyer, M. D. (2005). *Starting out on the Internet: A learning journey for teachers* (3rd ed.). Boston, MA: Pearson.

Roblyer, M. D., & Doehring, A. (2010). *Integrating educational technology into teaching* (5th ed.). Boston, MA: Pearson Education.

Solomon, G., & Schrum, L. (2007). Web 2.0: New tools, new schools. Washington D.C.: ISTE Books.

Turner, R. (2006). Super searchers go to school: Sharing online strategies with K-12 students, teachers, and librarians. *New Library World, 107*(3/4), 168–171.

Van Gorp, L. (2007). Must-see websites for busy teachers. Huntington, CA: Shell Education.

Wells, J., & Lewis, L. (2006). Internet access in U.S. public schools and classrooms: 1994–2005 U.S. Department of Education (NCES 2007-020). Available at http://nces.ed.gov/pubsearch/pubsinfo.asp?pubid=2007020.

Electronic Resources

http://42explore.com/
(42explore: Thematic Pathfinders for All Ages)

http://www.loc.gov/index.html
(Library of Congress)

http://school.discoveryeducation.com/schrockguide/yp/iypabout.html
(Kathy Schrock's Guide for Educators: About the Internet)

http://school.discoveryeducation.com/schrockguide/eval.html
(Discovery Education: Kathy Schrock's Guide for Educators: Critical Evaluation Information)

http://digiteen.wikispaces.com/
(Digiteen Wikispaces: Digital Citizenship in Education)

http://socialnetworksined.wikispaces.com/
(Social Networks in Education: Wikispaces)

http://www.ikeepsafe.org/
(iKeep Safe Coalition)

http://www.safekids.com/
(Safe Kids: Internet Safety and Civility)

http://www.kidsclick.org/
(KidsClick! Web Search for Kids by Librarians)

http://webquest.org/index-resources.php
(WebQuest Portal: Useful WebQuest Resources)

11

Integration of Distance Education to Support Learning

Source: Cindy Charles/PhotoEdit.

KEY WORDS AND CONCEPTS

Distance education
Synchronous
Asynchronous
Hybrid/blended learning
Audio teleconferencing

Video conferencing
Podcast
Webinar
Computer mediated communication
Online learning/e-learning

CHAPTER OBJECTIVES

After reading and studying this chapter, you will be able to:

↗ Define distance education, and identify the needs it addresses.

↗ Compare and contrast audio-based, video-based, and computer-based distance education technologies on the basis of capabilities, advantages, and limitations.

↗ Describe examples of the use of audio-based, video-based, and computer-based distance education technologies for K-12 education.

↗ Identify basic guidelines for the use of distance education technologies in teaching and learning including planning, implementation, and assessment considerations.

↗ Discuss issues related to the use of distance education in K-12 education.

In the two preceding chapters, we explored how to integrate computers and the Internet into the classroom. In this chapter, we continue to examine the classroom integration of technologies. This chapter focuses on distance education technologies. Distance education is growing rapidly today, and a variety of distance education technologies are available for use in the classroom. This chapter summarizes information about distance education technologies and their applications in the classroom.

 ## INTRODUCTION

Miranda Allen is a high school Spanish teacher. While planning for a unit in her Advanced Spanish class, she was looking for a way to provide her students with an authentic educational experience. Her class was going to be studying the culture of Mexico by reading articles about various regions of Mexico, and browsing the Web to look at various sites including Mexican newspapers online. Miranda thought it would be ideal to cap off the unit by providing her students with the opportunity to converse directly with native speakers of Spanish living in Mexico. She was talking about this in the teachers' lounge, and a colleague suggested she might be able to use technology to make it happen.

Miranda remembered an old college friend, Señora Diego, a high school English teacher who lived in Mexico City. She decided to e-mail Señora Diego to ask if she might be interested in having the students in her English class converse with the students in Miranda's Spanish class. Señora Diego was enthusiastic about the idea and agreed to participate if Miranda could make the arrangements. Miranda then checked with her principal, Mr. Taylor, to make sure it would be all right. He told Miranda that as long as there was no extra cost to the school, he would support it.

What options do you think Miranda might have to make a connection between her students and Señora Diego's students in Mexico? What options would best help her students to improve their Spanish abilities? What will she need to know about distance education and available technologies? What will she need to consider when planning for and implementing a classroom activity with a distance education component? As you study this chapter, think about Miranda's class and other situations where education might be enhanced by the ability to bridge distances using technology. This chapter presents information about distance education, available distance education technologies, and ways to plan, implement, and evaluate the use of distance education.

TECHNOLOGY INTEGRATION PROCESS: PREPARING TO INTEGRATE DISTANCE EDUCATION IN THE LEARNING EXPERIENCE

As you have learned in the previous chapters, planning is an important precursor to any instructional activity. However, planning becomes even more important in distance education. In a typical classroom, the teacher can often adjust learning activities "on the fly." For example, Miranda Allen, the Spanish teacher introduced earlier, might change a planned whole-class activity in her Advanced Spanish class by having her students get into small groups to practice conversational skills with one another. However, if Miranda were teaching students at a distance, perhaps via an online course or television to students in another district, she could not simply decide on the spur of the moment to ask students to work in groups. She would need to prepare in advance a way for them to be able to work together, such as by creating an Internet chat room where they could interact with one another or by scheduling groups to take turns using a two-way video connection to talk with one another. So, a key to successful distance education is careful advanced planning.

As with any learning experience, in distance education you must prepare your learners, the learning environment, and the learning materials. Distance education may be unfamiliar to your students. Therefore, learners should be informed of what to expect during a distance education experience. They may need to know how to use whatever technology is being used (e.g., switching on a microphone to make a comment or ask a question, controlling a video conferencing camera,

Careful advanced preparation is a key to successful distance education.
Source: David Young-Wolff/PhotoEdit.

using an asynchronous discussion board in an online course). The learners also need to know expectations and norms for participation (e.g., how to ask a question from a remote site, etiquette for participating in an online discussion), and they need to prepare themselves to participate (e.g., jotting down questions to ask during an audio teleconference). Of course, the learning environment must be arranged to facilitate the distance education experience. Technical support staff may be needed to set up the distance education technology to be used (e.g., a satellite video linkage with remote site). For an online course, learners may need to adjust their browser settings so that the course management software works properly. Finally, learning materials must be prepared in advance so that the learners at the remote sites will have them in time for the distance education experience.

When implementing a distance education lesson, the teacher should seek opportunities to allow the students to interact with the content, interact with the each other, and interact with the teacher. In distance education, these interactions are usually mediated by technology. This makes distance education more complex for the teacher who must focus not only on implementing the lesson but also on adapting the lesson to the distance education technology being used. It is particularly important for the teacher to use available communication channels to check for learners' comprehension and engagement. In a classroom, it is relatively easy for the teacher to monitor learners' understanding by observing facial expressions and body language. However, these cues may be absent in a distance education environment, so it is important for the teacher to ask questions and actively check for understanding.

Finally, following a distance education learning experience, you and your students should take time to evaluate the success of the experience. Because of the separation of teacher and learners, this can be more challenging than in the traditional classroom. Therefore, it is important for the teacher to plan in advance to gather evaluative information in a distance education environment, for example, by asking students to e-mail their questions or post their reflections using a blog or discussion forum.

 # WHAT IS DISTANCE EDUCATION?

Think about the convenience of shopping at a modern grocery store. Goods are brought to the store to save you from traveling to many locations around town, as your grandparents and great grandparents did, or even around the world to get the items you want to buy. On the store shelves, you can find coffee from Colombia, cheese from Wisconsin, fruit from Florida, meat from a butcher, bread from a bakery, rice from Asia, and produce from California or central America. Fresh goods from throughout the world are brought to one location where you can pick and choose from what is available. Just as a grocery store brings items from around the world to one location, distance education brings teaching and learning resources from afar into your classroom or the student's home. Without having to travel, learners can get educational materials and experiences that may come from another city, another state, or another country. Distance education can deliver a complete set of instructional materials and experiences to the learner, substituting for what might ordinarily take place in a classroom, or it can supplement and enrich what learners experience in a traditional education setting. Like a grocery store for learning, distance education makes it convenient for learners to get the education that they want without having to travel to get it.

Distance education refers to "any instructional situation in which learners are separated in time or space from the point of origination, characterized by limited access to the teacher or other learners" (Smaldino, Lowther, & Russell, 2007). Figure 11–1 shows a matrix of educational settings formed by crossing the factors of both place and time. Traditional classroom instruction involves teacher and learners meeting at the same time and in the same place. Time-shifted classroom instruction occurs when teacher and students meet in the same place but at different times, such as when a teacher videotapes a lesson for an absent student to view the next day. **Synchronous** distance education refers to situations where teacher and students meet at

	Same Place	**Different Place**
Same Time	Traditional Classroom	Synchronous Distance Education
Different Time	Time-Shifted Classroom	Asynchronous Distance Education

FIGURE 11–1 Matrix of educational settings based on time and place.

the same time but in different places, as in a live video broadcast or an audio teleconference. **Asynchronous** distance education refers to circumstances in which both time and place are different, as is the case with most Web-based distance education.

Distance education addresses problems of educational access. Obviously, distance can be a major barrier to educational access. Just as people in rural or remote locations often have more limited selections at the grocery store than those in urban areas, educational access may also be limited in rural or remote locations. Resources may be scarce, and, in the worst cases, there may not be teachers for certain subjects. For example, a small, rural school may not have a teacher to teach advanced physics or Chinese to the handful of students who might be interested in the subject. Problems of access may be manifested in other ways as well. For example, learners who are homebound due to illness or physical disability may not be located far from a school, but they are effectively isolated if they cannot physically attend school. Time can also be a barrier. For example, a college-bound high school student might want to take advanced level course work for college placement but be unable to fit it into his or her regular school and work schedule. Distance education can overcome many of these problems of access and provide educational opportunities.

> **PEARSON** **myeducationkit**™ Go to the Assignments and Activities section of Chapter 11 in MyEducationKit and complete the activity entitled "Benefits of Virtual School." As you view this video, think about the needs that virtual schooling is addressing for these students and their families.

Traditionally, distance education has referred to educational experiences that are apart from conventional in-class learning experiences. People often think of distance education as an instructor at one site teaching learners at another site or sites via television, the Internet, or another communication channel. As a teacher, you might have the opportunity to teach students at other locations this way, or you might be the recipient of distance education by taking a teacher professional development class from a university at a distance. However, distance education technologies are increasingly being used to supplement traditional classroom instruction. **Hybrid** or **blended learning** combines elements of face-to-face teaching and learning with elements of distance education. This approach is becoming common on college campuses, in corporate training settings, and increasingly in K–12 education as well. As a teacher, you might use Web-based instruction or asynchronous online discussion, for example, to encourage your students to study or discuss topics from the classroom during the after school hours. The term **distributed education**, while sometimes used interchangeably with distance education, might better

capture this notion of using learning resources, which can be distributed in space and time, to support learners who may be situated locally or at a distance. Figure 11–2 provides descriptions of distance and blended/hybrid learning and gives examples of their use in K-12 education.

> **PEARSON** **myeducationkit**™ Go to the Assignments and Activities section of Chapter 11 in MyEducationKit and complete the activity entitled "Approaches to Online Learning." As you view this video, consider how an approach that blends online and face-to-face learning supports student learning and success.

DISTANCE EDUCATION TECHNOLOGIES

The earliest efforts at distance education involved correspondence study in which individuals used self-study printed materials (Moore & Kearsley, 2005; Simonson, Smaldino, Albright, & Zvacek, 2006). In correspondence study, learners would receive materials via the postal mail, read and study them, and then send their work back to the teacher for grading through the mail. While useful and still in existence today, print-based correspondence study is limited, especially because of the limited interaction between instructor and learners. Over the years, various technologies have been employed to enhance distance education, including radio, television, the telephone, and recently, the Internet. A key element of these technologies is their ability to enhance communication between teacher and learners and among learners who may be at different locations. We look at three broad categories of distance education technologies: audio-based, video-based, and computer-based.

Audio-Based Technologies

Audio technologies have been used in distance education for many years. Options include audio cassettes and CDs, radio, and audio teleconferencing (see Figure 11–3). Audio technologies are familiar and readily available. While not as widely used as computer and video technologies, they offer a cost-effective alternative that can meet many distance education needs. However, audio technologies, except where supplemented with other technologies, lack visual elements and so are limited.

Video-Based Technologies

Video overcomes the lack of visual elements in audio-based distance education. Video may be delivered over distances using a variety of means including video cassettes and DVDs, broadcast television, satellite and microwave transmission, closed-circuit and cable systems, and today the Internet. Video technologies are familiar, widely available, and one of the most popular options

Type of Learning	Description	Examples
Distance learning	In a pure or fully distance learning situation, teacher and learners are physically separated and have little or no face-to-face interaction.	↗ A student wishing to study an advanced or specialized subject (e.g., mathematics, foreign language) unavailable in the local school takes a course from a teacher in another location via video and/or the Internet. ↗ A student homebound due to illness keeps up with school work by completing self-study units and by participating in classes via a two-way video link-up with the school. ↗ A teacher needing to participate in professional development for license renewal participates in an online course from a university using a computer and network connection at home.
Blended or hybrid learning	In blended or hybrid learning, elements of distance education are combined with elements of traditional face-to-face teaching and learning. The distance education components ordinarily augment or supplement face-to-face learning experiences.	↗ Students in a high school English class use an online discussion forum to extend the discussion about a novel they are reading outside of regular class time. ↗ A primary school teacher enriches a classroom unit on a storybook by inviting the book's author to talk with her second graders via an audio or video teleconference. ↗ Students in a seventh-grade social studies class working on a local history project use a wiki on the Internet, both in and out of class, to assemble their materials and develop their project.

FIGURE 11–2   Distance and blended/hybrid learning descriptions and examples.

Toolbox: Defining Distance Education

Conceptions of distance education vary even among experts in the field. Review the following websites that provide information about definitions of distance education.

Website	URL
Distance-Educator.com Knowledge Netbook (follow the definitions link)	http://www.distance-educator.com/knb/
Instructional Technology Council Definition of Distance Education	http://144.162.197.250/definition.htm
University of Idaho Engineering Outreach Distance Education at a Glance	http://www.uidaho.edu/eo/distglan.html
University of Wisconsin Distance Education Clearinghouse Definitions	http://www.uwex.edu/disted/definition.cfm

Based upon your review, answer the following questions:

↗ What are the common elements in most of the definitions of distance education?

↗ Why do you think there are differences of opinion in how distance education should be defined?

↗ How do you personally think distance education should be defined?

for distance education. However, the degree of interactivity available with various video distance education options varies. Some options have fairly limited interactivity (see Figure 11–4).

Video technologies are widespread, and the most advanced video technology, two-way video, is becoming more common in K–12 schools. A national survey of distance education in elementary and secondary schools

Technology	Description	Examples
Audio cassettes and CDs	Audio cassettes and CDs, often supplementing print material, provide a convenient, easy-to-use, and inexpensive way to deliver audio-based instruction asynchronously. They are often used for self-study or correspondence courses.	↗ Foreign language self-study programs ↗ "How-to" instructional modules ↗ Books on tape
Radio	Radio has the capability to reach a relatively broad geographical region at relatively low cost when compared to television. Radio broadcasts are a synchronous form of distance education; they adhere to a fixed schedule. Radio is also a one-way medium; it sends information from the instructor to the learners, but it does not allow learners to communicate back to the instructor.	↗ Educational programming on National Public Radio ↗ Instructional lectures to remote regions, commonly used in developing countries
Audio teleconferencing	***Audio teleconferencing*** extends a basic telephone call to permit instruction and interaction among individuals or groups at two or more locations. By using a speakerphone or more sophisticated audio equipment (e.g., microphones, amplifiers, high-quality speakers), members of the audience can both hear and be heard allowing for live, two-way interaction. It can be supplemented by print-based or graphical materials. ***Audiographics*** refers to the use of audio teleconferencing along with the transmission of still pictures or graphics via fax or computer.	↗ Question and answer session between elementary students and the author of a children's book recently read in class ↗ Dialogue between foreign language students and native speakers of the language ↗ Collaboration among students at two different schools on a common project
Podcasts	*See computer-based technologies following.*	

FIGURE 11–3 Audio-based distance education technologies.

Using a speakerphone, students can engage in an audio teleconference with individuals at a distance.
Source: John Underwood, Center for Instructional Services, Purdue University.

found that 55 percent of districts offering distance education courses used two-way interactive video (National Center for Education Statistics, 2005). However, it is important to recognize that this technology is still relatively new and can be complex and expensive to set up and operate. Two-way video transmission over network or telephone lines may require specialized equipment and can be subject to problems with sound and picture quality. However, the development of relatively easy-to-use Internet-based video conferencing equipment from companies such as Polycom (http://www.polycom.com) is making video conferencing more accessible. With a unit such as this, you can make a two-way video connection to another site equipped with a similar unit just by dialing the Internet address of the other site, similar to making a telephone call. The equipment is controlled with a simple remote control device much like a TV remote control. A room-to-room video conferencing unit includes a camera, microphone, and built-in codec (compressor/decompressor) for transmitting video over digital telephone lines or the Internet. Schools interested in exploring this technology should consult experts in the field for advice about equipment, options, and requirements.

Computer-Based Technologies

Computers are the newest tools for distance education. In addition to the use of packaged software as part of correspondence courses, the computer can be used as a

Technology	Description	Examples
Video cassettes and DVDs	Video cassettes and DVDs provide asynchronous distance education. Video cassettes, like their audio counterparts, are a convenient and easy-to-use technology. VCRs are commonplace, and video cassettes provide a familiar way to deliver instruction into students' homes. As DVDs replace VCRs, more educational materials are being released on this newer medium.	↗ Basic skills and literacy self-study courses (e.g., *Hooked on Phonics*) ↗ Musical instrument (e.g., guitar, piano) home study courses ↗ Computer skills training courses
One-way video	Broadcast video, like radio, is a synchronous technology that involves transmission of both audio and video information to a mass audience. It is a relatively cost-effective way to reach a broad geographical area. Its chief limitations are time dependence (i.e., programs are broadcast only at certain times) and the lack of interaction between instructor and learners.	↗ Educational programming on public television stations ↗ School-based offerings such as *Channel One* and *CNN Newsroom* ↗ Educational courses offered via local cable companies
One-way video with two-way audio	This technology combines one-way video with audio "talkback" capability, usually added by means of a simple telephone connection between the originating video location and the receiving sites. Students can call the instructor with questions or comments and so be active participants rather than passive receivers of a video program. Limitations include the added cost of talkback capability, the instructor's lack of visual contact with callers, and problems of access that can arise when many receiving sites attempt to call a single originating site.	↗ College and university courses (e.g., teacher professional development) broadcast live to multiple receiving sites ↗ Satellite teleconferences in which a small group of experts at one site presents information to and accepts input from various receiving sites
Two-way video	In two-way interactive video, also called **video conferencing,** both sending and receiving sites are equipped with cameras, microphones, and video monitors. Some means of transmission—satellite, microwave, cable, digital-grade telephone line, or the Internet—links the two (or sometimes more) sites together permitting a high level of interaction. This is the closest approximation to face-to-face instruction via technological means.	↗ Advanced foreign language course taught at one site by a teacher who teaches and interacts with both local students and students at another school ↗ Students at two different schools working on the same science project make live presentations to each other about their research findings

FIGURE 11–4   Video-based distance education technologies.

A two-way interactive video classroom, such as the one shown here, allows video and audio to be transmitted between two sites.
Source: Scott Cunningham/Merrill

This unit from Polycom supports video conferencing over digital telephone lines or the Internet.
Source: Polycom, Inc.

communication tool. **Computer-mediated communication (CMC)** is the term given to any use of the computer for communication between teacher and learners and among learners, often over distances. Common CMC applications include e-mail, chat/instant messaging, online discussions, and Web-based instruction (see Figure 11–5). Of course, the computer can also be used as a tool for gathering information and resources and for sharing information. As we discussed in Chapter 10, the World Wide Web is a huge repository of up-to-date information on nearly every topic imaginable, and it can also be a platform for students to share their work with one another.

The computer is now the most widely used platform for distance education delivery. In the past decade, online learning courses and virtual schools have grown rapidly. According to data from surveys conducted by the Sloan Consortium (http://www.sloan-c.org/), online enrollments in higher education more than doubled from 2002 to 2007 and now exceed 3.9 million (Allen & Seaman, 2008). Likewise, about three-fourths of U. S.

school districts reported having students taking online or blended/hybrid courses in 2007–08 with a total enrollment estimated to be over one million (Picciano & Seaman, 2009). In the fall of 2008, 44 states offered significant online learning opportunities for students, either full-time online programs, supplemental programs, or both (Watson, Germin, & Ryan, 2008). The reason for this dramatic increase is simple. Computer technologies have grown to encompass many of the other technologies that have traditionally been used in distance education. Computers and the World Wide Web can deliver textual information, graphics, audio, and even video to learners in remote classroom locations or in their own homes. Plus, the Web provides a communication channel between teacher and learners and among learners (see Figure 11–6). This technology makes education more accessible and more convenient than ever before. Further, recent research from the U.S. Department of Education (Means, Toyama, Murphy, Bakia, & Jones, 2009) indicates that online learning, on average, yields better learning outcomes than face-to-face instruction.

Technology	Description	Examples
Computer-based media	Like audio and video cassettes, computer media such as CD-ROMs or DVD-ROMs can be mailed to learners for asynchronous correspondence study on home computers. While Web-based instruction can often replace packaged software today, some bandwidth intensive applications, such as digital video, work better when delivered on computer-readable media.	↗ Technical skills courses, such as "how to" courses for using various computer applications (e.g., *The Video Professor*) ↗ Self-study courses in disciplines such as foreign language and business education
E-mail, chat, and instant messaging	E-mail, chat, and instant messaging support communication between teacher and learners, between teacher and parents, or among individual learners. While e-mail is asynchronous, chat and instant message allow for synchronous communication. Common e-mail, chat, and instant messaging applications can be used, and course support systems such as *Blackboard*, *Angel*, and *Moodle* have their own built-in e-mail and chat functions.	↗ Electronic communication between a teacher and students or parents ↗ Class discussions in a chat room or via an e-mail list ↗ Student interaction with a distant expert such as a NASA scientist ↗ Online "office hours" when distant students can contact their instructor
Online discussion forums	Online discussion forums, or computer conferencing systems, permit two or more individuals to engage in an asynchronous text-based dialogue. Individuals type messages and post them to the forum at any time, and the computer maintains and organizes the messages. An online discussion resembles conversation, in printed form, where participants can drop in and out at any time. Popular electronic course support systems such as *Blackboard*, *Angel*, and *Moodle* have built-in discussion forum capabilities.	↗ Online class discussions of class topics or common readings ↗ Online debates about issues related to class topics ↗ Sharing student works, such as papers or projects, to permit peer review and critique ↗ Student group collaboration on a project outside of school hours

FIGURE 11–5 Computer-based distance education technologies.

Podcasting	A *podcast* is a digital media file, most often audio, distributed via the Internet for playback on a portable media player, such as Apple's iPod, or computer. *Podcasting* is the process of making and distributing podcasts. Video podcasts, also called *vodcasts*, are also available. Podcasting, like radio and television, is way of broadcasting information widely. Unlike radio and TV, podcasts are not limited by geography but can reach anywhere that the Internet reaches.	↗ Students listen to recorded lectures as a way to catch-up because of absence or to study for an exam. ↗ The teacher records learning exercises, such as vocabulary words or foreign language comprehension activities, for student use outside of class.
Webinars	A *webinar* is a synchronous seminar or meeting conducted over the Web and supported by audio and shared images. It resembles an audio teleconference with audiographics. In most cases, one individual leads the meeting while the participants watch and listen to the live presentation at their computers. The audio may be delivered via the telephone or voice over IP (VoIP), Internet-based telephone, while the visuals are delivered via the Web.	↗ Live lectures or presentations to learners at remote sites ↗ Interactive meetings
Blogs and wikis	A *blog* is a personal online journal where individuals can post messages for others to read. A *wiki* is a type of software that allows people to collaboratively create and edit Web pages. See Chapter 10 for more information. In distance education, blogs and wikis are increasing used as tools for students to develop and share their work with the instructor and others.	↗ Student journals about readings and other class content ↗ Collaborative development of student projects and papers
Internet-based audio and video conferencing	Computers on the Internet can be used for audio and video conferencing, replacing other types of audiovisual equipment. Internet-based telephony or voice over IP (VoIP) supports telephone calls on the Internet; *Skype* is a popular tool for VoIP. **Desktop video conferencing** is the computer equivalent of video conferencing or what is sometimes called *video phone* technology. Software for Internet or IP-based video conferencing includes White Pine's *CUSeeMe,* Microsoft's *NetMeeting,* Adobe *Connect*, and proprietary packages from vendors such as Polycom, PictureTel, and others.	↗ See examples under audio-based and video-based technologies previously.
Web-based instruction	Web instruction, also known as **online learning** or **e-learning,** can present content, provide links to online information, and serve as a focal point for a distance education experience. Online course management systems, such as *Blackboard, Angel*, and *Moodle*, consolidate a number of functions (content presentation, discussion forums, chat, quizzes, and grading) that an instructor might desire (see "Toolbox: Course Management Systems" on page 219). Newer technologies, such as *Tegrity,* Articulate *Presenter,* and Adobe *Connect,* allow presentations to be captured and put on the Web. Software tools originally designed for collaborative work, such as Lotus *Notes* and *Groove,* can also support online learning.	↗ Complete courses on almost any topic ↗ Online supplements to traditional face-to-face courses

FIGURE 11–6 Products like Adobe Connect, shown here, support communication between teacher and learners via the Internet.
Source: Reprinted with permission of Adobe, Inc.

Distance education learners may have characteristics that are different from learners in traditional classrooms.
Source: iStockphoto.

PLANNING FOR DISTANCE EDUCATION

Distance education allows students to obtain learning experiences, from enrichments of traditional lessons to complete courses and degree programs, at places and often at times that are convenient for them. Distance education technologies can be used to meet many of the educational goals one would have in a typical classroom. However, sometimes modifications of traditional approaches may be necessary to be successful in the distance education environment, and distance education learners may differ in some ways from students in the traditional classroom.

Understanding the Distance Education Learner

Distance education technologies may be used across a variety of grade levels and subject matters. Because of this, there is no single profile that describes the typical distance education learner. However, learners who take courses taught at a distance tend to have characteristics that are different from those of learners in traditional educational settings (Simonson, Smaldino, Albright, & Zvacek, 2006). For example, in K–12 schools, distance education learners may tend to be either more advanced or lagging behind the average student, because distance education courses are often offered to meet advanced placement needs or as make-up courses for students who have already failed the subject (Picciano & Seaman, 2007). When planning for distance education, it is important to take into account the special characteristics of these learners.

↗ Some distance education learners, such as students pursuing advanced coursework (e.g., Advanced Placement courses), are likely to be highly motivated and self-directed because they are seeking out learning experiences to fulfill personal needs or wishes such as obtaining college credits. Those who pursue advanced coursework at a distance are often capable students who require more challenging work than the average student.

↗ Other distance education learners might include students who have been unsuccessful in traditional classroom settings and are completing remedial coursework at a distance. These students may have anxiety about their ability to perform, especially when first starting a distance education course or program. These students may have difficulty academically and require higher levels of support and assistance than the average student.

↗ Many distance education learners prefer learning opportunities that are flexible in terms of time and place. They may pursue distance education because other obligations (e.g., school or work schedules, family responsibilities) make it difficult for them to fulfill their goals via traditional forms of education. Therefore, providing options and remaining flexible are important.

↗ Distance education learners across all settings may be more prone than traditional learners to drop out or fail to complete a course/program because of competing obligations, the need to maintain self-direction when learning at a distance, and the difficulty of receiving adequate support at a distance. Teachers should be aware of this and integrate strategies for helping students to monitor their progress and stay on task when learning at a distance.

Preparing for Distance Education

Now that you have an understanding of distance learners, following are some things to consider as you plan and prepare the learning materials, the learning environment, and the learners for distance education.

Toolbox: Course Management Systems

Course management systems (CMSs) are software programs that integrate a variety of functions in support of teaching and learning activities in an online environment. Popular course management systems include *Blackboard, Angel,* and *Moodle* among others (see Figure 11–7). *Sakai* (http://sakaiproject.org/) is an open-source course management project that is gaining popularity. Most course management systems integrate multiple course support functions including:

↗ content organization and presentation,
↗ student record/grade management,
↗ communication tools (e.g., e-mail, chat, and asynchronous discussions),
↗ online quizzing/testing, and
↗ other tools for managing course content and activities.

In recent years, these systems have begun to migrate from higher education, where they are very popular for supporting online and blended/hybrid courses, to K–12 education. We can expect to see much greater use of CMSs in K-12 education in the future.

CMSs provide students with a central point of access for information about a course, and they give teachers the tools to make course content and information available to students through a secure Web interface. Unlike typical Web pages, where anyone on the Internet has access to the information, a course management system can restrict access to only those students who are actually enrolled in the course, because students must log in with an ID and password. In addition, features such as online testing and discussion boards provide new ways of performing typical classroom instructional activities. As these systems continue to evolve, we are likely to see an even greater range of functionality.

FIGURE 11–7   Screen from *Moodle,* a popular course management system.
Source: Reprinted with permission of Moodle.

Be sure to prepare the learning materials, the learning environment, and your learners for a distance learning experience.
Source: Polycom, Inc.

Preparing the Learning Materials

↗ Provide detailed information to learners including explicit directions, a clear timeline, guidelines for how to participate, grading information, what to do in the event of technical problems, and where to seek assistance. An extensive course syllabus, distance learning handbook, or website can provide the necessary information. When teaching online, create a frequently asked questions (FAQ) file for learners to access.

↗ Take advantage of the medium when preparing distance education materials. Video, for example, can be used to show action or zoom in on something of interest. However, when using video, avoid "talking heads" as this will quickly become very uninteresting. When teaching on the Web, take advantage of the ability to link to information resources and facilitate communication among learners; avoid static pages of Web content that offer no improvement over the pages of a book.

↗ Send materials to remote sites or make them available on the Web to ensure that learners have access to whatever they need.

↗ Make back-up plans in the event of technical problems, and be sure to inform the learners what to do in the event of unforeseen problems.

Preparing the Learning Environment

↗ Arrange for the use of the distance education technology well in advance of when you will need it. For example, some technologies, such as broadcast and two-way video, may require significant lead time to reserve a studio, obtain network time, and so on. With other technologies, such as IP-based video conferencing, it may be necessary to configure the school's Internet firewall to allow the connection. When using computer-based technologies, you must make sure that any necessary software in installed (e.g., *Skype* for doing Internet-based telephony).

↗ Prior to beginning a distance education lesson, test the equipment to make certain that it is working properly. If you are using Web resources, check links to make sure they still work. Make sure that browser settings are properly configured to use the resources you will access (e.g., *Java* may need to be enabled or pop-up windows may need to unblocked).

↗ If using audio or video technologies, adjust the audio and video levels so that all of the learners will be able to see and hear.

Preparing the Learners

↗ Inform learners of what to expect in advance of a distance education experience. Whether using an audio teleconference, two-way video conference, or online discussion forum, learners may be unfamiliar with distance education and could benefit from an orientation.

↗ Have students practice using the technology in advance so that they become familiar with how it works. If using video conferencing equipment, for example, arrange for a local connection that can be used for practice in advance of the real thing, or spend time during the first class having students practice. In an online course, have students do a nongraded activity, such as posting a personal biographical sketch to an online discussion forum, as a warm-up.

↗ Set expectations and establish norms for participation (e.g., inform users in an online discussion forum of when, how often, and in what ways they should contribute to the online discussion). Stick to these expectations, especially

early in the activity, and model appropriate behavior for the students.

↗ Make certain that learners at a distance have access to the resources that they need, know how to contact you or other sources of help, and know what to do in the event of problems. Be available to your students, perhaps through online office hours.

Problems and Pitfalls

↗ *Monetary cost.* All distance education technologies involve some real monetary cost. In the case of simpler technologies, such as audio teleconferencing, this may be as little as the cost of a long-distance telephone call. That alone, however, may be a barrier to implementation in some schools. More advanced distance education technologies, such as two-way interactive video that uses satellite or digital telephone line transmission, can be very costly. The required equipment is often expensive, and the recurring costs associated with actually connecting two sites can be quite high as well. Schools should weigh the costs of using particular technologies against the benefits.

↗ *Technical difficulty.* Distance education technologies can be technically complex, and this complexity may mean that teachers cannot manage on their own. Although an audio teleconference may not be too difficult to set up, video conferencing may require expert assistance and may involve the coordinated efforts of local personnel, vendors, network technicians, and others. This complexity also increases the chance that something may go wrong.

↗ *Need for planning.* As we have emphasized, distance education requires careful planning. This is true even for simpler forms of distance education. Advance scheduling of equipment and facilities may be required. Materials must be prepared in advance and may need to be sent to participants at remote sites. In many cases, teachers need to redesign materials and learning activities for the distance education medium.

↗ *Need for training and support.* Teachers may need training to effectively use distance education technologies. Learners may need assistance in learning via these unfamiliar means, and provisions for assisting learners need to be made. These may involve onsite coordinators, telephone help, e-mail, and so on. In short, distance education is complex; teachers and schools should be aware of the significant effort involved. As with any other educational enterprise, distance education requires time, effort, commitment, and resources. The technology is only a tool that helps schools meet existing needs.

↗ *Not all content works well.* Some content cannot effectively be taught at a distance. For example, you would *not* want to fly in a plane that has been serviced by a mechanic who has only learned about aircraft engines on the Internet. Hands-on experience would be essential!

IMPLEMENTING DISTANCE EDUCATION

Now that you are aware of the need for planning for distance education, we move on to consider some examples of ways that distance education technologies can be implemented for teaching and learning at a distance. Following these examples, we discuss strategies for teaching at a distance and utilization guidelines for distance education. Figure 11–8 gives a comparison of a traditional face-to-face class with a synchronous video-based distance education class and an asynchronous online distance education class, the most common forms of distance education.

Distance Education Examples

↗ A high school teacher offers a specialized class (e.g., advanced computer programming, Latin, Russian) to interested students in his own school as well as several other schools using a one-way video with two-way audio connection.

↗ A teacher invites an expert (e.g., book author, scientist, politician) at a distance to interact with her students via an audio teleconference using an available speakerphone.

↗ A high school student with a talent for mathematics would like to take advanced calculus, but a course in the subject is not offered at her school. She enrolls in a Web-based course from a nearby university and takes the class online using a computer at home.

↗ A museum in a major metropolitan center offers virtual field trips to classes in schools through a statewide two-way video network.

↗ Using desktop (computer-based) video conferencing and e-mail, preservice teachers at a college tutor elementary school students to help them improve their reading and mathematics skills.

↗ Searching for lesson ideas, an English teacher posts a question to an Internet discussion group and receives several helpful suggestions from other teachers around the country. She has an online chat with one of those teachers to learn more about a proposed lesson suggestion.

↗ Students in classes at two different middle schools work on a common project (e.g., investigating local water quality) and prepare presentations that they share with each other using Yugma, a webinar program (http://www.yugma.com).

↗ To get practice doing research and making presentations, sixth-graders prepare informational presentations on animals for second-grade learners. They make the presentations from a television studio in their school to several elementary classrooms simultaneously using a cable television network within the school district.

	Traditional Face-to-Face Class	**Synchronous Video Class**	**Asynchronous Online Class**
Characteristics	Teacher and students meet at the same time in the same classroom or other instructional space.	A teacher in one location uses video to present to and/or interact with students at other locations, often specially equipped video receiving sites.	A teacher and students in different locations use networked computers to participate whenever and wherever it is convenient for them.
Common instructional methods	Face-to-face presentation, demonstration, in-class discussion, cooperative learning, drill and practice, textbook readings, etc.	Video lectures and demonstrations, discussion (two-way video), out-of-class homework and projects, textbook readings, etc.	Web-based instruction, online discussion, chat, WebQuests and other online activities, textbook readings, etc.
Student-teacher and student-student interaction	Face-to-face interactions	Video-mediated interactions (two-way video), talk-back (one-way video), fax, e-mail, etc.	Computer-mediated interactions: email, chat, online discussion, etc.
Assessments	Live quizzes and exams, in-person homework and projects, etc.	Proctored quizzes and exams, mailed homework and projects, etc.	Online quizzes and exams, electronically submitted homework and projects, etc.

FIGURE 11–8   Comparison of face-to-face, synchronous video, and asynchronous online classes.

Strategies for Teaching at a Distance

In many ways, teaching at a distance is similar to teaching face-to-face. The same instructional methods that are commonly used in the traditional classroom—presentation, demonstration, discussion, cooperative learning, drill and practice, simulation, etc.—can also be used in distance education, although some modifications may be necessary. A class discussion, for example, can be conducted at a distance using audio teleconferencing or two-way video. However, the instructor may need to call on students at distant locations to engage them in the discussion. In an online class, a discussion could take place via chat or in an asynchronous discussion forum although individuals will type their contributions rather than speaking. A presentation or demonstration can be done at a distance, via one-way or two-way video, by sending a videotape to the learner, or by posting a *Tegrity*, Adobe *Connect*, or Articulate *Presenter* presentation (which combines *PowerPoint* with the accompanying video or audio) to a website (see Figure 11–9).

Cooperative learning can take place using two-way video or Internet-based collaboration tools.

In other ways, strategies for teaching at a distance depend on the particular technology being used. For example, when using video for distance education, it is important to be aware of the characteristics of the medium. Video is a visual medium, so it is important to use visuals (e.g., pictures, graphical organizers) to convey information. When creating visuals for video (e.g., *PowerPoint* slides), use a large font size and avoid the edges of the screen which are often cut off when converted to video. When teaching via video, make eye contact with the camera, and speak loudly and clearly. Avoid clothing that can cause visual effects on television (e.g., plaids, checks, all white). Camera shots and pacing should be varied and activities should be changed frequently to maintain the interest of the distant learners.

When teaching online, make resources available online; this may entail designing web pages or creating

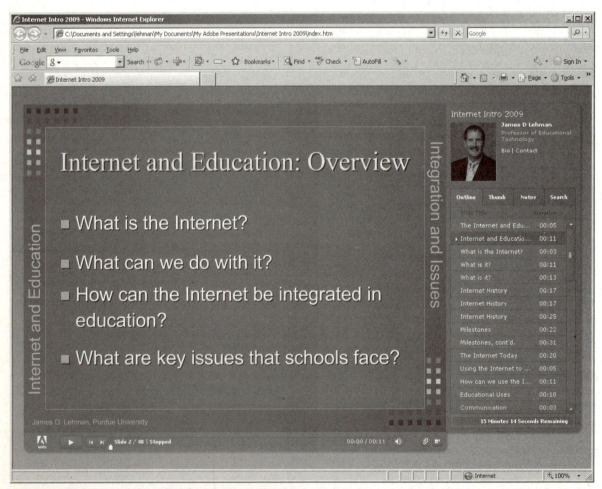

FIGURE 11–9   Adobe *Presenter*, shown here, is one of several programs that can package a *PowerPoint* presentation with audio or video to be posted on the Web.
Source: Reprinted with permission of Adobe Systems. Inc.

materials for a course management system such as *Blackboard*, *Angel*, or *Moodle*. Establish regular office hours so that distant learners can make contact by e-mail, chat, or telephone. When conducting online discussions, establish guidelines and norms for participation (e.g., set the time line for the discussion, set parameters for number and length of postings, model the types of contributions desired, establish guidelines for online etiquette). See the "Toolbox: Managing Asynchronous Discussions Online" given below for more information.

Assessing Student Performance in Distance Education

After planning and implementing distance education experiences, the next important part of the PIE model is to evaluate the instruction. One of the ways we evaluate whether our instruction is effective is by assessing the students. Approaches to assessing student performance at a distance, like approaches to teaching at a distance, are often no different from those used in face-to-face

Toolbox: Managing Asynchronous Discussions Online

A common feature of many online and blended/hybrid courses is asynchronous discussions (see Figure 11–10). Online discussions provide one of the only mechanisms for interaction and exchange in fully online courses. They not only replace traditional live discussions in a classroom, but often provide a vehicle for communicating information about the course and assignments, fostering collaborative learning, and sharing student work. In blended/hybrid courses, online discussions can increase student time on task by extending class discussions beyond ordinary class time. While asynchronous discussions naturally will vary depending on the specific topics discussed and the purposes of the discussion, some general tips for conducting online discussions are given here.

↗ Build discussions around specific topics from the course. This will help to provide focus and establish a clear schedule.

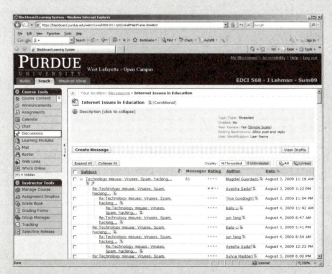

FIGURE 11–10 A screen from Blackboard *Vista* showing a discussion forum.
Source: Vista is a copyright of Blackboard, Inc. All rights reserved.

↗ Establish a clear time line for each online discussion, and be specific about the expectations for when and how often students should contribute. Set parameters for length and quantity of messages.

↗ Assess students on both the quantity and quality of their participation. If you value the discussion, students are more likely to value it as well.

↗ Establish basic ground rules for participation and etiquette in the online discussion, and model appropriate behavior. This can help to head off problems and misunderstandings.

↗ Create an open and welcoming atmosphere for the discussion. Refer to students by name and share relevant personal experiences to build a sense of community.

↗ Use techniques to structure the online discussion (e.g., case studies, debates, assigning roles to students).

↗ Encourage students to quote from the original message when making replies. This makes it easier for readers to follow the discussion thread.

↗ Allow students to take leadership at times by starting a discussion topic, developing a discussion question, or synthesizing comments from classmates.

↗ Monitor the discussion to make certain that students stay on the topic and do not get off on tangents. However, avoid intervening in a discussion too quickly; the pronouncement of the teacher can sometimes squelch further discussion.

↗ Ask good questions to stimulate thought and discussion. Occasionally summarize points from the ongoing discussion to help synthesize the topic. At the end of the discussion, bring closure by wrapping up the key points.

↗ Provide feedback to the learners. You need not acknowledge every message a student posts, but regular feedback is essential to let the students know how they are doing and that you are involved.

↗ Be available to students who might want to contact you outside of the discussion. Monitor e-mail and establish regular hours when you will be in your office or available online.

educational settings. However, just as teaching approaches must sometimes be modified for teaching at a distance, assessment techniques must sometimes be modified for effective use at a distance.

Traditional tests—whether multiple choice, true-false, short answer, or essay—are one of the most common forms of assessment in education. In the typical classroom setting, tests are administered by the instructor who monitors the students during the exam and enforces a specific time limit. Tests can also be used when learning occurs at a distance, although issues of identity authentication and test security must be addressed. When tests are not given face-to-face, there is the potential for cheating. One traditional solution to the testing problem in distance education has been the use of proctors at remote sites. Tests are mailed to a proctor, and students then take the test from the proctor in the usual way. This solution works well for distance learning situations in which a group of students is located at a single remote site, such as a video-based course that is transmitted to a remote school or workplace site.

The use of exam proctors is less suitable for online courses where individual students may be widely scattered. However, online testing is becoming an increasingly viable option. Course management systems such as *Blackboard*, *Angel*, and *Moodle*, as well as stand-alone testing software, can generate and administer quizzes and tests online (see Figure 11–11). Various options are available within most testing software packages to generate a set of questions of various types (e.g., multiple choice, true-false, short answer), draw test questions from the available set, randomize the order of questions, and so forth. In addition, online test taking can be limited to particular time frames and even particular Internet domains or addresses to limit access. The issue of authentication of student identification online can be addressed through system logins and the use of personal identification information (e.g., asking for an ID number or personal information), but one can never know for certain if an online learner working from home has a helper in the room or is using the textbook for assistance.

Many distance education instructors simply avoid the issue of online testing by using other means of assessment. For example, rather than giving timed exams, one can give students in a distance education course a take-home exam that stresses application, analysis, synthesis, and evaluation of course material rather than recall of content. Traditional in-class forms of assessment such as papers and projects can also be used in distance education. Alternative forms of assessment such as portfolios can be used at a distance just as well as in the traditional classroom. Thus, instructors have a full range of options available for assessing student performance in distance education.

UTILIZATION GUIDELINES FOR DISTANCE EDUCATION

↗ *Plan thoroughly in advance.* As we noted at the beginning of this chapter, good instruction always requires planning, but it is even more important in distance education. It is difficult, if not impossible, to teach "on the fly" at a distance. You need to set schedules in advance, prepare materials, ensure that distant students have access to necessary resources, arrange for synchronous connections, practice using the equipment, and so on. Careful advance planning is the single most important thing that you can do to ensure a successful distance education experience for yourself and your students.

↗ *Make contingency plans.* The technologies involved in distance education can and do fail. The speakerphone for an audio teleconference may not work, your video connection to a remote site may fail, or your connection to the Internet may go "down." Always have backup plans that you and your students can follow in the event things do not work as expected.

↗ *Use the medium.* Make effective use of your particular medium of communication. When using video-based distance education, you could prepare effective visuals, do demonstrations, and otherwise make use of what video offers. When teaching an online class, you could link to Web-based resources that your students can use and take advantage of the computer's ability to store materials and make them accessible at any hour of the day.

↗ *Encourage active participation.* Regardless of the particular medium of communication, encourage active student participation. During a synchronous audio or video conference, call on distant students by name. If a local class is listening to a speaker at a remote location, have each student prepare a question to ask the speaker. During asynchronous online discussions, respond directly to students' comments; use private e-mail if you need to prod a reluctant student to participate more fully.

↗ *Vary activities and approaches.* Almost nothing is as boring as a "talking head" lecture on video. Change your activities and instructional approaches to add variety and maintain students' interest. During audio or video conferencing, change activities frequently, especially if you have younger learners. Mix online and off-line activities. In Web-based instruction, use a variety of approaches such as self-study content modules, Web information retrieval, asynchronous discussion forums, synchronous chat sessions, and so on, to keep lessons interesting.

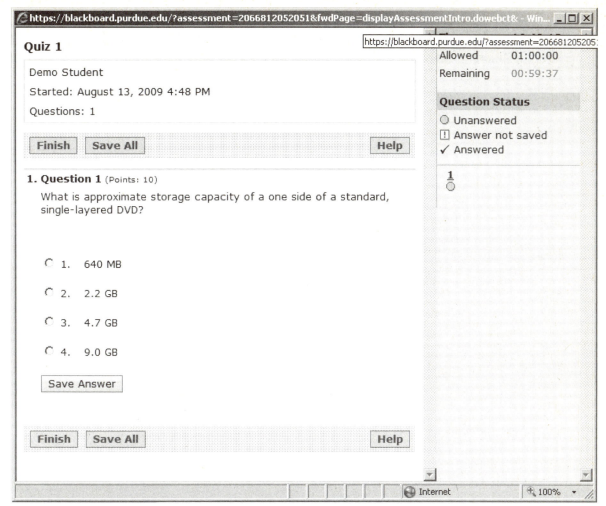

FIGURE 11–11   A screen of an interactive quiz in blackboard *vista*.
Source: Reprinted with permission from Blackboard, Inc.

 Guide your students. Students at a distance may feel isolated and out of touch. You can help them by providing explicit guidance. Provide a clear schedule of when things will be happening and when any assignments are due. Prompt students about proper forms and level of participation (e.g., asking questions during a video conference, posting comments to an online discussion board). Summarize audio/video conferencing sessions or online discussions to help students understand the main points.

 Use appropriate assessment methods. As with all instruction, match your assessments to your learning objectives. If traditional testing is called for, consider using proctors or testing online. Use other forms of assessment (e.g., take-home exams, papers, projects, portfolios) as appropriate to your content and the needs of your students.

ISSUES RELATED TO DISTANCE EDUCATION

Copyright

As you have learned, copyright refers to the legal rights applied to original works authored in a tangible medium of expression (Refer again to the information on copyright in Chapter 8). As a reminder, copyright law grants copyright owners certain exclusive rights including the rights to copy or make derivatives of a work, sell or distribute the work, and perform or display the work in public. These rights are balanced by certain limitations including fair use and the face-to-face teaching exemption, which allow teachers to make certain uses of copyrighted works without permission from the copyright owner.

In 2002, the Technology, Education, and Harmonization (TEACH) Act was passed by Congress and enacted into law. It extended many of the protections

Toolbox: Copyright and Distance Education

Copyright law can be confusing, especially to those unfamiliar with it. To learn more about copyright law and how it applies in distance education, check out the websites below.

Website	URL
Copyright Management Center at Indiana University Purdue University at Indianapolis	http://www.copyright.iupui.edu/
North Carolina State University Libraries TEACH Act Toolkit	http://www.lib.ncsu.edu/scc/legislative/teachkit/
University of Idaho Engineering Outreach Distance Education at a Glance Guide #12	http://www.uidaho.edu/eo/dist12.html
University of Wisconsin Distance Education Clearinghouse Intellectual Property and Copyright	http://www.uwex.edu/disted/intprop.html

Suppose a teacher you know tells you that she is planning to teach an online course at a nearby school and asks you how copyright applies.

↗ What would you tell her are the key things to know about copyright and distance education?
↗ What cautions would you give?

afforded by the face-to-face teaching exemption to distance education settings. Under the provisions of the TEACH Act, it is permissible when teaching at a distance (i.e., via transmission or digital networks) to perform or display reasonable and limited portions of legally acquired works, comparable to what would typically be displayed in the course of a live classroom session, as long as this occurs as a material part of instruction under the supervision of an instructor in a class at a nonprofit educational institution. However, the law requires that policies regarding copyright must be implemented by the institution, and students must be informed that materials used within the course may be subject to copyright protection. Further, to the extent technically feasible, any performance of copyrighted works in conjunction with distance education should be restricted to the students officially enrolled in the course (e.g., through logins), and measures should be employed to prevent retention or further dissemination of any copyrighted work beyond the class session (e.g., students may be able to view a video but not download the source file).

So, distance educators are allowed to do many of the same things as classroom instructors, but these permissions do have their limits. For example, one cannot simply put a copyrighted work on an unprotected web page as part of an online course, because individuals other than the students in the class could easily access and copy the work. Measures such as password protection must be employed to limit access to the students in the class and prevent unauthorized use. To learn more, see "Toolbox: Copyright and Distance Education" (given above).

Support

Support tends to be a critical component of successful distance education. Technical support is often necessary to get the delivery technology (e.g., video, Web) up and running. In addition, technical support staff may be needed to assist learners if problems arise during a distance education course or lesson. Because learners are often located far from the campus or school where a distance education course originates, support is needed to help students get enrolled and acquire books and other course materials. As we have noted, it may also be necessary to have support staff at remote sites to distribute materials, assist learners, or proctor examinations. Many institutions that do significant amounts of distance education have an entire support structure dedicated to the distance education enterprise. Schools that are considering launching new distance education initiatives should carefully examine support needs before proceeding. As with other aspects of distance education, planning for support is important for a successful experience.

PEARSON **myeducationkit** Go to the Assignments and Activities section of Chapter 11 in MyEducationKit and complete the activity entitled "Professional Development for Virtual Schools." As you view this video, consider how virtual school teachers are prepared and supported in this example, and think about what you would need to learn and the kinds of support you would need if you were to teach online in the future.

Policy Issues

Policy issues may also arise with respect to distance education. One fundamental issue is the certification or accreditation of distance education courses and programs. Although research has tended to demonstrate that learners at a distance perform as well as or even better than those in traditionally delivered courses (Bernard et al., 2004; Machtmes & Asher, 2000; Means, Toyama, Murphy, Bakia, & Jones, 2009; Neumann & Shachar, 2003; Russell, 1999), there has traditionally been doubt about the quality of distance education experiences in comparison with those delivered face-to-face. As a result, distance educators often must produce evidence showing that courses taught at a distance are equivalent to those taught face-to-face. As distance education has expanded in recent years, many state agencies and accrediting organizations have come to accept that distance education courses can be just as rigorous and just as effective as traditional courses.

Teacher issues can also arise in distance learning situations. For example, how is a distance education course factored into a teacher's load? If a teacher has 15 students in a class at his/her school and another 20 students at remote video receiving sites, is that counted as two classes or one? Is an online class with 25 students equivalent to a face-to-face class with the same number of students? Many teachers who teach at a distance report that distance education requires more time and effort than traditional instruction. This is an important issue that must be addressed by school policies.

Basic administrative issues, such as costs and revenues, also need to be addressed by school policy. How are costs determined and revenue distributed in programs involving distance education? Due to the costs of the delivery technology and support structures, distance education programs may be more expensive than traditional programs. Further, when distance education programs are delivered at remote sites, there may be costs associated with the remote sites (e.g., support staff, proctors). So, schools may need to develop funding models that differ from those in traditional education.

myeducationkit Go to the Assignments and Activities section of Chapter 11 in MyEducationKit and complete the activity entitled "Virtual Schools as an Alternative." As you view this video, consider the issues that the developers of this virtual school faced and what they did to try to ensure that it successfully helped students to learn.

TECHNOLOGY COORDINATOR'S CORNER

At the beginning of this chapter, you learned about Miranda Allen, a high school Spanish teacher who wanted to use distance education technologies to provide the students in her advanced Spanish course with an authentic language learning experience. After doing some preparatory work, Miranda went to her school's technology coordinator, Donald Simpson, to see what could be done. Miranda explained to Mr. Simpson that her goal was to have her students get experience speaking to native speakers of Spanish, and she hoped they could arrange a live video connection between their schools in the United States and Mexico. Mr. Simpson agreed to investigate options, confer with the support staff in Señora Diego's school, and report back to Miranda.

A few days later, Mr. Simpson explained the options to Miranda. He said, "You have a few options. I looked into the possibility of a video teleconference. While we have satellite uplink capability, Señora Diego's school does not have a satellite receiver. The class would have to go to a university receiving site, which might be a problem. The other catch is that it would be very expensive. Then, I looked into the possibility of an Internet-based video conference. Unfortunately, Señora Diego's school has a relatively slow Internet connection. We could use a small PC-based video camera, but the quality would not be very good, especially for a whole class of students. Your other option would be to do an audio teleconference, either by making a long distance telephone call or using something like *Skype* over the Internet. That really just involves the use of a speakerphone to make the phone call. You'd have the cost of the phone call, but it would give your students the chance to speak to native Spanish speakers."

After weighing her options, Miranda decided to try an audio teleconference. Mr. Taylor, the principal, okayed the idea when the Spanish Club raised the funds to pay for the call. Mr. Simpson advised Miranda to consider several things in planning the activity. He pointed out the time difference, and he advised Miranda to have her students prepare for the audio teleconference by preparing questions in advance. He also advised Miranda to have a backup lesson plan in case things didn't work.

About a week later, using a speakerphone borrowed from the media center, Miranda called Señora Diego at the arranged time. Her students took turns asking their prepared questions and answering questions from the students in Mexico. Miranda's kids spoke Spanish, and Señora

Diego's kids spoke English. It was pretty crazy, but somehow they all managed to understand each other. As a follow-up activity, Miranda's students and Señora Diego's students became e-pals (e-mail pen pals). So, the students got to practice their writing skills as well as their speaking skills. They were motivated to do well because they were communicating with real students at the other school. It turned out to be a great way to harness the power of distance education technologies to make the classroom learning experience more real, more engaging, and just plain fun.

SUMMARY

In this chapter, we examined distance education, any organized instructional program in which the teacher and learners are physically separated. Distance education addresses problems of educational access caused by distance, disability, or work and family obligations, among others. Technology is often used in distance education to facilitate communication between teacher and learners. We examined the characteristics of three categories of distance education technologies: audio-based, video-based, and computer-based.

Planning is especially important for successful distance education. When planning for a distance education lesson, you should take advantage of the benefits of the technology, understand the characteristics of distance education learners, prepare for the experience, and avoid problems and pitfalls. Examples of distance education were presented, and strategies for implementing distance education were described. Assessment of student performance at a distance was considered, and utilization guidelines for distance education were presented.

Issues associated with distance education were also presented. These issues include copyright, the need for support, and issues related to policy.

PEARSON **myeducationkit™** To check your comprehension of the content covered in this chapter, go to the MyEducationKit for this book and complete the Study Plan for Chapter 11. Here you will be able to take a chapter quiz, receive feedback on your answers, and then access resources that will enhance your understanding of chapter content.

SUGGESTED RESOURCES

Print Resources

Allen, I. E. & Seaman, J. (2008). *Staying the course: Online education in the United States, 2008*. Needham, MA: Sloan Consortium (Sloan-C).

Beldarrain, Y. (2006). Distance education trends: Integrating new technologies to foster student interaction and collaboration. *Distance Education, 27*(2) 139–153.

Bernard, R. M., Abrami, P. C., Lou, Y., Borokhovski, E., Wade, A., Wozney, L., Wallet, P. A., Fiset, M., & Huang, B. (2004). How does distance education compare with classroom instruction? A meta-analysis of the empirical literature. *Review of Educational Research, 74*(3), 379–439.

Blomeyer, R., & Cavanaugh, C. (2007). *What works in K-12 online learning*. Washington, DC: ISTE Books.

Bonk, C. J., & Zhang, K. (2008). *Empowering online learning: 100+ activities for reading, reflecting, displaying, and doing*. San Francisco, CA : Jossey-Bass.

Cole, C., Ray, K., & Zanetis, J. (2009). Videoconferencing for K-12 classrooms. Washington, DC: ISTE Books.

Cyrs, T. E. (1997). *Teaching at a distance with the merging technologies: An instructional systems approach*. New Mexico State University: Center for Educational Development.

Dawley, L. (2007). *The tools for successful online teaching*. London: Idea Group.

Donaldson, A., & Conrad, R. (2004). *Engaging the online learner: Activities and resources for creative instruction*. Jossey-Bass.

Ko, S., & Rossen, S. (2008). *Teaching online: A practical guide*. Boston, MA: Houghton Mifflin.

Machtmes, K., & Asher, J. W. (2000). A meta-analysis of the effectiveness of telecourses in distance education. *The American Journal of Distance Education, 14*(1), 27–46.

Means, B., Toyama, Y., Murphy, R., Bakia, M., & Jones, K. (2009). *Evaluation of evidence-based practices in online learning: A meta-analysis and review of online learning studies*. Washington, DC: U.S. Department of Education, Office of Planning, Evaluation, and Policy Development.

Moore, M., & Kearsley, G. (2005). *Distance education: A systems view* (2nd ed.). Belmont, CA: Thomson Wadsworth.

Neumann, Y., & Shachar, M. (2003, October). Differences between traditional and distance education academic performances: A meta-analytic approach. *International Review of Research in Open and Distance Learning, 4*(2). Available at http://www.irrodl.org/content/v4.2/shachar-neumann.html.

Picciano, A. G., & Seaman, J. (2009). *K–12 online learning: A follow-up of the survey of U.S. school district administrators*. Needham, MA: Sloan Consortium (Sloan-C).

Ray, K., & Zanetis, J. (2008). *Interactive videoconferencing*. ISTE Books.

Rice, K. (2006). A comprehensive look at distance education in the K-12 context. *Journal of Research on Technology in Education, 38*(4), 425–448.

Russell, T. L. (1999). *The no significant difference phenomenon*. Available at http://www.nosignificantdifference.org/.

Simonson, M., Smaldino, S., Albright, M., & Zvacek, S. (2006). *Teaching and learning at a distance: Foundations of distance education* (3rd ed.). Upper Saddle River, NJ: Pearson Education.

Smaldino, S. E., Lowther, D. L., & Russell, J. D. (2008). *Instructional technology and media for learning* (9th ed.). Upper Saddle River, NJ: Pearson Education, Inc.

Watson, J., Germin, G., & Ryan, J. (2008). Keeping pace with K-12 online learning: A review of state-level policy and practice. Evergreen, CO: Evergreen Consulting Associates. Available: http://www.kpk12.com/.

Zandberg, I., & Lewis, L. (2008). *Technology-based distance education courses for public elementary and secondary school students: 2002-03 and 2004-05* (NCES 2008-008). Washington, DC: U.S. Department of Education, National Center for Education Statistics.

Electronic Resources

http://www.adec.edu/
(American Distance Education Consortium)

http://www.uidaho.edu/evo/distglan
(Distance Education at a Glance, University of Idaho Engineering Outreach)

http://www.uwex.edu/disted/index.cfm
(Distance Education Clearinghouse, University of Wisconsin-Extension)

http://www.distance-educator.com/k12/
(Distance-Educator.com)

http://www.educationworld.com/a_tech/archives/distance.shtml
(Education World: Distance Learning)

http://teams.lacoe.edu/
(TEAMS: Center for Distance and Online Learning, Los Angeles County Office of Education)

http://www.mivhs.org/
(Example of K-12 Online School: Michigan Virtual High School)

http://www.techlearning.com/section/Elearning
(Tech & Learning: eLearning Resources)

http://www.usdla.org/
(United States Distance Learning Association)

http://www.trainingshare.com/resources/12Reference.htm
(Online Resources from Dr. Bonk's Empowering Online Learning Book)

ENSURING SUCCESSFUL TECHNOLOGY-ENHANCED LEARNING EXPERIENCES

Evaluation and assessment are, and probably always will be, anxiety provoking. That is, most of us feel a little nervous when someone says, "Next week, you will be tested on . . ." or "It's time to assess your skill level in . . ." or even "Demonstrate how well you've mastered the goal of. . . ." Why? Because evaluation and assessment are the major ways we receive information about levels of our personal competency and skill and/or how well our programs are working—and that information may reveal some inadequacies. In a commercialized world that constantly promotes perfection, being shown that you or one of the programs are less than perfect is not something we like to hear.

If evaluation and assessment are that unpleasant, why bother? Although many students may think that tests are created merely as a way for teachers to inflict pain and suffering, in most cases, there are good reasons for their use. Those reasons center on the *feedback* they provide. By obtaining feedback about your current level of performance, you can make the changes needed to reach your specific goal. Likewise, feedback about how well an instructional lesson facilitates learning offers guidance in how the lesson can be improved. Reread the title of this section: "Ensuring Successful Technology-Enhanced Learning Experiences." Evaluation is a key step in making sure that success is achieved.

When individuals realize the value of feedback, student assessment and program evaluation become desirable tools for facilitating improvement. Think about an experience you may have had with someone who is an expert at something (e.g., cooking, teaching, managing people, art). In all cases (at least all that we can think of), those experts have mastered the art of self-assessment. Their goal is to change or eliminate small imperfections early on, so they do not become big problems later. This is the true essence of assessment—helping learners to assess where they are and then envisioning what their next steps might be.

In Chapter 12, the focus is on evaluation as a tool for improvement. It looks at evaluating instructional materials and assessing student learning. In both cases, we discuss various instruments you can use to supply feedback *as* learning is occurring (or supposed to be occurring) as well as *after* learning has occurred. Additionally, you will see how the computer can be an important assistant in your evaluation process.

12 Evaluation of Instructional Materials and the Assessment of Student Learning

Source: Sharie Kennedy/Corbis.

KEY WORDS AND CONCEPTS

Evaluation

Assessment

Cycle of continuous improvement

Pretest

Embedded test

Posttest

Transfer

Pilot test

Formative evaluation

Summative evaluation

Triangulation

Assessment rubric

CHAPTER OBJECTIVES

After reading and studying this chapter, you will be able to:

↗ Describe the purposes of evaluating the effectiveness of the instructional materials before, during, and after a learning experience.

↗ Describe the purposes of assessing student learning before, during, and after a learning experience.

↗ Identify and describe a variety of techniques for evaluating instruction and assessing students and describe their advantages and limitations.

↗ Use a list of developmental guidelines to construct and/or evaluate a set of evaluation and assessment instruments.

INTRODUCTION

We often find ourselves evaluating the world around us; it is a common activity. As an example, recall the last time that you took a shower. Did you just take off your clothes, step in, turn on the water, lather up, rinse off, and step out? Probably not. Most of us have learned not to stand in front of a shower and then turn it on. Instead, we first stand off to the side, run the water for a moment, and then check its temperature with our hand or foot. If the water is too hot or too cold, we adjust it until it feels "just right." Likewise, during the shower, we monitor the temperature and adjust it whenever it feels too hot or too cold. During a typical shower, we may also find ourselves thinking about whether we have rinsed all the soap off, left enough hot water for the next person in the family, and stayed in the shower long enough to wake up, sing, and think about the day's activities.

This example illustrates the basic purpose of evaluation: to make sure that we are getting what we want and, if not, to figure out what we can do so that we can get what we want in the near future.

In this chapter, we describe evaluation in terms of *what* it is, *why* you should do it, and *how* it should be done. As shown in Figure 12–1, evaluation of both learners and the instructional materials is a key piece in the jigsaw puzzle of planning and delivering valuable learning experiences. Recall that the vision of this text is to provide the foundations for enhanced learning experiences (see Chapter 1). Through the process of evaluation, we help to ensure that those learning experiences are of the quality that will lead to the greatest levels of learning.

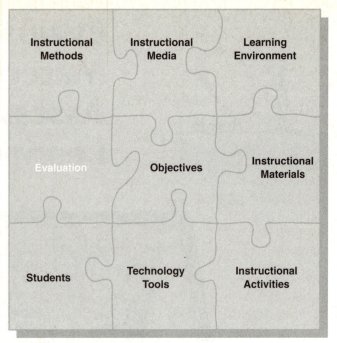

FIGURE 12–1   The "Evaluation and Assessment" piece is a key part of understanding the full design, development, and implementation procedures.

 WHAT IS EVALUATION?

Evaluation is the process of gathering information from multiple sources in order to judge the merit or worth of a program, project, or entity (Rossi, Lipsey, & Freeman, 2004). With that information, the goal is to improve the instruction's development and implementation. An essential source of data when completing an evaluation of a set of instructional materials or some type of learning experience is the data gathered from the target audience of learners. **Assessment** is the process of gathering evidence of what learners know and can do. Assessing student performance is critical to gaining a full understanding of the merit of specific instructional materials. Within this chapter we will focus on the general process of evaluating of instructional materials and specifically the role of student assessment within that overall evaluation.

Within education, evaluation is an ongoing process. Recall again, from the opening description of adjusting the water temperature for a shower, about how needed adjustments to the temperature are determined. Note that evaluation in this case did not occur at a single point in time. Evaluation occurred before, during, and after the shower. This is typical of good evaluation, in the classroom as well as the bathroom.

In Chapter 1, we described evaluation as a time to reflect on both successes and problems, resulting in information you can use to improve the quality of instruction. Seen in this way, a thorough evaluation considers all instructional components—objectives, activities, methods,

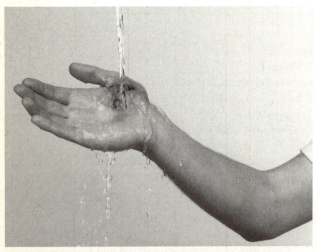

Just as evaluating the water temperature in a shower ensures a comfortable, safe, and reliable experience, so too the evaluation of instructional materials ensures a successful learning experience.
Source: Andy Crawford/Dorling Kindersley Media Library.

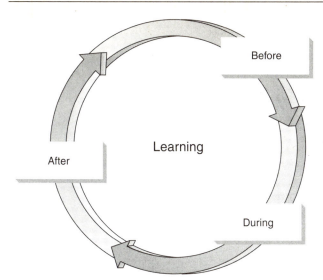

FIGURE 12–2 The cycle of continuous improvement.

media, and materials—as well as the way you combine and present them to students to help them learn. This reflection can occur at any point in the learning process. This translates into a **cycle of continuous improvement**, represented graphically in Figure 12–2.

There are three important characteristics of this cycle. First, evaluation is an integral part of planning and implementing instruction, rather than something that simply gets tacked on to the end of the process. Evaluation is an important part of "reflection in action" (Schön, 1983), in which instructional experts continually monitor their efforts to help their students learn, looking for and incorporating ways to better match instruction to the students.

Second, evaluation allows you to make adjustments as you move from one part of the learning process to the next. You can use the information as the input for the next part of the process, following it with more evaluation and adjustment. This cycle repeats throughout the instructional process. Naturally, evaluation takes a somewhat different form at different points in the cycle. Evaluation *before* instruction has a future orientation: **How will it work?** This encourages *pre*planning by providing a framework for making conscious estimates about the effectiveness, efficiency, and appeal of instruction. Evaluation *during* instruction has a present orientation: **How is it working?** Continuing the evaluation during the lesson allows you to revise instruction in time to benefit current students. Evaluation *after* the instruction has a past orientation: **How did it work?** This encourages conscious reflection about the effectiveness, efficiency, and appeal of the instruction so you can improve it for the next time.

Third, evaluation can focus on both the students and the instruction. We commonly think of teachers assessing their students in order to give them grades. But teachers also naturally evaluate their own instruction. As a result, evaluation can focus on determining both how

well students have learned the desired material and how effectively the instruction helped them learn.

 WHY EVALUATE?

This is not always as simple a question as it seems. Sometimes, evaluations indicate that "all is well." However, evaluations often point out problems and weaknesses, and indicate the time and effort that you must devote to making changes. This is not always something to look forward to.

So, if evaluation often points out your weaknesses and increases your workload, why would you want to do it? The answer lies is that evaluation provides information you can use to guide your efforts to improve. In addition, the amount of information increases as you repeat the cycle. Throughout the cycle, the consistent purpose of the evaluation is to increase the amount of student learning that takes place by continually evaluating the instruction in terms of its effectiveness (does it lead students to their learning goals?), efficiency (does it make good use of available time and resources?), and appeal (does it hold students' interest and maintain their motivation?). As you repeat the cycle, your evaluation gains power, like the proverbial snowball rolling downhill. It should come as no surprise that instruction that has been used (and evaluated) several times often works better than instruction being used for the first time. Through repeated evaluation, information accumulates and trends—both positive and negative—become identifiable. Based on emerging trends, you can update content; revise methods, media, activities, and materials; and add new ones. Thorough and continuous evaluation contributes to this in the following ways:

- Identifying areas of the content that are unclear, confusing, or otherwise not helpful
- Identifying areas of the content that have the highest priority for revision because they are (1) the most critical aspects, (2) the most difficult to learn, or (3) likely to have the greatest impact on learning
- Providing a rationale and evidence in support of making specific revisions

Thinking like an evaluator, therefore, means that you view evaluation as a way to improve and that you seek, rather than avoid, opportunities to evaluate your efforts. Evaluation takes on slightly different purposes depending on whether the focus is on the students or the instruction. We focus first on evaluating the instructional materials.

Evaluating the Instruction

Each semester, Mrs. Singleton teaches a twelfth–grade U.S. history course to about 25 students. One of the units in the course focuses on the broad impact of various social issues that took shape during the 1960s, including desegregation and civil rights, the Cold War, poverty and the Great Society, and the space race. As part of her research, Mrs. Singleton previewed the *American History* CD-ROM produced by the Instructional Resources Corporation. The CD contains a collection of photographs, short videos, and audio clips that can be randomly accessed and placed within presentation programs such as *PowerPoint*. The photographs and video clips are arranged chronologically and described in an accompanying catalog. Mrs. Singleton thinks the images on the CD will help make her presentation of the events of the 1960s less abstract and will stimulate discussion among her students.

Before the lesson (often called a **pilot test**), Mrs. Singleton discusses the visual images she has selected with Ms. Fellows, who also teaches history at the school. They discuss which issues might be most interesting to students, which most likely would create confusion, and what possible directions students might take in their discussion of the issues. Based on this conversation, Mrs. Singleton decides to add a few images to her initial presentation and to identify a second set of images that matches the directions students are likely to take in their discussion.

During the lesson (often called **formative evaluation**), Mrs. Singleton begins by showing a few selected images related to each issue, briefly describing each image. She begins the discussion by asking, "Which of these events had the greatest impact on American society during the 1960s?" Mrs. Singleton closely monitors the discussion as it progresses. She uses images from the CD, including the second set she had selected, to focus the discussion when it gets off track, to provide additional information when students request it, and to provide visual support to students making critical points.

After the lesson (often called **summative evaluation**), Mrs. Singleton assigns students the task of selecting one of the issues presented in class and writing an essay about the breadth and depth of its impact. As she reads the essays, she notes that, in general, they are thoughtful and insightful and that they include more specific references to people, places, and events than had been the case when she had taught the lesson without the CD. She determines from this that the presentation is worth trying again, and she decides to expand its use. She considers using the CD in American history to link the social issues of the 1960s and the 1930s to encourage students to compare the two periods. She makes notes on her lesson plan about the issues and questions that generated a lot of discussion, the types of images that might help bridge the two periods, and possible adaptations to the essay assignment.

Before she teaches the lesson during the next year, Mrs. Singleton reviews her notes and incorporates them into a revised instructional plan, emphasizing the link between the 1960s and the 1930s. She selects a new set of photographs and video clips to show to students, revises the question she will ask to begin the discussion, and modifies the essay assignment.

Assessing Student Learning

During a recent parent-teacher conference, Ms. Sara Powley, the ninth-grade English teacher at McCutcheon High School, explained some of the assignments and tests her students had completed. Her comments focused on the first essay examination. She explained that, for many students, this was the first exam they had taken that relied entirely on essay questions. She described how well the students had done and to what extent they had achieved the intended objectives. This particular assessment method, Ms. Powley explained, had been helpful in a number of different ways. First, she thought that it had served as a great motivator. It gave students a reason to think about what they had discussed in class and to assimilate information from many different topics. Second, it provided information about how well students were able to recall, analyze, and integrate critical information. Third, students' answers provided an indication of their writing skills. Fourth, the exam gave students the chance to determine how well their study habits were working. By comparing *how* they had studied with *what* had been asked on the exam, they could judge if their efforts had been successful. Finally, the exam provided Ms. Powley with a way to give students useful feedback. Her extensive comments on the essays highlighted strengths and weaknesses of students' work.

Before instruction, a student assessment (often called a **pretest**) can serve the following purposes:

➤ Identify students' preinstructional knowledge and skill levels. This indicates (1) whether students have the prerequisite knowledge and skills and (2) whether they already know the lesson content.

➤ Focus learners' attention on the important topics you will cover. In this way, the students are primed to notice those important topics when they come up during the instruction (Fleming, 1987).

➤ Establish a point of comparison with postinstruction knowledge and skills. One word of caution: Tell your students that you predict lower scores on a pretest since they are taking it prior to the lesson. Be sure they understand that you are not holding them responsible for content you have not yet taught them.

For example, our English teacher, Ms. Powley, could have given her English class an essay pretest as a way of identifying the students' prerequisite knowledge and showing the students what they would be expected to learn. For those students who had already mastered the content, Ms. Powley could have provided some enrichment activities.

During instruction, assessment (often called an **embedded test**) serves the following purposes:

➚ Determine what students have learned to that point. Both teachers and students can use this information to determine if new content can be introduced or if additional practice is needed to master the previous content.

➚ Supply feedback as the learning process occurs. This feedback can both increase students' confidence by indicating that they have mastered content to that point and correct problems *before* they become thoroughly ingrained.

➚ Identify when and what type of additional practice may be needed. As students progress, assessment ensures that they are integrating the new knowledge and skills with previously learned information and that they can apply this learning when needed.

➚ Refocus students' attention. In the event that students lose sight of their goals and objectives, a formative assessment can be an effective tool for refocusing their attention.

For example, Ms. Powley assessed how well students were learning new information throughout the course. Her formative assessments often consisted of asking students to write a paragraph or two summarizing a new topic. As Ms. Powley pointed out, her reasons for assessing during instruction were to (1) find out how well students were assimilating the information and (2) encourage the students to monitor their own learning.

After instruction, assessment (often called a **posttest**) serves the following purposes:

➚ Measure what students have learned. This is the most frequent use of formal assessment. Along with demonstrating their learning, a posttest gives students the opportunity to think about and synthesize what they have learned.

➚ Make specific decisions about grades, accreditation, advancement, or remediation.

➚ Review important knowledge and skills and **transfer** them to new and different situations. The value of new knowledge and skills increases when it can be used in a variety of contexts and a summative assessment can facilitate this transfer.

For example, Ms. Powley used the essay exam to determine how well her students could perform following instruction. The exam indicated how much improvement they had made and whether they could advance to the next unit of instruction.

Figure 12–3 summarizes the key questions that you should consider when evaluating the instruction and assessing the students before, during, and after the instruction.

	Evaluating Instruction	Assessing Learning
Before instruction	How well is the instruction likely to work? Will the instruction hold student interest? Is there an alternative way to organize the instruction to make better use of available time and resources?	Do students have the prerequisite knowledge and skills? Do students already know the content they are slated to learn? What is the students' current level of performance (baseline)?
During instruction	What obstacles are students encountering and how can they be overcome? What can be done to maintain student motivation? How can these students be helped to better progress through the instruction?	Are students ready for new content or is additional practice and feedback needed? In what specific areas do students need additional practice and feedback? What types of remediation or enrichment activities may be necessary for students?
After instruction	What improvements could be made in the instruction for future use? What revisions have the highest priority? Did students find the instruction interesting, valuable, and meaningful? Were the selected instructional methods, media, activities, and materials effective in helping students learn?	Have students learned what was intended? Can students be accredited or "passed"? What will be needed to help students generalize what they have learned and transfer it to new situations?

FIGURE 12–3   Key questions for evaluating instruction and assessing learning.

PEARSON myeducationkit™ Go to the Assignments and Activities section of Chapter 12 in MyEducationKit and complete the activity entitled "Exploring Assessments." Go to the website listed and then review the video "An Introduction to Comprehensive Assessment" on that site and note the various types of student assessment that are described. Reflect on the need for the various types of assessments – why are all of these different types needed? What is their value?

HOW TO EVALUATE

Now that you understand what evaluation is and why you should do it, we look at specific techniques you can use to conduct the actual evaluation. There are three basic principles to keep in mind as you select and use these techniques. First, continuous improvement requires continuous information. Recall that the purpose of evaluation is to increase the amount of student learning through ongoing self-renewal. This kind of continuous improvement depends on a steady stream of information flowing before, during, and after every period of instruction. Over time, this information may become increasingly detailed and the refinements in the instruction may become increasingly small, but these small refinements are no less important to student learning than the earlier, larger refinements (for a full discussion, see Stiggins, 2007).

Second, encourage and teach students how to evaluate for themselves. We most often think of evaluation as being done by the teacher. Teachers, as instructional experts, are responsible for evaluation. However, throughout the evaluation cycle, students can often assess their own learning and the instruction implemented to help them learn. They may need help in identifying the best techniques to use and guidance in how to use those techniques, but they can often be effective evaluators.

Before the lesson, students can ask, "What will work best for me?" This will encourage them to think strategically, identifying the instructional methods, media, activities, and materials that are most likely to help them achieve the learning goals. *During* the lesson, students can ask, "Is this working for me?" This will encourage them to think about what they are learning and what they are having trouble with, thus helping to identify where they need additional information and/or different study techniques. *After* the lesson, students can ask, "Did this work for me?" This will encourage them to think about their own skills as learners and about the learning strategies they use. They can then make a conscious effort to add to their repertoire of learning strategies and become more effective learners. Finally, *before* the next lesson, students can ask, "What will work best for me now?" This will encourage them to think ahead about their newly developed learning skills and strategies, identifying ways

the instructional methods, media, activities, and materials can be matched to their particular skills and strategies.

Third, information will carry more weight when it has been "triangulated" or based on many sources (Morrison, Ross, & Kemp, 2007). **Triangulation** refers to the process of obtaining information from multiple techniques or sources. All information is useful. However, information is strengthened when supported by information from other techniques or sources. Similarly, information is weakened when contradicted by information from other techniques or sources. Therefore, rather than relying on a single source of information, when possible gather information from several different sources.

Techniques to Evaluate Instruction

In this section, we describe a collection of techniques that you can use to generate information in order to evaluate your instruction.

Tests   We use the term *test* here in a generic sense to refer to any of the variety of standard and alternative assessment techniques you can use to assess students' knowledge and skills. As noted, assessment techniques can identify what students know before beginning instruction, assess their growing knowledge and skills during instruction, and measure what they have learned at the end of instruction. Because assessment techniques focus primarily on student learning, which is invariably the purpose of instruction, they provide a direct measure of a lesson's effectiveness. As a result, it is usually beneficial to use test results as a part of evaluating your own teaching.

As an example, Ms. Estes has her fourth-grade students play the computer game *Where in the World is Carmen Sandiego?* At the beginning of the lesson, Ms. Estes gives students a pretest, an assortment of matching, multiple-choice, and short-answer items, to find out how much they already know about geography.

A young student takes a pretest to assess his knowledge prior to the start of the learning experience.
Source: Bob Daemmrich Photography.

Then, at the end of the lesson, when everyone has completed the game, she gives them a posttest to find out how much their knowledge of geography has grown. Ms. Estes finds that virtually all students score much higher on the posttest than on the pretest. She determines from this that the game has been a valuable addition to her students' learning experience and decides to make it a permanent part of the lesson.

Student Tryout   A **student tryout** refers to having a "test run" of some instructional activity, method, media, or material with a small group of students before using it on a large scale. In a sense, a tryout is a rehearsal or practice run intended to identify any problems that might come up when you actually teach using the particular lesson. A tryout has two distinct advantages. First, it is an opportunity to test your assumptions about the usefulness of the materials. Second, it helps you find any problems in the materials so you can "fix" them before using the materials in the "real" classroom.

Mr. Hughes has developed a board game to use in his eighth-grade social studies class. However, before he uses the game in the class, he decides to try it out. He enlists the help of his 14-year-old daughter and several of her friends, asking them to play the game as though they were his students. He notices from this that the rules of the game are clear and that the game seems to engage their interest. However, he also notices that his tryout learners seem to become bored with the game if it slows down for any reason. He determines from this that the game is potentially useful as long as sessions are kept brief, so he decides to use it as a relatively short review activity.

Direct Observation   As may be clear from the term, **direct observation** refers to watching students as they go through some part or parts of the lesson, often when group activities are involved. The primary advantage of

observing students is that you gain information about the process of your instruction as well as the products of their learning. With careful observation, you will learn how students actually use materials and how they respond to different parts of the lesson, and can identify places where you may need to give them more information or guidance.

Students in Mr. Lockwood's high school art appreciation class are learning about the different forms of creative art through a cooperative learning activity. Mr. Lockwood has divided the students into groups. Each group contains a student who plays a musical instrument, a student who paints, and a student who sculpts. The students' task is to use research, as well as their own experience, to identify the similarities and differences among these art forms. From this, they are to identify the essential characteristics of the concept "art." Much of their research occurs outside of class, but the groups meet during the class period to discuss what they have found. Mr. Lockwood routinely listens as they talk, making sure that he spends time with each group. For the most part, he lets the students do their own work. However, because individual students have different experiences, each group is examining somewhat different issues and coming to different conclusions. As a result, Mr. Lockwood is modifying the activity "on the fly" and pushing the groups in somewhat different ways. He challenges some groups to incorporate a broader range of creative arts to test their emerging definition. He helps other groups narrow their focus on the important similarities among the arts as a way of developing a definition.

Talking with Students   Talking with students may take a variety of forms. It may involve a relatively formal discussion with a student or group of students, or it may consist of a relatively informal chat with them. Whether

A small group of target students evaluate the quality of the instructional materials.
Source: Ellen B. Senisi/The Image Works.

Observing a group of students as they experience the lesson and noting how well it works and what needs to be adapted or deleted.
Source: Frank Siteman.

formal or informal, talking with students has the advantage of going straight to the source to find out what they think about instruction. As a result, it is an excellent source of information about the appeal of particular materials. You can learn a great deal, from the students' perspective, about how well the materials worked and how interesting they were. This encourages students to reflect on their own learning and to think about what helps them learn. It also helps communicate to your students your interest in them. Students get the message that you are committed to helping them learn.

The fifth-grade Ecology Club is taking a field trip to a creek near the school, and the club's advisor decides to ask club members to research the source of oil floating in the water and to determine what may be done about it. Each member of the group is given a specific task to perform. After completing the research, preparing a report, and delivering it to the public health department, the advisor decides to spend a club meeting discussing the project. He asks members specific questions to identify which parts of the project were easy and challenging, fun and boring, and informative and uninformative. Based on the discussion, the advisor determines that the project is a useful learning experience for students and decides that the club should do similar projects on a regular basis.

Peer Review   **Peer review** refers to asking a colleague or colleagues to examine all or part of the materials for a lesson, to comment on their usefulness, and to suggest ways to improve the lesson. This is a little like getting a second opinion before having surgery. The idea is to have another set of eyes look at the materials. This has two distinct advantages. First, it helps identify trouble spots that you may miss. Sometimes you aren't sure what to look for when a lesson is relatively new. On the other hand, sometimes you are so familiar with a lesson that you look past existing problems, just as you can sometimes read past your own spelling errors. In either case, you may overlook inaccuracies, inconsistencies, and other potential problems. Second, a review by a colleague will provide a fresh perspective on the materials, offering new insights on student responses to the lesson, ways to update the content, and so on.

Mr. Crawford has developed a *PowerPoint* digital story presentation for his fifth- and sixth-grade Spanish class. He included the pictures he took during his trip to Spain and has added Spanish music and his own audio narration clips describing the various people, places, and activities he photographed. Before showing the presentation to his class, Mr. Crawford invites Mrs. Rivera, who also teaches Spanish, to review the presentation. Mr. Crawford is particularly interested in whether he has created a story that will be interesting to students, whether he has adequately matched the pictures and his narration, and whether the technical quality of

Other teachers can give relevant information and insights about the improvement of the instructional materials.
Source: Michael Newman/PhotoEdit.

the presentation is sufficient. Mrs. Rivera agrees that the pictures add a personal touch to the lesson, which will increase its relevance to the students. However, in some parts she feels the students will become confused by the lack of explanation about locations and landmarks. Based on this review, Mr. Crawford decides to rearrange the presentation slides and to add more narration clips at several points.

Classroom Observation   **Classroom observation** refers to inviting a colleague into the classroom to watch the lesson in process, comment on how well the materials and activities work, and suggest improvements. Like peer review, classroom observation provides another set of eyes that can offer a different perspective and help find problems in the implementation of the instruction that you may otherwise overlook.

Nancy Foust uses a presentation with a larger-than-life model to teach her vocational school students how an automobile carburetor works. Because this is a relatively new part of the lesson, Nancy is interested in getting some feedback, so she asks Ted Morrison to observe her presentation. Ted, who teaches construction methods, frequently uses models in his classes, and Nancy is particularly interested in how effectively she uses the model carburetor during her presentation. After observing Nancy's class, Ted makes a number of suggestions that allow Nancy to improve this specific presentation and her use of models in general.

Teacher Preview   Regardless of the content area, a variety of instructional materials may already be available from several different sources. Some have been produced commercially, some have been produced by teachers and published in professional journals or on the Internet, and some you may have produced yourself during previous terms. **Previewing** materials refers to the process of reading or working through specific instructional materials to appraise their quality and usefulness prior to their actual classroom implementation (Smaldino, Lowther, & Russell, 2008). In Chapter 8, we described the instructional materials acquisition process, noting that your students, content, instructional method, and instructional setting are all important considerations when selecting materials. A thorough preview is the necessary first step in determining how well specific materials match these considerations and, therefore, in deciding whether to use the materials as they are, use a part or parts of them, use them with some modifications or adaptations, or not use them at all.

Mr. McCormick has found computer software titled *Discover—A Science Experiment,* which he thinks would be useful in his first-year high school biology class. However, before he makes a final decision, he previews the software by working through the entire program himself. As he works through the exercises in the program, he makes notes on a preview form for computer software. He is particularly interested in how well the program matches the objectives he has for the lesson, encourages collaborative hypothesis testing, and presents realistically complex problems, as well as how likely it is to hold his students' interest. Based on his preview, Mr. McCormick determines that the exercises in the software match his learning objectives and are engaging, interesting, and reasonably complex. He decides to use it in class, adding only his own introduction to the lesson and the software.

Reflection   In many cases, experience is the best gauge of whether something worked. As described in Chapter 1, *reflection* refers to the process of thinking back over what happened during a lesson, using your own experience and expertise to identify the parts of the lesson that did and did not work.

For example, in her middle school U.S. history class, Mrs. Chan uses a debate as part of a lesson. She selects two teams of students and asks them to debate the question, "Were the causes of the Civil War primarily economic or political?" The rest of the class observes the debate, evaluates the two teams on their presentation of facts and arguments, and selects a "winner." Later in the term, Mrs. Chan reflects on this activity. She reviews the notes she had made on her lesson plan, specifically considering the clarity and scope of the debate topic, the time allotted to the debate, and the amount of participation of students who were not on one of the debate teams. From her reflection, Mrs. Chan determines that, while it had been interesting, there had been too many students in the class not involved in the debate. She concludes that this activity is not a good match for the large classes she often teaches, so she decides to save the activity for a time when she has a smaller class.

Figure 12–4 presents guidelines to consider when using these evaluation techniques.

Summary of Techniques to Evaluate Instruction

We have suggested a number of techniques you can use to evaluate how well your instruction has helped students learn. Your students, too, can use these techniques. Review the information found in Figure 12–5, relating evaluation of the instruction to our PIE model. What needs to occur during planning, implementation, and actual evaluation? These questions are focused on the instruction and what you can do to improve it.

Techniques to Assess Student Learning

It would be wonderful if all learners could be plugged into a machine that would tell us when learning had occurred. Although it is not quite that easy, there are means that you can use to help identify when, and to what degree, learning has occurred.

This section will give you an overview of different techniques you can use to assess student learning, some of their advantages and limitations, and some guidelines for their selection and use. The first group of techniques will focus on traditional means of gathering assessment data (e.g., multiple-choice, essay, and true-false items), and the second will be devoted to alternative assessment techniques (e.g., portfolios, logs, journals). We have included both types for a very important reason: Different techniques will provide different types of information. Just as we have shown the need for you to know a variety of instructional methods and media to ensure the appropriate learning of individual students, you need to know different forms of assessment to be able to determine which will deliver the best possible information. You must understand the types from which to choose and under which conditions each is most appropriate. For example, many educators feel that standard assessment

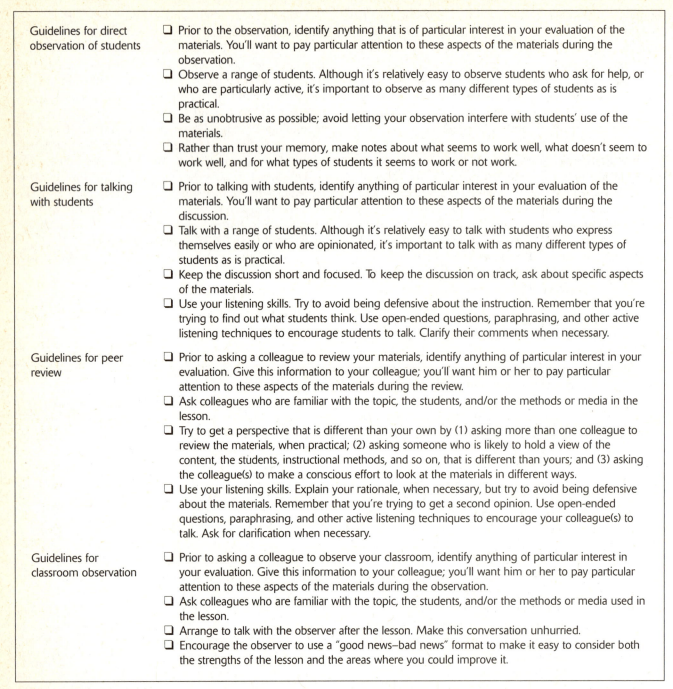

Guidelines for direct observation of students	❏ Prior to the observation, identify anything that is of particular interest in your evaluation of the materials. You'll want to pay particular attention to these aspects of the materials during the observation.
	❏ Observe a range of students. Although it's relatively easy to observe students who ask for help, or who are particularly active, it's important to observe as many different types of students as is practical.
	❏ Be as unobtrusive as possible; avoid letting your observation interfere with students' use of the materials.
	❏ Rather than trust your memory, make notes about what seems to work well, what doesn't seem to work well, and for what types of students it seems to work or not work.
Guidelines for talking with students	❏ Prior to talking with students, identify anything of particular interest in your evaluation of the materials. You'll want to pay particular attention to these aspects of the materials during the discussion.
	❏ Talk with a range of students. Although it's relatively easy to talk with students who express themselves easily or who are opinionated, it's important to talk with as many different types of students as is practical.
	❏ Keep the discussion short and focused. To keep the discussion on track, ask about specific aspects of the materials.
	❏ Use your listening skills. Try to avoid being defensive about the instruction. Remember that you're trying to find out what students think. Use open-ended questions, paraphrasing, and other active listening techniques to encourage students to talk. Clarify their comments when necessary.
Guidelines for peer review	❏ Prior to asking a colleague to review your materials, identify anything of particular interest in your evaluation. Give this information to your colleague; you'll want him or her to pay particular attention to these aspects of the materials during the review.
	❏ Ask colleagues who are familiar with the topic, the students, and/or the methods or media in the lesson.
	❏ Try to get a perspective that is different than your own by (1) asking more than one colleague to review the materials, when practical; (2) asking someone who is likely to hold a view of the content, the students, instructional methods, and so on, that is different than yours; and (3) asking the colleague(s) to make a conscious effort to look at the materials in different ways.
	❏ Use your listening skills. Explain your rationale, when necessary, but try to avoid being defensive about the materials. Remember that you're trying to get a second opinion. Use open-ended questions, paraphrasing, and other active listening techniques to encourage your colleague(s) to talk. Ask for clarification when necessary.
Guidelines for classroom observation	❏ Prior to asking a colleague to observe your classroom, identify anything of particular interest in your evaluation. Give this information to your colleague; you'll want him or her to pay particular attention to these aspects of the materials during the observation.
	❏ Ask colleagues who are familiar with the topic, the students, and/or the methods or media used in the lesson.
	❏ Arrange to talk with the observer after the lesson. Make this conversation unhurried.
	❏ Encourage the observer to use a "good news–bad news" format to make it easy to consider both the strengths of the lesson and the areas where you could improve it.

FIGURE 12–4   Guidelines for evaluating the effectiveness of instructional materials.

techniques (e.g., multiple-choice or true-false items) will not always produce the best information about student learning during the learning process. In some cases, then, alternative techniques (e.g., portfolios, journals) may prove more beneficial. Again, you must understand the students, the situation, and the type of information that you want before you can choose a proper assessment technique. In all cases, however, you are in a much better position when you know the different techniques and their individual strengths and limitations.

Standard Assessment Techniques

True-False. This technique consists of statements in which a choice is made between two alternatives—generally either true or false, agree or disagree, or yes or no. Examples:

↗ Slavery was the main cause of the American Civil War.
↗ In the sentence, "The old woman and her husband walked slowly up the stairs," the word *slowly* is an adjective.

FIGURE 12–5 Evaluation of instruction within the PIE model.

Planning	❏ Was the planning of the instructional materials effective and efficient?
	❏ How could you have planned the instructional experience in a better/more efficient/effective manner?
Implementation	❏ How well was the instructional experience carried out?
	❏ Did the feedback from students indicate that they were motivated by the materials?
	❏ Did students achieve the desired results?
Evaluation	❏ How could you have improved the instructional materials?
	❏ Were the materials evaluated properly?
	❏ Were the correct criteria for evaluation used?

Advantages of true-false items:

↗ These items and their answers tend to be short, so you can ask more items within a given time period.

↗ Scoring is relatively easy and straightforward.

Limitations of true-false items:

↗ There is no real way to know why a student selected the incorrect answer; thus it is difficult to review students' responses and diagnose learning problems.

↗ There is a tendency to emphasize rote memorization. It is difficult to design true-false items that measure comprehension, synthesis, or application.

Matching. In this type of assessment, students are asked to associate an item in one column with a number of alternatives in another column. Example:

Match the following wars with their main causes.

Wars

_____ 1. American Revolutionary War

_____ 2. American Civil War

_____ 3. Spanish-American War

Main Causes

a. Failure of the British to sign commercial agreements favorable to the United States.

b. Use of yellow journalism to sway public opinion about the need for humanitarian intervention and the annexation of Cuba by the United States.

c. The Nullification Controversy, in which South Carolina declared the U.S. tariff laws null and void.

d. Imposition of taxation without proper representation of those being taxed.

Advantages of matching items:

↗ Matching items are well suited for measuring students' understanding of the association between pairs of items.

↗ Students can respond rapidly, thus allowing for more content coverage.

Limitations of matching instruments:

↗ They are frequently used to associate trivial information.

↗ They measure students' ability to recognize, rather than recall, the correct answer.

Completion/Short Answer. This type of item asks students to recall a particular short answer or phrase. Completion and short-answer items are similar. A completion item requires students to finish a sentence with a word or short phrase; a short-answer item poses a question they can answer in a word or phrase. Examples:

↗ A major cause of the American Civil War was the _____.

↗ The Nullification Controversy was a major cause of which American war? _____

Advantages of completion and short-answer items:

↗ These items work well when students are expected to recall specific facts such as names, dates, places, events, and definitions.

↗ The possibility of guessing a correct answer is eliminated.

↗ More items can be used because this type of item usually takes less time to read and answer than other types. This allows you to cover a larger amount of content.

Limitations of completion and short-answer items:

↗ It is difficult to develop items that measure higher-level cognitive skills.

↗ They can be difficult to score. For example, which is the correct answer for the following item? Abraham Lincoln was born in _____ (Kentucky, a bed, a log cabin, 1809).

Multiple-Choice. The multiple-choice item is one of the most frequently used evaluation techniques. Each item is made up of two parts: a stem and a number of options or alternatives. The **stem** sets forth a problem, and the list of options contains one alternative that is the correct or "best" solution. All incorrect or less appropriate alternatives are called **distractors,** or **foils.** Examples:

↗ Which of the following was a major cause of the American Civil War?
  a. Failure of the British to sign commercial agreements favorable to the United States.
  b. Use of yellow journalism to sway public opinion about the need for humanitarian intervention and the annexation of Cuba by the United States.
  c. The Nullification Controversy, in which South Carolina declared the U.S. tariff laws null and void.
  d. Imposition of taxation without proper representation of those being taxed.
↗ If one frequently raises the cover of a container in which a liquid is being heated, the liquid takes longer to boil because
  a. boiling occurs at a higher temperature if the pressure is increased.
  b. escaping vapor carries heat away from the liquid.
  c. permitting the vapor to escape decreases the volume of the liquid.
  d. the temperature of a vapor is proportional to its volume at constant temperature.
  e. permitting more air to enter results in increased pressure on the liquid.

Advantages of multiple-choice items:

↗ You can use them with objectives ranging from simple memorization tasks to complex cognitive manipulations.
↗ You can use them to diagnose student learning problems if incorrect alternatives are designed to detect common errors.
↗ You can construct them to require students to select among alternatives that vary in degree of correctness. Thus, students are allowed to select the "best" alternative and aren't left to the absolutes required by true-false or matching instruments.

Limitations of multiple-choice items:

↗ They are often difficult and time-consuming to write. Determining three or four plausible distractors is often the most arduous part of the task.
↗ Students may feel there is more than one defensible alternative. This may lead to complaints of the answer being too discriminating or "picky."

Essay. The essay item asks students to write a response to one or more questions. For elementary students an answer may consist of a single sentence. For older students, the responses may range from a couple of sentences to several pages. Essay items can be used to compare, justify, contrast, compile, interpret, or formulate valid conclusions—all of which are higher-level cognitive skills. Examples:

↗ Why does the single issue of slavery fail to explain the cause of the American Civil War?
↗ Describe the role of the Nullification Controversy in the debate over national versus states' authority prior to the start of the American Civil War?

Advantages of essay items:

↗ You can use them to measure desired competency at a greater depth and in greater detail than with most other items.
↗ They give students the freedom to respond within broad limits. This can encourage originality, creativity, and divergent thinking.
↗ They effectively measure students' ability to express themselves.

Limitations of essay items:

↗ They are difficult and time-consuming to score, and scoring can be biased, unreliable, and inconsistent.
↗ They may be difficult for students who misunderstand the main point of the question, who tend to go off on tangents, or who have language and/or writing difficulties.
↗ They provide more opportunity for bluffing.

Figure 12–6 presents guidelines for developing these standard types of evaluation items.

PEARSON myeducationkit™ Go to the Assignments and Activities section of Chapter 12 in MyEducationKit and complete the activity entitled "Interactive Assessments." Review the linked information about the various forms of classroom response systems (often referred to as "clickers"). Consider how you might use such classroom response systems within your classroom. Think about when and how this type of assessment might be both useful and appropriate.

Alternative Assessment Techniques Alternatives are available to the traditional assessment techniques described previously. In particular, the performance and portfolio techniques have gained popularity in recent years. Here we outline their purpose, advantages and limitations, and some guidelines for their use. Following this, we describe additional techniques: interviews, journals, writing samples, open-ended experiences, and long-term projects (see Stiggins, 2007, for more on all of these alternatives).

Performance. The purpose of a performance assessment is to measure skills (usually psychomotor or

General guidelines	❏ Relate all items to an objective.
	❏ Provide clear, unambiguous directions.
	❏ Make sure all options appear on the same page.
	❏ Make sure the vocabulary is suitable for students.
	❏ Avoid lifting statements verbatim from the instructional materials.
True-false	❏ Select items that are unequivocally true or false. Avoid words such as *always, all,* and *never.*
	❏ Avoid multiple negatives (e.g., "It was not undesirable for the First Continental Congress to meet in response to the Intolerable Acts of the British Parliament").
	❏ Make sure the evaluation has approximately the same number of true and false answers.
Matching	❏ Explain to students the basis for matching and whether options may be used more than once or if more than one option is given for any of the questions.
	❏ Provide extra alternatives in the answer column to avoid selection by elimination.
	❏ Provide between six and eight associations within a single question.
	❏ Arrange the answer choices in a logical manner (alphabetical, chronological, etc.).
Multiple choice	❏ Avoid opinion items.
	❏ Include graphics, charts, and tables within items whenever possible.
	❏ Present one problem or question in the stem, and make sure it presents the purpose of the item in a clear and concise fashion.
	❏ Make sure the stem contains as much of the question or problem as possible. Do not repeat words in each option that you could state once in the stem.
	❏ Use negatives sparingly. If the word *not* is used in the stem, highlight it to make sure students do not overlook it.
	❏ Provide only one correct or clearly best answer.
	❏ All alternatives should be homogeneous in content and length and grammatically consistent with the stem.
	❏ Provide three to five alternatives for each item.
	❏ Write alternatives on separate lines beginning at the same point on the page.
	❏ Ensure that all alternatives are plausible.
	❏ Compose incorrect alternatives by including common misconceptions.
Completion and short answer	❏ Write the item specifically enough that there is only one correct answer.
	❏ Omit only key words from completion items.
	❏ Put the blanks near the end of the statement rather than at the beginning.
	❏ Avoid writing items with too many blanks.
	❏ Require a one-word response or at most a short phrase of closely related words.
	❏ Use blanks of the same length to avoid providing clues as to the length of the correct response.
Essay	❏ Phrase each question so students clearly understand what you expect. For example, include specific directions using terms such as *compare, contrast, define, discuss,* or *formulate.*
	❏ Provide as many essay items as students can comfortably respond to within the time allowed.
	❏ Avoid using items that focus on opinion and attitudes—unless the learning goal is to formulate and express opinions or attitudes.
	❏ Begin, when possible, with a relatively easy and straightforward essay item.
	❏ Minimize scoring subjectivity by preparing a list of key points, assigning weights to each concept, scoring all papers anonymously, and scoring the same question on all papers before moving on to the next question.

FIGURE 12–6   Development guidelines for standard evaluation items.

physical) needed to accomplish a specific task. Within a performance situation, students are required to perform some feat or demonstrate some skill they have learned, such as delivering a persuasive speech, calculating an arithmetic average, performing a successful ceiling shot in racquetball, or parallel parking a car. Unlike the previous techniques, learners in this situation must demonstrate not only that they know *what* to do but also that they know *how* to do it. Regarding the Civil War topic previously presented, for example, you may ask a student to present a persuasive speech explaining why the southern states were justified in seceding from the Union. Figure 12–7

Toolbox: Automated Testing

All types of assessments and evaluations take time. Often one of the leading reasons why they are not completed has to do with the time that is involved in the process. Individuals are constantly examining methods that could be used to obtain the needed evaluation and assessment information and feedback, but make the process as reliable, valid, and efficient as possible. Technology has been viewed as one possibility for helping in the area of efficiency. For example, testing (especially of large numbers of test takers) can be impacted in a number of ways: the production of the test, the distribution of the test, the monitoring of the testing, the manner in which the test is taken, how the test is collected, analyzed, and the results are distributed. To get a small idea of the impact of technology in this area do the following:

1. Go to a website that offers online testing. For example www.4tests.com is a website that offers all types of short tests that can cover a wide variety of topics.
2. Select one of the provided tests. Examine the types of questions used (e.g., true-false or multiple-choice questions).
3. Complete the short test and submit it.
4. Examine the feedback that is provided.
5. Reflect on the following questions:
   a. What advantages and limitations do you think this kind of assessment has for the instructor? For the student?
   b. How might you use this kind of assessment in a class that you're taking now?

FIGURE 12–7   Performance checklist for evaluating the front crawl swimming stroke.

Source: Courtesy of the American Red Cross. All rights reserved in all countries.

Swimming stroke: **Front Crawl**	
Component	Level V
Body Position	❏ Body inclined less than 15°
Arms	❏ Elbow high during recovery
	❏ Hand enters index finger first
	❏ Arm fully extended at finish of pull
	❏ Arms pull in "S" pattern
Kick	❏ Emphasis on downbeat
	❏ Relaxed feet with floppy ankles
Breathing/Timing	❏ Head lift not acceptable during breathing
	❏ Continuous arm motion in time with breathing

shows a performance checklist used by water safety instructors to assess swimming performance.

Advantages of performance assessment:

↗ This technique allows for the objective evaluation of a performance or product, particularly when using a checklist.

↗ Students actually get to demonstrate, rather than simply describe, the desired performance.

↗ With the use of a performance checklist, students can practice the performance before the test and receive reliable feedback from other students, parents, teachers, or themselves.

Limitations of performance assessment:

↗ This format can be time-consuming to administer (usually one student at a time).

↗ It may require several individuals or judges (e.g., skating and diving competitions) to assess the abilities of the performers.

↗ Increased setup time with specialized equipment at a specialized location is often required.

Portfolio. Arter and Spandel (1992) define the student **portfolio** as "a purposeful collection of student work that tells the story of the student's efforts, progress, or achievement" (p. 36). The portfolio is a rich collection of work that demonstrates what students know and can do. For years, artists have used portfolios to highlight the depth and breadth of their abilities. Similarly, students may use portfolios to illustrate their unique problem-solving or critical-thinking skills, as well as their creative talents (e.g., writing, drawing, design). Additionally, portfolios can be used to demonstrate the evolution students went through to achieve their current performance level. Unlike the end-of-the-unit objective evaluation, the portfolio is designed to capture a greater range of students' capabilities and to indicate how those capabilities developed and grew over time. Not only does the portfolio convey to others the students' progression, but it also serves as a vehicle for students to gauge their own development and to envision what additional things they might learn. In our discussion of constructivist theory in Chapter 2, we explained that this theory deals with the creation of meaning and understanding by the student. Portfolios (as well as journals, logs, long-term projects, etc.) can effectively show how and to what degree that meaning and understanding have developed. Moreover, the portfolio itself offers a means by which learners can reflect and gain greater insights as they think about what they have accomplished and what additional things they can do.

As suggested by D'Aoust (1992), portfolios may be structured around the exemplary "products" of students' work (i.e., including only those of the best quality) or around the "process" by which students arrived at current levels of performance (i.e., pieces from the beginning, middle, and end of the course that show the progression of students' abilities), or they could include a mixture of both. In either case, a major benefit comes from actually putting it together. "Students cannot assemble a portfolio without using clearly defined targets (criteria) in a systematic way to paint a picture of their own efforts, growth, and achievement. This is the essence of assessment. Thus, portfolios used in this manner provide an example of how assessment can be used to improve achievement and not merely monitor achievement" (Arter & Spandel, 1992, p. 37).

Within the classroom setting, the portfolio is becoming more and more accepted as a means of student assessment. Some states now have a mandated statewide portfolio assessment program.

Advantages of portfolio assessment:

↗ It provides a broad picture of what students know and can do.
↗ It can portray both the process and the products of student work, as well as demonstrate student growth.
↗ It actively involves students in assessing their own learning and actively promotes reflection on their work and abilities.

Limitations of portfolio assessment:

↗ The work in the portfolio may not be totally representative of what students know and can do.
↗ The criteria used to critique the product may not reflect the most relevant or useful dimensions of the task.
↗ The conclusions drawn from the portfolio can be heavily influenced by the person doing the assessment.

Figure 12–8 presents a set of guidelines to consider when developing either performance or portfolio assessment instruments.

There are many advantages for using portfolios. The problems that often occur, however, have to do with two basic questions. First, is the portfolio constructed in a manner that is usable and valuable for student assessment? Second, once it is assembled, how is it stored so that it can be expanded and used whenever needed?

myeducationkit Go to the Assignments and Activities section of Chapter 12 in MyEducationKit and complete the activity entitled "Integrating Visuals within Portfolios." As you watch the video, and note how teachers and students can use e-portfolios to showcase and assess their learning. In addition note how the teachers across grade levels and content areas work collaboratively to help students learn. Identify the strategies the teachers use to determine what and how they will teach, as well as how the learning will be assessed via the portfolio.

Today several software programs are available to assist in the development of **electronic portfolios** (Baron, 2004; Bullock & Hawk, 2005). *Chalk and Wire* (www.chalkandwire.com), for example, is a program to develop an electronic cumulative record that can be used for each student every year, from prekindergarten through grade 12. Within programs such as this, you or your students can build the portfolio from within the program itself or import work from other programs or through scanned images. Once stored, the portfolio can be searched and sorted based on a table of contents, by subject, project, or theme.

With this program, you can include images and photographs of the student and sample work, include videos of the student as well as videos produced by the student, and record all of the information that is standard in a cumulative record. This capacity enables you to capture and monitor both the learning process and samples of work within the same portfolio. The electronic portfolio provides teachers, students, and parents with access to rapid evaluation of student progress and comprehensive capacities for reporting and monitoring student performance. The program provides you with the ability to transfer selected pieces or entire portfolios onto VHS videotape for presentation in the classroom, to pass on to next year's teachers, or to be viewed at home.

As shown in Figure 12–9, a popular portfolio software program for preservice teachers is *TaskStream: Tools for Engagement.* This software not only facilitates the development of portfolios, but also provides website development software, design tools to create lesson plans, **assessment rubrics**, standards integration wizards, and communication tools that provide e-mail, discussion boards, and so on.

Performance test guidelines	❑ Specify exactly what learners are to do (through a demonstration and/or explanation), the equipment and materials that will be needed, and how performances will be assessed.
	❑ Develop and use a checklist based on acceptable performance standards. In most cases, the checklist should include some type of scoring system.
	❑ Make sure the checklist outlines all the critical behaviors that should be observed. List behaviors that should *not* be observed on a separate part of the checklist.
	❑ Be sure that, if a sequence of behaviors is needed to complete a task successfully, it is highlighted in some way.
	❑ Keep the scoring system as simple as possible.
	❑ Give a copy of the checklist and scoring system to students before they begin to practice the skill. Have them refer to it as they are learning the skill.
	❑ Use video- and/or audiotape to record performances. This may be extremely helpful when behaviors occur very quickly or in rapid succession. The tapes are also an effective means for supplying feedback to students.
Portfolio guidelines	❑ Many different skills and techniques are needed to produce an effective portfolio. Students need models of finished portfolios as well as examples of how others develop and reflect on them.
	❑ Students should be involved in selecting the pieces to be included in their portfolios. This promotes reflection on the part of students.
	❑ A portfolio should convey the following: *rationale* (purpose for forming the portfolio), *intents* (its goals), *contents* (the actual displays), *standards* (what are good and not-so-good performances), and *judgments* (what the contents tell us).
	❑ Portfolios should contain examples that illustrate growth.
	❑ Student self-reflection and self-evaluation can be promoted by having students ask, What makes this my best work? How did I go about creating it? What problems did I encounter? What makes my best piece different from my weakest piece?
	❑ All pieces should be dated so that progress can be noted over time.
	❑ Students should regularly be given time to read and reorganize their portfolios.
	❑ The portfolio should be organized, inviting, and manageable. Plan a storage system that is convenient for both you and your students.
	❑ Students should be aware of the criteria used for evaluating the portfolio.

FIGURE 12–8   Development guidelines for performance and portfolio evaluation.

FIGURE 12–9   *TaskStream: Tools of Engagement* electronic portfolio development software.

Source: Reprinted with permission from TaskStream, LLC. © TaskStream, LLC 2004. All rights reserved.

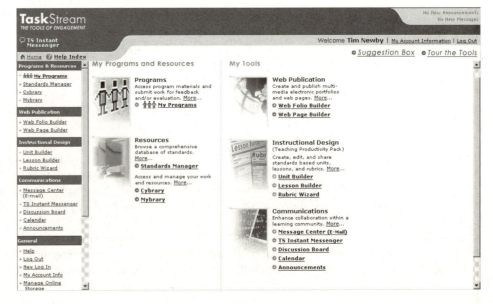

Today, storage of the portfolio has also become more simplified. Where once you had to create folders of materials for each student and store them in some file drawer or closet, much of the information can now be stored electronically on CD-ROM or DVD-ROM. The CD-R (CD-Recordable) and CD-RW (CD-Rewritable) formats, as well as comparable DVD formats, are capable of storing huge amounts of information. A CD-R allows the user to select information and "burn" or write it on the CD, while a CD-RW permits information to be written, erased, and rewritten. CD-R, CD-RW, and DVD recorders are now found as standard equipment on most computers. This technology allows you to record huge amounts of written text, scanned pictures, other digital images, and even videos. With this amount of storage space, it is possible for you to place on a single CD-ROM the entire school portfolio of a student from kindergarten to twelfth grade. Recordable DVD formats provide even greater storage capacity. So, storage capacity is no longer a barrier to maintaining student portfolios.

Interviews and Oral Assessments. Interviews and oral assessments are generally conducted face-to-face, with one person asking questions and the other responding. To conduct an interview or oral assessment, first design a set of questions covering a specific set of objectives. The questions may be very structured (i.e., requiring a specific response) or fairly unstructured (i.e., open-ended questions that allow for lengthy, detailed answers). As with the questions for an essay evaluation, the person conducting the interview or oral assessment (typically you, the teacher) asks a question and allows the student to respond. For purposes of clarification, students may take (or be asked to take) the opportunity to explain their answers in more depth and detail. You may record the response on video- or audiotape, or transcribe the main points. Because this form of assessment is conducted orally between two or more individuals, you can also conduct it over the telephone. Adaptations that incorporate e-mail technology and online surveys have also become prevalent. Interviews allow for more in-depth, on-the-spot questioning if needed. However, they can take a lot of time to complete and they may be somewhat unreliable.

Logs and Journals. Logs and journals are written records that students keep as they work through a long-term experience. For example, students in a discussion group might take time at the end of each session to write out their thoughts and experiences about what happened in the group. How well was the topic covered? What feelings did the discussion provoke? There is value in organizing one's thoughts and presenting them logically in writing. There is also value in rereading the journal later and reflecting. Just as students can reflect on their experiences, you can use the journal or log as a

means to evaluate what they experienced. This is a good instrument to use during the formative stages of learning. The use of electronic web logs, or **blogs**, has now become a common way to keep a journal or log for many individuals.

Writing Samples. This assessment technique is frequently combined with the portfolio. It generally consists of the student selecting one or more samples from different writing assignments and submitting them for evaluation. The samples may be selected as the student's "best work" as a means to demonstrate the progression that has occurred over a specific period of time. This technique is frequently used by businesses and by graduate school selection committees.

Open-Ended Experiences. This type of assessment technique generally is not focused on a single "correct" answer. With this, students are placed in a novel situation that requires a performance, and that performance is judged by how they respond and react. Many results from a continuum of possible "correct" outcomes may be produced. Examples include mock trials, debates, and different types of simulated experiences.

Long-Term Projects. Term papers, science fair projects, and unit activities (e.g., mini-societies, dramatic reenactments, trade fairs) are all examples of long-term projects. They can require extended research and library work and often involve the use of cooperative groups. As stated by Blumenfeld et al. (1991), "Within this framework, students pursue solutions to nontrivial problems by asking and refining questions, debating ideas, making predictions, designing plans and/or experiments, collecting and analyzing data, drawing conclusions, communicating their ideas and findings to others, asking new questions, and creating artifacts" (p. 371). This technique generally requires the use of checklists with important attributes that must be exhibited within the project. Frequently, the effectiveness of this project is enhanced through the use of journals or logs.

PEARSON
myeducationkit Go to the Assignments and Activities section of Chapter 12 in MyEducationKit and complete the activity entitled "Exploring Assessments." Review the video "Assessment for Understanding." Reflect on the various alternative type of assessment techniques. How could such techniques be incorporated within your future teaching? Will there be difficulties in integrating such assessments? Why or why not?

Figure 12–10 gives application examples of this and other alternative evaluation instruments.

Alternative Assessment Instrument	Application Examples
Portfolio	Assess the improvement of writing skills over the course of a semester by having eleventh-grade English students create a portfolio of their best writing samples at the end of the first week, at the end of the first nine weeks, and at the end of the semester.
	Have student teachers compile a portfolio of their teaching philosophy with accompanying documents and examples to illustrate the implementation of their philosophy during the semester of classroom teaching.
Interviews and Oral Assessments	Interview third-year Spanish students about different cultural aspects of Mexico. All questions and responses are to be given in Spanish.
	Ask preschool children to complete a sorting task and then explain how they actually accomplished the task.
Logs and Journals	Have students within a fifth-grade "Conflict Resolution" program keep a journal about what they learned in class and how they used the techniques with their family and friends.
	Have students in a high school psychology class keep a daily journal of interactions between themselves and their friends, including descriptions of the "most significant interaction to happen each day" and thoughts on why it was important.
Writing Samples	Assess potential graduate student applicants' writing and organizational skills by having them submit three or four papers from their undergraduate classes.
	Assess the abilities of candidates for the school newspaper by having them submit short articles about recent school events.
Open-Ended Experiences	Assess students on their ability to research and then debate the pros and cons of corporal punishment (e.g., spankings) used within the school systems of other countries.
	Assess student understanding of the concept of supply and demand by having them set up a classroom store and demonstrate what would happen given different conditions (e.g., competition from other classes, lack of product, increased costs of product).
Long-Term Projects	In a project on the Native American tribes of Indiana, group students into tribes of Miami, Potawatomi, and Delaware Indians and have them develop reports and skits on the village life of their tribe. This could include designing a model of the village, preparing food similar to what their tribe would eat, and dressing in authentic attire.
	After a science unit on sound, have students in a fourth-grade class develop different ways in which the principles of frequency and pitch can be demonstrated.

FIGURE 12–10   Examples of the application of different alternative assessment instruments.

Planning the Assessment   After considering different types of assessment instruments, we are ready to plan the assessment. In Chapter 4, we emphasized the importance of planning so that your final instructional materials accomplish the desired learning goals. Likewise, forethought and planning are required to properly measure learning. The following suggestions outline important considerations for planning and implementing an assessment. Do not interpret the following to be a "cut-in-stone" prescription of exact steps to follow. These are guidelines, proven helpful in the past, that you can adapt to your specific situation.

1. Ask yourself the following question: What is it that students are supposed to have learned? The easiest and quickest way to answer this question is to refer to the objectives. As explained in Chapter 4, objectives, instruction, and evaluations should all be parallel. This means that the assessment instruments should measure what you taught during your instruction and that instruction should be developed from the objectives.

2. Determine the relative importance of each objective. Make decisions on how many questions to ask related to the different objectives and how much time you will need to assess each one. In most cases, those decisions are closely aligned with the relative importance of each objective.

3. Based on the objectives, select the most relevant assessment technique(s) and construct the

assessment items. These items should reflect the principles of good item construction discussed earlier. It is critical that the conditions and the behaviors mentioned in the objectives match those within the assessment item. Be sure to consider other techniques you could use to assess the given objective.

4. Assemble the complete assessment. As you bring together all of the individual items, it is important to consider the following:

    a. Group questions according to item type (e.g., multiple-choice, true-false) so students do not have to continuously shift response patterns.

    b. Do not arrange items randomly. Try to list items in the order the content was covered or in order of difficulty. When possible, place easier questions first to give students confidence at the outset of the test.

    c. Avoid using a series of interdependent questions in which the answer to one item depends on knowing the correct answer to another item.

    d. Reread the assessment and make sure items do not provide clues or answers to other items.

5. Construct the directions for the complete assessment and any subparts. Make sure you include the full directions on the type of response required. You may also wish to include information regarding the value of each item or subpart of the evaluation. This is useful to students as they determine how much emphasis they should place on any one item.

6. If possible, have a content expert or another teacher check the items to be sure they are accurate and valid. This is helpful with both the items and the directions.

7. If possible, try out the exam on a few students who are similar to the ones you are actually assessing. This tryout will ensure that the directions are clear, that the vocabulary is at the correct level, that the test length is appropriate, and that the scoring system is adequate.

8. Finally, consider what will occur after the assessment is over. Evaluate the assessment. Ask yourself the following questions: How well did the students do? Were there any particular problems? What should I change before using this assessment again? How should this assessment and the suggested changes be filed and retrieved when I need it in the future?

Summary of Student Assessment Techniques We have suggested a number of different techniques that you can use to assess what your students have learned. It is important, however, to realize that, in most cases,

this information is most effectively used by the learners themselves. For the cycle of continuous improvement to function appropriately, students must know how well they are performing and what adjustments they need to make in order to achieve your learning objectives. These assessment techniques will help learners gain that information if they are constructed and delivered in the proper manner, at the proper time, and coupled with timely feedback about the results.

TECHNOLOGY COORDINATOR'S CORNER

Anne Ramirez was worried about the quality of information that some of her sixth-grade students were obtaining for their recent English research papers. For the most part, it sounded good, but she knew that most of it was coming from various Internet websites and that her students really did not know how to determine if the information was reliable or not—they simply accepted what they found. What brought it to the forefront was that two of her students found conflicting information about a similar topic they were investigating. They had come to her to determine which source "was right."

In a conversation with Jan Ingrahm, the technology coordinator for her building, Jan had indicated that this is a question that many students are now facing—whether the students realize it or not. Many had been schooled over the years to trust the information they found in their textbooks and other written reference materials. Learning now to question Internet website information was not an easy task for them to accept, and they quickly found out that it was more work to question a source than it was to just accept it as fact.

Jan suggested that Anne invest some time in teaching her students the skills needed to effectively evaluate materials they find on the Internet (see discussion in Chapter 10). She suggested that they start with five traditional evaluation criteria suggested by Alexander and Tate (1999) in their book *Web Wisdom: How to Evaluate and Create Information Quality on the Web*. When Jan returned to her office, she e-mailed Anne a short synopsis of the key things she had gleaned from *Web Wisdom* that may serve as a foundation on what could be taught to Anne's students about learning to evaluate websites. Her e-mail included:

↗ **Accuracy** (Is the information reliable and free from error?)

↗ **Authority** (Who actually produced the material on the website? Do they identify themselves and do they have the background and qualifications to provide reliable information?)

↗ **Objectivity** (Is the information presented in an unbiased fashion or is there an attempt to convey a specific point of view?)

↗ **Currency** (How old is the material? Has a publication date as well as revision dates been printed on the website? Has the website been updated in the last few days, weeks, or months?)

↗ **Coverage** (To what degree is the subject explored? Is there some depth to the topic being presented?)

As a final note, Jan also suggested that she could develop a short presentation on this topic that would help the students understand the need to develop their website evaluation skills. She suggested that one way to catch their attention would be to expose them to one of the many hoax sites on the Internet (for a listing of hoax sites, one can visit www.museumofhoaxes.com) and have them use their evaluation skills to determine why such information should be examined closely before accepting it as fact.

SUMMARY

In this chapter, we described evaluation as a "cycle of continuous improvement" in which you can use a variety of evaluation techniques before, during, and after a learning experience. We discussed different techniques to evaluate both how much students have learned (including both standard and alternative assessment techniques) and the effectiveness of your instruction. For each technique, we described its advantages and offered a set of practical guidelines for its use.

PEARSON myeducationkit™ To check your comprehension of the content covered in this chapter, go to the MyEducationKit for this book and complete the Study Plan for Chapter 12. Here you will be able to take a chapter quiz, receive feedback on your answers, and then access resources that will enhance your understanding of chapter content.

SUGGESTED RESOURCES

Print Resources

Ainsworth, L., & Viegut, D. (2006). *Common formative assessments: How to connect standards-based instruction and assessment*. Thousand Oaks, CA: Corwin.

Bernhardt, V. (2004). *Data analysis for continuous school improvement*. Larchmont, NY: Eye on Education.

Butler, S., & McMunn, N. (2006). *A teacher's guide to classroom assessment: Understanding and using assessment to improve student learning*. San Francisco, CA: John Wiley & Sons.

Falchikov, N. (2005). *Improving assessment through student involvement: Practical solutions for aiding learning in higher and further education*. Abingdon, Oxon: RoutledgeFalmer.

Gareis, C. & Grant, L. (2008). *Teacher-made assessments: How to connect curriculum, instruction, and student learning*. Larchmont, NY: Eye On Education.

Hiebert, J., Morris, A., Berk, D., & Jansen, A. (2007). Preparing teachers to learn from teaching. *Journal of Teacher Education, 58*(1), 47–61.

Lang, S., Stanley, T., & Moore, B. (2008). *Short-cycle assessment: Improving student achievement through formative assessment*. Larchmont, NY: Eye On Education.

Nicol, D., & Milligan, C. (2006). Rethinking technology-supported assessment practices in relation to the seven principles of good feedback practice. In C. Bryan & K. Clegg. *Innovative assessment in higher education.* (pp. 64–78). Abingdon, Oxon: Routledge.

Pelligrino, J., Chudowsky, N., & Glaser, R. (2001). *Knowing what students know: The science and design of educational assessment*. National Academy Press, Washington, DC.

Popham, W. (2008). *Transformative assessment*. ASCD Publishing.

Ross, J., & Bruce, C. (2007). Teacher self-assessment: A mechanism for facilitating professional growth. *Teaching and Teacher Education, 23*(2), 146–159.

Stiggins, R. (2007). Introduction to student-involved assessment for learning (5th ed.). Prentice Hall.

Tuttle, H. (2009). *Formative assessment: Responding to your students*. Larchmont, NY: Eye On Education.

Yang, H. (2008). Blogfolios for student-centered reflection and communication. In M. Iskander (Ed.). *Innovative techniques in instruction technology, e-learning, e-assessment, and education.* (pp. 179–182). Springer Science + Business Media B.V.

Electronic Resources

http://www.neirtec.org/evaluation/
(Northeast & the islands regional technology in education consortium: Collaborative evaluation)

http://www.edutopia.org/creating-culture-student-reflection
(Edutopia | Creating a Culture of Student Reflection: Self-Assessment Yields Positive Results)

http://www.edutopia.org/assessment
(Edutopia | Educational Assessment Articles, Videos, and Resources)

http://www.edutopia.org/teacher-development
(Edutopia | Teacher Development Articles, Videos, and Resources)

http://teacher.scholastic.com/professional/selfassessment/checklist/index.htm
(Scholastic | Teachers' Timely Topics: Self-Assessment Checklist)

http://www.jeanmcniff.com/booklet1.html
(jeanmcniff.com | Action Research for Professional Development: Concise Advice for New Action Researchers)

http://teachereducation.merlot.org/teach.html
(MERLOT: Teacher Education Portal – Teaching Resources and Community)

http://www.pbs.org/teachers/librarymedia/tech-integration/index.html
(PBS Teachers | Technology Integration: Research and Best Practices)

SECTION V

TECHNOLOGY AND LEARNING TODAY AND TOMORROW

Throughout this textbook, we have discussed how you can use educational technology to identify principles and processes, as well as hardware products that both you and your students can use to increase learning effectiveness, efficiency, transfer, impact, and appeal. We have attempted to demonstrate the importance of such tools for both you and your learners. When considering the individual differences in learners, the varying content, environment, and constraints in today's world, learning is an ever increasingly complex activity. During the twenty-first century, that complexity will not diminish. Individuals will require skills with advanced instructional tools and techniques to succeed, to be able to function and solve the complex problems of an advanced society.

Where are we going? What skills and tools will you need to be successful in the future? To be prepared, it is important that you have a vision of the future. We conclude the text with a look at the present and on into the future of educational technology. Reviewing the past and our present help to illustrate how we have progressed to our current state, but even more importantly, they help us predict the challenges and needs of the future. Although predicting

exactly what the future will bring is not a simple task, of this you can rest assured: Change will be a constant, and you will need to continually learn.

New problems and issues will confront us as we go about teaching and learning now and in the future; likewise, new tools and techniques will be introduced. It is up to us to develop the mindset and skills needed to confront the challenges, make the needed changes, and find creative solutions. Educational technology will play a vital role in providing tools and techniques to facilitate learning so that we can solve all upcoming problems no matter how complex.

Chapter 13 begins by focusing on the current issues that are increasingly confronted as we learn to integrate technology within our classrooms. Although not all answers are available, suggestions and guidance are provided in order to help us in our quest for answers and our attempts to not repeat problems of the past. The text concludes with a look at the future of educational technology. Reviewing where we are helps us to project the changes that are on the horizon. This is a great asset as we envision and plan for the future.

13 Integrating Technology— Issues, Trends, and Horizons

Source: Shutterstock.

KEY WORDS AND CONCEPTS

Library/media specialist
Technology coordinator
Digital divide
Hackers
Computer virus
Plagiarism Detection Services
Artificial intelligence (AI)

Intelligent tutoring system
Speech recognition
Semantic-aware applications
Smart phone
Cloud computing
Virtual reality (VR)
Ubiquitous computing

CHAPTER OBJECTIVES

After reading and studying this chapter, you will be able to:

↗ Identify significant trends in educational technology and speculate about their impact in the future.
↗ Identify the barriers that commonly inhibit the integration of technology and describe how a

technology integration plan, training, and support address those barriers.
↗ Identify other issues (e.g., equity, privacy, security, plagiarism, isolationism) that have been produced or enhanced because of the integration of technology and describe how these issues can be effectively addressed.

↗ Explain the key benefits of investing time, energy, and money for the integration of technology within the classroom and other learning environments.

↗ Describe at least three "horizon technologies," those that are emerging in importance, and discuss how they might impact education.

↗ Describe a vision for education and schooling in the future, based on the changes now occurring in technology.

Previous chapters of this text have highlighted various forms of technology and how they could potentially impact learners. For the most part, technology has been shown as a means to accomplish the desired end of enhanced levels of learning. Just as a boat that glides across a still lake leaves a wake of disturbance behind it, the use of technology changes the environment in which it is implemented. These changes may be necessary in some cases, but they may also create problems and challenges to address and solve. Within this chapter, we will discuss several issues created by the integration of technology within the learning environment.

 ## INTRODUCTION

On a recent hiking/camping experience with a group of 11-year-olds, an adult leader noticed that one young man had quickly fallen behind the main group of hikers as they moved up the high mountain trail. When asked about his slow progress, the young hiker complained about the work involved in "all the walking." At the first opportunity to take a break, the leader asked what he was carrying in his large backpack. The boy responded that he had included just the normal list of required camping gear and a "couple of other things." Upon examination—besides the needed sleeping gear, cover, eating utensils, and food—the leader found several extra pounds of candy, two heavy cans of pork and beans (the boy's favorite), three rolls of toilet paper, a giant flashlight with extra batteries, an extra pair of hiking boots, as well as a pair of tennis shoes, three school textbooks (in case he had extra time to get some homework done), and a handheld electronic game (with extra batteries). His oversized pack was weighed down by an extra 15 to 20 pounds of those "other things." Although each item may have seemed like a good idea to include, their combined weight actually inhibited the boy from being able to adequately participate in the hike. Instead of learning about the joy of hiking and camping, he was learning only about how painful such an experience could be. Those extras needed to be removed from his backpack so that he could focus on the goals of the hiking experience.

Similar to this hiker, many of us today find the use of technology has created a number of issues. These issues are often considered as "extra things" that are

Just as planning can help ensure a successful hiking experience, it also ensures productive and enjoyable technology integration.
Source: Courtesy of the National Park Service.

continually added to our daily load. At times, they may come to overburden us to the point that they inhibit our performance. In fact, if not careful, we may lose sight of our purpose for using the technology. With better initial planning and by identifying and removing (or at least redistributing) the heavy weight of these "extra things," we should be able to address issues and obstacles created by the technology so that we can experience the benefits of its use.

Teachers in typical schools of today face many challenges as they attempt to enhance their students' learning through the integration of technology. What types of issues do schools face as they attempt to integrate instructional technology? Here are some key questions to consider.

1. Where are we today in terms of technology integration?
2. What are today's relevant technology trends?
3. What barriers to integration of technology have been encountered?
4. How can we address and overcome the barriers to integration?
5. What additional issues does the integration of technology create?
6. Why invest the time, energy, and cost in the integration of technology?
7. What "horizon" technologies may potentially facilitate student learning?

The remaining sections of this chapter address each of these questions in detail. Although perfect solutions have not been found in every case, these discussions should help you identify ways that solutions may be uncovered for your specific situation.

WHERE ARE WE TODAY IN TERMS OF TECHNOLOGY INTEGRATION?

Educational technology is evident in schools today as never before. Of course, the instructional process has always been there. Teachers have long been seen as instructional experts, even if many in the past may not have viewed the process from a perspective such as the PIE model (see Chapter 1, pg. 11). However, in days past, teachers had few tools available. Today, computers and other educational technologies are commonplace in schools in the U.S. and many other countries.

In the "typical" school of today in the U.S., you will find one computer for about every three or four students, on average. However, the numbers vary by state and community. The ratio tends to be a little worse in schools with greater numbers of poor and minority students and many schools have older computers that may not run modern multimedia applications, but at the same time many schools are launching 1:1 computing initiatives. About seven out of every 10 computers belong to the Windows/Intel family from various vendors; Apple Macintosh computers make up most of the remainder. Many of the computers are likely to be found concentrated in labs, although having one or more computers in the classroom is now the norm rather than the exception.

The "typical" school is likely to have a relatively fast, dedicated connection to the Internet, and in most schools, network connectivity extends to nearly all instructional rooms. Interactive whiteboards are becoming common classroom fixtures in many schools. Video technologies are also evident; most schools have one or more VCRs or DVD players, and cable TV is common. Access to instructional technologies in the typical school of today is much better than it was in the past, but it is still a long way from ideal. Teachers continue to cite the lack of access as one of the major barriers to effective use of technology in the schools.

Having access to certain technologies, of course, does not guarantee their use. Whereas almost all teachers with access to computers now report using them for administration purposes, only about half to three-quarters of teachers report using computers for instruction to a moderate or large extent. When they do use computers, the most common instructional applications include relatively basic applications such as word processing, Internet research, drill and practice on basic skills such as mathematics facts, and problem solving/data analysis. Actual instructional time involving the use of computers and the Internet may amount to only a few hours per week on average. However, schools do help to address a "digital divide" among students; use of computers and the Internet is less common among poor and minority students, and many disadvantaged students are only able to access the Internet at school.

The availability and use of technology in the "typical" school has improved greatly in the past decade. However, given the wide variety of applications available for teaching and learning that we have introduced in this book, the picture of the typical school of today remains somewhat disappointing. A lot of the potential of educational technologies is going untapped. However, some schools are trying to change all that.

Today, many schools are exploring the benefits of a technology-enhanced learning environment. For example, the New Technology High School in Napa, California, developed a model program, now being replicated in many other sites across the country, which relies on a challenging project-based learning curriculum, linked to authentic problems, involving engagement with the community, and supported by extensive use of state-of-the-art technology. Students work on projects, usually in collaboration with other students, which often span significant blocks of time. They use technology routinely as a tool for research, data gathering, and writing and to collaboratively create products that may include written essays, digital photo essays, websites, and *PowerPoint* presentations. Assessment is performance-based, and students often present their work to other students, teachers, and members of the community. Teachers function as collaborators and guides as students take significant responsibility for their own learning.

A number of schools, such as the Cincinnati (Ohio) Country Day School, have experimented with 1:1 computing by equipping students with laptops or, more recently, tablet computers. Providing such a high level of computer access to students has shown a number of benefits. Students who have access to portable computing devices consistently use their computers and access the Internet more frequently than their counterparts who do not have such technology, even when availability of desktop computers is the same. Students using laptops spend more time on homework and use computers at home for a wider array of subjects and tasks than their peers. There is at least some evidence that they write better. Teachers in schools with 1:1 computing programs increase their use of computers for specific academic purposes, shift toward more use of student-led inquiry and collaborative work, and decrease their reliance on direct instruction. These results mirror those found in other model technology projects.

What can we learn from these examples? In these settings, the barrier of lack of access to educational technology was removed, and the results were strikingly similar. The process of teaching and learning itself became

Toolbox: Technology-Using Schools of Today

Learn more about model technology-using schools of today. Visit the websites of schools or school-based projects that have been recognized as being exemplary users of technology. Some examples are provided in the table below. Feel free to seek other examples on the Web.

School	URL
Cincinnati Country Day School (Cincinnati, Ohio)	http://www.countryday.net/
Generation Yes Project (Olympia, Washington)	http://www.genyes.org/
Lemon Grove Middle School (Lemon Grove, California)	http://www.lgsd.k12.ca.us/lgms/
Napa New Technology High School (Napa, California)	http://newtechhigh.org
Newsome Park Elementary School (Newport News, Virginia)	http://npes.nn.k12.va.us/

What uses of technology are featured in these exemplary technology-using schools/projects? How do these projects tend to view the role of technology in teaching and learning? What do you think we can learn from schools like these?

transformed. These model school technology projects have the following in common:

- ↗ Technology is used as a tool for creative expression, information access, communication, and collaboration.
- ↗ Teachers are models, guides, collaborators, and sometimes learners.
- ↗ Students are active and collaborative learners, and sometimes teach others.
- ↗ Assessments are performance-based (e.g., projects, portfolios).

As access to technology continues to expand, and schools take advantage of technology, we can probably expect to see these characteristics in more classrooms in the future.

 ## WHAT ARE TODAY'S RELEVANT TECHNOLOGY TRENDS?

Educational technology continues to grow and evolve. Today we can see a number of trends that will help us to project where the field might be headed in the future.

- ↗ *Evolution of learning perspectives.* In Chapter 2, we introduced you to some of the basic theoretical perspectives of learning and their implications for instruction. The field was founded by researchers who took a behavioral approach to learning. However, beginning in the 1960s and 1970s, cognitive theories of learning, such as the information processing perspective, began to hold sway. Today, constructivism is the focus of much research. Although the application of the constructivist perspective to the practice of designing, implementing, and evaluating instruction

is not always clear, there is a shift today from a more teacher-centered perspective to a more learner-centered perspective.

- ↗ *Media convergence.* Where once media developed separately—each with its own technological basis, vocabulary, and experts—today all media are converging in the computer. Media have gone digital! The advantages of this development are considerable. Digital media can be reproduced flawlessly. They can be recorded on computer-readable media such as CD-ROMs and DVDs or distributed anywhere in the world by computers over the Internet. Additionally, computers can be used to process, transform, or otherwise manipulate the media in myriad ways.
- ↗ *Increasing computing power with decreasing size and cost.* Continuing developments in computing are affecting more than just media. Moore's Law, which predicts a doubling of microchip power about every 18 months, has remained in effect since the birth of the microprocessor. This has allowed personal computers to become more powerful, more compact, and less expensive over time. Microchips are powering a host of new educational devices in addition to computers such as **smart phones**, which are already providing new educational opportunities. In addition, advances in related technologies continue. For example, storage capacities are increasing, and wireless technologies make it possible for people to access the Internet without being tethered to a wired connection.
- ↗ *The growth of the Internet.* The emergence of the Internet as the Information Superhighway is another key trend of today. While personal computers were once isolated desktop machines, networking is

common today and increasing globally at a phenomenal rate. It is as though our planet is growing its own nervous system. The Internet brings unprecedented opportunities for teaching and learning. It brings up-to-the-minute multimedia resources into classrooms and homes; it provides a vehicle for communication among teachers, learners, and their communities; it provides a forum for students to publish their work; and it makes available a wide variety of applications and tools for doing work. Computers and the Internet are bringing tremendous new educational opportunities.

Today, educational technology is the focus of great attention. In the military and business training settings, the systematic design and implementation of instruction has been widely embraced, and the use of mediated instruction delivered via video, multimedia computer software, intranets, and the Internet is widespread. Schools are investing millions of dollars in the "nuts and bolts" of educational technology—computers and allied technologies. But people wonder about the value of educational technology for K–12 education. Is the large investment in technology worth it? Some schools are moving forward with innovative programs, but others seem mired in nineteenth-century approaches in the twenty-first century. What is the status of educational technology in schools today?

WHAT BARRIERS TO INTEGRATION OF TECHNOLOGY HAVE BEEN ENCOUNTERED?

Effective planning helps to identify needs as well as to establish goals and means whereby school administrators, teachers, and individual students can come to reliably achieve desired levels of technology integration. However, along the journey to integration, barriers that inhibit, and at times stop, progression with integration are often encountered. A key issue within educational technology is being able to know and understand the ramifications of these barriers. Some may be quickly addressed through the acquisition of specific tools, but others may require extensive training, time, and experience to overcome.

Barriers to technology integration have been categorized in a number of ways (Ertmer, 1999). One type relates to problems created by such things as equipment difficulties, time restrictions, or inadequate training, support, and funding. These are frequently outside, or external to, the teacher's control. A different category of barrier is that which is more internally oriented for the teacher. These barriers are "typically rooted in teachers' underlying beliefs about teaching and learning" (Ertmer, 1999, p. 51). They are often produced when the use of technology conflicts in some way with an individual's teaching philosophy. For example, A teacher who frequently utilizes a classroom discussion method may find it a challenge to integrate certain types of computer Web searches and tutorials that can require a more individualized approach to learning.

In order to better understand these barriers and ways to address them, we discuss several of the key issues that underlie each.

What Are the Costs Involved?

As pointed out by Tiene and Ingram (2001), several categories of cost are incurred when attempting to integrate technology. No longer can we just consider the hardware costs and leave it at that. As shown in Figure 13–1, the integration of technology requires one to consider all potential costs.

Cost estimates for technology expenses in order to reach a target level of one computer for every five students "would require an annual investment of somewhere between $10 and $20 billion for an unspecified period of time" (Healy, 1998, p. 80). Questions have been and will continue to be raised about those expenses and if that money would see greater utility in other areas. Although computers are becoming more available and are being utilized to a greater degree, indications are that those gains may come at the expense of other programs (e.g., art, music, physical education). A significant question should be, "Can we afford the technology when it comes at a cost to these other important areas of study?"

A second area of cost that also must be considered is the additional time involved in planning, implementing, and evaluating the effectiveness of the integration of technology within an instructional unit or lesson (Chuang, Thompson, & Schmidt, 2003a). This cost of time can be viewed from three different perspectives. First, those developing the instructional experience need to understand when and why specific technology can and should be used. Understanding what various types of technology have to offer, the benefits and challenges of each, and how to make a proper selection all require time to determine. Second, expertise in using the technology for both the teacher and the student requires time to develop. Training and practice are often required in order to gain the needed skill to use the technology to the desired level of effectiveness and reliability. Finally, time also must be invested in the management of the technology. There is always time needed to schedule and access the equipment and facilities, make certain that all technology will work properly, and that everything is stored correctly following the lesson. To illustrate, imagine teaching a group of students how to creatively write and report a personal autobiography. If the assignment allowed for the creation of a video autobiography,

Hardware	Computers, Monitors, Projectors, Scanners, Digital Cameras, etc.
Software	Programs used to run on the computers and other hardware. These programs may include productivity software such as Microsoft *Office*, but may also include all instructional software used for student learning and exercises.
Infrastructure	May include things such as the rooms and furniture used to house and support the technology. In addition, networks and wiring also are considered part of this cost category.
Maintenance	It is often necessary to repair and periodically update hardware and software. Upkeep of the technology requires time, skill, as well as money.
Personnel	With the complexity and quantity of computer systems being used within school systems, it is now important to have individuals who understand the hardware and the software to ensure its proper implementation and maintenance. Moreover, individuals to secure and staff computer labs may be needed to ensure their availability and proper care.
Materials	With all hardware, there are always a number of ancillary items that need to be purchased in order to make sure the hardware functions properly. These would include storage devices (e.g., DVDs, external storage devices such as flash drives), cables, printer supplies (e.g., ink cartridges, paper), technical manuals, and so forth.
Training	Without an understanding of the technology and how that technology should/could be integrated within the classroom, the technology will not be viewed as a benefit. In fact, without proper training, individual teachers can come to view technology as a major waste of time, money, and effort.
Services and Utilities	Electricity service, as well as Internet service provider fees, room fees, and so on are all expenditures that have to be considered when operating technology as a learning tool.

FIGURE 13–1   Costs of Educational Technology (adapted from Tiene & Ingram, 2001, p. 124).

additional time would be needed by the students to plan the project, determine the types of software and hardware to use, as well as learn how the technology works. There will also be time required to ensure that the video works and that schedules will be allowed for it to be delivered at the proper time and in the desired manner.

In addition to the financial barriers, other types of barriers may be encountered by the classroom teacher. For example, some individuals may feel that their teaching is just as (or even more) effective without the problems associated with the addition of technology. Reflect back on the chapter involving the various instructional methods (see Chapter 6) or the one that described the various media (see Chapter 7). In both cases, we presented a list of various methods and media, all of which are effective some of the time—but few of which are optimally effective all of the time. The same type of selection and integration philosophy applies to the use of the computer or other technology within a specific lesson experience that you desire for your students. We want you to understand not only how integration occurs but, more important, when and why it should occur. There will be times in all learning when the integration of computers or other technology may not be the optimal thing to do. By understanding the strengths and limitations, the benefits and the costs, a proper selection can be made.

Some educators (both new and experienced) may be reluctant to integrate technology because it is new and different. Change increases anxiety and allows for

mistakes and other problems to occur. Again, we would suggest that you look closely at your audience, your objectives, the content, and the environment to help determine if it would be advantageous to integrate technology. Here are several questions that you could reflect on when determining if the integration of technology may be worth the effort and time. Ask yourself if the integration would help your students:

- ↗ Understand the material to a greater degree?
- ↗ Gain the needed understanding in a faster, more efficient manner?
- ↗ Transfer the new information to a greater degree?
- ↗ Gain increased levels of insight (see things not previously seen, be more open to new ideas, etc.) about the material?
- ↗ Experience the material through different means that will perhaps help them grasp it in a more memorable fashion?
- ↗ Be motivated by increasing their curiosity, levels of confidence, excitement, and/or interest in the content?

Once an opportunity for integration, as well as any potential barriers, has been identified, several specific tactics may be utilized to facilitate the potential integration effort. Ertmer (1999) suggests, "(a) talking to others at the same grade level, or in the same content area, to share ideas about how and when to use technology, (b) developing creative ways to address logistical and technical problems during early stages of use (e.g., team teaching; soliciting parent volunteers as classroom helpers; grouping students to include a more knowledgeable student in each group), (c) starting small—incorporating technology into the curriculum, one lesson at a time, and (d) working with others at the school, district, and state levels to incorporate technology competencies into existing curriculum guidelines" (pp. 55–56).

We need to emphasize several of these points. First, as suggested above, start small. You and your students need to see success early on, and that can readily be achieved through a small integration experience. Once experience with the smaller project has been accomplished, then it will be possible to move to other more complex integration efforts. In addition, the small efforts will help you begin to see the possibilities (and the potential barriers) that will help facilitate the success of the larger integration efforts. Second, if at all possible, get help from others. Those individuals who have worked in your school's computer labs and who have attempted projects in the past should have relevant information about the integration process that is specific to your situation. It is always helpful to know what works and what doesn't within your own setting.

HOW CAN WE ADDRESS AND OVERCOME THE BARRIERS TO INTEGRATION?

Successful schools have technology specialists who can help teachers with the process of implementing instructional technology. Until recently, most of the specialized work related to instructional media in the schools was performed by **library/media specialists**. Library/media specialists help students and teachers become effective users of ideas and information by providing access to materials, providing instruction to develop users' interest as well as competence in finding and using information and ideas, and working with teachers to design learning strategies to meet the needs of individual students.

Over the past decade or so, a new category of specialist has emerged in the schools—the computer or technology coordinator. The **technology coordinator** is a specialist and resource person who handles computers and related technologies for a school building or district. In some school districts, the position of technology coordinator is a full-time post. Indeed, some larger school districts employ a technology support staff of several individuals. Many schools today also support building-level coordinators. At the building level, and at the district level in smaller school districts, it is common for the technology coordinator to be a teacher who has expertise in the use of computers and who assumes these duties on a part-time basis. Part-time coordinators usually receive some release time

and/or extra compensation for their activities. Perhaps you will find yourself serving as a part-time coordinator one day.

The job of a technology coordinator varies considerably from school to school. It is common for such a coordinator to do any or all of the following:

- Work with administrators and the district's technology committee to develop and implement a technology plan
- Work with teachers to support and promote technology integration
- Plan and oversee hardware and software purchases and installations
- Install and maintain the school's computer network
- Maintain up-to-date records of the school's hardware and software
- Arrange for, or conduct, repairs of equipment
- Assemble and disseminate information about instructional technologies
- Write grants to seek support for the school's technology activities
- Provide in-service training for faculty and staff

Although typical schools today devote only a small portion of their technology budgets to faculty and staff training, regular in-service education is needed to keep teachers up to date in educational technology. In-service training should be considered as part of overall technology planning. It should be regular and ongoing. It should derive from the school's technology plan. It should help teachers to utilize technology effectively within the framework of both the plan and their own classroom goals and objectives.

Several approaches to in-service education for instructional technology are common. Single, focused presentations or workshops on a topic (sometimes referred to as "one-shot" in-service sessions) can be useful for raising faculty awareness and stimulating interest, but they are unlikely to have a long-term impact without follow-up activities. More successful programs involve a series of activities, with opportunities for guided practice, exploration, and feedback. Better in-service training experiences use local computer experts and teachers, provide hands-on experience, are conducted in a nonthreatening environment and at convenient times for teachers, present information in steps with opportunities for practice and mastery, and provide follow-up support and feedback. Good in-service education is a key component of successful implementation of instructional technology in schools today. In addition, positive results have been shown for the establishment of groups of individuals (teachers and students) into learning communities where the focus is on mentoring each other through the integration process (Chuang, Thompson, & Schmidt, 2003b).

Teachers learning together in technology in-service training.
Source: Phil McCarten/PhotoEdit.

Training, planning, and support are all critical issues that have to be addressed by anyone attempting to integrate technology. Ignoring these issues will lead to increased levels of frustration by the teacher and students, as well as lower levels of accomplishment. In addition, when future efforts at integration are required or even suggested, apprehension based on these earlier frustrations can develop into another issue that could taint and inhibit that future success.

Other issues have also been created and/or heightened, extended, and so on by the integration of technology. Several of these have been discussed in earlier chapters. One example would be copyright (see Chapter 8). As technology has made it easier to duplicate and produce instructional materials, the need to understand copyright has come to the forefront. In the next section we highlight several additional key issues that should be considered by the classroom teacher, administrator, parent, and student.

WHAT ADDITIONAL ISSUES MAY THE INTEGRATION OF TECHNOLOGY CREATE?

Equity and Other Issues of Access

Equity is another key issue for all schools planning for instructional technology. It seems likely that access to technology and opportunity to learn to use it appropriately will be a key factor for individual students' economic success both now and in the future. Unfortunately, socioeconomic differences have the potential to create a serious gap when it comes to technology. This "gap"

between those who have access to technology and those who do not is often referred to as the "**digital divide**." While students from wealthier households are likely to have access to a computer at home today, this is not as true for students from poorer households. Schools have a responsibility to help remedy this problem by providing access to all students.

As reflected in Figure 13–2, the situation in U.S. schools mirrors that of society as a whole. Poorer school districts and those with higher percentages of minority students have fewer computers per capita and are less likely to have Internet connections than wealthier districts. Fortunately, the ratio of students to computers continues to improve, and efforts to bring the Internet to every school in the United States have been very successful. Of course, this is a problem that schools cannot solve alone. Government, communities, and businesses must help schools provide needed access to technology.

However, even when access is not an issue, there are concerns about equity within schools. Less–wealthy and less–able students are more likely to experience computers as a tool for things such as remediation and drill and practice over basic skills, while more affluent and more capable students tend to have more opportunities to use computers in creative and open-ended ways. Schools and teachers need to avoid the stereotype that certain students cannot use technology in creative ways. *All* students can benefit from such applications.

In the past, there have also been reported gender inequities in regard to technology. Boys tended to be more involved with computers, both in school and out, than girls, and girls tended to exhibit less confidence with computers than boys. There is some evidence (refer to Figure 13–2) that these tendencies have been ameliorated through the involvement of girls with computers at an early age and through the maintaining of that involvement throughout the school curriculum. Schools need to plan their curricula so that both girls and boys have opportunities to be involved with instructional technology throughout their schooling.

Schools and teachers also need to guard against other biases in access to technology. In some schools, available computers are monopolized by a small percentage of users. This may result from preferential laboratory scheduling for certain classes, historical patterns of use, or other reasons. To some extent, this is natural. But when prioritizing access to available equipment, schools should make an effort to encourage a spectrum of users. Teachers, too, sometimes unconsciously stack the deck against certain students. Some teachers, for example, may provide access to a classroom computer as a reward for students getting their work done early. While this may occasionally be all right, it can create a pattern where the same speedier students are rewarded time after time, and other students are left out. Teachers must take care to provide equitable access to all students.

Characteristics	Using Computers (%)	Using the Internet (%)
Total (persons age 5–17)	91	59
Student characteristics		
Sex		
Female	91	61
Male	91	58
Race		
White	93	67
Black	86	47
Hispanic	85	44
Asian	91	58
American Indian	86	47
Family & household characteristics		
Family income		
Under $20,000	85	41
$20,000–$34,999	87	50
$35,000–$49,999	93	62
$50,000–$74,999	93	66
$75,000 or more	95	74

FIGURE 13–2   Percentage of children and adolescents who use computers and the Internet by student and family/household characteristics (DeBell & Chapman, 2006).

Legal, Ethical, and Security Issues

Schools and teachers must also be concerned with a range of potential legal and ethical issues associated with instructional technologies. For example, in Chapters 8, 9, and 11 we discussed one of these—copyright—and how it affects teachers and schools. Schools should have a clearly stated policy regarding copyright, and this policy should be made known to every teacher and student. Schools and teachers have a responsibility to model proper use of educational technology within the confines of copyright law. This includes the use of copyrighted materials and application of fair use guidelines. Certainly, an important part of this modeling also includes a stance of zero tolerance for software piracy, the illegal copying of computer software, digital music, pictures, and videos. Teachers have often been guilty of illegally copying software, often rationalizing that limited school budgets and high software costs make it justified. It does not! Illegal copying of software is theft. Teachers must not do it, and they must educate their students about illegal copying.

Teachers must also help students learn to use computers and other technologies in proper ways. This can sometimes be difficult when the computer culture glorifies questionable behavior. **Hackers**, individuals who gain access to computer systems without authorization, usually for the intellectual challenge and thrill, are viewed as heroes—sort of latter-day Robin Hoods—by many members of the computing community. Although hackers are often not malicious, they can create problems on accessed computer systems, either intentionally or unintentionally. In addition, it is a small step from hacking into a computer for fun to hacking into one for the purpose of stealing information or committing some other type of computer crime. Schools and teachers need to help students understand that this type of activity is wrong.

Computer viruses represent another threat in the school computer environment. While school–age students are rarely responsible for creating viruses, they can certainly be responsible for infecting school computers. Viruses are easily spread from infected storage devices such as flash drives to school computers, and they can often unknowingly be downloaded from sites on the Internet. To avoid virus problems, both schools and individuals should use antivirus software. For more information on viruses and virus protection, see the "Toolbox: Computer Viruses" on page 266.

Plagiarism   When an individual copies an original idea or piece of work and attempts to pass it off as his or her own, a problem known as plagiarism occurs. Plagiarism is wrong because it robs the work's originator of the acknowledgment that he/she deserves for its production. It is dishonest, because those who plagiarize misrepresent something as their original creation when it is not.

Technology has played an interesting role in the world of plagiarism. First, plagiarism generally involves the copying of something. In today's digital world, the copy feature found in almost all software allows for

Toolbox: Computer Viruses

Computer viruses can create significant problems both for individual users and in school laboratories. In the biological realm, viruses are tiny particles that infect organisms; they can be benign or disease causing. A virus invades a cell, taking it over to make more viruses, and releasing the copies to start a new cycle of infection. In the computer world, the term *virus* refers to a computer program that functions in a manner similar to a biological virus. A computer virus invades software, usually without any overt sign, and directs the computer to copy the virus and pass it on. Like natural viruses, computer viruses can have effects ranging from fairly benign (e.g., a prankish message appears on the infected computer's screen) to quite serious (e.g., the contents of the computer's hard disk are damaged or erased). Computer viruses have become a common problem for computer users in many settings, including schools.

Take the following precautions to reduce problems due to computer viruses:

↗ Use antivirus software (e.g., *Norton Internet Security, Trend Micro ("PC-cillin") Internet Security Suite, ESET NOD 32 Antivirus System, McAfee VirusScan*) on personal and school computers to check for and eliminate known viruses and spyware, as well as provide a firewall, filter spam, and even provide parental controls. Regularly update this software, because antivirus programs have limited effectiveness against new or unknown viruses.

↗ Avoid downloading software from bulletin boards and Internet sites that may not be trustworthy, and never open e-mail attachments from sources you do not know; these are common sources of infection. If you do download software, scan the downloaded files with antivirus software before use.

↗ In schools, establish practices that reduce the spread of viruses. Discourage or prohibit students from bringing their own software to school. Restart each computer between users, and set up your antivirus software to perform a scan automatically when the computer starts up or when an external storage device is inserted.

Many viruses pose real threats to computer data. However, there are also many reports of viruses, often circulated on the Internet, that are groundless. These virus hoaxes warn of catastrophic results often from just reading an e-mail message with a particular subject heading (e.g., Good Times, Pen-pal Greetings). While some security problems with popular e-mail programs have been reported, manufacturers have patched many of these potential security holes, and there have been few reports of viruses that can infect a computer through the simple act of reading an e-mail message. E-mail attachments, on the other hand, can contain executable programs, and these can be infected by a virus, such as the Code Red and Code Red II virus of 2001, which had a massive corrupting effect on personal, educational, and corporate computers in the United States and many other countries. It was estimated that more than two billion dollars was spent repairing the damage from these two viruses alone (DeLong, 2001). It is good practice to scan e-mail attachments with antivirus software before use. For more information about real viruses and virus hoaxes, visit the Cyber Incident Response Capability website operated by the U.S. Department of Energy (http://www.doecirc.energy.gov/).

---

exact duplicates to be created in fast, efficient, and extremely cost-effective ways. Second, plagiarism requires access to original items and works. Again, in today's information age, access to all types of digital information via the Internet has allowed individuals unprecedented access to sources of information. Coupling these elements together, you have a means to access and copy huge amounts of information, figures, video, music, and so on. This has produced an environment that easily allows individuals to copy and paste information. When used appropriately, these elements can facilitate the learning experience; when used inappropriately, they may lead to individuals finding ways to misrepresent original work.

What can be done to help address the problems of plagiarism? Here is a list based upon the work of McCullen (2002):

1. Educate students about the concepts of *intellectual property, plagiarism,* and the problems associated with plagiarism.

2. Show examples of intentional and unintentional plagiarism.

3. Highlight why plagiarism cannot be tolerated and indicate your expectations and policies.

4. Teach how to utilize one or more note-taking techniques (e.g., Cornell method) that help to ensure students use only their own original work and proper citations are given to the work of others.

5. Provide students' examples of proper citation methods.

6. Develop activities where the students can practice gathering information, taking notes, developing drafts, and creating proper citations.

7. Demonstrate for the students how you will use electronic means to monitor their use of improperly cited references and works (see "Toolbox: Electronic Plagiarism Detection Tools" on page 268).

For more information on plagiarism and techniques that can help students overcome associated problems, a multitude of websites can readily be found on the Internet using key words such as "plagiarism" in regular search engines (e.g., Google). One such site that has information on this topic and other writing subject matter is the Purdue University Online Writing Lab (OWL) (http://owl.english. purdue.edu/handouts/print/research/r_plagiar.html).

In addition to problems created by plagiarism, when someone accesses and steals the work of others, educators are faced with students accessing services that for a price will sell work to students. Imagine a student faced with a social studies paper that requires 10 pages of writing about a topic that the student does not have the time and/or motivation to complete. Instead of failing the assignment, students have found it possible to access websites that will provide access to databases of previously completed work that may be similar to the student's assignment. For a price, papers within the database can be obtained. Examples of such services include Thousands of Papers (www.termpapers-on-file.com) and School Sucks (www.schoolsucks.com). Frequently these services are advertised as research assistance for students, where papers on various topics and subjects can be purchased to be used as research and help for the student's own work. However, educators complain that, frequently, these papers are used in their entirety with only a name change being completed. To overcome these problems, instructors can again inform students of their policies, use plagiarism detection services, and have students turn in various drafts of their work to monitor the students' progression through the development process.

Security Schools must address issues related to privacy and security. Certainly, one concern that has been around for a number of years is security of student data. Schools and teachers often keep grades and other student records on the computer. These should not be accessible to students. But perhaps a bigger concern today is the access to personal information that is possible through the Internet. Many Internet sites collect personal information; this is of such concern that lawmakers have drafted legislation to make it illegal for websites to collect information from children. Individuals bent on exploitation may try to gather information from young people in chat rooms or online forums. Finally, schools that post information about students on the school website may inadvertently allow pedophiles or others to locate the students. Care must be exercised. Students should be educated about the risks of giving out information on the Internet and taught to use precautions. Schools and teachers should not post student information or products to a website without first getting the approval of both the students and their parents/guardians. Inadvertently, information about a student may be obtained by individuals who could use that for other purposes. For example, cases have occurred in which student health information was transmitted via an unsecured

e-mail transmission, which was unknowingly electronically monitored and filtered by a third party. Later, health insurance services were denied to the student's family because of information gained via that e-mail. When it comes to protecting privacy, it is best to err on the side of caution. For additional information (e.g., lesson plans, activities) on security issues that pertain to parents, teachers, and technology coordinators, see the Center for Education and Research in Information Assurance and Security (http://www.cerias.purdue.edu/K-12).

Finally, schools today must be concerned with how, students access information and what information they access on school computers. Probably the most important example today is the Internet. As we pointed out in Chapter 10, there is much on the Internet that is unsuitable for school children and has much potential for misuse. As a result, it is incumbent upon schools to educate students and to develop and implement acceptable use policies regarding the Internet.

Questioning the Benefits of Technology Integration

Within this chapter (and throughout other sections of this text), we have touched on several issues involving technology that will have an impact on not only how technology is integrated but also how that technology will impact our daily lives. In some cases, those changes are important and beneficial; however, they also frequently produce impacts that may not be viewed as desired.

Listed following are a number of topics that identify various technological changes that have occurred in recent years. Each topic has several reflective questions for you to consider. Although most of these topics reflect readily accepted technology integration changes, the questions highlight discussion issues that should be discussed and addressed.

- *Information access on the Internet.* What is the impact on students who now have access to the vast quantities of information available on the Internet? Is there a problem for students having access to information that may or may not be correct? Should the freedom of expression be limited in some way on the Internet? Should filters be used to stop students from accessing certain types of information?
- *Cross-cultural comparisons.* In what ways can technology facilitate cross-cultural comparisons? Will this type of comparison increase levels of understanding or could it highlight differences and subsequently increase levels of animosity?
- *Isolationism.* If we can shop, get educated, be entertained, and complete our job assignments all from the confines of our own home, is there a need for us to ever go out? Are we missing anything by

Toolbox: Electronic Plagiarism Detection Tools

Although plagiarism has never been a difficult task, technology has made it even easier (e.g., through efficient access, copying, and pasting of information). Electronic tools, however, have now been developed to help identify and document when plagiarism has taken place. These tools are used to compare the submitted document with documents from huge electronic databases and the Internet. In fractions of seconds, millions of comparisons can be made and matches can be identified, highlighted, and cited. For teachers that means that suspicious work can be quickly and efficiently scanned and a documented report generated showing if proper citations have been attributed; likewise, for students such scanning can help identify places within their work where potential problems may exist and what they need to do to ensure that no plagiarism has transpired.

TYPES OF DETECTION TOOLS
Simple Detection
A very simple form of this tool would involve the use of a common Internet search engine (e.g., Google). Simply copy a suspect phrase, sentence, or paragraph and place it within quotation marks within the search window of the search engine. The search should highlight Web documents with similar statements that are found on the Internet.

Advanced Detection Services
Several commercial **plagiarism detection services** are now available (generally for a small fee; however, there are some free services available) where a suspected document can be submitted and within a short period of time, a report will be generated about the document (see Figure 13–3) that highlights suspect plagiarized areas of the paper and gives citation of similar works. Examples of companies that provide such tools include:

- Turnitin.com (www.turnitin.com)
- SafeAssign by Blackboard (safeassign.com)
- EVE2 (www.canexus.com/eve/index.shtml)

In most cases, free sample searches or free trial days are offered by these services. A free service (WCopyfind) is offered at http://plagiarism.phys.virginia.edu/.

Benefits and Challenges of the Use of Detection Tools
Benefits include:

- Fast, efficient identification of work that has been plagiarized. Evidence can be shown to the student in an efficient manner so that appropriate actions can be taken.
- Educating students about such tools and then indicating that they will be used often has the effect of students taking extra effort to ensure that plagiarism is held to a minimum.
- It allows writers to use the tool with their own work to mark potential problems that may have been inserted unintentionally.

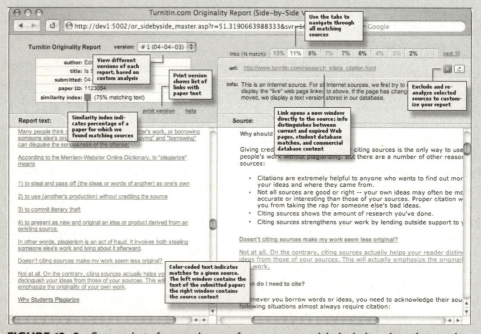

FIGURE 13–3 Screen shot of a sample page from a commercial plagiarism detection service.
Source: Reprinted with permission from Melissa Lipscomb, co-founder and vice president of iParadigms, LLC.

(continued)

Toolbox: Electronic Plagiarism Detection Tools (continued)

Challenges include:

➤ Cost of the service may be prohibitive to individual teachers.

➤ In some cases (e.g., turnitin.com), the submitted student papers are kept in a database by the detection service and used as reference for later comparisons. Questions about copyright infringement have been raised.

➤ All material that is found matching other sources is highlighted in many cases—even sources that are properly cited.

➤ The search may be limited so plagiarized materials are not detected.

➤ Trust between student and teacher may suffer because of the feeling that all work is suspect and thus must be examined.

ADDITIONAL REFERENCES RELEVANT TO PLAGIARISM DETECTION

Current Issues and Resources. Center for Intellectual Property. Retrieved July 28, 2009, from University of Maryland University College website: http://www.umuc.edu/distance/odell/cip/links_plagiarism.shtml

---

not shopping at the store, interacting with classmates in a school classroom, or working with coworkers in real time at a central work location?

➤ *Communications.* Is technology allowing us to develop and use new ways of effectively communicating with others? Are we learning ways that enhance the quality of person-to-person communication? In what ways have social norms been impacted by technology and how has the technology impacted the quality of our interactions?

➤ *Research methodology.* In what ways has technology allowed for new research methodologies to be developed and used? For example, can access to a wider variety of individuals (e.g., via the Internet) be helpful or does it cause problems for researchers?

➤ *Technology dependency.* Are there times that we can become so dependent on technology that we begin to lose or not develop needed skills? For example, are spell checkers helping our ability to spell words correctly or hindering our development of good spelling techniques? Similarly, are calculators helping us develop basic math skills or inhibiting our math development?

➤ *"Keeping up with the Joneses."* Is there a need to always have the latest and greatest technology? Is it possible (and possibly desirable) to skip certain generations of new machines and software?

➤ *Quantity versus quality.* If the technology allows us to produce more efficiently and/or effectively, why do individuals still seem to not have enough time to get things done? Is the technology helping to make our lives "better" or just more demanding?

➤ *Spurning technology.* Are there times when the use of technology should not be used? Under what situations should we begin to think about eliminating technology or at least inhibiting its integration?

WHY INVEST THE TIME, ENERGY, AND COST INTO THE INTEGRATION OF TECHNOLOGY?

This is a critical question for many individuals. With billions of dollars being spent on technology and technology integration and maintenance within our schools each year, a strong, convincing rationale needs to be given. A recent report from the U.S. Department of Education, Office of Educational Technology (Culp, Honey, & Mandinach, 2003) presented findings about why the investment is justified.

Technology as a Means to Address Difficulties in Teaching and Learning

As pointed out in Chapter 1 of this text, the demands placed on learners over the past century have shifted dramatically. Development of technology in some ways has produced and intensified some of these demands and at the same time has come to provide a means for accomplishing needed learning. For example, in a world demanding greater levels of problem-solving skills within complex learning environments, technology offers students a variety of ways to access, analyze, synthesize, and communicate their methods and potential solutions. Moreover, technology can be used to enhance the learning experience in order to help the learner grasp the problem, practice needed skills, present relevant answers, and assess the quality of the learning. In other situations, technology can increase the effectiveness of instruction by reaching those students who may have been previously inhibited geographically, physically, or even socially. Finally, technology tools offer a way to add greater levels of diversity. Through advanced communications, students can now more readily access timely information from a multitude of relevant sources (e.g., content experts, professional organizations, other students, teachers, and administrators from around the world) who may offer a more expansive view of specific learning situations.

> **PEARSON myeducationkit** Go to the Assignments and Activities section of Chapter 13 in MyEducationKit and complete the activity entitled "Online Connections." Review the web links presented in this activity and think about how you could connect students in your classrooms with others in a global community. What would be the benefits of doing so?

Technology as a Change Agent

Another rationale for the value of technology integration is the impact it has on how teachers design and carry out their instructional lessons. Assimilating technology in a learning situation often triggers "changes away from lecture-driven instruction and toward constructivist, inquiry-oriented classrooms" (Culp et al., 2003, p. 5). That is, teachers who integrate and utilize technology effectively often find the need to first make their lessons "more flexible, more engaging, and more challenging for students" (Culp et al., 2003, p. 5). In this role, the integration of technology facilitates how learning is viewed and subsequently how the optimal learning experience is designed and implemented.

Technology as a Means to Maintain Economic Competitiveness

Rapid shifts toward a global economy have dictated the need for many individuals to obtain, maintain, and enhance their skills with technology. For example, within the manufacturing industry, technology is central to being able to increase productivity while decreasing the time and costs involved with that production. As labor and material costs increase, ways of using technology to reduce expensive person-hours and material scrap are constantly being sought. This continuous implementation and adaptation of technology requires a workforce that understands the need to constantly learn and upgrade their skills. Likewise, within education, technology impacts how, when, and why we learn. That does not mean that you will no longer be able to learn without the use of some form of technology; however, technology can provide for greater access to information, broader and more realistic learning experiences, increased quantity and quality of practice, or even greater levels of in-depth feedback that produce more

efficient and effective learning. Learners may find that the use of technology allows them to ask questions, see novel perspectives, explore and discover solutions to more complex problems, and be able to adapt more readily to change. All of these qualities are fundamental to the success of living and learning within an information society.

"These three rationales for investing in educational technology surface again and again throughout the last twenty years. They are also highly interconnected. At their core, each of these rationales is based on recognition that technology is the embodiment and the means of much of the social and economic change of the past century. There is also an acknowledgement that integrating technologies into the instructional fabric of teaching and learning in our society requires commitment, focus, and resources from multiple stakeholders" (Culp et al., 2003, p. 6)

WHAT HORIZON TECHNOLOGIES MAY POTENTIALLY FACILITATE STUDENT LEARNING?

Predicting the future is always a risky business. Conditions change, new developments occur, and old patterns fail to hold true. Nonetheless, developments in educational technology over the past 100 years certainly do suggest some trends. We noted some of these earlier new perspectives on learning, media convergence, continuing computer developments, and growth of the Internet. If we assume that these trends will continue, then we are able to make some predictions. The implications of these trends may not always be clear, but it is possible, at least in some cases, to see the direction in which we are headed. And knowing which way we are going helps us to chart our course.

A number of technologies are emerging in importance today. Many of these technologies are not yet fully functional or widely implemented. But the nature of these technologies suggests that they could become increasingly important to teaching and learning. We call these *horizon technologies*, because, like the horizon, we can see them in the distance but we are not altogether sure what they will look like when we get closer. We examine some of these horizon technologies following.

Artificial Intelligence (AI)

Artificial Intelligence (AI) is a branch of computer science concerned with the design of computers and software that are capable of responding in ways that mimic human thinking. Although AI has been around as a field of study for a long time now, the early promise of "intelligent" machines that can truly think like people has not been realized. However, the field has borne fruit, and we expect to see further developments in the future. One successful result of AI research has been the development of *expert systems*, programs that embody the knowledge and skills of an expert in a particular discipline. They have already proven to be successful in fields as diverse as oil exploration and medical diagnosis. In education, the concept of the expert system has led to the development of **intelligent tutoring systems**, sometimes called *intelligent computer-assisted instruction* (ICAI). These programs have been developed in mathematics, geography, and computer science, to name just a few subjects. For example, *Cognitive Tutor* is intelligent tutoring software in secondary mathematics from Carnegie Learning (http://www.carnegielearning.com), an outgrowth of AI research at Carnegie Mellon University, that is now used in a number of school districts across the country. Intelligent tutoring systems usually combine detailed information about the subject area and a database of common student mistakes with a model of student performance to diagnose a given student's level of understanding and provide instruction tailored to meet that student's specific needs. They embody the expertise of a tutor within a particular content domain. We may see more of these programs in the future as well as the adaptation of techniques from these programs to more common instructional software.

Speech and Handwriting Recognition

An outgrowth of AI research has been developments in speech and handwriting recognition. **Speech recognition** systems translate speech into text that the computer can manipulate, and some support basic computer commands (e.g., opening or closing applications) issued by voice. Several speech recognition systems are on the market now. Examples include Nuance's *Dragon Naturally Speaking* and *IBM ViaVoice*. Microsoft includes a speech recognition and speech synthesis engine in *Windows*, and Apple built speech recognition and synthesis software into *MacOS*. In addition to these, several vendors produce speech recognition products for telephony applications and access to the World Wide Web via spoken commands. As developments continue, the day when we can routinely communicate with our computers via spoken language, just like on *Star Trek*, may not be far off. Handwriting recognition software is now part of the operating system on Tablet PCs. This software translates handwritten notes into text that can be saved and edited on the computer. A related development that is emerging today is **semantic-aware applications**. These applications take advantage of computer processing capabilities to determine the meaning, or semantics, of information on the Internet to make connections and answer questions that would otherwise take much time and effort.

Tablet PCs support basic handwriting recognition.
Source: © 2005 SMART Technologies Inc.

Mobile Technologies

Since their inception, computing devices have grown steadily more compact and more mobile. Today, many schools have moved away from desktop computers and toward laptops and tablet PCs. Students may also possess **personal digital assistants (PDAs)** and/or cell phones. Of particular interest are so-called **smart phones,** such as Apple's iPhone that combines the functionality of a cell phone with the versatility of a handheld computer. These devices, which are small enough to fit in a pocket or purse, can be tools for note-taking, calculating, reading material, working with productivity applications, and browsing the Web. As they continue to grow more capable, mobile devices promise to become valuable educational tools that in many cases will replace larger and more expensive computers while also freeing the user from being tethered to power and network connections.

PEARSON myeducationkit™ Go to the Assignments and Activities section of Chapter 13 in MyEducationKit and complete the activity entitled "Tablet Computers." Watch how the history teacher uses the tablet to draw on a series of maps. Reflect on how these maps on the computer help to guide the presentation and highlight the key concepts that are being presented. What benefits do you see from this approach to using the tablet computer? Are there any potential problems with this approach?

PEARSON myeducationkit™ Go to the Assignments and Activities section of Chapter 13 in MyEducationKit and complete the activity entitled "Wireless in the Classroom." As you watch this video, consider how these wireless devices promote student collaboration and engagement in this activity.

Apple iPhone is an example of smart phone technology.

Source: Andrew Vaughan/The Canadian Press/AP Images.

Cloud Computing

An emerging technology related to the growth and development of the Internet is so-called **cloud computing**. Cloud computing refers to the distribution of applications, processing power, and storage across many computers accessible via the Internet. In the past, if you had a personal computer, in most cases, you did your work using applications on that computer, using the computer's processing capabilities, and you stored whatever you produced on that computer. Today, the proliferation of Internet applications and services makes it possible for you to do all of your work in the "cloud." You can use applications available on the Internet, take advantage of processing capabilities provided by a cluster of computers, and store your work on a server that is out in cyberspace somewhere. This approach frees you and your work from being tied to a particular computer. Instead, as long as you have a connection to the Internet, even through a simple computer such as a **netbook**, you can effectively do your work. The downside of cloud computing is that you may not be able to access your work if your Internet connection is unavailable, or if the companies that provide the services should go out of business. Despite the possible drawbacks, cloud computing is clearly a growing trend.

Virtual Reality

Another emerging area of computer development is virtual reality. **Virtual reality (VR)** refers to a computer-generated, three-dimensional, visual representation of an environment that responds to the user's motion within it. Today, VR systems often consist of a computer linked to special headgear and bodysuits or gloves worn by the user. The headgear projects the image of a three-dimensional world before the user and senses the motion of the user's head so that as the head turns, the image the user sees also turns appropriately. With a sensor-equipped glove, the user can reach out and touch or grab objects in the virtual environment. For example, a student studying organic chemistry might be able to reach and rotate an

One day, virtual reality gear like this may allow students to take virtual field trips.
Source: Georgia Tech Communications.

organic molecule in three dimensions to better understand its structure and function. While VR technology can be crude now, it has already gained popularity, and developments are continuing rapidly. For example, newer stereo projection systems allow for similar imaging without the special headgear. As VR technology improves, we can envision a variety of educational applications. It may be possible for students to take virtual field trips—re-creations of historical events, travel to faraway places, or journeys inside the human body. In addition, students may be able to perform virtual tasks such as mixing dangerous chemicals or learning how to perform an operation without the risk and expense of the real thing. Virtual reality could make simulations incredibly lifelike. The possibilities are truly exciting.

PEARSON **myeducationkit** Go to the Assignments and Activities section of Chapter 13 in MyEducationKit and complete the activity entitled "Virtual Reality." Review the Web links presented in this activity and think about how you could use virtual reality in your curriculum. What would be the benefits of doing so?

Ubiquitous Computing

Ubiquitous computing, sometimes called pervasive computing or distributed intelligence, refers to situations in which computer processing power is embedded, often invisibly, in objects in the everyday environment. The idea, which was originally developed by researchers at the Xerox Palo Alto Research Center, is in some ways the opposite of virtual reality. Whereas virtual reality puts the user in a computer-generated environment, in ubiquitous computing, the environment is imbued with computer

processing power. Given the low cost and widespread availability of powerful processors today, it is not a stretch to envision a day when many devices will contain "smart" computer chips. Cars, microwave ovens, and other consumer appliances already contain processors. In the future, we might imagine computer chips in our clothing that alert us to excess exposure to harmful ultraviolet radiation, a sensor in a wristwatch that continuously monitors glucose levels in a diabetic individual, or chips embedded in the walls of a house that sense the presence of people in a room and automatically adjust temperature and lighting. Educational applications might include "smart" museum exhibits that automatically provide customized content when visitors approach. As ubiquitous computing grows, computing power will increasingly fade into the background, invisibly playing an important role in our work and our lives.

SCHOOLING AND EDUCATION IN THE FUTURE

How will these predicted changes affect education and schooling in the future? This is the most difficult question of all to answer; our crystal ball is growing cloudy! The difficulty lies in the fact that education is a complex social, cultural, and political phenomenon. While it is relatively simple to predict that present technological trends will one day result in a computer capable of responding to human vocal commands, it is far less certain how, if at all, such a development may impact the educational enterprise. It may help to remember that we are all about the business of learning, and we must stay focused on how technology developments may impact what we and our students do to promote learning. So, with trepidation, let us forge ahead.

In many ways, public education in the United States has been a tremendous success. Yet despite this success—or perhaps because of it—the history of education and schooling shows remarkable resistance to change. If you have ever seen a picture of a nineteenth-century classroom, you probably noticed a teacher in the front of the room, students with books at neat rows of benches and worktables, and a potbellied stove in the corner. Except for the use of individual desks and more modern heating systems, not a lot has changed in many present-day classrooms. Most classrooms today still look like and to a large extent function as they did over one hundred years ago. Even the summer vacation common to most school calendars is a vestige of a bygone era when children were needed during the summer to work on the family farm. Do schools today prepare students for the Information Age that is upon us?

Over the years, many educational innovations with promises of dramatic change have come and gone. Instructional television is certainly a case in point. During the 1950s, advocates of instructional television envisioned

Toolbox: Exploring Horizon Technologies

Information about emerging technologies is available from a number of sources on the Internet. You can use these sources to research future developments in computing that may impact education. Use the following websites to explore trends in emerging technologies.

Site	URL
Horizon Project, New Media Consortium	http://www.nmc.org/horizon
EDUCAUSE Forum for the Future of Higher Education	http://www.educause.edu/forum/
MIT's Media Lab at the Massachusetts Institute of Technology	http://www.media.mit.edu
Xerox Palo Alto Research Center	http://www.parc.com/
Ziff Davis net, a website supporting information technology topics	http://www.zdnet.com/

What emerging technologies are commonly mentioned across the various sites? Which ones seem likely to have an impact in the next few years or in the next few decades? Which ones do you foresee having a significant impact on education? Why?

Classrooms of today do not look much different from this classroom of the nineteenth century.
Source: Scott Cunningham/Merrill Education.

a radical change in education and schooling as a result of this innovation. Although instructional television did not disappear, it never lived up to the expectations created by early advocates. Today, some critics think that computers and related technologies represent a similarly overhyped innovation for schools. Clifford Stoll, author of *High-Tech Heretic*, has argued that computers detract from the most important things in education, including students' interactions with teachers and peers, and so should be used only minimally in schools. Mark Bauerlein,

author of *The Dumbest Generation*, suggests that use of digital technologies has actually been harmful to the current generation of students. Respected educator Larry Cuban, author of *Oversold and Underused: Computers in the Classroom*, has repeatedly pointed out that the historical and organizational contexts of education lead to resistance of many technical innovations, such as computers, and as a result these innovations are underutilized and/poorly utilized in schools. So, on the one hand, there is evidence that computers and other educational technologies are having little impact in schools and perhaps we should quit investing in them.

Yet, it is clear that technology is bringing dramatic changes to society. The Information Age is here now. Computers have brought about significant changes in the workplace, and they are becoming common in homes. Media convergence is well under way, and there is no denying that major corporations are investing significant sums of money to get on and make use of the Information Superhighway. Some authors have suggested that dramatic changes are occurring. Dan Tapscott, author of *Grown Up Digital*, argues that today's students, the so-called net generation, are truly different from their predecessors, and we must embrace the new technologies that they utilize in their daily lives. Clayton Christensen, author of *Disrupting Class*, argues that new technologies will take root with today's learners and become a disruptive force that will change the educational system as we know it. So, on the other hand, computers and other educational technologies might literally transform education.

What will happen? Of course, no one knows. While educational technologies might fade away as unimportant or revolutionize education as we know, we envision a more moderate course. It is clear that learning is already developing into a lifelong commitment. The days when a person could expect to get a high school diploma, go to work for the local company, and retire 45 years later without ever having cracked a book again are long gone. It is also clear that the tools are here now, or will be here soon, to free learning from the confines of the school building. Soon the world's knowledge will be available to nearly every household via a thin fiber-optic cable or through the airways. Will this mark the demise of schooling and education as we have known it? While it could, the social and political ramifications of such an eventuality would be considerable. Alternatively, this may provide the impetus needed to truly change schools to become centers of lifelong learning for the Information Age.

We envision a future where teachers and learners embrace and integrate educational technology and use it to improve both teaching and learning. To be sure, this will mean that there must be some important changes in education. The following are possible outcomes of this process of change:

- Learners and teachers alike will have access to powerful, portable computing devices that will be wirelessly connected to network resources.
- Multimedia learning resources, available via information networks, will proliferate and become available for education anytime and anyplace.
- Learning increasingly will take place in authentic contexts and focus on authentic tasks. Students will find answers to real problems using technology as a tool.
- Students will be active learners, collaborating with one another and with more experienced members of society, to seek out information and gain knowledge.
- Teachers' roles will tend to shift from "the sage on the stage" to the "guide on the side." Instead of conveying information, they will help learners make use of new information tools to find, analyze, and synthesize information; to solve problems; to think creatively; and to construct their own understandings.
- Education will become a lifelong process, important and accessible to all, and schools will become centers of learning—not just for children, but for all members of the community.
- Education will focus increasingly on authentic performance-based forms of assessment. Students will be judged by their ability to find and use information to solve genuine problems.
- The boundaries separating schools from each other and from the community will blur or disappear. Students will learn from teachers at other locations and collaborate with students at other locations. Teachers will learn alongside students. Students will

learn from other students or from members of the community. Communities themselves will change as technology enables collaboration over distances.

This is a future that is not just about educational technology. Education and schooling are bigger than that. However, without educational technology, it will be very hard for us to get where we need to go. We see a future that is *enabled* by educational technology.

TECHNOLOGY COORDINATOR'S CORNER

Not long ago, Donna Owens, a middle school math teacher, stopped by the office of her district's computer coordinator, Maria Cavazos. Donna and Maria chatted about the future of technology in education, a topic that came up because Donna had read an article that predicted future developments including continuous network connectivity, virtual environments, and computers in eyeglasses.

Maria pointed out that these developments, while seeming somewhat far-fetched, were evident in the trends of today. She noted that the district had installed wireless access points throughout Donna's school the year before last, students liked to play a virtual reality game at the arcade in the local shopping mall, and PDAs, while not small enough to fit in eyeglasses, packed the power that was once in desktop computers into a very small package. Maria remarked that it was not hard to imagine these trends continuing and leading to exciting new developments.

Donna agreed that the new developments in technology were exciting, but she also found them to be a little intimidating. She commented to Maria that technology, unlike the curriculum in her math classroom, seemed to change every year. Technology, she noted, seemed to require that she learn something new all of the time, and she found it difficult to keep up. She asked Maria for advice on how to learn about new developments in the field.

Maria explained that there was not any secret to it. She told Donna to approach learning about technologies the way she approached learning anything. This is what she suggested. Spend time gathering information about new developments. Look for opportunities to try out new technologies to see what they might have to offer. Think about how new technologies replace, build upon, or go beyond what has been available in the past. Reflect on how any new technology might be applied to teaching and learning. Additional specific suggestions include the following:

- Read about new developments in technology. Magazine articles often provide a nice overview of trends, and articles in professional journals are a good source of ideas for integrating technology into teaching practice. You

(continued)

can also find a lot of useful information about new developments on the Internet.

↗ Take workshops or courses. Having someone else lead you through learning about a new technology can be one of the quickest ways to gain some expertise.

↗ Attend professional conferences in your discipline. Presentations at conferences are where you are apt to hear the most up-to-date ideas about using technology in the classroom. Also technology vendors often display their products at professional conferences. That is a great place to try out things that you think you might want to use in the classroom. For a real technology experience, go to a conference that focuses on technology in education such as the International Society for Technology in Education (ISTE) Conference.

↗ When you get new software or other new technology in the classroom, take advantage of the tutorials, online support, and other forms of help that often come with it. You might not remember how to do something such as a mail merge using an *Excel* data file if you seldom do it but the built-in help files can walk you through the process.

↗ Talk to other teachers. You can learn a lot about new developments by talking to other teachers or school technology coordinators. One quick way to gain insights is to get online and review various blogs written by teachers about technology that they are finding effective in their classrooms.

↗ Finally, do not be afraid to learn from your students. Students have a lot of time to explore computers and other new technologies, and they seem to pick it up very quickly. Make students your resident technology experts in the classroom, and let them teach you. You will benefit, and they will get a feeling of pride and accomplishment from being acknowledged as experts in the class.

Maria concluded by advising Donna that she should not feel like she needed to become knowledgeable about every new development. There will always be new developments in technology, and no one can be an expert in all of them. She suggested that Donna just try to keep up with the developments in her own field, learn the things she would need in order to do her job productively, and find ways to integrate technology in her classroom that complement her personal teaching style. For any teacher learning about new technologies, that is good advice.

SUMMARY

Today, instructional design, educational media, and educational computing are all established disciplines and are converging through the capabilities of the computer. Media are becoming digital, and the computer offers new capabilities for planning, implementing, and evaluating instruction. While the typical school of today has a fair amount of technology, it may not be used fully. Model schools suggest how things might change if all schools made better use of available technology. In particular, technology is a means to address and overcome specific challenges faced by learners; a way to help teachers design, develop, and implement learning experiences that engage learners to a greater degree and create more complex, realistic learning experiences for their learners; as well as a means to help individual learners be productive and competitive in a rapidly shifting world economy.

Although the integration of technology has been important to accomplish, that integration has also introduced several issues. For instance, (a) the ramifications for learners who come from different socioeconomic backgrounds and cultures and their varying levels of technology access; (b) the increased need to identify and implement privacy and security measures; and (c) the implications of legal and ethical issues such as heightened levels of plagiarism or even the purchase of completed projects and assignments.

As schools move toward the future, we see trends that are likely to continue in the future. There will be even greater convergence of instructional design, media, and computing. Computer networking will expand, and computer capabilities will grow. While education and schooling may ultimately either ignore these innovations or become totally transformed by them, we see a middle course in which instructional technology empowers both teachers and learners.

PEARSON myeducationkit™ To check your comprehension of the content covered in this chapter, go to the MyEducationKit for this book and complete the Study Plan for Chapter 13. Here you will be able to take a chapter quiz, receive feedback on your answers, and then access resources that will enhance your understanding of chapter content.

SUGGESTED RESOURCES

Print Resources

Bailey, G., & Ribble, M. (2007). *Digital citizenship in schools*. Washington, DC: International Society for Technology in Education.

Bauerlein, M. (2008). *The dumbest generation: How the digital age stupefies young American and jeopardizes our future (or, don't trust anyone under 30)*. New York: Tarcher.

Brooks-Young, S. (2006). *Critical technology issues for school leaders*. Thousand Oaks, CA: Corwin.

Christensen, C., Horn, M., & Johnson, C. (2008). *Disrupting class: How disruptive innovation will change the way the world learns*. New York: McGraw-Hill.

Cuban, L. (2001). *Oversold & underused: Computers in the classroom.* Harvard University Press: London.

Fogg, B. (2003). *Persuasive technology: Using computers to change what we think and do.* San Francisco, CA: Morgan Kaufmann.

Fogg, B. (2007). *Mobile persuasion: 20 perspectives of the future of behavior change.* Stanford Captology Media.

Forum on Education Statistics. (2002). *Technology in schools: Suggestions, tools, guidelines for assessing technology in elementary and secondary education.* National Center for Education Statistics. U.S. Department of Education: Washington, DC. Available at http://nces.ed.gov/pubs2003/2003313.pdf

Frazier, M., & Bailey, G. (2004). *The technology coordinator's handbook.* Eugene, OR: International Society for Technology in Education.

Hendron, J. (2007). *RSS for educators: Blogs, newsfeeds, podcasts, and wikis.* Washington, DC: International Society for Technology in Education.

Kelly, F., McCain, T., & Jukes, I. (2009). *Teaching the digital generation: No more cookie-cutter high schools.* Thousand Oaks, CA: Corwin.

Kolb, L. (2008). *Toys to tools: Connecting student cell phones to education.* Washington, DC: International Society for Technology in Education.

Mantgem, M. (2007). *Tablet PCs in K-12 education.* Washington, DC: International Society for Technology in Education.

Moe, T., & Chubb, J. (2007). *Librating learning: Technology, politics, and the future of American education.* San Francisco, CA: John Wiley & Sons.

Morrison, G., Ross, S., & Lowther, D. (2009). Technology as a change agent in the classroom. In L. Moller, J. Huett, & Harvey, D. (Eds.). *Learning and instructional technologies for the 21st century: Visions of the future.* (pp. 151–174). New York: Springer Science+Business Media, LLC.

Nitko, A. J., & Brookhart, S. M. (2007). Educational Assessment of Students (5th Ed.). Upper Saddle River, NJ: Pearson/Merrill/Prentice Hall.

Shamburg, C. (2009). *Student-powered podcasting.* Washington, DC.: International Society for Technology in Education.

Solomon, G., & Schrum, L. (2007). *Web 2.0: New tools, new schools.* Washington, DC: International Society for Technology in Education.

Stoll, C. (2000). *High tech heretic: Why computers don't belong in the classroom and other reflections by a computer contrarian.* New York City: Anchor Books/Random House, Inc.

Tapscott, D. (2008). *Grown up digital: How the net generation is changing your world.* New York: McGraw-Hill Professional.

Tiene, D., & Ingram, A. (2001). *Exploring current issues in educational technology.* Boston: McGraw Hill.

Wagner, T. (2008). *The global achievement gap: Why even our best schools don't teach the new survival skills our children need – and what we can do about it.* New York: Basic Books.

Electronic Resources

http://www.ikeepsafe.org/
(iKeepSafe: Internet Safety Coalition)

http://ed-web3.educ.msu.edu/outreach/k12out/internationalization07Toolkit.htm
(Toolkit | Preparing Our Students for a Place in the World: Internationalizing Michigan Education)

http://emergingtech.ittoolbox.com/
(IT Toolbox Emerging Technologies)

http://www.media.mit.edu/
(MIT's Media Lab)

http://ed.fnal.gov/lincon/staff_rubric.shtml
(LInC | District Technology Plan Rubric)

http://www.ed.gov/about/offices/list/os/technology/plan/2004/site/edlite-default.html
(National Education Technology Plan Website: Resources and Information)

http://eduscapes.com/tap/evidence.html
(Teacher Tap: Evidence-based Practice and Educational Technology)

http://etoolkit.org/etoolkit/
(School 2.0 eToolkit | Project commissioned by the Office of Educational Technology, U.S. Department of Education)

http://www.edutopia.org/project-learning
(Edutopia | Project Based Learning Resources and Information)

http://www.digitaldivide.org
(Digital Divide: Ushering in the Second Digital Revolution)

http://www.edutopia.org/digital-divide-where-we-are-today
(Edutopia | The Digital Divide: Where We Are Today)

http://www.cited.org/index.aspx?page_id=60&current_level=0&mf_value0=79&mf_id0=2
(CITEd Learn Center | Center for Implementing Technology in Education: Address Social, Legal, and Ethical Issues)

http://www.accessibletech4all.org/self_assessment/index.cfm
(Leadership and District Technology Plan Development)

Teacher Resource
A

The ISTE National Educational Technology Standards (NETS-T) and Performance Indicators for Teachers

Effective teachers model and apply the National Educational Technology Standards for Students (NETS-S) as they design, implement, and assess learning experiences to engage students and improve learning; enrich professional practice; and provide positive models for students, colleagues, and the community. Teachers have standards that they must meet as well, the NETS-T, that present the necessary educational technology knowledge and performance indicators. All teachers should meet the following standards and performance indicators. Teachers:

1. **Facilitate and Inspire Student Learning and Creativity**

   Teachers use their knowledge of subject matter, teaching and learning, and technology to facilitate experiences that advance student learning, creativity, and innovation in both face-to-face and virtual environments. Teachers:

   a. promote, support, and model creative and innovative thinking and inventiveness

   b. engage students in exploring real-world issues and solving authentic problems using digital tools and resources

   c. promote student reflection using collaborative tools to reveal and clarify students' conceptual understanding and thinking, planning, and creative processes

   d. model collaborative knowledge construction by engaging in learning with students, colleagues, and others in face-to-face and virtual environments

2. **Design and Develop Digital-Age Learning Experiences and Assessments**

   Teachers design, develop, and evaluate authentic learning experiences and assessments incorporating contemporary tools and resources to maximize content learning in context and to develop the knowledge, skills, and attitudes identified in the NETS-S. Teachers:

   a. design or adapt relevant learning experiences that incorporate digital tools and resources to promote student learning and creativity

   b. develop technology-enriched learning environments that enable all students to pursue their individual curiosities and become active participants in setting their own educational goals, managing their own learning, and assessing their own progress

   c. customize and personalize learning activities to address students' diverse learning styles, working strategies, and abilities using digital tools and resources

   d. provide students with multiple and varied formative and summative assessments aligned with content and technology standards and use resulting data to inform learning and teaching

3. **Model Digital-Age Work and Learning**

   Teachers exhibit knowledge, skills, and work processes representative of an innovative professional in a global and digital society. Teachers:

   a. demonstrate fluency in technology systems and the transfer of current knowledge to new technologies and situations

b. collaborate with students, peers, parents, and community members using digital tools and resources to support student success and innovation

c. communicate relevant information and ideas effectively to students, parents, and peers using a variety of digital-age media and formats

d. model and facilitate effective use of current and emerging digital tools to locate, analyze, evaluate, and use information resources to support research and learning

4. **Promote and Model Digital Citizenship and Responsibility**
   Teachers understand local and global societal issues and responsibilities in an evolving digital culture and exhibit legal and ethical behavior in their professional practices. Teachers:

   a. advocate, model, and teach safe, legal, and ethical use of digital information and technology, including respect for copyright, intellectual property, and the appropriate documentation of sources

   b. address the diverse needs of all learners by using learner-centered strategies and providing equitable access to appropriate digital tools and resources

   c. promote and model digital etiquette and responsible social interactions related to the use of technology and information

   d. develop and model cultural understanding and global awareness by engaging with colleagues and students of other cultures using digital-age communication and collaboration tools

5. **Engage in Professional Growth and Leadership**
   Teachers continuously improve their professional practice, model lifelong learning, and exhibit leadership in their school and professional community by promoting and demonstrating the effective use of digital tools and resources. Teachers:

   a. participate in local and global learning communities to explore creative applications of technology to improve student learning

   b. exhibit leadership by demonstrating a vision of technology infusion, participating in shared decision making and community building, and developing the leadership and technology skills of others

   c. evaluate and reflect on current research and professional practice on a regular basis to make effective use of existing and emerging digital tools and resources in support of student learning

   d. contribute to the effectiveness, vitality, and self-renewal of the teaching profession and of their school and community

NETS for Teachers: National Educational Technology Standards for Teachers, Second Edition © 2008 ISTE® (International Society for Technology in Education), www.iste.org. All rights reserved. Used with permission.

Meeting the NETS-T Standards

The following activities are based on the ISTE NETS-T standards rubric. All activities are aimed at achieving the proficient or transformative levels for each standard. References to the most useful chapters for each activity are listed under "Resources."

Overall Recommendation

One of the main teacher NET standards is focused on professional growth and development: "Teachers continuously improve their professional practice, model lifelong learning, and exhibit leadership in their school and professional community by promoting and demonstrating the effective use of digital tools and resources." Therefore, we recommend to meet this standard, as well as to provide evidence of meeting the remaining standards, teachers should keep online journal/blogs or electronic portfolios describing their growth. This delivery mechanism should be used to reflect on the readings, respond to the activities listed following, and upload artifacts to provide evidence that they have met all the NET teacher standards.

Educational technology is most useful when teachers perceive it as being relevant. Therefore, most of the activities are designed to incorporate individual teachers' subject areas, grade levels, and various local and state education requirements.

1a

This activity addresses standard 1a: Promote, support, and model creative and innovative thinking and inventiveness.

Sometimes, in order to solve a problem, you need to see the problem in a different way. This is often the case when we encounter large amounts of data. Charts and graphs can show a clearer depiction than just the numbers. Or grouping items in a Venn diagram can help make decisions. Regardless of the specific vehicle, visual representations of concept development and problem solving can help students understand. In addition, technology can also help create these visual representations. For example, a simulation of the die experiment can help students understand a normal curve (http://statlab0 .fon.bg.ac.yu/eng/eng/apletieng/resources/resources4 .html). In another example, comparing temperatures over the course of a year for several different cities might be complex with just numbers. However, using those numbers to create a graph may result in easier interpretation.

Level 1: Can you think of a situation for your specific grade/subject that might use visual representation to increase student understanding? In a journal entry, describe this application and what technology tools you might use to create that visual representation.

Level 2: Using the example expressed in Level 1, actually create that visual representation for your students (or a student sample is that is more applicable).

Special Note: *It is important that all of your instructional materials are age-appropriate.*

Resources: *Chapter 3 (Productivity tools). Be sure to also view the reference list at the end of this chapter for additional assistance.*

1b and 4d

This activity addresses standard 1b: Engage students in exploring real-world issues and solving authentic problems using digital tools and resources, and standard 4d: Develop and model cultural understanding and global awareness by engaging with colleagues and students of other cultures using digital-age communication and collaboration tools.

From Chapter 13, you have learned that one of the emerging trends in educational technology is the ability to collaborate and engage with people and ideas from around the world. Chapters 10 and 11 also provided information on how the Internet and distance education are making these connections more possible. In addition, Chapter 2 discussed the importance of shifting to a learner-centered classroom, and provided information, from a constructivist perspective, on how technology can be used to make this happen.

Therefore, you decide it is important for your students to collaborate with others from around the world to develop global awareness. In addition, you find that engaging students in real-world problems really enhances their motivation (Chapter 4) and will help them solve future real-world problems. Based on all this knowledge, you decide to assign students to complete a real-world project by collaborating with others around the world to help solve their problem. For both of the levels following, answer the following questions in your online journal/blog or electronic portfolio:

1. List the state standards this project addresses.
2. Briefly describe the project in your own words.
3. How will you locate global partners?
4. Briefly describe how you will collaborate with your global partners.
5. Describe the end product of this project.
6. What are the benefits of engaging with these global partners? (support responses with information from the book)
7. What are the benefits of engaging students in this real-world problem? (support responses with information from the book)

Level 1: Find a global project for your students to participate in that aligns with a specific state standard within the curriculum/grade level you (intend to) teach. Provide a link to the idea and describe why this activity is a good fit for you and your (prospective) students.

Level 2: Develop an idea for a global project for your students to participate in that aligns with a specific state standard within the curriculum/grade level you (intend to) teach. Produce a short, one-page journal entry describing this project and why this activity is a good fit for you and your (prospective) students.

Special Note: *It is important that all of your instructional materials are age-appropriate. In other words, make sure to check that level of reading (i.e., don't use big words for younger students) and requirements match the abilities of your learners (see Chapter 4 for more information on learners).*

Resources: *Chapter 2 (A shift in the roles of teachers and students), Chapter 2 (Constructivist perspective), Chapter 10 (all), Chapter 11 (all), and Chapter 13 (all). Be sure to also view the reference lists at the end of these chapters for additional assistance.*

1c

This activity addresses standard 1c: Promote student reflection using collaborative tools to reveal and clarify students' conceptual understanding and thinking, planning, and creative processes.

When students are required to reflect on their thoughts, it can provide them with an opportunity to clarify their own thinking. One method for student reflection can occur through collaboration. Students are required to think about their own knowledge before engaging in collaborative activities. As we learned about in Chapter 2, constructivist learning perspective capitalizes on student collaboration, because it helps them test and refine their understanding. In a journal entry, describe an opportunity for your (future) students; how might they use a wiki or other collaborative tools to enhance their understanding of a topic. Here is one idea: Wikipedia is a popular online encyclopedia that gathers its content from the collaboration of experts across the world. Students can research a particular topic and then visit the Wikipedia site for that topic. Students can add information and resources to support their claims on Wikipedia. For another example of student collaboration and reflection using a wiki, visit the Horizon Project 2008 (http://horizonproject2008.wikispaces.com/).

Special Note: *It is important that all of your instructional materials are age-appropriate. For example, if you are teaching kindergarten, students may not be literate or able to type, thus limiting their abilities to collaborate via a wiki. However, they could still collaborate by using images or parent helpers.*

Resources: *Chapter 2 (Constructivist perspective), Chapter 10 (Internet applications for information publishing), and Chapter 12 (Logs and journals). Be sure to also view the reference lists at the end of these chapters for additional assistance.*

1d

This activity addresses standard 1d: Model collaborative knowledge construction by engaging in learning with students, colleagues, and others in face-to-face and virtual environments.

As we learned in Chapters 10 and 11, technology has the ability to make communication easier across vast distances. Using your lesson plan from 1b/4d, what technology tools might you use to make this a synchronous and/or asynchronous online activity? In a journal entry, describe why you selected these technology(ies). Be sure to address the benefits and limitations of your choice(s).

Special Note: *It is important that all of your instructional materials are age-appropriate. For instance, younger students may have difficulties with typing. Video conferencing may be a more appropriate solution.*

Resources: *Chapter 10 (Internet applications for communication), Chapter 11 (What is distance education?), and Chapter 11 (Distance education technologies). Be sure to also view the reference lists at the end of these chapters for additional assistance.*

2a

This activity addresses standard 2a: Design or adapt relevant learning experiences that incorporate digital tools and resources to promote student learning and creativity.

You have been learning how to design instructional materials and use technology to increase the effectiveness, efficiency, transfer, impact and appeal of your instruction (Chapter 1 – Why is the study of learning important?). With the advent of the Internet, searching and locating information has become an important skill for students to develop (Chapter 10 – Internet applications for information retrieval). To develop this skill in your students, you assign a research project where they must use technology to search, collect, and analyze information. In addition to searching for information, you ask students to create a final report or presentation or other product that can be shared with an audience.

Level 1: Although your goal is to enable students to conduct these searches on their own, you recognize that students sometimes need scaffolds or helpful reminders. Create an Internet "cheat sheet" that provides helpful hints on how to search.

Level 2: Students often create better products when they have an example of what the teacher expects. Create a

student example of a research project specific to your grade/subject.

Level 3: Because finding information online is sometimes difficult for students, you want to establish links that your students can use to help locate relevant information for their research project. Create a wiki that provides all these resources and links or produce a WebQuest if the research project is more narrowly defined.

Special Note: *It is important that all of your instructional materials are age-appropriate.*

Resources: *Chapter 10 (Internet applications for information retrieval) and Chapter 10 (Internet applications for information publishing). Be sure to also view the reference list at the end of this chapter for additional assistance.*

2b

This activity addresses standard 2b: Develop technology-enriched learning environments that enable all students to pursue their individual curiosities and become active participants in setting their own educational goals, managing their own learning, and assessing their own progress.

Learner-centered classrooms provide many opportunities for students to assess their own learning. When students are actively involved in assessing their own learning, it actively promotes reflection on their work and abilities (Chapter 12). There are many ways to use technology to enable students to manage and assess their own learning (e.g., Toolbox: Course management systems – Chapter 11). For example, many K-2 teachers use stations to facilitate math or reading skills. This allows them to differentiate learning for varying abilities and students can complete tasks on their own. However, students (and teachers) need a way to track this information. Another example could be for middle school science students who were asked to complete a science project with specific requirements. In a journal entry, discuss what technology tools could help students in both of these situations manage and assess their own progress?

Resources: *Chapter 12 (How to evaluate) and Chapter 11 (Course management systems). Be sure to also view the reference lists at the end of these chapters for additional assistance.*

2c

This activity addresses standard 2c: Customize and personalize learning activities to address students' diverse learning styles, working strategies, and abilities using digital tools and resources.

The most cost-effective way to incorporate instructional materials into a lesson is to use existing materials. There is an abundance of materials available from various software companies and free materials on the Internet (Chapter 8). However, more likely than not, the instructional material will not directly meet your needs and all of your students' needs. Students can have a variety of differences that may need to be accommodated for (Chapter 4): learning style (visual, auditory, or kinesthetic), technology literacy (varying student technology skills), culture and ethnicity, existing knowledge of the content. Each of these characteristics may influence your need as a teacher to adapt or modify an existing instructional material. For example, if you are presenting a new concept of the sun, earth, and moon "orbiting" to your students with a video, kinesthetic learners may not grasp the concept as they need to manipulate items to understand the concept.

To provide evidence that you can use technology as a teacher to customize and personalize learning activities to address students' diverse needs:

Level 1: There are many existing instructional materials made available from a variety of software companies. Some are free, others have free trials, and some require payment. You will need to conduct an Internet search to find these, or check out your local library. Once you have located an appropriate software that aligns with the grade level/subject area you (intend to) teach, explore this software and its capabilities. In a journal/blog entry, or as a reflection in your electronic portfolio, describe how this software can accommodate for a variety of students' diverse needs (Chapter 4).

Level 2: Locate and select an existing appropriate instructional material from the Internet based on the grade level/subject area you (intend to) teach. Adapt the instructional material to meet one of the characteristics (all learning styles, various levels of technology literacy, various levels of content knowledge, various cultures or ethnicities). For example, elementary students may have different levels of literacy and the instructional materials need to be altered in three different ways to meet the wide variety of student reading abilities in your classroom. Once you have finished adapting the instructional materials, in a journal/blog entry, or as a reflection in your electronic portfolio, describe how you adapt the materials and why this will address the specified variety of students' diverse needs (Chapter 4).

Resources: *Chapter 4 (Students), Chapters 6 and 7 (depending on your adaptation), Chapter 8 (Determining the value of instructional materials), Chapter 8 (Where do we acquire instructional materials?), Chapter 8 (Locating, adapting, creating, and evaluating instructional materials: How can technology help?), Chapter 8 (Locating relevant instructional materials), and Chapter 9 (Software evaluation and acquisition). Be sure to also view the reference lists at the end of these chapters for additional assistance.*

2d

This activity addresses standard 2d: Provide students with multiple and varied formative and summative assessments aligned with content and technology standards and use resulting data to inform learning and teaching.

One of the larger policy initiatives associated with the No Child Left Behind Act is the notion of data-driven decision-making. Teachers use student assessment data to make instructional decisions. For example, after Mrs. Robinson assessed her students' knowledge on a mathematics test, she finds that most seem to have done well on the long-division questions, while a few are still having difficulty. Therefore, she uses this information to revisit long-division with a few of her students while the others practice more complex long-division problems on their own.

Level 1: According to the No Child Left Behind Act, teachers typically have access to the following categories of data from electronic student data systems to make instructional decisions: attendance, student course grades, current year's state standardized test scores, previous year's state standardized test scores, online assessments. Because this is an important requirement, administration considers this activity a high priority for teachers: Because you are capable of using technology to analyze data and make instructional decisions. Therefore, your principal asks that you compose a memo to the other teachers in the building, describing how you would use this data to make instructional decisions. Make sure to include specific examples.

Level 2: Locate a unit plan (describe the difference) that aligns with your grade level/subject area. In a journal/blog entry, or as a reflection in your electronic portfolio, provide a list of formative assessments that could be included throughout the unit plan to check student learning.

Level 3: Select one standard from your state standards that aligns with your grade level/subject area. Based on this standard, in a journal/blog entry, or as a reflection in your electronic portfolio, brainstorm and describe several different types of formatives and summative student assessments that would target this particular standard to assess students' learning. Also, describe which assessments would be the most valuable and why. For extra credit, try designing one or several of these assessments using technology.

Resources: *Chapter 12 (all). Be sure to also view the reference list at the end of this chapter for additional assistance.*

3a and 5a

This activity addresses standard 3a: Demonstrate fluency in technology systems and the transfer of current knowledge to new technologies and situations, and standard 5a: Participate in local and global learning communities to explore creative applications of technology to improve student learning.

In Chapter 3, we introduced basic hardware and software, many of which you may have already known about. How do you currently learn about a new technology? When Facebook first became popular, how did you learn that this technology existed? Most likely, you heard about it through a friend. How did you learn how to use it? You may have consulted friends or explored it on your own.

One of the difficulties with using the most effective technology in the classroom to improve student learning is that technology is constantly changing. Everyday, new hardware, software, and websites are being developed that can be utilized in the classroom. To be the most effective teacher possible, you need to be aware of technology that can improve your teaching and student learning. What are some ways that you can keep current with new, developing technologies?

Teachers often have to fill out individual professional development plans stating their goals for improving themselves professionally and how they plan to achieve these goals. For example, all Rhode Island educators can renew their certification by creating and maintaining a professional development plan. Teachers propose professional development goals appropriate to their current certification that will help them become better teachers. The plan is then approved by the Rhode Island Department of Education and teachers have five years to show they have met these goals through professional development activities (self-study, workshops, conferences, professional networks, etc.). (See http://www.ride.ri.gov/EducatorQuality/iplans.aspx.)

Many teachers include technology as one of their professional development goals. Try answering the following questions to establish your own professional development plan focusing on technology goals:

↗ Personal interest and growth
  ↗ What educational issues or areas interest me?
  ↗ What knowledge or skill of my practice do I need to improve or expand?
  ↗ What do I want to learn about?
  ↗ What new knowledge do I wish to learn; what new skills do I wish to develop?
↗ Impact of goals
  ↗ What needs do my students and school community need to work on? How can what I learn help my students and my school district?
  ↗ How would I use the knowledge or skills in my everyday professional practice?
  ↗ What changes would I make in my professional practice and how would those changes affect my students or my school/district community?

↗ Achievement of goals
  ↗ What are the best ways to achieve these goals?
  ↗ How will I know if I have achieved these goals?

Special Note: *Try using technology to address the goals. New and creative applications of technology are constantly being thought up by teachers around the world. To discover all the different ways to use technology, you may need to explore technology to come up with your own creative applications of technology. However, it is also just as important to utilize other teachers' creative applications of technology. Explore teacher networks around the world to find one that will help you address your own professional development goals.*

Resources: *Chapter 3 (Understanding computer systems), Chapter 3 (Computer productivity tools), and Chapter 13 (all). Be sure to also view the reference lists at the end of these chapters for additional assistance.*

3b

This activity addresses standard 3b: Collaborate with students, peers, parents, and community members using digital tools and resources to support student success and innovation.

Level 1: It is sometimes difficult to manage collaboration in your classroom; technology can sometimes help to support collaboration. One of your colleagues wants to try a group project with technology, but does not know how to go about managing this collaboration. In Chapters 10 and 11, you learned about how technology can be used to facilitate teaching and learning. In an e-mail, can you give him/her some advice on how to set up a collaboration activity with technology?

Level 2: One of the most common teacher uses of technology is for communicative purposes. In Chapters 10 and 11, you learned how technology can help the teaching and learning process. Listed following are a number of forms of telecommunications. Think about each and then generate one or more ways in which each could be used to increase interaction between teacher and students, between students and students, between parents and teachers, and between teachers and other teachers.

Wiki

Teacher-to-student collaboration:
Student-to-student collaboration:
Teacher-to-teacher collaboration:

Electronic mail

Teacher-to-student collaboration:
Student-to-student collaboration:
Teacher-to-teacher collaboration:

Discussion boards found in most course management systems (e.g., Blackboard, Moodle, Angel)

Teacher-to-student collaboration:
Student-to-student collaboration:
Teacher-to-teacher collaboration:

Live synchronous meetings (e.g., video conferencing, skype)

Teacher-to-student collaboration:
Student-to-student collaboration:
Teacher-to-teacher collaboration:

Resources: *Chapter 10 (Internet applications for communication), and Chapter 11 (all). Be sure to also view the reference lists at the end of these chapters for additional assistance.*

3c

This activity addresses standard 3c: Communicate relevant information and ideas effectively to students, parents, and peers using a variety of digital-age media and formats.

Student learning is truly a partnership between the teacher, the student, and the parents. Within your classroom, communication with students and parents can be critical to supporting this partnership and ensuring it runs properly. Technology can be a great facilitator of communication. How could you use technology to communicate specific information to your students and their parents? At the beginning of the year, teachers typically host open houses or send home documents describing how their classrooms operate. You wish to provide background information on how you expect your students and their parents to communicate with you. Should they e-mail you with a question or call your phone? Are there certain hours when they are more likely to reach you? If a student forgets a homework assignment, what should they do? Possible communication topics you may want to address are: parental concerns (i.e., student behavior, grades, attendance, assignments); student assignments (i.e., where to turn in, expectations, descriptions, due dates); upcoming class/school events (i.e., needing parent volunteers, descriptions, dates, field trip permission slips and checklist).

Level 1: Construct a newsletter detailing your expectations for student and parent communication. Make sure to address the topics mentioned above.
Level 2: Construct an open house presentation detailing your expectations for student and parent communication. Make sure to include pages covering the topics mentioned previously.

Level 3: Construct a class website detailing your expectations for student and parent communication. Make sure to include pages covering the topics mentioned previously.

Special Note: *Look around at other classroom websites: What other items did we forget to mention that might be important in student/parent communication efforts?*

Resources: *Chapter 10 (Internet applications for communication), and Chapter 11 (Distance education technologies & Course management systems). Be sure to also view the reference lists at the end of these chapters for additional assistance.*

3d

This activity addresses standard 3d: Model and facilitate effective use of current and emerging digital tools to locate, analyze, evaluate, and use information resources to support research and learning.

As discussed in Chapter 10 (Evaluating the quality of websites), anyone can put anything on a website. Therefore, it is important for students to learn to judge the quality of information on the Web. Complete one of the following activities.

Level 1: Create a handout (using desktop publishing software) or a wiki/website page for your students to guide them on evaluating the quality of websites. Make sure to include links to helpful websites. (Use the Chapter 10 resources to help you).
Level 2: Also in Chapter 10 (Scavenger hunts), scavenger hunts were introduced as a method for teaching students how to find and use information resources on the Internet. Design a scavenger hunt (using a wiki/website page) to help your students learn ways to locate, analyze, evaluate, and use information resources to support research and learning.

Special Note: *It is important that all of your instructional materials are age-appropriate. For example, use websites that are at your students' reading levels.*

Resources: *Chapter 10 (Evaluating the quality of websites & scavenger hunts). Be sure to also view the reference list at the end of this chapter for additional assistance.*

4a

This activity addresses standard 4a: Advocate, model, and teach safe, legal, and ethical use of digital information and technology, including respect for copyright, intellectual property, and the appropriate documentation of sources.

One of the main student NET standards focuses on ethical, safe, and legal uses of digital information. As the teacher, you will be responsible for advocating, modeling, and teaching safe, legal, and ethical uses of digital information and technology. Following are some activities you can do to provide evidence of your abilities to meet these standards:

Level 1: Create a handout to provide to your students, educating them on how to be responsible digital citizens with one of the following aspects: copyright, appropriate documentation of sources, cyberbullying, privacy issues, security issues (e.g., spam, spyware, firewalls).

Level 2: Design (or locate and augment) a lesson plan to specifically teach students how to be responsible digital citizens with one of the following aspects: copyright, appropriate documentation of sources, cyberbullying, privacy issues, security issues (e.g., spam, spyware, firewalls).

Level 3: To ensure your students know how to be responsible digital citizens, you assign them to create a promotional video, educating the other students in school on how to be responsible digital citizens with one of the following aspects: copyright, appropriate documentation of sources, cyberbullying, privacy issues, security issues (e.g., spam, spyware, firewalls). In order to show them what is expected for the project, you will need to create an example video on one of the topics and create a rubric for evaluating these projects.

Special Note: *It is important that all of your instructional materials are age-appropriate. In other words, make sure to check that level of reading (i.e., don't use big words for younger students) and requirements match the abilities of your learners (see Chapter 4 for more information on learners).*

Resources: *Chapter 8 (Copyright issues), Chapter 10 (Issues involved in the use of the Internet in the classroom), Chapter 11 (Issues related to distance education), and Chapter 13 (Legal, ethical, and security issues). Be sure to also view the reference lists at the end of these chapters for additional assistance.*

4a

This activity addresses standard 4a: Advocate, model, and teach safe, legal, and ethical use of digital information and technology, including respect for copyright, intellectual property, and the appropriate documentation of sources.

In Chapter 10, you learned briefly about Acceptable Use Policies (AUPs). You can also find some additional information in the references section of Chapter 10. Locate 3 different AUPs on the Web. You can typically obtain this from the school's or school district's website. Answer the following questions for each AUP:

1. What are the strengths of this AUP? How will it help promote responsible digital citizenship and technology use?

2. What are the weaknesses of this AUP? Why would these aspects not promote responsible digital citizenship and technology use?

3. What elements do you feel are important to address within an AUP for your future school/classroom?

For extra practice, develop your own AUP for your (future) school or classroom or create a journal entry that includes your lists and how you would model those behaviors if you were teaching in one of that school district's elementary schools. Would what and how you model differ if you were teaching at a secondary school level? Why or why not?

Special Note: *It is important that all of your materials are age-appropriate. For example, if you teach kindergarten, you may not need to include illegal installation of copyrighted software.*

Resources: *Chapter 10 (Acceptable use policies). Be sure to also view the reference list at the end of this chapter for additional assistance.*

4b

This activity addresses standard 4b: Address the diverse needs of all learners by using learner-centered strategies providing equitable access to appropriate digital tools and resources.

As you learned (Chapter 4), you will have many students with special instructional needs due to disabilities. Therefore, you have to be able to adapt your lesson plans to address those special needs. Many teachers do this using assistive technology (Chapter 3).

Level 1: Select a lesson plan you have created or find one on the Internet (Chapter 5 resources). You will next need to adapt this lesson plan for one student with special needs. You may select any of the following disabilities, but note that there must be some adaptation due to the individual's disability: learning disabilities (ADD – attention deficit disorder); behavior disorder, communication disorder (stuttering); perception problems (loss of vision or hearing); motor problems (cerebral palsy); or health problems (asthma). In your online journal/blog or electronic portfolio, describe the adaptations you would make to this particular lesson plan.

Level 2: Create a two-column table on your online journal/blog or electronic portfolio. On one side, list several types of special needs of students that teachers in your field may encounter. In the other column, brainstorm and list several types of technologies that may be used to assist students with those special needs.

Special Note: *Make sure to select a lesson plan that aligns with your content/grade level focus. In addition, make* *sure to explore all options of assistive technology for the particular learning disability (Chapter 3 – Resources).*

Resources: *Chapter 2 (A shift in the roles of teachers and students), Chapter 3 (Assistive technology), Chapter 3 (Resources), Chapter 4 (Special needs), Chapter 5 (Resources), and Chapter 13 (Technology as a means to address difficulties in teaching and learning). Be sure to also view the reference lists at the end of these chapters for additional assistance.*

4c

This activity addresses standard 4c: Promote and model digital etiquette and responsible social interactions related to the use of technology and information.

Just as with anything else in the classroom, student use of technology in the classroom requires guidelines and rules. Although your students have been using technology (most likely) since they were young they were not typically taught how to responsibly use technology (both face-to-face and virtual). Therefore, you may find it necessary to provide some guidelines on how to responsibly use technology. Create a desktop publishing document for guidelines outlining netiquette or responsible social interaction guidelines for your (future) students.

Special Note: *It is important that all of your instructional materials are age-appropriate.*

Resources: *Chapter 10 (Netiquette) and Chapter 11 (Utilization guidelines for distance education). Be sure to also view the reference lists at the end of these chapters for additional assistance.*

4d

See 1b.

5a

See 3a.

5b

This activity addresses standard 5b: Exhibit leadership by demonstrating a vision of technology infusion, participating in shared decision making and community building, and developing the leadership and technology skills of others.

In Chapter 13 (How can the integration of technology be effectively accomplished?), we discussed how schools could plan to use instructional technology. The first task in any plan is to not just identify what resources are needed, but how those resources should be used. Although you may not be the director of the school or

district technology committee, you are still the director of your own classroom (or soon will be). Using the "Creating the Technology Integration Vision," try developing your own vision plan for technology integration in your own classroom. Describe how you see technology being used in your classroom.

Special Note: *It is important that all of your instructional materials are age-appropriate.*

Resources: *Chapter 13 (How can the integration of technology be effectively accomplished?). Be sure to also view the reference list at the end of this chapter for additional assistance.*

5c

This activity addresses standard 5c: Evaluate and reflect on current research and professional practice on a regular basis to make effective use of existing and emerging digital tools and resources in support of student learning.

Mr. Auer teaches the same grade/subject as you and is apprehensive about using technology in his class. He knows you have taken an educational technology course and has approached you for advice on how technology could be used in his class. One of the things that intimidate him the most is how quickly technology and resources change. He remembered using a fantastic website last year that is no longer present, and the new changes in his word processing system have made it very difficult to use. Please compose an e-mail to Mr. Auer explaining (1) your view on the best ways to use technology in your specific grade/subject; and (2) how you keep up to date on effective use of existing and emerging digital tools and resources in support of student learning.

Special Note: *It is important that your suggestions should be primarily grade and subject specific. In part two, make sure to include how you can use technology to keep current.*

Resources: *Chapter 8 (Determining the value of instructional materials), Chapter 8 (Where do we acquire instructional materials?), Chapter 8 (Formative evaluation of instructional materials), and Chapter 8 (Locating, adapting, creating, and evaluating instructional materials: How can technology help?). Be sure to also view the reference list at the end of this chapter for additional assistance.*

5d

This activity addresses standard 5d: Contribute to the effectiveness, vitality, and self-renewal of the teaching profession and of their school and community.

Your principal wants to start sharing best practices using technology (to improve student learning) at faculty meetings. This will help contribute to the effectiveness of technology use within the classroom and will open a dialogue for discussion. Because you have taken an educational technology class, your principal has asked you to be the first to share some of your own success stories with technology in the classroom. Create a five-minute presentation showcasing your own best practices with regards to technology; include reflections on why these are best practices and support with rationale from the various chapters in this book.

Special Note: *It is important that all of your instructional materials are age-appropriate.*

Resources: *May vary depending on answer. Chapter 6 (Which method(s) to use?), Chapter 7 (Which medium?), Chapter 8 (Determining the value of instructional materials), Chapter 8 (Locating, adapting, creating, and evaluating instructional materials: How can technology help?), and Chapter 12 (How to evaluate). Be sure to also view the reference lists at the end of these chapters for additional assistance.*

Teacher Resource
B

Kevin Spencer's Sample Lesson Plan (Civil War Unit)

Created by Anne Ottenbreit-Leftwich, Indiana University

BACKGROUND INFORMATION

(required for planning, but not included in the plan itself)

Students

Twenty-three sixth-graders in a suburban public school in a predominantly blue-collar neighborhood:

Gender—13 boys and 10 girls

Ethnicity—10 white, 6 African American, 2 Asian, and 5 Hispanic

SES—7 students qualify for free or reduced price lunch (definition of low SES)

Learning preferences—16 primarily visual, 5 primarily auditory, and 2 primarily kinesthetic

Special needs—1 visually impaired student; 1 student with epilepsy, controlled by medication; and 1 student who works with a reading teacher 1 hour a week

Technology literacy—Students are all able to use MS *Word, PowerPoint,* and Internet *Explorer*

Learning Environment

The learning environment is a traditional classroom with 25 movable student desks, arranged in 5 rows of 5 with a teacher's desk at the front of the room.

A teacher's computer, at the front of the room, is connected to a data projector.

Against the back wall are 4 computers with broadband Internet connections.

Along one side of the room is a bank of windows with book shelves underneath. Along the opposite side is a bulletin board covering the wall. A chalkboard covers the wall behind the teacher's desk. Two pull-down maps are located above one side of the chalkboard. A pull-down screen is located above the center of the chalkboard.

THE LESSON PLAN

Grade—sixth-grade social studies
Topic—U.S. Civil War
Time frame—10 days

Standards—from NCHS Era 5: Civil War and Reconstruction (1850–1877)

Standard 2:	The course and character of the Civil War and its effects on the American people.
Standard 2A:	The student understands how the resources of the Union and Confederacy affected the course of the war.
Standard 2B:	The student understands the social experience of the war on the battlefield and homefront.

Objectives

1. Given a WebQuest containing information about the Civil War, students will be able to create an online blog journal that (1) is written in the first person from the perspective of the assigned character, (2) uses historically accurate language, and (3) refers to historically important events.

2. Given a WebQuest containing information about the Civil War and working with a small group of peers, students will be able to create either a digital storytelling presentation that (1) is at least 5 minutes long,

(2) tells a story from the perspective of the assigned character, (3) uses historically accurate language, and (4) refers to historically important events.

Instructional Activities Introduction (motivation/orientation activity)
Allotted time—10 minutes

Method—discussion
Media—projected visuals
Equipment and materials required—computer with Internet access and a data projector.

1. Show a short series of photographs of people from the Civil War era, one at a time. (Possible sources—http://www.civilwarphotos.net or http://memory.loc.gov/ammem/cwphtml/cwphome.html). The pictures should vary as much as possible: man-woman-child; black-white; city-rural; military-civilian.
2. With each photograph, briefly identify the person and ask the students—What do you think life was like for this person? How do you think the war affected him/her? In what ways do you think life was different than for the previous person?
3. Explain that this lesson will explore what life was like for various people during the Civil War. Outline the objectives, emphasizing that the students will use the story-telling presentation to teach the rest of the class about how the war affected various people. This will help create a transition to the next activity.

Digital video presentation
Allotted time—10 minutes

Method—presentation
Media—multimedia; projected visuals
Equipment and materials required—computer connected to a data projector; digital storytelling example

1. Briefly introduce a sample storytelling presentation. Explain that this is an example of what the students will be creating in this lesson. Point out 2 or 3 things that they should pay particular attention to as they watch the presentation.
2. Show a digital storytelling presentation created by a previous group of students (if available) or the teacher.
3. Briefly discuss the presentation by asking the students about the things you pointed out in your introduction.

Development of a KWL chart (orientation activity)
Allotted time—5–10 minutes per group for collaborative activity, 15 minutes for discussion

Method—collaborative activity; discussion
Media—multimedia; projected visuals

Equipment and materials required—computer with Internet access and a data projector; KWL chart template on wikispaces

This new lesson should build on what the students already know. Create a starting point for the lesson by asking the students to contribute to a know-want-learn (KWL) chart, based on previous Civil War lessons.

1. Show the blank KWL chart on wikispaces and explain what information should be put in each column. The K column (KNOW) should be where they enter what they already know about the Civil War. In the W column (WANT) should include descriptions of what they would most like to learn about the Civil War. The L column (LEARNED) should be left blank. The entries in the chart can be short bullet points, but make sure that each entry is accurate and that everyone understands it.
2. Separate the students into groups of 3-4 and allows these groups to visit the computer work stations. Students can add to the KWL chart on wikispaces. They can work together to add information to both the K and W columns.
3. After all students have had the opportunity to add to the KWL chart wiki, engage students in a discussion of these elements (revisit the KNOW points to make sure everyone remembers this information and clarify the WANT points to ensure your instruction can target these areas). Also, point out the still blank L column and say that we will fill that column in at the end of the lesson.

Overview of important events (information activity)
Allotted time—10 minutes

Method—presentation
Media—projected visuals
Equipment and materials required—computer with Internet access and a data projector; timeline handouts (or use Web resource: http://www.historyplace.com/civilwar/index.html)

The purpose of this activity is not to provide a lengthy description of these events, but to provide an overview of the time period to help students organize the information that they may gather from the WebQuest.

1. Show a timeline of key events that took place during the Civil War—include events from both the battlefield and the home front.
2. Briefly describe each key event. One thing to emphasize during this presentation is the chronological relationships among the events. For example, point out any events that take place at the same time or that follow one another in time.

Introduction to WebQuest search (orientation activity)
Allotted time—20 minutes

Method—presentation
Media—multimedia
Equipment and materials required—computer with Internet access and a data projector; scoring rubric on handouts (attached)

1. Use the following list and ask the students to pick the character they would most like to learn about. Students may choose a character that is not on the list, with teacher approval.

Southern farmer	Northern farmer
Southern plantation owner	Northern storekeeper
Southern belle	Northern woman
Southern newspaper reporter	Northern newspaper reporter
Female African American slave	African American freeman
Confederate infantry soldier	Union infantry soldier
Southern abolitionist	Northern railroad engineer

2. Introduce the WebQuest and demonstrate how to access it.
3. Describe the expectations for the online blog journal assignment. Explain that this assignment is intended to help the students learn what it was like to live during the Civil War. They are to gather as much information as possible about their character and to write in their blogs as though they were writing in people's journals. Encourage students to also include links in their blogs that help support their ideas. Remind the students of the key events included in the timeline discussed previously and suggest that they look at these events from their character's point of view: How did it affect that character; what did it mean to that character. Through this use of the blog, you (and other students) can comment directly on each entry.
4. Present the scoring rubric and explain it. Emphasize that the online blog journals must use historically accurate language and historically accurate descriptions of events. Each day in the classroom will be one month during the Civil War.

WebQuest search (information activity)
Allotted time—30 minutes a day

Method—discovery
Media—multimedia
Equipment and materials required—computers with Internet access

1. Provide students with time during each class period to search the WebQuest and write in their blogs.

2. During the search periods, meet with individual students to answer questions and help them make sense of the information they find.

Preparation of student presentations (application activity)
Allotted time—30 minutes a day

Method—collaborative learning
Media—multimedia
Equipment and materials required—computers loaded with Microsoft *Word* and *PowerPoint*

1. Assign students to groups of 3 or 4. You can group common roles together to provide more depth to one viewpoint, or include a variety of characters in a group to provide more breadth.
2. Describe the expectations for the assignment. The primary sources of information for the assignment are the students' blogs. Their digital storytelling presentation must be at least 5 minutes long.
3. Present the scoring rubric and explain it. Emphasize that the journals must use historically accurate language and historically accurate descriptions of events.
4. Provide the students with time during each class session to meet with their groups and prepare their presentations. The main message that each presentation should convey is what life was like for that character. Emphasize that the presentations must use historically accurate language and historically accurate descriptions of events.
5. Throughout the preparation, meet with each group to answer questions, correct any misconceptions, and provide guidance.

Student presentations (application/ evaluation activity)
Allotted time—60 minutes

Method—presentation; discussion
Media—multimedia
Equipment and materials required—computers loaded with Microsoft *Word* and *PowerPoint* and connected to a data projector; scoring rubric on handouts (attached)

1. Briefly remind the students of the assignment.
2. Ask the groups of students to give their presentations.
3. Briefly discuss the presentations, when they are all done. Ask the students questions such as:
   - What did you learn about your character from the other presentations?
   - Based on what you saw in the presentations, how did the _____ (insert one of the key events from the timeline activity) affect your character?

- What events had the biggest effect on the most people?
- What other characters were affected most by the war and how were they affected?

4. Evaluate each presentation, using the scoring rubric for this assignment.

Summary (information/orientation activity)
Allotted time—10 minutes

Method—discussion
Media—projected visuals

Equipment and materials required—data projector; KWL chart from the earlier activity

1. Show the KWL chart from the earlier activity and briefly review the K and W columns.
2. Ask the students to provide information for the L column, describing what they learned about the Civil War from this lesson. Enter this information into the chart. The entries can be short bullet points, but make sure that everyone understands each entry.
3. Close the lesson by briefly describing the subject of the next lesson.

Rubric for WebQuest Journaling Blog Assignment

	4	3	2	1
Ideas	Ideas were expressed in a clear and organized fashion. The writer showed thoughtful interpretation of characters.	Ideas were expressed in a clear manner, but the interpretation of the characters could have been better.	Ideas were somewhat organized, but were not very clear. It took more than one reading to figure out what the character was feeling.	The journal seemed to be a collection of unrelated sentences. It was very difficult to figure out what the character was thinking.
Content accuracy	The journal entry contains at least 5 accurate facts about the topic. At least one link is provided.	The journal entry contains 3–4 accurate facts about the topic.	The journal entry contains 1–2 accurate facts about the topic.	The journal entry contains no accurate facts about the topic.
Historical language	Historically accurate language was used.	Some historically accurate language was used.	Little historically accurate language was used.	Historically accurate language was not used.
Grammar	There were no spelling or grammar mistakes.	There were 1–3 spelling or grammar mistakes.	There were 4–6 spelling or grammar mistakes.	There were more than 6 spelling or grammar mistakes.
Total	_____/16 = _____ %			
Comments				

Rubric for Digital Storytelling Presentation Assignment

	4	3	2	1
Historical accuracy	The story and images contain historically accurate information and create an accurate portrayal of life during the Civil War according to the specific character.	The story and images contain historically accurate information, although some incorrect interpretations are presented. The final product is a somewhat accurate portrayal of life during the Civil War according to the specific character.	The story and images contain historically accurate information, although many incorrect interpretations are presented. The final product is not a very accurate portrayal of life during the Civil War according to the specific character.	The story and images did not contain historically accurate information and the final product did not present an accurate portrayal of life during the Civil War according to the specific character.
Detail	The story is told with perfect detail. It does not seem too short or too long.	The story is good, though it seems to drag or it needs more detail.	The story is satisfactory, but it is too long or too short in more than one section.	The story needs work. It is too long or too short to be interesting.
Images	Images are chosen to match different parts of the story. There was a specific purpose for each picture.	Some images are chosen to match different parts of the story. There was a purpose for almost every picture.	Few images are chosen to match different parts of the story. There was no purpose for some of the pictures.	No images are chosen to match different parts of the story. There was no purpose for some of the pictures.
Point of view	Establishes an idea and maintains a focus throughout.	Establishes an idea early on and maintains focus for a majority of the presentation.	There are a few parts which lack focus, but the idea is fairly clear.	It is difficult to distinguish the idea behind the presentation.
Voice	Voice is audible and the narration makes sense.	Voice is audible throughout a majority of the presentation and the narration makes sense.	Voice is audible throughout some of the presentation and most of the narration makes sense.	Voice is audible throughout some of the presentation and some of the narration makes sense.
Length	The presentation was at least 5 minutes long.	The presentation was at least 4 minutes long.	The presentation was at least 3 minutes long.	The presentation was less than 2 minutes long.
Total	_____ /24 = _____ %			
Comments				

Teacher Resource
C

PIE Checklist

Planning Phase

1. **Learners – Chapter 4**
   ☐ Give a general description of your learners (e.g., age, gender, culture, socioeconomic status).
   ☐ Describe the general background knowledge, skills, and attitudes they already possess about the to-be-learned content.
   ☐ Describe each of the following characteristics of your learners that could impact their learning:
   Level of motivation
   Level of technology literacy
   Learning style
   Special needs
   Other: _____

2. **Objectives – Chapter 4**
   ☐ Briefly describe what you want your learners to know or do. That is, what is the goal of the learning experience?
   ☐ Explain how your learners will demonstrate that the needed learning has actually occurred.
   ☐ Develop and list each of the learning objectives.

***Note:** include the 3 key elements of conditions, performance, and criteria (e.g., Given the [conditions], the students will be able to [performance], based on [criteria].).*

3. **Learning Environment – Chapter 4**
   ☐ Describe where the learning is designed to occur.
   ☐ List and describe what resources are available within the selected learning environment (e.g., technology available, equipment, furniture).
   ☐ Describe any ways that this learning environment could hinder/challenge learning from occurring (e.g., high level of noise or other distractions, improper heating/cooling/lighting, location).

4. **Developing the initial draft outline – Chapter 4**
   ☐ Complete background research (e.g., review relevant research, Internet sites, previously published instructional materials).
   ☐ Based on each objective:
   Complete a draft outline
   Develop a set of planning/storyboard cards
   Develop a flowchart

5. Instructional Activities – Chapter 5

☐ For each of the following instructional activities, review the questions and reflectively consider how the various activities and strategies can be incorporated within the instructional materials:

Motivation Activities

What strategies will you use to hold students' attention throughout the lesson?

What strategies will you use to help students see the relevance of the information?

What strategies will you use to increase students' confidence in learning?

What strategies will you use to increase students' satisfaction in learning?

Orientation Activities

What will you do to help students understand the objectives of the current lesson?

What will you do to link the lesson to previous lessons?

What will you do to form transitions?

What will you do to summarize the lesson and link it to future lessons?

Information Activities

What major content ideas will you present? In what sequence? Using what examples?

What will you do to help students understand and remember those ideas?

What will you do to help students see the relationships among the ideas?

What will you do to help students understand when and why the ideas will be useful?

Application Activities

What will you do to give students an opportunity to apply their new knowledge or skill?

How much guidance will you provide and what form will that guidance take?

In what way will you give students feedback about their performances during practice?

Evaluation Activities

What will you do to determine whether students have achieved the learning objectives?

How will you give students feedback about their performances during the evaluations?

☐ Create additional planning cards that include and explain the selected activities and include those within the previously developed set.

6. Instructional Methods – Chapter 6

☐ Select all instructional methods that apply to the instruction and provide a short description of how each selection will be used.

Check Methods to Incorporate	Provide Short Description
☐ Presentation	
☐ Demonstration	
☐ Discussion	
☐ Drill and Practice	
☐ Tutorial	
☐ Instructional Games	
☐ Cooperative Learning	
☐ Simulations	
☐ Discovery	
☐ Problem Solving	

☐ Indicate within the planning card set what method, as well as when each of the selected methods will be integrated within the instruction.

7. Instructional Media – Chapter 7

☐ Select all instructional media that apply to the instruction and provide a short description of how each selection will be used.

Check Media Used	Provide Short Description
☐ Video	
☐ Visuals	
☐ Audio	
☐ Text	
☐ Real objects and/or models	
☐ Multimedia	

☐ Indicate within the planning card set which media, as well as when each of the selected media will be integrated within the instruction.

8. Instructional Materials – Chapter 8

☐ Identify ways in which technology could be integrated to facilitate the development of the instructional materials.

☐ Outline the steps involved to develop the draft instruction.

☐ Based on your planning cards, outline, and flowchart develop the initial draft of your materials.

☐ Review your draft materials for any possible copyright infringement.

☐ Have members of the target audience and other stakeholders (e.g., teachers, content experts) review and evaluate the draft materials.

Implementation Phase

1. Instructional Delivery – Chapters 9, 10, and 11

☐ Identify the various ways that the instruction may be delivered (e.g., face-to-face, computer-based, online).

☐ Determine the optimal manner for delivering your instruction.

☐ Revise your instruction to be delivered in the proper manner.

2. Instructional Management – Chapters 9, 10, and 11

☐ Describe the role of the teacher and the learners before, during, and after the learning experience.

☐ Determine and describe the procedures needed to effectively implement the instructional experience.

☐ Revise your instruction so it can be managed properly.

Evaluation Phase

Continuous Cycle of Improvement – Chapter 12

☐ Implement the revised instructional materials with a selected group of target learners.

☐ Review the revised materials with both content and teaching experts (e.g., subject matter experts and other teachers).

☐ Based on the data collected from those reviewing the draft instruction, describe what went well, as well as what difficulties were encountered.

☐ Based on the evaluation data, complete a "final" version of the instructional materials.

Teacher Resource
D

Preview Forms for the Review of Instructional Materials

Preview Form: Real Objects and Models

Title/Description _____   Producer _____

Source _____   Date _____   Cost _____

Criteria	Comments
Relevance to objectives	
Likely to arouse/maintain interest	
Sturdy, stable, not easily broken	
Ease of use, manipulable	
Ease of storage	
Not dangerous (real objects)	
Shelf life (real objects)	
Degree of realism (models)	
Accuracy (models)	

Preview Form: Text

Title _____   Producer _____

Source _____   Date _____   Cost _____

Criteria   *Comments*

Photographs, diagrams, drawings

Use of color, layout

Relevance to course objectives

Up-to-date, accurate (copyright date)

Free of objectionable bias

Reading level (easy to read)

Likely to stimulate/maintain student interest

Table of contents, glossary, index

Special features

Adjunct materials (student manual, teacher's guide)

Organization, scope, and sequence

Chapter summaries/reviews

Study questions

References (complete and up-to-date)

Preview Form: Visuals

Title _____   Producer _____

Source _____   Date _____   Cost _____

Criteria	Comments
Relevance to objectives	
Authenticity/accuracy of visual	
Likely to arouse/maintain interest	
Likely to be comprehended clearly	
Technical quality (durability)	
Legibility for use (size and clarity)	
Simplicity (clear, unified design)	
Appropriate use of color	
Appropriateness of accompanying verbal information	
Timeliness (avoids out-of-date elements, such as dress)	

Preview Form: Audio

Title _____   Producer _____

Source _____   Date _____   Cost _____

Minutes _____

Criteria	Comments
Relevance to objectives	
Accuracy of information	
Likely to arouse/maintain interest	
Technical quality	
Promotes participation/involvement	
Evidence of effectiveness (e.g., field-test results)	
Free from objectionable bias	
Pacing appropriate for audience	
Clarity of organization	
Appropriate vocabulary level	

Preview Form: Video

Title _____   Producer _____

Source _____   Date _____   Cost _____

Format _____   Minutes _____

Criteria	*Comments*
Relevance to objectives	
Accuracy of information	
Likely to arouse/maintain interest	
Technical quality	
Promotes participation/involvement	
Evidence of effectiveness (e.g., field-test results)	
Free from objectionable bias	
Pacing appropriate for audience	
Use of cognitive learning aids (e.g., overview, cues, summary)	

Preview Form: Computer Software

Title _____   Producer _____

Source _____   Date _____   Cost _____

Format _____   Equipment needed _____   Minutes _____

Criteria   *Comments*

Relevance to objectives

Accuracy of information

Likely to arouse/maintain interest

Ease of use

Appropriate color, sound, graphics

Frequent, relevant practice (active participation)

Feedback provides remedial branches

Free of technical flaws (e.g., dead ends, infinite loops)

Clear, complete documentation

Evidence of effectiveness (e.g., field-test results)

Preview Form: Multimedia

Title _____   Producer _____

Source _____   Date _____   Cost _____

Format _____

Equipment Required _____

Criteria	Comments
Relevance to objectives	
Accuracy of information	
Likely to arouse/maintain interest	
Ease of use	
Level of interactivity	
Appropriate use of color, graphics, sound	
Appropriate use of individual media	
Coordination of visuals, sound, text	
Technical quality	
Evidence of effectiveness	

Preview Form: Web Pages/Sites

Title _____   Producer _____

Source _____   Date _____   Cost _____

Criteria   *Comments*

Material appropriate for students

Content relevant to objectives

Information reliable, up-to-date, and accurate

Value of content vs. glitz ("bells and whistles")

Ease of navigation

Appropriate reading level for users

Site supporters

Author cites other authorities

Site provides useful links to other sites. *Note:* You may also want to refer to Chapter 9, Table 9–6, "Guidelines for Designing Web Pages/Sites" for other criteria.

GLOSSARY

Acceptable use policy   An agreement signed by all participants defining proper Internet usage guidelines.

Acronym   A type of mnemonic in which a single word is made up of the first letters of a group of words.

Acrostic   A type of mnemonic in which letters in the new information are used as the first letters of the words in a sentence or phrase.

Advance organizer   An outline, preview, or other such preinstructional cue used to promote retention of content to be learned.

Algorithm   A series of steps needed to solve a particular problem or perform a particular task.

Analogy   A statement that likens something new to something familiar. Analogies are typically used either to make abstract information more concrete or to organize complex information.

Antecedent   An event, object, or circumstance that prompts a behavior.

Application activity   A type of instructional activity that provides students with an opportunity to practice using what they are learning.

Applications   Software programs designed to perform a specific function for the user, such as processing text, performing calculations, and presenting content lessons.

Artificial intelligence (AI)   A branch of computer science concerned with the design of computers and software that are capable of responding in ways that mimic human thinking.

ASCII format   American Standard Code for Information Interchange; a standard way of representing text, which allows different computer brands to "talk" to one another. It is sometimes referred to as plain text or unformatted text.

Assessment   The process of gathering evidence of what learners know and can do.

Assessment rubric   A set of guidelines used to reliably appraise or judge products or performances.

Assistive technology   Computer hardware and software that supports students with special needs.

Asynchronous   Not occurring at the same time.

Attachments   E-mail additions; may be documents, graphics, or software.

Attention   The process of selectively receiving information from the environment.

Attitudes   A type of learning that refers to feelings, beliefs, and values that lead individuals to make consistent choices when given the opportunity.

Audio   Spoken words or sounds, either live or recorded.

Audiographics   The use of audio teleconferencing accompanied by the transmission of still pictures and graphics via slow-scan video, fax, or an electronic graphics tablet.

Audiotape   Acetate on which sounds are recorded using magnetic signals, usually stored in a cassette case.

Audio teleconferencing   A distance education technology that uses a speakerphone to extend a basic telephone call and permits instruction and interaction between individuals or groups at two or more locations.

Authoring software   Computer programs used to develop multimedia or Web applications.

Backbone   The set of high-speed data lines connecting the major networks that make up the Internet.

Behavior   A response made by an individual.

Bit   The smallest amount of information that the CPU can deal with; a single binary digit.

Bitmapped graphics   Sometimes called paint or raster graphics, in which each pixel directly corresponds to a spot on the display screen. When scaled to larger sizes, this type of graphic looks jagged.

Blended learning   See hybrid learning.

Blog   Short for web log, a website where an individual can post information for others to access; entries on a topic are usually posted in reverse chronological order.

Blu-Ray disc   High definition DVD format.

Bookmark   A way to store addresses of frequently used websites on your computer.

Browser   A computer application for accessing the World Wide Web.

Bulletin board system   A computer network software tool that allows individuals to "post" messages and to read messages posted by others.

Byte   A collection of eight bits, equivalent to one alphanumeric character.

Case study   A type of problem solving that requires students to actively participate in real or hypothetical problem situations that reflect the types of experiences actually encountered in the discipline under study.

CD   See Compact disc.

CD-ROM (Compact disc–read-only memory)   Digitally encoded information permanently recorded on a compact disc.

Cell   A single block in a spreadsheet grid, formed by the intersection of a row and a column.

Chat   A synchronous form of Internet communication in which individuals type messages to one another.

Chat room   On computer networks, a location for person-to-person real-time (synchronous) interaction by typing messages.

Classroom observation   A form of evaluation that involves having a knowledgeable person come into the classroom to watch a lesson in process, to comment on how well the materials and activities work, and to make suggestions for improvements.

Clip art   Previously created graphics designed to be added to word processing or desktop publishing documents or to computer-based instruction.

Cloud computing   Term for the distribution of applications, processing power, and storage across many computers accessible via the Internet.

Cognitive overload   Inhibited functioning created by excessive demands being placed on memory and/or other cognitive processes.

Compact disc (CD)   A 4.72-inch-diameter disc on which a laser has digitally recorded information such as audio, video, or computer data.

Computer   A machine that processes information according to a set of instructions.

Computer-assisted instruction (CAI)   See Computer-based instruction.

Computer-assisted learning (CAL)   See Computer-based instruction.

Computer-based instruction (CBI)   The use of the computer in the delivery of instruction.

Computer conferencing   An asynchronous communication medium in which two or more individuals exchange messages using personal computers connected via a network or telephone lines.

Computer gradebook   A computer database program that can store and manipulate students' grades.

Computer program   A set of instructions that tells the computer how to do something.

Computer software   See Software.

Computer system   A collection of components that includes the computer and all of the devices used with it.

Computer virus   See Virus.

Computer-managed instruction (CMI)   The use of the computer in the management of instruction, including applications such as student recordkeeping, performance assessment, and monitoring students' progress.

Computer-mediated communication (CMC)   The use of the computer as a device for mediating communication between teacher and students and among students, often over distances. Electronic mail and computer conferencing are two types of application software commonly used in CMC.

Concept map   A graphical representation of interrelated concepts that students can use as a learning aid or that teachers can use as an aid in content organization.

Conditional information   A type of information that describes the potential usefulness of facts, concepts, and principles.

Conditions   A portion of the instructional objective that indicates under what circumstances students are expected to perform.

Consequence   An event, object, or circumstance that comes after a behavior and is attributable to the behavior.

Contingencies   The environmental conditions that shape an individual's behavior.

Cooperative learning   An instructional method that involves small heterogeneous groups of students working toward a common academic goal or task. Its use promotes positive interdependence, individual accountability, collaborative/social skills, and group processing skills.

Copyright   The legal rights to an original work produced in any tangible medium of expression, including written works, works of art, music, photographs, and computer software.

Corrective feedback   Feedback that tells students specifically what they can do to correct their performance.

CPU   The central processing unit, or brain, of the computer, which controls the functions of the rest of the system and performs all numeric calculations.

Criteria   A portion of the instructional objective that indicates the standards that define acceptable performance.

CRT   Television-like display screen that uses a cathode ray tube.

Culture   Refers to the attitudes, values, customs, and behavior patterns that characterize a social group (Banks, 1997).

Cursor   A highlighted position indicator used on the computer screen.

Cycle of continuous improvement   The continuous evaluation of instruction before, during, and after implementation, which leads to continual revision and modification in order to increase student learning.

Database   An organized collection of information, often stored on the computer.

Database management system (DBMS)   Software that enables the user to enter, edit, store, retrieve, sort, and search through computer databases.

Datafile   The collection of all related records in a database.

Declarative information   A type of information that includes facts, concepts, principles, and the relationships among them.

Demonstration   An instructional method that involves showing how to do a task as well as describing why, when, and where it is done. Provides a real or lifelike example of the skill or procedure to be learned.

Designing instruction   The process of "translating principles of learning and instruction into plans for instructional materials" and activities (Smith & Ragan, 1999, p. 2).

Desktop publishing (DTP)   Computer application software that gives users a high degree of control over the composition and layout of material on a printed page, including both text and graphics.

Digital camera   A camera that stores pictures in computer-compatible digital format rather than on film.

Digital divide   A term used to describe the gap between those individuals who have access to technology such as computer software, the Internet, and so on and those who do not.

Digital storytelling   Use of the computer to orchestrate text, images, audio, and video to support a storytelling narrative with multimedia.

Digitizer   A device that allows analog audio or video to be captured in a form that the computer can use.

Direct observation   A form of evaluation that involves watching students as they work through some part(s) of the lesson.

Discovery   An instructional method that uses an inductive, or inquiry, method to encourage students to find "answers" for themselves through the use of trial-and-error problem-solving strategies.

Discussion   A dynamic instructional method in which individuals talk together, share information, and work cooperatively toward a solution or consensus. This method encourages classroom rapport and actively involves students in learning.

Display boards   Classroom surfaces used for writing and displaying information, including chalkboards, multipurpose boards, bulletin boards, magnetic boards, and flip charts.

Displayed visuals   Category of visuals that are generally exhibited on display boards, (e.g., multipurpose boards, bulletin boards) and are not projected.

Distance education   An organized instructional program in which the teacher and learners are physically separated by time or by geography.

Distractors   The incorrect or less appropriate alternative answers for a given multiple-choice question. Also called *foils*.

Distributed education   Similar to distance education, the notion of supporting learners, who may be situated locally or at a distance, with learning resources that may be distributed in space and time.

Domain   A major category of locations on the Internet. Major domains include com (company), edu (educational institution), gov (government), mil (military), net (network), and org (organization).

Downloading   Receiving information over a network from another computer.

Drill and practice   A series of practice exercises designed to increase fluency in a new skill or to refresh an existing one. Use of this approach assumes that learners have previously received some instruction on the concept, principle, or procedure to be practiced.

DVD   A compact disc format for storing motion video and computer data. Sometimes called digital video disc or digital versatile disc.

Educational computing   The use of the computer in the teaching and learning process.

Educational media   Channels of communication that carry messages with an instructional purpose; the different ways and means by which information can be delivered to or experienced by a learner.

Educational technology   The "application of technological processes and tools which can be used to solve problems of instruction and learning" (Seels & Richey, 1994, p. 4).

Electronic mail (e-mail)   Electronically transmitted private messages that can be sent from individuals to other individuals or groups.

Electronic whiteboard   Classroom display that allow teachers or students to interact with the computer through a touch sensitive board on which the computer screen is projected.

E-learning   Online learning.

E-mail   See Electronic mail.

E-mail address   A unique electronic address for an individual or organization, analogous to a postal address.

Emoticons   Combinations of type characters that resemble human faces when turned sideways. Used to indicate emotion or intent on e-mail or in chat rooms.

Encoding   The process of translating information into some meaningful form that can be remembered.

Ergonomics   A field of study focusing on the design of technology systems that align with human characteristics, needs, and capabilities.

Ethnicity   The manner in which individuals identify themselves based on their (or their ancestors') country of origin.

Evaluation   The third phase in the Plan, Implement, Evaluate model. Focus is on assessment techniques used to determine the level of learning students have achieved and/or the effectiveness of the instructional materials.

Evaluation activity   A type of instructional activity designed to determine how well students have mastered lesson objectives.

Event driven   Computer actions or programs, such as hypermedia software, that respond to events in the environment; for example, a mouse action event that occurs when the user clicks on a button.

Fair Use   "A policy established by the courts interpreting copyright law that allows parts of a copyrighted work to be used free of charge by educators, under certain very specific conditions having largely to do with the amount of the work used and the degree to which this use would financially penalize the copyright owner" (Tiene & Ingram, 2001, p. 310).

FAQ   Acronym for "frequently asked questions." Used on the Internet to disseminate basic information and to reduce repetitive queries.

Feedback   Information provided to students regarding how well they are doing during practice.

Field   Each individual category of information recorded in a database.

File server   A computer dedicated to managing a computer network and providing resources to other computers on the network (the clients). The file server is usually faster and has larger storage capabilities than the client machines.

Floppy disk/diskette   A magnetic storage medium for computer data that allows users to randomly access information.

Flowcharting   A graphical means of illustrating the logical flow of a computer program.

Focusing question   A question typically used at the beginning of a lesson to direct students' attention to particularly important aspects of the new information.

Foils   See Distractors.

Font   The appearance of the text itself, which can be altered through the selection of various typefaces and sizes of type. These include many typefaces common to the printing field, such as Times, Helvetica, Geneva, and Courier.

Formative evaluation   A form of assessment that indicates whether or not students have learned what they must know before progressing to the next portion of the instruction.

Formula   A mathematical expression that directs an electronic spreadsheet to perform various kinds of calculations on the numbers entered in it.

FTP (file transfer protocol)   The standard method for sending or retrieving electronic files on the Internet.

Game   An activity in which participants follow prescribed rules as they strive to attain a goal.

Gigabyte   Approximately a billion bytes, or 1,000 megabytes.

Grammar checker   Ancillary feature of word processors that identifies a range of grammatical and format errors such as improper capitalization, lack of subject-verb agreement, split infinitives, and so on.

Graphic   Any pictorial representation of information such as charts, graphs, animated figures, or photographic reproductions.

Graphical user interface (GUI)   The use of graphical symbols instead of text commands to control common computer functions such as copying programs and disks.

Graphics tablet   A computer input device that permits the development of graphic images by translating drawing on the tablet into onscreen images.

Hacker   An individual who gains access to computer systems without authorization.

Hard copy   A printed copy of computer output.

Hard disk   A large-capacity magnetic storage medium for computer data. Also called a fixed disk, it remains sealed within the case of most computers to protect it from dust, smoke, and other contaminants.

Hardware   The physical components of the computer system.

Heuristic   A rule of thumb or flexible guideline that can be adapted to fit each instructional situation.

High-level language   A computer language that contains instructions that resemble natural language and that does not require knowledge of the inner workings of the computer to use successfully.

Highlighting   Various techniques designed to direct attention to certain aspects of information, including the use of **bold**, underlined, or *italicized* print; color, labels, and arrows for pictorial information; and speaking more loudly or more slowly to highlight verbal information.

Home page   The preliminary or main web page of a particular website.

HTML   See Hypertext Markup Language.

Hybrid learning   Instructional format that combines elements of face-to-face teaching and learning with elements of distance education. Also known as blended learning.

Hypermedia   A system of information representation in which the information—text, graphics, animation, audio, and/or video—is stored in interlinked nodes.

Hypertext   An associational information-processing system in the text domain. In a hypertext system, text information is stored in nodes, and nodes are interconnected to other nodes of related information.

Hypertext Markup Language (HTML)   The authoring language used to define web pages.

I/O device   Any computer input or output device.

Icon   A small pictorial or graphical representation of a computer hardware function or component, or a computer software program, commonly associated with a graphical user interface.

IM   See Instant Messaging.

Image capture   The software capability to copy images from web pages or computer applications and store them on your own computer.

Imagery   A type of mnemonic in which mental pictures are used to represent new information.

Implementation   The second phase of the Plan, Implement, Evaluate model. Focus is on the use of instructional materials and activities designed to help students achieve the outcomes specified in the instructional plan.

Individualized education program (IEP)   An instructional plan for an individual student (usually one with special needs) that describes the student's current level of proficiency and also establishes short- and long-term goals for future focus. An IEP

is typically developed through a conference with the student's teachers and parents and other appropriate individuals.

Information activity   A type of instructional activity designed to help students understand, remember, and apply new information.

Inkjet printer   A type of printer that forms letters on the page by shooting tiny electrically charged droplets of ink.

Input   Information entered into the computer for processing.

Input device   Hardware such as a keyboard, mouse, or joystick through which the user sends instructions to the computer.

Instant Messaging (IM)   Generally one-to-one synchronous or real-time interaction using computers in which individuals interact by typing messages back and forth to one another.

Instruction   The selection and arrangement of information, activities, methods, and media to help students meet predetermined learning goals.

Instructional activity   An activity completed during a lesson to help students learn. There are five types of instructional activities: motivation, orientation, information, application, and evaluation activities.

Instructional appeal   The interest, or value, that instructional materials or activities have for the learner.

Instructional design   "The systematic process of translating principles of learning and instruction into plans for instructional materials and activities" (Smith & Ragan, 1999, p. 2).

Instructional effectiveness   A measure of the difference between what learners know before and after instruction; for example, Posttest – Pretest = Achievement.

Instructional efficiency   A measure of how much learners achieve per unit of time or dollar spent; for example, (Posttest – Pretest)/Time, or (Posttest – Pretest)/Cost.

Instructional game   An instructional approach that provides an appealing environment in which learners invest effort to follow prescribed rules in order to attain a challenging goal.

Instructional materials   The specific items used in a lesson and delivered through various media formats, such as video, audio, print, and so on.

Instructional method   A procedure of instruction selected to help learners achieve objectives or understand the content or message of instruction (e.g., presentation, simulation, drill and practice, cooperative learning).

Instructional plan   A blueprint for instructional lessons based on analyses of the learners, the context, and the task to be learned. Planning involves "the process of deciding what methods of instruction are best for bringing about desired changes in student knowledge and skills for a specific course content and a specific student population" (Reigeluth, 1983, p. 7). The instructional plan also includes the selection of appropriate media.

Instructional technology   "Applying scientific knowledge about human learning to the practical tasks of teaching and learning" (Heinich et al., 1993, p. 16).

Integrated learning system (ILS)   A single networked delivery system that combines sophisticated computer-assisted instruction (CAI) with computer-managed instruction (CMI).

Intellectual skills   A type of learning that refers to a variety of thinking skills, including concept learning, rule using, and problem solving.

Intelligence   The adaptive use of previously acquired knowledge to analyze and understand new situations.

Intelligent tutoring system   Combines detailed information about a subject area and common student mistakes with a model of student performance to diagnose a given student's level of understanding. Also provides instruction designed to meet that student's individual needs. Sometimes called intelligent computer-assisted instruction (ICAI).

Interactive media   Media formats that allow or require some level of physical activity from the user, which in some way alters the sequence of presentation.

Interactive multimedia   Multimedia that allows user interactions so that the user can determine the direction of the program or presentation.

Interface   An electronic go-between by which the computer communicates with a peripheral device.

Internal memory   Storage inside the computer. The CPU in a personal computer retrieves and deposits information in the computer's internal memory. Also called *main memory.*

Internet   A network of computer networks that links computers worldwide.

Intrinsic motivation   Motivation in which the act itself is the reward.

Java   A computer language, often associated with the Internet, designed to create applications capable of operating across different hardware platforms.

Keyboard   The most common input device; resembles the key layout of a typewriter.

Key word   A type of mnemonic in which an unfamiliar new word is linked to a similar-sounding familiar word, which is used to create a visual image that incorporates the meaning of the new word.

Knowledge   A type of learning that refers to the ability to recall specific information.

Label   Text used to name parts of an electronic spreadsheet.

Laser printer   A printer that combines laser and photocopying technology to produce very high-quality output, comparable to that produced in typesetting. Laser printers can produce text as well as high-quality graphics and can achieve print densities of up to 1,200 dots per inch for very finely detailed images.

LCD projector   A liquid crystal display device used with a computer or VCR for large-group display.

LCD screen   Liquid crystal display screen, commonly used in computers and also in conjunction with display panels and projectors as large-group display devices.

Learner-centered instruction   "Actively collaborating with learners to determine what learning means and how it can be enhanced within each individual learner" (Wagner & McCombs, 1995, p. 32). An emphasis is placed on drawing on the learner's own unique talents, capacities, and experiences.

Learning   "Learning is a persisting change in human performance or performance potential [brought] about as a result of the learner's interaction with the environment" (Driscoll, 1994, pp. 8–9). To change (or have the capacity to change) one's level of ability or knowledge.

Learning environment   The setting or physical surroundings in which learning takes place, including the classroom, science or computer laboratory, gymnasium, playground, and so on.

Learning in context   The application of knowledge to solve problems or complete tasks that are realistic and meaningful.

Learning style   An individual's preferred ways for "processing and organizing information and for responding to environmental stimuli" (Shuell, 1981, p. 46).

Learning theory   A set of related principles explaining changes in human performance or performance potential in terms of the causes of those changes.

Library/media specialist   A school specialist who helps students and teachers to become effective users of ideas and information by providing access to materials, providing instruction, and working with teachers to design learning strategies to meet the needs of individual students.

Liquid crystal display (LCD)   See LCD screen.

Listserv   Also called a *mail server,* this is the computer or software that operates an e-mail discussion list on the Internet. Interested individuals subscribe to the list and subsequently receive all e-mail that is sent to the listserv.

Local-area network (LAN)   A computer network covering a limited geographical area, such as a single building or even a single room within a building.

Logo   A computer language developed by Seymour Papert and based on the learning theories of Jean Piaget; it is used in schools, particularly at the elementary level.

Macro   A shortcut to encoding a series of actions in a computer program. Provides the means to perform a number of separate steps through a single command.

Mailing list   Software that uses e-mail to deliver topic-specific information to a targeted group of respondents.

Mass storage   Input/output devices that provide for storage and retrieval of programs and other types of data that must be stored over a long period of time. Also referred to as *external* or *auxiliary* memory.

Medium/media   See Educational media.

Megabyte   Approximately a million bytes, or 1000 kilobytes.

Memory   Within a computer, this is an area that stores instructions (programs) and information that can be readily accessed by the processor.

Methods   See Instructional methods.

Microprocessor   A single silicon chip that contains all of the CPU circuits for a computer system.

Mnemonic   Any practical device used to make information easier to remember, including rhymes, acronyms, and acrostics.

Model   A three-dimensional representation of a real object; it may be larger, smaller, or the same size as the object represented.

Modem   A combination input and output device that allows a computer to communicate with another computer over telephone or cable TV lines. A modem (short for *modulator-demodulator*) converts digital computer information into sound (and vice versa) for transmission over telephone lines.

Monitor   A video or computer display device. The most common output device for personal computers.

Motivation   An internal state that leads people to choose to work toward certain goals and experiences. Defines what people will do rather than what they can do (Keller, 1983).

Motivation activity   A type of instructional activity that leads students to want to learn and to put in the effort required for learning.

Motor skills   A type of learning that refers to the ability to perform complex physical actions in a smooth, coordinated manner.

Mouse   A pointing device used to select and move information on the computer display screen. When the mouse is moved along a flat surface such as a desktop, an arrow moves across the display screen in the same direction. The mouse typically has one to three buttons that may be used for selecting or entering information.

Multimedia   Sequential or simultaneous use of a variety of media formats in a single presentation or program. Today, this term conveys the notion of a system in which various media (e.g., text, graphics, video, and audio) are integrated into a single delivery system under computer control.

Netbook   A small laptop or notebook computer designed primarily to access the Internet.

Netiquette   Rules for polite social behavior while communicating over a network.

Newsgroup   On computer networks, a discussion group created by allowing users to post messages and read messages among themselves.

Objective   A statement of what learners will be expected to do when they have completed a specified course of instruction, stated in terms of observable performances.

One-computer classroom   Classroom equipped with a single computer.

Online learning   Course of study or training generally delivered via the Internet.

OOPS   Object-oriented programming systems, where each thing that one sees on the computer screen is treated as an object, and each object can have a programming code associated with it.

Operating system (OS)   The master control program for a computer system.

Orientation activity   A type of instructional activity that helps students understand what they have previously learned, what they are currently learning, and what they will be learning in the future.

Output   Information that comes out of the computer.

Output device   The hardware that receives and displays information coming from the computer.

Overhead transparencies   Acetate sheets whose images are projected by means of a device that transmits light through them and onto a screen or wall.

Packet   A chunk of information routed across the Internet.

PDA   See Personal digital assistant.

Peer review   A form of evaluation that involves asking a colleague to examine all or part of an instructional lesson and make suggestions for improvement.

Performance   A portion of the instructional objective that indicates what students will do to demonstrate what they have learned.

Peripheral   Any of various devices that connect to the computer, including input devices, output devices, and mass storage devices.

Personal computer   A computer intended for use by an individual.

Personal digital assistant (PDA)   A handheld mobile electronic device that provides users access to calendars, e-mail, contact information, and even some applications programs such as word processing and spreadsheets.

Photo CD   A CD format developed by Kodak that can store high-quality images made from 35-millimeter photographic negatives or slides.

Pilot test   An evaluation of instruction conducted before implementing the instruction.

Pixel   A single dot, or picture element, on the computer screen.

Plagiarism detection services   Companies and organizations (e.g., Turnitin.com) that offer services to help identify if, and to what degree, potential plagiarism has occurred within written documents.

Planning   The first phase of the Plan, Implement, Evaluate model. Focus is on the design of instructional materials based on the learners, content, and context.

Plug-in   Small software program that works with a Web browser to perform tasks that the browser cannot perform on its own.

Podcast   A digital media file, most often audio, distributed via the Internet for playback on a portable media player, such as Apple's iPod, or a computer.

Portfolio   "A purposeful collection of student work that tells the story of the student's efforts, progress, or achievement" (Arter & Spandel, 1992, p. 36).

Posttest   An assessment of students' knowledge or skills given after instruction.

PowerPoint   Microsoft Office presentation software. Also a common term to refer to a type of projected visual (slide) that is created within presentation software.

Prerequisite   The knowledge and skills students should have at the beginning of a lesson.

Presentation   An instructional method involving a one-way communication controlled by a source that relates, dramatizes, or otherwise disseminates information to learners, and includes no immediate response from, or interaction with, learners (e.g., a lecture or speech).

Presentation software   Computer software designed for the production and display of computer text and images, intended to replace the functions typically associated with the slide projector and overhead projector.

Pretest   Preinstructional evaluation of students' knowledge and/or skills to determine students' level of performance before instruction.

Preview   A form of evaluation that involves reading, viewing, and/or working through specific instructional materials prior to using them (Heinich et al., 1999).

Printed visual   Nonprojected drawings, charts, graphs, posters, and cartoons that are commonly found in printed sources such as textbooks, reference materials, newspapers, and periodicals.

Printer   A device that provides printed output from the computer.

Printer driver   Software that ensures an application's formatting commands are translated correctly into printer actions. Most operating systems provide a number of different printer drivers to support different models of printers.

Problem solving   An instructional method in which learners use previously mastered skills to reach resolution of challenging problems. Based on the scientific method of inquiry, it typically involves the following five steps: (1) defining the problem and all major components, (2) formulating hypotheses, (3) collecting and analyzing data, (4) deriving conclusions/solutions, and (5) verifying conclusions/solutions.

Problem-solving software   Computer applications designed to foster students' higher-order thinking skills, such as logical thinking, reasoning, pattern recognition, and use of strategies.

Processor   The "brain" of the computer that controls the functions of the rest of the system and manipulates information in various ways. See CPU.

Programming   The process of creating a computer program. See Computer program.

Programming language   A set of instructions that can be assembled, according to particular rules and syntax, to create a working computer program.

Projected visual   A drawing, chart, graph, and so on that is presented in a projected fashion (e.g., overhead transparencies, projected *PowerPoint* slides).

Public Domain   Materials (e.g., book, song, artwork) that are not protected by intellectual property laws (e.g., copyright) and may be freely copied and distributed without first getting permission.

RAM   See Random-access memory.

Random-access memory (RAM)   The computer's working memory. In a personal computer, RAM provides a temporary work space that allows the user to change its contents, as needed, to perform different tasks. Common RAM is volatile, which means that its contents disappear as soon as the power is turned off (or otherwise interrupted).

Read-only memory (ROM)   The permanent memory that is built into the computer at the factory, referred to as "read only" because the computer can read the information that is stored there but cannot change that stored information. ROM contains the basic instructions the computer needs to operate.

Real objects   Actual materials, not models or simulations.

Record   A collection of related fields that is treated as a logical unit in a database.

Reinforcing feedback   Feedback used to recognize good performance and encourage continued effort from students. Takes the form of verbal praise or a "pat on the back."

Relational database   A type of computer database that permits the interrelation of information across more than one datafile.

Reliability   "The degree to which a test instrument consistently measures the same group's knowledge level of the same instruction when taking the test over again" (Gentry, 1994, p. 383).

Retrieval   Identifying and recalling information for a particular purpose.

Rhyme   A type of mnemonic that uses words spoken in a rhythm or in verse to help remember information.

ROM   See Read-only memory.

Router   A computer that regulates Internet traffic and assigns data transmission pathways.

Rubric   See Assessment rubric.

Scan converter   A device that converts computer output for display on a television or video monitor.

Scanner   A device that uses technology similar to a photocopying machine to take an image from a printed page and convert it into a form the computer can manipulate.

Search and replace   A common feature of word processors that allows the user to locate the occurrence of any word or phrase within a document and substitute something else.

Search engine   A website that maintains a database of Internet-accessible information that can be searched to locate information of interest.

Semantic aware applications   Computer applications that determine the meaning, or semantics, of information on the Internet to make connections and answer questions that would otherwise take much time and effort.

Serious games   Games, usually video or computer games, which have an overtly educational purpose as opposed to games designed purely for entertainment.

Server   See File server.

SES   See Socioeconomic status.

Simulation   An instructional method involving a scaled-down approximation of a real-life situation that allows realistic practice without the expense or risks otherwise involved. Similar to problem solving, simulations often include case studies and/or role-plays.

Slides   A small-format (e.g., 35mm) photographic transparency individually mounted for one-at-a-time projection.

Smart phone   A mobile telephone with computer-like functionality often including e-mail, Web browsing, and ability to run applications.

Socialization   The process by which we learn the rules, norms, and expectations of the society in which we live.

Social networking   Web applications, such as Facebook and MySpace, that allow individuals to share information and interests in an online community.

Socioeconomic status (SES)   One's perceived rank or standing in a society based on a variety of factors, which may include family income, parents' occupations, and the amount of formal education completed.

Software   The programs or instructions that tell the computer what to do, often stored on diskette or CD-ROM.

Special needs students   Individuals who require special educational services to help them reach their potential.

Speech recognition   Artificial-intelligence-based computer technology in which oral speech is converted by the computer into text.

Spelling checker   A common ancillary feature of word processors that searches through a document and reports any instances of text that do not match a built-in dictionary.

Spreadsheet   A general-purpose computer calculating tool based on the paper worksheet used by accountants.

Stem   The part of a multiple-choice assessment instrument that sets forth the problem that will be "answered" by one option from a list of alternatives.

Storyboarding   A technique for illustrating, on paper, what the screen displays in a computer program will look like before they are actually programmed.

Structural information   Information that refers to the relationships that exist among ideas and concepts (e.g., it allows one to understand how items are related).

Structured programming   A set of programming conventions designed to result in organized, easy-to-read, and correct programs. It relies on a top-down method, modular program design, a limited set of program constructs, and careful documentation of the program.

Student tryout   A "test run" of an instructional activity, approach, media, or materials with a small group of students before using it on a large scale (Mager, 1997).

Summative evaluation   Assessment that occurs after instruction that measures what students have learned.

Synchronous   Occurring at the same time.

Syntax   Rules for using computer languages.

Systems software   The basic operating software that tells the computer how to perform its fundamental functions.

Tags   Elements of HTML that are used to define properties of web pages; for example, the tags, <B>. and, </B>. denote the beginning and end of boldfaced text.

TCP/IP   Transmission Control Protocol/Internet Protocol—the communication standard used by computers on the Internet.

Technology   "The systematic application of scientific or other organized knowledge to practical tasks" (Galbraith, 1967, p. 12). Technology performs a bridging function between research and theory on one side and professional practice on the other.

Technology coordinator   A specialist and resource person who handles computers and related technologies for a school building or district.

Technology literacy   The ability to understand and use various forms of technology.

Technology plan   Organized set of goals, objectives, and steps that outline how an individual or organization will acquire and maintain specific levels of technology hardware and software (e.g., computers).

Template   A prepared layout designed to ease the process of creating a product in certain computer applications; for example, a slide design and color scheme for presentation software or a spreadsheet with appropriate labels and formulas but without the data.

Test generator   A computer program used to create assessment instruments.

Text   A combination of alphanumeric characters and numbers used to communicate.

Theory   A set of related principles explaining observed events/relationships. Theories typically make predictions in the form of "If . . . , then . . . " statements that can be tested.

Top-down approach   An approach to problem solving and computer programming that begins by outlining the basic solution at a fairly high level of abstraction and then breaks that outline down into its component parts until they can be coded.

Transfer   The use of prior knowledge in new situations or as it applies to new problems.

Triangulation   The process of obtaining information from more than one technique or source in order to strengthen individual findings.

Tutorial   An instructional method in which a tutor—in the form of a person, computer, or special print materials—presents the content, poses a question or problem, requests learner response, analyzes the response, supplies appropriate feedback, and provides practice until the learner demonstrates a predetermined level of competency.

Two-way interactive video   A distance education technology in which sending and receiving sites are equipped with cameras, microphones, and video monitors and linked via some means of transmission (e.g., satellite, microwave, cable, fiber-optic cable).

Type style   Application of different features to any word-processing font, including **boldface,** *italics,* underline, and others.

Ubiquitous computing   Sometimes called pervasive computing or distributed intelligence, it refers to situations in which computer processing power is embedded, often invisibly, in objects in the everyday environment.

Undo   A software feature that allows the user to recover from an error; for example, if you select and delete the wrong block of text, the undo command restores the text to the document.

Uniform Resource Locator (URL)   The unique address for every Internet site or World Wide Web page containing the protocol type, the domain, the directory, and the name of the site or page.

Universal design   An approach to the design of products and environments, developed in part from assistive technology, that emphasizes usability for all people.

Uploading   Sending information over a network to another computer.

URL   See Uniform resource locator.

Vector graphics   Also called *draw graphics,* in which the computer "remembers" the steps involved in creating a particular graphic image on the screen, independent of a particular screen location or the graphic's size.

Video   The display of recorded pictures on a television-like screen. Includes videotapes, videodiscs, and CDs.

Video conferencing   A distance education technology that uses two-way audio and two-way video between sites.

Video digitizer   An add-on device for the computer that takes video from analog video sources and captures it as a computer graphic or motion video.

Videodisc   An analog video storage medium composed of recorded images and sound, similar to the CD. Depending on format, a videodisc can hold from 30 to 60 minutes of motion video images, up to 54,000 still images, or a combination of motion and still images. As with the CD, the videodisc can be indexed for rapid location of any part of the material.

Videotape   A video storage medium in which video images and sound are recorded on magnetic tape. Popular sizes include one-inch commercial tape, three-quarter-inch U-matic, half-inch VHS or S-VHS, 8-millimeter, and digital miniDV.

Virtual reality (VR)   A computer interface that simulates an interactive environment that appears to the observer as another reality. A VR system uses special hardware and software to project a three-dimensional visual representation of an environment and responds to the user's motion within that environment.

Virus   A computer program that infects a computer system, causing damage or mischief. Like a biological virus, it causes the host computer to make copies of the virus, which can then spread to other computers over networks, through online services, or via infected diskettes.

Vision   How one perceives the future could/should be (e.g., technology vision—how technology should be used in the future).

Visual   Combination of graphics and text presented in a two-dimensional format.

Vodcast   A video podcast.

Web   See World Wide Web.

Web 2.0   Umbrella term for second-generation web technologies that allow for communication and collaboration of people in Web-based communities.

Web browser   Application program designed to access the Internet and navigate its nonsequential pathways.

Webinar   Short for web seminar, an interactive and synchronous meeting or presentation format which is conducted over the Web.

Web page   A hypertext document on the World Wide Web, somewhat analogous to a printed page.

WebQuest   A form of inquiry-oriented activity, first developed by Bernie Dodge and Tom March at San Diego State University, in which some or all of the information used by learners is drawn from resources on the Web.

Web server   A computer connected to the Internet that makes web pages and websites available to other computers.

Website   A set of interrelated Web pages usually operated by a single entity (e.g., company, school, organization, or individual).

Web use policy   See Acceptable use policy.

Wide-area network (WAN)   A computer network covering a broad geographical area, such as between buildings, campuses, or even across hundreds or thousands of miles. Often involves the interconnection of multiple local-area networks.

Wiki   A website that permits individuals to collaborative with others to easily create and edit Web pages using a Web browser.

Word processing   Using a word processor.

Word processor   A computer program for writing that supports the entry, editing, revising, formatting, storage, retrieval, and printing of text.

World Wide Web (WWW or the Web)   An information retrieval system on the Internet that relies on a point-and-click hypertext navigation system.

WYSIWYG   What You See Is What You Get—a standard for word processor displays where what shows on the computer display is what the document will look like when it is printed.

REFERENCES

Abbitt, J., & Ophus, J. (2008). What we know about the impacts of WebQuests: A review of research. *AACE Journal 16*(4), 441–456.

Achinstein, B., & Barrett, A. (2004). (Re)framing classroom contexts: How new teachers and mentors view diverse learners and challenges of practice. *Teachers College Record, 106*(4), 716–746.

Ackerman, E., & Hartman, K. (2002). *Learning to use the Internet and World Wide Web.* Wilsonville, OR: Franklin, Beedle, & Associates.

Ainsworth, L., & Viegut, D. (2006). *Common formative assessments: How to connect standards-based instruction and assessment.* Thousand Oaks, CA: Corwin.

Alexander, J. E., & Tate, M. A. (1999). *Web wisdom: How to evaluate and create information quality on the Web.* Mahwah, NJ: Lawrence Erlbaum Associates.

Allen, I. E. & Seaman, J. (2008). *Staying the course: Online education in the United States, 2008.* Needham, MA: Sloan Consortium (Sloan-C).

Alvarado, A. E., & Herr, P. R. (2003). *Inquiry-based learning using everyday objects: Hands-on instructional strategies that promote active learning in grades 3-8.* Thousand Oaks, CA: Sage.

American Society for Training and Development (2008). *Instructional design & implementation: The tools for creating training program curriculum (vol 2).* Danvers, MA: Infoline and ASTD Press.

Anderson, P. (2006). *Psychology in learning and instruction.* Upper Saddle River, NJ: Merrill/Prentice Hall.

Anglin, G. J. (Ed.). (1991). *Instructional technology: Past, present, and future.* Englewood, CO: Libraries Unlimited.

Arter, J. A., & Spandel, V. (1992). Using portfolios of student work in instruction and assessment. *Educational Measurement: Issues and Practice, 11*(Spring), 36–44.

Asimov, I. (1984). *Asimov's guide to science* (2nd ed.). New York: Basic Books.

Ausubel, D. P., Novak, J. D., & Hanesian, H. (1978). *Educational psychology: A cognitive view.* New York: Holt, Rinehart & Winston.

Ayersman, D. J. (1996). Reviewing the research on hypermedia-based learning. *Journal of Research on Computing in Education, 28*(4), 500–525.

Bailey, G., & Ribble, M. (2007). *Digital citizenship in schools.* Washington, DC: International Society for Technology in Education.

Baker, J. E. & Sugden, S. J. (2003). Spreadsheets in education: The first 25 years. *Spreadsheets in Education, 1*(1), 18–43.

Bangert-Drowns, R. L. (1993). The word processor as an instructional tool: A meta-analysis of word processing in writing instruction. *Review of Educational Research, 63*(1), 69–93.

Banks, J. (1997). Multicultural education: Characteristics and goals. In J. Banks & C. Banks (Eds.), *Multicultural education: Issues and perspectives* (3rd ed.) (pp. 3–32). Boston: Allyn & Bacon.

Barell, J. (1995). *Teaching for thoughtfulness: Classroom strategies to enhance intellectual development.* White Plains, NY: Longman.

Baron, C. L. (2004). *Designing a digital portfolio.* Indianapolis, IN: New Riders.

Bauerlein, M. (2008). *The dumbest generation: How the digital age stupefies young American and jeopardizes our future (or, don't trust anyone under 30).* New York: Tarcher.

Bayraktar, S. (2001). A meta-analysis of the effectiveness of computer-assisted instruction in science education. *Journal of Research on Technology in Education, 43*(2), 173–188.

Beldarrain, Y. (2006). Distance education trends: Integrating new technologies to foster student interaction and collaboration. *Distance Education, 27*(2) 139–153.

Bell, A. (2005). *Creating digital video in your school: How to shoot, edit, produce, distribute, and incorporate digital media into the curriculum.* Worthington, OH: Linworth.

Benjamin, A. (2005). *Differentiated instruction using technology: A guide for middle and high school teachers.* Larchmont, NY: Eye on Education, Inc.

Bernard, R. M., Abrami, P. C., Lou, Y., Borokhovski, E., Wade, A., Wozney, L., Wallet, P. A., Fiset, M., & Huang, B. (2004). How does distance education compare with classroom instruction? A meta-analysis of the empirical literature. *Review of Educational Research, 74*(3), 379–439.

Bernhardt, V. (2004). *Data analysis for continuous school improvement.* Larchmont, NY: Eye on Education.

Bigge, M., & Shermis, S. (2003). *Learning theories for teachers.* Allyn & Bacon.

Blanchard, J., & Marshall, J. (2004). *Web-based learning in K-12 classrooms: Opportunities and challenges.* New York: The Haworth Press.

Blomeyer, R., & Cavanaugh, C. (2007). *What works in K-12 online learning.* Washington, DC: ISTE Books.

Bloom, B. S. (1956). *Taxonomy of educational objectives: Book 1, Cognitive domain.* New York: Longman.

Blumenfeld, P. C., Soloway, E., Marx, R. W., Krajcik, J. S., Guzdial, M., & Palinscar, A. (1991). Motivating project-based learning: Sustaining the doing, supporting the learning. *Educational Psychologist, 26,* 369–398.

Bonk, C., & Zhang, K. (2006). Introducing the R2D2 model: Online learning for the diverse learners of this world. *Distance Education, 27*(2), 249–264.

Bonk, C. J., & Zhang, K. (2008). *Empowering online learning: 100+ activities for reading, reflecting, displaying, and doing.* San Francisco, CA : Jossey-Bass.

Borich, G. (2007). *Effective teaching methods: Research-based practice* (6th ed.). Upper Saddle River, NJ: Pearson/Merrill/Prentice Hall.

Borko, H., & Livingston, C. (1992). Cognition and improvisation: Differences in mathematics instruction by expert and novice teachers. *American Educational Research Journal, 26,* 473–498.

Boss, S., & Krauss, J. (2007). *Reinventing project-based learning: Your field guide to real world projects in the digital age.* Washington, DC: International Society for Technology in Education.

Bransford, J. D., Brown, A. L., & Cocking, R. R. (2000). *How people learn: Brain, mind, experience, and school.* Washington, DC: National Academy Press.

Brooks-Young, S. (2006). *Critical technology issues for school leaders.* Thousand Oaks, CA: Corwin.

Brown, A., Green, T., & Bray, M. (2004). *Technology and the diverse learner: A guide to classroom practice.* Thousand Oaks, CA: Corwin Press.

Brown, J. S., Collins, A., & Duguid, P. (1989). Situated cognition and the culture of learning. *Educational Researcher, 18*(1), 32–42.

Bruer, J. T. (1993). *Schools for thought: A science of learning in the classroom.* Cambridge, MA: MIT Press.

Bruner, J. S. (1961). The act of discovery. *Harvard Education Review, 31*(1), 21–32.

Brunner, C. & Bennett, D. (1997). Technology and gender: Differences in masculine and feminine views. *NASSP Bulletin, 81*(592), 46–51.

Bull, G. (2005). *Teaching with digital images: Acquire, analyze, create, communicate.* Washington, DC: International Society for Technology in Education.

Bullock, A. A., & Hawk, P. P. (2005). *Developing a teaching portfolio: A guide for preservice and practicing teachers.* Upper Saddle River, NJ: Pearson/Merrill/Prentice Hall.

Butler, S., & McMunn, N. (2006). *A teacher's guide to classroom assessment: Understanding and using assessment to improve student learning.* San Francisco, CA: John Wiley & Sons.

Butzin, S. (2005). *Joyful classrooms in an age of accountability: The Project CHILD recipe for success.* Bloomington, IN: Phi Delta Kappa International.

Carlson, G. (2004). *Digital media in the classroom.* San Francisco: CMP Books.

Carr-Chellman, A. (2010). I*nstructional design for teachers: Improving classroom practice.* New York: Routledge.

Chen, I., & Thielemann, J. (2008). *Technology application competencies for K-12 teachers.* Hershey, PA: IGI group

Chen, P., & McGrath, D. (2003). Moments of joy: Student engagement and conceptual learning in the design of hypermedia documents. *Journal of Research on Technology in Education, 35*(3), 402–422.

Christensen, C., Horn, M. & Johnson, C. (2008). *Disrupting class: How disruptive innovation will change the way the world learns.* New York: McGraw-Hill.

Chuang, H., Thompson, A., & Schmidt, D. (2003a). Issues and barriers to advanced faculty use of technology. Paper presented at the *Society for Information Technology and Teacher Education International Conference (SITE),* Albuquerque, NM.

Chuang, H. H., Thompson, A. D., & Schmidt, D. (2003b). Faculty technology mentoring programs: Major trends in the literature. *Journal of Computing in Teacher Education, 19*(4), 101–106.

Clark, R. (2008). *Developing technical training: A structured approach for developing classroom and computer-based instructional materials.* San Francisco, CA: Pfeiffer.

Clark, R. C., & Lyons, C. (2004). *Graphics for Learning.* San Francisco, CA: Pfeiffer.

Clark, R. C., & Mayer, R. E. (2008). *E-Learning and the science of instruction* (2nd ed). San Francisco, CA: Pfeiffer.

Cochran-Smith, M. (1991). Word processing and writing in elementary classrooms: A critical review of related literature. *Review of Educational Research, 61*(1), 107–155.

Cole, C., Ray, K., & Zanetis, J. (2009). *Videoconferencing for K-12 classrooms.* Washington, DC: ISTE Books.

Collins, A., Brown, J. S., & Holum, A. (1991). Cognitive apprenticeship: Making thinking visible. *American Educator, 15*(3), 6–11, 38–46.

Collis, B. (1990). *The best of research windows: Trends and issues in educational computing.* Eugene, OR: International Society for Technology in Education. (ERIC Document Reproduction Service No. ED 323 993).

Coyne, M., Kame'enui, E., & Carnine, D. (2007). *Effective teaching strategies that accommodate diverse learners* (3rd ed.). Upper Saddle River, NJ: Merrill.

Crews, K. D. (2003). New copyright law for distance education: The meaning and importance of the TEACH Act. Retrieved December 9, 2004, from http://www.copyright.jupui.edu/teachsummary.htm.

Crews, K. D. (2006). *Copyright Law for Librarians and Educators* (2nd ed). Chicago, Ill.: American Library Association.

Cronje, J. (2006). Paradigms regained: Toward integrating objectivism and constructivism in instructional design and the learning sciences. *Educational Technology Research and Development, 54*(4), 387–416.

Cuban, L. (2001). *Oversold & underused: Computers in the classroom.* Cambridge, MA: Harvard University Press.

Culp, K. M., Honey, M., & Mandinach, E. (2003). *A retrospective on twenty years of education technology policy.* U.S. Department of Education, Office of Educational Technology: Washington DC. Retrieved November 3, 2004, from www.nationaledtechplan.org/participate/20years.pdf.

Cyrs, T. E. (1997). *Teaching at a distance with the merging technologies: An instructional systems approach.* New Mexico State University: Center for Educational Development.

Dallmann-Jones, A. S. (1994). *The expert educator: A reference manual of teaching strategies for quality education.* Fond du Lac, WI: Three Blue Herons.

D'Aoust, C. (1992). Portfolios: Process for students and teachers. In K. B. Yancey (Ed.), *Portfolios in the writing classroom* (pp. 39–48). Urbana, IL: National Council of Teachers of English.

Davis, M. (2008). *The teacher's guide to copyright.* Shreveport, LA: Buzzgig, LLC.

Dawley, L. (2007). *The tools for successful online teaching.* London: Idea Group.

Deason, C. (2007). *Culturally sensitive computer environments for pedagogy: A review of the literature.* In C. Crawford et al. (Eds.), Proceedings of Society for Information Technology and Teacher Education International Conference 2007 (pp. 1965–1967). Chesapeake, VA: AACE.

Deaux, K. (1984). From individual differences to social categories: Analysis of a decade's research on gender. *American Psychologist, 39,* 105–116.

DeBell, M., & Chapman, C. (2003). *Computer and Internet use by children and adolescents in 2001: Statistical analysis report*. National Center for Education Statistics. U.S. Department of Education: Washington, DC. Retrieved October 15, 2009 from nces.ed.gov/pubs2004/2004014.pdf.

DeLong, D. F. (2001). Code red virus—Most expensive in history of Internet. NewsFactor Network. Retrieved November 2, 2004, from www.newsfactor.com/perl/story/12668.html#story-start.

deMarrais, K., & LeCompte, M. (1999). *The way schools work* (3rd ed.). New York: Longman.

Derry, S., & Murphy, D. A. (1986). Designing systems that train learning ability: From theory to practice. *Review of Educational Research, 56*(1), 1–39.

Dewey, J. (1897). My pedagogic creed. *School Journal, 54,* 77–80.

Dick, W., & Reiser, R. A. (1996). *Planning effective instruction*. Upper Saddle River, NJ: Prentice Hall.

Dieterle, E., & Clarke, J. (2008). Multi-user virtual environments for teaching and learning. In M. Pagani (Ed.), *Encyclopedia of multimedia technology and networking* (2nd ed.). Hershey, PA: Idea Group.

Dockerman, D. (2003). *Great teaching with video: TSP's guide to using the VCR and videodisc player in the classroom*. Watertown, MA: Tom Snyder Productions.

Donaldson, A., & Conrad, R. (2004). *Engaging the online learner: Activities and resources for creative instruction*. San Francisco, CA: Jossey-Bass.

Driscoll, M. P. (2005). *Psychology of learning for instruction* (3rd ed.). Boston: Allyn & Bacon.

Duffy, T. M., Lowyck, J., & Jonassen, D. H. (1993). Introduction. In T. M. Duffy, J. Lowyck, & D. H. Jonassen (Eds.), *Designing environments for constructive learning* (pp. 1–5). Berlin: Springer-Verlag.

Dynarski, M., Agodini, R., Heaviside, S., Novak, T., Carey, N., Campuzano, L., Means, B., Murphy, R., Penuel, W., Javitz, H., Emery, D. & Sussex, W. (2007). *Effectiveness of Reading and Mathematics Software Products: Findings from the First Student Cohort*. Washington, DC: U.S. Department of Education, Institute of Education Sciences.

Eggen, P., & Kauchak, D. (2001). *Educational psychology: Windows on classrooms* (5th ed.). Upper Saddle River, NJ: Merrill.

Ehrman, L., Glenn, A., Johnson, V., & White, C. (1992). Using computer databases in student problem solving: A study of eight social studies teachers' classrooms. *Theory and Research in Social Education, 20*(2), 179–206.

Ertmer, P. A. (1999). Addressing first- and second-order barriers to change: Strategies for technology integration. *Educational Technology Research and Development, 47*(4), 47–61.

Ertmer, P. A., Hruskocy, C., & Woods, D. M. (2003). *The worldwide classroom: Access to people, resources, and curricular connections*. Upper Saddle River, NJ: Prentice Hall.

Ertmer, P. A., & Newby, T. J. (1993). Behaviorism, cognitivism, constructivism: Comparing critical features from an instructional design perspective. *Performance Improvement Quarterly, 6*(4), 50–72.

Falchikov, N. (2005). *Improving assessment through student involvement: Practical solutions for aiding learning in higher and further education*. Abingdon, Oxon: RoutledgeFalmer.

Farkas, B. GT. (2006). *Secrets of podcasting*. (2nd ed.). Berkeley, CA: Peachpit Press.

Fenrich, P. (2005). *Creating instructional multimedia solutions: Practical guidelines for the real world*. Santa Rosa, CA: Informing Science Press.

Fleming, M. L. (1987). Displays and communication. In R. M. Gagné (Ed.), *Instructional technology: Foundations* (pp. 233–260). Hillsdale, NJ: Lawrence Erlbaum Associates.

Fogg, B. (2003). *Persuasive technology: Using computers to change what we think and do*. San Francisco, CA: Morgan Kaufmann.

Fogg, B. (2007). *Mobile persuasion: 20 perspectives of the future of behavior change*. Stanford Captology Media.

Forcier, R., & Descy, D. (2007). *The computer as an educational tool: Productivity and problem solving* (5th ed.). Upper Saddle River, NJ: Prentice Hall.

Forum on Education Statistics. (2002). *Technology in schools: Suggestions, tools, guidelines for assessing technology in elementary and secondary education*. National Center for Education Statistics. U.S. Department of Education: Washington, DC. Available at http://nces.ed.gov/pubs2003/2003313.pdf.

Foshay, W. R., Silber, K. H., & Stelnicki, M. B. (2003). *Writing training materials that work: How to train anyone to do anything*. Jossey-Bass/Pfeiffer: San Francisco, CA.

Frazel, M. (2009). *Digital storytelling guide for educators*. Washington, DC: ISTE Books.

Frazier, M., & Bailey, G. (2004). *The technology coordinator's handbook*. Eugene, OR: International Society for Technology in Education.

Frei, S., Gammill, A., & Irons, S. (2007). *Integrating technology into the curriculum: Practical strategies for successful classrooms*. Huntington Beach, CA: Shell Education.

Gagné, R. M. (Ed.). (1987). *Instructional technology: Foundations*. Hillsdale, NJ: Lawrence Erlbaum Associates.

Gagné, R. M., Wager, W. W., Golas, K., & Keller, J. M. (2005). *Principles of instructional design* (5th ed.). Belmont, CA: Wadsworth.

Galbraith, J. K. (1967). *The new industrial state*. Boston: Houghton Mifflin.

Gardner, H. (1985). *The mind's new science: A history of the cognitive revolution*. New York: Basic Books.

Gareis, C. & Grant, L. (2008). *Teacher-made assessments: How to connect curriculum, instruction, and student learning*. Larchmont, NY: Eye On Education.

Gee, J. P. (2003). *What video games have to teach us about learning and literacy*. New York: Palgrave/St. Martin's.

Gee, J. P. (2007). *Good video games and good learning: Collected essays on video games, learning and literacy*. New York: Peter Lang Publishing.

Gentry, C. G. (1994). *Introduction to instructional development: Process and technique*. Belmont, CA: Wadsworth.

Giles, J. (2005). Internet encyclopaedias go head to head. *Nature, 438,* 900–901.

Goodstein, A. (2007). *Totally wired: What teens and tweens are really doing online*. New York: St. Martin's Press.

Gredler, M. E. (2001). *Learning and instruction: Theory into practice*. Upper Saddle River, NJ: Merrill/Prentice Hall.

Gronlund, N., & Brookhart, S. (2008). *Gronlund's writing instructional objectives* (8th ed.). Upper Saddle River, NJ: Prentice Hall.

Hannafin, R., & Foshay, W. R. (2008). Computer-based instruction's (CBI) rediscovered role in K-12: An evaluation case study of one high school's use of CBI to improve pass rates on high-stakes tests. *Educational Technology Research and Development, 56*(2), 147–160.

Hanor, J. H. (1998). Concepts and strategies learned from girls' interactions with computers. *Theory into Practice, 37*(1), 64–71.

Harasim, L. (2009). *Learning theory, design and educational technology.* Routledge.

Harper, G. K. (2001). The TEACH Act finally becomes law. The UT System Copyright Crash Course. Retrieved December 9, 2004, from http://www.utsystem.edu/OGC/IntellectualProperty/teachact.htm

Hattie, J., & Timperley, H. (2007). The power of feedback. *Review of Educational Research, 77*(1), 81–112.

Healy, J. M. (1998). *Failure to connect: How computers affect our children's minds—for better and worse.* New York: Simon & Schuster.

Heide, A., & Stilborne, L. (2004). *The teacher's Internet companion.* Markham, Ontario: Trifolium Books.

Heinich, R., Molenda, M., Russell, J. D., & Smaldino, S. (1993). *Instructional media and technologies for learning* (4th ed.). Upper Saddle River, NJ: Merrill/Prentice Hall.

Heinich, R., Molenda, M., Russell, J. D., & Smaldino, S. (1999). *Instructional media and technologies for learning* (6th ed.). Upper Saddle River, NJ: Merrill/Prentice Hall.

Hendron, J. (2008). *RSS for educators: Blogs, newsfeeds, podcasts, and wikis in the classroom.* Washington DC: ISTE Books.

Herring, J. E. (2004). *The Internet and information skills: A guide for teachers and school librarians.* New York: Neal Schuman.

Hiebert, J., Morris, A., Berk, D., & Jansen, A. (2007). Preparing teachers to learn from teaching. *Journal of Teacher Education, 58*(1), 47–61.

Hill, M., & Epps, K. (2009). Does physical classroom environment affect student performance, student satisfaction, and student evaluation of teaching in the college environment? *Proceedings of the Academy of Educational Leadership, 14*(1), 15–19. Retrieved on June 9, 2009 from http://www.alliedacademies.org/public/Proceedings/Proceedings24/AEL%20Proceedings.pdf.

Holden, J., & Westfall, P. (2005). *An instructional media selection guide for distance learning.* United States Distance Learning Association. Available at www.usdla.org/html/resources/2._USDLA_Instructional_Media_Selection_Guide.pdf.

Houtz, L. E., & Gupta, U. G. (2001). Nebraska high school students' computer skills and attitudes. *Journal of Research on Computing in Education, 33*(3).

Howell, D. D., Howell, D. K., & Childress, M. (2006). *Using PowerPoint in the classroom.* Thousand Oaks, CA: Corwin Press.

Hunter, M. (1982). *Mastery teaching.* El Segundo, CA: TIP.

Ivers, K., & Barron, A. (2005). *Multimedia projects in education: Designing, producing, and assessing* (5th ed.). Libraries Unlimited.

Jacobsen, D. A., Eggen, P., & Kauchak, D. (2006). *Methods for Teaching: Promoting Student Learning* (7th Ed.). Upper Saddle River, NJ: Merrill/Prentice Hall.

Johnson, R. T., Johnson, D. W., & Stanne, M. B. (1985). Effects of cooperative, competitive, and individualistic goal structures on computer-assisted instruction. *Journal of Educational Psychology, 77*(6), 668–677.

Joliffe, W. (2007). *Cooperative learning in the classroom: Putting it into practice.* London: Paul Chapman Publishing.

Jonassen, D. H. (1991). Evaluating constructivist learning. *Educational Technology, 31*(9), 28–33.

Jonassen, D. (Ed.). (2004). *Handbook of research for educational communication and technology.* Mahwah, NJ: Lawrence Erlbaum Associates.

Jonassen, D. H. (2006). *Modeling with technology: Mindtools for conceptual change* (3rd ed.). Upper Saddle River, NJ: Allyn & Bacon.

Jonassen, D., Howland, J., Marra, R. M., & Crismond, D. (2008). *Meaningful learning with technology* (3rd ed.). Upper Saddle River, NJ: Pearson/Merrill/Prentice Hall.

Jonassen, D. H., Peck, K. L., & Wilson, B. G. (1999). *Learning with technology: A constructivist approach.* Upper Saddle River, NJ: Merrill/Prentice Hall. (Chapter 1)

Jones, F., Jones, P., & Lynn, J. (2007). *Fred Jones tools for teaching: Discipline, instruction, motivation.* Fredric H. Jones & Associates.

Kafai, Y. (2008). How computer games help children learn. *Science Education, 92*(2), 378–381.

Kauchak, D., & Eggen, P. D. (1989). *Learning and teaching: Research based methods.* Boston: Allyn & Bacon.

Kauchak, D. & Eggen, P. (2008). *Introduction to teaching: Becoming a professional* (3rd ed). Upper Saddle River, NJ: Pearson/Merrill/Prentice Hall.

Ke, F. (2008). Computer game application within alternative classroom goal structures: Cognitive, metacognitive, and affective evaluation. *Educational Technology Research and Development, 56*(5/6), 539–556.

Kearny, C., Newby, T., & Stepich, D. (1995). Building bridges: Creating instructional analogies. Presentation at the Annual Convention of the National Society for Performance and Instruction, Atlanta, GA, March.

Keller, J. (2008). First principles of motivation to learn and e3-learning. *Distance Education, 29*(2), 175–185.

Keller, J. M. (1983). Motivational design of instruction. In C. M. Reigeluth (Ed.), *Instructional design theories and models: An overview of their current status* (pp. 383–434). Hillsdale, NJ: Lawrence Erlbaum Associates.

Keller, J. M. (1987). Development and use of the ARCS model of instructional design. *Journal of Instructional Development, 10*(3), 2–10.

Kelly, F., McCain, T., & Jukes, I. (2009). *Teaching the digital generation: No more cookie-cutter high schools.* Thousand Oaks, CA: Corwin.

Kim, D., & Gilman, D. A. (2008). Effects of text, audio, and graphic aids in multimedia instruction for vocabulary learning. *Educational Technology & Society, 11*(3), 114–126.

Kirschner, P., & Erkens, G. (2006). Cognitive tools and mindtools for collaborative learning. *Journal of Educational Computing Research, 35*(2), 199–209.

Kizlik, B. (2009) How to write learning objectives to meet demanding behavioral criteria. *Education Information for New and Future Teachers.* Available at http://www.adprima.com/objectives.htm.

Kizlik, B. (2009). A rationale for learning objectives that meet demanding behavioral criteria. *Education Information for New and Future Teachers.* Available at http://www.adprima.com/objectives2.htm.

Kizlik, B. (2009). Examples of student activities using behavioral verbs. *Education Information for New and Future Teachers*. Available at http://www.adprima.com/examples.htm.

Kleiner, A., & Lewis, L. (2003). *Internet access in U.S. public schools and classrooms: 1994–2002*. Washington, DC: U.S. Department of Education, National Center for Education Statistics.

Ko, S., & Rossen, S. (2008). *Teaching online: A practical guide*. Boston, MA: Houghton Mifflin.

Kolb, L. (2008). *Toys to tools: Connecting student cell phones to education*. Washington, D.C.: International Society for Technology in Education.

Kozma, R. (1991). Learning with media. *Review of Educational Research, 61*(2), 179–211.

Kozma, R. B., Belle, L. W., & Williams, G. W. (1978). Methods of Teaching. Schooling, Teaching and Learning American Education. (pp. 210–211). St. Louis, Missouri: C.V. Mosby Co.

Kulik, J. A. (2003). *Effects of using instructional technology in elementary and secondary schools: What controlled evaluation studies say*. Arlington, VA: SRI International. Available: http://www.sri.com/policy/csted/reports/sandt/it.

Kulik, C. C., & Kulik, J. A. (1991). Effectiveness of computer-based instruction: An updated analysis. *Computers in Human Behavior, 7,* 75–94.

Lang, S., Stanley, T., & Moore, B. (2008). *Short-cycle assessment: Improving student achievement through formative assessment*. Larchmont, NY: Eye On Education.

Lee, J. (1999). Effectiveness of computer-based instructional simulation: A meta-analysis. *International Journal of Instructional Media, 26,* 71–85.

Lengel, J. G., & Lengel, K. M. (2006). Integrating technology: A practical guide. Boston: Allyn & Bacon.

Lenhart, A., & Madden, M. (2007, January). *Social networking sites and teens: An overview. PEW Internet & American Life Project.* Washington, DC: Pew Charitable Trusts. Retrieved March 9, 2010, from www.pewinternet.org/PPF/r/230/report_display.asp

Leshin, C. B., Pollock, J., & Reigeluth, C. M., (1992). *Instructional design strategies and tactics*. Englewood Cliffs, NJ: Educational Technology.

Lever-Duffy, J. and McDonald, J. B. (2008). *Teaching and learning with technology* (3rd ed.). Boston: Allyn & Bacon.

Lewis, P. (2006). *Spreadsheet magic*. Washington D.C.: ISTE Books.

Lewis, P. (2007). *Database magic*. Washington D.C.: ISTE Books.

Lewis, P. (2008). *PowerPoint magic*. Washington D.C.: ISTE Books.

Lou, Y., Abrami, P. C., & d'Apollonia, S. (2001). Small group and individual learning with technology: A meta-analysis. *Review of Educational Research, 71*(3), 449–521.

Machtmes, K., & Asher, J. W. (2000). A meta-analysis of the effectiveness of telecourses in distance education. *The American Journal of Distance Education, 14*(1), 27–46.

Macionis, J. (1997). *Sociology* (5th ed.). Upper Saddle River, NJ: Prentice Hall.

Mager, R. F. (1997). *Preparing instructional objectives* (3rd ed.). Belmont, CA: Pitman.

Mantgem, M. (2007). *Tablet PCs in K-12 education*. Washington, D.C.: International Society for Technology in Education.

Maor, D., & Taylor, P. C. (1995). Teacher epistemology and scientific inquiry in computerized classroom environments. *Journal of Research in Science Teaching, 32*(8), 839–854.

Market Data Retrieval. (2003). *Technology in education 2003*. Shelton, CT: Author.

Marzano, R., & Kendall, J. (2008). *Designing and assessing educational objectives: Applying the new taxonomy*. Thousand Oaks, CA: Corwin.

Matzen, N. & Edmunds, J. (2007). Technology as a catalyst for change: The role of professional development. *Journal of Research on Technology in Education, 39*(4), 417–430.

Mayer, R. E. (2008, 2nd ed.) *Learning and Instruction*. Upper Saddle River, NJ: Pearson/Merrill/Prentice Hall.

McCullen, C. (2002). Preventing digital plagiarism. *Technology & Learning, 22*(9), 8.

McCutcheon, G. (1980). How do elementary school teachers plan? The nature of planning and influences on it. *Elementary School Journal, 81*(1), 4–23.

McKeachie, W. J. (1994). Why classes should be small, but how to help your students be active learners even in large classes. In W. J. McKeachie (Ed.), *Teaching tips* (pp. 197–210). Lexington, MA: Heath.

McKeachie, W. J., & Svinicki, M. (2006). *Teaching Tips: Strategies, Research, and Theory for College and University Teachers, 11th ed.* Houghton Mifflin: Boston.

Means, B., Toyama, Y., Murphy, R., Bakia, M., & Jones, K. (2009). *Evaluation of evidence-based practices in online learning: A meta-analysis and review of online learning studies*. Washington, DC: U.S. Department of Education, Office of Planning, Evaluation, and Policy Development.

Mehlinger, H., & Powers, S. (2002). *Technology and teacher education: A guide for educators and policymakers*. Boston: Houghton-Mifflin.

Merrill, M., Barclay, M., & van Schaak, A. (2008). Prescriptive principles for instructional design. In J. Spector, M. Merrill, J. vanMerrienboer, & M. Driscoll. *Handbook of research on educational communications and technology* (3rd ed.) (pp. 173–184). New York: Lawrence Erlbaum Associates.

Milem, J. F. (2003). The educational benefits of diversity: Evidence from multiple sectors. In M. J. Chang, D. Witt, J. Jones, & K. Hokuta (Eds.), *Compelling interest: Examining the evidence on racial dynamics in colleges and universities* (pp. 126–169). Stanford, CA: Stanford University Press.

Moe, T., & Chubb, J. (2007). *Librating learning: Technology, politics, and the future of American education*. San Francisco, CA: John Wiley & Sons.

Moll, O., Amanti, C., Neff, D., & Gonzalez, N. (1992). Funds of knowledge for teaching: Using a qualitative approach to connect homes and classrooms. *Theory into Practice, 31*(2), 132–141.

Moore, M., & Kearsley, G. (2005). *Distance education: A systems view* (2nd ed.). Belmont, CA: Thomson Wadsworth.

Moreno, R. (2006). Does the modality principle hold for different media? A test of the method-affects-learning hypothesis. *Journal of Computer Assisted Learning, 22*(3), 149–158.

Moreno, R. (2006). Learning with high tech and multimedia environments. *Current Directions, 15,* 63–67.

Morrison, G. R., Ross, S. M., & Kemp, J. E. (2004). *Designing effective instruction*. Hoboken, NJ: John Wiley & Sons.

Morrison, G., Ross, S., & Lowther, D. (2009). Technology as a change agent in the classroom. In L. Moller, J. Huett, & Harvey, D. (Eds.). *Learning and instructional technologies for the 21st century: Visions of the future.* (pp. 151–174). New York: Springer Science+Business Media, LLC.

Muthukumar, S. (2005). Creating interactive multimedia-based educational courseware: Cognition in learning. *Cognition, Technology & Work, 7*(1), 46–50.

National Center for Education Statistics. (2000, September). *Teacher's tools for the 21st century.* Washington, DC: U.S. Department of Education. Available on the World Wide Web: http://nces.ed.gov/.

National Center for Education Statistics. (2002, September). *Internet access in U.S. public schools and classrooms: 1994–2001.* Washington, DC: U.S. Department of Education. Available on the World Wide Web: http://nces.ed.gov/.

National School Boards Association. (2007). *Creating and connecting: Research and guidelines on online social – and educational – networking.* Available at http://www.nsba.org/site/docs/41400/41340.pdf.

Neumann, Y., & Shachar, M. (2003, October). Differences between traditional and distance education academic performances: A meta-analytic approach. *International Review of Research in Open and Distance Learning, 4*(2). Available at http://www.irrodl.org/content/v4.2/shachar-neumann.html.

Newby, T. & Lewandowski, J. (2009). *Teaching and learning with Microsoft Office 2007 and Expression Web: A multilevel approach to computer integration* (2nd ed.). Boston, MA: Pearson Education.

Nicol, D., & Milligan, C. (2006). Rethinking technology-supported assessment practices in relation to the seven principles of good feedback practice. In C. Bryan & K. Clegg. *Innovative assessment in higher education.* (pp. 64–78). New York: Routledge.

Nielsen, J. (2000). *Designing Web usability.* Indianapolis, IN: New Riders Publishing.

Niemiec, R., & Walberg, H. J. (1987). Comparative effects of computer-assisted instruction: A synthesis of reviews. *Journal of Educational Computing Research, 3*(1), 19–37.

Nitko, A. J., & Brookhart, S. M. (2007). *Educational Assessment of Students* (5th Ed.). Upper Saddle River, NJ: Pearson/Merrill/Prentice Hall.

November, A. (2008). *Web literacy for educators.* Thousand Oaks, CA: Corwin Press.

O'Bannon, B., Puckett, K., & Rakes, G. (2006). Using technology to support visual learning strategies. *Computers in the Schools, 23*(1/2), 125–137.

Ogbu, J. (1992). Understanding cultural diversity and learning. *Educational Researcher, 21*(8), 5–14.

Ogbu, J., & Simons, H. (1998). Voluntary and involuntary minorities: A cultural-ecological theory of school performance with some implications for education. *Anthropology & Education Quarterly, 29*(2), 155–188.

O'Grady, J., & O'Grady, K. (2008). *The information design handbook.* Cincinnati, OH: How.

Orey, M. (Ed.). (2001). Emerging perspectives on learning, teaching, and technology. Retrieved June 9, 2009 from http://projects.coe.uga.edu/epltt/.

Orlich, D., Harder, R., Callahan, R., Trevisan, M., & Brown, A. (2009). *Teaching strategies: A guide to effective instruction.* Boston, MA: Wadsworth.

Ormrod, J. E. (1995). *Educational psychology: Principles and applications.* Upper Saddle River, NJ: Merrill/Prentice Hall.

Ormrod, J. E. (2008). *Human learning* (5th ed.). Upper Saddle River, NJ: Pearson/Merrill/Prentice Hall.

Palinscar, A. S. (1986). Metacognitive strategy instruction. *Exceptional Children, 53*(2), 118–124.

Paske, R. (2005). Hypermedia: A brief history and progress report. *Technological Horizons in Education.*

Pelligrino, J., Chudowsky, N., & Glaser, R. (2001). *Knowing what students know: The science and design of educational assessment.* National Academy Press, Washington, DC.

Perelman, L. J. (1992). *School's out.* New York: Avon.

Phillion, J., Johnson, T., & Lehman, J. D. (2004). Using distance education technologies to enhance teacher education through linkages with K–12 schools. *Journal of Computing in Teacher Education, 20*(2), 63–70.

Phillips, D. C. (1995). The good, the bad, and the ugly: The many faces of constructivism. *Educational Researcher, 24*(7), 5–12.

Picciano, A. G. & Seaman, J. (2009). *K–12 online learning: A follow-up of the survey of U.S. school district administrators.* Needham, MA: Sloan Consortium (Sloan-C).

Pintrich, P. R., & Schunk, D. H. (1996). *Motivation in education: Theory, research, and applications.* Englewood Cliffs, NJ: Merrill/Prentice-Hall.

Popham, W. (2008). *Transformative assessment.* ASCD Publishing.

Project Tomorrow. (2007). *Speak Up 2007 for Students, Teachers, Parents & School Leaders.* Available at http://www.tomorrow.org/speakup/speakup_reports.html.

Provenzo, E. F. (2004). *The Internet and online research for teachers.* Boston: Allyn & Bacon.

Ray, K., & Zanetis, J. (2008). *Interactive videoconferencing.* ISTE Books.

Reigeluth, C. M. (1983). Instructional design: What is it and why is it? In C. M. Reigeluth (Ed.), *Instructional-design theories and models: An overview of their current status* (pp. 3–36). Hillsdale, NJ: Lawrence Erlbaum Associates.

Reigeluth, C. M. (1999). *Instructional design theories and models: A new paradigm of instructional theory, vol. 2.* Hillsdale, NJ: Lawrence Erlbaum Associates.

Reiser, R. A., & Dick, W. (1996). *Instructional planning: A guide for teachers.* Boston: Allyn & Bacon.

Reynolds, A. (1992). What is competent beginning teaching? A review of the literature. *Review of Educational Research, 62*(1), 1–35.

Rice, K. (2006). A comprehensive look at distance education in the K-12 context. *Journal of Research on Technology in Education, 38*(4), 425–448.

Richardson, W. (2008). *Blogs, wikis, podcasts, and other powerful web tools for classrooms.* Thousand Oaks, CA: Corwin Press.

Rieber, L. P. (1994). *Computers, graphics, and learning.* Madison, WI: Brown & Benchmark.

Rieber, L. (2005). Multimedia learning in games, simulations, and microworlds. In R. E. Mayer (Ed.), *The Cambridge Handbook of Multimedia Learning* (pp. 549–567). New York: Cambridge University Press.

Roblyer, M. D. (2005). *Starting out on the Internet: A learning journey for teachers* (3rded.). Boston, MA: Pearson.

Roblyer, M. D., & Doehring, A. (2010). *Integrating educational technology into teaching* (5th ed.). Boston, MA: Pearson Education.

Rogoff, B. (1990). *Apprenticeship in thinking: Cognitive development in social context.* New York: Oxford University Press.

Ross, J., & Bruce, C. (2007). Teacher self-assessment: A mechanism for facilitating professional growth. *Teaching and Teacher Education, 23*(2), 146–159.

Rossi, P. H., Lipsey, M. W., & Freeman, H. E. (2004). *Evaluation: A systematic approach* (7th ed.). Thousand Oaks, CA: Sage publications, Inc.

Rothwell, W. J., & Kazanas, H. C. (1992). *Mastering the instructional design process: A systematic approach.* San Francisco: Jossey-Bass.

Russell, T. L. (1999). *The no significant difference phenomenon.* Available at http://www.nosignificantdifference.org/.

Saettler, P. (1990). *The evolution of American educational technology.* Englewood, CO: Libraries Unlimited.

Salend, S. J. (2005). *Creating inclusive classrooms: Effective and reflective practices for all students* (5th ed.). Upper Saddle River, NJ: Merrill/Prentice Hall.

Sapon-Shevin, M. (2001). Schools fit for all. *Educational Leadership, 58*(4), 34–39.

Sardo-Brown, D. (1990). Experienced teachers' planning practices: A U.S. survey. *Journal of Education for Teaching, 16*(1), 57–71.

Schmitt, M. S., & Newby, T. J. (1986). Metacognition: Relevance to instructional design. *Journal of Instructional Development, 9*(4), 29–33.

Schön, D. A. (1983). *The reflective practitioner: How professionals think in action.* New York: Basic Books.

Schunk, D. H., (2008, 5th ed.). *Learning theories: An educational perspective.* Upper Saddle River, NJ: Pearson/Merrill/Prentice Hall.

Schunk, D. H., Pintrich, P. R., & Meece, J. L. (2008). *Motivation in Education: Theory, Research, and Applications.* Upper Saddle River, NJ: Pearson/Merrill/Prentice Hall.

Schunk, D. H., & Zimmerman, B. J. (Eds.) (1998). *Self-regulated learning: From teaching to self-reflective practice.* New York: Guilford Press.

Seels, B. B., & Richey, R. C. (1994). *Instructional technology: The definition and domains of the field.* Washington, DC: Association for Educational Communications and Technology.

Shamburg, C. (2009). *Student-powered podcasting.* Washington, DC: International Society for Technology in Education.

Sharan, S. (Ed.) (1990). *Cooperative learning: Theory and research.* Westport, CT: Praeger.

Shelly, G. B., & Cashman, T. J. (1984). *Computer fundamentals for an information age.* Brea, CA: Anaheim.

Shelly, G. B., Cashman, T. J., Gunter, R. E. & Gunter, G. A. (2008). *Teachers discovering computers: Integrating technology and digital media in the classroom* (5th ed.). Boston, MA: Thompson Learning.

Shuell, T. J. (1981). Dimensions of individual differences. In F. H. Farley & N. J. Gordon (Eds.), *Psychology and education: The state of the union* (pp. 32–59). Berkeley, CA: McCutchan.

Simkins, M., Cole, K., Tavalin, F., & Means, B. (2002). *Increasing student learning through multimedia projects.* Alexandria, VA: Association for Supervision and Curriculum Development.

Simmons, C. & Hawkins, C. (2009). *Teaching ICT: Developing as a reflective secondary teacher.* London: Sage.

Simonson, M., Smaldino, S., Albright, M., & Zvacek, S. (2006). *Teaching and learning at a distance: Foundations of distance education* (3rd ed.). Upper Saddle River, NJ: Pearson Education.

Skinner, B. F. (1968). *The technology of teaching.* New York: Appleton-Century-Crofts.

Skinner, B. F. (1984). The shame of American education. *American Psychologist, 39,* 947–954.

Smaldino, S. E., Lowther, D. L., & Russell, J. D. (2008, 9th ed.). *Instructional technology and media for learning.* Upper Saddle River, NJ: Pearson/Merrill/Prentice Hall.

Smith, P. L., & Ragan, T. J. (2005). *Instructional design* (3rd ed.). San Francisco: John Wiley & Sons/Jossey-Bass.

Smith, G., & Throne, S. (2007). *Differentiating instruction with technology in K-5 classrooms.* Washington, D.C.: International Society for Technology in Education.

Snow, R., Corno, L., & Jackson, D., III (1996). Individual differences in affective and cognitive functions. In D. Berliner & R. Callee (Eds.), *Handbook of educational psychology* (pp. 243–310). New York: Simon & Schuster Macmillan.

Solomon, G. (2004). Drafting a customized tech plan: An up-to-the-minute design. *Technology & Learning, 24*(7), 34–35.

Solomon, G., & Schrum, L. (2007). *Web 2.0: New tools, new schools.* Washington DC: ISTE Books.

Spector, J., & Merrill, M. (2008). Editorial. *Distance Education, 29*(2), 123–126.

Steel, N., & Dijkstra, S. (2004). *Curriculum, plans, and processes in instructional design: International perspectives.* Mahwah, NJ: Lawrence Erlbaum.

Stepich, D. A., & Newby, T. J. (1988). Analogical instruction within the information processing paradigm: Effective means to facilitate learning. *Instructional Science, 17,* 129–144.

Stiggins, R. (2007). *Introduction to student-involved assessment for learning* (5th ed.). Prentice Hall.

Stoll, C. (1996). *Silicon snake oil: Second thoughts on the information highway.* New York: Doubleday.

Stoll, C. (2000). *High tech heretic: Why computers don't belong in the classroom and other reflections by a computer contrarian.* New York: Doubleday.

Swain, S. L., & Harvey, D. M. (2002). Single-sex computer classes: An effective alternative. *TechTrends, 46*(6), 17–20.

Tapscott, D. (2008). *Grown up digital: How the net generation is changing your world.* New York: McGraw-Hill Professional.

Taylor, J., Van Scotter, P., & Coulson, D. (2007). Briding research on learning and student achievement: The role of instructional materials. *Science Educator, 16*(2), 44–50.

Taylor, R. P. (Ed.). (1980). *The computer in the school: Tutor, tool, tutee.* New York: Teachers College Press.

Taylor, R. (2003). The computer in the school: Tutor, tool, and tutee. *Contemporary Issues in Technology and Teacher Education, 3*(2), 241–252.

Terenzini, P. T., Cabrera, A. F., Colbeck, C. L., Bjorklund, S. A., & Parente, J. M. (2001). Racial and ethnic diversity in the classroom: Does it promote learning. *The Journal of Higher Education, 72*(5), 509–531.

Tessmer, M. (1990). Environment analysis: A neglected state of instructional design. *Educational Technology, 38*(1), 55–64.

Thompson, N., & McGill, T. (2008). Multimedia and cognition: Examining the effect of applying cognitive principles to the design of instructional materials. *Journal of Educational Computing Research, 39*(2), 143–159.

Thorndike, E. L. (1931). *Human learning*. New York: Century.

Thorsen, C. (2008). *Techtactics: Technology for teachers*. (3rd ed.). Boston: Allyn & Bacon.

Tiene, D., & Ingram, A. (2001). *Exploring current issues in educational technology*. Boston: McGraw Hill.

Tileston, D. (2004). *What every teacher should know about learning, memory, and the brain*. Thousand Oaks, CA: Corwin.

Tondreau, B. (2009) *Layout essentials: 100 design principles for building grids*. Beverly, MA: Rockport.

Turner, R. (2006). Super searchers go to school: Sharing online strategies with K-12 students, teachers, and librarians. *New Library World, 107*(3/4), 168–171.

Tuttle, H. (2009). *Formative assessment: Responding to your students*. Larchmont, NY: Eye On Education.

U.S. Department of Commerce. (1998). *Current population survey, 1997*. Washington, DC: Bureau of the census.

U.S. Department of Education. (1996). *Getting America's students ready for the 21st century*. Washington, DC: U.S. Department of Education.

Van Gorp, L. (2007). *Must-see websites for busy teachers*. Huntington, CA: Shell Education.

Vaughan, T. (2008). *Multimedia: Making it work*. New York: McGraw-Hill.

Vercauteren, D. (2008). *Teacher feedback to primary school students: Do they get the message?* VDM Verlag.

Villegas, A. M., & Lucas, T. (2002). *Educating culturally responsive teachers: A coherent approach*. Albany, NY: State University of New York Press.

Vogel, J., Vogel., D., Cannon-Bowers, J., Bowers, C., & Wright, M. (2006). Computer gaming and interactive simulations for learning: A meta-analysis. *Journal of Educational Computing Research, 34*(3), 229–243.

Wagner, E. D., & McCombs, B. L. (1995, March–April). Learner centered psychological principles in practice: Designs for distance education. *Educational Technology, 35,* 32–35.

Wagner, T. (2008). *The global achievement gap: Why even our best schools don't teach the new survival skills our children need – and what we can do about it*. New York: Basic Books.

Wasserman, S. (1992). *Asking the right question: The essence of teaching*. Bloomington, IN: Phi Delta Kappa.

Watson, J., Germin, G., & Ryan, J. (2008). *Keeping pace with K-12 online learning: A review of state-level policy and practice*. Evergreen, CO: Evergreen Consulting Associates. Available at http://www.kpk12.com/.

Watson, J. B. (1924). *Behaviorism*. New York: Peoples' Institute.

Wells, J., & Lewis, L. (2006). *Internet access in U.S. public schools and classrooms: 1994–2005* U.S. Department of Education (NCES 2007–020). Available at http://nces.ed.gov/pubsearch/pubsinfo.asp?pubid=2007020.

West, C. K., Farmer, J. A., & Wolff, P. M. (1991). *Instructional design: Implications from cognitive science*. Upper Saddle River, NJ: Merrill/Prentice Hall.

Westwood, P. (2008). *What teachers need to know about teaching methods*. Victoria, Australia: ACER.

White, R., & Downs, T. (2008). *How computers work* (9th ed.). Indianapolis, IN: Que Publishing.

Williams, M., & Linn, M. C. (2002). WISE inquiry in fifth grade biology. *Research in Science Education, 32,* 415–436.

Wittrock, M. C. (1990). Generative processes of comprehension. *Educational Psychologist, 24,* 345–376.

Woolfolk, A. E. (1990). Generative processes of comprehension. *Educational psychology* (4th ed.). Upper Saddle River, NJ: Merrill/Prentice Hall.

Woolfolk, A. E. (2010, 11th ed.). *Educational psychology*. Upper Saddle River, NJ: Pearson/Merrill/Prentice Hall.

Yang, H. (2008). Blogfolios for student-centered reflection and communication. In M. Iskander (Ed.). *Innovative techniques in instruction technology, e-learning, e-assessment, and education*. (pp. 179–182). Springer Science+ Business Media B.V.

Yelon, S. L. (1991). Writing and using instructional objectives. In J. L. Briggs, K. L. Gustafson, & M. H. Tillman (Eds.), *Instructional design: Principles and applications* (2nd ed.) (pp. 75–122). Englewood Cliffs, NJ: Educational Technology.

Yelon, S. L. (1996). *Powerful principles of instruction*. White Plains, NY: Longman.

Young, B. (2000). Gender differences in students' attitudes toward computers. *Journal of Research on Computing in Education, 33*(2).

Zandberg, I., & Lewis, L. (2008). *Technology-based distance education courses for public elementary and secondary school students: 2002–03 and 2004–05* (NCES 2008–008). Washington, DC: U.S. Department of Education, National Center for Education Statistics.

Zheng, R. (2008). *Cognitive effects of multimedia learning*. Hershey, PA: Information Science Reference.

NAME INDEX

SUBJECT INDEX